Urban Issues

Urban Issues

CQ PRESS

A Division of SAGE
Washington, D.C.

FIFTH EDITION

SELECTIONS FROM CQ RESEARCHER

CQ Press
2300 N Street, NW, Suite 800
Washington, DC 20037

Phone: 202-729-1900; toll-free, 1-866-4CQ-PRESS (1-866-427-7737)

Web: www.cqpress.com

Cover design: Judy Myers, Graphic Design
Cover photo: © James Leynse/Corbis

♾ The paper used in this publication exceeds the requirements of the American National Standard for Information Sciences—Permanence of Paper for Printed Library Materials, ANSI Z39.48-1992.

Printed and bound in the United States of America

14 13 12 11 10   1 2 3 4 5

A CQ Press College Division Publication

Executive director	Brenda Carter
Editorial director	Charisse Kiino
Development editor	Dwain Smith
Marketing manager	Christopher O'Brien
Composition	C&M Digitals (P) Ltd.
Managing editor	Stephen Pazdan
Production editor	Belinda Josey
Production manager	Paul Pressau

Library of Congress Cataloging-in-Publication Data

Urban issues: selections from CQ researcher. — 5th ed.
    p. cm.
    Includes bibliographical references.
    ISBN 978-1-60871-707-1 (pbk.: alk. paper) 1. Urban policy—United States. 2. Social problems—United States. I. CQ Press. II. CQ researcher.

HT123.U74564 2011
307.760973—dc22

2010041666

Contents

Annotated Contents

The 12 *CQ Researcher* reports reprinted in this book have been reproduced essentially as they appeared when first published. In the few cases in which important developments have since occurred, updates are provided in the overviews highlighting the principal issues examined.

EDUCATION

Fixing Urban Schools

African-American and Hispanic students — largely in urban schools — lag far behind white students, who mostly attend middle-class suburban schools. Critics argue that when Congress reauthorizes the 2002 No Child Left Behind Act (NCLB), it must retarget the legislation to help urban schools tackle tough problems, such as encouraging the best teachers to enter and remain in high-poverty schools, rather than focusing on tests and sanctions. Some advocates propose busing students across district lines to create more socioeconomically diverse student bodies. But conservative analysts argue that busing wastes students' time and that permitting charter schools to compete with public schools will drive improvement. Meanwhile, liberal analysts point out that successful charter programs are too costly for most schools to emulate, and that no one has yet figured out how to spread success beyond a handful of schools, public or private. In 2010, the education debates have steered toward favoring economic considerations over racial equity in the face of a severe recession, mixed results of nationwide test scores, a three-year delay in reauthorizing NCLB, and a 2007 Supreme Court ruling on school desegregation.

LAW ENFORCEMENT AND HOMELAND SECURITY

Fighting Crime

Efforts to reduce violent crime are succeeding in some, but not all, areas of the country. The number of violent crimes fell by about 2 percent during the first half of 2007. But crime still grips parts of cities large and small, where guns remain plentiful and many young men are caught up in a cycle of attack and revenge. In Washington, D.C., for example, there were 181 killings in 2007, up from 169 in 2006. But in the capital and elsewhere, homicide rates are significantly lower than durin '90s. Experts attribute some of the improvement to better policing techniques, such as closely tracking neighborhood crime and quickly responding to upticks. But a countertrend of persistent violent crime is plaguing impoverished inner cities, where city officials and grassroots activists are struggling to keep young men from joining the ranks of victims and perpetrators.

Disaster Preparedness

The flawed response to Hurricane Katrina by local, state and federal officials has experts worried that the nation is unprepared for another major disaster. Nearly every emergency-response system broke down in the days immediately following the monster storm — the costliest disaster in American history. Some disaster experts say the government's preoccupation with terrorism — including the deployment of thousands of National Guard and Reserve troops in Iraq — has jeopardized domestic emergency-response capabilities. Nearly four years after President Bush signed the Post-Katrina Emergency Management Reform Act into law in 2006, critics charge that FEMA has not fully implemented the provisions of the reform act. Moreover, the Office of Emergency Communications was created to help multiple responders from different jurisdictions more effectively operate in disaster situations, but significant shortcomings still persist in the office's communications plan.

LAND USE AND URBAN DEVELOPMENT

Rapid Urbanization

About 3.3 billion people — half of Earth's inhabitants — live in cities, and the number is expected to hit 5 billion within 20 years. Most urban growth today is occurring in developing countries, where about a billion people live in city slums. Delivering services to crowded cities has become increasingly difficult, especially in the world's 19 "megacities" — those with more than 10 million residents. Moreover, most of the largest cities are in coastal areas, where they are vulnerable to flooding caused by climate change. Many governments are striving to improve city life by expanding services, reducing environmental damage and providing more jobs for the poor, but some still use heavy-handed clean-up policies like slum clearance. Researchers say urbanization helps reduce global poverty because new urbanites earn more than they could in their villages. The global recession could reverse that trend, however, as many unemployed city dwellers return to rural areas. But most experts expect rapid urbanization to resume once the economic storm has passed.

Aging Infrastructure

The deadly collapse in August 2007 of Minneapolis' Interstate I-35 West bridge over the Mississippi River tragically underscored the condition of the nation's highways, dams, wastewater treatment systems, electrical transmission networks and other infrastructure. Many facilities and systems are 50–100 years old, and engineers say they have been woefully neglected. Decades ago taxpayers, lawmakers and private companies found it relatively easy to ante up the huge sums needed to build vital infrastructure, but money for repairs and maintenance has been far tougher to come by in recent years. Federal and state lawmakers today often prefer to spend public dollars on high-profile convention centers and sports arenas, and anti-tax groups often fight tax hikes or utility-rate increases to pay for maintenance. But now lawmakers are debating whether aging infrastructure merits higher taxes or other measures, such as turning more highways into privately run toll roads.

Mass Transit Boom

Pressed by rising gas prices, highway gridlock and global-warming concerns, cities are spending unprecedented amounts on public transit systems — from streetcars and other "light-rail" lines to commuter trains and rapid-transit buses. They also are experimenting with "congestion-pricing" plans that impose tolls on motorists to induce them to use transit or alter driving habits. While traffic congestion is partly behind the transit boom, it is not the only force driving it. Some light-rail projects are built hand-in-hand with "transit-oriented developments" — walkable, mixed-use projects designed to attract residents, shoppers and office workers to urban neighborhoods. Cities from Portland, Ore., to Charlotte, N.C., have embraced rail projects, but critics argue that such ventures aren't boosting ridership or reducing traffic. Some worry, too, that they benefit the wealthy at the expense of low-income residents whose needs may not be well-served by new rail lines.

Property Rights

State and local governments are under increasing criticism for using the long-established power of eminent domain to acquire private property not only for highways and other government projects but also for private developments. Financially strapped cities say eminent domain, or condemnation, is sometimes the only way to assemble large tracts of land for upscale residential and commercial development that will enhance urban life and bring in needed tax revenue. Property-rights advocates and other critics say the government should not force home and business owners to turn over their property to other private parties.

Downtown Renaissance

After World War II, suburban job and population growth in the United States far outstripped that of cities, leading many to worry that downtowns were doomed. In recent years, however, many cities have revived their fortunes by fashioning downtowns that are attractive and — for the first time in decades — drawing in new residents. Once-forlorn urban centers from San Diego to Philadelphia are now busy construction zones that are filling up with trendy shops and restaurants. But despite the good news, downtowns are still grabbing only a tiny fraction of metropolitan growth. Some skeptics worry that the downtown renaissance is fragile, largely built on upscale shopping and entertainment — relatively new trends that could

easily change. But others believe downtowns, having once again become the most vital parts of many cities, will provide a model for future development — even in the suburbs.

RACE, CLASS AND ETHNICITY
Housing the Homeless

The face of homelessness is changing in the United States. In the past, the homeless typically were single men and women who lived on the street or in shelters; many were mentally ill or drug addicts, or both. But today's homeless may well be a suburban couple with children who lost their home to foreclosure and are staying with relatives or living at a shelter. As the recession continues to ravage the middle class and the working poor, job losses and medical emergencies add to the number of homeless Americans. Advocates for the homeless also cite a shortage of affordable housing. A 2008 federal government survey showed a one-year 9 percent increase in families relying on homeless shelters. In recent months, local governments and school districts have been reporting homelessness cases more than doubling this year. But funding shortages may force agencies that help the homeless to curtail services.

Domestic Poverty

Despite sweeping welfare reforms in the 1990s and generally healthy economic growth in recent years, domestic poverty remains intractable. Moreover, signs are emerging that so-called deep poverty is growing sharply — most significantly among children. U.S. poverty is fueled by a long list of problems, including Katrina's devastation, immigration, the growing income gap between rich and poor, the subprime mortgage fallout and education disparities. Conservatives say solutions must emphasize personal responsibility, higher marriage rates and fewer out-of-wedlock births. Liberals focus on the negative effects of government budget cuts for anti-poverty programs, tax cuts benefiting the wealthy and the need for more early-childhood-development programs. The Democratic Congress is making poverty a priority issue. President Bush himself acknowledged the gap between rich and poor, raising hopes that a bipartisan effort would be found to reduce poverty.

Mortgage Crisis

More than 2 million borrowers will lose their homes to foreclosure because of subprime mortgage lending in recent years. With the housing market booming, lenders enticed many lower-income people into buying homes they couldn't afford by offering adjustable-rate mortgages (ARMs) with temptingly low initial teaser interest rates. Many loans didn't require down payments or documented proof of income. Moreover, with real-estate prices rising many homeowners used the higher value of their homes to get second mortgages to pay for extras like remodeled kitchens. But the housing market crashed and the party ended: The low teaser loans reset at higher interest rates, and many borrowers defaulted on their new, higher mortgage payments. When the dust settles, investors who bought mortgage-based securities stand to lose $160 billion or more. Congress and officials in the executive branch are debating how to help borrowers keep their homes and whether tough, new lending standards are warranted.

Immigration Debate

The number of illegal immigrants in the country has topped 12 million, making immigration once again a central topic of debate. Moreover, with undocumented workers spreading far beyond traditional "gatekeeper" states such as California and Texas, complaints about illegal immigrants have become a daily staple of talk radio. Debate about tougher enforcement policies, a dominant theme of the 2008 presidential campaign, has become ever more contentious in the wake of Arizona's Republican Gov. Jan Brewer signing the nation's toughest immigration enforcement law in April 2010. While Congress deliberates removing "birthright citizenship" (favored by Republicans) from the 14th Amendment or the Development, Relief and Education of Alien Minors (DREAM) Act (favored by Democrats), states like South Carolina and Michigan are pushing for state immigration bills.

Preface

As the daily news constantly reminds us, coming to terms with the full complexity and variety of issues that confront America's urban areas is no small feat. Can inner-city crime be significantly reduced? Should the government bail out floundering borrowers? Can cities cope with rampant growth? To promote change and hopefully reach viable resolution, scholars, students and policymakers must strive to understand the context and content of each of these urban issues. It is such understanding that eventually enables students to define their roles as active participants in urban policy.

With the view that only an objective examination that synthesizes all competing viewpoints can lead to sound analysis, this fifth edition of *Urban Issues* provides comprehensive and unbiased coverage of today's most pressing policy problems. This book is a compilation of 12 recent reports from *CQ Researcher*, a weekly policy backgrounder that brings into focus key issues on the public agenda. It enables instructors to fairly and comprehensively uncover opposing sides of each issue and illustrate just how significantly these issues impact citizens and the government they elect. *CQ Researcher* fully explains difficult concepts in plain English. Each article chronicles and analyzes past legislative and judicial action as well as current and possible future maneuvering. Each report addresses how issues affect all levels of government—local, state and federal—and also the lives and futures of citizens. *Urban Issues* is designed to promote in-depth discussion, facilitate further research and help readers think critically and formulate their own positions on these crucial issues.

This collection is organized into four subject areas that span a range of important urban policy concerns: Education; Law Enforcement and Homeland Security; Land Use and Urban Development; and Race, Class and Ethnicity. These pieces were chosen to expose students to a wide range of issues, from the current state of U.S. infrastructure to the efficacy of cities' eminent domain powers. We are gratified to know that *Urban Issues* has found a following in a wide range of departments of political science, sociology, public administration and urban planning, and we hope that this new edition continues to meet readers' needs.

CQ RESEARCHER

CQ Researcher was founded in 1923 as *Editorial Research Reports* and was sold primarily to newspapers as a research tool. The magazine was renamed and redesigned in 1991 as *CQ Researcher*. Today, students are its primary audience. While still used by hundreds of journalists and newspapers, many of which reprint portions of the reports, the *Researcher*'s main subscribers are now high school, college and public libraries. In 2002, *Researcher* won the American Bar Association's coveted Silver Gavel award for magazine excellence for a series of nine reports on civil liberties and other legal issues.

Researcher staff writers — all highly experienced journalists — sometimes compare the experience of writing a *Researcher* report to drafting a college term paper. Indeed, there are many similarities. Each report is as long as many term papers — about 11,000 words — and is written by one person without any significant outside help. One of the key differences is that writers interview leading experts, scholars and government officials for each issue.

Like students, staff writers begin the creative process by choosing a topic. Working with the *Researcher*'s editors, the writer identifies a controversial subject that has important public policy implications. After a topic is selected, the writer embarks on one to two weeks of intense research. Newspaper and magazine articles are clipped or downloaded, books are ordered and information is gathered from a wide variety of sources, including interest groups, universities and the government. Once the writers are well informed, they develop a detailed

outline, and begin the interview process. Each report requires a minimum of 10 to 15 interviews with academics, officials, lobbyists and people working in the field. Only after all interviews are completed does the writing begin.

CHAPTER FORMAT

Each issue of *CQ Researcher*, and therefore each selection in this book, is structured in the same way. Each begins with an overview, which briefly summarizes the areas that will be explored in greater detail in the rest of the chapter. The next section chronicles important and current debates on the topic under discussion and is structured around a number of key questions, such as "Is a new approach needed to help the poorest Americans?" and "Is the U.S. ready for another major disaster?" These questions are usually the subject of much debate among practitioners and scholars in the field. Hence, the answers presented are never conclusive but rather detail the range of opinion on the topic.

Next, the "Background" section provides a history of the issue being examined. This retrospective covers important legislative measures, executive actions and court decisions that illustrate how current policy has evolved. Then the "Current Situation" section examines contemporary policy issues, legislation under consideration and legal action being taken. Each selection concludes with an "Outlook" section, which addresses possible regulation, court rulings and initiatives from Capitol Hill and the White House over the next 5 to 10 years.

Each report contains features that augment the main text: two to three sidebars that examine issues related to the topic at hand, a pro versus con debate between two experts, a chronology of key dates and events and an annotated bibliography detailing major sources used by the writer.

CUSTOM OPTIONS

Interested in building your ideal CQ Press *Issues* book, customized to your personal teaching needs and interests? Browse by course or search for specific topics or issues from our online catalog of more than 200 *CQ Researcher* issues at http://custom.cqpress.com.

ACKNOWLEDGMENTS

We wish to thank many people for helping to make this collection a reality. Tom Colin, managing editor of *CQ Researcher,* gave us his enthusiastic support and cooperation as we developed this fifth edition. He and his talented staff of editors and writers have amassed a first-class library of *Researcher* reports, and we are fortunate to have access to that rich cache. We also thankfully acknowledge the advice and feedback from current readers and are gratified by their satisfaction with the book.

Some readers may be learning about *CQ Researcher* for the first time. We expect that many readers will want regular access to this excellent weekly research tool. For subscription information or a no-obligation free trial of *CQ Researcher,* please contact CQ Press at www.cqpress.com or toll-free at 1-866-4CQ-PRESS (1-866-427-7737).

We hope that you will be pleased by the fifth edition of *Urban Issues.* We welcome your feedback and suggestions for future editions. Please direct comments to Charisse Kiino, Editorial Director, College Division CQ Press, 2300 N Street, N.W., Suite 800, Washington, DC 20037, or *ckiino@cqpress.com.*

—The Editors of CQ Press

Contributors

Thomas J. Colin, managing editor of *CQ Researcher,* has been a magazine and newspaper journalist for more than 30 years. Before joining Congressional Quarterly in 1991, he was a reporter and editor at the *Miami Herald* and *National Geographic* and editor in chief of *Historic Preservation.* He holds a bachelor's degree in English from the College of William & Mary and in journalism from the University of Missouri.

Thomas J. Billitteri is a *CQ Researcher* writer and editor with more than 30 years' experience covering business, nonprofit institutions and public policy for the *St. Petersburg Times, The Chronicle of Philanthropy* and other publications. His recent *CQ Researcher* reports include "Youth Violence," "Afghanistan's Future" and "Financial Literacy." He holds a BA in English and an MA in journalism from Indiana University.

Charles S. Clark is a veteran Washington freelancer who writes for *The Washington Post, National Journal* and other publications. He previously served as a staff writer at *CQ Researcher* and writer-researcher at Time-Life Books. He graduated in political science from McGill University.

Marcia Clemmitt is a *CQ Researcher* staff writer and a veteran social-policy reporter who previously served as editor in chief of *Medicine & Health* and staff writer for *The Scientist.* She has also been a high school math and physics teacher. She holds a liberal arts and sciences degree from St. John's College, Annapolis, and a master's degree in English from Georgetown University. Her recent reports include "Gridlock in Washington" and "Health-Care Reform."

Alan Greenblatt is a freelance writer in St. Louis and former staff writer at *Governing* magazine. He previously covered elections, agriculture and military spending for *CQ Weekly*, where he won the National Press Club's Sandy Hume Award for political journalism. He graduated from San Francisco State University in 1986 and received a master's degree in English literature from the University of Virginia in 1988. His recent *CQ Researcher* reports include "Future of the GOP" and "State Budget Crisis."

Kenneth Jost, associate editor of *CQ Researcher,* graduated from Harvard College and Georgetown University Law Center. He is the author of the *Supreme Court Yearbook* and editor of *The Supreme Court from A to Z* (both from CQ Press). He was a member of the *CQ Researcher* team that won the American Bar Association's 2002 Silver Gavel Award. His previous reports include "Bilingual Education vs. English Immersion" and "Testing in Schools." He is also author of the blog Jost on Justice (http://jostonjustice.blogspot.com).

Peter Katel is a *CQ Researcher* staff writer who previously reported on Haiti and Latin America for *Time* and *Newsweek* and covered the Southwest for newspapers in New Mexico. He has received several journalism awards, including the Bartolomé Mitre Award from the Inter-American Press Association for coverage of drug trafficking. He holds an AB in university studies from the University of New Mexico. His recent reports include "New Strategy in Iraq," "Rise in Counterinsurgency" and "Wounded Veterans."

Patrick Marshall is a freelance writer in Seattle, Wash., and contributing writer for *CQ Researcher* who writes about public policy and technology issues. He is a computer columnist for *The Seattle Times* and holds a BA in anthropology from the University of California at Santa Cruz and an MA in international studies from the Fletcher School of Law & Diplomacy at Tufts University.

Pamela M. Prah, a former *CQ Researcher* staff writer, is now political editor at Stateline.org. She has also written for Kiplinger's *Washington Letter* and the Bureau of National Affairs. She holds a MA degree in government from Johns Hopkins University and a BA degree in magazine journalism from Ohio University.

Jennifer Weeks is a *CQ Researcher* contributing writer in Watertown, Mass., who specializes in energy and environmental issues. She has written for *The Washington Post, The Boston Globe Magazine* and other publications, and has 15 years' experience as a public-policy analyst, lobbyist and congressional staffer. She has an AB degree from Williams College and master's degrees from the University of North Carolina and Harvard University.

Urban Issues

1

Fixing Urban Schools

Marcia Clemmitt and Charles S. Clark

Philadelphia police officers guard West Philadelphia High School on March 12, 2007, where a teacher was attacked by three students three days earlier. Experts suggest that a "behavior gap" between black and white students parallels the academic achievement gap between high- and low-performing students.

From *CQ Researcher*,
April 27 2007 (updated August 5, 2010).

"I didn't go to school much in elementary, and they saw me as a bad girl" who skipped class, says Jeanette, a Houston high-school student who dropped out several times but is struggling to get a diploma. After her parents divorced when she was in grade school, she fell into a pattern typical of urban students, repeatedly "switching schools," sometimes living with her mother, sometimes her father and sometimes with an aunt who "didn't make us go to school" at all.[1]

In middle school, Jeanette began taking drugs but later got involved in sports, which motivated her to try, sometimes successfully, to keep up her grades and stay off drugs. Some teachers have tried hard to help her, but like many troubled urban kids, she pulls back. "If I need help . . . I don't say anything. . . . They have to ask me." Still, Jeanette is determined to avoid the fate of her parents, who dropped out of school when they had her. At the time, her mother was only 13. "I don't want to live like them. I want to have a better life," she says.

Jeanette typifies the daunting challenge that urban schools face in promoting academic achievement among children whose lives have been disordered and impoverished.

Most middle-class families with children have moved to the suburbs, leaving urban schools today overwhelmingly populated by low-income, African-American and Hispanic students. "Nationally, about 50 percent of all black and Latino students attend schools in which 75 percent or more of the students are low-income, as measured by eligibility for free and reduced-price lunch," according to the Center for Civil Rights at the University of North Carolina.

Minority Districts Often Get Less Funding

In 28 states, school districts with high-minority enrollments received less per-pupil funding (shown as a negative number, top map) than districts with low-minority levels. For example, in Illinois, the highest-minority districts received an average of $1,223 less per student than the lowest-minority districts. In 21 states, the highest-minority districts received more per pupil (shown as a positive number, bottom map), than the districts with the lowest-minority enrollments. For example, in Georgia, the highest-poverty districts received $566 per student more than the lowest-poverty districts.

Minority Funding Gaps by State, 2004

States where high-minority districts received less funding than low-minority districts

-$2,000+
-$1,001 to -$2,000
-$500 to -$1,000
-$1 to -$500

States where high-minority districts received more funding than low-minority districts

$0 to $500
$500 to $1,000
$1,001 to $2,000
$2,000+

Note: Hawaii is not shown because data are not available.

Source: Funding Gaps 2006, The Education Trust, 2006

Only 5 percent of white students attend such high-poverty schools.[2] (*See graph, p. 7.*)

These schools, mostly urban, aren't making the grade, even in the context of lagging achievement in American schools overall.

Although states show significant variations, nationwide "71 percent of eighth-graders are not reading at grade level," and the percentage shoots up to between 80 and 90 percent for students of color, says former Gov. Bob Wise, D-W.Va., now president of the Alliance for Excellent Education, a broad-based coalition that advocates for academically stronger high schools.

Furthermore, of the approximately 15,000 U.S. high schools, 2,000 — mostly in cities — account for half of the nation's school dropouts, says Wise.

When President George W. Bush joined Massachusetts Sen. Edward M. Kennedy and other congressional Democrats to enact the No Child Left Behind Act (NCLB) in 2002, a key aim was requiring states to report achievement scores for all student groups. That ensured that lagging scores of low-income and minority students wouldn't be masked by having only state or district overall average scores reported.[3]

This year, Congress is expected to provide funding to keep the law in operation, but there's considerable disagreement about where federal education law should go next, and lawmakers may wait until next year to consider revisions (*See p. 20*).

NCLB's test-score reporting requirements "make it more possible to look at whether schools are doing well just for more affluent students or for poor students" as well, and that's valuable, says Jeffrey Henig, professor of political science and education at Columbia University's Teachers College.

But some supporters, including President Bush, say the NCLB has done more than just improve data-gathering, arguing that the law itself has pushed achievement upward. "Fourth-graders are reading better. They've made more progress in five years than in the previous 28 years combined," he said on March 2.[4]

Many education analysts disagree with that rosy assessment. The small improvement in fourth-grade reading and mathematics scores is part of a long-term trend, which began years before NCLB was even enacted, said Harvard University Professor of Education Daniel M. Koretz. "There's not any evidence that shows anything has changed" since NCLB, he said.[5]

And for urban schools, the post-NCLB picture is especially grim.

Of the non-achieving schools in New York state, for example, 90 percent are in cities and 80 percent in the state's five biggest cities, says David Hursh, an associate professor of teaching and curriculum at the University of Rochester's Margaret Warner Graduate School of Education.

The gap between average reading scores of black and white fourth-graders narrowed by only one point on the 500-point National Assessment of Educational Progress test (NAEP) between 2002 and 2005, and the narrowing appears to be part of a long-term trend, since it narrowed by three points between 1998 and 2005. Between 2002 and 2005, the reading-score gap between white and black eighth-graders actually widened, from 25 points to 28 points.[6]

The continuing severe achievement gap, newly high-lighted by NCLB's data-reporting requirements, leaves lawmakers and educators scratching their heads about what to do next.

Some analysts say lagging achievement in urban schools demonstrates that poor families in poor

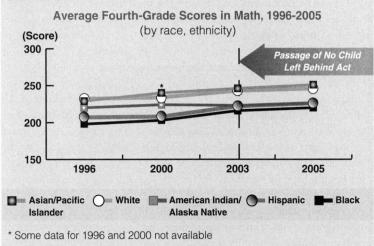

All Racial/Ethnic Groups Improved on Test

Fourth-graders in all racial and ethnic groups began modestly improving in math on the National Assessment for Educational Progress several years before passage of the No Child Left Behind Act.

Average Fourth-Grade Scores in Math, 1996-2005 (by race, ethnicity)

* Some data for 1996 and 2000 not available

Source: U.S. Department of Education, National Center for Education Statistics

communities require much more intense interventions than middle-class students, including better teachers and longer school days as well as improved health care, nutrition and parenting education.

A public school enrolling mainly middle-class white students has a one-in-four chance of producing good test scores, across years and in different subject matter, according to Douglas N. Harris, assistant professor of education policy at the University of Wisconsin, Madison. A school with a predominantly low-income minority population has a 1-in-300 chance of doing so.[7]

Experts blame the poor outcome on the fact that urban schools, like all schools, are staffed and organized to provide substantial extra help to only 15 percent of students and curriculum enrichment to another 15, while "the students in the middle are supposed to take care of themselves," says Robert Balfanz, associate research scientist at the Johns Hopkins University Center on the Social Organization of Schools and associate director of the Talent Development High School program, a reform initiative in 33 schools nationwide. The formula for extra help fits most suburban schools, "but in urban schools

50 to 60 percent, and sometimes up to 80 percent, of the kids are 'high-needs,' defined as English-as-a-second-language students, special-education students or students below grade level or with severe attendance problems.

"We're not set up to respond when that many kids need one-on-one tutoring, monitoring of their attendance on a daily basis, [or] people calling up to say, 'Glad you came today,'" Balfanz says.

One of the biggest problems is the kind of "student mobility" experienced by Jeanette, the Houston dropout.

"Homelessness is much underreported," says James F. Lytle, a professor at the University of Pennsylvania and former school superintendent in Trenton, N.J. "Statistics are based on who's in shelters and on the streets. But 20 to 30 percent of our kids were living in 'serial households' on a day-to-day basis," or moving about from parents to grandparents to relatives to friends — not living in the same house all the time.

Inner-city schools have a 40 to 50 percent student-mobility rate, which means up to half the students change schools at least once a year because of parents losing or changing jobs, evictions and other factors, says Columbia University's Henig. That disrupts students' ability to keep up with work and build relationships with the adults in a school.

In addition, city students miss school for a wide range of reasons, including high asthma rates; lack of school buses, forcing kids to get to school on their own, often through unsafe neighborhoods; and family responsibilities, like caring for younger siblings.

"Imagine the teacher's dilemma in a classroom where the population is different every day," says Balfanz.

But some conservative analysts argue that a large proportion of high-needs students is still no reason for schools to fail.

"Schools frequently cite social problems like poverty . . . and bad parenting as excuses for their own poor performance," said Jay P. Greene, a senior fellow at the Manhattan Institute, a conservative think tank. "This argument that schools are helpless in the face of social problems is not supported by hard evidence. . . . The truth is that certain schools do a strikingly better job than others," including public, private and charter schools.[8]

Some educators say one solution for low-quality urban schools is establishing publicly funded "charter" schools and awarding vouchers for private-school tuition.[9] When choice is expanded, "urban public schools that once had a captive clientele must improve the education they provide or else students . . . will go elsewhere," said Greene.[10]

But others argue that lessons from successful urban schools, including charters, demonstrate that raising low-income students' achievement requires resources and staff commitment that may be tough for the nation to muster.

"Teachers in high-poverty urban schools are as much as 50 percent more likely to . . . leave than those in low-poverty schools," in part because of the intensity of the work, according to researchers at the University of California, Santa Cruz.[11]

A second-grade teacher fluent in Spanish who reported working 10 hours a day, six days a week said she'd probably stop teaching when she had children: "It's too time-consuming and energy-draining," she said.[12]

"None of the teachers in our sample could conceive of being a successful urban teacher without an extraordinary — perhaps unsustainable — commitment to the work," the researchers commented.[13]

Not just schools but communities must help in the effort to improve students' performance.

"There ought to be a parade through the heart of town" every time a student achieves an academic goal, says Hugh B. Price, a fellow at the Brookings Institution, a liberal think tank. "We need to wrap and cloak kids in this message of achievement." That's how the military successfully trains soldiers, Price says. "They will praise anything that's good."

Schools and communities also have a role in helping parents better equip their children for school, says Mayor Douglas H. Palmer of Trenton, N.J., president of the National Conference of Democratic Mayors. "You don't have to be rich to talk to your child, help her build vocabulary and learn to reason and negotiate," as psychologists recommend, he says. "We can help parents with these skills."

As educators and lawmakers debate the next steps to improving urban schools, here are some of the questions being asked:

Has the No Child Left Behind law helped urban students?

NCLB was intended to improve overall academic achievement and raise achievement for minority and low-income students, in particular, mainly by requiring more student testing, getting schools to report test data separately for student groups including minorities and the poor and requiring schools to employ better-qualified teachers.

The law, scheduled for reauthorization this year, gets praise for focusing attention on the so-called achievement gap between minority and low-income students and their middle-class counterparts. But critics say the legislation doesn't do enough to assure that low-performing urban schools get the excellent teachers they need.

Student achievement also has improved slightly under the law, some advocates point out. "Is NCLB really paying off? The answer is yes," U.S. Chamber of Commerce Senior Vice President Arthur J. Rothkopf told a joint House-Senate committee hearing on March 13. While current testing data is still "abysmal," it nevertheless "represents improvement from where this nation was" before the law.

The law has benefited urban schools by raising reading scores for African-American and Hispanic fourth- and eighth-graders and math scores for African-American and Hispanic fourth-graders to "all-time highs." Achievement gaps in reading and math between white fourth-graders and African-American and Hispanic fourth-graders also have diminished since NCLB, he noted.[14]

NCLB's data-reporting requirements have "lifted the carpet" to reveal two previously unrecognized facts about American education — "the continuing under-performance of the whole system and the achievement gap" for low-income and minority students, says Daniel A. Domenech, senior vice president and top urban-education adviser for publisher McGraw-Hill Education and former superintendent of Virginia's vast Fairfax County Public Schools.[15]

And while some critics complain that NCLB gave the federal government too much say over education — traditionally a state and local matter — "there needs to be a strong federal role for these kids" in low-income urban schools "because they have been left behind," says Gary Ratner, a public-interest lawyer who is founding executive director of the advocacy group Citizens for Effective Schools. "States and localities have not stepped up."

Now NCLB "has got the country's attention," and when Congress reauthorizes the law, "the federal role can be redirected to focus on Title I schools" — those serving a large proportion of disadvantaged students — "and do more of the things that professional educators support," Ratner says.

NCLB's requirement that every school "have very qualified teachers is good," says Gary Orfield, a professor of social policy at the Harvard Graduate School of Education and director of The Civil Rights Project.

But critics argue that NCLB doesn't put muscle behind the high-quality teacher requirement and sets unrealistic goals and timetables for school progress.

NCLB actually "incentivizes teachers to leave failing schools," the last thing lawmakers intended, says Jennifer King-Rice, an economist who is associate professor of education policy at the University of Maryland, College Park. "Teachers say, 'I can't produce the AYP [average yearly progress] results'" the law calls for in low-performing schools with few resources and, frustrated, go elsewhere, she says. Nevertheless, it's still unclear whether and how the government can enforce the qualified-teacher rule. (*See graphs, p. 6.*)

The law provides no additional funding to help schools meet the teacher-quality goal, said Richard J. Murnane, professor of education and society at the Harvard Graduate School of Education. "Teaching in these schools is extremely difficult work," and "very few school districts provide extra pay or other inducements to attract talented teachers to these schools.[16]

"As a result, all too often these schools are left with the teachers other schools don't want," he continued. "And the teachers who do have options exercise seniority rights to leave . . . as soon as they can."[17]

The achievement targets set by NCLB are panned by many. The main goal schools must meet is moving kids over a standardized-testing threshold from "basic" or "below basic" understanding of reading and math to a "proficient" level or above. But focusing on that narrow goal as the key measure by which schools are judged created bad incentives to game the system, many analysts say.

Rather than concentrating on raising overall achievement or trying to give the most help to students who score lowest, many schools concentrate "on students who are on the bubble" — those who need to raise their scores by only a few points to move into the "proficient" range — and "forget the others," says Patrick McQuillan, an associate professor of education at Boston College's Lynch

Minority Enrollment and Teacher Quality

In Illinois, 88 percent of the schools that were virtually 100 percent minority ranked in the lowest quartile of the state's Teacher Quality Index (graph at left). By comparison, only 1 percent of the all-minority schools ranked in the highest quartile (right). High-quality teachers have more experience, better educations and stronger academic skills. Similar patterns are found in most other states.

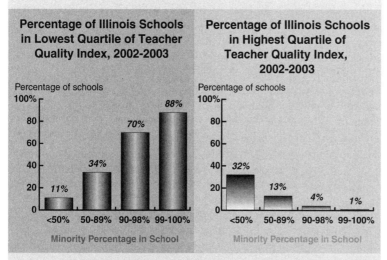

Percentage of Illinois Schools in Lowest Quartile of Teacher Quality Index, 2002-2003

Percentage of schools

<50%	50-89%	90-98%	99-100%
11%	34%	70%	88%

Minority Percentage in School

Percentage of Illinois Schools in Highest Quartile of Teacher Quality Index, 2002-2003

Percentage of schools

<50%	50-89%	90-98%	99-100%
32%	13%	4%	1%

Minority Percentage in School

Source: "Teaching Inequality: How Poor and Minority Students Are Shortchanged on Teacher Quality," The Education Trust, June 2006

School of Education. Schools that succeed at pushing the scores of "bubble" students up by a few points are deemed successful, according to current NCLB standards, even if they leave the neediest students even farther behind, he says.

The law's pronouncement that 100 percent of U.S. students will test at the "proficient" level is simply unrealistic, some critics say.

"We've never fully funded education in the United States," and achievement continues to lag far below the "proficient" level, especially for low-income students, says Domenech. So "let's not kid around and say that by 2014" all students will be academically proficient, he says. "That's like saying, 'I'm going to push you out the window, and I know you can fly.' "

Furthermore, NCLB's focus on a handful of standardized tests as the sole measures of children's progress puts teachers in an ethical bind that "definitely lowers their morale," says Marshalita Sims Peterson, an

associate professor of education at Atlanta's Spelman College, an historically black school for women.

Teachers in training are taught that students are individuals with a wide variety of learning styles, and that no single assessment can define a student, says Peterson. The NCLB's excessive focus on a single measurement of achievement "leaves the teacher in an awful position" she says. "You need to keep the job, but when you are actually completing that form" stating the single score "for a third-grader, you're asking, 'Is that all there is to this child?' "

Should governments make schools more racially and economically diverse?

Today, most African-American and Latino students attend urban schools with a high concentration of low-income students and very few white classmates.

Some advocates argue that the country has backtracked to an era of separate but unequal schools and say government programs aimed at creating more racially and socioeconomically diverse schools are good tools for narrowing the achievement gap. Opponents of government interference with children's attendance at neighborhood schools argue that with residential neighborhoods increasingly segregated by race and income, school integration is unrealistic, and that governments should focus instead on improving achievement in urban schools.[18]

"The effort to get the right racial balance is misguided" and represents a kind of "liberal racism — a belief that black children need to be in school with white children to learn," says Stephan Thernstrom, a history professor at Harvard University and a fellow at the conservative Manhattan Institute.

If integration "can be managed naturally, that's fine, but there is no clear correlation that can be drawn from data" showing it's important for closing the achievement gap, Thernstrom says. He rejects as incomplete and flawed studies that suggest integration does make a big difference. Furthermore, "if you need a white majority to learn," learning will soon be impossible in America, since Hispanic, Asian and African-American populations are growing faster than the current white majority, he notes.

Racial concentration is not the same as segregation and doesn't stand in the way of achievement, said his wife, Manhattan Institute Senior Fellow Abigail Thernstrom. School districts are powerless to change housing demographics, making it highly unlikely that racial concentration of students ever could be ended, she said.[19]

Some school districts are attempting to integrate lower-income and higher-income students, rather than integrating schools based on race. But Abigail Thernstrom argued that giving children a longer commute to schools outside their neighborhoods, for any reason, simply wastes time better spent in the classroom. "Busing doesn't raise the level of achievement," she told C-SPAN. "Now they're going to start busing on the basis of social class. And I have a very simple view of that. Stop moving the kids around and teach them."[20]

Meanwhile, some charter schools — such as the Knowledge Is Power Program (KIPP), begun in Houston — are making great strides in reducing the urban achievement gap, and for the most part those schools are not racially integrated, wrote *New York Times Magazine* features editor Paul Tough last year.

Most of the 70 schools that make up the three charter networks he observed have "only one or two white children enrolled, or none at all," he noted. Leaders of the networks, all of them white, actually intend to educate their students separately from middle-class students, according to Tough. However, unlike those who've argued that schools can be "separate but equal," the successful high-intensity charter schools aim for "separate but better." Their founders argue that

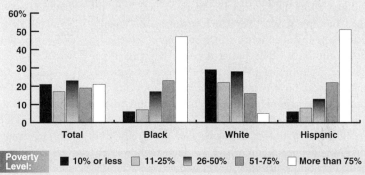

Blacks, Hispanics Attend High-Poverty Schools

Black and Hispanic students are more likely to be concentrated in high-poverty schools than white students. Forty-seven percent of black and 51 percent of Hispanic fourth-graders were in the highest-poverty schools in 2003 vs. 5 percent of white fourth-graders. By contrast, only 6 percent of black and Hispanic fourth-graders were in the lowest-poverty schools compared with 29 percent of whites.

Source: "The Condition of Education 2004 in Brief," National Center for Education, June 2004

"students who enter middle school significantly behind grade level don't need the same good education that most American middle-class students receive; they need a better education," he said.[21]

But many advocates argue that data show a proven way to improve education for thousands of low-income students rather than for the handful that attend the highly successful charter schools is integration of minority and poor students with middle-class children.

School desegregation by race "has clear academic benefits," wrote R. Scott Baker, an associate professor of education at Wake Forest University. Data from Charlotte, N.C., show that the longer both black and white students spent in desegregated elementary schools, the higher their standardized test scores in middle and high school. Research also suggests that "where school desegregation plans are fully and completely implemented," local housing also becomes more integrated.[22]

In the 1960s and '70s some federal courts mandated programs to help urban minority families move to middle-class white suburbs. Long-term data from those cases show that children who moved did better than those who stayed behind, according to Howell S. Baum, a professor of urban studies and planning at the University of Maryland. In St. Louis, 50 percent of the black students who moved to the suburbs graduated from high school, compared to 26 percent of those who remained in the high-minority, low-income urban schools.[23]

Many policy analysts agree that segregating low-income children in some public schools "perpetuates failure," wrote the Century Foundation's Task Force on the Common School. Nevertheless, there is an "equally durable political consensus that nothing much can be done about it." The panel argued that this must change: "Eliminating the harmful effects of concentrated school poverty is the single most important step that can be taken for improving education in the United States."[24]

"Dozens of studies" dating back to the 1960s "find that low-income children have . . . larger achievement gains over time when they attend middle-class schools," said the panel.[25]

"The tragedy right now is that places that were once forced to [integrate their schools] now aren't allowed to," says Orfield of The Civil Rights Project. "That will be seen as a cosmic blunder" for white Americans as well, he said. "We're not preparing ourselves for the multiracial society and world" of the 21st century.

Are teachers prepared to teach successfully in urban classrooms?

Urban schools have high teacher turnover, low test scores and many reported discipline problems. Furthermore, most of America's teaching force still consists of white, middle-class women, while urban schoolchildren are low-income minorities, creating a culture gap that may be hard to bridge.

Consequently, some analysts argue that today's teachers aren't prepared to teach successfully in urban classrooms for a variety of reasons, from discipline to second-language issues. Others, however, point to sterling examples of teachers and schools that do succeed and argue that the real problem is teachers not following good examples.

Fifth-grade teacher Rafe Esquith, at the Hobart Elementary School in central Los Angeles, routinely coaches his urban Korean and Central American-immigrant students to top standardized-test scores. Furthermore, his classes produce Shakespearean plays so impressive they've been invited to perform with Britain's Royal Shakespeare Company, said Abigail Thernstrom.[26]

But despite Esquith's success, "nobody copies him," even in his own school, said Thernstrom. "I went to the fifth-grade [classroom] next door [to Esquith's] one day," and "it was perfectly clear nothing was going on." When Thernstrom suggested the teacher might copy Esquith's methods — which include beginning class as early as 6 a.m. and working with students at his home on weekends — he remarked that "it's an enormous amount of work."[27]

Today, around the country, "we do have shining examples" of schools that succeed at urban education, says Timothy Knowles, executive director of the University of Chicago's Center for Urban School Improvement and a former deputy school superintendent in Boston.

Ratner, of Citizens for Effective Schools, agrees. "I spent time in an elementary school in Chicago a few years ago where all the teachers were teaching reading," even at the upper grades, equipping students with the vocabulary and comprehension skills needed for future academic work, he says. "They had a good principal, and they were showing that it can be done."

But while successful urban schools and classrooms are out there, many education analysts say the know-how and resources needed to spread that success to millions of students are sorely lacking.

Some individual schools are closing the achievement gap for needy students, but "very few, if any" entire school districts have had equivalent success, says Knowles.

Charter schools also haven't seen their successes spread as widely as many hoped.

Out of Ohio's "300-plus charter schools," for example, "some . . . are indeed excellent, but too many are appalling," wrote analysts Terry Ryan and Quentin Suffran of the conservative Thomas B. Fordham Foundation in a recent report.[28]

There are reasons for that, said Mark Simon, director of the Center for Teacher Leadership at Johns Hopkins University, in Baltimore. "Teaching lower-class kids well is tougher than teaching middle-class kids." Furthermore, "it is surprising how little we know about teaching practices that cause students to succeed, particularly in high-poverty schools."[29]

"You have poverty in many districts, but in urban schools you have a concentration of it" that makes teaching successfully there much harder than in middle-class suburbs, says Timothy Shanahan, professor of urban education at the University of Illinois at Chicago and president of the International Reading Association. Schools are traditionally set up to deal with 15 to 20 percent of a student body having very high needs, says Shanahan. But urban schools usually have 50 percent or more of their students needing special attention of some kind, "and that's a huge burden on the teachers," he says.

"Literally, we have 5-year-olds who come into the Chicago school system not knowing their own names," he says. "I know local neighborhoods with gang problems, where the kids are up all night. Their mothers are hiding them under the bed to protect them from shootings in the street. Then teachers can't keep them awake in class."

The nation's rapidly growing Hispanic population is heavily concentrated in urban schools. That new phenomenon presents another tough obstacle for the urban teaching force, because "older teachers know nothing about working with non-native English speakers," says McQuillan of Boston College.

Not just language but race complicates urban-school teaching. As many as 81 percent of all teacher-education students are white women.[30]

"Those most often entering teaching continue to be white, monolingual, middle-class women," wrote Jocelyn A. Glazier, assistant professor of education at the University of North Carolina at Chapel Hill.[31]

Many teachers, especially white women, shy away from making tough demands on African-American students, according to a survey of urban community leaders by Wanda J. Blanchett, associate professor of urban special education at the University of Wisconsin, Milwaukee. "Especially with African-American males, you hear the teachers say, 'Oh, he is such a nice kid.' But . . . this irks me when teachers baby their students to death instead of pushing. . . . I get that a lot when you have white teachers who have never worked with black students from the urban environment."[32]

Many entering education students at Indiana University-Purdue University, in Indianapolis, balked at the school's fieldwork and student-teaching venues, which were in urban schools, wrote Professor Christine H. Leland and Professor Emeritus Jerome C. Harste. "They saw our program's urban focus as an obstacle to their career goals" of teaching in schools like the suburban ones most had attended.[33]

Some viewed urban students as an alien race they didn't want to learn to know. "Students rarely felt the need to interrogate their underlying assumption that poor people deserve the problems they have" or "spent any time talking or thinking about issues such as poverty or racism," Leland and Harste wrote. After student teaching, however, some students changed their plans and applied to become urban teachers.[34]

Race is a taboo subject in America, which some analysts say compounds urban teachers' difficulties. Many teacher-preparation programs center on an effort not to see or at least not to acknowledge race differences, according to Glazier. But "by claiming not to notice [race], the teacher is saying that she is dismissing one of the most salient features of a child's identity."[35]

"Many teachers believe that if they recognize a student's race or discuss issues of ethnicity in their classroom, they might be labeled as insensitive and racist," wrote Central Michigan University graduate student in education Dreyon Wynn and Associate Dean Dianne L. H. Mark. But white teachers' deliberate color-blindness ignores students "unique culture, beliefs, perceptions, [and] values," blocking both learning and helpful student-teacher relationships, Mark and Wynn argue.[36]

BACKGROUND

Educating the Poor

American education has long struggled with providing equal education for the poor, racial minorities and non-English-speaking immigrants. Until recently, however, even people who never made it through high school could usually find a good job. A new, global, technical economy may be changing that.

In the earliest years in the United States, schooling wasn't widespread. A farm-based economy made extensive education unnecessary for most people. In 1805, more than 90 percent of Americans had completed a fifth-grade education or less, and education for richer people was often conducted by private tutors.[37]

1950s-1960s *Concerns grow over student achievement and racially segregated schools.*

1954 Supreme Court rules in *Brown v. Board of Education* that separate schools are inherently unequal.

1965 Title I of the new Elementary and Secondary Education Act (ESEA) targets the largest pool of federal education assistance to help schools serving disadvantaged students.

1966 Sociologist James S. Coleman's "Equality of Educational Opportunity" report concludes that disadvantaged African-American students do better in integrated classrooms.

1969 National Assessment of Educational Progress (NAEP) tests launched but report statewide average scores only, allowing states to mask lagging achievement among poor and minority students.

1970s-1980s *Latinos are becoming most segregated minority in U.S. schools. "Magnet schools" are established. School integration efforts gradually end.*

1973 Supreme Court rules in *San Antonio Independent School District v. Rodriguez* the Constitution does not guarantee equal education for all children. . . . In *Keyes v. School District No. 1*, the court bans city policies that segregate Denver schools.

1990s-2000s *Steady gains in African-American students' test scores over the past two decades begin to taper off by decade's end. . . . Poverty concentrates in cities. . . . Governors lead efforts to raise education standards.*

1990 New Jersey Supreme Court rules in *Abbott v. Burke* the state must provide more funding for poor schools than for richer ones.

1991 Minnesota enacts first charter-school law.

1994 In reauthorizing ESEA, Congress requires states receiving Title I funding for disadvantaged students to hold them to the same academic standards as all students.

1995 Knowledge Is Power Program charter schools launched in Houston and New York City. . . . Boston

creates Pilot School program to research ideas for urban-school improvement.

1999 Florida establishes first statewide school-voucher program.

2000 Countywide, income-based school integration launched in Raleigh, N.C.

2002 Cambridge, Mass., schools begin integration based on income.

2002 No Child Left Behind Act (NCLB) requires states to report student test scores "disaggregated" by race, income and gender to avoid masking the failing scores of some groups. . . . U.S. Supreme Court rules in favor of Ohio's school-voucher program, which allows public funding for tuition at Cleveland parochial schools. . . . State takes over Philadelphia's bankrupt school system, allows private companies to run some schools.

2005 Hoping to halt isolation of the lowest-income students in inner-city schools, Omaha, Neb., tries but fails to annex neighboring suburban districts.

2006 Department of Education admits that few students in failing city schools receive the free tutoring NCLB promised and that no states have met the 2006 deadline for having qualified teachers in all classrooms. . . . Government Accountability Office finds that nearly one-third of public schools, most in low-income and minority communities, need major repairs.

2007 Gov. Deval L. Patrick, D-Mass., puts up $6.5 million to help schools lengthen their hours. . . . Democratic Mayor Adrian Fenty, of Washington, D.C., is the latest of several mayors to take control of schools. . . . New York City Schools Chancellor Joel Klein says he will fire principals of schools with lagging test scores. . . . Teachers' unions slam report calling for all high-school seniors to be proficient in reading and math by 2014. . . . Houston school district calls for state to replace NCLB-related standardized periodic testing on math and reading with traditional end-of-course subject-matter exams.

2007

June 2007 — U.S. Supreme Court invalidates school-attendance-zone plans used in Seattle and Louisville to achieve greater racial diversity. The 5-4 ruling in *Parents Involved in Community Schools v. Seattle Dist. No. 1* said the Seattle School District's plan to use race as a consideration in student assignments was unconstitutional.

2008

Nov. 26, 2008 — Washington, D.C., School Chancellor Michelle Rhee appears on the cover of *Time*.

2009-2010

Educational reforms have been made by 28 states under the administration's $4 billion state grant education initiative, Race to the Top. The number of reforms is triple that of the previous two years.

2009 — Education Secretary Arne Duncan rescinds pending scholarships under the D.C. Opportunity Scholarship Program, and Congress declines to reauthorize.

2010 — Obama administration unveils its blueprint to overhaul No Child Left Behind Act. . . . In the District of Columbia in June, school officials and the teachers' union finalize a contract that, in addition to granting a retroactive pay increase, requires all teachers in the system to be evaluated in part on whether their students' test scores improve, and offers sizable pay increases to teachers who opt for and succeed in a special new pay-for-performance arrangement. . . . Civil Rights Project at UCLA reviews school integration efforts and calls on the Obama administration to issue guidance on how race can be considered in public education. . . . Washington, D.C., School Chancellor Rhee dismisses 241 teachers.

State legislatures were just beginning to debate whether to establish free tax-funded schools for all children.[38] Nevertheless, even in those early days, some religious and other charitable groups considered it a moral duty to educate the poor. In New York City, for example, the Association of Women Friends for the Relief of the Poor opened a charity school in 1801. By 1823 the group was providing free elementary education for 750 children, with some public assistance. Similar charity schools sprang up in most other major cities.

But as all states began establishing public education systems — between the late 18th and the mid-19th century — questions over equality in education arose, first for black students and later for immigrants. "When public schools opened in Boston in the late 18th century, black children were neither barred nor segregated," wrote Derrick Bell, a visiting professor at the New York University School of Law. "But by 1790, racial insults and mistreatment had driven out all but three or four black children."[39]

Later, some black families joined with white liberals to form black-only schools in Massachusetts and in other states. But complaints about poor conditions and poor teaching in those schools led others to sue for integrated education.

Even in the early 19th century, some courts were bothered by race-based inequities in education, said Bell. A federal court struck down a Kentucky law directing that school taxes collected from white people would maintain white schools, and taxes from blacks would operate black schools. "Given the great disparities in taxable resources" this would result in an inferior education for black children, the court said.[40]

Around the 1820s, waves of non-English immigration began, raising new controversies over educating poor children of sometimes-despised ethnicities.

Before 1820, most U.S. immigrants were English, and a few were Dutch. But between 1820 and 1840 Irish immigrants became the first in a long parade of newcomers judged inferior by the predominantly English population. A rising tide of immigration in the late 19th and early 20th centuries included many non-English-speakers — Italians, Germans, Chinese, Russians, Poles and many others — who posed new challenges for schools and were looked down on by many citizens.

The new immigrants generally clustered in cities, the economic engines of the time, and overcrowded city schools were charged with integrating them into American life. Critics charged that the urban schools used rigid instruction and harsh discipline to control classrooms

Dropouts' Problems Often Begin Early

Clear warning signs appear, such as skipping class.

With the baby-boom generation on the verge of retirement, sustaining the American workforce and economy depends on having a cadre of new young workers to replace them, says former Gov. Bob Wise, D-W.Va., now president of the Alliance for Excellent Education. But with jobs in the fastest-growing economic sectors now requiring at least a high-school diploma and, often, two years or more of post-high-school training, coming up with an adequately trained new workforce won't be easy, Wise says.

The annual graduation rate has risen from a little over 50 percent per year in the late 1960s to 73.9 percent in 2003. If it's to rise higher, however, the improvement must come among poor and minority students, mostly in urban schools, who are far less likely than others to earn diplomas.[1]

For example, while about two-thirds of all students who enter ninth grade graduate four years later, on-time graduation rates for minority and low-income students, especially males, are much lower. In 2001, for example, only about 50 percent of African-American students and 51 percent of Latino students graduated on time, compared to 75 percent of white students and 77 percent of Asian and Pacific Islanders.[2]

Students with family incomes in the lowest 20 percent dropped out of school at six times the average rate of wealthier students.[3]

In about a sixth of American high schools, the freshman class routinely shrinks by 40 percent or more by the time students reach senior year. For the most part, those schools serve low-income and minority students. Nearly half of African-American students, 40 percent of Latino students and 11 percent of white students attend high schools where

graduation is not the norm. A high school with a majority of students who are racial or ethnic minorities is five times more likely to promote only 50 percent or fewer freshmen to senior status within four years than a school with a white majority.[4]

Meanwhile, the earning power of dropouts has been dropping for three decades. For example, the earnings of male dropouts fell by 35 percent between 1971 and 2002, measured in 2002 dollars. Three-quarters of state prison inmates and 59 percent of federal inmates are dropouts. In 2001, only 55 percent of young adult dropouts were employed. Even the death rate is 2.5 times higher for people without a high-school education than for people with 13 years or more of schooling.[5]

But if the consequences are known, the cures may be harder to pinpoint.

Many educators say dropping out starts early. "Disengagement doesn't start in the ninth grade. It starts in fifth," says James F. Lytle, a University of Pennsylvania professor and former superintendent of the Trenton, N.J., public schools. For on-track students in middle-class schools, "middle school has the most interesting, exciting stuff in class" — science experiments, readings about interesting people in history and studies "of how the world works" — he says.

But once students are judged to be reading behind grade level, as happens with many urban fifth-graders, middle schools turn to "dumbed-down remedial work" that's below students' real intellectual level and leaves them bored and dispirited, Lytle says. It doesn't have to be that way, he says. "But I wish that educational courseware was farther down the road" of providing ways to combine skills teaching with subject matter that is at students' actual age level.

bursting with 60 or more children, many of whom spoke no English.

Two Tracks

In the economy of the early 20th century, however, there remained little need for most students to learn more than basic reading and writing, so the failure of poor urban schools to produce many graduates wasn't seen as a problem.

In current debates over U.S. education, "people aren't looking at education historically" and therefore expect American schools to do things they were never designed to do, says Ratner of Citizens for Effective Schools.

"We consciously decided to have a two-track system," he says. In the early 20th century, education experts generally agreed that "in the industrial age there are lots of immigrants and poor people, and most are going to

"Kids disengage early," says Lalitha Vasudevan, an assistant professor at Columbia University's Teachers College who works in an education program for young African-American males who've been diverted from jail and are mostly dropouts. "Often, early on, they've had teachers say things to them that they interpret as, 'You don't really care that I'm here,'" she says.

Dropping out "is not a decision that is made on a single morning," says a report from the Bill & Melinda Gates Foundation. In an extensive survey of dropouts, researchers found that "there are clear warning signs for at least one-to-three years" before students drop out, such as frequently missing school, skipping class, being held back a grade or frequently transferring among schools.[6]

Some key factors cited by the dropouts in the Gates study: Schools don't respond actively when students skip class and don't provide an orderly and safe environment. "In middle school, you have to go to your next class or they are going to get you," said a young male dropout from Philadelphia. "In high school, if you don't go to class, there isn't anybody who is going to get you. You just do your own thing."[7]

Lytle says cities could also establish post-dropout academies, like the Dropout Recovery High School he started in Trenton, which helped increase that city's graduation numbers.

"Rather than defining the whole problem as stopping dropouts, we can also reach out to those who already have," he says. "There are a slew of people around" who are out of school and would like to go back, from teenage mothers caring for their children to 60-year-olds, he says. "They need a school that is built around their lives. I simply don't understand why urban districts haven't been more imaginative" about this.

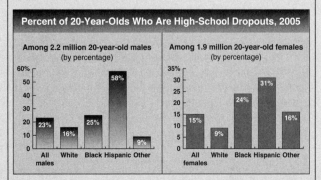

Majority of Dropouts Are Hispanic, Black

More than 50 percent of 20-year-old male high-school dropouts are Hispanic or African-American (graph at left). By comparison, 55 percent of the females are black or Hispanic (graph at right).

Percent of 20-Year-Olds Who Are High-School Dropouts, 2005

Among 2.2 million 20-year-old males (by percentage): All males 23%, White 16%, Black 25%, Hispanic 58%, Other 9%

Among 1.9 million 20-year-old females (by percentage): All females 15%, White 9%, Black 24%, Hispanic 31%, Other 16%

Source: "The Costs and Benefits of an Excellent Education for All of America's Children," Teachers College, Columbia University, January 2007

[1] Nancy Martin and Samuel Halperin, *Whatever It Takes: How Twelve Communities are Reconnecting Out-of-School Youth,* American Youth Policy Forum, www.aypf.org/publications/WhateverItTakes/WITfull.pdf.

[2] *Ibid.*

[3] *Ibid.*

[4] Robert Balfanz and Nettie Legters, "Locating the Dropout Crisis," Center for Social Organization of Schools, Johns Hopkins University, June 2004.

[5] Martin and Halperin, *op. cit.*

[6] John M. Bridgeland, John J. DiIulio, Jr. and Karen Burke Morison, *The Silent Epidemic: Perspectives of High School Dropouts*, Bill & Melinda Gates Foundation, March 2006.

[7] Quoted in *ibid.*

work on the assembly line, so how about if we create an academic track and a general/vocational track" mostly for the poor?

The school system that we have "was never set up to educate all students to the levels of proficiency now being asked for," Ratner says.

"I graduated exactly 40 years ago, and then about half the kids — 52 percent — were graduating," says Wise of the Alliance for Excellent Education. "And the non-graduates could still get good jobs."

But today "the fastest-growing sectors of the economy require two years of post high-school training," says Daniel J. Cardinali, president of Communities In Schools, a dropout-prevention group that helps school districts bring services like tutoring and health care to needy students.

The "Behavior Gap" Between Black and White Students

Many educators blame a system that's middle-class and white-centered.

Data from around the country indicate that black students, especially males, are cited much more often for disciplinary infractions than whites. The resulting "behavior gap" parallels the much-talked-about academic achievement gap.

Many analysts blame the phenomenon in part on a "culture clash" between black students, many poor, and an education system that's white-centered and middle-class. But there's little agreement about exactly what the gap means and what to do about it.

"You find the gap in all schools," including wealthy ones, says Clara G. Muschkin, a researcher at the Duke University Center for Child and Family Policy. Nevertheless, some evidence suggests there may also be a behavior gap between richer and poorer students, which accounts for just under a third of the black-white gap, Muschkin says.

In North Carolina schools, the racial gap "is persistent at all the grades" but is widest in seventh grade, says Muschkin. About 30 percent of black seventh-graders and 14 percent of whites have at least one disciplinary infraction reported during the school year.

African-American male students have the highest rates of suspensions and expulsions in most metropolitan areas around the country, according to Denise L. Collier, a doctoral candidate in education at California State University, Los Angeles. In New York, for example, where African-American males are 18 percent of the student population, they account for 39 percent of school suspensions and 50 percent of expulsions. In Los Angeles, black males make up 6 percent of the population but account for 18 percent of suspensions and 15 percent of expulsions.[1]

Some educators say that many urban African-American students don't learn at home the kinds of communication behaviors that are the norm for the middle class, and that this lack of background accounts for much of the gap.

"Americans of a certain background learn . . . early on and employ . . . instinctively" techniques like sitting up straight, asking questions and tracking a speaker with their eyes in order to take in information, said David Levin, a founder of the Knowledge Is Power Program (KIPP) charter schools, which serve mainly black and Hispanic students in several cities.[2]

When students in one Levin class were asked to "give us the normal school look," they responded by staring off into space and slouching, recounted *New York Times Magazine* editor Paul Tough in an article last year on successful urban charter schools. "Middle-class Americans know intuitively that 'good behavior' is mostly a game with established rules; the KIPP students seemed to be experiencing the pleasure of being let in on a joke," Tough observed.[3]

Behavior like a proper in-school work ethic has to be taught "in the same way we have to teach adding fractions with unlike denominators," said Dacia Toll, founder of the Amistad Academy charter school in New Haven, Conn. "But once children have got the work ethic and the commitment to others and to education down, it's actually pretty easy to teach them."

The academic gap that puts many black students in remedial instruction as they move through school may worsen the problem, says Robert Balfanz, associate research scientist at the Johns Hopkins University Center on the Social Organization of Schools. "In traditional remedial

Calls in the 1990s for higher academic standards by groups like The Business Roundtable brought widespread attention to the problems of low student achievement, especially in low-income schools.

Today few question the premise that all students should attain higher levels of literacy, mathematical problem-solving and critical thinking. Many who work in schools

argue that simply setting higher standards isn't nearly enough, however, especially for urban schools where most students already are behind grade level.

As standards rise, for example, "ninth-graders are increasingly placed in introductory algebra classes . . . despite skill gaps in fundamental arithmetic," wrote Balfanz and Ruth Curran Neild, research scientists at the instruction, I assume you know nothing, so I teach the times table" and basic reading skills like letter sounds, he says. "But the majority of kids behind can actually read at a basic level. What they're missing is comprehension skill, vocabulary. So they get bored and frustrated."

Middle-class education majors student-teaching in urban schools found that using books about topics their students personally had encountered — including homelessness, racism and poverty — decreased discipline problems, even though the teachers initially resisted the books as inappropriate for children, according to Professor Christine H. Leland and Professor Emeritus Jerome C. Harste of Indiana University-Purdue University, Indianapolis. Once the student teachers broached the tough subject matter, they began reporting "fewer discipline problems . . . the children listened carefully and engaged in thoughtful discussions when they perceived that the issues being discussed were worth their attention."[4]

Many African-American student discipline problems involve "defiance" issues such as acting threatening or making excessive noise rather than activities like drug use or leaving the classroom without permission, according to University of Virginia Assistant Professor Anne Gregory.[5]

Seventy-five percent of African-American disciplinary referrals were for "defiance" behaviors in a study Gregory cites, many more than for other ethnic groups. That may suggest that teachers judge African-American students' behavior more "subjectively" than that of other students, Gregory says. Based on their past feelings of being restricted and excluded, some African-American students may be more likely to act out when they perceive that teachers are being unfair, Gregory suggests.

"If I was this little Caucasian boy or this preppy girl, she wouldn't talk with me that way. I am like the opposite. I am this little thug . . . I mean, she don't know," one student in Gregory's study said of a teacher perceived to be unfair.[6]

Avoiding excessive discipline battles in urban schools requires a seemingly contradictory set of characteristics that not everyone can muster, said Franita Ware, a professor of education at Spelman College, a historically black school for women in Atlanta. Teachers who succeed tend to be "warm demanders," those whom "students believed . . . did not lower their standards" but also "were willing to help them."[7]

"Sometimes I mean-talk them in varying degrees of severity," one teacher told Ware. But "sometimes you have to go back and say, 'What was really going on with you when I yelled at you? I'm just so sorry.'"[8]

Often the adult is the provocateur in the behavior situation, even if they don't realize it, such as when a student finds the nurse's office door locked at 3:02 and starts pounding on it, says James F. Lytle, a professor at the University of Pennsylvania and former school superintendent in Trenton, N.J.

"A lot of it is just the way you talk to people — respect," Lytle says. "Many are so accustomed to being denigrated. The kids have so little that the protection of one's ego is very important."

---

[1] Denise L. Collier, "Sally Can Skip But Jerome Can't Stomp: Perceptions, Practice, and School Punishment (Preliminary Results)," paper presented at the American Educational Research Association annual meeting, San Francisco, Calif., April 2006.

[2] Quoted in Paul Tough, "What It Takes To Make a Student," *New York Times Magazine*, Nov. 26, 2006, p. 51.

[3] *Ibid.*

[4] Christine H. Leland and Jerome C. Harste, "Doing What We Want to Become: Preparing New Urban Teachers," *Urban Education*, January 2005, p. 67.

[5] Anne Gregory, "Justice and Care: Teacher Practices To Narrow the Racial Discipline Gap," paper presented at the American Educational Research Association annual conference, San Francisco, Calif., April 2006.

[6] Quoted in *ibid.*

[7] Franita Ware, "Warm Demander Pedagogy: Culturally Responsive Teaching that Supports A Culture of Achievement for African-American Students," *Urban Education*, July 2006, p. 427.

[8] Quoted in *ibid.*

Johns Hopkins University Center on the Social Organization of Schools.

But few resources exist to help kids catch up, "nor are there many curriculum materials that specifically target the spotty skills of urban ninth-graders," the Johns Hopkins researchers said. And when students reading behind grade level enter middle and high school, their "secondary-certified English teachers" — educated to teach high-school-level literature and composition — "are generally unprepared" to diagnose reading problems or to teach the comprehension strategies and background vocabulary they need. Science and history teachers are even less prepared to help, Balfanz and Neild said.[41]

AP Photo/Mike Derer

Edwin Bradley listens to his fifth-grade daughter Antoinette read at the South Street School library in Newark, N.J. One of the poorest in the state, the school district has been encouraged under a new program to support parental involvement in an attempt to improve student performance.

Retooling the school system to support higher standards may seem daunting, but "a quick walk through history" shows that it wouldn't be the first time the United States has made heroic efforts on education, says Wise. For example, "after World War II, you had soldiers coming home in need of better skills, and you had the GI Bill" to help them continue their educations.

Then "in the civil rights era we said, 'We believe that every child should be able to enter school,' and that happened," Wise says. "Now we're saying that every child should graduate."

For a time, the civil rights era seemed to be accelerating growing academic parity in learning, at least between black and white students. Following World War II, standardized test scores for black students began moving closer to white students' scores. The years from the 1960s to the '80s saw fully half of the black-white academic achievement gap eliminated, says The Civil Rights Project's Orfield.

In the late '80s, however, the progress of African-American students in closing the gap stalled, and between 1988 and 1994, average test scores for black students actually began falling.[42]

Minority Schools

U.S. schools briefly became more integrated after the civil rights battles of the 1950s and '60s, but shifting housing patterns have caused the concentration of poor, minority and non-English-speaking students in urban schools to rise for the past 25 years.

"One thing that's not fully understood is that, through a long historical process, we've concentrated our most needy students in a small subset of schools and districts" in rural and, mostly, urban areas, vastly increasing the burden those schools face in raising academic achievement, says Balfanz.

In its landmark 1954 *Brown v. Board of Education* ruling, the Supreme Court declared it illegal to intentionally segregate schools by race.[43] In 1964, Congress passed the Civil Rights Act, outlawing discrimination in any institution that received federal funds, including schools.[44] As a result, more schools accommodated lower-income students along with middle-class students, white students and students from other ethnic groups.

The civil rights era lasted a scant 20 years, however, and housing patterns and new waves of immigration soon led to concentrations of poor and minority students in many urban school districts again.

As early as 1974, the Supreme Court effectively set limits on how far racial integration of students could go. The court ruled in *Milliken v. Bradley* that the remedy to racial segregation in Detroit could not include moving children to schools in the surrounding suburbs.[45]

Then, in the 1980s, federal efforts to desegregate schools effectively ended. During the presidency of Ronald Reagan (1981-1989), the U.S. Justice Department backed off forcing states to comply with desegregation mandates. Two Supreme Court decisions in the early 1990s effectively declared the goal of black-white school integration had been addressed, as the court ruled that school districts could be excused from court-ordered busing if they had made good-faith efforts to integrate, even if they had not fully complied with court orders.[46]

At the same time, however, Hispanic students were becoming a new minority that concentrated in schools with bigger academic challenges than others, such as teaching English-language learners.

The segregation of Latino students soared during the civil rights era. In 1973, in *Keyes v. School District No. 1*, the Supreme Court outlawed policies in Denver that had the effect of segregating Hispanic and African-American children into separate schools. In ensuing years, however, this somewhat complex ruling was only spottily enforced, according to civil rights advocates.[47]

Today Latinos "are America's most segregated minority group," said Orfield. The average Latino student goes to a school that is less than 30 percent white, has a majority of poor children and an "increasing concentration" of students who don't speak English.[48]

Poor in School

Until around the 1970s, children of all races and classes attended urban schools, and their average achievement levels didn't draw the same alarmed attention as today. Urban sprawl and white flight from cities over the past three decades have not only increased the number of urban schools with high minority populations but also increased the concentration of urban poverty as well, increasing the burden on urban schools.

"Sprawl is a product of suburban pulls and urban pushes," said the University of Maryland's Baum. "Families move to the suburbs for good housing, open space. They leave cities to avoid bad schools, threats to safety . . . contact with other races and poor public services."[49]

Furthermore, minority children are more concentrated in urban areas than the general population, largely because white families with children move to suburbs while childless whites are more likely to remain in the city, said Baum. Nationally, in nearly all school districts with more than 25,000 students, interracial contact has declined since 1986.[50]

Even more than ethnic minorities, poor people have concentrated in cities, says Balfanz. Over the past 20 years, even in periods when overall poverty has dropped, "the cities have gotten poorer and the concentration of poverty there deeper."

Between 1960 and 1987, the national poverty rate for people in central cities rose from 13.4 percent to 15.7 percent. At the same time, the poverty rate for rural residents fell by one-half and for suburban residents by one-third. By 1991, 43 percent of people with incomes below the federal poverty line lived in central cities.[51]

"The nation's student population is two-thirds middle class (not eligible for federally subsidized lunches), yet one-quarter of American schools have a majority of students from low-income households," according to The Century Foundation.[52]

Among the burdens urban schools bear are poverty-related learning deficiencies children bring to school with them, regulations and economic barriers that limit urban-school resources, and a historical role as job providers in inner cities.

A large body of research shows that many low-income parents interact with their children in ways that hinder them in school, wrote Tough last year in *The New York Times Magazine*. For example, professional parents speak to their young children about two-and-a-half more times in an hour than poor parents do and encourage them verbally about six times more often than they discourage them; low-income parents discourage their children about three times as often as they encourage them, he said.

Unlike poor parents, middle-class parents also encourage their children to question, challenge and negotiate. In short, "in countless ways, the manner in which [poor children] are raised puts them at a disadvantage" in a school culture, Tough noted.[53]

For a variety of reasons, urban schools also have a much harder time keeping good teachers. "Many thousands — perhaps millions — of urban students don't have permanent, highly qualified teachers, ones with the skill to communicate important stuff to kids," says Kitty Kelly-Epstein, a professor of education at the Fielding Graduate University in Santa Barbara, Calif. In California, at least, state rules force some urban school districts to rely on temporary teachers because not enough applicants have required certifications, she says. "There never has been a time when low-income schools were fully staffed," she says.

With joblessness high in cities, especially for minority applicants, it's also "not uncommon" for school districts to be the major job source in the area, according to Johns Hopkins University Associate Professor of Education Elaine M. Stotko and colleagues. In a tradition that dates back to patronage systems in the early 20th century, urban politicians often interfere with schools' hiring the best managerial and teaching candidates by pressuring them to hand out jobs "as political favors."[54]

The Supreme Court is due to rule by the end of June in two race-based integration cases. With a new conservative majority, the court is widely expected to rule in favor of the white parents who are seeking to end race-based school integration in Seattle and Louisville, Ky. Decisions against the school districts could end many similar programs around the country, many of which were court-ordered in the past.[55]

But some school districts still worry that schools with high concentrations of minority and poor students harm achievement. Over the past several years, a few districts, including Raleigh, N.C., and Cambridge, Mass., have experimented with integrating students by socioeconomic

The Knowledge Is Power Program (KIPP) charter school in the Bronx, N.Y., boasts the highest test scores in the area. Although most KIPP schools are not racially integrated, they are reducing achievement gaps between black and white students.

status. In 2000, for example, the school board in Wake County, N.C., which includes Raleigh and its suburbs, replaced its racial integration system with the goal that no school should have 40 percent of students eligible for free or reduced-price lunch.[56]

Raleigh's effort was simpler politically than most, because the school district contains both the area's low-poverty and high-poverty schools. If the higher-income suburbs had been outside the district, political push-back would have made the program a tougher sell.

Some early Raleigh results look promising. On the state's 2005 High School End of Course exams, 63.8 percent of the low-income students passed, as did 64.3 percent of its African-American seniors, compared to pass rates in the high-40 and low 50-percent range for the state's other urban districts.[57]

CURRENT SITUATION

Congress Divided

The No Child Left Behind Act (NCLB), enacted in 2002, is intended to push American schools to raise achievement for all students, including low-income and minority children. As such, it represents one more step down a road that Congress embarked on in its 1994 reauthorization of the Elementary and Secondary Education Act — exerting federal influence to ensure that all students meet higher academic standards.

With NCLB up for reauthorization, Congress is struggling to figure out its next steps, with little apparent agreement on the horizon. With the press of other business, and strong disagreements in Congress about the education law, it's not clear that it will be reauthorized this year. The new congressional Democratic majority has already begun to hold hearings, however.

U.S. businesses have become increasingly involved in education policy, and many business leaders are urging Congress to continue and strengthen federal efforts to raise academic standards and provide incentives for states and localities to extensively retool their school systems to improve student achievement.

"Unless we transform the American high school, we will limit economic opportunities for millions of Americans," declared Microsoft Chairman Bill Gates at a Senate Health, Education, Labor and Pensions Committee hearing on March 7.[58]

Meanwhile, a group of conservative congressional Republicans has introduced legislation that would replace most of the NCLB achievement and reporting requirements that determine funding with block-grant funding that states could get whether they met NCLB standards or not. The measure would restore states and localities to their traditional role as prime overseers of schools, said Rep. Peter Hoekstra, R-Mich., who sponsored the legislation. "President Bush and I just see education fundamentally differently," he said. "The president believes in empowering bureaucrats in Washington, and I don't."[59]

But many congressional Democrats argue that a strengthened federal hand in education is warranted, partly because NCLB data now clearly reveal that the state-run systems of old have left so many poor and minority children disastrously behind.

Rep. George Miller, D-Calif., and Sen. Kennedy, key supporters of NCLB and chairs of the House and Senate committees that govern it, have both held pre-authorization hearings this year. Both say they're committed to increasing resources for struggling schools in a new bill, especially by supporting the hiring and training of more and better teachers.

"We know the law has flaws, but we also know that with common-sense changes and adequate resources, we can improve it by building on what we've learned," said Kennedy in a statement.

Would raising teacher pay help struggling schools?

YES — Patty Myers
Technology Coordinator, Great Falls (Montana) Public Schools

From Testimony on Behalf of the National Education Association before U.S. Senate Committee on Finance, March 20, 2007

Ensuring a highly qualified teacher in every classroom is critical to closing achievement gaps and maximizing student learning. No single factor will make a bigger difference in helping students reach high academic standards. . . .

Unfortunately, difficulty in attracting quality teachers and high turnover rates severely hamper the ability to maintain a high-quality learning environment. Approximately one-third of the nation's new teachers leave the profession during their first three years, and almost one-half leave during their first five years. And turnover in low-income schools is almost one-third higher than the rate in all schools.

The teaching profession has an average national starting salary of $30,377. Meanwhile, computer programmers start at an average of $43,635, public accounting professionals at $44,668 and registered nurses at $45,570.

Annual pay for teachers has fallen sharply over the past 60 years in relation to the annual pay of other workers with college degrees. The average earnings of workers with at least four years of college are now over 50 percent higher than the average earnings of a teacher. Congress should reward states that set a reasonable minimum starting salary for teachers and a living wage for support professionals working in school districts. NEA recommends that all teachers in America enter the classroom earning at least $40,000 annually.

NEA also supports advancing teacher quality at the highest-poverty schools by providing $10,000 federal salary supplements to National Board Certified Teachers. Congress also should fund grants to help teachers in high-poverty schools pay the fees and access professional supports to become certified.

Often schools with the greatest needs and, consequently, the most challenging working conditions have the most difficulty retaining talented teachers. . . . Many hard-to-staff schools are high-poverty inner-city school or rural schools that, as a consequence of their location in economically depressed or isolated districts, offer comparatively low salaries and lack [the] amenities with which other districts attract teachers.

NEA strongly supports federal legislation with financial incentives for teaching in high-poverty schools, such as the Teacher Tax Credit Act introduced in the 109th Congress. The bill would provide a non-refundable tax credit to educators who work at schools that are fully eligible for federal Title I funds for disadvantaged students and would help hard-to-staff schools retain the quality teachers they need to succeed.

NO — Jay P. Greene
Senior Fellow, Manhattan Institute

Posted on the Web, 2006

The common assertion that teachers are severely underpaid is so omnipresent that many Americans simply accept it as gospel. But the facts tell a different story.

The average teacher's salary does seem modest at first glance: about $44,600 in 2002 for all teachers. But when we compare it to what workers of similar skill levels in similar professions are paid, we find that teachers are not shortchanged.

People often fail to account for the relatively low number of hours that teachers work. Teachers work only about nine months per year. During the summer they can either work at other jobs or use the time off however else they wish. Either way, it's as much a form of compensation as a paycheck.

The most recent data indicate that teachers average 7.3 working hours per day, and that they work 180 days per year, or about 1,314 hours. Americans in normal 9-to-5 professions who take two weeks of vacation and another 10 paid holidays put in 1,928 hours. This means the average teacher's base salary is equivalent to a full-time salary of $65,440.

In 2002, elementary-school teachers averaged $30.75 per hour and high-school teachers $31.01 — about the same as architects, civil engineers and computer-systems analysts. Even demanding, education-intensive professions like dentistry and nuclear engineering didn't make much more per hour.

Some argue that it's unfair to calculate teacher pay on an hourly basis because teachers perform a large amount of work at home — grading papers on the weekend, for instance. But people in other professions also do off-site work.

Many assume that teachers spend almost all of the school day teaching. But in reality, the average subject-matter teacher taught fewer than 3.9 hours per day in 2000. This leaves plenty of time for grading and planning lessons.

It is well documented that the people drawn into teaching these days tend to be those who have performed least well in college. If teachers are paid about as well as employees in many other good professions, why aren't more high performers taking it up?

One suspects that high-performing graduates tend to stay away because the rigid seniority-based structure doesn't allow them to rise faster and earn more money through better performance or by voluntarily putting in longer hours. In any case, it's clear that the primary obstacle to attracting better teachers isn't simply raising pay.

Retooling NCLB?

Education analysts have no shortage of changes to suggest.

President Bush is looking at "tinkering" with NCLB in a reauthorization, but Democrats are "interested in something broader," says Cardinali of Communities in Schools. "The [current] law is too fixated on academics," he says. After 30 years of experience helping students get additional services they need like tutoring and health care, "we've learned that student services are a critical component," he says.

"The brutal truth is that there is only one institution in America where you can get to kids in a thoughtful way — the school," he says. "Let's make that the center" where parents and children can get needs met that are critical for learning readiness. "Are we trying to make public education something it's not? No. It's a holistic view" of what it takes to educate a child.

One gap the University of Chicago's Knowles would like to see rectified: In NCLB's reporting requirements "the unit of analysis is the kid, the school and the district, and there's a stunning absence there if we really believe that instruction is at the heart of learning." Research indicates, he says, that individual classroom teachers may be the strongest in-school influence on student achievement.

However, "Democrats' strong ties to labor" helped keep teacher accountability out of the bill, he says.

In addition, "higher ed has been given pretty much a free pass," Knowles says. A future bill should focus attention on which education schools are producing the best-quality teachers.

Low-achieving schools shouldn't be punished, but given the tools to do better, says Knowles. Supports like teacher development and well-integrated extra services like social workers, closely targeted on high-need schools, are a "precondition" for improvement, he says.

Another key: additional flexibility for leaders of low-achieving schools to hire and fire and set policy and schedules. Principals say, "Yeah, you give me the hiring and firing of teachers and I'll give you the better results," and they're correct, says Knowles.

Reporting data for accountability isn't the problem. It's the very narrowly focused reporting requirement, many analysts say.

"Replace the overreliance on standardized testing with multiple measures," such as attendance figures and accurate dropout rates, says the University of Rochester's Hursh.

The federal government should also support strong, unbiased research on what improves instruction, especially in the middle- and high-school years, which are federally funded at a tiny fraction of the level of elementary schools and colleges, says Wise of the Alliance for Excellent Education. "No state or local district has the money for this," he says.

OUTLOOK

Agreeing to Disagree

There's growing agreement that schools should be educating all students to a higher standard. However, there's still disagreement about how much and what kind of help schools would need to do it.

An ideal outcome would be for institutions that are the most lasting presence in cities, such as business groups like the Chamber of Commerce, local hospitals and colleges to take ownership of urban education to drive change, says Balfanz of Johns Hopkins. A movement in that direction may be beginning, he says. "For awhile, there were mainly rhetorical reports," but today groups like the Chamber of Commerce are producing more potentially useful policy work, he says.

"The climate is shifting" toward the conclusion that everyone needs a diploma, says Balfanz. "You can't even find an employer who says, 'I'll hire people who aren't high-school graduates.'" So when students drop out, "it just feeds the next generation of poverty," he says.

There's currently an opportunity to revise NCLB in a way that helps low-achieving schools, says the University of Chicago's Knowles. Nevertheless, "people have already formed hard opinions," and debate could turn solely partisan, he says.

Lawmakers must aim for a delicate balance on federal initiatives, says Columbia's Henig. Federal interventions must aim at "making local processes work," since local on-the-ground actions are ultimately what make or break schools, he says.

The University of Pennsylvania's Lytle fears that privatization may be on the verge of overwhelming education, with potentially disastrous consequences for low-income families.

"I think the K-12 education business is in the process of deconstructing," he says. "The middle class is looking outside the schools" to private tutoring companies and Internet learning for academics. "More and more, for them, schools are amounting to expensive child care." Some states are aggressively pioneering "virtual" online charter schools and charters granted to home-schoolers, he says.

"The cost side and the efficacy side of education are on a collision course, and I think Congress will end up endorsing fairly radical experimentation" with vouchers, for example, Lytle says. "They'll say, 'There's no evidence that reducing class size or other expensive measures helps, so let's let American ingenuity work. Where does that leave urban kids? Out of luck," Lytle says. "You've got to be pretty sophisticated to make market forces work for you."

But "there's been progress in the last decade with whole-school reform," says Balfanz. "The big question now is how we [change] whole school districts. It's a big job but within human capacity," he says.

UPDATE

An array of forces has slowed long-sought progress in narrowing the minority-student achievement gap among urban schools. Those forces include mixed results in nationwide test scores, three years of delay in reauthorizing the federal No Child Left Behind Act and a pivotal 2007 Supreme Court ruling on school desegregation, which, combined with a severe recession, has steered the education debate toward favoring economic considerations over racial equity.

"As a nation we decided long ago against separate but equal, but the reality is we're moving fast to becoming a majority-minority population," former West Virginia Gov. Bob Wise, president of the Alliance for Excellent Education, said in a recent interview. "So we need to focus on each child having a quality school no matter where they live." Because the modern economy now requires success by poor children as well as by those bound for higher-paying jobs, Wise said, education reform must link both economic performance and social justice.

The economic pressure on schools continues. A recent study by labor economist Anthony Carnevale of Georgetown University found that two-thirds of the 47 million new jobs he expects the U.S. economy to create between 2008 and 2018 will require workers who have at least some college education.[60] That is a sea change from a half-century ago when nearly two-thirds of jobs were filled by those with only a high school diploma.

The latest student test scores from the nation's urban K-12 schools show some noteworthy but unspectacular improvements. According to a new experimental index of urban student performance in the reading portion of the National Assessment of Educational Progress (NAEP), average reading scores for students in large-city school districts in grades four and eight rose by several points on the proficiency scale between 2003 and 2009, a change that narrowed the achievement gap to 10 points when compared with the national sampling.[61]

Lagging in Math

In math, according to a March analysis of NAEP scores and state tests by the Council of the Great City Schools, 79 percent of districts increased the percentage of fourth-graders who scored at or above proficient between 2006 and 2009, with a fourth of the districts raising scores by more than 10 percent.[62] Yet "despite significant gains in performance and faster rates of improvement than their states," the assessment said, "the majority of urban school districts continue to score below state averages on fourth- and eighth-grade mathematics assessments."

The decades-old assumption that school districts should actively pursue racial integration was challenged by a June 2007 U.S. Supreme Court ruling that invalidated school-attendance-zone plans used in Seattle and metropolitan Louisville to achieve greater diversity. In a 5-4 ruling in *Parents Involved in Community Schools v. Seattle Dist. No. 1*, the majority, in an opinion written by Chief Justice John G. Roberts Jr., said, "The way to stop discrimination on the basis of race is to stop discriminating on the basis of race."[63] Roberts deplored what he saw as an "ends justify the means" approach to achieving integration. "[R]acial classifications," he argued, "are simply too pernicious to permit any but the most exact connection between justification and classification."

The dissent by the court's liberal justices argued that Roberts' opinion undermined the promise of integrated schools the court set down in its 1954 landmark decision in *Brown v. Board of Education*, a change that Justice

Davis Guggenheim, director of "Waiting for Superman," a documentary about the public school system in America, and Michelle Rhee, D.C. Public Schools Chancellor, attend the Silverdocs Festival in Silver Spring, Md.

John Paul Stevens called "a cruel irony." Justice Anthony Kennedy, in a concurring opinion, left open the possibility of a more modest consideration of race in drawing school boundaries.

The court's ruling was hardly the last word, however. In a June 2010 review of school integration efforts since the Supreme Court decision, the Civil Rights Project at UCLA said the "divided decision confused many educators and it was somewhat unclear what did remain legal."[64] It noted that "economic pressure is forcing school districts to make deep cuts in services, which is another potential constraint for integration efforts," and it called on the Obama administration to issue new guidance on how race can be considered.

One of the nation's most troubled urban districts, the District of Columbia, in spring 2010 became the scene for ratification of a highly innovative teachers' contract. For nearly three years, national attention had focused on the controversial tenure of D.C. Public Schools Chancellor Michelle Rhee. Her efforts at reforming the system's bureaucracy and sweeping away incompetent teachers — she appeared on the Nov. 26, 2008, cover of *Time* holding a broom — had put her at odds with the local branch of the American Federation of Teachers.

Her reputation for tough management has attracted private foundation money to help the D.C. schools, and her future in the job became an issue in the current mayoral race.

Further roiling the waters was Rhee's firing of 241 teachers this summer, including 165 who received poor appraisals under a new evaluation system based in part on students' standardized test scores.[65]

Paying for Success

But in June 2010, school officials and the teachers' union finalized a contract that, in addition to granting a retroactive pay increase, requires all teachers in the system to be evaluated in part on whether their students' test scores improve, and it offers sizable pay increases to teachers who opt for and succeed in a special new pay-for-performance arrangement.[66]

D.C.'s special constitutional status that gives Congress a major say in its education policies continued to play a role in the district's efforts to improve results. Since 2004, Congress has funded the D.C. Opportunity Scholarship Program, a unique, federally funded voucher option favored by many conservatives that has given some 3,700 students $7,500 per year to attend any accredited private school that will accept them.[67]

But the Democratic takeover of Congress and the election of President Obama brought a change in priorities. Education Secretary Arne Duncan in 2009 rescinded the pending scholarships, and Congress declined to reauthorize them. An Education Department report found that the voucher program had not demonstrated much impact on test scores, though graduation rates for students in the program topped those of other students in D.C. Public Schools.[68]

Virtually every tool in the school reform grab bag — from charter schools to new teacher-accountability rules to dropout-prevention efforts — will be affected by the long-delayed reauthorization of the Elementary and Secondary Education Act (ESEA), known since 2002 as No Child Left Behind. The law has long been the center of disputes over reliance on student test scores. Its deadlines for improving student proficiency are seen by many as unrealistic, and critics have considered its funding levels inadequate. The bill has run into a new set of obstacles in the Obama era.

A Call for Flexibility

In a March 15, 2010, "blueprint" to overhaul No Child Left Behind, the Obama team argued that the law had "created incentives for states to lower their standards; emphasized punishing failure over rewarding success; focused on absolute scores, rather than recognizing growth and progress; and prescribed a pass-fail, one-size-fits-all series of interventions for schools that miss their goals." It called for greater flexibility in methodology to turn around some 5,000 schools labeled as underperforming.

But the reauthorization, though the subject of a dozen or more hearings this year in the House and Senate, has continued to divide Congress. One reason is the attention devoted to Obama's competitive $4 billion state grant education initiative, called Race to the Top. It is viewed by some as highly successful in providing incentives to states to enact reforms. Though only Delaware and Tennessee have won grants so far, 28 states have made reforms in 2009 and 2010, or triple the number during the previous two years, according to *Education Week*.[69] Yet in a surprise twist, the ravages to state and local budgets wrought by the current recession prompted the House to pass an emergency jobs bill that would shift funds from Race to the Top to preserve current teacher salaries.

In another division among education reformers, the teachers' unions want to make the rewrite of the law less "punitive" toward teachers and more cognizant of family income disparities. "Today, students' success in school depends in large part on the zip code where they live," National Education Association president Dennis Van Roekel told Congress. "Students who struggle the most in impoverished communities too often don't attend safe schools with reliable heat and air conditioning; too often do not have safe passage to and from school; and far too often do not have access to great teachers on a regular and consistent basis."[70]

Former Gov. Wise worries that if the reauthorization is not completed this year, the nation must continue with the existing No Child Left Behind, which he sees as inflexible and short on help for high schools. The law "focused on where the problems are, and a light has been shined on the fact that students of color or low economic status are not making it," Wise says. "But the law does not have adequate remedies. It's like a compact disc in an iPod world."

NOTES

1. Quoted in Judy Radigan, "Reframing Dropouts: The Complexity of Urban Life Intersects with Current School Policy," paper presented at the Texas Dropout Conference, Houston, Oct. 6, 2006.

2. "The Socioeconomic Composition of the Public Schools: A Crucial Consideration in Student Assignment Policy," University of North Carolina Center for Civil Rights, Jan. 7, 2005, www.law.unc.edu/PDFs/charlottereport.pdf.

3. For background, see Barbara Mantel, "No Child Left Behind," *CQ Researcher*, May 7, 2005, pp. 469-492.

4. Quoted in David J. Hoff and Kathleen Kennedy Manzo, "Bush Claims About NCLB Questioned," *Education Week*, March 9, 2007, www.edweek.org.

5. Quoted in *ibid.*

6. "The Nation's Report Card: Reading 2005," U.S. Department of Education Institute of Education Sciences, www.nationsreportcard.gov.

7. Douglas N. Harris, "Ending the Blame Game on Educational Inequity: A Study of 'High-Flying' Schools and NCLB," Education Policy Studies Laboratory, Arizona State University, March 2006.

8. Jay P. Greene, "Education Myths," The American Enterprise Online, American Enterprise Institute, August 2006.

9. For background, see Charles S. Clark, "Charter Schools," *CQ Researcher*, Dec. 20, 2002, pp. 1033-1056; Kenneth Jost, "School Vouchers Showdown," *CQ Researcher*, Feb. 15, 2002, pp. 121-144.

10. Greene, *op. cit.*

11. Brad Olsen and Lauren Anderson, "Courses of Action: A Qualitative Investigation Into Urban Teacher Retention and Career Development," *Urban Education*, January 2007, p. 5.

12. Quoted in *ibid.*, p. 14.

13. *Ibid.*

14. Arthur J. Rothkopf, "Elementary and Secondary Education Act Reauthorization: Improving NCLB To Close the Achievement Gap," testimony before the Senate Committee on Health, Education, Labor, and Pensions and the House Committee on Education and Labor, March 13, 2007.

15. For background, see Kenneth Jost, "Testing in Schools," *CQ Researcher*, April 20, 2001, pp. 321-344.

16. Richard J. Murnane, "Improving the Education of Children Living in Poverty," unpublished paper, Jan. 25, 2007.

17. *Ibid.*

18. For background, see Kenneth Jost, "School Desegregation," *CQ Researcher*, April 23, 2004, pp. 345-372.

19. Quoted in "Center on Race and Social Problems Commemorates *Brown v. Board of Education*," University of Pittsburgh School of Social Work, May 7, 2004.

20. Quoted in Brian Lamb, "No Excuses: Closing the Racial Gap in Learning," transcript, "Booknotes," C-SPAN, Feb. 1, 2004.

21. Paul Tough, "What It Takes To Make a Student," *The New York Times Magazine*, Nov. 26, 2006, p. 70.

22. R. Scott Baker, "School Resegregation: Must the South Turn Back?" *Journal of Southern History*, November 2006, p. 993.

23. Howell S. Baum, "Smart Growth and School Reform: What If We Talked About Race and Took Community Seriously?" *Journal of the American Planning Association*, winter 2004, p. 14.

24. "Divided We Fail: Coming Together Through Public School Choice," Task Force on the Common School, The Century Foundation Press, 2002, p. 3.

25. *Ibid.*, p. 13.

26. Quoted in Lamb, *op. cit.*

27. *Ibid.*

28. Terry Ryan and Quentin Suffren, "Charter School Lessons from Ohio," *The Education Gadfly*, Thomas B. Fordham Foundation, March 15, 2007, www.edexcellence.net.

29. Mark Simon, "What Teachers Know," *Poverty & Race*, September/October 2004, www.prrac.org.

30. Dreyon Wynn and Dianne L. H. Mark, "Book Review: Educating Teachers for Diversity: Seeing With a Cultural Eye," *Urban Education*, May 2005, p. 350.

31. Jocelyn A. Glazier, "Moving Closer to Speaking the Unspeakable: White Teachers Talking About Race," *Teacher Education Quarterly*, winter 2003.

32. Wanda J. Blanchett, "Urban School Failure and Disproportionality in a Post-*Brown* Era," *Remedial and Special Education*, April 2005, p. 70.

33. Christine H. Leland and Jerome C. Harste, "Doing What We Want to Become: Preparing New Urban Teachers," *Urban Education*, January 2005, p. 60.

34. *Ibid.*, p. 62.

35. Glazier, *op. cit.*

36. Wynn and Mark, *op. cit.*

37. For background, see Wayne J. Urban and Jennings L. Wagoner Jr., *American Education: A History* (2003); Stanley William Rothstein, *Schooling the Poor: A Social Inquiry Into the American Educational Experience* (1994).

38. For background, see Kathy Koch, "Reforming School Funding," *CQ Researcher*, Dec. 10, 1999, pp. 1041-1064.

39. Derrick Bell, *Silent Covenants:* Brown v. Board of Education *and the Unfulfilled Hopes for Racial Reform* (2004), p. 88.

40. *Ibid.*, p. 91.

41. Ruth Curran Neild and Robert Balfanz, "An Extreme Degree of Difficulty: The Educational Demographics of Urban Neighborhood High Schools," *Journal of Education for Students Placed at Risk*, spring 2006, p. 135.

42. V. W. Ipka, "At Risk Children in Resegregated Schools; An Analysis of the Achievement Gap," *Journal of Instructional Psychology*, December 2003, p. 294.

43. The case is *Brown v. Board of Education of Topeka*, 347 U.S. 483 (1954).

44. For background, see Jost, "School Desegregation," *op. cit.*; Gary Orfield and John T. Yun, "Resegregation in American Schools," The Civil Rights Project,

Harvard University, June 1999, www.civilrightsproject
.harvard.edu/research/deseg/reseg_schools99.php.

45. The case is *Milliken v. Bradley*, 418 U.S. 717 (1974).

46. Ipka, *op. cit.* The cases are *Board of Education of
Oklahoma City v. Dowell*, 498 U.S. 237 (1991) and
Freeman v. Pitts, 498 U.S. 1081 (1992).

47. Gary Orfield and Chungmei Lee, "Racial
Transformation and the Changing Nature of
Segregation," The Civil Rights Project, Harvard
University, January 2006, www.civilrightsproject
.harvard.edu; *Keyes v. School District No. 1*, Denver,
Colorado, 413 U.S. 189 (1973).

48. Gary Orfield and Susan E. Eaton, "Back to
Segregation," *The Nation*, March 3, 2003, p. 5.

49. Baum, *op. cit.*

50. *Ibid.*

51. Neild and Balfanz, *op. cit.*, p. 126.

52. "Divided We Fail," *op. cit.*, p. 17.

53. Tough, *op. cit.*

54. Elaine M. Stotko, Rochelle Ingram and Mary Ellen
Beaty-O'Ferrall, "Promising Strategies for Attracting
and Retaining Successful Urban Teachers," *Urban
Education*, January 2007, p. 36.

55. Patrick Mattimore, "Will Court Put Integration on
Hold?" *San Francisco Examiner*, Dec. 8, 2006, www
.examiner.com. The cases — argued on Dec. 4,
2006 — are *Meredith v. Jefferson County Board of
Education*, 05-915; and *Parents Involved in Community
Schools v. Seattle School District No. 1*, 05-908.

56. Richard Kahlenberg, "Helping Children Move
from Bad Schools to Good Ones," The Century
Foundation, 2006, www.tcf.org/list.asp?type=PB&
pubid=565.

57. *Ibid.*

58. Quoted in Michael Sandler, "Minding Their
Business," *CQ Weekly*, April 2, 2007, p. 952.

59. Quoted in Jonathan Weisman and Amit R. Paley,
"Dozens in GOP Turn Against Bush's Prized 'No
Child' Act," *The Washington Post*, March 15, 2007, p. A1.

60. Written testimony of Anthony P. Carnevale, Director,
Georgetown University Center on Education and the
Workforce, U.S. Senate Committee on Health,
Education, Labor and Pensions, Feb. 24, 2010,
http://help.senate.gov/imo/media/doc/Carnevale
.pdf.

61. Council of the Great City Schools, press release,
May 20, 2010, www.cgcs.org/pressrelease/ TUDA_
Reading2010.pdf.

62. "Beating the Odds: Analysis of Student Performance
on State Assessments and NAEP," Council of the
Great City Schools, March 2010.

63. Linda Greenhouse, "Justices Limit the Use of Race
in School Plans for Integration," *The New York
Times*, June 28, 2007, p. A1.

64. Civil Rights Project, University of California at Los
Angeles, www.civilrightsproject.ucla. edu/research/
deseg/school-integration-three-years-after-parents-
involved.pdf.

65. Bill Turque, "Rhee dismisses 241 D.C. teachers;
union vows to contest firing," *The Washington Post*,
July 24, 2010, p. A1, www.washingtonpost.com/
wp-dyn/content/article/2010/07/23/AR2010072
303093.html.

66. Bill Turque, "D.C. Teachers' Contract Passes Its
Final Hurdle; Council Unanimously Approves Pact
that Bases Pay on Results," *The Washington Post*,
June 30, 2010.

67. "Opportunity Denied," editorial, *The Washington
Post*, June 23, 2010.

68. "Evaluation of the DC Opportunity Scholarship
Program: Final Report," U.S. Department of
Education, June 2010, http://ies.ed.gov/ncee/pubs/
20104018/pdf/20104018.pdf.

69. Chad Adelman, "How Race to the Top Could
Inform ESEA Reauthorization," *Education Week*,
June 28, 2010.

70. Testimony before Senate Health, Education, Labor
and Pensions Committee, March 9, 2010.

BIBLIOGRAPHY

Books

Kozol, Jonathan, *The Shame of the Nation: The
Restoration of Apartheid Schooling in America*, **Three
Rivers Press, 2006.**

A longtime education writer and activist reports on his five-year journey to closely observe 60 schools in 11 states. He describes almost entirely resegregated urban schools with dilapidated buildings, dirty classrooms and a dearth of up-to-date textbooks.

Rothstein, Richard, *Class and Schools: Using Social, Economic, and Education Reform to Close the Black-White Achievement Gap*, Economic Policy Institute, 2004.

A research associate at a think tank concerned with low- and middle-income workers and families argues that raising the achievement of urban students requires public policies that address students' multiple social and economic needs.

Thernstrom, Abigail, and Stephan Thernstrom, *No Excuses: Closing the Racial Gap in Learning*, Simon & Schuster, 2004.

A husband and wife who are senior fellows at the conservative Manhattan Institute for Public Policy Research argue that charter schools and the No Child Left Behind Act's focus on holding schools accountable for poor student achievement can close the achievement gap for urban students.

Articles

Boo, Katherine, "Expectations," *The New Yorker*, Jan. 15, 2007, p. 44.

A reform-minded superintendent closes Denver's lowest-achieving high school, hoping its students will accept the offer to enroll in any other city school, including some with mainly online classes. Mostly Latinos from the city's poorest families, the displaced students struggle with losing their old school, which has provided many with a sense of community, and with new choices that confront them, as well as the ever-present choice of dropping out.

Moore, Martha T., "More Mayors Are Moving To Take Over School System," *USA Today*, March 21, 2007, p. A1.

Albuquerque's mayor is among those who believe they could run schools better than their local school boards.

Saulny, Susan, "Few Students Seek Free Tutoring or Transfers From Failing Schools," *The New York Times*, April 6, 2006, p. 20.

The No Child Left Behind Act promises free tutoring for many students in low-achieving schools, but few of those students' families know about the option or have been able to enroll their children in good-quality tutoring programs.

Tough, Paul, "What It Takes To Make a Student," *The New York Times Magazine*, Nov. 26, 2006, p. 44.

A handful of charter schools are making strides against the achievement gap. But largely because low-income and minority students arrive at school with smaller vocabularies and far less knowledge about how to communicate with adults and behave in a learning situation, the work requires extra-long school hours and intense teacher commitment.

Reports and Studies

***Beating the Odds: An Analysis of Student Performance and Achievement Gaps on State Assessments: Results from the 2005-2006 School Year*, Council of the Great City Schools, April 2007.**

A group representing 67 of the country's largest urban school districts examines in detail the recent performance of urban students on state tests.

***Divided We Fail: Coming Together Through Public School Choice*, Task Force on the Common School, The Century Foundation, 2002.**

Basing its discussion on the idea that race- and class-segregated schools have proven a failure, a nonpartisan think tank explores the possibility of encouraging cross-district integration of low-income and middle-income students by methods like establishing high-quality magnet schools in cities.

***Engaging Schools: Fostering High School Students' Motivation to Learn*, Committee on Increasing High School Students' Engagement and Motivation to Learn, National Research Council, 2003.**

A national expert panel examines methods for re-engaging urban high-school students who have lost their motivation to learn, a problem they say is widespread but solvable.

Bridgeland, John M., John J. DiIulio, Jr., and Karen Burke Morison, *The Silent Epidemic: Perspectives of High School Dropouts*, Bill & Melinda Gates Foundation, March 2006.

Nearly half of high-school dropouts say they left school partly because they were bored. A third of the students left because they needed to work, and more than a fifth said they left to care for a family member.

Levin, Henry, Clive Belfield, Peter Muennig and Cecilia Rouse, "The Costs and Benefits of an Excellent

Education for All of America's Children," Teachers College, Columbia University, January 2007; www .cbcse.org/media/download_gallery/Leeds_Report_ Final_Jan2007.pdf.
A team of economists concludes that measures to cut the number of school dropouts would pay for themselves with higher tax revenues and lower government spending.

For More Information

Achieve, Inc., 1775 I St., N.W., Suite 410, Washington, DC 20006; (202) 419-1540; www.achieve.org. An independent bipartisan group formed by governors and business leaders to promote higher academic standards.

Alliance for Excellent Education, 1201 Connecticut Ave., N.W., Suite 901, Washington, DC 20036; (202) 828-0828; www.all4ed.org. A nonprofit research and advocacy group seeking policies to help at-risk high-school students.

The Center for Education Reform, 910 17th St., N.W., Suite 1120, Washington, DC 20006; (301) 986-8088; www.edreform.com. A nonprofit advocacy group that promotes school choice in cities.

The Century Foundation, 41 E. 70th St., New York, NY 10021; (212) 535-4441; www.tcf.org. Supports research on income inequality and urban policy.

Citizens for Effective Schools, 8209 Hamilton Spring Ct., Bethesda, MD 20817; (301) 469-8000; www .citizenseffectiveschools.org. An advocacy group that seeks

policy changes to minimize the achievement gap for low-income and minority students.

Council of the Great City Schools, 1301 Pennsylvania Ave., N.W., Suite 702, Washington, DC 20004; (202) 393-2427; www.cgcs.org. A coalition of 67 urban school systems dedicated to improving urban schools.

Education Next, Harvard Kennedy School, 79 JFK St., Cambridge, MA 02138; www.educationnext.org. A quarterly journal on education reform published by a conservative think tank.

The Education Trust, 1250 H St., N.W., Suite 700, Washington, DC 20005; (202) 293-1217; www2.edtrust .org. Dedicated to closing the achievement gap in learning and college preparation for low-income and minority students.

National Center for Education Statistics, 1990 K St., N.W., Washington, DC 20006; (202) 502-7300; http:// nces.ed.gov. A Department of Education agency that provides statistics and analysis on U.S. schools, student attendance and achievement.

2

Fighting Crime

Peter Katel

A Los Angeles policeman detains suspected members of the Rolling 60's, an affiliate of the nationwide Crips gang. Violent crime in the United States fell by about 2 percent in the first half of 2007, but crime still grips many inner cities, where young men are often caught up in a cycle of attack and revenge and joblessness, family dysfunction and inadequate schools are endemic. Many communities also face what Attorney General Michael Mukasey calls a "terrible gang problem."

From *CQ Researcher*, February 8, 2008.

Ronald Moten and Jauhar Abraham are standing near a street corner in Washington, D.C.'s tough Southeast district, outside the office of Peaceoholics. The two ex-drug dealers (Abraham is also a U.S. Army veteran) founded the grassroots group four years ago to get young people in Washington's inner-city neighborhoods to quit shooting each other.

It's a tall order. Before 2008 was a month old, an 18-year-old girl was shot dead and a 17-year-old friend was wounded as they walked home from school in a Washington suburb. A separate drive-by shooting killed a 17-year-old youth in the city. And eight young people and an adult were wounded in two separate shootings.[1]

Now Moten and Abraham worry the city will soon have another tragedy. They have just gotten word that teenagers in the Saratoga neighborhood are gunning for a group of high-school basketball players who reportedly had "dissed" — disrespected — a Saratoga youth. "It got back to the dudes in the 'hood,'" Moten says. "So boys from Saratoga were going to kill basketball players." The Peaceoholics were trying to talk to people on both sides.

The recent shootings have Moten and Abraham worried, along with Mayor Adrian Fenty and other city officials, that the city is in the grip of a new wave of violence. The shootings followed a year in which the number of Washington homicides went up by 7 percent over the previous year, to 181 killings.[2]

The nation's capital is not alone. A number of cities saw upticks in homicide or other violent crimes in 2007, including Atlanta, Baltimore, Dallas, New Orleans and Miami.[3]

By comparison, the most recent national statistics, covering only the first six months of 2007, show a national drop-off of 1.8 percent for the same period in 2006.[4]

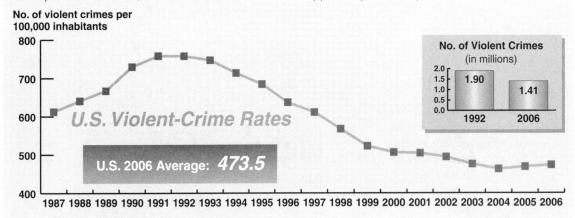

Violent-Crime Rate Steadily Decreasing

In the past two decades, the nation's violent-crime rate dropped 23 percent; it peaked in 1991 at 758.2.

Source: "Uniform Crime Report," Federal Bureau of Investigation, 2006

The biggest cities, New York, Chicago and Los Angeles, reflected that national trend. But an independent survey of cities and counties by the Police Executive Research Foundation (PERF) show homicide increases in 22 of these jurisdictions, and decreases in 28.[5]

Citing increases in various cities, Attorney General Michael Mukasey promised a gathering of mayors on Jan. 24 that the Bush administration will ask Congress for $200 million for cities fighting rising violent crime. "We'll be able to send targeted resources where they are needed the most," he told the U.S. Conference of Mayors. "The nature of crime varies not only from one city to another, but even from one block to the next."[6] Response ranged from tepid to highly critical from mayors and federal lawmakers who call that proposal inadequate. They have been fighting for five years against what they call Bush administration short-changing of local police assistance, including to Midwestern states hit by a methamphetamine manufacturing and addiction boom.

Today's up-and-down crime rates contrast with a period in which violent crime dropped nationwide. Following an urban crime explosion in the 1980s and early '90s sparked by a boom in crack cocaine, crime dramatically declined. Throughout the 1990s and into the new century, the United States enjoyed the longest spell of falling crime rates since the end of World War II.

The rate fell annually from 747 per 100,000 population in 1993 to 463 per 100,000 in 2004.[7]

Now, the country is returning to its natural condition of varied crime rates, some specialists argue. "Divergence, over the vast social differences and geography of the United States, is much more normal than the tight, everybody-marching-to-the-same-trend experience we had in the '90s," says Franklin E. Zimring, a criminologist at the University of California law school at Berkeley. Zimring authored a recent book on crime rates in the 1990s.[8]

For police in cities fighting to keep crime under control, the emergence and disappearance of national patterns matter less than they do to academics. "We think about this differently than traditional criminologists, who wait for long-term trends," says Chuck Wexler, executive director of PERF. "We're not as interested in that as we are in what's happening in the short term. Police departments are focused more than ever on accurate, timely information."

But while some of those trends take time to identify, they may still signal urgent issues.

"Where the problem is, is among black underclass youth in cities," says James A. Fox, a professor at Northeastern University's College of Criminal Justice in Boston. "This has been the pattern since 2002. If we don't respond appropriately, the problem in poor, black communities could further spiral out of control. We have no hesitancy to spend millions on preventing terrorism but just don't seem to want to spend money on preventing street violence that plagues millions of Americans."

Increasingly, however, popular culture is echoing that conclusion. HBO's "The Wire," a fictional treatment of crime, race and urban decay set in Baltimore, depicts a veteran African-American detective telling a fellow cop: "If 300 white people were killed in this city every year, you think they wouldn't send in the 82nd Airborne?"[9]

The slow-motion crisis in African-American inner cities is hardly a secret to residents. "Three of our former students have been killed," says Karen Falcon, founder and director of Jubilee School, a private elementary school in Philadelphia. "One of them was in an argument with a friend and the friend killed him. Three years before that, his mother, a good friend of mine, was just walking down the street and got caught in cross fire and died. The son of a neighbor across the street died in gun violence. We have a former student who was riding the school bus home and saw yellow tape on her father's block. Her father had been killed."

Jubilee students have been working to develop a Web site that young people can use to write about violent episodes that have touched their lives. "I'm in a horrible neighborhood," says Daria Ross, the 12-year-old sixth-grader who is the project's sparkplug. "Someone got shot in front of my door last night."

That victim survived his wounds. But an analysis of Centers for Disease Control statistics by the Violence Policy Center, a gun-control advocacy organization, shows that homicide is the leading cause of death for black young people ages 15 to 34, with 90 percent of them shot to death. Among African-Americans 15-24, 42 percent of all deaths were homicides. For whites — 8.5 percent. "The devastation homicide inflicts on black teens and adults is a national crisis, yet it is all too often

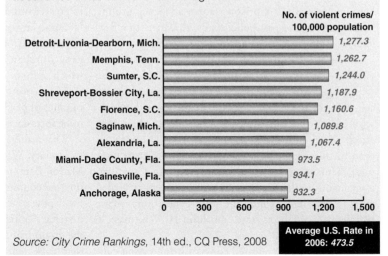

Detroit Area Had Highest Violent-Crime Rate

Three cities had violent crime rates of more than 1,200 in 2006, or about three times the national average.

No. of violent crimes/ 100,000 population

Detroit-Livonia-Dearborn, Mich.	1,277.3
Memphis, Tenn.	1,262.7
Sumter, S.C.	1,244.0
Shreveport-Bossier City, La.	1,187.9
Florence, S.C.	1,160.6
Saginaw, Mich.	1,089.8
Alexandria, La.	1,067.4
Miami-Dade County, Fla.	973.5
Gainesville, Fla.	934.1
Anchorage, Alaska	932.3

Source: City Crime Rankings, 14th ed., CQ Press, 2008

Average U.S. Rate in 2006: *473.5*

ignored outside of affected communities," the center concluded in a study released in January that was based on 2005 statistics, the most recent available.[10]

In Philadelphia, 70 percent of the 406 murder victims in 2006 were black men. "If it were anything else, an explosion or a health outbreak, the federal government would have our city on lockdown trying to find out what's going on," said newly elected Mayor Michael Nutter." "It's ripping the heart out of the city."[11]

If the homicide rate among blacks constitutes an emergency today, the explosion of crack-linked homicides in an earlier era amounted to a catastrophe. Beginning in the mid-1980s, the federal response to the crack epidemic included the expansion of a massive imprisonment policy that was already under way — helping to raise the nation's prison and jail population to 2.2 million inmates by 2007.[12]

Crime experts of varying political persuasions say the incarceration boom undoubtedly contributed to the crime decline of the 1990s. But even law-and-order types, such as David Mulhausen, a senior policy analyst at the conservative Heritage Foundation, say that government's shrinking purse requires a more refined approach to imprisonment. "Prison is a scarce resource," he says. "Incarcerate the worst first."

In 2007, 26 state legislatures undertook a variety of measures to soften or study sentencing laws. " 'Tough-on-crime' policies that previously dominated the criminal-justice legislative agenda have ceded ground," said the Sentencing Project, a prison-reform advocacy group. "The fiscal cost of past policies now threatens to affect vital state services."[13]

Seven of the states expanded programs to assist convicts leaving prison, or decided to study whether to do so. The state lawmakers acted as crime and prison experts across the country pointed to the frequency with which released convicts wind up back behind bars. The ripple effects of so many men cycling in and out of prison go even further. "Certain lower-socioeconomic areas produce clients for the criminal-justice system in a way that is analogous to the way that the welfare system created a cycle of first- and second- and third-generation welfare recipients," said Texas state Sen. John H. Whitmire, a Houston Democrat.[14]

Inevitably, newly released convicts bring prison culture back home. The spread of the "no-snitching" code is an example — one that Washington's Peaceoholics is battling. (*See Sidebar, p. 42.*) The group's $3 million budget comes from foundation grants and contracts with city agencies.

But co-founder Abraham acknowledges that citizens who do alert police to crimes can't always count on police protection from retaliation. Many inner-city residents feel they have to take care of themselves in a world where violence is commonplace. "I may be talking with a 19-year-old who takes off his jacket and a gun falls out," Abraham says. "He'll tell me that to come see me he had to cross three neighborhoods where he's got problems with people."

As city officials, law-enforcement personnel and concerned citizens confront inner-city crime, here are some of the questions being asked:

Can violent crime be significantly reduced in inner cities?

Anyone familiar with U.S. demographics can't help but be struck by the common theme that runs through the list of cities both large and small battling to keep violent crime under control. From Atlanta to Miami, most are cities with large, concentrated populations plagued by joblessness, family dysfunction and inadequate schools — the classic foundation of persistent crime. Small and medium-sized cities may share those problems, even if homicide and other violent crimes occur in greater numbers in major urban centers.

Some law-enforcement officials and politicians also cite what Attorney General Mukasey calls a "terrible gang problem" in some communities — a matter on which opinions are divided. (*See "At Issue," p. 45.*)

"There is no question that there is a disproportionate number of black victims of homicide, and murder tends to be intra-racial," says Wexler of PERF.

That reality is a familiar one among African-Americans. In January, Washington councilman and former mayor Marion Barry called for 300 black men to serve as mentors and counselors for young men in one of the toughest, most poverty-stricken neighborhoods in his Southeast district. "This is a great beginning," Barry said of the group half that size that answered his plea. "It shows that black men can really come out when we care. We're going to save these young guys, not just today but in the long run."[15]

The councilman was taking a page from Philadelphia Police Commissioner Sylvester Johnson. In September 2007, shortly before retiring, Johnson proposed that 10,000 men — mainly blacks — retake city streets from criminals. "It's time for African-American men to stand up," Johnson said. "We have an obligation to protect our women, our children and our elderly."[16]

How successful such efforts can be — especially in an era of reduced government spending on social projects — is in dispute.

"Every year, you find the same group of cities at the top of the list — Atlanta, New Orleans, Baltimore, Washington, Detroit," says Northeastern University's Fox. All of those are cities with substantial communities of poor African-Americans.

Some community activists argue that judging how far cities can go in improving public safety is difficult in the absence of political will. "There needs to be a permanent, ongoing approach," says the Rev. David Bowers, who founded the grassroots group No Murders DC and was a driving force behind the creation in December 2006 of the city's Comprehensive Homicide Elimination Strategy Task Force. "The effort to end murder is bigger than any one sector or agency; it's much more than

Homicide Is Leading Killer of Young Blacks

Homicide is the leading cause of death among black teens and young adults, according to 2005 data, the most recent available. Among black males and females ages 15-24, 42 percent of all deaths were homicides. In comparison, homicide was the third-leading cause of death for whites ages 15-24. Black homicide victims in the United States in 2005 outnumbered whites.

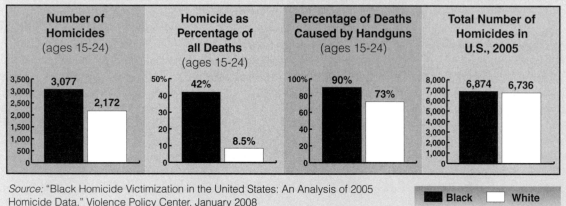

Source: "Black Homicide Victimization in the United States: An Analysis of 2005 Homicide Data," Violence Policy Center, January 2008

■ Black ☐ White

a law-enforcement initiative. One is mental health. People say you've got to get people jobs or a good education, and that's good. But we may be trying to educate someone who is walking around bitter, sad, angry — someone who's 16 years old and knows three or five who've been killed. The mental component is so critical and has been missing."

But programs of any kind may make few changes, says the Heritage Foundation's Mulhausen. To be sure, he agrees that broken families and failing schools — longtime characteristics of inner-city neighborhoods — tend to create circumstances in which young people drift into crime.

Mulhausen argues, though, that making long-lasting inroads against crime in poor neighborhoods requires more than simply improving social conditions. He adds that faith in social programs may be misplaced. "People make the mistaken assumption that just because you have a crime increase, it's because you have a certain policy," Mulhausen says. "Crime declines in a particular city, and all the politicians are going to say they're responsible, but maybe two-thirds of the time it was the result of conditions we don't understand yet."

The University of California's Zimring agrees that conventional explanations may not unlock the reasons behind rises and falls in crime rates. But experience shows, he says, that crime can be reduced even in violence-plagued inner cities.

For Zimring, the proof is in New York City's dramatic decline in crime rates that began in the 1990s and is continuing today. "In lousy neighborhoods with bad middle schools, the chances of the males who were doing badly in those schools getting involved in life-threatening violence went down by 70-80 percent in 15 years," he says. "The notion of the inevitability of high rates of interpersonal violence as part of the modern American city is being effectively challenged."

New York enjoys some uncommon advantages, Zimring adds. Among them, a compact geography — as opposed to Los Angeles' suburban-style sprawl — that benefit police looking for potential trouble, or for criminals.

But Andrew Karmen, a sociologist at New York's John Jay College of Criminal Justice, notes that while crime may have lessened in New York, it still runs strongest in poor neighborhoods populated by ethnic or racial minorities. The only way to attack the problem at its roots, he argues, is to ensure that residents of those neighborhoods get the tools to improve their lives.

Cops Focus on "Hot Spots"

Monitoring crime hot spots is the most effective approach to reducing violent crime, according to nearly two-thirds of the law-enforcement agencies polled.

Programs/Policies Implemented in Response to Increases in Violent Crime

Programs/Policies	Percentage of agencies implementing policy/program
Hot-spots enforcement	63%
Community-oriented initiative	44
Problem-solving policing	37
Cooperation with other departments	37
Gang suppression (enforcement)	37
Shifts in police resources	28
Drug enforcement	23
Targeting repeat offenders	22
Hiring/recruiting more officers	20
Federal grant programs (Weed & Seed, etc.)	17
Technology (cameras, computer systems, etc.)	15
School resource officers	12
"Zero tolerance" for low-level disorder	12
Juvenile crime programs	10
Creation of anti-gang unit	9

Source: "Violent Crime in America: A Tale of Two Cities," Police Executive Research Forum, November 2007

Are "stop-and-frisk" programs the best way to cut gun violence?

"Guns don't kill people, people kill people," goes the old pro-gun rights slogan. Whether people or their weapons are to blame, crime statistics make unmistakably clear that guns are a big part of the story of recent crime increases — and that reducing the number of guns on the street seems to have played some part in New York's crime drop.

In 2007, slightly more than half of the 56 police chiefs and sheriffs surveyed by PERF cited increased availability of firearms as one of the causes of violent-crime increases in their cities and towns. "We need to talk about national policies with guns, because that's what's killing inner-city youths today," said Garry McCarthy, police director of Newark, N.J. "If the guns weren't available, the shootings wouldn't be occurring at the rates that they're occurring. It's a lot harder to kill somebody with a golf club than it is with a gun."[18]

McCarthy's comments came seven weeks after the horrific Aug. 4 execution-style slaying of three college students in a Newark playground; a fourth student, a young woman, also shot at point-blank range, survived. Using her eyewitness account, fingerprint evidence and word from the neighborhood grapevine, police within weeks had arrested six people, including three juveniles. All were Latin American immigrants, one of them without legal status. They apparently had planned to rob the victims.[19]

One is access to higher education, he says, citing a statistical finding that only 8 percent of New York murder victims in 1989 attended college. But New York, he says, may phase out its present minimal-cost public colleges. Nationwide, programs to improve elementary and high-school education are also threatened. "Most elected officials want a quick fix that can take place while they're in office," argues Karmen, who authored a book examining reasons for New York's crime drop.[17] "If there's improvement in the schools and you have to wait 14 years for the effects, that doesn't appeal to elected officials, unfortunately."

How to keep guns out of the hands of criminals has long ranked as one of the most troublesome issues in U.S. law enforcement. The legal debate over gun laws aside, police face the practical question of how to disarm gun-toting bad guys before they open fire. As in other aspects of crime fighting, New York City changed the nature of the debate. In 1994, Mayor Rudolph

Giuliani's celebrated police chief, William J. Bratton, directed the 400-officer Street Crime Unit to aggressively target people suspected of carrying guns. One of their tactics was to stop and search young men — typically members of minority groups — known as "stop and frisk."[20]

The approach was controversial from the start. Criticism that the cops were overly confrontational seemed validated by the 1999 shooting of a West African immigrant from Guinea, Amadou Diallo, who turned out to be unarmed. (*See "Background," p. 44.*) And statistics showed that searches far outnumbered gun seizures — 18,023 searches in 1997, for 4,899 guns; and 27,061 searches in 1998, yielding 4,647 firearms.[21]

Giuliani turned to the courts as well. New York Mayor Michael Bloomberg is still pursuing a lawsuit that his predecessor began, seeking tens of millions of dollars from more than a dozen gun manufacturers and distributors, on the grounds that they didn't do enough to keep guns out of criminals' hands.[22]

Some criminologists note that street seizures were especially effective in a city whose strict gun laws made it hard for criminals to buy replacement guns or steal them from lawful owners. "There were a lot of guns on the street and none in apartments," says Zimring of the University of California.

Still, another set of statistics stands out as well. As New York cops zeroed in on guns, firearm crime plummeted. From 1988 to 1998 (the last year of Giuliani's first term), gun homicides dropped from 1,330 to 376.[23]

For some crime scholars, those ends justify the aggressive means. "Gun carrying in those neighborhoods where violence is endemic provides an incentive for a preemptive strike. If the other guy is going to get you, you're going to get him first," says criminologist Alfred Blumstein, a professor of urban systems and operations

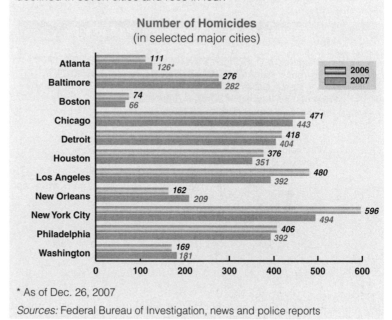

Big Cities Battle Homicide With Mixed Results

Homicide remains a serious problem in parts of many major cities, where guns are often plentiful. In the sample below, homicides declined in seven cities and rose in four.

Number of Homicides
(in selected major cities)

2006 / 2007

- Atlanta: 111 / 126*
- Baltimore: 276 / 282
- Boston: 74 / 66
- Chicago: 471 / 443
- Detroit: 418 / 404
- Houston: 376 / 351
- Los Angeles: 480 / 392
- New Orleans: 162 / 209
- New York City: 596 / 494
- Philadelphia: 406 / 392
- Washington: 169 / 181

* As of Dec. 26, 2007

Sources: Federal Bureau of Investigation, news and police reports

research at Carnegie-Mellon University's H. John Heinz III School of Public Policy and Management, in Pittsburgh.

Blumstein acknowledges that the aggressive policing involved in seizing guns endangers civil rights. But, he notes, Nutter won election last year as mayor of Philadelphia based in part on promises to implement a New York-style campaign against gun violence. "My sense, and the election bears it out, is that the public would rather have safety than an avoidance of stop-and-frisk."

Some Philadelphians disagree. "It plays into racial profiling," says Jubilee School founder Falcon, who calls for tougher laws against gun ownership. "As long as guns are so available, you can take the guns away all you want; they're just going to be replaced. I don't think it's the stop-and-frisk that stopped the guns in New York. They have very strict gun laws."

The Diallo shooting gave pause even to some stop-and-frisk advocates. "Bratton did that very well in New York City; then it got out of control," says George L. Kelling, a

Violent Crime Rose Most in Bismarck, N.D.

Although nationwide crime only rose by 1 percent between 2005 and 2006, methamphetamine use and gangs have contributed to big crime increases in relatively small, rural communities like Bismarck, N.D.

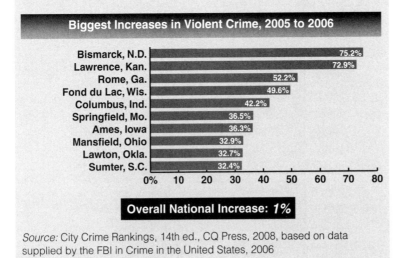

Biggest Increases in Violent Crime, 2005 to 2006

Bismarck, N.D.	75.2%
Lawrence, Kan.	72.9%
Rome, Ga.	52.2%
Fond du Lac, Wis.	49.6%
Columbus, Ind.	42.2%
Springfield, Mo.	36.5%
Ames, Iowa	36.3%
Mansfield, Ohio	32.9%
Lawton, Okla.	32.7%
Sumter, S.C.	32.4%

Overall National Increase: *1%*

Source: City Crime Rankings, 14th ed., CQ Press, 2008, based on data supplied by the FBI in Crime in the United States, 2006

professor at Rutgers University's School of Criminal Justice in Newark, who advised Bratton when he headed New York's transit police. Kelling co-authored "Broken Windows," a 1982 article that still influences policing across the country. (The article argued that if police and city officials cracked down on minor crimes and problems, such as fixing broken windows and arresting vagrants, more serious crimes would also be reduced.)[24]

Kelling blames the Diallo shooting on inexperience. "That was the first time those guys had worked together; they were relatively inexperienced," he says. If you're going to use special units for gun tactics, you need officers who are highly trained, mature and who have worked together for a long time."

But Minneapolis Police Chief Tim Dolan questions the tactic. "I don't think we'd get much support here if we were stopping and frisking without at least reasonable suspicion or some articulable reason," he says.

Dolan does encourage his officers to look for guns. But — unlike in New York — seized guns are easy to replace. Criminals can obtain weapons through middlemen who buy them legally. And purchases at flea markets and the like are unregulated, Dolan says.

Does joblessness cause crime?

The drumbeat of news about U.S. and international economic woes makes clear that the atmosphere in which crime debates are taking place has changed. Starting in 2007, real estate prices began tumbling, and holders of "subprime" mortgages began defaulting. Those developments spooked consumers, who held back on spending during the all-important Christmas buying season.[25]

Statistics released in November showed that 1.4 million people, 20 percent of the nation's unemployed, hadn't found work within 27 weeks of losing their jobs, the point at which most unemployment benefits run out. "The economy is operating at stall speed," Mark Zandi, chief economist of Moody's Economy .com, a research firm in West Chester, Pa., told the *Los Angeles Times.* "Either something is going to revive it quickly or else we're going to get into a vicious cycle of declining spending and even weaker job growth."[26]

In Minneapolis, Chief Dolan worries about the repercussions from a wave of home foreclosures that has hit his city's highest-crime neighborhoods. "Some intersections that were once problematic now look like ghost towns," he says. The worry is that whoever eventually rents those now-shuttered homes could lack stable employment, he says, which could lead to crime motivated by desperation.

Criminologists have long puzzled and argued over the relationship between economic changes and crime trends. Whatever the precise nature of that relationship, the University of California's Zimring says the economic climate in which the recent crime decline occurred has to be considered as a factor. "What is beyond controversy is the extraordinary and sustained growth of the American economy during all but the first year or two of the 1990s" — the exact time when the crime rate plummeted.

The course that crime rates take amid the country's current economic woes may test the two major sociopolitical schools of thought about crime.

In broad terms, the debate pits "root cause" liberals against "individual responsibility" conservatives. The "root cause" school argues that most offenders start down the road of crime because they were born into and grew up amid socioeconomic deprivation. The "responsibility" advocates say that most poor people aren't criminals and that blaming crime on unemployment and other economic conditions amounts to excusing criminal behavior.

Lately, the lines between the camps have blurred somewhat, although the argument between the two schools persists. Some liberals now allow for the role of individual decisions, and some conservatives acknowledge economic circumstances can influence someone to start a life of crime.

Police officials tend to fall into the conservative camp. But exceptions exist. Minneapolis' Dolan says flatly that "economic disparity is what brings crime." He adds, "Whoever is struggling in that lower economic group is who you're going to find is involved in crime, for the most part."

Dolan acknowledges that first-generation, working-class immigrants, often poor and often destined to stay that way, tend to be law-abiding. But their U.S.-born children and grandchildren often don't inherit their elders' optimism and respect for the rules. "We'll see some crime if they're stuck in those lower-income areas," Dolan says. "They go to inner-city schools and tend to band together." Minneapolis' immigrants include Somalis, Hmong from Laos and Latinos from various countries.

The Rev. Bowers, the stop-homicide advocate in Washington, might be expected to embrace a "root cause" view, as do many grassroots activists. But without completely discounting the effects of socioeconomic environment, he argues against a simple poverty-causes-crime analysis. "If you talk to folks from older generations, they'll say there were times when folks were a lot poorer and didn't have this level of violence," he says.

Looking back to the years of the crack boom, Bowers finds more support for his view that poverty alone can't explain crime. Competition between rival groups of criminals — drug traffickers, for instance — accounts for much crime, he says. "The years when we had the highest number of murders — was that because someone's poor? No, it was turf wars."

To some extent, the criminological version of the "nature versus nurture" debate depends on how broadly poverty is defined. If it's simply a matter of not having a lot of money, most crime experts tend to discount poverty as a crime cause. But if 'poverty' signifies a constellation of conditions that may include broken families and educational deprivation, some crime-trend watchers do point to it as a major causative factor.

"You can suppress crime, bottle it up to some degree, but the long-range solution has to include job training; decent jobs — jobs that pay a living wage — for all who want to work; constructive recreational activities, especially during nights and summers; and help for families that are dysfunctional," says Karmen of the John Jay College of Criminal Justice.

From the conservative wing, Kelling, the former adviser to Police Chief Bratton, argues that the relationship between crime and socioeconomic conditions is more complicated and dynamic than "root cause" advocates acknowledge. "Unemployment in some neighborhoods could cause crime to increase," he says. "But in other neighborhoods, where people who worked in the auto industry have been laid off, you now have guardians in the neighborhood — crime decreases, homes are not going to be burglarized."

BACKGROUND

Crackdown

The two sides in the debate over crime — what causes it and how to stop it — are reflected in the Great Society programs of President Lyndon B. Johnson, 1963-1969, and the tough-on-crime laws of the Ronald Reagan administrations of 1981-1989.[27]

The view that crime has to be attacked at its root economic and social causes emerged as a key part of the Great Society. In a 1968 message to Congress, Johnson said: "To speak of crime only in terms of the work of the police, the courts and the correctional apparatus alone is to refuse to face the fact that widespread crime implies a widespread failure by society as a whole." As *Time* magazine paraphrased, "crime is often one visible effect of poverty, and economic deprivation in youth sows a huge harvest of blighted promise and lost opportunity."[28]

Those who dismiss that view tend to regard Reagan as their philosopher king. Following Reagan's death in 2004, Sen. Jeff Sessions, R-Ala., said crime went down in the

Peaceoholics co-founder Jauhar Abraham, right, and a colleague plan a meeting with teenagers in Washington's tough Southeast district. Several recent shootings have left the anti-crime group worried that the city is in the grip of a new wave of violence.

1990s "because we went back to the fundamental precepts of crime and punishment. Some people are just dangerous. They need to be incarcerated. They need to be removed from society for the protection of society."[29]

The arrival of crack cocaine on America's inner-city streets in the early 1980s ignited a crime wave of historic proportions that took the entire country — liberals, and conservatives — by surprise. Contributing factors included huge demand for the highly addictive drug, the ready availability of young marketers who saw no future for themselves in conventional society and the enormous profits to be made. Drug traffickers vying to control open-air drug markets that sprang up across the country often settled their conflicts violently.

An exhaustive 1997 study of homicide in eight cities hit hard by crack included examinations of homicides of black men ages 18-24. "In Washington, D.C., the rate climbed from less than 100 [homicides] per 100,000 [population] in 1985 to more than 400 in 1988 and nearly 800 in 1991 before declining to about 600 per 100,000 in 1994," the National Institute of Justice found.[30]

Cops, courts and lawmakers responded with an iron fist. From 1985 to 1999, the nation's prison and jail population grew 130 percent, to nearly 2 million. And after Congress ratcheted up sentences for drug offenses in 1986, the number of drug convicts behind bars skyrocketed 400 percent in the next 10 years. Congress imposed

"mandatory minimum" sentences for crack that exceeded those for powder cocaine by a multiple of 100: selling 50 grams of crack brought 10 years in prison, the same penalty as selling 5,000 grams of cocaine powder.[31]

The sentencing disparity was widely seen as discriminating against blacks, who were the principal sellers of crack. The U.S. Sentencing Commission has authorized early release for those who received these sentences, but Congress hasn't changed the law.[32] (*See "Current Situation," p. 46.*)

The impact of the crack epidemic rippled far beyond prison walls. By 1992, emergency rooms near inner cities came to resemble combat surgery units. At the Martin Luther King Jr./Drew Medical Center in Los Angeles, gunshot victims increased from 19 percent of patients in 1985 to 51 percent in 1991. In that year, homicide skyrocketed in the African-American community, becoming the No. 1 cause of death of teenage males. The American Medical Association grew so alarmed it launched a public-health campaign against gun violence.[33]

Even young children weren't immune. In Los Angeles, King/Drew and Childrens Hospital in Hollywood treated 65 children 14 and younger for gunshot wounds from 1981 to 1991. Such was the level of violence that a psychiatrist at the University of California, Los Angeles, found a high incidence of untreated post-traumatic stress disorder among high-school students.[34]

The havoc crack wreaked extended beyond bodies and minds to society itself — especially in African-American communities. As many activists, writers and politicians have despairingly observed, poor African-Americans paid by far the biggest price for the crack epidemic, in part because inner-city streets invariably were the drug marketplaces.

"The metaphor of a raging fire or a cancer comes to mind," sociologist Elijah Anderson wrote in 1999. "Crack leads to illness, death, the proliferation of homeless children, crack babies, teenage pregnancy, violence, high rates of incarceration and other social problems."[35]

Crime Drops

The crack epidemic began burning itself out in most cities in the early 1990s, and crime rates dropped. But the stepped-up street enforcement and tough sentences generated by the crime boom ensured that the imprisoned population continued to grow. And the racial dimension of the prison boom was every bit as marked as the racial element of the preceding increase.

C H R O N O L O G Y

1960s-1984 *Johnson and Reagan administrations produce sharply contrasting crime-and-punishment policies.*

1968 President Lyndon B. Johnson tells Congress that crime grows out of poverty and reflects failure by society.

1982 Influential "Broken Windows" essay argues that focusing police attention on vandalism and similar low-level crimes makes streets safer.

1984 President Ronald Reagan denounces "coddling criminals" and pushes for tougher federal sentences. . . . Police begin encountering "crack," a cheap, smokable and highly addictive form of cocaine.

1985-1990 *Crack boom devastates inner cities, prompting crackdown.*

1985 Drug-abuse experts predict crack-cocaine epidemic.

1986 Crack sparks explosion in violent crime; Congress enacts long mandatory-minimum sentences for selling small amounts of the drug.

1988 Homicide rate for black men in hard-hit Washington, D.C., quadruples in three years. . . . New York City police officer killed while protecting drug-case witness. . . . Congress creates grants to state and local police for targeting violent drug criminals.

1990-2000 *Crack wave peaks, then ebbs, and violent crime begins declining nationwide; New York City — home to a series of policing innovations — leads the way.*

1990 New York homicides peak at 2,245 murders. . . . New transit Police Chief William J. Bratton begins cracking down on "broken windows" and other "quality of life" offenses.

1991 Half of patients at King-Drew Medical Center in Los Angeles are gunshot victims. . . . Homicide becomes leading cause of death for African-American males. . . . Number of homicides nationwide peaks at 24,703.

1993 Crime begins long decline with decrease of 0.3 percent from previous year.

1994 Congress enacts Clinton administration's Community Oriented Policing Services, designed to add 100,000 local police nationwide. . . . Bratton becomes New York City police chief, institutes "compstat" system of holding local commanders accountable for crime upticks; also targets gun-toting criminals.

1996 Homicides fall to 984 in New York and to 16,645 nationwide.

1998 New York gun homicides fall to 376, a 71 percent drop over 10 years.

1999 New York gun squad provokes firestorm after killing unarmed man, Amadou Diallo.

2000-Present *Violent crime remains low nationwide but upsurges crop up, especially in inner cities, prompting anti-violence activism.*

2002 New York shuts down controversial street-crime unit.

2003 Congressional lawmakers and local police chiefs oppose Bush administration's law-enforcement priorities, protest proposed cut in grants fund.

2004 Crime rates continue decline — longest such period since end of World War II.

2005 National crime decline ends with a 2.5 percent increase over previous year. . . . Lawmakers from districts hit hard by methamphetamine epidemic step up fight against Bush administration funding cuts to state and local law enforcement.

2007 Outgoing Philadelphia Police Chief Sylvester Johnson urges African-American men to reclaim the city's streets from criminals. . . . Legislatures in 26 states take steps toward liberalizing sentencing laws. . . . Majority of police chiefs blame easy access to guns for crime upsurges.

2008 Attorney General Michael Mukasey proposes $200 million in anti-crime aid for state and local law enforcement. Some lawmakers and city officials criticize administration's proposed cuts in crime-fighting aid for cities and states.

Crime Not a Campaign Issue This Time

But past candidates rode it to the White House.

In 1968, tough talk about rising street crime and riots in the streets helped Richard M. Nixon win the White House. In 1988, a commercial accusing the Democratic nominee, Gov. Michael Dukakis, D-Mass., of letting a rapist out of prison is credited with contributing to his defeat by Vice President George H.W. Bush.

But in 2008 crime is simply not an issue in the presidential race. And that's because crime as an issue isn't resonating with voters this year.

After more than a decade of decline, crime rates are largely stable, and voters have bigger concerns on their minds. In fact, crime and personal safety don't even register when pollsters ask voters about their top priorities, displaced by the economy, health care and the war in Iraq.

"Crime is just not that far up on the agenda," says Vincent J. Webb, dean of the College of Criminal Justice at Sam Houston State University in Huntsville, Texas.

Since the 9/11 attacks, terrorism has supplanted crime as the button candidates are most likely to push if they want to show they're tough or their opponents are weak when it comes to personal security.

"It's no longer about street crime or drugs," says Christopher Bracey, a law professor at Washington University School of Law in St. Louis.

Crime's lower profile as a campaign issue isn't necessarily a bad thing, given how candidates usually exploit public fears rather than engaging in an enlightening debate about public safety, says Richard Rosenfeld, a professor of criminology and criminal justice at the University of Missouri, St. Louis. "We're all the better for it," he says. "The way in which these issues are discussed and debated doesn't do anyone much good."

To be sure, an unforeseen school shooting this year could propel crime and gun control back to the top of the agenda. But thus far, crime is only an issue in certain places, such as California, where prison overcrowding is becoming acute, and Philadelphia and Newark, N.J., where urban violence remains high.

That's consistent with much of American history, when crime was considered a local political issue, says Rosenfeld. That changed, Rosenfeld says, with the 1964 presidential campaign of Sen. Barry Goldwater, R-Ariz., and the 1966 California gubernatorial race where a former actor named Ronald Reagan successfully campaigned against crime and campus disorder among students protesting the Vietnam War. By 1968, both Nixon and former Gov. George Wallace, D-Ala., both ran on law-and-order platforms at a time of rising public fear.

In 1999, Justice Department data showed that one in four African-Americans born that year would serve time in prison — while the comparable figure for all Americans was one in 20. In 1996, 8.3 percent of black men ages 25 to 29 were jailed or imprisoned, compared with 0.8 percent of whites.[36]

As for violent crime, the national trend was unmistakable. In 1991-97, robberies declined by 17 percent — an enormous drop in a field usually characterized by minuscule changes upward or downward. And the drop in homicides — 31 percent — was even starker. Two scholars at the National Development and Research Institutes in New York traced the shift directly to the end of the crack boom. Inner-city youths, they wrote, "clearly do not want to emulate their parents, older siblings, close relatives or other associates in their neighborhoods who were enmeshed with crack."[37]

But in a seemingly contradictory trend, the population of imprisoned drug convicts continued to expand. For one thing, a growing number of ex-prisoners were jailed again for violating parole. And the toughened penalties for drug offenses assured that drug convictions led to prison sentences.

On a slightly positive note, however, the growth of the federal and state prison population slowed. In 1999, the increase was 3.4 percent, the lowest rate since 1979 and well below the average increase for the decade, 6.5 percent. At its highest, in 1994, the growth rate reached 8.7 percent. [38]

"Broken Windows"

New York City's experience with crime in recent decades exemplifies the nationwide boom and retreat.

Both candidates blamed Democrats — and their appointees to the Supreme Court led by Chief Justice Earl Warren — for tying the hands of police with a series of decisions that bolstered criminal defendants' rights.

The last election where crime is credited with playing a decisive role was 1988, when a campaign advertisement tarred Gov. Dukakis because he had allowed a prisoner out for a weekend furlough, during which he committed armed robbery and rape.

The ad's focus on the rapist, Willie Horton, an African-American, was criticized for trying to exploit racial fears. At the time, surging violence associated with the rise of crack cocaine was blamed on African-Americans living in inner cities.

This year, however, the candidates aren't talking much about crime — not on the campaign stump and not even on their Web sites.

Bracey points out that Sen. Barack Obama, D-Ill., sprinkled his proposals for addressing law-enforcement issues such as racial profiling and narrowing disparities in the length of prison sentences under other headings such as civil rights in the plan outlining his policy agenda he calls, "Blueprint for Change."[1]

He says Democratic candidates have good reason to avoid talking about issues that might wind up alienating voters, such as gun control. "The leading candidates are just not going to go there," says Bracey. "These issues prove too nettlesome and create cleavages among constituents."

Two Republican candidates who emphasized their crime-related credentials flamed out early. Sen. Sam Brownback of Kansas has been the chief backer of legislation aimed at helping ease prisoners' transition back to the broader society. Rudy Giuliani trumpeted his record fighting crime as New York City mayor.

Nor did former Govs. Mike Huckabee (Arkansas) and Mitt Romney (Massachusetts) have much success attracting voters when they traded charges about who was tougher on clemency and the death penalty.

"It just doesn't have any traction right now," says Rosenfeld.

But Stephen Handelman, director of the Center on the Media, Crime and Justice at the John Jay College of Criminal Justice in New York, says crime might have greater resonance than candidates think. A recent survey by the center suggests the public would actually like to hear candidates talk a little more about crime.[2]

"The message is politicians would be misguided and shortsighted to ignore the fact the public still worries about crime," says Handelman.

— *Seth Stern, staff reporter,*
Congressional Quarterly

---

[1] www.barackobama.com/pdf/ObamaBlueprintForChange.pdf.

[2] www.jjay.cuny.edu/extra/symposium/John%20Jay%20POLL%20 Presentation.11%2029%2007.pdfs.

Beginning in the 1970s, the city was widely viewed as out of control. Robbers and fare-jumpers seemed to be taking over the subway system. Drugs were openly sold in many neighborhoods; and it was open season on parked cars, which were routinely broken into for their sound systems.

The public demand to reclaim public space — and restore a decent quality of life, free from fear — grew into a major political issue. Anticipating it, criminologist Kelling and conservative crime scholar James Q. Wilson offered a solution in a 1982 *Atlantic* magazine article that's still cited today.

"Arresting a single drunk or a single vagrant who has harmed no identifiable person seems unjust, and in a sense it is," they wrote. "But failing to do anything about a score of drunks or a hundred vagrants may destroy an entire community. Just as physicians now recognize the importance of fostering health rather than simply treating illness, so the police — and the rest of us — ought to recognize the importance of maintaining, intact, communities without broken windows."[39]

New York's crime wave came to a head in 1990, when a record 2,245 murders were recorded. Mayor David Dinkins, who took office the same year, embarked on a strategy of "community policies" alternately praised for strengthening police ties to the public and ridiculed for trying to turn cops into social workers.[40]

Still, crime began declining during Dinkins' tenure as well as the two-term administration of Giuliani, who in January ended his campaign for the Republican presidential nomination.

As mayor, Giuliani, along with his top police officials, began claiming much of the credit for the crime decline, setting off a debate that is still under way.

"Stop-Snitching" Street Code Hampers Police

Most Chicago murders remain unsolved.

"If someone did something to your mother and you tell on them, is that snitching?" Ronald Moten asks young people in Washington, D.C.'s toughest neighborhoods. They shake their heads "no." But, "If a white man came to your community and did a drive-by [shooting], would you tell?" The typical response: "Hell yeah!"

Moten, a co-founder of the anti-violence group Peaceoholics, has a simple, but controversial message: "Stop snitching" may sound like righteous street conduct, but there are built-in exceptions. In fact, he explains, it's only criminals who traditionally are discouraged from ratting out a crime buddy. "That code is not supposed to apply to law-abiding citizens, which is what most people are," Moten says.

But even young people who admit that talking to the police isn't always bad still need persuading that providing tips about crimes is a good thing, even when the victims aren't their mothers. "They've been brainwashed that there's something wrong with being a good citizen," Moten says.

In recent years, police and prosecutors in D.C. and other cities around the country have been running into stone walls because of uncooperative witnesses in inner-city neighborhoods.

In Chicago, police blame their inability to solve some two-thirds of local murders on a "no-snitching" code revved up by an underground media campaign using all the tools of modern marketing. A man wearing a T-shirt bearing the image of a tombstone and the words "RIP Snitches" was ejected from a Chicago courthouse in the summer of 2007, the *Chicago Sun-Times* reported.[1]

That was the same year in which police solved only 36 percent of the city's 443 murders, roughly the same percentage as the year before. "A lot of people will not cooperate with the police because it is not the thing to do," said Maria Maher, the Chicago Police Department's chief of detectives.[2]

The year before, in Pittsburgh, the alleged victim of an attempted murder was wearing a "stop-snitching" T-shirt as he was about to take the witness stand. When prosecutor Lisa Pellegrini told him to reverse the shirt, he refused and walked out of the courthouse. The judge threw out the case.[3]

Baltimore produced one of the most notorious examples of "no-snitch" propaganda — a rough-hewn 2004 video that's still circulating on DVD. "Stop Snitching" featured a gun-toting man who raps: "They're giving evidence to the pigs. I'll . . . destroy your house like you had 100 elephants in your crib."[4]

The makers of the DVD knew whereof they spoke. Cameraman Akiba M. Matthews was later convicted and sent to prison for intent to distribute heroin. Baltimore police made a point of noting that the DVD got them interested in Matthews — a sign of how much the video infuriated Maryland law-enforcement officials. "Think how bold criminals must be to make a DVD," Baltimore Circuit Judge John M. Glynn said. "It shows that threatening snitches has become mainstream — so much so that they make a DVD joking about it."[5]

Indeed, Rodney Bethea, the independent Baltimore-based producer behind the video, reportedly has made a sequel, set for release this year. According to *The Baltimore Sun*, the new video features a small boy exclaiming, "We don't know who snitches are, but when we find out, we gonna bust a cap," or shoot the snitches.[6]

Word of the "stop snitching" code didn't remain in the underground media. In 2007, rap star Cam'ron told interviewer Anderson Cooper on CBS' "60 Minutes" that he wouldn't

---

"Increases usually are not the policeman's fault," said criminologist Marcus Felson, a colleague of Kelling's at Rutgers, in 1995. "And decreases are not [to] his credit."[41]

But David C. Anderson, a journalist specializing in criminal justice, suggested in 1997 that the magnitude of the drop-off lent credibility to police claims. "Homicides for 1996 totaled 984, an astounding 57 percent below the 1990 figure," Anderson wrote. "Success probably attributable to the new police management deals a serious blow to skeptics."[42]

Anderson was referring to moves made by Giuliani and his first chief, Bratton. In fact, Giuliani's predecessor, Dinkins, also hired Bratton first, as chief of the transit

Legendary rapper Chuck D of Public Enemy has spoken out forcefully against the "stop snitching" campaign.

tell police even if he knew a serial killer was living next door. After a furor erupted, Cam'ron added fuel to the fire by saying that tipping police to a crime would hurt his business. The rapper then proclaimed a change of heart, saying he understood that earlier comments might offend crime victims.[7]

Some hip-hoppers, however, took a strong anti-crime line from the beginning. A founding father of the genre, Chuck D of Public Enemy, has denounced the "stop snitching" campaign. Writing on the group's Web site, he condemns "violent drug thug crime dogs, who've sacrificed the black community's women and children."[8]

But Moten adds that another motive not to snitch often comes into play, one that is understandable. "They feel that something might happen to them — which is a good reason not to tell." One of the most notorious cases of retaliation against witnesses occurred in Baltimore in 2002, when seven members of a family died in an arson fire at their home after they reported neighborhood drug dealing to police.[9]

Police have to take those fears into account, Moten wrote in *The Washington Post* last year. "Showing up in uniform and knocking on someone's door could get an innocent person killed. If police are clumsy in their investigations and let word out about who is cooperating, that can also lead to more bloodshed."[10]

But making people feel secure if they do the right thing is not easy, he says. "Me and you both know that if a person in [affluent] Georgetown is a witness, they're not about to have to sell their house [to leave the neighborhood]. But we also know that in Georgetown, 50 people will talk. In our communities, you only get one or two people who want to speak. The culture can intimidate people."

[1] See Annie Sweeney, "Police blame 'no snitching' for unsolved murders," *Chicago Sun-Times*, Jan. 22, 2008, p. A13.

[2] Quoted in *ibid.*

[3] See Rick Hampson, "Anti-snitch campaign riles police, prosecutors," *USA Today*, March 29, 2006, p. A1.

[4] Quoted in Julie Bykowicz, "Another weapon in war on witnesses," *The Baltimore Sun*, Dec. 12, 2004, p. A1.

[5] Quoted in *ibid.*

[6] See Julie Bykowicz, "Thug life — the sequel," *The Baltimore Sun*, Dec. 23, 2007, p. B1; Lynn Anderson, "'Stop Snitching' cameraman arrested," *The Baltimore Sun*, March 3, 2005, p. B1.

[7] See Peter Katel, "Debating Hip-Hop," *CQ Researcher*, June 15, 2007, pp. 529-552.

[8] Quoted in Hampson, *op. cit.*

[9] See Ryan Davis, "Homemade DVDs about informing gave police clues," *The Baltimore Sun*, Dec. 4, 2004, p. A1.

[10] See Ronald Moten, "The Real Meaning of 'Snitching,'" *The Washington Post*, Aug. 19, 2007, p. B2.

police, who are responsible for law and order on subways and buses. He ordered a crackdown on petty offenses, including evading fares, to create a more orderly environment. The strategy proved popular.[43]

One of Bratton's advisers in his subway years was Kelling, the "Broken Windows" theorist. Once Giuliani was in office and Bratton was chief, both became known for their enthusiastic embrace of the "Broken Windows" thesis. Despite its intuitive appeal, the strategy and whatever role it may have played in the New York turnaround has its skeptics.

Bernard E. Harcourt, a University of Chicago law professor, wrote in 2006 that the strategy had been oversold: "Those precincts that experienced the largest drops in crime in the 1990s were the ones that experienced the largest increases in crime during the city's crack epidemic of the mid- to late-1980s. What goes up must come down — and it would have come down even if New York had not embarked on its quality-of-life initiative."[44]

But such debates came later. As Giuliani's top cop, Bratton introduced a strategy known as "compstat" — from "computerized statistics." Police began gathering daily and hourly data on newly committed crimes. When computers crunched the numbers, they would reveal, for instance, pockets of lawlessness in a given precinct. At daily 7 a.m. meetings at headquarters, precinct commanders would be challenged to come up with ways to deal with the new crime outbreaks.[45]

Out on the street, Bratton expanded the strategy he had launched on subways and buses, ordering beat cops to crack down on so-called quality of life offenses. And he assigned a special squad to hunt down violent criminals — especially those carrying guns.

The Street Crime Unit (motto: "We Own the Night") used two tactics. Initially, officers began confronting people drinking on the street or committing other relatively minor offenses. Violators who could produce an ID were given a summons for a court date. Others were arrested — providing legal cause for a search. The tactic also produced the arrests of a sizable number of bail jumpers and other wanted criminals, some charged with serious crimes.[46]

A later tactic was to stop and frisk people — almost invariably young men, usually from minority groups — who had aroused "reasonable suspicion" — the standard set out in a 1968 U.S. Supreme Court decision.[47]

The unit, made up of detectives who worked in street clothes, soon earned a reputation for aggressiveness and for disdaining civil rights — and, its toughest critics said, for human life. In 1999, a four-man squad from the unit killed African immigrant Diallo after challenging him while he stood in the doorway of his apartment building. Police opened fire — shooting him 41 times — after he reached into a pocket, leading the cops to think he was going for a gun. He was trying to find his wallet. The officers were indicted for murder but acquitted by an Albany, N.Y., jury in 2000.[48]

Under Giuliani's successor, Mayor Michael Bloomberg, the unit was disbanded by Police Commissioner Raymond W. Kelly. "There is not a change in function," Kelly told reporters. "It is a change in title because we no longer have anything called street crime."[49]

CURRENT SITUATION
Crime vs. Terrorism

The Bush administration's 2009 federal budget proposal would slash the amount of federal aid to state and local law-enforcement agencies to $400 million — down dramatically from the $2.3 billion Congress appropriated for this year.

The $400 million includes the new $200 million grant program for targeting violent crime that Mukasey promised the mayors and $200 million in grants for prosecuting and rehabilitating drug offenders, plus three other programs. Bush is also seeking $285 million in grants to combat juvenile crime and violence against women.

The Bush package is getting harsh reviews from lawmakers, the latest chapter in a years-long fight for more federal aid for local crime-fighting. In previous appropriations battles, lawmakers more than doubled what the administration proposed for law enforcement, but less than they themselves wanted.[50]

Among the programs funded was the Clinton-era Community Oriented Policing Services (COPS), designed to boost police manpower; it got $587 million. In 1994, Congress had launched COPS with a $8.8 billion appropriation.[51] The most recent sum amounts to gutting the program, Sen. Joseph Biden, D-Del., its original author, told Mukasey.

"The COPS program was essentially all but eliminated," Biden told a Senate Judiciary Committee hearing on Jan. 30, with Mukasey sitting at the witness table.

"The single biggest bang for the buck, based upon all the data your office has acknowledged in the past — the more cops we have on the street, the further the violent crime drops," Biden said. "As old Ronald Reagan used to say, 'If it ain't broke, don't fix it.' It was working. You guys broke it."[52]

Mukasey left Biden's charge hanging and responded in general terms. "I agree with you that the strategy is not to tolerate any level of violent crime," he said. "What we are trying to do is to target grants to go where the need is and to gather information on what works best and to get it out to the people who need it."[53]

Do street gangs represent a growing national problem?

YES
Robert S. Mueller III
Director, Federal Bureau of Investigation

From statement before House Judiciary Committee, July 26, 2007

Violent gangs are a nationwide plague that is no longer limited to our largest cities. Since 2001, our violent gang caseload has more than doubled.

We [created] the National Gang Intelligence Center (NGIC) in Washington, D.C., to support our law-enforcement partners on the front lines. The NGIC shares information and analysis concerning the growth, migration, criminal activity and association of gangs that pose a significant threat to communities across the United States.

In Los Angeles we have come together on a task force with the Los Angeles Police Department and a number of other federal agencies to address gang violence. There has been a substantial reduction in gang violence in Los Angeles as a result of the joint efforts.

In support of the president's strategy to combat criminal gangs from Central America and Mexico, such as MS-13, the FBI has forged partnerships with anti-gang officials in El Salvador, Honduras and Guatemala, among other countries. We are working with the U.S. Department of State and the Department of Homeland Security to support the FBI's Central American Fingerprint Exploitation (CAFE) initiative, which collects gang members' fingerprints in [these] countries, allowing the United States to deny entry to the country even if they utilize aliases. There are many thousands of persons associated with MS-13 in the United States, in Guatemala, in Mexico, [and] quite obviously El Salvador and several other countries. And the threat is not just limited to Los Angeles but [extends] throughout the United States.

Approximately a year ago, some 600 MS-13 individuals were arrested not only in the United States but in El Salvador and Guatemala, Mexico and Honduras in a coordinated takedown. A gang such as this that crosses borders is a function of globalization, which requires us to work cooperatively and build allegiances and alliances with our counterparts overseas, if we are to effectively address the scourge of gang activity.

Currently, we have more than 2,800 pending investigations into gangs and gang-related activities. The number of agents working such cases has increased by 70 percent. We routinely work with our state and local partners to combat this pervasive threat. Of our 188 Safe Streets Task Forces, 135 are dedicated to identifying, prioritizing and targeting violent gangs. We now have more than 600 agents serving on those task forces, along with more than 1,100 officers from state and local law enforcement. Last year, they convicted nearly 2,200 violent gang members.

NO
Sheila Bedi
Executive Director, Justice Policy Institute

Written for *CQ Researcher*, January 2008

Nationwide gang membership is at its lowest level in three decades, and there is no evidence that gang activity is growing. The myth of a growing gang menace is primarily fueled mainly by media sensationalism and the misuse of law-enforcement gang statistics.

Concern has spread from neighborhoods with longstanding gang problems to communities with historically low levels of crime, and some policymakers declare the arrival of a national gang "crisis."

An effective response to the perceived "gangs crisis" requires a more realistic grasp of the challenges that gangs pose.

Research shows that despite law-enforcement reports, most gang members are not youth of color, and most young people outgrow their gang affiliation within the first year, without law-enforcement or gang-intervention programs. Gang members play a relatively small role in the national crime problem. And gangs themselves play an even smaller role, since most crime committed by gang members is self-directed and not committed for the gang's benefit.

Therefore, the objective should not be to eradicate gangs — an impossible task — but rather to promote community safety and reduce youth violence, which continues to be a problem in some communities. Experience, research and advances in criminal justice have taught us a lot about gangs, allowing us to identify effective approaches to crime reduction.

Suppression remains the most popular response to gang activity despite research showing that such tactics can strengthen gang cohesion and increase tension between law enforcement and communities. African-American and Latino communities bear the brunt of the cost of failed gang-enforcement initiatives and are targeted for surveillance, arrest and incarceration, while whites — who make up a significant share of gang members — rarely show up in accounts of gang-enforcement efforts. City and state officials have spent billions of dollars on more police, more prisons and more punitive measures, with few results. The cost of uninformed policymaking — including thousands of lives lost to violence or imprisonment — is simply too high.

Effective public-safety strategies include proven, evidence-based practices that reduce youth crime and lower barriers to the reintegration into society of former gang members. Such policies promote jobs and education and create safer, healthier communities. Rather than play to the false fears embodied in some legislative responses to youth violence, we should build upon the positive approaches that we know work with youth.

A second major bone of contention arose between the administration and senior lawmakers over the Edward Byrne State and Local Law Enforcement Assistance Grant Program. Named after a New York City police officer killed in the line of duty in 1988, "Byrne grants" are designed to finance upgrades in efforts to detect, arrest, prosecute and rehabilitate violent drug offenders.[54]

In February, the administration proposed appropriating $200 million for Byrne grants and three other programs. But a bipartisan group of senators led by Sens. Tom Harkin, D-Iowa, and Christopher S. Bond, R-Mo., the group plans to add $660 million in Byrne grant funding to an emergency war-funding bill. Byrne grants alone were funded at $170 million in fiscal 2007 and at $520 million the year before.[55]

Harkin has played a key role in the fight over anti-crime funding. "This is a shared priority," Harkin spokeswoman Jennifer Mullin said. "We don't expect for the state budgets to be able to bear the entire cost of these programs."[56]

Harkin and other Midwestern lawmakers are seeking, among other things, to stem an epidemic in methamphetamine manufacturing, addiction and crimes. In 2005, the Congressional Caucus to Fight and Control Methamphetamine — better known as the "meth caucus" — became the engine of opposition to cuts in the Byrne grants.[57]

The grants have been the focus since 2003 of fights over anti-crime versus anti-terrorism funding. Lawmakers and their constituents insist that continued federal anti-crime help is essential. "You can't tell me to put more officers on the street for homeland security and tell me to cut my budget," Craig Steckler, police chief in the Silicon Valley suburb of Fremont, Calif., said in 2003. Declining tax revenues forced him to lay off some of his force.[58]

President Bush has consistently said the administration's major mission has to be the fight against terrorists. In his 2008 State of the Union speech, he didn't mention domestic crime.

In the most recent round of the conflict, Harkin said proposed Byrne cuts would be "devastating" because "the Byrne program is the only source of federal funding for multi-jurisdictional efforts to fight crime and drugs."[59]

But in 2005, the White House's Office of Management and Budget recommended scrapping the grants. "The program funds a variety of potential local law-enforcement activities rather than a clearly defined, specific or existing problem, interest, or need," the OMB said. "There are no meaningful goals for the program. Performance measures are still under development. Grantees are not required to report on performance."[60]

In a strange-bedfellows twist, the administration has won the support of a leading anti-drug-war advocacy organization, the Drug Policy Alliance, which said the Byrne program had financed at least one notoriously botched drug investigation — in Tulia, Texas, where an undercover policeman committed perjury to make cases against 38 black townspeople whose convictions were later overturned.[61]

Mukasey's comments aroused another opposition front as well. He devoted part of his talk to opposing early release of thousands of federal prisoners sentenced under the highly controversial mandatory minimums for offenses involving crack cocaine. The U.S. Sentencing Commission approved standards in December that would allow the early releases of as many as 19,500 convicts, about 85 percent of them black.

"Before we take that step, we need to think long and hard," Mukasey said. "A sudden influx of criminals from federal prison into your communities could lead to a surge in new victims with a tragic but predictable result."[62]

Critics of the crack-sentencing laws expressed outrage. "In the grand sweep of the nation's criminal-justice system, the release of this minuscule number of prisoners will not affect crime rates," said Paul Cassell, a professor at the University of Utah law school and a former federal judge. "It will, however, significantly improve the perceived fairness of our federal criminal-justice system."[63]

War on Gangs

Congress is considering two competing approaches to combating criminal gangs. A bill passed by the Senate last fall would authorize a tough, enforcement-oriented strategy that includes the creation of new federal laws covering gang-related offenses. A pending House bill takes a more rehabilitation-oriented tack.

The extent to which gangs present a growing nationwide menace is a matter of some dispute. The Justice Department's National Youth Gang Center reported in 2004 that 760,000 gang members and 24,000 gangs were active in more than 2,900 jurisdictions. But the center said in a separate report that those numbers represented a decline from earlier surveys. And 53 percent of law-enforcement agencies said their gang problems were "getting better" or "staying about the same."[64]

Nonetheless, a study by the liberal Justice Policy Institute concluded that while gang activity as a national problem is largely overblown, gangs are a real menace in some cities, including Chicago and Los Angeles. But in Los Angeles, the report said, "Spending on gang enforcement has far outpaced spending on prevention programs or on improved conditions in communities where gang violence takes a heavy toll."[65]

The Gang Abatement and Prevention Act, which senators approved by voice vote on Sept. 21, 2007, would appropriate $1 billion over five years for anti-gang enforcement. Sponsored by Sens. Dianne Feinstein, D-Calif., and Orrin Hatch, R-Utah, the bill would create several new federal crimes, including interstate interference with witnesses in state court proceedings; recruiting criminal street-gang members; and illegal activities by a criminal street gang. Rep. Adam B. Schiff, D-Calif., introduced a companion bill in the House.[66] Other House bills take similar approaches.[67]

But the House also has produced another strategy for dealing with gangs, the Youth Prison Reduction through Opportunities, Mentoring, Intervention, Support, and Education (Youth PROMISE) Act, sponsored by Rep. Robert C. Scott, D-Va. The legislation would authorize communities with gang problems to form councils that would come up with local strategies to keep young people out of gangs and criminal activity.

"For years, we have been codifying slogans and sound bites that do nothing to reduce crime," Scott said in a press release. "This legislation implements the recommendations of researchers, practitioners, analysts and law-enforcement officials from across the political spectrum concerning evidence- and research-based strategies to reduce gang violence and youth crime."[68]

The Senate's Abatement Act won the endorsement of a law-enforcement rock star: Bratton, now chief in Los Angeles, a city notorious for its deeply rooted, violent gangs. Bratton told the Senate Judiciary Committee that his department forced gang-related crimes down from 2,521 in 2006 to 2,382 by late 2007. "The LAPD firmly believes that prevention, intervention and suppression are the keys to curbing gang violence," he said.[69]

Amid praise from other officials, including Los Angeles Mayor Antonio Villaraigosa, Judiciary Chairman Sen. Patrick Leahy, D-Vt., sounded a note of caution. "I do not believe that sweeping new federal crimes, which federalize the kind of street crime that states have traditionally addressed, and can address well with the adequate resources, are the right way to go," he said.[70]

The competing approach embodied by Scott's bill has been endorsed by some 47 organizations, including the American Civil Liberties Union, the NAACP and the National Association of Criminal Defense Lawyers. They laud its proposed investment in "prevention and intervention rather than in more costly and ineffective prosecution and incarceration."[71]

OUTLOOK

Economic Ripple Effect?

Liberals, conservatives, police chiefs, academics, neighborhood activists — everyone with a professional interest in crime — agree on one point if on few others: Lawbreaking will never go away. Theorizing on the future focuses on whether rates will rise or fall, whether prevention or punishment will dominate the law-enforcement approach and what new sorts of crimes might accompany new forms of technology.

But because the future depends on the present, one veteran scholar wonders whether there is much room for speculation that the next 10 years will bring any major changes.

"I suspect the picture will look largely as it does now," says Blumstein of Carnegie-Mellon University. "While resources are being drained in foreign adventures, major new investments in social services, job opportunities and job training are going to be tough to come by."

And if today's economic conditions worsen, "The major burden will be felt in state and local governments, which will cut back further on social services, and policing," Blumstein says.

Wexler of PERF argues that demography may play just as big a role in the future of crime. A bulge in the number of juveniles could well push crime rates up, he says, touching on a topic that criminologists have long been debating and analyzing — the influence of population shifts on crime rates.

However, Wexler notes, "As the economy becomes more electronic, as we use cash for fewer transactions, that may result in fewer opportunities for crimes involving cash." But immigrants, who typically rely on cash, would become even more vulnerable.

What would the law-enforcement consequences be of an upsurge in, say, robberies and burglaries? The University of California's Zimring notes that revenue shortfalls are already forcing some states to cut back on imprisonment. In any event, he argues, the value of prison may have passed the point of diminishing returns.

"We've probably been making our biggest bets on the wrong thing," Zimring says. "I suspect that emphasizing the front end of law enforcement — putting a steering-wheel lock on a car, keeping streets under observation, creating emergency-response procedures — works better than shipping people off to the gulag."

In any event, Zimring says, "Lethal violence isn't part of [the system of] distribution of income, isn't part of any fundamental economic processes. It is a byproduct of social values and patterns of free time and non-productivity. When a kid's arrest rate goes down, it's when he stops hanging out with male friends and starts hanging out with a significant other and gets a job. Then he only has time for lethal violence when he gets drunk on Friday night."

But "Broken Windows" co-author Kelling of Rutgers argues that the major elements of homicide are the drug trade and high-powered weapons, and the likelihood of making big inroads against either is slim.

"These are gun-carrying, drug-dealing youths who are killing each other," Kelling says, arguing that street confrontations over perceived disrespect are largely diminishing. "Increasingly, it's not just the 'dis' but the planned targeting," that leads to homicides, he says. Add to that the "no-snitching" rule, and one killing is likely to trigger retaliation, he notes.

While others in the field bemoan the use of resources for the Iraq War that might otherwise fund social services, Kelling sees at least one street-level benefit. Citing the counterinsurgency campaign that began in 2007 under Gen. David H. Petraeus, Kelling says, "We're starting to learn that if you want to police these tough crime areas you've got to take the risks of working closely with the community. You can't have officers in cars or in a bivouacked area; you have to become part of the community."

Kelling's vision of inner cities as a domestic version of Iraq mirrors, to some extent, the democracy-building focus of Peaceoholics co-founder Abraham. In the inner city, he says, "Most people don't understand what it takes to be a citizen" — that is, a full member of the larger society, with rights and responsibilities.

Meanwhile, Abraham has another grim concern: the ripple effects of the economic downturn, which he sees as likely to spark an upsurge in crime. "The average American has not begun to feel the blow," he says. "If you don't have money and a job, you've got to go get something. Nobody's living anywhere for free. Even if you're living with your mother and you're grown, you've got to bring something to the table."

NOTES

1. See Allison Klein and Theolo Labbé, "3 Students From Ballou High Wounded in Shooting Nearby," *The Washington Post*, Jan. 23, 2008, p. B1; Nelson Hernandez and Candace Rondeaux, "Teen Shot in Drive-By Near High School Dies," *The Washington Post*, Jan. 11, 2008, p. B2; Petula Dvorak, "Youth Had Just Turned 17 When He Was Fatally Shot," *The Washington Post*, Jan. 10, 2008, p. B2; Keith L. Alexander, "Suspect Being Held Without Bond," *The Washington Post*, Jan. 26, 2008, p. B5.

2. Allison Klein, "Killings in D.C. Up After Long Dip," *The Washington Post*, Jan. 1, 2008, p. A1.

3. See Joseph A. Gambardello and Barbara Boyer, "Slayings in city down, but still high," *The Philadelphia Inquirer*, Jan. 1, 2008, www.philly.com/inquirer/local/20080101_Slayings_in_city_down__but_still_high.html; Colleen Long, "Historic low in NYC, Chicago homicides," usatoday.com (The Associated Press), Dec. 28, 2007, www.usatoday.com/news/nation/2007-12-29-big-city-homicides_N.htm?csp=34.

4. See "Table 2 — Percent Change by Geographic Region, January-June 2007," "Uniform Crime Report, Preliminary January through June 2007," FBI, January 2008, www.fbi.gov/ucr/prelim2007/table2.htm.

5. See "Violent Crime in America: 'A Tale of Two Cities,'" Police Executive Research Forum, November, 2007, p. 6, www.policeforum.org/upload/VC%20Summit%2007_full_148192123_1272007111812.pdf.

6. See "Prepared Remarks of Attorney General Michael B. Mukasey at the U.S. Conference of Mayors," Jan.

24, 2008, www.usdoj.gov/ag/speeches/2008/ag_speech_080124.html.

7. "Crime in the United States by Volume and Rate per 100,000 Inhabitants, 1987-2006," Department of Justice, FBI, September 2007, www.fbi.gov/ucr/cius2006/data/table_01.html. For background see Marc Leepson, "Cocaine: Drug of the Eighties," Aug. 27, 1982, and Mary H. Cooper, "The Business of Illicit Drugs," May 20, 1988, both in *Editorial Research Reports*, available at *CQ Researcher Plus Archive*, http://library.cqpress.com.

8. Franklin E. Zimring, *The Great American Crime Decline* (2007).

9. "Unconfirmed Reports," "The Wire," Season 5, Episode 2, HBO.

10. "Black Homicide Victimization in the United States: An Analysis of 2005 Homicide Data," Violence Policy Center, January, 2008, p. 1, www.vpc.org/studies/blackhomicide08.pdf.

11. Daryl Fears, "City to Take New Tack to Curb Gun Violence," *The Washington Post*, Dec. 23, 2007, p. A3, www.washingtonpost.com/wp-dyn/content/article/2007/12/22/AR2007122200384_pf.html.

12. See Richard B. Schmitt and David G. Savage, "Chipping at tough crack sentencing," *Los Angeles Times*, Dec. 30, 2007, p. A16. For background see Peter Katel, "Prison Reform," *CQ Researcher*, April 6, 2007, pp. 289-312.

13. See Ryan S. King, "The State of Sentencing 2007: Developments in Policy and Practice," The Sentencing Project, January, 2008, p. 1, http://sentencingproject.org/Admin/Documents/publications/sl_state sentencingreport2007.pdf.

14. Quoted in Solomon Moore, "Trying to Break Cycle of Prison at Street Level," *The New York Times*, Nov. 23, 2007, p. A28.

15. Quoted in Sylvia Moreno, "Spreading a Message of Peace in Troubled Barry Farm," *The Washington Post*, Jan. 27, 2008, p. C4.

16. Quoted in Dave Davies, "Commish: I need 10,000 black men," *Philadelphia Daily News*, Sept. 12, 2007, www.philly.com/dailynews/ local/20070912_Commish__I_need_10_000_black_men.html.

17. Andrew Karmen, *New York Murder Mystery: The True Story Behind the Crime Crash of the 1990s* (2000).

18. Quoted in "Violent Crime in America: 'A Tale of Two Cities,' " *op. cit.*, p. 22.

19. For background, see Peter J. Boyer, "The Color of Politics," *The New Yorker*, Feb. 4, 2008, p. 38. See also Janet Frankston Lorin, "Newark mayor says student slayings weren't planned," The Associated Press, Aug. 21, 2007; Kareem Fahim and Andrew Jacobs, "Man and Youth Held in Killings Of 3 in Newark," *The New York Times*, Aug. 10, 2007, p. A1.

20. See David C. Anderson, "Crime Stoppers," *The New York Times Magazine*, Feb. 9, 1997, p. 47.

21. See David Kocieniewski, "Success of Elite Police Unit Exacts a Toll on the Streets," *The New York Times*, Feb. 15, 1999, p. A1.

22. See Diane Cardwell, "Bloomberg Begs to Differ With Giuliani on Gun Suit," *The New York Times*, Sept. 25, 2007, p. B2.

23. See Karmen, *op. cit.*, p. 65.

24. See James Q. Wilson and George L. Kelling, "Broken Windows," *The Atlantic*, March, 1982, www.theatlantic.com/ideastour/archive/windows.mhtml.

25. For background, see Marcia Clemmitt, "Mortgage Crisis," *CQ Researcher*, Nov. 2, 2007, pp. 913-936.

26. Quoted in Peter Gosselin, "Job slump latest omen of recession," *Los Angeles Times*, Jan. 5, 2008, p. A1. See also Michael A. Fletcher, "Highly Skilled and Out of Work," *The Washington Post*, Jan. 21, 2008, p. A1.

27. For additional background, see Sarah Glazer, "Declining Crime Rates," *CQ Researcher*, April 4, 1997, pp. 289-312.

28. "To Redeem the Worst, to Better the Best," *Time*, Feb. 17, 1967, www.time.com/time/magazine/article/0,9171,839436-2,00.html.

29. Sen. Jeff Sessions, "Tribute to former President Ronald Reagan," June 9, 2004, http://sessions.senate.gov/pressapp/record.cfm?id=222498.

30. See Pamela K. Lattimore, *et al.*, "Homicide in Eight U.S. Cities: Trends, Context and Policy Implications," National Institute of Justice, December,

1997, p. 33, www.whitehousedrugpolicy.gov/publi cations/pdf/homicide_trends.pdf.

31. For background, see Kenneth Jost, "Sentencing Debates," *CQ Researcher*, Nov. 5, 2004, pp. 925-948.

32. See Timothy Egan, "War on Crack Retreats, Still Taking Prisoners," *The New York Times*, Feb. 28, 1999, p. A1.

33. See Dennis Cauchon, "Murder a National 'Epidemic,'" *USA Today*, June 10, 1992, p. A1.

34. See David Freed, "Guns, Violence Exact a Toll on L.A.'s Youngest Victims," *Los Angeles Times*, May 21, 1992, p. A1.

35. See Anderson, *op. cit.*, p. 235.

36. See Egan, *op. cit.*

37. Quoted in Fox Butterfield, "Decline of Violent Crimes is Linked to Crack Market," *The New York Times*, Dec. 28, 1998, p. A18.

38. See Fox Butterfield, "Number in Prison Grows Despite Crime Reduction," *The New York Times*, Aug. 10, 2000, p. A10.

39. Wilson and Kelling, *op. cit.*

40. For murder statistic see Karmen, *op. cit.*, p. 23.

41. Quoted in Jim Newton, "The NYPD: Bigger, Bolder — Is It Better?" *Los Angeles Times*, Dec. 24, 1995, p. A1.

42. See Anderson, *op. cit.*, p. 48.

43. See Calvin Sims, "For Subway Police, a New Pride Over Duty in 'the Hole,'" *The New York Times*, March 1, 1991, p. B1.

44. Bernard E. Harcourt, "Bratton's 'Broken Windows,'" *Los Angeles Times*, April 20, 2006, p. B13.

45. See Newton, *op. cit.*

46. See David C. Anderson, *op. cit.*; and David Kocieniewski, "Success of Elite Police Unit Exacts a Toll on the Streets," *The New York Times*, Feb. 15, 1999, p. A1.

47. *Terry v. Ohio*, 392 U.S. 1 (1968). See Karmen, *op. cit.*, pp. 118-120.

48. See Kevin Flynn, "Shooting in the Bronx: The Overview," *The New York Times*, Feb. 14, 1999, p. A1; Robert D. McFadden, "Four Officers Indicted for Murder in Killing of Diallo, Lawyer Says," *The*

New York Times, March 26, 1999, p. A1; Robert D. McFadden, "The Diallo Verdict: The Reaction," *The New York Times*, Feb. 26, 2000, p. A1.

49. Quoted in William K. Rashbaum and Al Baker, "Police Commissioner Closing Controversial Street Crime Unit," *The New York Times*, April 10, 2002, p. B1.

50. See Caitlin Weber, "Senators Seeking Emergency Funding for Law Enforcement Grants," *CQ Today*, Jan. 30, 2008. "Justice Department," Office of Management and Budget, www.whitehouse.gov/ omb/budget/fy2009/justice.html.

51. See Christopher S. Koper, "Putting 100,000 Officers on the Street: A Survey-Based Assessment of the Federal COPS Program," Urban Institute, Justice Policy Center, October 2002, pp. 2-1, www.sas .upenn.edu/jerrylee/research/cops_levels.pdf.

52. See "Senate Judiciary Committee Holds Hearing on Oversight of the Department of Justice," *Congressional Transcripts*, Jan. 30, 2008.

53. *Ibid.*

54. See Weber, *op. cit.*; and "Edward Byrne State and Local Law Enforcement Assistance Grant Program," Bureau of Justice Assistance, Department of Justice, undated, www.ojp.us doj.gov/BJA/grant/byrne.html.

55. Weber, *op. cit.*

56. Quoted in Nigel Duara, "Cutbacks threaten anti-drug campaign," *Des Moines Register*, Jan. 20, 2008, www.desmoinesregister.com/apps/pbcs.dll/ article?AID=/20080120/NEWS01/801200337/-1/ archive.

57. See Stephen Bodzin, "Power of 'Meth Caucus' Grows," *Los Angeles Times*, Jan. 23, 2005, p. A20.

58. Quoted in Nick Anderson and Christine Hanley, "Bush Fails to Sell Congress on Terror Spending Goals," *Los Angeles Times*, Feb. 22, 2003, p. A15.

59. Quoted in Weber, *op. cit.*

60. "Program Assessment, Multipurpose Law Enforcement Grants," Office of Management and Budget, 2005, www.whitehouse.gov/omb/expect-more/summary/10003806.2005.html.

61. See Duara, *op. cit.* Also, Simon Romero with Adam Liptak, "Texas Court Acts to Clear 38 in Town-Splitting

Drug Case," *The New York Times*, April 2, 2003, http://query.nytimes.com/gst/fullpage.html?res=9B04E5DF1E39F931A35757C0A9659C8B63.

62. Quoted in Richard B. Schmitt, "Mukasey sees risk in early release," *Los Angeles Times*, Jan. 25, 2008, p. A27.

63. *Ibid.*

64. See "Frequently Asked Questions Regarding Gangs," National Youth Gang Center, undated, www.iir.com/NYGC/faq.htm#q3; and "Highlights of the 2004 National Youth Gang Survey," Office of Juvenile Justice and Delinquency Prevention, Department of Justice, April 2006, www.ncjrs.gov/pdffiles1/ojjdp/ fs200601.pdf. For background, see William Triplett, "Gang Crisis," May 14, 2004, pp. 421-444, and Charles S. Clark, "Youth Gangs," Oct. 11, 1991, pp. 753-776, both in *CQ Researcher*, available at *CQ Researcher Plus Archive*, http://library.cqpress.com.

65. See Judith Greene and Kevin Pranis, "Gang Wars: The Failure of Enforcement Tactics and the Need for Effective Public Safety Strategies," Justice Policy Institute, July 2007, p. 3, www.justicepolicy.org/images/upload/07-07_ REP_GangWars_GC-PS-AC-JJ.pdf.

66. See Seth Stern, "Senate Passes Legislation Designed to Deter and Crack Down on Gang Violence," *CQ Today*, Sept. 21, 2007.

67. The lawmakers outlined their bills at a House Judiciary Committee meeting. See "Gang Crime Prevention," House Judiciary Committee testimony, Oct. 2, 2007.

68. "Rep. Scott Introduces Youth PROMISE Act," press release, Oct. 16, 2007, www.house. gov/apps/list/press/va03_scott/pr_071016.html.

69. See "The Gang Abatement and Prevention Act of 2007," Senate Judiciary Committee testimony, June 5, 2007.

70. *Ibid.*

71. "Support for the Youth PROMISE Act," Jan. 23, 2008, www.house.gov/scott/pdf/ Promise_Act_support_080123.pdf.

BIBLIOGRAPHY

Books

Anderson, Elijah, *Code of the Street: Decency, Violence, and the Moral Life of the Inner City*, W.W. Norton, 1999.
A Yale University sociologist tells how residents of poor African-American neighborhoods navigate around the many obstacles in their path, including criminal violence.

Bratton, William, with Peter Knobler, *Turnaround: How America's Top Cop Reversed the Crime Epidemic*, Random House, 1998.
The former New York City police chief, now Los Angeles' top cop, claims his leadership and methods reduced New York's crime rate.

Karmen, Andrew, *New York Murder Mystery: The True Story Behind the Crime Crash of the 1990s*, New York University Press, 2000.
Partisan explanations for New York's anti-crime success story get skeptical analysis by a sociologist at the John Jay College of Criminal Justice.

Venkatesh, Sudhir, *Gang Leader for a Day: A Rogue Sociologist Takes to the Streets*, Penguin Press, 2008.
A young academic shadows a crack-gang leader for seven years to study the gang's organizational structure and culture.

Zimring, Franklin E., *The Great American Crime Decline*, Oxford University Press, 2007.
A veteran criminologist at the University of California, Berkeley, analyzes the crime drop of the 1990s.

Articles

Benn, Evan S., "Assault weapons multiply, take a deadly toll," *The Miami Herald*, Jan. 14, 2008, p. A1.
South Florida criminals are taking up high-powered firearms in growing numbers, and police are worried.

Boyer, Peter J., "The Color of Politics," *The New Yorker*, Feb. 4, 2008, p. 38.
Newark Mayor Cory Booker's challenges include the aftermath of one of last year's most notorious crimes: the execution killing of three African-American college students by Latino criminals.

Bykowicz, Julie, "Searching for answers; the numbers look bleak for city mired in murder," *The Baltimore Sun,* **Dec. 30, 2007, p. A1.**
Drug-linked crimes in Baltimore have outlasted all efforts at solution.

Cramer, Maria, "2007 drop in crime buoys hub leaders, but troubling trends remain," *The Boston Globe,* **Jan. 1, 2008, p. B1.**
Officials take heart from a recent decrease, but violent crime remains at a high level.

Gurwitt, Rob, "Bratton's Brigade," *Governing,* **August 2007.**
Disciples of Los Angeles Police Chief William J. Bratton are deploying his data-driven, quick-reaction strategies.

Pierre, Robert E., "Brokering Peace," *The Washington Post,* **Jan. 14, 2007, p. C1.**
The grassroots group Peaceoholics is working the streets to calm some of Washington's toughest neighborhoods.

Rubin, Joel, and Duke Helfand, "L.A. gang-related killings plunge 27%," *Los Angeles Times,* **Jan. 11, 2008, p. B3.**
A heartening reduction in gang-related homicides hasn't ended the debate over long-range anti-crime strategies.

Schmitt, Richard B., and David G. Savage, "Chipping at tough crack sentencing," *Los Angeles Times,* **Dec. 30, 2007, p. A16.**
Debate is intensifying over the disparate sentence requirements for crack and powder cocaine.

Reports and Studies

Greene, Judith, and Kevin Pranis, "Gang Wars: The Failure of Enforcement Tactics and the Need for Effective Public Safety Strategies," Justice Policy Institute, July 2007, www.justicepolicy.org/images/upload/07-07_REP_GangWars_GC-PS-AC-JJ.pdf.
Analysts at a liberal think tank argue that the menace of gangs has been overblown.

"National Methamphetamine Threat Assessment 2008," National Drug Intelligence Center, Department of Justice, December 2007, www.usdoj.gov/ndic/pubs26/26594/26594p.pdf.
The latest, annual, region-by-region report includes a look at enforcement efforts.

Webster, Daniel W., *et al.,* **"How Cities Can Combat Illegal Guns and Gun Violence," Center for Gun Policy and Research, Johns Hopkins Bloomberg School of Public Health, Oct. 23, 2006, www.jhsph.edu/gunpolicy/How%20Cities%20Can%20Combat%20Illegal%20Guns.pdf.**
The think tank lays out strategies and tactics, including the building of databases to track the origins of guns used in crimes.

"Violent Crime in America: 'A Tale of Two Cities,' " Police Executive Research Forum, November 2007, www.policeforum.org/upload/VC%20Summit%2007_full_148192123_1272007111812.pdf.
The think tank presents data and police chiefs' commentary on America's disparate crime picture.

For More Information

Bureau of Justice Statistics, 810 7th St., N.W., Washington, DC 20531; (202) 307-0765; www.ojp .usdoj.gov/bjs. Justice Department agency publishes statistics on all aspects of crime and punishment.

Criminal Justice Policy Foundation, 8730 Georgia Ave., Suite 400, Silver Spring, MD 20910; (301) 589-6020; www.cjpf.org. Liberal group advocates easing crack cocaine sentences.

The Homicide Report, *Los Angeles Times*, http://latimes-blogs.latimes.com/homicidereport. Describes every violent death reported by the Los Angeles County coroner.

Justice Mapping Center, 155 Washington Ave., Brooklyn, NY 11205; (888) 816-8117; www.justicemapping.org/ home. Uses computers to map clusters of recently paroled people and other detailed graphics relevant to criminal-justice policy.

Los Angeles Police Department blog, www.lapdblog.type pad.com. Records police-related news events including gang killings, pointing lasers at the eyes of police helicopter pilots and transporting Britney Spears to a hospital.

Manhattan Institute for Policy Research, 52 Vanderbilt Ave., New York, NY 10017; (212) 599-7000; www.manhattan-institute.org. Conservative think tank publishes crime-control studies supporting the "Broken Windows" thesis co-authored by institute senior fellow George L. Kelling.

Peaceoholics, 61 Raleigh Pl., S.E., Washington, DC 20032; (202) 562-1895; www.peaceoholics.org/prod1 .html. Works to defuse inner-city violence and to train young people in conflict resolution.

Police Executive Research Forum (PERF), 1120 Connecticut Ave., N.W., Suite 930, Washington, DC, 20036; (202) 466-7820; www.policeforum.org. A think tank on law-enforcement strategy that examines the reasons for disparities in urban-crime rates

3

Disaster Preparedness

Pamela M. Prah and Patrick Marshall

Hundreds of shipping containers, recreational vehicles and motorboats litter a residential area of Gulfport, Miss., after Hurricane Katrina hit. The storm killed more than 1,300 people in Louisiana, Alabama and Mississippi, and racked up $200 billion in property damage and relief expenses, making it the costliest storm in U.S. history.

AFP/Getty Images/Paul J. Richards

From *CQ Researcher*,
November 18, 2005 (updated August 6, 2010).

Six days before Hurricane Katrina tore through the Gulf Coast, Wal-Mart swung into action. As the deadly storm barreled toward New Orleans, the world's biggest retailer dispatched a fleet of tractor-trailer trucks loaded with generators, dry ice, thousands of cases of bottled water and other vitally needed supplies to nearby staging areas.[1]

Federal, state and local authorities also saw Katrina coming — but their delayed and deeply flawed response became a national scandal.

President Bush declared a state of emergency for Louisiana on Aug. 27, two days before the storm struck, making it eligible for federal assistance. When Katrina made landfall on Aug. 29, Bush issued a federal "declaration of emergency," activating the country's disaster plan. The $64,000 question is why it took so long for federal authorities to act.

Michael Brown, director of the Federal Emergency Management Agency (FEMA), was deemed so inept he was called back to Washington mid-disaster. Local officials were overwhelmed by the scope of the devastation and unsure who was in charge. More than 1,300 people died, and at one point more than 300,000 evacuees were housed in shelters in 40 states.[2] And politicians at all levels bickered openly about who was to blame for the horrific catastrophe that was unfolding on live TV for the world to see.

Critics charged that little thought had been given to helping people without the means to evacuate on their own — the elderly, disabled and poor.

55

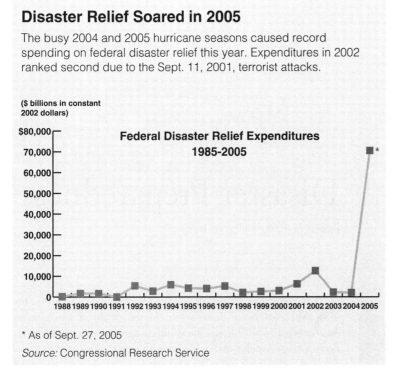

Disaster Relief Soared in 2005

The busy 2004 and 2005 hurricane seasons caused record spending on federal disaster relief this year. Expenditures in 2002 ranked second due to the Sept. 11, 2001, terrorist attacks.

($ billions in constant 2002 dollars)

Federal Disaster Relief Expenditures 1985-2005

* As of Sept. 27, 2005

Source: Congressional Research Service

history," wrote Donald F. Kettl, director of the Fels Institute of Government at the University of Pennsylvania."[4]

The fabled Big Easy suffered such extensive damage that some officials questioned the wisdom of rebuilding. (*See sidebar, p. 68.*)

Disaster experts blame much of the flawed response to Katrina on inadequate communications technology. Emergency-phone systems in different jurisdictions were "interoperable." Nearly forty 911 centers were knocked out, leaving citizens no way to call for help. New Orleans Mayor Ray Nagin was stuck in a hotel without a phone for two days while Louisiana Gov. Kathleen Blanco, a Democrat, reportedly couldn't get through to President Bush for two crucial days.

While looting was extensive, wildly exaggerated reports of mayhem and murder added to the sense of an out-of-control city. Even the arrival of more than 50,000 National Guard and 20,000 active-duty troops turned controversial, because critics said they came too late or were ordered not to stop the looters.

When Hurricane Rita hit Texas and Louisiana three weeks later, the response was better. But the system again faltered in late October when Hurricane Wilma — as predicted — hit Key West and Fort Lauderdale, forcing thousands of Floridians to wait in lines for water, gas, ice and insurance help.

Emergency experts and administration critics were particularly concerned about the bungled 2005 storm responses because hurricanes come with plenty of advance warning, but terrorist attacks, tornadoes and earthquakes don't.

"If we can't get Katrina right, how on Earth are we going to get a dirty bomb right, a bioterrorist attack right, the avian flu right?" asks Kathleen Tierney, director of the Natural Hazards Center at the University of Colorado in Boulder.

And most homeland security experts say another terrorist attack on the United States is all but inevitable.

As for New Orleans, experts have long known the below-sea-level city was a catastrophe waiting to happen.

As a result, residents who had banked on government help were left to fend for themselves. In New Orleans, levees broke, and as floodwaters rose thousands of residents huddled on rooftops. The 20,000 people who took refuge in the Superdome found inadequate food and water, scant medical help and toilets that quickly were overwhelmed. Outside the disaster zone, government doctors stood by hundreds of empty cots, watching for patients who never arrived. Paltry resources were predeployed, or arrived late. Experts fear that sick and injured victims died for lack of timely care.

"If the federal government would have responded as quickly as Wal-Mart, we could have saved more lives," said Jefferson Parish Sheriff Harry Lee.[3]

Hurricane Katrina ranks as the most destructive storm in U.S. history. It destroyed some 200,000 homes in New Orleans alone and cost as much as $200 billion. Katrina directly affected more than a half-million people in Louisiana, Mississippi and Alabama. More than that, Katrina revealed what was widely seen as a shocking lack of readiness for another major catastrophe.

"The government's response to Katrina ranks as perhaps the biggest failure of public administration in the nation's

The federal government in 2001 ranked the potential damage to New Orleans from a hurricane as among the three likeliest, most catastrophic disasters facing this country.[5] Engineers said the city's levees would not withstand the strongest of hurricane winds. Indeed, when FEMA and Louisiana authorities practiced responding to a severe mock hurricane in July 2004, they anticipated conditions eerily similar to those wrought by Katrina: the evacuation of a million people, overflowing levees and the destruction of up to 600,000 buildings.[6]

Critics say the country should have been better prepared, particularly after the Sept. 11, 2001, terrorist attacks revealed that communications systems used by emergency workers from different jurisdictions often did not work with one another. Yet three years after the attacks, emergency equipment used in more than 80 percent of America's cities was still not interoperable with federal agencies, and 60 percent of the cities did not have communication systems that meshed with state emergency centers.[7]

The White House and Congress are both investigating the government's botched response to Katrina, but they had better act fast. Experts at the National Hurricane Center warn that the country has entered a new weather cycle that will produce more frequent "super-hurricanes" for the next 20 years, threatening cities even as far north as New York.[8]

"Houston, Galveston, Tampa Bay, southwest Florida, the Florida Keys, southeast Florida, New York City, Long Island and, believe it or not, New England, are all especially vulnerable," Max Mayfield, director of the National Hurricane Center's Tropical Prediction Center, told a Senate panel on Sept. 20.

The picture isn't much brighter for earthquakes, which threaten 75 million Americans in 39 states.[9] Experts say the United States has been lucky that recent earthquakes have occurred relatively far from populated areas, but that a major quake eventually is going to hit a big city like San Francisco.

Katrina Was Costliest U.S. Disaster

By far the most expensive disaster in the nation's history, Katrina is expected to cost at least three times more than the second-costliest U.S. disaster, the 1988 heat wave and drought.

Ten Costliest U.S. Natural Disasters
(1980-2005)

Year	Cost ($ in billions)	Disaster	Location
2005	$200 (est.)	Hurricane Katrina	Gulf Coast
1988	$61.6	Heat wave, drought	Central, Eastern U.S.
1980	$48.4	Heat wave, drought	Central, Eastern U.S.
1992	$35.6	Hurricane Andrew	South Florida, Louisiana
1993	$26.7	Floods	Midwest
1994	$25	Earthquake	Northridge/San Francisco, Calif.
2004	$14	Hurricane Charley	Florida, S.C., N.C.
1989	$13.9	Hurricane Hugo	S.C., N.C.
2004	$12	Hurricane Ivan	Florida, Alabama
1989	$10	Earthquake	Loma Prieta, Calif.

Sources: National Climatic Data Center, National Oceanic and Atmospheric Administration; Insurance Information Institute

FEMA has long been criticized as a dumping ground for White House political appointees. A report on the agency's blunders in responding to Hurricane Andrew in 1992 noted, "Currently, FEMA is like a patient in triage. The president and Congress must decide whether to treat it or let it die."[10]

But even FEMA critics concede that part of the problem is that many Americans mistakenly see the agency as a national fire-and-rescue squad, equipped with its own fire trucks, personnel and advanced technology. FEMA actually is a tiny agency — only 2,500 employees — charged with coordinating all the federal help available to states and localities.

"The federal government is never going to be the nation's first-responder. We shouldn't be, we don't have the capability to be, and we won't be," said White House homeland security adviser Frances Fragos Townsend, who is spearheading a review of the federal government's response to Katrina.[11]

Some, including President Bush and the U.S. Conference of Mayors, ask whether the military should take the lead in disaster response.[12] Others still champion FEMA but say that budget cuts and changes

Katrina flooded three-quarters of New Orleans and revealed gaping weaknesses in the nation's disaster-response system. Many experts question the government's ability to deal with future catastrophes.

following 9/11 — and the country's preoccupation with terrorism — have jeopardized FEMA's effectiveness. For example, nearly three out of every four grant dollars that the Department of Homeland Security (DHS) handed out to first-responders in 2005 were for terrorism-related activities.[13]

"It's like we've adopted the philosophy that if you are prepared for a terrorist event, then you are prepared for any event that could possibly affect the people of the United States," says Albert Ashwood, director of Oklahoma's Department of Emergency Management.

As politicians debate the effectiveness of FEMA and lessons learned from Katrina, here are some questions being discussed:

Is the United States prepared for another major disaster?

Many emergency-management experts say the country is ready for the next "disaster," but not for another "catastrophe" like Katrina. Others say the country falls woefully short on both counts.

In disasters, not everyone in the affected area is a victim, explains John R. Harrald, director of the Institute for Crisis, Disaster and Risk Management at George Washington University, in Washington, D.C. Typically, roads, communications and medical systems are still in good enough shape for first-responders to get in and help. For example, three blocks from the collapsed Twin Towers on Sept. 11, New Yorkers still had electricity and phones.

In a "catastrophic event" like Katrina, however, all systems fail. Entire swaths of the Gulf Coast had no communications; city halls and police stations were destroyed; power, water and sewer systems ceased functioning. New Orleans lost virtually its entire infrastructure — transportation, telecommunications, energy and medical systems.

Disaster experts say preparedness depends on the locale. California is prepared for earthquakes, Florida for hurricanes (notwithstanding recent problems after Wilma), and the Northeast and Midwest for major snowstorms, experts say. These areas are prepared because they have learned from experience. "If you do something a number times, you get good at it," says David Aylward, secretary of the ComCARE Alliance, an organization of safety groups, first-responders and medical professionals.

But Tierney of the Natural Hazards Center worries that the country is not only unprepared for catastrophes but also ill-equipped for "ordinary" disasters, largely because of the latest reorganization of the country's disaster management system.

After the 2001 terrorist attacks, the federal government realized its response plan for "extreme events" needed to be revamped to deal with the terrorism threat. But Tierney wonders if local officials fully understand the revised 426-page National Response Plan — released in December 2004 — or their roles in it.[14] "We don't know the extent to which states and local governments have absorbed the new response philosophies under the national response plan," she says. "If Hurricane Katrina is any indication, we're in deep trouble."

Critics say the new plan focuses almost exclusively on terrorism rather than natural disasters. For instance, of the 15 emergency scenarios that the plan recommends states and localities train and prepare for — 13 are terrorist events.

Likewise, terrorism prevention now receives the lion's share of federal emergency-preparedness dollars. In 2005 some $180 million was allocated nationwide for state and local governments to fund emergency management, but it was in the form of 50-50 matching grants, which require local governments to supply a dollar for every federal dollar received. At the same time, the federal government dispersed $2.3 billion for anti-terrorism measures, with no matching funds required, explains Ashwood.

But supporters of the new federal plan point out that even before Sept. 11, FEMA had provided funds for "all-hazards" emergency preparedness. The Government Accountability Office (GAO) concluded this year that while most funding today is targeted at preventing terrorist attacks, the all-hazards approach is generally working, training first-responders for skills needed for both kinds of disasters.[15]

However, says Aylward, the country spends far too little on emergency medicine — only $3.5 million in 2005 for states to build up medical-trauma capacity. A flu pandemic, for example, could send 2.3 million Americans to hospitals, many in need of respirators — but there are only 105,000 respirators available in U.S. hospitals, and most are already in constant use.[16]

"We've pumped billions of dollars into preparedness since 9/11, but virtually none of that has gone to the one place where we know 80 percent of patients go first," said Rick Blum, president of the American College of Emergency Physicians.[17]

Most agree that the country falls particularly short in emergency communications. Many communities do not have technology that allows first-responders, government officials and others to stay in contact with each other. And local, state and federal officials also do not have systems in place enabling them to communicate with one another during an emergency.

In the aftermath of Katrina, some rescuers finally got a radio system that let them talk to one another — only after FedEx technical adviser Mike Mitchell of Memphis realized while watching Katrina TV coverage that a broken FedEx radio antenna in New Orleans could be adapted with some spare parts, a generator and radios. He made his way to the city, and atop a 54-story building near the convention center he installed a new nine-foot FedEx radio antenna that an Army helicopter lowered to him.[18]

The independent commission that investigated the 9/11 attacks recommended that more spectrum, or airwaves, be reserved for public-safety use, but Congress has yet to act. "We know, looking back at 9/11, that lives were lost because we didn't have interoperability and didn't have access to public radio spectrum," former Sen. Timothy J. Roemer, D-Ind., a 9/11 Commission member, told Congress.[19] "We know that lives were lost in New Orleans because we didn't have this capability."

The Homeland Security department's study on interoperability won't be finished until summer 2006, and a Federal Communications Commission (FCC) report on the need for additional spectrum is due in December.[20]

"If something knocks out phones, electricity, the Internet and radio towers, is there a backup so that responders can still communicate?" Aylward asks. "To my knowledge, no one has done that."

In addition to first-responders' radios, Katrina knocked out 40 call centers that provide 911 assistance, and more than 20 million telephone calls did not go through the day after the hurricane struck.[21] The hurricane also knocked 80 percent of the radio stations and 70 percent of the TV stations off the air.[22] Hundreds of thousands of hurricane victims were unable to receive news and emergency information, and emergency workers and public safety officials had difficulty coordinating their efforts. The New Orleans Police Department, for example, was severely crippled for three days following the storm.[23]

FCC Chairman Kevin Martin told Congress that Katrina made the commission realize that when 911 call centers go down, "there's not even a standard protocol" for rerouting the calls. So when Hurricane Rita followed shortly after, federal authorities made sure 911 centers knew to contact telephone companies with backup plans.

Satellite-phone companies did not lose service during Katrina and were able to provide phone and video links to police, emergency personnel and news outlets. Ironically, when the storm hit, New Orleans was one of 25 cities taking part in an "integrated wireless network" program spearheaded by the departments of Justice, Homeland Security and Treasury designed to usher in the next generation of radio systems for federal law enforcement.[24]

Ashwood, of the National Emergency Management Association, says that while enabling responders to

Hurricane Katrina's Unprecedented Impact

Katrina affected an area roughly the size of Great Britain and will cost an estimated $200 billion.

During the relief effort:

- 72,000 federal workers and 50,000 National Guard troops were deployed;

- 33,000 people were rescued by the Coast Guard;

- 300,000 evacuees were sheltered in more than 40 states;

- 717,000 households received $1.5 billion in federal aid;

- 27 million hot meals were served by the Red Cross; and

- 93 Disaster Recovery Centers were operated.

Source: Dept. of Homeland Security

communicate with one another is extremely important, it pales in comparison to the need for first-responders to know each other and what each one does.

"If you want to talk about the big communications problem in this country, that's it," says Ashwood. "It has nothing to do with radios."

Should the military play the lead role in disaster response?

President Bush has asked Congress to consider allowing the military to take the lead in certain disaster responses. "It is now clear that a challenge on this scale requires greater federal authority and a broader role for the armed forces — the institution of our government most capable of massive logistical operations on a moment's notice," Bush said in a Sept. 15 televised speech from New Orleans.[25]

Indeed, after Katrina, the public saw the military as the only government entity that seemed able to restore order swiftly. Bush tapped Coast Guard Vice Adm. Thad

W. Allen to temporarily head the government's response to Katrina. And no-nonsense Lt. Gen. Russel Honoré, the military's task force commander, epitomized why the military should take the lead. Mayor Nagin called him a "John Wayne dude" who can "get some stuff done."[26]

But many officials vehemently oppose tapping the military to lead the federal response to disasters. Governors in particular don't want to lose control of their National Guard troops, whom they call up for natural disasters, crowd control and quelling civil violence. Moreover, active-duty soldiers are prohibited from enforcing civilian laws or providing police services by the 1878 *Posse Comitatus* Act.*

Of 38 governors asked by *USA Today* about Bush's idea, only Republicans Mitt Romney of Massachusetts and Tim Pawlenty of Minnesota supported it.[27] Even the president's brother, Gov. Jeb Bush, R-Fla., opposes more federal involvement. "Federalizing emergency response to catastrophic events would be a disaster as bad as Hurricane Katrina," Gov. Bush told Congress in October. "Just as all politics are local, so too are disasters. The most effective response is one that starts at the local level and grows with the support of surrounding communities, the state and then the federal government."[28]

Typically, active-duty soldiers are called in only if local, state and other federal resources are overwhelmed and the lead federal agency — typically FEMA — requests help. Under the Stafford Act, the president can declare a federal emergency or disaster and deploy troops, but only to help deliver aid.[29] Lt. Gen. Honoré reminded his soldiers that New Orleans wasn't Iraq and to keep their guns pointed down.

To seize control of the Katrina mission, President Bush would have had to invoke the Insurrection Act, which allows federal troops to suppress a rebellion and enforce federal laws. Bush's father invoked the law in 1992 during riots in south-central Los Angeles following the acquittal of police officers charged in the beating of Rodney King.

Pentagon leaders are waiting for completion of a Defense Department review before making recommendations on whether to amend current laws prohibiting the

---

* Posse Comitatus ("power to the county" in Latin) was passed after the Civil War to end the use of federal troops in Southern states.

military from policing local communities. The Pentagon reportedly is considering creating new "rapid response" units trained to respond to domestic catastrophes. The units would be used rarely and would quickly transfer responsibilities to civilian authorities.[30]

Defense Secretary Donald H. Rumsfeld stressed in September that the current system "works pretty well" for dealing with most natural disasters, but that Hurricane Katrina was "distinctly different" because "the first-responders [were] victims themselves, and as such, somewhat overwhelmed by the catastrophic nature of Hurricane Katrina and the floods" that followed.[31]

The New Orleans Police Department was unable to account for 240 officers on its 1,450-member force following Hurricane Katrina and has since fired more than 50 officers for desertion.[32]

Actually, military officials began deploying ships and personnel before receiving specific requests from the DHS or FEMA. In fact, they began preparing responses a week before Katrina hit.[33]

A day after the hurricane struck, the DHS declared Katrina an "incident of national significance," which under the new National Response Plan should trigger a coordinated federal response. By the following day, the amphibious assault ship *USS Bataan* arrived with supplies off New Orleans, but not until Sept. 5 — a week after Katrina hit — did troops arrive.[34]

The governors of Louisiana and Mississippi had both declared states of emergency before Katrina made

Are You Prepared?

Disasters can wipe out basic services — water, gas, electricity or telephones. Often emergency personnel cannot reach everyone right away. Experts stress the importance of individuals being prepared to take care of themselves for at least three days or until basic services are restored or help arrives.

Create a Family Disaster Plan

- Establish two places to meet in the event your home is damaged or roads are blocked — one near the home and one outside of the immediate area.
- Arrange a way to contact each other should you be separated during a disaster. Since local phone calls may be impossible, designate an out-of-state person as the "family contact."
- Plan for an urgent evacuation. Keep a backpack or duffle bag packed in advance with:
  - First aid kit, prescription drugs for three days and extra eyeglasses (copies of the drug and eyeglass prescriptions).
  - Flashlight, batteries, battery-powered radio, bottled water.
  - A change of clothes, a sleeping bag or bedroll and pillow for each household member.
  - Car keys (and keys to where you are going if it is a friend's or relative's house).
  - Checkbook, cash, credit cards, driver's license or personal identification, Social Security card, proof of residence (deed or lease), insurance policies, birth and marriage certificates, stocks, bonds and other negotiable certificates, wills, deeds and copies of recent tax returns.

"Sheltering in Place"

Have an Emergency Preparedness Kit (preferably stored in waterproof containers) prepared in advance with sufficient supplies for your family to survive in your home for at least three days without power or municipal services, including:

- The same supplies you would take with you when evacuating. (*See above.*)
- Water (a gallon per person per day).
- Foods that do not require refrigeration or cooking.
- Special items or medical equipment for infants and family members.
- Sanitation supplies: toilet paper, towelettes, soap, hand sanitizer, toothbrush, contact lens supplies, feminine supplies, garbage bags.
- Tool kit with matches in waterproof container, pliers, paper/pencil, map of the area.
- Non-electronic entertainment, games, books.

For more information, contact www.prepare.org or www.redcross.org. Fact sheets and a 204-page guide from FEMA are available at www.fema.gov/areyouready/.

Sources: American Red Cross, FEMA

Ousted FEMA Director Michael Brown answers lawmakers' questions about the agency's response to Hurricane Katrina. Brown defended his agency's performance, blaming many of the problems in Louisiana on state and local authorities.

landfall, but many of their National Guard units were deployed overseas. Within 10 days of the hurricane hitting, National Guard personnel from all 50 states had joined in the relief operations, an unprecedented effort.[35]

Some wonder whether lives would have been saved in New Orleans if the military had been in charge from the beginning. "When you have a disaster that overwhelms state and local government and requires a federal response, the Department of Defense is the agency best positioned to do it," said Lawrence Korb, former assistant secretary of Defense for manpower and personnel during the Reagan administration.[36]

Sen. John W. Warner, R-Va., chairman of the Senate Armed Services Committee, supported an expanded military role in emergencies even before Katrina hit, calling for a change in the *Posse Comitatus* law.[37] "The current framework of law did not in any way render less

effective the inner working of the [National] Guard and active forces in this Katrina situation," Warner said in September. "But who knows about the next one?"[38]

Mayors also would like the military to take a more active role in relief — at least in the first few days after a disaster — and want to get military help without needing the state's approval.[39] But the military is already stretched thin with deployments in Iraq and Afghanistan, and many question whether adding more domestic tasks would undermine military readiness.[40] Plus, it would depart from the longstanding tradition of keeping the U.S. military out of civilian affairs.

"Putting full-time warriors into a civilian policing situation can result in serious collateral damage to American life and liberty," said Gene Healy, a defense expert at the libertarian Cato Institute.[41]

Expanding the military's role was also explored after Hurricane Andrew ripped through South Florida in 1992. At Congress' request, the National Academy of Public Administration studied the proposition and eventually opposed it. Essentially, the academy concluded current structure allows the military to provide support to civilian authorities, such as logistics and humanitarian aid, but that ultimately civilians must maintain decision-making authority.[42]

States and localities should be able to turn to the military, but disaster response is "entirely a civilian function," says George Washington University's Harrald.

The key, according to state and local officials, is better coordination. "Hurricane Katrina, and to some extent Rita, revealed the need for improved intergovernmental response to catastrophic disasters," Audwin M. Samuel, mayor pro tem of Beaumont, Texas, told Congress.[43]

Robert W. Klein, director of the Center for Risk Management at Georgia State University, does not oppose a military-led response, but, he says, ideally a "properly staffed, properly charged and properly oriented" FEMA would take the lead role. But in either scenario, he says the military role should happen automatically. "The disaster czar or disaster general shouldn't be waiting for a phone call."

Does politics reduce FEMA's effectiveness?

Some experts say that structural changes were made at FEMA after Sept. 11 strictly for political reasons — and that the country's preparedness has suffered. Others contend that incompetence — not politics — is a bigger factor at FEMA.

Former FEMA Director Brown told the special House panel investigating Katrina he didn't want to make the problems surrounding the response partisan. But noting he didn't have problems evacuating Alabama and Mississippi, Brown added, "I can't help that Alabama and Mississippi are governed by Republican governors, and Louisiana is governed by a Democratic governor."[44]

Brown largely blamed post-Katrina missteps on strained relations between Gov. Blanco and Mayor Nagin — both Democrats. "I very strongly personally regret that I was unable to persuade [them] to sit down, deal with their differences and work together. I just couldn't pull that off," he said.[45]

For their part, neither Blanco nor Nagin had anything positive to say about FEMA or the White House. After the storm, Blanco reportedly was unable to reach either President Bush or his chief of staff and had to plead for help via a message left with a low-level adviser.[46] Nagin angrily complained on national television that federal officials "don't have a clue what's going on down here" and called on them to "get off your asses and do something."[47]

Some speculate that Bush was reluctant to step in and take control in a Southern state run by a Democrat, and a woman at that. "Can you imagine how it would have been perceived if a president of the United States of one party had pre-emptively taken from the female governor of another party the command and control of her forces?" a senior administration official told *The New York Times*.[48]

But in 17 years of emergency management, Ashwood says he has never seen politics enter into decisions. "It's after-the-fact finger-pointing," he says. "It's people saying, 'Well, I might have made mistakes, but I didn't make as many as that guy.'"

George Washington [University's] Harrald agrees: "I don't think anyone intentionally, for political reasons, made bad decisions. Bad decisions and inaction were a matter of competence, not intent."

Some experts point out that in the mid-1990s — after its disastrous response to Hurricane Andrew — FEMA overcame its reputation for being slow and bureaucratic, but that post-9/11 changes have undermined the agency's ability to respond to natural disasters. "The system that exists today is nothing like the emergency-management system that had been built up over

the last 30 years," says Tierney of the Natural Hazards Center in Colorado. "Those patterns were radically reversed after 9/11. All this talk about FEMA, FEMA, FEMA" misses the point. "We're operating under a homeland-security policy system now, not a comprehensive emergency-management system."

For example, when FEMA was incorporated into the new DHS after Sept. 11, it lost its status as an independent agency with direct access to the president. Instead, the agency and its 2,500 employees became one of 22 agencies folded into the 180,000-employee DHS.

"The driving force behind the creation of DHS was the need of elected officials to . . . be seen as responding to the attacks of Sept. 11, 2001," said Kettl at the University of Pennsylvania.[49] But in the process, he said, FEMA's role in disaster response was weakened.

Richard W. Krimm, a former senior FEMA official for several administrations, agreed. "It was a terrible mistake to take disaster response and recovery . . . and put them in Homeland Security," he said.[50]

Critics say it is now impossible for FEMA to implement the four steps that make up comprehensive emergency management. The first is mitigation, which is the ongoing effort to reduce the potential impact disasters can have on people and property, such as engineering bridges to withstand earthquakes and enforcing effective building codes to protect property from hurricanes. The other steps are preparedness, response and recovery.

"These four steps should be seamlessly integrated," says Tierney. But since Sept. 11, "The comprehensive emergency-management approach has been broken up."

Moreover, key FEMA posts were not filled by people experienced in emergency management. James Lee Witt, the Clinton administration FEMA director who was widely credited with turning FEMA around, previously had headed the Office of Emergency Services in Arkansas. Ousted FEMA Director Brown had little emergency-management experience, having joined the agency as legal counsel after several years at the International Arabian Horse Association.

"You get the impression that for higher-level appointments at FEMA, political connections weighed heavier than qualifications," says Klein of Georgia State University. Indeed, of the eight top officials at FEMA, only two had experience with fire and emergency services, and they were not used early on in the Katrina response, according to

William Killen, president of the International Association of Fire Chiefs. "The coordination would have been a lot better if there had been more people with operational experience in emergency response in position," Killen told a House panel.[51]

Brown also lacked the same access to the president that Witt had enjoyed under Clinton. "That direct relationship to the White House is crucial," former Gov. Bob Wise, D-W.Va., told Congress. "All the other federal agencies must know that the FEMA director and the president communicate directly and that there isn't anyone between them."[52]

The reorganization of FEMA required Brown to send budget and policy requests to the DHS secretary, who would then pitch FEMA's issues to the president. After being fired as FEMA director, Brown complained bitterly to the House panel that his budget requests had never made it to the president and that his budget and staff were cut.

Experts outside the agency agree that many competent FEMA officials left the agency out of frustration or were contracted out after the reorganization, leaving key posts without expertise. In fact, many of the DHS employees assigned to the Gulf Coast after Katrina had to first spend two to three days studying federal emergency-management rules, including the types of aid available to hurricane victims.[53]

"The organization just wasn't there. We lost that and didn't really realize it," says Harrald. "There was not an awareness that the system was collapsing."

The new emphasis on terrorism also undercut FEMA. "After Sept. 11, they got so focused on terrorism they effectively marginalized the capability of FEMA," said George D. Haddow, a former Clinton administration FEMA official.[54]

BACKGROUND

FEMA's Roots

The federal government hasn't always taken an active role in natural disasters.

The Congressional Act of 1803, considered the first piece of disaster legislation, provided federal assistance to Portsmouth, N.H., following a huge fire.

Over the next century, Congress passed more than 100 measures in response to hurricanes, earthquakes, floods and other natural disasters, but those actions were ad hoc, often overlapping and disjointed.[55] Local communities, on the whole, were expected to handle disaster relief.

Even the 1900 hurricane that killed 6,000 people in Galveston, Texas — the most deadly U.S. natural disaster — triggered only a limited federal response. The Army Corps of Engineers helped build a new sea wall, but it was up to the locals to help survivors and rebuild the flattened city.[56]

The efforts of future President Herbert Hoover in Florida following two deadly hurricanes in the late 1920s probably helped the then-secretary of Commerce win the presidency in 1928.[57] In 1926, a hurricane hit South Florida, killing about 240 people. Two years later, less than two months before the election, another hurricane hit Lake Okeechobee, killing 2,500. Hoover visited the area following both storms and was instrumental in the push for new channels and levees. Since then, presidents have found that their own responses to natural disasters can affect the outcome of an election, with some historians dubbing the phenomenon as "The Photo-op Presidency."[58]

During the Depression, President Franklin D. Roosevelt initiated a more active federal role in disaster response. For instance, he authorized the Reconstruction Finance Corporation, established by Hoover in 1932 to bolster the banking industry, to make reconstruction loans for public facilities damaged by earthquakes, and later, other disasters. In 1934 the Bureau of Public Roads was given authority to provide funding for highways and bridges damaged by natural disasters. The Flood Control Act of 1936, which gave the Army Corps of Engineers greater authority to implement flood control projects, also became law during FDR's era.

This piecemeal approach lasted until the 1960s and early '70s, when a series of hurricanes and earthquakes spurred the federal government to become more involved. In 1961, the Kennedy administration created the Office of Emergency Preparedness inside the White House to deal with natural disasters. Then in 1968, Congress created the National Flood Insurance Program (NFIP), which offered new flood protection to homeowners. The insurance was available only to those in communities that adopted and enforced a federally approved-plan to reduce flood risks.

The Disaster Relief Act of 1974 laid out the formal process that permits a president to declare "disaster areas," which are eligible for federal assistance, including money

CHRONOLOGY

1800-1950s *President Franklin D. Roosevelt increases federal government's role in disasters.*

1803 The first federal disaster relief law, the Congressional Act of 1803, provides assistance to Portsmouth, N.H., after an extensive fire.

May 31,1889 Johnstown, Pa., is devastated by the worst flood in the nation's history, killing more than 2,200 residents.

Sept. 8, 1900 Hurricane destroys Galveston, Texas, killing 6,000 residents.

Sept. 16, 1928 Hurricane kills 2,500 in South Florida.

1933-34 The Reconstruction Finance Corporation and Bureau of Public Roads are authorized to make disaster loans.

1936 Flood Control Act of 1936 gives Army Corps of Engineers greater authority to implement flood control projects.

1960s-1970s *Washington boosts federal role in disaster preparedness and response.*

1961 John F. Kennedy administration creates the Office of Emergency Preparedness inside the White House to deal with natural disasters.

1974 Disaster Relief Act permits president to declare "disaster areas," thus providing federal help to states.

Sept. 16, 1978 President Jimmy Carter creates Federal Emergency Management Agency (FEMA).

1980s-1992 *FEMA comes under fire.*

Aug. 7, 1978 Carter declares a federal emergency at Love Canal, the neighborhood near Niagara Falls, N.Y., contaminated by hazardous wastes.

1980 FEMA is accused of stretching its authority by responding to Cuban refugee crisis in Miami.

1985 FEMA director resigns amid charges of misusing government funds; the agency is lampooned in the comic strip "Doonesbury."

1989 FEMA's sluggish response to Hurricane Hugo prompts Sen. Ernest Hollings, D-S.C., to call the agency "the sorriest bunch of bureaucratic jackasses" he had ever seen.

1992 FEMA's response to Hurricane Andrew in Florida is bungled; Congress considers abolishing FEMA.

1993-2001 *FEMA is rehabilitated under Clinton.*

1992 President Bill Clinton picks James L. Witt, a 14-year veteran of Arkansas' emergency services, as FEMA director and makes him a Cabinet member.

1993-94 Witt streamlines disaster relief-and-recovery operations; FEMA wins praise for efforts in 1993 flooding in Midwest and the 1994 Northridge, Calif., earthquake.

1995 The Murrah Federal Building in Oklahoma City is bombed, killing 168 and raising questions about FEMA's role in responding to terrorist attacks.

Sept. 11, 2001 The World Trade Center and Pentagon are attacked; nearly 3,000 people are killed.

2001-2005 *Budget cuts, reorganization and loss of experienced employees weaken FEMA's ability to respond to disasters.*

March 1, 2003 FEMA becomes part of the Department of Homeland Security, losing its independence and Cabinet status.

August-September 2004 Four hurricanes hit Florida, a pivotal state in the ongoing presidential campaign. President George W. Bush quickly declares the state a disaster area, making it eligible for federal assistance.

August-September, 2005 Numerous hurricanes are spawned in the Atlantic, including Katrina, which strikes the Gulf Coast on Aug. 29, causing massive flooding and destruction. FEMA's poor response prompts Congress and the White House to review the nation's preparedness.

2006

Oct. 6 — President George W. Bush signs Post-Katrina Emergency Reform Act, significantly reorganizing FEMA to address gaps evident in Hurricane Katrina response.

Dec. 18 — President Bush signs Pandemic and All-Hazards Preparedness Act, aimed at improving public-health security and response to public hazards.

2007

March 31 — FEMA begins administering Center for Domestic Preparedness, in Anniston, Ala., for training emergency responders.

July 18 — Congress provides $1 billion for public-safety communications.

2008

May 22-Aug. 29 — Nearly 2,800 individual fires burn more than 1 million acres of land in northern and central California.

Aug. 31 — Hurricane Gustav makes landfall in Louisiana after leaving a trail of death in the Caribbean.

Sept. 13 — Hurricane Ike strikes Texas coast after ravaging Haiti, Cuba and other locales.

2009

Jan. 27 — National Emergency Center Act authorizes Department of Homeland Security to set up network of FEMA camp facilities to house U.S. citizens in case of a national emergency.

Oct. 15 — Nearly 7 million people participate in "Great California ShakeOut" earthquake preparedness drill.

2010

January — Government Accountability Office finds FEMA unprepared for recovery efforts following a potential incident of nuclear terrorism.

Jan. 12 — Haiti is hit by 7.0-magnitude earthquake.

Feb. 27 — An 8.8-magnitude earthquake strikes off the coast of Chile.

April 20 — Explosion on BP's Deepwater Horizon oil rig results in largest oil spill in U.S. history.

July 15 — Cap contains BP oil spill. "Static kill" — intended to close down the broken well for good — begins soon thereafter.

Aug. 5 — BP begins pumping cement into the well to seal it.

Aug. 10 — Relief well nears completion.

---

for state and local governments to make repairs, clear debris and provide temporary housing and unemployment and cash assistance for individuals. The law was amended in 1988 and renamed the Robert T. Stafford Disaster Relief and Emergency Act, after its chief sponsor, a Republican senator from Vermont. It remains the main federal disaster law.

In the late 1970s, hazards associated with nuclear power plants and the transportation of hazardous substances were added to the list of potential disasters. Eventually, more than 100 federal agencies were authorized to deal with disasters, hazardous incidents and emergencies. Similar programs and policies existed at the state and local level, further complicating disaster-relief efforts.

Frustrated with the overlapping programs and confusing bureaucracy, the nation's governors urged President Jimmy Carter to centralize federal emergency functions. Carter responded with a 1979 executive order that merged some 100 separate disaster-related responsibilities into a new agency — FEMA.[59]

For the first time, Carter said, "key emergency-management and assistance functions would be unified and made directly accountable to the president and Congress."[60] As the federal government's lead disaster agency, FEMA established official relationships with organizations such as Catholic Charities, the United Way, the Council of Jewish Federations and the American Red Cross.

The Red Cross is the only relief organization chartered by Congress "to maintain a system of domestic and international disaster relief." In fact, the National Response Plan specifically calls on the Red Cross to provide local relief. During Katrina, the Red Cross provided hurricane survivors with nearly 3.42 million overnight stays in more than 1,000 shelters. And, in coordination with the Southern Baptist Convention, it served nearly 27 million hot meals to victims.

Political Storms

In addition to natural disasters, FEMA handled the 1970s cleanup of Love Canal, near Niagara Falls, N.Y., contaminated by buried toxic wastes; the 1979 accident at the Three Mile Island nuclear power plant, near Harrisburg, Pa., and the 1980 "Mariel boat lift" crisis, in which 125,000 Cuban refugees converged on South Florida. Carter declared all the affected regions disaster areas, although critics said the refugee crisis was not, technically, a disaster.

In the early and mid-1980s, FEMA also faced political and legal disasters. During the Reagan administration, Congress, the Justice Department and a grand jury investigated senior FEMA political officials on a variety of charges, including misuse of government funds. FEMA Director Louis O. Guiffrida resigned in 1985, and the agency was repeatedly lampooned in the comic strip "Doonesbury."[61]

In its early years, FEMA was, like much of the federal government, preoccupied with protecting Americans from the threat of the Soviet Union. "When I entered this profession 17 years ago, FEMA and emergency management in general were quasi-military, [trying to] figure out where a nuclear attack was going to take place and how to relocate the nation's citizens," Oklahoma's Ashwood recently told Congress.[62]

But just as the Cold War was ending in the late 1980s and early '90s, a pair of hurricanes and an earthquake put FEMA — then plagued by morale problems, poor leadership and conflicts with its state and local partners — in a negative national spotlight.[63]

FEMA was widely criticized for its slow response to Hugo, the 1989 hurricane that devastated Charleston, S.C. Sen. Ernest Hollings, D-S.C., described FEMA as "the sorriest bunch of bureaucratic jackasses" he had ever encountered in the federal government.[64] Hugo caused $7 billion in damage in the United States, making it the costliest hurricane in U.S. history at that time.

Less than a month later, San Francisco was hit by the Loma Prieta earthquake — the largest quake along the San Andreas Fault since the 1906 San Francisco earthquake. Although FEMA was unprepared for the quake — which

caused nearly $6 billion in damage and 63 deaths — California was ready, thanks to "good mitigation practices in building codes and construction . . . and some good luck," wrote former FEMA official Haddow.[65]

When Hurricane Andrew struck in 1992, it further devastated FEMA's credibility along with parts of South Florida and Louisiana. The agency's response to the disaster, which caused $25 billion in damage and left thousands without shelter and water for weeks, was blasted as disorganized.

"Where in the hell is the cavalry on this one?" asked Miami-Dade County Emergency Management Director Kate Hale.[66] "They keep saying we're going to get supplies. For God's sake, where are they?"

President George H. W. Bush, who was running for re-election, then dispatched federal troops, mobile kitchens and tents. Within a week, nearly 20,000 troops were in South Florida.[67] Nonetheless, many analysts say FEMA's poor performance cost Bush votes in the 1992 election, in which he was defeated by Democrat Bill Clinton.

Some three weeks after Andrew, one of the most powerful hurricanes in Hawaiian history hit Kauai. This time, FEMA sent disaster teams to Hawaii even before Iniki struck.

After Andrew and Iniki, some critics proposed abolishing FEMA and giving the military a bigger disaster role. The National Academy of Public Administration, however, recommended establishing a White House Domestic Crisis Monitoring Unit to ensure "timely, effective and well coordinated" federal responses to catastrophes.[68]

Reforming FEMA

President Clinton gave the agency a shot in the arm when he nominated Witt as FEMA director — the first with experience as a state emergency manager. Clinton elevated the post to Cabinet level, and Witt urged governors to similarly elevate their state emergency-management directors.[69]

Witt is credited with streamlining disaster relief and recovery operations and focusing workers on "customer service." When floods ravaged the Midwest in 1993 and an earthquake shook Los Angeles the next year, FEMA crisis-management teams quickly delivered aid to the injured. After the floods, Witt persuaded the federal government to buy flood-prone properties in the Midwest

Should New Orleans Be Rebuilt?

President Bush has vowed to rebuild New Orleans, and Congress has already started doling out reconstruction funds. But is that a good idea? Hurricane Katrina put 80 percent of the city under water, destroying some 200,000 homes.

House Speaker J. Dennis Hastert, R-Ill., came under withering criticism, particularly from Democratic lawmakers who represent New Orleans, when he said rebuilding "doesn't make sense," adding, it "looks like a lot of that place could be bulldozed." Hastert later said he was not "advocating that the city be abandoned or relocated."[1]

But some experts argue that rebuilding a city below sea level, on land that is sinking, near a large lake and in a hurricane-prone area is simply another disaster waiting to happen — and taxpayers shouldn't have to keep picking up the tab.

"Should we rebuild New Orleans . . . just so it can be wiped out again?" asked Klaus Jacob, a geophysicist and adjunct professor at Columbia University's School of International and Public Affairs. Even strengthening the levee system isn't the answer, Jacob said. "The higher the defenses, the deeper the floods that will inevitably follow," he wrote.[2]

"It is time to face up to some geological realities and start a carefully planned deconstruction of New Orleans," Jacob continued, "assessing what can or needs to be preserved, or vertically raised and, if affordable, by how much."

The city is nestled in a so-called bowl, sandwiched between levees holding back Lake Pontchartrain to the north and the Mississippi River to the south. Some places are up to 10 feet below sea level; areas nearer the river generally are higher in elevation.

Traditional homeowner insurance policies do not cover losses from floods, so homeowners, renters and businesses that want insurance must turn to the National Flood Insurance Program (NFIP) for coverage. Nationwide, about half of eligible properties are covered by flood insurance.[3]

Many people wrongly believe that the U.S. government will take care of their financial needs if they suffer damage due to flooding. In fact, federal disaster assistance is only available if the president formally declares a disaster, which he did for Katrina. But often, federal disaster-assistance loans must be repaid. That is on top of any mortgage loans that people may still owe on the damaged property.

Katrina was the largest and costliest flood disaster in U.S. history. FEMA estimates flood insurance payouts for 225,000 claims from hurricanes Katrina and Rita could hit $23 billion, far exceeding the $15 billion that has been paid out since the NFIP program began in 1968.[4]

While FEMA collects the premiums, it lacks reserves and must borrow from the U.S. Treasury to meet the

and relocate businesses and residents, saving taxpayers millions of dollars when floods struck again in 1995.[70]

FEMA also won praise for its response to a 1994 earthquake in Northridge, Calif., a modern urban environment generally designed to withstand earthquakes. Although $20 billion in damages resulted, few lives were lost.

The Oklahoma City bombing on April 19, 1995, raised questions about FEMA's role in responding to terrorist attacks. Debates raged among officials at FEMA and the Justice and Defense departments over who should be the first-responder — fire, police, emergency management or emergency medical services? Terrorism was part of FEMA's "all-hazards" approach to emergency management, but it lacked the resources and

technologies to address specific terrorism issues such as weapons of mass destruction.[71]

When George W. Bush became president, like Clinton he appointed a close friend to head FEMA, Joe Allbaugh, Bush's former chief of staff as governor of Texas and his campaign manager during the 2000 presidential race. Allbaugh's lack of emergency-management experience was not an issue during his confirmation hearings.[72]

In a speech the day before the 9/11 attacks, Allbaugh outlined firefighting, disaster mitigation and catastrophic preparedness as his top priorities.[73] Ironically, on Sept. 11 Allbaugh and other FEMA senior leaders were in Montana, attending the annual meeting of the National Emergency Management Association, whose members payouts. Congress in September temporarily increased the amount FEMA could borrow to $3.5 billion from $1.5 billion and is considering upping that to $8.5 billion under a measure pending in Congress.[5]

Private insurers are expected to pay about $40 billion in Katrina damage, according to Robert P. Hartwig, chief economist at the Insurance Information Institute.[6] The institute said the percentage of homes with flood insurance affected by Hurricane Katrina varied in Louisiana from nearly 58 percent in some areas down to 7 percent. In many areas, homeowners and business owners were not required, or even encouraged, by their banks or their insurance companies to purchase flood insurance, partly because outdated floodplain maps were used.

Critics say taxpayers are too often left holding the bag for those who continually build in flood-prone or other risky areas. "Are we going to continue to bail out people who will continue to build in very, very hazardous areas?" asked Sen. Richard Shelby, R-Ala., chairman of the Banking, Housing and Urban Affairs Committee, which examined the NFIP program in October.[7]

Congress in 2004 approved a pilot program that would impose higher insurance premiums for property owners at severe risk of suffering repeated flood damage.

Rather than allowing rebuilding in lowlying areas, some suggest more radical approaches: "Moving the city is clearly going to be an option," said John Copenhaver, a former FEMA Southeast regional director. "It would be an unbelievably expensive and difficult proposition, but it has to be on the table."[8]

And such a solution is not unprecedented. The government has helped move entire towns following disasters, including Soldiers Grove, Wis., after a 1979 flood. And businesses were moved in several communities — including Valmeyer, Ill., and Pattonsburg, Mo. — after floods in 1993.[9]

Hastert said undoubtedly New Orleans residents would rebuild, adding, however: "We ought to take a second look at it. But you know, we build Los Angeles and San Francisco on top of earthquake fissures, and they rebuild, too. Stubbornness."[10]

[1] The Associated Press, "Hastert: Rebuilding New Orleans 'doesn't make sense to me,'" Sept. 2, 2005.

[2] Klaus Jacob, "Time for a Tough Question: Why Rebuild?" *The Washington Post*, Sept. 6, 2005, p. A25.

[3] Testimony of William Jenkins, Government Accountability Office, before Senate Banking, Housing and Urban Affairs Committee on National Flood Insurance Program, Oct. 18, 2005.

[4] Testimony of David Maurstad, Acting Mitigation Division Director, FEMA, before U.S. Senate Banking Housing and Urban Affairs Committee on National Flood Insurance Program, Oct. 18, 2005.

[5] Liriel Higa, "FEMA Would Get Second Boost in Borrowing Authority Under House Bill," *CQ Weekly*, Oct. 31, 2005, p. 2925.

[6] Peter Whoriskey, "Risk Estimate Led to Few Flood Policies," *The Washington Post*, Oct. 17, 2005, p. A1.

[7] Transcript of hearing of Senate Banking, Housing and Urban Affairs Committee on National Flood Insurance Program, Oct. 18, 2005.

[8] Seth Borenstein and Pete Carey, "Experts debate rebuilding New Orleans," *The* [San Jose] *Mercury News*, Sept. 1, 2005.

[9] FEMA Region X press release, "New Planning Guide Helps Communities Become Disaster-Resistant," April 26, 1999.

[10] The Associated Press, *op. cit.*

are state emergency officials. FEMA immediately activated the Federal Response Plan.

Some elements of the response to 9/11 — particularly the communication problems — revealed major weaknesses in the country's ability to respond to terrorism and raised questions about the capabilities and appropriate role of states and localities in managing a massive disaster. Less than a week later, President Bush announced the formation of a Homeland Security Office, and a year later, on Nov. 25, 2002, Congress approved the Homeland Security Act, consolidating 22 federal agencies, including FEMA, into the new Department of Homeland Security — the largest government reorganization in 50 years.

When FEMA was officially transferred to DHS on March 1, 2003, it lost its Cabinet-level status and its independence. It also lost some of its personnel and funding to another new agency, the Office of Domestic Preparedness. In addition, $80 million was transferred from FEMA's coffers to help pay for DHS's overhead, and in 2003 and 2004 FEMA lost $169 million to DHS for other purposes, including funds FEMA was supposed to have saved from being folded into DHS.[74]

Since then, up to a third of the staff has been cut from FEMA's five Mobile Emergency Response Support detachments — teams that deploy quickly to set up communications gear, power generators and life-support equipment to help federal, state and local officials coordinate disaster response.[75]

Hurricane victims slog past a police officer standing guard in flooded downtown New Orleans. Water was up to 12 feet high in some areas. The storm forced more than 300,000 people to evacuate their homes, mainly in Louisiana and Mississippi.

"Over the past three-and-a-half years, FEMA has gone from being a model agency to being one where . . . employee morale has fallen, and our nation's emergency management capability is being eroded," veteran FEMA staffer Pleasant Mann told Congress in 2004.

The Bush administration also cut Corps of Engineers' flood control funds. "For the first time in 37 years, federal budget cuts have all but stopped major work on the New Orleans area's east bank hurricane levees," the New Orleans *Times-Picayune* reported in June 2004.[76]

Meanwhile, the natural disasters continued. Nine tropical systems affected the United States in 2004, causing some $42 billion in damage.[77] President Bush issued 68 major disaster declarations — the most for a single year in nearly a decade.[78]

In 2004 — as Bush was running for re-election — an unprecedented four hurricanes (Charley, Frances, Ivan and Jeanne) slammed into Florida, which had been a pivotal state in Bush's race for the White House in 2000. Careful to avoid his father's delays after Hurricane Andrew in 1992, Bush quickly declared the state a federal disaster area, making it eligible for federal assistance. Less than two days later the president was touring hard-hit neighborhoods in southwest Florida.[79]

Bush handled the next storm, Frances, in a similar fashion, drawing partisan allegations that he was using the

hurricane as a photo opportunity. The president was "touting a $2 billion aid package that has already been promised to Florida as a result of Hurricane Charley," complained Rep. Robert Wexler, a Democrat from West Palm Beach.[80] The aid package was not without controversy. At least 9,800 people from Miami-Dade County received more than $21 million in assistance, even though Frances hit 100 miles away and inflicted little damage in the county.

Still, the 2004 hurricane destruction in Florida was unprecedented. An estimated one in five Florida homes was damaged, and 117 people died.[81]

Two months later, Bush won the state and the presidency.

CURRENT SITUATION

Katrina Aftershocks

In the wake of Hurricane Katrina, the DHS is "re-engineering" its disaster preparedness; Congress is trying to figure out what went wrong and how to pay for the damage; and states and localities are reviewing their emergency plans.

Katrina ignited weeks of contradictory testimony, finger-pointing and conflicting reports from federal, state and local officials. There's no argument, however, that all three levels of government were ill prepared for a deadly storm they all knew was coming.

"It turned out we were all wrong," said White House homeland security adviser Townsend. "We had not adequately anticipated."[82] The review of the disaster being spearheaded by Townsend is expected to make recommendations by the end of 2005.

Homeland Security Secretary Michael Chertoff also acknowledged to lawmakers that Katrina overwhelmed FEMA and promised to revamp the agency and hire more experienced staff.[83] "Dealing with this kind of an ultra-catastrophe . . . requires a lot of work beforehand, months beforehand," Chertoff said in October.[84]

Several Democrats, including Sen. Hillary Rodham Clinton, N.Y., say Chertoff's proposed changes don't go far enough and that the administration's changes in the agency have gutted it. "The bureaucracy created by moving FEMA under the Department of Homeland Security is clearly not working," she said in introducing legislation restoring FEMA to Cabinet-level rank.[85]

The Democrats have boycotted Congress' probe into the Katrina relief efforts and called for an independent commission similar to the panel that investigated the 9/11 attacks. But Senate Majority Leader Bill Frist, R-Tenn, noted in a letter to Democratic Minority Leader Harry Reid of Nevada that it took longer than a year for Congress to form an outside commission to investigate the federal government's handling of the Sept. 11 attacks. Such a delay now, Frist wrote, "would put more people at risk for a longer time than is necessary."[86]

The administration is pressing ahead with its own reforms. Chertoff, for example, said FEMA needs to learn from the military and private companies that were able to keep communication lines open. DHS is setting up "emergency reconnaissance teams" that will be deployed to catastrophes to provide up-to-the-minute reports to federal planners, who can then send the appropriate resources.[87]

Meanwhile, FEMA continues to come under fire for spending $236 million to temporarily house Katrina victims and emergency workers on cruise ships. FEMA also was criticized for handing out $2,000 checks to hurricane victims. In three Louisiana parishes, for example, FEMA issued more checks than there are households, at a cost of at least $70 million.[88]

Katrina-related contracts have also stirred controversy, including a $500 million debris-removal contract awarded to AshBritt Environmental, which has ties to Mississippi Gov. Haley Barbour, a former Republican National Committee chairman.[89] And former FEMA Director Allbaugh and his wife founded a company that has received federal contracts for Gulf Coast cleanup.[90] Homeland Security Inspector General Richard Skinner said in October he is investigating "all the contracting activities that took place immediately following this disaster from day one."[91]

Contracting questions aside, many emergency-management experts worry most about communication problems between federal, state and local authorities. Chertoff said his department is reviewing emergency-operations plans for every major urban area to ensure they are clear, detailed and up-to-date. "That includes a hard, realistic look at evacuation planning ranging from earthquakes to subway bombings," he said.

Thousands wait for food, water and medical aid outside the New Orleans Convention Center on Sept. 1, 2005 — three days after Hurricane Katrina struck New Orleans.

Local Reviews

Every city in the country is looking at its evacuation plan" in the aftermath of Katrina, says Aylward of the ComCare Alliance.

States and localities aren't always finding what they expected. A week before Hurricane Wilma hit, Gov. [Jeb] Bush touted Florida's hurricane readiness before a House panel. "Local and state governments that fail to prepare are preparing to fail," he said.[92]

The next week, however, when Wilma struck, "We did not perform to where we want to be," Bush said, noting that many residents failed to prepare and ended up overwhelming local government water-and-ice distribution sites. "People had ample time to prepare. It isn't that hard to get 72 hours' worth of food and water," he said, repeating the advice officials gave days before the storm.[93]

But enabling all levels of government to communicate with one another has been harder. "Since 9/11, enormous investments of time, effort and taxpayer money have been made to craft a system in which all levels of government can communicate and coordinate for the most effective response possible, whether to a natural disaster or a terrorist attack. That did not occur with Katrina," said Sen. Susan Collins, R-Maine, chairwoman of a Senate panel that examined FEMA's recovery efforts.[94]

Indeed, fire chiefs who responded to Katrina told Congress there was an "utter lack of structure and communication at

Did race play a role in the government's slow response to Hurricane Katrina?

YES

The Rev. Jesse L. Jackson Sr.
*Founder and President, National Rainbow/
PUSH Coalition*

Written for the *CQ Researcher*, November 2005

Race played a role in who was left behind. Race seems to be a factor in who will get back in. Class played a role in who was left behind. Class may play a role in who is let back in.

Incompetence and cronyism played a role, especially in the slowness of the response. No-bid contracts to out-of-state corporations suggest that role has not yet ended.

The hurricane hit the whole region, without concern for skin color or wealth — but Katrina's impact was multiplied if you were African-American or poor — and so many facing the worst flooding were both.

We can't forget that years of neglect and disinvestment in public goods and services — after years of politically motivated attacks on the role of government in our society — left the people of New Orleans defenseless. Some had the individual resources to escape; many did not. And race and class are heavily correlated with those who did not.

Then there is the war. Tax money spent on invading Iraq, rather than for needed goods and services at home, such as levees. National Guard troops stuck in Baghdad, not saving lives in Biloxi.

The whole world watched in horror as helpless people were stranded and neglected in the wealthiest, most powerful nation ever to exist. It must never happen again.

Let's rebuild New Orleans. Instead of experimenting on real people in trouble with an agenda based on right-wing economic ideology, we should rebuild, reinvest in and revitalize all of New Orleans.

The rescue is not over yet. People continue to need relief, shelter, food. They want jobs, living wages and the chance to come back home. Small businesses and contractors want to help do the rebuilding. New housing must be built in Louisiana, and affordable housing provided in the meantime, near people's jobs and neighborhoods. Families and communities must be reunified.

Reconstruction must be bottom-up, not top-down, and include everyone. Reconstruction should emphasize public investment to rebuild levees, construct mass transit and sewers, open up new schools and parks. I have suggested a Civilian Reconstruction Corps to provide former residents with work, training and a chance to be part of rebuilding their homes and their city.

Too many people were abandoned during Katrina. Surely we will not abandon them again, by not bringing them home and helping them participate in the rebirth of their own beloved New Orleans.

NO

John McWhorter
Senior Fellow, Manhattan Institute

Written for the *CQ Researcher*, November 2005

The almost all-black crowds sweltering, starving and dying in the Convention Center after Hurricane Katrina showed us that in New Orleans, as in so many other places, by and large to be poor is to be black. This is the legacy of racism, although opinions will differ as to whether that racism is in the past or the present.

But to claim that racism is why the rescue effort was so slow is not a matter of debate. It is, in fact, absurd.

To say "George Bush doesn't care about black people" is to honestly believe that if it were the white poor of Louisiana who happened to live closest to the levees, then barely anyone would have even gotten wet, and 50,000 troops would have been standing at the ready as soon as Katrina popped up on meteorologists' radar screens. The National Guard would have magically lifted the long-entrenched bureaucratic restrictions that only allow states to assign troops when it is proven that they are needed. Suddenly, against all historical precedent, just for that week, the Federal Emergency Management Agency would have morphed into a well-organized and dependable outfit.

But what about the hurricane that Katrina displaced as the third strongest on record to hit America — Andrew in 1992 — which left 250,000 people homeless? Ground zero for this one was Homestead, Fla., where whites were a big majority. So help was pouring in as soon as the rain stopped, right?

Well, not exactly. "Where in the hell is the cavalry on this one?" asked Kate Hale, Miami-Dade County emergency-management director, on national television. People went without electricity or food and dealt with looters for five days, just like in New Orleans. FEMA was raked over the coals for the same bureaucratic incompetence that is making headlines now.

Is it so far-fetched to admit that the problem after Katrina as well was the general ineptness of America's defenses against unforeseen disasters? A little event called 9/11 comes to mind. Two presidential administrations neglected increasingly clear signs that Osama bin Laden was planning to attack us on our shores. In general, bureaucracies are notoriously bad at foresight and long-term planning, and FEMA has never exactly been a counter-example.

Of course, there will be those who will insist, no matter what the evidence, that racism slowed down the rescue effort. But this is essentially the way a certain kind of person affirms their sense of importance when they lack healthier ones.

any level of government in the first 10 days."[95] As for former FEMA Director Brown, he was in an area totally cut off from communications when the hurricane hit and "probably would have been better off staying in Washington," says Harrald of George Washington University.

Some relief may be on the way. The proposed budget savings package working through Congress would free up spectrum for emergency responders and provide between $500 million and $1 billion in grants to local government to buy "interoperable" communication equipment.[96]

Congress is considering creating a national alert office capable of disseminating warnings of natural disasters and terrorist attacks using a wide range of media, including cell phones, cable and satellite TV, and radio and PDAs (personal digital assistants). A Senate panel on Oct. 20 approved a measure sponsored by Sen. Jim DeMint, R-S.C., chairman of the Commerce Subcommittee on Disaster Prevention and Prediction. "Without a proper way to alert those in danger, even the most accurate disaster prediction is useless," he said.[97] The House does not have a companion bill.

Congress has approved more than $62 billion in emergency aid following Katrina, but more than $40 billion remained unspent as of late October. The White House wants to shift $17 billion of the unspent portion to levee reconstruction, road repairs and other basic infrastructure work in the region.[98]

Lawmakers already have shifted $750 million from FEMA to a program that lends money to local governments to maintain essential services such as police and fire protection. The measure was signed shortly after New Orleans Mayor Nagin announced plans to lay off 3,000 city employees because of funding shortfalls.

Cleaning up after Katrina is expected to dwarf clean-up expenses of past disasters. For example, about 150 million cubic yards of debris will have to be removed from four Gulf Coast states — 10 times more than Hurricane Andrew left behind in Florida in 1992, which was several times greater

Worst-Case Scenarios

Scientists and storm chasers always have their sights on the next disaster. Experts at the National Hurricane Center, for example, say Katrina won't be the last major hurricane to strike a big city, forecasting that even New York City is vulnerable. Other catastrophes that scientists think could occur include:

- Gulf Coast tsunami (generated by a fault line in the Caribbean)
- East Coast tsunami (caused by asteroid falling into the Atlantic Ocean)
- Heat waves (as the population ages, urban areas get hotter and electricity systems are strained)
- Midwest earthquake
- Colossal volcanic eruption at Yellowstone National Park could destroy life for hundreds of miles and bury half the country in ash up to 3 feet deep
- Los Angeles tsunami (generated by an earthquake fault off Southern California)
- Asteroid impact
- New York City hurricane
- Pacific Northwest megathrust earthquake (could cause a tsunami like the 2004 tsunami in South Asia)

Source: Live Science, http://livescience.com

than the amount hauled away (at a cost of $1.7 billion) after the World Trade Center Twin Towers collapsed.[99]

While Congress is debating how to pay this year's hurricane bill, some argue that now is the time to develop a more coherent disaster policy. "The response to the disaster has been to open up the wallet and dump it out," said U.S. Rep. Dennis Cardoza, D-Calif.[100]

David Moss, a Harvard Business School economist who studies disaster financing, agrees. "Right now we cover major disaster losses mainly on an ad hoc basis," he says. "We wait until the disaster strikes, and then we spend whatever seems necessary to relieve the victims."

Natural disasters also batter the insurance industry. It estimates Katrina alone is likely to cost at least $34.4 billion in insured property losses.[101]

Florida Insurance Commissioner Kevin McCarty has asked government officials nationwide to support a "national catastrophe fund." One of its supporters is Rep. Mark Foley, R-Fla., who has sponsored a bill to amend the federal tax code to allow insurance companies to voluntarily set aside, on a tax-deferred basis, reserves to pay for future catastrophic losses. And Sen. Kay Bailey

Hutchinson, R-Texas, proposes setting up an emergency reserve fund for domestic disasters and emergencies.

Moss says insurers could also include a "catastrophe rider" on every insurance policy covering losses stemming from terrorism and natural disasters, and the federal government could also offer some sort of "backstop" covering losses above a certain level, such as $100 billion.

Homeowners' insurance policies do not cover flood damage caused by the storm surges that accompany hurricanes. Experts estimate that Katrina caused $44 billion in flood damage. Flood insurance is available through the National Flood Insurance Program, but it is expensive, and many homeowners do not buy it. In addition, the New Orleans maps used to determine if a home is in a floodplain were apparently out of date, and many homeowners whose homes flooded had been told that they were not in danger of being flooded.

OUTLOOK

Just Talk?

While there is a lot of talk about improving disaster preparedness and response, few experts expect radical changes any time soon.

"The investigations are focusing on individual blame, rather than system failures," says George Washington University's Harrald. "The hubris in Washington is that we can solve everything by passing a law or reorganizing something inside the Beltway. It's a little more complicated."

Ashwood, director of emergency management in Oklahoma, agrees. "All we are doing right now is just talking. Nobody is doing anything else." He adds that while it's all good that people in Washington want answers, some of the scrutiny is misdirected. He notes that 90 auditors have been sent to monitor the 72 full-time FEMA employees who work on disaster recovery. "Ninety auditors covering 72 people," he says. "That's ridiculous."

Meanwhile, on Capitol Hill, many lawmakers — particularly Democrats —feel the Katrina investigations are losing steam. "In the case of 9/11, it took a while to develop, and only after intense political pressure from the families," said former Rep. Lee Hamilton, D-Ill., who co-chaired the 9/11 Commission. "I don't see anything comparable" happening for the Katrina disaster.[102]

The fact that FEMA reacted quicker to hurricanes Rita and Wilma also may dampen the urgency for action, experts say. Others worry that the attention on Katrina may give short shrift to future floods, earthquakes and other disasters. "That is part of the human experience. We react to the last disaster," Harrald says.

While homeland security adviser Townsend admits that a "failure of communication" within the federal government and with state and local officials was the "single most important" contributor to the Katrina breakdown, some disaster experts aren't optimistic that even that situation will change.[103]

"The federal government needs to take a leadership role to pull the agencies together," said Priscilla Nelson, a former National Science Foundation executive. "That really hasn't happened yet . . . [and] I don't have a reasonable expectation it will. People are organized in a way that doesn't promote integration or accountability or authority."[104]

The University of Pennsylvania's Kettl says the federal government's "lack of imagination" — cited by the 9/11 Commission as a reason for the government's failure in 2001 — contributed to its poor performance after Katrina. The United States has failed to "build the capacity to deal with costly, wicked problems that leave little time to react," he wrote, and instead is "trying to solve the most important challenges of the 21st century by retreating back to models from the past."[105]

Aylward of ComCare says the discussions sparked by Hurricane Katrina miss a key point. "There's a real mistaken idea that disasters are somehow different from day-to-day events. But these are the same firemen, the same police, all the same people on the ground using the same radios, same computers," he says. "We ought to be focusing on improving the day-to-day response of emergency agencies."

For her part, the University of Colorado's Tierney hopes individual citizens will become more prepared. "The ultimate first-responders in any disaster are members of the public," she says. "If we want to be prepared for the future terrorist attack, for the future disasters in this country, we have to build within neighborhoods and through local community organizations to help people to be self-sufficient, to help others when disaster strikes. Katrina certainly taught us that."

UPDATE

Major disasters have ravaged Louisiana twice in five years — Hurricane Katrina in August 2005 and the unprecedented BP oil spill this spring and summer — but the Federal Emergency Management Agency (FEMA) has played starkly different roles in each.

FEMA was in charge after Katrina hit the Gulf Coast and came under heavy fire for its poor preparation before and lackluster performance after the hurricane, which in New Orleans alone destroyed thousands of homes and much of the city's infrastructure.

In the case of the BP oil spill, which dumped an estimated 4.9 million barrels of crude into the Gulf of Mexico, the federal government's role has been to monitor, rather than lead, the response. Unlike Katrina, which as a natural disaster brought in FEMA, the oil spill was caused by a private enterprise, so BP has been responsible for cleanup and compensation of victims. The U.S. Coast Guard has been the lead federal agency overseeing BP's response, and FEMA has played only a supporting role.

FEMA officials may be excused if they're breathing a sigh of relief for not being on the hook for the BP spill. Ever since Hurricane Katrina made landfall, the agency has been under the microscope in Congress and the court of public opinion.

After a series of hearings, Congress responded to the agency's shortcomings in 2006 with the Post-Katrina Emergency Management Reform Act, signed into law by President George W. Bush on Oct. 4. The legislation increased FEMA's responsibilities and gave it more autonomy within the Department of Homeland Security.

Emergency Management Overhaul

The legislation also overhauled other emergency-management areas that were seen as weak during Hurricane Katrina. For example, the act requires the development of a National Emergency Communications Plan to improve emergency communications coordination among different first responding agencies.

Still, nearly four years after the FEMA overhaul, some critics charge that Congress and the Department of Homeland Security have put too much money into buying emergency equipment and too little into training.

"Billions have been spent in an effort to make America safer, but the big question still remains whether the push has benefited the men and women on the ground or if it has primarily supported a burgeoning homeland security industrial complex," said Bill Buzenberg, executive director of the nonprofit Center for Public Integrity, a journalistic watchdog group in Washington. "While a host of agencies are now outfitted with the latest technologies . . . , many of them lack the training and skills to use them efficiently."[106] At least some members of Congress have sought more fundamental changes than the 2006 act created. A draft report of the Senate Homeland Security and Governmental Affairs Committee, written when the 2006 act was under discussion, called for FEMA to be abolished and a new disaster-response agency created from scratch.[107] And in 2009 Rep. James L. Oberstar, D-Minn., introduced legislation to move FEMA out of the Department of Homeland Security and made a free-standing agency. In introducing the bill, Oberstar said that oversight hearings had shown a "clear correlation between the absorption of FEMA into [the Department of Homeland Security] and deterioration of FEMA's effectiveness." He charged that "FEMA's emergency management mission has been distorted by a focus on terrorism."[108]

In May 2009, however, the Obama administration made it clear that FEMA would remain within the Department of Homeland Security.

Sen. Susan Collins, R-Maine, an author of the Post-Katrina Emergency Management Reform Act, applauded the administration's position, saying, "Today's FEMA is not the same agency it was in 2005. Rather than splintering apart agencies that work together well now, the president has wisely chosen to allow FEMA to rebuild itself into the best disaster preparedness and response agency in the world."[109]

Praise for FEMA

Collins praised FEMA's response to a string of post-Katrina disasters, including two 2008 hurricanes. "As we have seen from its response to Hurricanes Gustav and Ike, the California wildfires, flooding in the Midwest and winter storms in Maine, FEMA has made a great deal of progress since passage of the Post-Katrina Emergency Management Reform Act," she said.

An oil slick forms near the Chandeleur Islands in the Gulf of Mexico as cleanup operations continue from the April 20, 2010, BP Deepwater Horizon platform explosion.

Not everyone has given FEMA such high marks for its efforts since 2005, however.

In February 2008, FEMA came under fire from Congress and the media for its handling of formaldehyde contamination in trailers provided to residents made homeless by Katrina.[110]

FEMA was not blamed for the contamination itself but rather for its handling of the contamination issue after it emerged.

The agency also faced criticism for its treatment of residents in Texas made homeless by Hurricane Ike, which struck on Sept. 13, 2008. In the months following the storm, according to The Associated Press, FEMA turned down nearly 90 percent of aid requests. An attorney for a homeowner denied aid said that it seemed that the agency had "hired a bunch of people, basically just anybody, and put them on the street after one day of training."[111]

FEMA declined to comment on that charge. But Harvey E. Johnson, FEMA deputy administrator, had previously conceded that the agency's performance in the aftermath of Hurricane Ike had been less than stellar, telling a reporter that "we need to box some ears."[112]

Uneven Progress

A report by a federal watchdog agency released in April 2009 found that while FEMA had made some progress since Katrina, the agency had failed to implement fully the provisions of the 2006 reform act.

"The roles and responsibilities of key officials involved in responding to a catastrophe have not been fully defined and, thus, cannot be tested in exercises," the Government Accountability Office (GAO) reported.

"The lack of clarity in response roles and responsibilities among the diverse set of responders contributed to the disjointed response to Hurricane Katrina and highlighted the need for clear, integrated disaster preparedness and response policies and plans. Although best practices for program management call for a plan that includes key tasks and their target completion dates, FEMA does not have such a plan."[113]

FEMA's inspector general, Richard L. Skinner, echoed that assessment in congressional testimony in July 2009. Skinner said that while "FEMA continues to perform well responding to non-catastrophic or 'garden variety' disasters . . . it still has much to do to become a cohesive, efficient, and effective organization to prepare for and respond to the next catastrophic event."[114]

Skinner put most of the blame for the shortcomings on a lack of resources. "FEMA does not have sufficient tools, operational procedures, and legislative authorities to aggressively promote the cost-effective repair of housing stocks, which would increase the amount of housing available and likely limit increases in the cost of housing, particularly rental rates," he said.

The GAO again took FEMA to task in January 2010, when it found the agency unprepared for recovery efforts following a potential incident of nuclear terrorism. "FEMA . . . has not developed a national disaster recovery strategy, as required by law, or issued specific guidance to coordinate federal, state, and local government recovery planning for . . . radiological-dispersal-device and . . . improvised-nuclear-device incidents, as directed by executive guidance," the GAO reported. "To date, most federal attention has been given to developing a response framework, with less attention to recovery.[115]

On February 26, a letter signed by the entire Senate Homeland Security and Government Affairs Committee was sent to Homeland Security Secretary Janet Napolitano complaining of the agency's failure to fully implement the 2006 reform act. The senators specifically cited inadequacies in a recently released FEMA draft disaster-recovery plan. "The act gave FEMA and its administrator elevated and expanded roles, including in recovery, and the draft fails to implement this statutory role," the senators wrote.[116]

Communication Shortcomings

While critics of federal disaster-response capabilities have focused mainly on FEMA, they also have pointed to vulnerability in the nation's emergency communications systems. During Katrina, emergency communications equipment was not "interoperable" — in other words, equipment used by multiple responders, such as police, firefighters and other first responders from different jurisdictions could not operate effectively with each other. Moreover, nearly forty 911 centers were knocked out by the storm, and the mayor of New Orleans was without telephone communications for two days.

Under the 2006 reform act, Congress created the Office of Emergency Communications in the Department of Homeland Security and required it to improve the survivability and interoperability of emergency communications at all levels of government. The office began operations in April 2007, and in July 2008 the Department of Homeland Security released the "National Emergency Communications Plan," a strategic document for improving emergency communications nationwide.

A GAO report in June 2009 found that these efforts had resulted in some improvement but that significant shortcomings persisted. "Limited collaboration and monitoring jeopardize federal emergency communications efforts, even as the federal government has taken strategic steps to assist first responders," the GAO wrote.[117]

Although Congress provided $1 billion in 2007 for public safety communications interoperability grants, and more than $50 million in 2008 and 2009 each, Rep. David Price, D-N.C., noted in opening recent hearings that "the interoperability problem is far from being solved."[118]

Meanwhile, a debate has erupted within the Obama administration over the Federal Communications Commission's plan to auction off a block of wireless broadband spectrum to the private sector. Many public safety officials, including Attorney General Eric Holder, have argued that the spectrum should instead be used for an emergency broadband network.[119]

NOTES

1. Devin Leonard, "The Only Lifeline Was the Wal-Mart," *Fortune*, Oct. 3, 2005, p. 74.

2. Testimony of David Paulison, acting under secretary for emergency preparedness, before Senate Homeland Security and Governmental Affairs Committee, Oct. 6, 2005.

3. Leonard, *op. cit.*

4. Donald F. Kettl, "The Worst is Yet to Come: Lessons from September 11 and Hurricane Katrina," University of Pennsylvania, Fels Institute of Government, September 2005.

5. Eric Berger, "The foretelling of a deadly disaster in New Orleans," *The Houston Chronicle*, Dec. 1, 2001. See also Dean E. Murphy, "Storm Puts Focus on Other Disasters in Waiting," *The New York Times*, Nov. 13, 2005, p. A1.

6. FEMA press release, "Hurricane Pam Exercise Concludes," July 23, 2004. See also Joel K. Bourne, Jr. "Gone with the Water," *National Geographic*, October 2004.

7. U.S. Conference of Mayors, "Report on Interoperability," June 28, 2004.

8. Prepared testimony of Max Mayfield, director, National Hurricane Center, before Senate Commerce Committee's Disaster Prediction and Prevention Subcommittee, Sept. 20, 2005.

9. Fact sheet, U.S. Geological Survey, Earthquake Hazards Program.

10. National Academy of Public Administration, "Coping With Catastrophe: Building an Emergency Management System to Meet People's Needs in Natural and Manmade Disaster," February 1993.

11. White House transcript, "Press Briefing by Homeland Security and Counterterrorism Adviser Frances Fragos Townsend," Oct. 21, 2005.

12. White House transcript, "President's Remarks During Hurricane Rita Briefing in Texas," Sept. 25, 2005.

13. U.S. Government Accountability Office, "Homeland Security: DHS' Efforts to Enhance First Responders' All Hazards Capabilities Continue to Evolve," July 2005.

14. The National Response Plan is available at www.dhs .gov/interweb/assetlibrary/NRP_FullText.pdf.

15. *Ibid.*

16. Jerry Adler, "The Fight Against the Flu," *Newsweek*, Oct. 31, 2005, p. 39.

17. *Ibid.*

18. Ellen Florian Kratz, "For FedEx, It Was Time To Deliver," *Fortune*, Oct. 3, 2005, p. 83.

19. Testimony before House Energy and Commerce Subcommittee on Telecommunications and the Internet, Sept. 29, 2005.

20. Testimony of David Boyd, director of SAFECOM Program, Department of Homeland Security, before House Energy and Commerce Subcommittee on Telecommunications and the Internet, Sept. 29, 2005.

21. Testimony of Kevin Martin, chairman, Federal Communications Commission, before House Subcommittee on Telecommunications and the Internet, Sept. 29, 2005.

22. *Ibid.*

23. Testimony of Chuck Canterbury, National President, Fraternal Order of Police, before House Homeland Security Subcommittee on Emergency Preparedness, Science and Technology, Sept. 29, 2005.

24. Transcript of House Energy and Commerce Subcommittee on Telecommunications and the Internet, Sept. 29, 2005.

25. White House transcript, "President Discusses Hurricane Relief in Address to the Nation," Sept. 15, 2005

26. CNN, "Lt. Gen. Honore a 'John Wayne dude,'" Sept. 3, 2005.

27. Bill Nichols and Richard Benedetto, "Govs to Bush: Relief our job," *USA Today*, Oct. 3, 2005.

28. Prepared testimony of Gov. Jeb Bush before U.S. House Committee on Homeland Security, Oct. 19, 2005.

29. Congressional Research Service, "Hurricane Katrina: DOD Disaster Response," Sept. 19, 2005.

30. Barbara Starr, "Military ponders disaster response unit," CNN, Oct. 11, 2005, and Ann Scott Tyson,

"Pentagon Plans to Beef Up Domestic Rapid-Response Forces," *The Washington Post*, Oct. 13, 2004, p. A4.

31. The Associated Press, "NOPD Fires 51 for Desertion," CBS News, Oct. 28, 2005.

32. Department of Defense news briefing, Sept. 27, 2005.

33. Congressional Research Service, *op. cit.*

34. *Ibid.*

35. *Ibid.*

36. "NewsHour with Jim Lehrer," "Using the Military at Home," Sept. 27, 2005.

37. Congressional Research Service, "The Posse Comitatus Act and Related Matters: A Sketch," June 6, 2005.

38. Anne Plummer, "Change in 'Posse' Law Unwise, Say Critics," *CQ Weekly*, Sept. 26, 2005, pp. 2550-2551.

39. U.S. Conference of Mayors, "The U.S. Conference of Mayors Hold Special Meeting on Emergency Response and Homeland Security," Oct. 24, 2005.

40. For background see Pamela M. Prah, "War in Iraq," *CQ Researcher*, Oct. 21, 2005, pp. 881-908, and Pamela M. Prah, "Draft Debates," *CQ Researcher*, Aug. 19, 2005, pp. 661-684.

41. Gene Healy, "What of 'Posse Comitatus'?" *Akron Beacon Journal*, Oct. 7, 2005, reprinted on Cato Institute Web site, www.cato.org/pub_display .php?pub_id=5115.

42. National Academy of Public Administration," *op. cit.*

43. Testimony before U.S. House Committee on Homeland Security, Oct. 19, 2005.

44. Transcript of House Select Katrina Response Investigation Committee, Sept. 27, 2005.

45. *Ibid.*

46. *Time*, "4 places Where the System Broke Down," Sept. 18, 2005, p. 38.

47. CNN, "Mayor to Feds: Get Off Your Asses," Sept. 2, 2005, www.cnn.com/2005/US/09/02/nagin .transcript/.

48. Eric Lipton, Eric Schmitt and Thom Shanker, "Political Issues Snarled Plans for Troop Aid," *The New York Times*, Sept. 9, 2005, p. A1.

49. Kettl, *op. cit.*

50. Peter G. Gosselin and Alan C. Miler, "Why FEMA was Missing in Action," *Los Angeles Times*, Sept. 5, 2005.

51. Testimony before Homeland Security Subcommittee on Emergency Preparedness, Science and Technology, Sept. 29, 2005.

52. Transcript, House Transportation and Infrastructure Subcommittee on Development, Public Buildings and Emergency Management, Oct. 6, 2005.

53. Rebecca Adams, "FEMA Failure a Perfect Storm of Bureaucracy, *CQ Weekly*, Sept. 12, 2005, p. 2378.

54. Frank James and Andrew Martin, "Slow response bewilders former FEMA officials," *Chicago Tribune*, Sept. 3, 2005, p. A1.

55. "FEMA History," www.fema.gov/about/history.shtm.

56. James O'Toole, "U.S. help for disaster victims goes from nothing to billions," *Pittsburgh Post-Gazette*, Oct. 2, 2005.

57. Ken Rudin, National Public Radio, "The Hurricane and the President (Hoover, That Is)," Oct. 5, 2005.

58. Aaron Schroeder, Gary Wamsley, and Robert Ward, "The Evolution of Emergency Management in America: From a Painful Past to a Promising but Uncertain Future," in *Handbook of Crisis and Emergency Management* (2001), p. 364.

59. "FEMA History," *op. cit.*

60. White House statement, June 19, 1978.

61. George D. Haddow and Jane A. Bullock, *Introduction to Emergency Management* (2003), p. 8.

62. Testimony before House Transportation and Infrastructure Subcommittee on Economic Development, Public Buildings and Emergency Management, Oct. 6, 2005.

63. Haddow and Bullock, *op. cit.*

64. *Ibid.*

65. http://seismo.berkeley.edu/faq/1989_0.html

66. *CQ Historic Documents 1993*, "President George Bush on Disaster Relief for Florida and Louisiana After Hurricane Andrew," Aug. 24, 1992.

67. Ali Farazmand, *Handbook of Crisis and Emergency Management* (2001), p. 379.

68. National Academy of Public Administration," *op. cit.*

69. Haddow and Bullock, *op. cit.*

70. Adams, *op. cit.*

71. Haddow and Bullock, *op. cit.*, p. 12.

72. Haddow and Bullock, *op. cit.*, p. 12.

73. *Ibid*, p. 13.

74. Justin Rood, "FEMA's decline: an agency's slow slide from grace," www.govexec.com, Sept .28, 2005.

75. *Ibid.*

76. Dick Polman, "A possible sea change on federal spending," *The Philadelphia Inquirer*, Sept. 7, 2005.

77. www.ncdc.noaa.gov/oa/climate/research/2004/hurricanes04.html.

78. www.fema.gov/news/newsrelease_print.fema?id=15967.

79. Charles Mahtesian, "How FEMA delivered Florida for Bush," Govexec.com, *National Journal*, Nov. 3, 2004.

80. Adam C. Smith, "Hurricanes roil the political waters," *St. Petersburg Times*, Sept. 8, 2004.

81. www.ncdc.noaa.gov/oa/climate/research/2004/hurricanes04.html.

82. White House transcript, "Press Briefing by Homeland Security and Counterterrorism Advisor Fran Townsend," Oct. 21, 2005

83. Transcript, House Select Katrina Response Investigation Committee, Oct. 19, 2005.

84. *Ibid.*

85. Statement, Sept. 6, 2005 http://clinton.senate.gov/news/statements/details.cfm?id=24526&&.

86. Susan Ferrechio and Martin Kady II, "Little Headway on Compromise for Select Panel to Examine Katrina Response," *CQ Today*, Sept. 20, 2005.

87. *Ibid.*, transcript, Oct. 19, 2005.

88. Sally Kestin, Megan O'Matz and John Maines, "FEMA's waste continues as millions in extra payments given out for Katrina," *Sun-Sentinel*, Oct. 20, 2005.

89. Eamon Javers, "Anatomy of a Katrina Cleanup Contract," *Business Week*, Oct. 27, 2005.

90. Leslie Wayne and Glen Justice, "FEMA Director Under Clinton Profits From Experience," *The New York Times*, Oct. 10, 2005, and Jonathan E. Kaplan, "Former FEMA chief Albaugh in the middle," *The Hill*, Sept. 30, 2005. See also "Profiting from Katrina: The contracts," Center for Public Integrity, www.publicintegrity.org/katrina.

91. Transcript, House Transportation and Infrastructure Subcommittee on Economic Development, Public Buildings and Emergency Management Hearing on FEMA After Katrina, Oct. 6, 2005.

92. Testimony before House Committee on Homeland Security, Oct. 19, 2005.

93. The Associated Press, "Gov. Bush Criticizes State's Storm Effort," Oct. 27, 2005.

94. Transcript of Senate Homeland Security and Governmental Affairs Committee Hearing on Status Report on FEMA Recovery Efforts, Oct. 6, 2005.

95. Killen, *op. cit.*

96. Amol Sharma, "Senate Panel Approves Bill That Would Create A National Alert Office, *CQ Weekly*, Oct. 20, 2005.

97. Tim Starks, "Unpromising Prospects for First Responders," *CQ Weekly*, Nov. 14, 2005, p. 3034.

98. Liriel Higa and Stephen J. Norton, "Louisiana Senators Remain Disappointed with Bush's Rebuilding plan," *CQ Today*, Oct. 28, 2005.

99. Spencer S. Hsu and Ceci Connolly, "La. Wants FEMA to Pay for Majority of Damage to State Property," *The Washington Post*, Oct. 28, 2005, p. A14.

100. Edmund L. Andrews, "Emergency Spending as a Way of Life," *The New York Times*, Oct. 2, 2005, p. A4.

101. Insurance Information Institute, "Catastrophes: Insurance Issues," November 2005.

102. Tim Starks, "Critics Expecting Little from Hurricane Probes," *CQ Today*, Oct. 18, 2005.

103. White House transcript, Townsend briefing, Oct. 21, 2005.

104. Brain Friel and Paul Singer, "Gaps remain in government strategy for handling natural disasters," *National Journal*, Govexec.com, Oct. 28, 2005.

105. Kettl, *op. cit.*

106. "Report: Federal Cash Hasn't Bought Interoperability," *CQ Homeland Security*, Feb. 17, 2010.

107. Eric Lipton, "Senate Committee Leaders Urge FEMA Dismantling," *The New York Times*, April 27, 2006, p. A22.

108. Daniel Fowler, "Oberstar Seeks Independent FEMA, Despite Napolitano Revelation," *CQ Homeland Security*, May 14, 2009.

109. "Final Word from President Obama: FEMA Stays in Department of Homeland Security," *U.S. Fed News*, May 14, 2009.

110. "Formaldehyde Foul-Up," editorial, *The New York Times*, Feb. 15, 2008, p. A22.

111. "FEMA is Faulted on Aid After Hurricane Ike," *The New York Times*, Feb. 9, 2009, p. A12.

112. "After Hurricane Ike; FEMA Admits Shortcomings and Tried to Fix Them," editorial, *The Washington Post*, Nov. 10, 2008.

113. "National Preparedness: FEMA Has Made Progress, but Needs to Complete and Integrate Planning, Exercise, and Assessment Efforts," General Accountability Office, April 2009, GAO-09-369.

114. http://homeland.house.gov/SiteDocuments/20090708101404-71881.pdf.

115. "Combating Nuclear Terrorism: Actions Needed to Better Prepare to Recover from Possible Attacks Using Radiological or Nuclear Materials," General Accountability Office, Jan. 29, 2010, GAO-10-204.

116. Matt Korade, "FEMA Draft Recovery Plan Misses Mark, Senators Say," *CQ Homeland Security*, March 2, 2010.

117. "Emergency Communication: Vulnerabilities Remain and Limited Collaboration and Monitoring Hamper Federal Efforts," General Accountability Office, June 2009, GAO-09-604.

118. "Price Opening Statement: Hearing on DHS Interoperable Communications," Congressional Documents and Publications, March 17, 2009.

119. Edward Wyatt, "A Face-Off Over Sale of Spectrum by FCC," *The New York Times*, June 16, 2010, p. B1.

BIBLIOGRAPHY

Books

Bea, Keith, *Federal Disaster Polices After Terrorists Strike*, Nova Science Publishers, 2003.
Prepared at the request of members of Congress, this book is primarily about terrorism, but it provides a good introduction to the Robert T. Stafford Disaster Relief and Emergency Assistance Act, the country's main federal disaster-assistance law.

Farazmand, Ali, (ed.), *Handbook of Crisis and Emergency Management*, Marcel Dekker, 2001.
A professor of public administration at Florida Atlantic University has compiled essays and case studies of crisis and emergency management, as well as a good primer on Federal Emergency Management Agency history.

Haddow, George D., and Jane A. Bullock, *Introduction to Emergency Management*, Butterworth-Heinemann, 2003.
Two former FEMA officials provide background on the history of disaster response and preparedness and strategies for improving planning and mitigation.

Articles

"FEMA: A Legacy of Waste," *South Florida Sun-Sentinel*, Sept. 18, 2005, p. A1.
A team of *Sun-Sentinel* reporters examined 20 disasters nationwide and found a pattern of mismanagement and fraud at FEMA.

"4 Places Where the System Broke Down," *Time*, Sept. 19, 2005, pp. 28-42.
A team of *Time* reporters shows how confusion, incompetence and fear of making mistakes hobbled the government at all levels in the New Orleans relief efforts, laying blame on the mayor, governor, FEMA director and secretary of Homeland Security.

Adams, Rebecca, "FEMA Failure a Perfect Storm of Bureaucracy," *CQ Weekly*, Sept. 12, 2005.
The reporter provides an overview of FEMA's challenges and pending proposals in Congress in the wake of the agency's sluggish response to Hurricane Katrina.

O'Toole, James, "U.S. help for disaster victims goes from nothing to billions," *Pittsburgh Post-Gazette*, Oct. 2, 2005.
The federal government has been assuming an increasing role in trying to make individuals, businesses and local governments whole after natural disasters, but there is no plan to budget for natural disasters.

Rood, Justin, "FEMA's decline: an agency's slow slide from grace," www.govexec.com, Sept. 28, 2005.
This article from a magazine for government executives discusses the budget and staffing cuts that FEMA has experienced in recent years and concludes that FEMA "was not the agency it once was" when Katrina struck.

Sappenfield, Mark, "Military wary of disaster role," *The Christian Science Monitor*, Sept. 29, 2005.
In some respects, the greatest opponent of giving the military more authority in U.S. disaster relief is the military itself.

Reports

Government Accountability Office, "Hurricane Katrina: Providing Oversight of the Nation's Preparedness, Response and Recovery Activities," Sept. 28, 2005.
This report to Congress includes a 10-page list of past GAO studies related to hurricanes and other natural disasters, including preparedness, the military's role and insurance.

Insurance Information Institute, "Catastrophes: Insurance Issues," November 2005.
A leading insurance industry group explains in simple language how catastrophes affect the insurance industry and how Katrina is prompting a re-examination of how the country pays for natural disasters.

Kettl, Donald, "The Worst is Yet to Come: Lesson from September 11 and Hurricane Katrina," University of Pennsylvania Fels Institute of Government, September 2005.
A professor of public policy specializing in state issues and homeland security concludes that policymakers need to pull FEMA out of the Department of Homeland Security and establish better communications systems.

National Academy of Public Administration, "Coping with Catastrophe: Building an Emergency Management System to Meet People's Needs in Natural and Manmade Disasters," February 1993.

A panel of experts that convened in the wake of the slow federal response to Hurricane Andrew in 1992 recommends that the military not take the lead in disaster responses.

National Academy of Public Administration, "Review of Actions Taken to Strengthen the Nation's Emergency Management System," March 1994.

This follow-up report, requested by FEMA Director James L. Witt, concluded that progress was being made but that FEMA needed fewer political appointees in leadership positions and that the president should establish a Domestic Crisis Monitoring Unit.

For More Information

American Red Cross, 2025 E St., N.W., Washington, DC 20006; (202) 303-5000; www.redcross.org. The congressionally chartered nonprofit provides disaster relief nationwide. Its Web site tells how to prepare for disasters.

Centers for Disease Control and Prevention, 1600 Clifton Road, Atlanta, GA 30333; (800) 232-4636; www.bt.cdc.gov. Provides information on emergency preparedness for bioterrorism, chemical and radiation emergencies, natural disasters and contagious diseases.

Department of Homeland Security, Washington, DC 20528; (202) 646-4600; www.dhs.gov. The principal agency charged with preventing terrorist attacks within the United States and minimizing the damage from attacks and natural disasters.

Federal Emergency Management Agency, 500 C St., S.W., Washington, DC 20472; (202) 566-1600; www.fema.gov. Provides information on preparedness, emergency response, the National Flood Insurance Program, how to apply for disaster relief, latest details on Katrina and a copy of the National Response Plan. A list of all 50 state emergency-management offices is at www.fema.gov/fema/statedr.shtm.

National Emergency Management Association, P.O. Box 11910, Lexington, KY 40578; (859) 244-8000; www.nemaweb.org. Represents state emergency-management directors.

National Hurricane Center, National Centers for Environmental Prediction, 11691 S.W. 17th St, Miami, FL 33165-2149; (305) 229-4470; www.nhc.noaa.gov. Tracks and forecasts hurricanes.

Insurance Information Institute, 110 William St., New York, NY 10038; (212) 346-5500; www.iii.org. Represents the insurance industry and tracks the impact of catastrophes, floods and terrorist acts on the industry.

International Association of Emergency Managers, 201 Park Washington Court, Falls Church, VA 22046-4527; (703) 538-1795; www.iaem.com. Represents local emergency managers and tracks federal homeland security grants and policies that affect local emergency officials.

U.S. Geological Survey Earthquake Hazards Program, 12201 Sunrise Valley Dr., MS 905, Reston, VA 20192; 1-888-275-8747; http://earthquake.usgs.gov/. Provides information on worldwide earthquake activity and hazard-reduction. Web site lists the largest U.S. earthquakes.

4

Rapid Urbanization

Jennifer Weeks

Children scavenge for recyclables amid rubbish in the Dharavi slum in Mumbai, India. About a billion people worldwide live in slums — where sewer, water and garbage-collection services are often nonexistent. If impoverished rural residents continue streaming into cities at current rates, the world's slum population is expected to double to 2 billion within the next two decades, according to the United Nations.

From *CQ Researcher*,
April 2009.

India's most infamous slum lives up to its reputation. Located in the middle of vast Mumbai, Dharavi is home to as many as 1 million people densely packed into thousands of tiny shacks fashioned from scrap metal, plastic sheeting and other scrounged materials. Narrow, muddy alleys crisscross the 600-acre site, open sewers carry human waste and vacant lots serve as garbage dumps. There is electricity, but running water is available for only an hour or so a day. Amid the squalor, barefoot children sing for money, beg from drivers in nearby traffic or work in garment and leather shops, recycling operations and other lightly regulated businesses.

Moviegoers around the globe got a glimpse of life inside Dharavi in last year's phenomenally popular Oscar-winning film, "Slumdog Millionaire," about plucky Jamal Malik, a fictional Dharavi teenager who improbably wins a TV quiz-show jackpot. The no-holds-barred portrayal of slum life may have been shocking to affluent Westerners, but Dharavi is only one of Asia's innumerable slums. In fact, about a billion people worldwide live in urban slums — the ugly underbelly of the rapid and haphazard urbanization that has occurred in many parts of the world in recent decades. And if soaring urban growth rates continue unabated, the world's slum population is expected to double to 2 billion by 2030, according to the U.N.[1]

But all city dwellers don't live in slums. Indeed, other fast-growing cities presented cheerier faces to the world last year, from Dubai's glittering luxury skyscrapers to Beijing's breathtaking, high-tech pre-Olympic cultural spectacle.

World Will Have 26 Megacities by 2025

The number of megacities — urban areas with at least 10 million residents — will increase from 19 to 26 worldwide by the year 2025, according to the United Nations. The seven new megacities will be in Asia and sub-Saharan Africa. Most megacities are in coastal areas, making them highly vulnerable to massive loss of life and property damage caused by rising sea levels that experts predict will result from climate change in the 21st century.

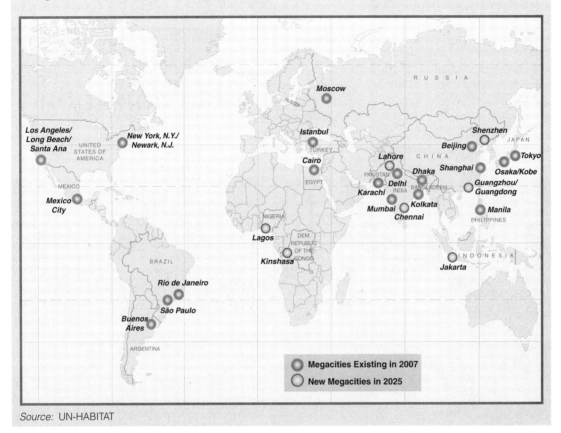

Source: UN-HABITAT

Today, 3.3 billion people live in cities — half the world's population — and urbanites are projected to total nearly 5 billion (out of 8.1 billion) worldwide by 2030.[2] About 95 percent of that growth is occurring in the developing world, especially in Africa and Asia.[3]

These regions are going through the same threefold evolution that transformed Europe and North America over a 200-year period between 1750 and 1950: the industrialization of agriculture, followed by rural migration to cities and declining population growth as life expectancy improves. But today's developing countries are modernizing much faster — typically in less than 100 years — and their cities are expanding at dizzying rates: On average, 5 million people in developing countries move to cities every month. As urban areas struggle to absorb this growth, the new residents often end up crowded into already teeming slums. For instance, 62 percent of city dwellers in sub-Saharan Africa live in slums, 43 percent in southern Asia, 37 percent in East Asia and 27 percent in Latin America and the Caribbean, according to UN-HABITAT, the United Nations agency for human settlements.[4]

UN-HABITAT defines a slum as an urban area without at least one of the following features:

- Durable housing,
- Adequate living space (no more than three people per room),
- Access to clean drinking water,
- Access to improved sanitation (toilets or latrines that separate human waste from contact with water sources), or
- Secure property rights.[5]

But all slums are not the same. Some lack only one basic necessity, while others lack several. And conditions can be harsh in non-slum neighborhoods as well. Thus, experts say, policies should focus on specific local problems in order to make a difference in the lives of poor city dwellers.[6]

Cities "are potent instruments for national economic and social development. They attract investment and create wealth," said HABITAT Executive Director Anna Tibaijuka last April. But, she warned, cities also concentrate poverty and deprivation, especially in developing countries. "Rapid and chaotic urbanization is being accompanied by increasing inequalities, which pose enormous challenges to human security and safety."[7]

Today, improving urban life is an important international development priority.[8] One of the eight U.N. Millennium Development Goals (MDGs) — broad objectives intended to end poverty worldwide by 2015 — endorsed by world leaders in 2000 was environmental sustainability. Among other things, it aims to cut in half the portion of the world's people without access to safe drinking water and achieve "significant

Tokyo Is by Far the World's Biggest City

With more than 35 million residents, Tokyo is nearly twice as big as the next-biggest metropolises. Tokyo is projected to remain the world's largest city in 2025, when there will be seven new megacities — urban areas with at least 10 million residents. Two Indian cities, Mumbai and Delhi, will overtake Mexico City and New York as the world's second- and third-largest cities. The two largest newcomers in 2025 will be in Africa: Kinshasa and Lagos.

Population of Megacities, 2007 and 2025
(in millions)

2007		2025 (projected)	
Tokyo, Japan	35.68	Tokyo, Japan	36.40
New York, NY/Newark, NJ	19.04	Mumbai, India	26.39
Mexico City, Mexico	19.03	Delhi, India	22.50
Mumbai, India	18.98	Dhaka, Bangladesh	22.02
São Paulo, Brazil	18.85	São Paulo, Brazil	21.43
Delhi, India	15.93	Mexico City, Mexico	21.01
Shanghai, China	14.99	New York, NY/Newark, NJ	20.63
Kolkata, India	14.79	Kolkata, India	20.56
Dhaka, Bangladesh	13.49	Shanghai, China	19.41
Buenos Aires, Argentina	12.80	Karachi, Pakistan	19.10
Los Angeles/Long Beach/ Santa Ana (CA)	12.50	Kinshasa, Dem. Rep. Congo	16.76
Karachi, Pakistan	12.13	Lagos, Nigeria	15.80
Cairo, Egypt	11.89	Cairo, Egypt	15.56
Rio de Janeiro, Brazil	11.75	Manila, Philippines	14.81
Osaka/Kobe, Japan	11.29	Beijing, China	14.55
Beijing, China	11.11	Buenos Aires, Argentina	13.77
Manila, Philippines	11.10	Los Angeles/Long Beach/ Santa Ana (CA)	13.67
Moscow, Russia	10.45	Rio de Janeiro, Brazil	13.41
Istanbul, Turkey	10.06	Jakarta, Indonesia	12.36
		Istanbul, Turkey	12.10
New megacities in 2025		Guangzhou/Guangdong, China	11.84
		Osaka/Kobe, Japan	11.37
		Moscow, Russia	10.53
		Lahore, Pakistan	10.51
Source: UN-HABITAT		Shenzhen, China	10.20
		Chennai, India	10.13

improvement" in the lives of at least 100 million slum dwellers.[9]

Global Population Is Shifting to Cities

Half a century ago, less than a third of the world's population lived in cities. By 2005, nearly half inhabited urban areas, and in 2030, at least 60 percent of the world's population will be living in cities, reflecting an unprecedented scale of urban growth in the developing world. This will be particularly notable in Africa and Asia, where the urban population will double between 2000 and 2030.

Worldwide Urban and Rural Populations

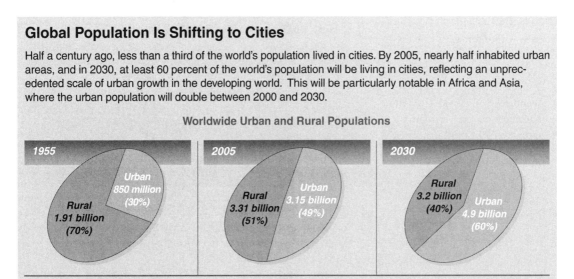

Source: U.N. Department of Economic and Social Affairs; U.N. Population Fund

Delivering even the most basic city services is an enormous challenge in many of the world's 19 megacities — metropolises with more than 10 million residents. And smaller cities with fewer than 1 million inhabitants are growing even faster in both size and number than larger ones.[10]

Many fast-growing cities struggle with choking air pollution, congested traffic, polluted water supplies and inadequate sanitation services. The lack of services can contribute to larger social and economic problems. For example, slum dwellers without permanent housing or access to mass transit have trouble finding and holding jobs. And when poverty becomes entrenched it reinforces the gulf between rich and poor, which can promote crime and social unrest.

"A city is a system of systems. It has biological, social and technical parts, and they all interact," says George Bugliarello, president emeritus of Polytechnic University in New York and foreign secretary of the National Academy of Engineering. "It's what engineers call a complex system because it has features that are more than the sum of its parts. You have to understand how all of the components interact to guide them."

Improving life for the urban poor begins with providing shelter, sanitation and basic social services like health care and education. But more is needed to make cities truly inclusive, such as guaranteeing slum dwellers' property rights so they cannot be ejected from their homes.[11]

Access to information and communications technology (ICT) is also crucial. In some developing countries, ICT has been adopted widely, particularly cell phones, but high-speed Internet access and computer use still lag behind levels in rich nations. Technology advocates say this "digital divide" slows economic growth in developing nations and increases income inequality both within and between countries. Others say the problem has been exaggerated and that there is no critical link between ICTs and poverty reduction.

Managing urban growth and preventing the creation of new slums are keys to both improving the quality of life and better protecting cities from natural disasters. Many large cities are in areas at risk from earthquakes, wildfires or floods. Squatter neighborhoods are often built on flood plains, steep slopes or other vulnerable areas, and poor people usually have fewer resources to escape or relocate.

For example, heavy rains in northern Venezuela in 1999 caused mudslides and debris flows that demolished many hillside shantytowns around the capital city of Caracas, killing some 30,000 people. In 2005 Hurricane Katrina killed more people in New Orleans' lower-income neighborhoods, which were located in a flood plain, than in wealthier neighborhoods of the Louisiana port city that were built on higher ground. As global warming raises sea levels, many of the world's largest cities are expected to be increasingly at risk from flooding.

Paradoxically, economic growth also can pose a risk for some cities. Large cities can be attractive targets for terrorist attacks, especially if they are symbols of national prosperity and modernity, such as New York City, site of the Sept. 11, 2001, attack on the World Trade Center. Last November's coordinated Islamic terrorist attacks in Mumbai followed a similar strategy: Landmark properties frequented by foreigners were targeted in order to draw worldwide media coverage, damage India's economy and send a message that nowhere in India was safe.[12]

Today the global economic recession is creating a new problem for city dwellers: Entry-level jobs are disappearing as trade contracts evaporate and factories shut down. Unable to find other jobs, many recent migrants to cities are returning to rural areas that are ill-prepared to receive them, and laborers who remain in cities have less money to send to families back home.[13]

As national leaders, development experts and city officials debate how to manage urban growth, here are some issues they are considering:

Does urbanization make people better off?

With a billion city dwellers worldwide trapped in slums, why do people keep moving to cities? Demographic experts say that newcomers hope to earn higher incomes and find more opportunities than rural areas can offer.

"Often people are fleeing desperate economic conditions," says David Bloom, a professor of economics and demography at Harvard University's School of Public Health. "And the social attractions of a city — opportunities to meet more people, escape from isolation or in some cases to be anonymous — trump fears about

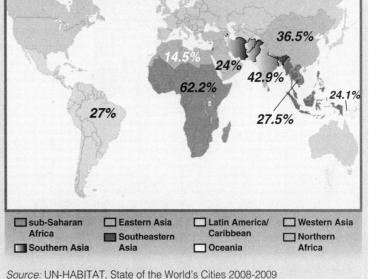

Most African City Dwellers Live in Slums

Most of the world's slum dwellers are in developing countries, with nearly two-thirds of sub-Saharan Africa's city dwellers living in slums.

Percentage of Urban Populations Living in Slums, by Region

36.5%
14.5%
24%
42.9%
62.2%
24.1%
27%
27.5%

- sub-Saharan Africa
- Southern Asia
- Eastern Asia
- Southeastern Asia
- Latin America/ Caribbean
- Oceania
- Western Asia
- Northern Africa

Source: UN-HABITAT, State of the World's Cities 2008-2009

difficult urban conditions. If they have relatives or friends living in cities already, that reduces some of the risk."

When nations attract foreign investment, it creates new jobs. In the 1990s both China and India instituted broad economic reforms designed to encourage foreign investment, paving the way for rapid economic growth. That growth accelerated as information technology advances like the Internet, fiber-optic networks and e-mail made it faster and cheaper to communicate worldwide in real time.[14] As a result, thousands of manufacturing and white-collar jobs were "outsourced" from the United States to India, China and other low-wage countries over the past decade.[15]

These jobs spurred major growth in some cities, especially in areas with educated, English-speaking work forces. The large southern Indian city of Bangalore became a center for information technology — dubbed "India's Silicon Valley." Other cities in India, Singapore and the Philippines now host English-language call centers that manage everything from computer technical support to lost-baggage complaints for airlines. In a

Packed buses in Dhaka take residents in the Bangladeshi capital to their homes in outlying villages on the eve of the Muslim holiday Eid al-Adha — the "Festival of Sacrifice." Rapidly growing cities have trouble keeping up with the transportation needs of residents.

twist on this model, the Chinese city of Dalian — which was controlled by Japan from 1895 through World War II and still has many Japanese speakers — has become a major outsourcing center for Japanese companies.[16]

Some observers say an increasingly networked world allows people to compete for global "knowledge work" from anywhere in the world instead of having to emigrate to developed countries. In his best-seller *The World Is Flat*, author and *New York Times* columnist Thomas Friedman cites Asian call centers as an example of this shift, since educated Indians can work at the centers and prosper at home rather than seeking opportunity abroad. While he acknowledges that millions of people in developing countries are poor, sick and disempowered, Friedman argues that things improve when people move from rural to urban areas.

"[E]xcess labor gets trained and educated, it begins working in services and industry; that leads to innovation and better education and universities, freer markets, economic growth and development, better infrastructure, fewer diseases and slower population growth," Friedman writes. "It is that dynamic that is going on in parts of urban India and urban China today, enabling people to compete on a level playing field and attracting investment dollars by the billions."[17]

But others say it's not always so simple. Educated newcomers may be able to find good jobs, but migrants

without skills or training often end up working in the "informal economy" — activities that are not taxed, regulated or monitored by the government, such as selling goods on the street or collecting garbage for recycling. These jobs are easy to get but come without minimum wages or labor standards, and few workers can get credit to grow their businesses. Members of ethnic minorities and other underprivileged groups, such as lower castes in India, often are stuck with the dirtiest and most dangerous and difficult tasks.[18]

And some countries have experienced urban growth without job growth. Through the late 1980s, many Latin American countries tried to grow their economies by producing manufactured goods at home instead of importing them from abroad.

"Years of government protection insulated these industries from outside competition, so they did not feel pressure to become more productive. Then they went under when economies opened up to trade," says Steven Poelhekke, a researcher with DNB, the national bank of the Netherlands. "In Africa, industrialization has never really taken off. And without job creation governments cannot deliver benefits for new urbanites."[19]

Meanwhile, when cities grow too quickly, competition for land, space, light and services increases faster than government can respond. Real estate prices rise, driving poor residents into squatter neighborhoods, where crowding and pollution spread disease. "When cities get too big, the downsides to city life are bigger than the benefits for vulnerable inhabitants," says Poelhekke.

Broadly, however, urbanization has reduced the total number of people in poverty in recent years. According to a 2007 World Bank study, about three-quarters of the world's poor still live in rural areas. Poor people are urbanizing faster than the population as a whole, so some poverty is shifting to cities. Yet, clearly, many of those new urbanites are finding higher incomes — even if they end up living in city slums — because overall poverty rates (urban plus rural) fall as countries urbanize. While the persistence of urban poverty is a serious concern, the authors concluded, if people moved to the cities faster, overall poverty rates would decline sooner.[20]

Many development advocates say policy makers must accept urbanization as inevitable and strive to make it more beneficial. "We need to stop seeing migration to cities as a problem," says Priya Deshingkar, a researcher at the Overseas Development Institute in Hyderabad, India. "These people were already vulnerable because they can't make a living in rural areas. Countries need to rethink their development strategies. The world is urbanizing, and we have to make more provisions for people moving to urban areas. They can't depend on agriculture alone."

Should governments limit migration to cities?

Many governments have tried to limit urban problems by discouraging migration to cities or regulating the pace of urban growth. Some countries use household registration policies, while others direct aid and economic development funds to rural areas. Political leaders say limiting migration reduces strains on city systems, slows the growth of slums and keeps villages from languishing as their most enterprising residents leave.

China's *hukou* system, for example, requires households to register with the government and classifies individuals as rural or urban residents. Children inherit their *hukou* status from their parents. Established in the 1950s, the system was tightly controlled to limit migration from agricultural areas to cities and to monitor criminals, government critics and other suspect citizens and groups.[21]

In the late 1970s China began privatizing farming and opened its economy to international trade, creating a rural labor surplus and greater demand for city workers. The government offered rural workers temporary residence permits in cities and allowed wealthy, educated citizens to buy urban *hukou* designations. Many rural Chinese also moved to cities without changing their registration. According to recent government estimates, at least 120 million migrant workers have moved to Chinese cities since the early 1980s.[22] Today *hukou* rules are enforced inconsistently in different Chinese cities, where many rural migrants cannot get access to health care, education, affordable housing or other urban services because they are there illegally.

Cities in Developing World Growing Rapidly

More than half the developing world's cities experienced fast annual growth in the 1990s, compared to just 6.3 percent of those in wealthier countries. Conversely, more than 80 percent of cities in the wealthier countries had slow or negative growth, compared to about a quarter of those in developing countries.

Urban Growth Rates, 1990s
(by percentage of cities)

	Accelerated	Rapid	Moderate	Slow	Negative
In developing countries (1,408 cities)	16.9%	35.9%	20.4%	16.7%	10.2%
In developed countries (1,287 cities)	1.0%	5.3%	11.2%	42.6%	39.9%

* Figures may not total 100 due to rounding.
Source: UN-HABITAT

Chinese officials say they must manage growth so all areas of the country will benefit. In a 2007 report to the 17th Communist Party Congress, President Hu Jintao promised to promote "a path of urbanization with Chinese characteristics" that emphasized "balanced development of large, medium-sized and small cities and towns."[23]

But critics say the *hukou* system has created an urban underclass and should be scrapped. When the municipality of Chongqing (which omits an estimated 4.5 million migrant workers from its official population figures) established November 4 as Migrant Workers' Day in 2007, the *Asia Times* commented, "By not changing the [*hukou*] system and instead giving the migrant workers a special holiday, it's a bit like showing starving people menus instead of feeding them."[24]

India and Vietnam also control migration to urban areas by requiring people to register or show local identity cards to access social services. "They're both trying to promote rural development and keep from overburdening urban areas," says Deshingkar at the Overseas Development Institute. "But it doesn't work. People move despite these regulations. It just makes it harder for them, and if they can access services it's at a price."

Many experts say governments should not try to halt rural-to-city migration because when migrant workers send large shares of their wages home to their families in the country it helps reduce rural poverty and inequality. In Dhaka, Bangladesh, for example, remittances from city workers provide up to 80 percent of rural households' budgets, according to the Coalition for the Urban Poor.[25]

Urban growth also helps rural economies by creating larger markets for agricultural products — including high-value products like meat, chicken and fish that people tend to add to their diets as their incomes rise. Cities can promote economic growth in surrounding areas by creating a demand for local farmers' products. For instance, South Africa's Johannesburg Fresh Produce Market offers vendors stalls, overnight storage space, business-skills training and financing; it also requires market agents to buy at least 10 percent of their produce from small, low-income farms.[26]

However, the rootless lifestyle adopted by so-called circular migrants — those who move back and forth between the city and the country — makes people vulnerable, Deshingkar points out. "There are roughly 100 million circular migrants in India now, and they're completely missed by official statistics because the government only counts permanent migrants," she says. "They can't get any insurance or social services, so they carry all the risk themselves."

Beyond the fact that anti-migration policies usually fail, experts say the biggest factor driving population increase in many fast-growing cities is not new residents moving in but "natural increase" — the rate at which people already living there have children. Natural increase accounts for about 60 percent of urban growth worldwide, while 20 percent comes from domestic and international migration and 20 percent results from reclassification of rural areas as urban.[27]

Family-planning programs helped reduce poverty rates in several developing Asian countries — including South Korea, Taiwan, Thailand, Singapore, Indonesia and Malaysia — where having smaller families increased household savings and reduced national education costs.[28] In contrast, artificial birth control is difficult to obtain in the Philippines, where the population is 80 percent Catholic and the government supports only "natural" family planning. Several professors at the University of the Philippines have calculated that if Filipinos had

followed Thailand's example on family planning in the 1970s, the Philippines would have at least 4 million fewer people in poverty and would be exporting rice rather than importing it. Instead, the Philippine government's opposition to family planning "contributed to the country's degeneration into Southeast Asia's basket case," said economist Arsenio Balisacan.[29]

Can we make large cities greener?

Many fast-growing cities are unhealthy places to live because of dirty air, polluted water supplies and sprawling waste dumps. City governments worldwide are increasingly interested in making their cities greener and more sustainable.

Greening cities has many up-front costs but can provide big payoffs. For example, energy-efficient buildings cost less to operate and give cities cachet as centers for advanced technology and design.

Green policies also may help cities achieve broader social goals. When Enrique Peñalosa was elected mayor of Bogotá, Colombia, in 1998, the city was overrun with traffic and crime. Wealthy residents lived in walled-off neighborhoods, while workers were squeezed into shanties on the city's outskirts. Under Peñalosa's rule, the city built hundreds of new parks and a rapid-transit bus system, limited automobile use, banned sidewalk parking and constructed a 14-mile-long street for bicyclists and pedestrians that runs through some of the city's poorest neighborhoods. The underlying goal of the programs: Make Bogotá more people-friendly for poor residents as well as the rich.

"[A]nything that you do in order to increase pedestrian space constructs equality," said Peñalosa, who now consults with city officials in other developing countries. "It's a powerful symbol showing that citizens who walk are equally important to those who have a car."[30] His administration also invested funds that might otherwise have been spent building highways in social services like schools and libraries. Air pollution decreased as more residents shifted to mass transit. Crime rates also fell, partly because more people were out on the streets.[31]

"Mobility and land use may be the most important issues that a mayor can address, because to unlock the economic potential of cities people have to be able to move from one area to another," says Polytechnic University's Bugliarello. "You also have to take care of water supplies and sanitation, because cities concentrate people and pathologies. Appropriate technologies aren't always the most expensive options, especially if cities get together and form markets for them."

For example, bus rapid transit (BRT) systems, which create networks of dedicated lanes for high-speed buses, are much cheaper than subways but faster than conventional buses that move in city traffic. By 2007 some 40 cities worldwide had developed BRT systems, including Bogotá; Jakarta, Indonesia; and Guayaquil, Ecuador. Many others are planned or under construction.[32]

Some developing countries are planning entire green cities with walkable neighborhoods, efficient mass transit and renewable-energy systems. Abu Dhabi, part of the United Arab Emirates on the Persian Gulf, is designing a $20 billion project called Masdar City, which it bills as the world's first carbon-neutral, zero-waste city. Located on the coast next to Abu Dhabi's airport, Masdar City will be a mixed-use community with about 40,000 residents and 50,000 commuters traveling in to work at high-tech companies. Plans call for the city to be car-free and powered mainly by solar energy.[33]

Abu Dhabi wants to become a global hub for clean technologies, according to Khaled Awad, property development director for the Masdar initiative. "It lets us leverage our energy knowledge [from oil and gas production] and our research and development skills and adapt them to new energy markets," he said.

"If we can do it there, we can do it anywhere," said Matthias Schuler, an engineer with the German climate-engineering firm Transsolar and a member of the international Masdar City design and planning team.[34] He points out that average daytime summer temperatures in Abu Dhabi are well over 100 degrees Fahrenheit, and coastal zones are very humid. "You can't find a harsher climate."

In China, meanwhile, green urban design is gaining support as a way to attract foreign investment and demonstrate environmental awareness. But some showpiece projects are falling short of expectations.

Huangbaiyu was supposed to be a sustainable "green village" that would provide new homes for a farming town of more than 1,400 in rural northeast China. But the master plan, produced by a high-profile U.S. green architecture firm, called for 400 densely clustered bungalows without enough yard space for livestock. This meant that villagers would lose their existing income from

backyard gardens, sheep flocks and trout ponds. The plan also proposed to use corncobs and stalks to fuel a biogas plant for heat, but villagers needed these crop wastes as winter feed for their goats.

By December 2008 the Chinese builder had constructed 42 houses, but only a few were occupied. The designer blamed the builder for putting up low-quality houses, but others said the plan did not reflect what villagers wanted or needed.[35] Planners "inadvertently designed an ecologically sound plan — from the perspectives of both birds and the green movement — that would devastate the local economy and bankrupt the households whose lives were to be improved," wrote Shannon May, an American graduate student who lived in the old village of Huangbaiyu for two years and wrote her dissertation on the project.[36]

Dongtan, a larger Chinese city designed as a green project with zero-carbon-emission buildings and transit systems, has also been sidetracked. Groundbreaking on the model city of 500,000 on a Manhattan-sized island near Shanghai is more than a year behind schedule. High-rise towers are sprouting up around the site, leading some observers to call the project expensive "greenwashing" — attempting to make lavish development acceptable by tacking on environmentally friendly features.

"'Zero-emission' city is pure commercial hype," said Dai Xingyi, a professor at Fudan University in Shanghai. "You can't expect some technology to both offer you a luxurious and comfortable life and save energy at the same time. That's just a dream."[37]

Construction is also under way on a new green city southeast of Beijing for 350,000 residents, co-developed by China and Singapore. Tianjin's features include renewable-energy sources, efficient water use and green building standards. Premier Wen Jiabao attended the 2008 groundbreaking.[38]

Although China's green development projects have a mixed record so far, "The government is starting to recognize that it has responsibility for environmental impacts beyond its borders, mainly by promoting renewable energy," says Alastair MacGregor, associate vice president of AECOM, an international design firm with large building projects in China. "Chinese culture is playing catch-up on sustainability."

More than 130 buildings designed to LEED (Leadership in Energy and Environmental Design)

China Aggressively Tackles Air Pollution

"No country in developing Asia takes those challenges more seriously."

China's large cities have some of the world's worst air pollution, thanks to rapid industrial growth, heavy use of coal and growing demand for cars.

The capital, Beijing, lost its 1993 bid to host the 2000 Summer Olympic Games partly because the city was so polluted. A chronic grey haze not only sullied Beijing's international image but also threatened to cause health problems for athletes and impair their performances.

When Beijing was chosen in 2001 to host the 2008 Summer Games, it pledged to put on a "green Olympics," which was widely understood to include clearing the air.

Between 2001 and 2007, however, China's economy grew beyond all predictions, with its gross domestic product expanding by up to 13 percent a year.[1] Beijing's air pollution worsened as new factories, power plants and cars crowded into the city. Winds carried in more pollutants from other burgeoning cities, including nitrogen oxides and sulfur dioxide — which contribute to acid rain and smog — and fine particulates, which can cause or worsen heart and lung problems.

With the Olympic deadline looming, many observers predicted Beijing would not meet its targets even if it relied heavily on authoritarian measures like shutting down factories and limiting auto use.[2] International Olympic Committee President Jacques Rogge said some outdoor endurance sports might have to be postponed if they occurred on high-pollution days — an embarrassing prospect for Chinese leaders.[3]

But China met its promised target, keeping Beijing's daily air pollution index — based on combined measurements of sulfur dioxide, nitrogen dioxide and fine particulates — below 100 during the month the Olympics took place. A 100 index score means air quality will not affect daily activities, compared to a maximum score of 500, when officials warn residents to stay indoors. In fact, during the Olympics in August 2008 Beijing's daily air pollution reached the lowest August measurements since 2000, sometimes even dropping into the 20s.[4]

"No country in Asia has bigger air quality challenges than China, but no country in developing Asia takes those challenges more seriously," says Cornie Huizenga, executive director of the Clean Air Initiative for Asian Cities (CAI-Asia), an international network based in the Philippines and founded by the Asian Development Bank, the World Bank and the U.S. Agency for International Development. "China has taken a whole series of long-term structural measures to address air pollution. The Olympics put a

standards — which measure energy efficiency and healthy indoor working conditions — are planned or under construction in Beijing, Shanghai, Chongqing, Wuhan and other Chinese cities.[39] Chinese investors see LEED buildings as premium products, not as an everyday model, said MacGregor.

Some Chinese cities are developing their own green standards. About half of worldwide new construction between 2008 through 2015 is projected to occur in China, so even greening a modest share of that development would be significant.

"China could end up being a sustainability leader just by virtue of its size," MacGregor predicted.[40]

BACKGROUND

From Farm to Factory

At the beginning of the 19th century only 3 percent of the world's population lived in cities, and only Beijing had more than a million inhabitants.[41] Then new technologies like the steam engine and railroads began to transform society. As the Industrial Revolution unfolded, people streamed from rural areas to manufacturing centers in Europe and the United States seeking a better income and life. This first great wave of urbanization established cities like London, Paris and New York as centers of global commerce.

magnifying glass on Beijing and made them focus there, but its programs are much bigger."

For instance, China continuously monitors air quality in more than 100 cities, requires high-polluting provinces and companies to close small, inefficient emission sources and install pollution-control equipment and has new-car emissions standards roughly equivalent to U.S. and Western European laws.

"For the Olympics China took temporary measures on top of those policies, like closing down large facilities and keeping cars off the roads. All of this plus good weather let Beijing deliver what it promised for the Games," says Huizenga.

Now China is further expanding air pollution regulations. During the Olympics, the Ministry of Environment announced that in 2009 it would start monitoring ultrafine particle and ozone pollution — persistent problems in many developed countries. And Beijing officials plan to increase spending on public transportation.

Local pollution sources, weather patterns and geography influence air pollution, so China's policies for cleaning up Beijing's air might not work in other large cities. Mexico City, for instance, also has tried to reduce its severe air pollution but is hampered by the city's high altitude (7,200 feet). Car engines burn fuel inefficiently at high altitudes, so they pollute more than at sea level. And while automobiles are the biggest emission sources, scientists also found that leaking liquefied petroleum gas (LPG) — which most Mexican households burn for cooking and heating — also contributes to Mexico City's air pollution.[5]

"We need better-harmonized air quality monitoring in developing countries before we can compare them," says Huizenga. "But other cities should be able to make progress on a large scale like Beijing. There's a lot of low-hanging fruit, such as switching to cleaner transportation fuels, getting rid of vehicles with [high-polluting] two-stroke engines, managing dust at construction sites and cutting pollution from coal-fired power plants. But to make them work, you also need effective agencies with enough people and money to carry [out] policies."

[1] Michael Yang, "China's GDP (2003-2007)," forum.china.org.cn, Nov. 10, 2008; "China Revises 2007 GDP Growth Rate to 13%," Jan. 15, 2009, http://english.dbw.cn.

[2] Edward Russell, "Beijing's 'Green Olympics' Test Run Fizzles," *Asia Times*, Aug. 10, 2007; Jim Yardley, "Beijing's Olympic Quest: Turn Smoggy Sky Blue," *The New York Times*, Dec. 29, 2007; David G. Streets, *et al.*, "Air Quality during the 2008 Beijing Olympic Games," *Atmospheric Environment*, vol. 41 (2007).

[3] "IOC President: Beijing Air Pollution Could Cause Events to Be Delayed During 2008 Olympics," The Associated Press, Aug. 7, 2007.

[4] "Summary: AQ in Beijing During the 2008 Summer Olympics," Clean Air Initiative for Asian Cities, www.cleanairnet.org/caiasia/1412/article-72991.html. Weather conditions are important factors in air pollution levels — for example, summer heat and humidity promote the formation of ground-level ozone, a major ingredient of smog — so to put conditions during the Olympics in context, scientists compared them to readings taken in August of previous years.

[5] Tim Weiner, "Terrific News in Mexico City: Air Is Sometimes Breathable," *The New York Times*, Jan. 5, 2001.

It also spawned horrific slums in factory towns and large cities. Tenement houses became a feature of working-class neighborhoods, with little access to fresh air or clean drinking water. Often whole neighborhoods shared a single water pump or toilet, and trash was usually thrown into the streets.[42]

German social scientist and a co-founder of communist theory Friedrich Engels graphically described urban workers' living conditions in cities like London and Manchester in 1844: "[T]hey are penned in dozens into single rooms. . . . They are given damp dwellings, cellar dens that are not waterproof from below or garrets that leak from above. . . . They are supplied bad, tattered or rotten clothing, adulterated or indigestible food. . . . Thus are the workers cast out and ignored by the class in power, morally as well as physically and mentally."[43]

Engels and his collaborator Karl Marx later predicted in *The Communist Manifesto* that oppression of the working class would lead to revolution in industrialized countries. Instead, public health movements began to develop in Europe and the United States in mid-century. Seeking to curb repeated cholera and typhoid epidemics, cities began collecting garbage and improving water-supply systems. A new medical specialty, epidemiology (the study of how infections are spread) developed as scientists worked to track and contain illnesses. Cities built

C H R O N O L O G Y

1700s-1800s *Industrial Revolution spurs rapid urban growth in Europe and the U.S. Expanding slums trigger reforms and public health laws.*

1804 World population reaches 1 billion.

1854 British doctor John Snow discovers the connection between contaminated drinking water and a cholera outbreak in London.

1897 Brazil's first *favela* (shanty town), is established outside Rio de Janeiro.

1900-1960s *Europe and the United States are the most urbanized. Africa and Asia begin gaining independence and struggle to develop healthy economies.*

1906 An earthquake and subsequent fire destroy much of San Francisco, killing more than 3,000 people.

1927 World population reaches 2 billion.

1949 Chinese communists defeat nationalists, establishing the People's Republic of China, which aggressively promotes industrial development.

1960 World population hits 3 billion.

1964 Tokyo becomes first Asian city to host the Olympic Games and soon after that displaces New York as the world's largest city.

1970s-1990s *Urbanization accelerates in Asia and Africa. Many U.S. and European cities shrink as residents move to suburbs.*

1971 East Pakistan secedes from West Pakistan and becomes the independent nation of Bangladesh; populations in Dhaka and other cities grow rapidly.

1974 World population reaches 4 billion.

1979 China initiates broad economic reforms, opens diplomatic and trade relations with the United States and starts to ease limits on migration to cities.

1985 An earthquake in Mexico City kills some 10,000 people and damages water-supply and transit systems.

1987 World population reaches 5 billion.

1991 India institutes sweeping market reforms to attract foreign investors and spur rapid economic growth.

1999 World population reaches 6 billion.

2000s *Most industrialized countries stabilize at 70-80 percent urban. Cities continue to grow in Asia and Africa.*

2000 International community endorses the U.N. Millennium Development Goals designed to end poverty by 2015, including improving the lives of slum dwellers.

2001 Many international companies shift production to China after it joins the World Trade Organization; migration from rural areas accelerates. . . . Terrorists destroy World Trade Center towers in New York City, killing thousands. . . . Taiwan completes Taipei 101, the world's tallest skyscraper (1,671 feet), superseding the Petronas Towers in Kuala Lumpur, Malaysia (1,483 feet).

2005 United Nations condemns Zimbabwe for slum-clearance operations that leave 700,000 people homeless.

2007 The nonprofit group One Laptop Per Child unveils a prototype $100 laptop computer designed for children in developing countries to help close the "digital divide" between cities and rural areas.

2008 More than half of the world's population lives in cities. . . . Beijing hosts Summer Olympic Games. . . . Coordinated terrorist attacks in Mumbai kill nearly 170 people and injure more than 300.

2009 A global recession leaves millions of urban workers jobless, forcing many to return to their home villages.

2030 World's urban population is expected to reach 5 billion, and its slum population could top 2 billion.

2070 About 150 million city dwellers — primarily in India, Bangladesh, China, Vietnam, Thailand, Myanmar and Florida — could be in danger due to climate change, according to a 2008 study.

green spaces like New York's Central Park to provide fresh air and access to nature. To help residents navigate around town, electric streetcars and subway trains were built in underground tunnels or on elevated tracks above the streets.

Many problems persisted, however. Homes and factories burned coal for heat and power, blanketing many large cities in smoky haze. Horse-drawn vehicles remained in wide use until the early-20th century, so urban streets were choked with animal waste. Wealthy city dwellers, seeking havens from the noise, dirt and crowding of inner cities, moved out to cleaner suburban neighborhoods.

Despite harsh conditions, people continued to pour into cities. Economic growth in industrialized countries had ripple effects in developing countries. As wealthier countries imported more and more raw materials, commercial "gateway cities" in developing countries grew as well, including Buenos Aires, Rio de Janeiro and Calcutta (now Kolkata). By 1900, nearly 14 percent of the world's population lived in cities.[44]

End of Empires

Worldwide migration from country to city accelerated in the early-20th century as automation spread and fewer people were needed to grow food. But growth was not uniform. Wars devastated some of Europe's major cities while industrial production swelled others. And when colonial empires dissolved after World War II, many people were displaced in newly independent nations.

Much of the fighting during World War I occurred in fields and trenches, so few of Europe's great cities were seriously damaged. By the late 1930s, however, long-range bombers could attack cities hundreds of miles away. Madrid and Barcelona were bombed during the Spanish Civil War, a prelude to intensive air attacks on London, Vienna, Berlin, Tokyo and elsewhere during World War II. In 1945 the United States dropped atomic bombs on the Japanese cities of Hiroshima and Nagasaki, destroying each. For centuries cities had walled themselves off against outside threats, but now they were vulnerable to air attacks from thousands of miles away.

After 1945, even victorious nations like Britain and France were greatly weakened and unable to manage overseas colonies, where independence movements were underway. As European countries withdrew from their holdings in the Middle East, Asia and Africa over the next 25 years, a wave of countries gained independence, including Indonesia, India, Pakistan, the Philippines, Syria, Vietnam and most of colonial Africa. Wealthy countries began providing aid to the new developing countries, especially in Asia and Latin America. But some nations, especially in Africa, received little focused support.

By mid-century most industrialized countries were heavily urbanized, and their populations were no longer growing rapidly. By 1950 three of the world's largest cities — Shanghai, Buenos Aires and Calcutta — were in developing countries. Populations in developing countries continued to rise through the late 1960s even as those nations struggled to industrialize. Many rural residents moved to cities, seeking work and educational opportunities.

In the 1950s and '60s U.S. urban planners heatedly debated competing approaches to city planning. The top-down, centralized philosophy was espoused by Robert Moses, the hard-charging parks commissioner and head of New York City's highway agency from 1934 to 1968. Moses pushed through numerous bridge, highway, park and slum-clearance projects that remade New York but earned him an image as arrogant and uncaring.[45] His most famous critic, writer and activist Jane Jacobs, advocated preserving dense, mixed-use neighborhoods, like New York's Greenwich Village, and consulting with residents to build support for development plans.[46] Similar controversies would arise later in developing countries.

By the 1960s car-centered growth characterized many of the world's large cities. "Circle over London, Buenos Aires, Chicago, Sydney, in an airplane," wrote American historian Lewis Mumford in 1961. "The original container has completely disappeared: the sharp division between city and country no longer exists." City officials, Mumford argued, only measured improvements in quantities, such as wider streets and bigger parking lots.

"[T]hey would multiply bridges, highways [and] tunnels, making it ever easier to get in and out of the city but constricting the amount of space available within the city for any other purpose than transportation itself," Mumford charged.[47]

Population Boom

In the 1970s and '80s, as populations in developing countries continued to grow and improved agricultural methods made farmers more productive, people moved to the cities in ever-increasing numbers. Some

Cities Need to Plan for Disasters and Attacks

Concentrated populations and wealth magnify impact.

Flash floods in 1999 caused landslides in the hills around Caracas, Venezuela, that washed away hundreds of hillside shanties and killed an estimated 30,000 people — more than 10 times the number of victims of the Sept. 11, 2001, terrorist attacks in the United States.

Because cities concentrate populations and wealth, natural disasters in urban areas can kill or displace thousands of people and cause massive damage to property and infrastructure. Many cities are located on earthquake faults, flood plains, fire-prone areas and other locations that make them vulnerable. The impacts are magnified when high-density slums and squatter neighborhoods are built in marginal areas. Political instability or terrorism can also cause widespread destruction.

Protecting cities requires both "hard" investments, such as flood-control systems or earthquake-resistant buildings, and "soft" approaches, such as emergency warning systems and special training for police and emergency-response forces. Cities also can improve their forecasting capacity and train officials to assess different types of risk.[1] Although preventive strategies are expensive, time-consuming and often politically controversial, failing to prepare for outside threats can be far more costly and dangerous.

Global climate change is exacerbating flooding and heat waves, which are special concerns for cities because they absorb more heat than surrounding rural areas and have higher average temperatures — a phenomenon known as the urban heat island effect. According to a study by the Organization for Economic Cooperation and Development (OECD), about 40 million people living in coastal areas around the world in 2005 were exposed to so-called 100-year floods — or major floods likely to occur only once every 100 years. By the 2070s, the OECD said, the population at risk from such flooding could rise to 150 million as more people move to cities, and climate change causes more frequent and ferocious storms and rising sea levels.

Cities with the greatest population exposure in the 2070 forecast include Kolkata and Mumbai in India, Dhaka (Bangladesh), Guangzhou and Shanghai in China, Ho Chi Minh City and Hai Phong in Vietnam, Bangkok (Thailand), Rangoon (Myanmar) and Miami, Florida. Cities in developed countries tend to be better protected, but there are exceptions. For example, London has about the same amount of flooding protection as Shanghai, according to the OECD.[2]

"All cities need to look at their critical infrastructure systems and try to understand where they're exposed to natural hazards," says Jim Hall, leader of urban research at England's Tyndall Centre for Climate Change Research. For example, he says, London's Underground subway system is vulnerable to flooding and overheating. Fast-growing cities planning for climate change, he adds, might want to control growth in flood-prone areas, improve water systems to ensure supply during droughts or build new parks to help cool urban neighborhoods. "Risks now and in the future depend on what we do to protect cities," says Hall.

In some cities, residents can literally see the ocean rising. Coastal erosion has destroyed 47 homes and more than 400 fields in recent years in Cotonou, the capital city of the West African nation of Benin, according to a local non-profit called Front United Against Coastal Erosion. "The sea was far from us two years ago. But now, here it is. We are scared," said Kofi Ayao, a local fisherman. "If we do not find a solution soon, we may simply drown in our sleep one day."[3]

national economies boomed, notably the so-called Asian tigers — Hong Kong, Singapore, Taiwan and South Korea — by focusing on manufacturing exports for industrialized markets and improving their education systems to create productive work forces. Indonesia, Malaysia, the Philippines and Thailand — the "tiger cubs" — went through a similar growth phase in the late 1980s and early '90s.

After China and India opened up their economies in the 1980s and '90s, both countries became magnets for foreign investment and created free-trade areas and special economic zones to attract business activity. Cities in those areas expanded, particularly along China's southeast coast where such zones were clustered.

As incomes rose, many Asian cities aspired to global roles: Seoul hosted the 1988 Summer Olympics, and

Social violence can arise from within a city or come as an attack from outside. For example, in 2007 up to 600 people were killed when urban riots erupted in Kenya after a disputed national election.[4]

Urban leaders often justify slum-clearance programs by claiming that poor neighborhoods are breeding grounds for unrest. Others say slums are fertile recruiting grounds for terrorist groups. Slums certainly contain many who feel ill-treated, and extreme

A Bangladeshi boy helps slum residents cross floodwaters in Dhaka. Rising waters caused by global warming pose a significant potential threat to Dhaka and other low-lying cities worldwide.

conditions may spur them into action. Overall, however, experts say most slum dwellers are too busy trying to eke out a living to riot or join terrorist campaigns.

"Poverty alone isn't a sufficient cause [for unrest]," says John Parachini, director of the Intelligence Policy Center at the RAND Corp., a U.S. think tank. "You need a combination of things — people with a profound sense of grievance, impoverishment and leaders who offer the prospect of change. Often the presence of an enemy nearby, such as an occupying foreign power or a rival tribal group or religious sect, helps galvanize people."

Last November's terrorist attacks in Mumbai, in which 10 gunmen took dozens of Indian and foreign hostages and killed at least 164 people, showed an ironic downside of globalization: Wealth, clout and international ties can make cities terrorist targets.

"Mumbai is India's commercial and entertainment center — India's Wall Street, its Hollywood, its Milan. It is a prosperous symbol of modern India," a RAND analysis noted. Mumbai also was accessible from the sea, offered prominent landmark targets (historic hotels frequented by

foreigners and local elites) and had a heavy media presence that guaranteed international coverage.[5]

But serendipity can also make one city a target over another, says Parachini. "Attackers may know one city better or have family links or contacts there. Those local ties matter for small groups planning a one-time attack," he says.

Developing strong core services, such as police forces and public health systems, can be the first step in strengthening most cities against terrorism, he says, rather than creating specialized units to handle terrorist strikes.

"Basic governance functions like policing maintain order, build confidence in government and can pick up a lot of information about what's going on in neighborhoods," he says. "They make it harder to do bad things."

[1] George Bugliarello, "The Engineering Challenges of Urban Sustainability," *Journal of Urban Technology*, vol. 15, no. 1 (2008), pp. 64-65.

[2] R. J. Nicholls, *et al.*, "Ranking Port Cities with High Exposure and Vulnerability to Climate Extremes: Exposure Estimates," *Environment Working Papers No. 1*, Organization for Economic Cooperation and Development, Nov. 19, 2008, pp. 7-8, www.olis.oecd.org/olis/2007doc .nsf/LinkTo/NT000058 8E/$FILE/JT03255617.PDF.

[3] "Rising Tides Threaten to Engulf Parts of Cotonou," U.N. Integrated Regional Information Network, Sept. 2, 2008.

[4] "Chronology: Kenya in Crisis After Elections," Reuters, Dec. 31, 2007; "The Ten Deadliest World Catastrophes 2007," Insurance Information Institute, www.iii.org.

[5] Angel Rabasa, *et al.*, "The Lessons of Mumbai," *RAND Occasional Paper*, January 2009.

Malaysia built the world's tallest skyscrapers — the Petronas Twin Towers, completed in 1998, only to be superseded by the Taipei 101 building in Taiwan a few years later.

Some Asian countries — including Malaysia, Sri Lanka and Indonesia — implemented programs to improve living standards for the urban poor and helped reduce poverty. However, poverty remained high in Thailand and the Philippines and increased in China and Vietnam.[48]

Cities in South America and Africa also expanded rapidly between 1970 and 2000, although South America was farther ahead. By 1965 Latin America was already 50 percent urbanized and had three cities with populations over 5 million (Buenos Aires, São Paulo and Rio de Janeiro) — a marker sub-Saharan Africa would not achieve for several decades.[49] Urban growth on both continents followed the "primacy" pattern, in which one city

Security officers forcibly remove a woman from her home during land confiscations in Changchun, a city of 7.5 million residents in northeast China, so buildings can be demolished to make way for new construction. Some rapidly urbanizing governments use heavy-handed methods — such as land confiscation, eviction or slum clearance — so redevelopment projects can proceed.

is far more populous and economically and politically powerful than all the others in the nation. The presence of so-called primate cities like Lima (Peru), Caracas (Venezuela) or Lagos (Nigeria) can distort development if the dominant city consumes most public investments and grows to a size that is difficult to govern.

Latin America's growth gradually leveled out in the 1980s: Population increases slowed in major urban centers, and more people moved to small and medium-sized cities.[50] On average the region's economy grew more slowly and unevenly than Asia's, often in boom-and-bust cycles.[51] Benefits accrued mostly to small ruling classes who were hostile to new migrants, and income inequality became deeply entrenched in many Latin American cities.

Africa urbanized quickly after independence in the 1950s and '60s. But from the mid-1970s forward most countries' incomes stagnated or contracted. Such "urbanization without growth" in sub-Saharan Africa created the world's highest rates of urban poverty and income inequality. Corruption and poor management reinforced wealth gaps that dated back to colonial times. Natural disasters, wars and the spread of HIV/AIDS further undercut poverty-reduction efforts in both rural and urban areas.[52]

New Solutions

As the 21st century began, calls for new antipoverty efforts led to an international conference at which 189 nations endorsed the Millennium Development Goals,

designed to end poverty by 2015. Experts also focused on bottom-up strategies that gave poor people resources to help themselves.

An influential proponent of the bottom-up approach, Peruvian economist Hernando de Soto, stirred debate in 2000 with his book *The Mystery of Capital: Why Capitalism Triumphs in the West and Fails Everywhere Else.* Capitalist economies did not fail in developing nations because those countries lacked skills or enterprising spirit, de Soto argued. Rather, the poor in those countries had plenty of assets but no legal rights, so they could not prove ownership or use their assets as capital.

"They have houses but not titles; crops but not deeds; businesses but not statutes of incorporation," de Soto wrote. "It is the unavailability of these essential representations that explains why people who have adapted every other Western invention, from the paper clip to the nuclear reactor, have not been able to produce sufficient capital to make their domestic capitalism work." But, he asserted, urbanization in the developing world had spawned "a huge industrial-commercial revolution" which clearly showed that poor people could contribute to economic development if their countries developed fair and inclusive legal systems.[53]

Not all experts agreed with de Soto, but his argument coincided with growing interest in approaches like microfinance (small-scale loans and credit programs for traditionally neglected customers) that helped poor people build businesses and transition from the "extra-legal" economy into the formal economy. Early microcredit programs in the 1980s and '90s had targeted mainly the rural poor, but donors began expanding into cities around 2000.[54]

The "digital divide" — the gap between rich and poor people's access to information and communications technologies (ICTs) — also began to attract the attention of development experts. During his second term (1997-2001), U.S. President Bill Clinton highlighted the issue as an obstacle to reducing poverty both domestically and at the global level. "To maximize potential, we must turn the digital divide among and within our nations into digital opportunities," Clinton said at the Asia Pacific Economic Cooperation Forum in 2000, urging Asian nations to expand Internet access and train citizens to use computers.[55] The Millennium Development Goals called for making ICTs more widely available in poor countries.

Some ICTs, such as mobile phones, were rapidly adopted in developing countries, which had small or unreliable landline networks. By 2008, industry observers predicted, more than half of the world's population would own a mobile phone, with Africa and the Middle East leading the way.[56]

Internet penetration moved much more slowly. In 2006 some 58 percent of the population in industrial countries used the Internet, compared to 11 percent in developing countries and only 1 percent in the least developed countries. Access to high-speed Internet service was unavailable in many developing regions or was too expensive for most users.[57] Some antipoverty advocates questioned whether ICTs should be a high priority for poor countries, but others said the issue was not whether but when and how to get more of the world's poor wired.

"The more the better, especially broadband," says Polytechnic University's Bugliarello.

While development experts worked to empower the urban poor, building lives in fast-growing cities remained difficult and dangerous in many places. Some governments still pushed approaches like slum clearance, especially when it served other purposes.

Notoriously, in 2005 President Robert Mugabe of Zimbabwe launched a slum-clearance initiative called Operation Murambatsvina, a Shona phrase translated by some as "restore order" and others as "drive out the trash." Thousands of shacks in Zimbabwe's capital, Harare, and other cities across the nation were destroyed, allegedly to crack down on illegal settlements and businesses.

"The current chaotic state of affairs, where small-to-medium enterprises operated outside of the regulatory framework and in undesignated and crime-ridden areas, could not be countenanced much longer," said Mugabe.[58]

But critics said Mugabe was using slum clearance as an excuse to intimidate and displace neighborhoods that supported his opponents. In the end, some 700,000 people were left homeless or jobless by the action, which the United Nations later said violated international law.[59] Over the next several years Mugabe's government failed to carry out its pledges to build new houses for the displaced families.[60]

CURRENT SITUATION

Economic Shadow

The current global economic recession is casting a dark cloud over worldwide economic development prospects. Capital flows to developing countries have declined

Slum Redevelopment Plan Stirs Controversy

Conditions for the 60,000 families living in Mumbai's Dharavi neighborhood (top) — one of Asia's largest slums — are typical for a billion slum dwellers around the globe. Slums often lack paved roads, water-distribution systems, sanitation and garbage collection — spawning cholera, diarrhea and other illnesses. Electric power and telephone service are usually poached from available lines. Mumbai's plans to redevelop Dharavi, located on 600 prime acres in the heart of the city, triggered strong protests from residents, who demanded that their needs be considered before the redevelopment proceeds (bottom). The project has stalled recently due to the global economic crisis.

sharply, and falling export demand is triggering layoffs and factory shutdowns in countries that produce for Western markets. But experts say even though the overall picture is sobering, many factors will determine how severely the recession affects cities.

In March the World Bank projected that developing countries would face budget shortfalls of $270 billion to $700 billion in 2009 and the world economy would

Reflecting China's stunningly rapid urbanization, Shanghai's dramatic skyline rises beside the Huangpu River. Shanghai is the world's seventh-largest city today but will drop to ninth-place by 2025, as two south Asian megacities, Dhaka and Kolkata, surpass Shanghai in population.

shrink for the first time since World War II. According to the bank, 94 out of 116 developing countries were already experiencing an economic slowdown, and about half of them already had high poverty levels. Urban-based exporters and manufacturers were among the sectors hit hardest by the recession.[61]

These trends, along with an international shortage of investment capital, will make many developing countries increasingly dependent on foreign aid at a time when donor countries are experiencing their own budget crises. As workers shift out of export-oriented sectors in the cities and return to rural areas, poverty may increase, the bank projected.

The recession could mean failure to meet the Millennium Development Goals, especially if donor countries pull back on development aid. The bank urged nations to increase their foreign aid commitments and recommended that national governments:

- Increase government spending where possible to stimulate economies;
- Protect core programs to create social safety nets for the poor;
- Invest in infrastructure such as roads, sewage systems and slum upgrades; and
- Help small- and medium-size businesses get financing to create opportunities for growth and employment.[62]

President Barack Obama's economic stimulus package, signed into law on Feb. 17, takes some of these steps and contains at least $51 billion for programs to help U.S. cities. (Other funds are allocated by states and may provide more aid to cities depending on each state's priority list.) Stimulus programs that benefit cities include $2.8 billion for energy conservation and energy efficiency, $8.4 billion for public transportation investments, $8 billion for high-speed rail and intercity passenger rail service, $1.5 billion for emergency shelter grants, $4 billion for job training and $8.8 billion for modernizing schools.[63]

Governments in developing countries with enough capital may follow suit. At the World Economic Forum in Davos, Switzerland, in January, Chinese Premier Wen Jibao announced a 4 trillion yuan stimulus package (equivalent to about 16 percent of China's GDP over two years), including money for housing, railways and infrastructure and environmental protection. " 'The harsh winter will be gone, and spring is around the corner,' " he said, predicting that China's economy would rebound this year.[64]

But according to government figures released just a few days later, more than 20 million rural migrant workers had already lost their jobs in coastal manufacturing areas and moved back to their home towns.[65] In March the World Bank cut its forecast for China's 2009 economic growth from 7.5 percent to 6.5 percent, although it said China was still doing well compared to many other countries.[66]

In India "circular migration" is becoming more prevalent, according to the Overseas Development Institute's Deshingkar. "Employment is becoming more temporary — employers like to hire temporary workers whom they can hire and fire at will, so the proportion of temporary workers and circular migrants is going up," she says. "In some Indian villages 95 percent of migrants are circular. Permanent migration is too expensive and risky — rents are high, [people are] harassed by the police, slums are razed and they're evicted. Keeping one foot in the village is their social insurance."

Meanwhile, international development aid is likely to decline as donor countries cut spending and focus on their own domestic needs. "By rights the financial crisis shouldn't undercut development funding, because the total amounts given now are tiny compared to the national economic bailouts that are under way or being debated in developed countries," says Harvard economist

Bloom. "Politically, however, it may be hard to maintain aid budgets."

At the World Economic Forum billionaire philanthropist Bill Gates urged world leaders and organizations to keep up their commitments to foreign aid despite the global financial crisis. "If we lose sight of our long-term priority to expand opportunity for the world's poor and abandon our commitments and partnerships to reduce inequality, we run the risk of emerging from the current economic downturn in a world with even greater disparities in health and education and fewer opportunities for people to improve their lives," said Gates, whose Bill and Melinda Gates Foundation supports efforts to address both rural and urban poverty in developing nations.[67]

In fact, at a summit meeting in London in early April, leaders of the world's 20 largest economies pledged $1.1 trillion in new aid to help developing countries weather the global recession. Most of the money will be channeled through the International Monetary Fund.

"This is the day the world came together to fight against the global recession," said British Prime Minister Gordon Brown.[68]

Slum Solutions

As slums expand in many cities, debate continues over the best way to alleviate poverty. Large-scale slum-clearance operations have long been controversial in both developed and developing countries: Officials typically call the slums eyesores and public health hazards, but often new homes turn out to be unaffordable for the displaced residents. Today development institutions like the World Bank speak of "urban upgrading" — improving services in slums instead of bulldozing them.[69]

This approach focuses on improving basic infrastructure systems like water distribution, sanitation and electric power; cleaning up environmental hazards and building schools and clinics. The strategy is cheaper than massive demolition and construction projects and provides incentives for residents to invest in improving their own homes, advocates say.[70]

To do so, however, slum dwellers need money. Many do not have the basic prerequisites even to open bank accounts, such as fixed addresses and minimum balances, let alone access to credit. Over the past 10 to 15 years, however, banks have come to recognize slum dwellers as potential customers and have begun creating microcredit

Two-thirds of sub-Saharan Africa's city dwellers live in slums, like this one in Lagos, Nigeria, which has open sewers and no clean water, electric power or garbage collection. About 95 percent of today's rapid urbanization is occurring in the developing world, primarily in sub-Saharan Africa and Asia.

programs to help them obtain small loans and credit cards that often start with very low limits. A related concept, micro-insurance, offers low-cost protection in case of illness, accidents and property damage.

Now advocates for the urban poor are working to give slum dwellers more financial power. The advocacy group, Shack/Slum Dwellers International (SDI), for example, has created Urban Poor Funds that help attract direct investments from banks, government agencies and international donor groups.[71] In 2007 SDI received a $10 million grant from the Gates foundation to create a Global Finance Facility for Federations of the Urban Poor.

The funds will give SDI leverage in negotiating with governments for land, housing and infrastructure, according to Joel Bolnick, an SDI director in Cape Town, South Africa. If a government agency resists, said Bolnick, SDI can reply, " 'If you can't help us here, we'll take the money and put it on the table for a deal in Zambia instead.' "[72]

And UN-HABITAT is working with lenders to promote more mortgage lending to low-income borrowers in developing countries. "Slum dwellers have access to resources and are resources in themselves. To maximize the value of slums for those who live in them and for a city, slums must be upgraded and improved," UN-HABITAT Executive Director Tibaijuka said in mid-2008.[73]

Will redevelopment of the Dharavi slum improve residents' lives?

YES
Mukesh Mehta
Chairman, MM Project Consultants

Written for *CQ Researcher,* April 2009

Slum rehabilitation is a challenge that has moved beyond the realm of charity or meager governmental budgets. It requires a pragmatic and robust financial model and a holistic approach to achieve sustainability.

Dharavi — the largest slum pocket in Mumbai, India, and one of the largest in the world — houses 57,000 families, businesses and industries on 600 acres. Alarmingly, this accounts for only 4 percent of Mumbai's slums, which house about 7.5 million people, or 55 percent of the city's population.

Mumbai's Slum Rehabilitation Authority (SRA) has undertaken the rehabilitation of all the eligible residents and commercial and industrial enterprises in a sustainable manner through the Dharavi Redevelopment Project (DRP), following an extensive consultative process that included Dharavi's slum dwellers. The quality of life for those residents is expected to dramatically improve, and they could integrate into mainstream Mumbai over a period of time. Each family would receive a 300-square-foot home plus adequate workspace, along with excellent infrastructure, such as water supply and roads. A public-private partnership between the real estate developers and the SRA also would provide amenities for improving health, income, knowledge, the environment and socio-cultural activities. The land encroached by the slum dwellers would be used as equity in the partnership.

The primary focus — besides housing and infrastructure — would be on income generation. Dharavi has a vibrant economy of $600 million per annum, despite an appalling working environment. But the redevelopment project would boost the local gross domestic product to more than $3 billion, with the average family income estimated to increase to at least $3,000 per year from the current average of $1,200. To achieve this, a hierarchy of workspaces will be provided, including community spaces equivalent to 6 percent of the built-up area, plus individual workspaces in specialized commercial and industrial complexes for leather goods, earthenware, food products, recycling and other enterprises.

The greatest failure in slum redevelopment has been to treat it purely as a housing problem. Improving the infrastructure to enable the local economy to grow is absolutely essential for sustainable development. We believe this project will treat Dharavi residents as vital human resources and allow them to act as engines for economic growth. Thus, the DRP will act as a torchbearer for the slums of Mumbai as well as the rest of the developing world.

NO
Kalpana Sharma
Author, Rediscovering Dharavi:
Stories from Asia's Largest Slum

Written for *CQ Researcher,* April 2009

The controversy over the redevelopment of Dharavi, a slum in India's largest city of Mumbai, centers on the future of the estimated 60,000 families who live and work there.

Dharavi is a slum because its residents do not own the land on which they live. But it is much more than that. The settlement — more than 100 years old — grew up around one of the six fishing villages that coalesced over time to become Bombay, as Mumbai originally was called. People from all parts of India live and work here making terra-cotta pots, leather goods, garments, food items and jewelry and recycling everything from plastic to metal. The annual turnover from this vast spread of informal enterprises, much of it conducted inside people's tiny houses, is an estimated $700 million a year.

The Dharavi Redevelopment Plan — conceived by consultant Mukesh Mehta and being implemented by the Government of Maharashtra state — envisages leveling this energetic and productive part of Mumbai and converting it into a collection of high-rise buildings, where some of the current residents will be given free apartments. The remaining land will be used for high-end commercial and residential buildings.

On paper, the plan looks beautiful. But people in Dharavi are not convinced. They believe the plan has not understood the nature and real value of Dharavi and its residents. It has only considered the value of the land and decided it is too valuable to be wasted on poor people.

Dharavi residents have been left with no choice but to adapt to an unfamiliar lifestyle. If this meant a small adjustment, one could justify it. But the new form of living in a 20-story high-rise will force them to pay more each month, since the maintenance costs of high-rises exceed what residents currently spend on housing. These costs become unbearable when people earn just enough to survive in a big city.

Even worse, this new, imposed lifestyle will kill all the enterprises that flourish today in Dharavi. Currently, people live and work in the same space. In the new housing, this will not be possible.

The alternatives envisaged are spaces appropriate for formal, organized industry. But enterprises in Dharavi are informal and small, working on tiny margins. Such enterprises cannot survive formalization.

The real alternative is to give residents security of tenure and let them redevelop Dharavi. They have ideas. It can happen only if people are valued more than real estate.

Nevertheless, some governments still push slum clearance. Beijing demolished hundreds of blocks of old city neighborhoods and culturally significant buildings in its preparations to host the 2008 Olympic Games. Some of these "urban corners" (a negative term for high-density neighborhoods with narrow streets) had also been designated for protection as historic areas.[74] Developers posted messages urging residents to take government resettlement fees and move, saying, "Living in the Front Gate's courtyards is ancient history; moving to an apartment makes you a good neighbor," and "Cherish the chance; grab the good fortune; say farewell to dangerous housing."[75]

Beijing's actions were not unique. Other cities hosting international "mega-events" have demolished slums. Like Beijing, Seoul, South Korea, and Santo Domingo in the Dominican Republic were already urbanizing and had slum-clearance programs under way, but as their moments in the spotlight grew nearer, eviction operations accelerated, according to a Yale study. Ultimately, the study concluded, the benefits from hosting big events did not trickle down to poor residents and squatter communities who were "systematically removed or concealed from high-profile areas in order to construct the appearance of development."[76]

Now the debate over slum clearance has arrived in Dharavi. Developers are circling the site, which sits on a square mile of prime real estate near Mumbai's downtown and airport. The local government has accepted a $3 billion redevelopment proposal from Mukesh Mehta, a wealthy architect who made his fortune in Long Island, N.Y., to raze Dharavi's shanties and replace them with high-rise condominiums, shops, parks and offices. Slum dwellers who can prove they have lived in Dharavi since 1995 would receive free 300-square-foot apartments, equivalent to two small rooms, in the new buildings. Other units would be sold at market rates that could reach several thousand dollars per square foot.[77]

Mehta contends his plan will benefit slum residents because they will receive new homes on the same site. "Give me a better solution. Until then you might want to accept this one," he said last summer.[78] But many Dharavi residents say they will not be able to keep small businesses like tanneries, potteries and tailoring shops if they move into modern high-rises, and would rather stay put. (See "At Issue," p. 102.)

"I've never been inside a tall building. I prefer a place like this where I can work and live," said Usman Ghani, a potter born and raised in Dharavi who has demonstrated against the redevelopment proposals. He is not optimistic about the future. "The poor and the working class won't be able to stay in Mumbai," he said. "Many years ago, corrupt leaders sold this country to the East India Company. Now they're selling it to multinationals."[79]

OUTLOOK
Going Global

In an urbanizing world, cities will become increasingly important as centers of government, commerce and culture, but some will be more influential than others. Although it doesn't have a precise definition, the term "global city" is used by city-watchers to describe metropolises like New York and London that have a disproportionate impact on world affairs. Many urban leaders around the world aspire to take their cities to that level.

The 2008 *Global Cities Index* — compiled by *Foreign Policy* magazine, the Chicago Council on Global Affairs and the A. T. Kearney management consulting firm — ranks 60 cities on five broad criteria that measure their international influence, including:

- Business activity,
- Human capital (attracting diverse groups of people and talent),
- Information exchange,
- Cultural attractions and experiences, and
- Political engagement (influence on world policy making and dialogue).[80]

The scorecard is topped by Western cities like New York, London and Paris but also includes developing-country cities such as Beijing, Shanghai, Bangkok, Mexico City and São Paulo. Many of these cities, the authors noted, are taking a different route to global stature than their predecessors followed — a shorter, often state-led path with less public input than citizens of Western democracies expect to have.

"Rulers in closed or formerly closed societies have the power to decide that their capitol is going to be a

In addition to Dubai's glittering, new downtown area filled with towering skyscrapers, the city's manmade, palm-tree-shaped islands of Jumeirah sport hundreds of multi-million-dollar second homes for international jetsetters. Development has skidded to a temporary halt in the Arab city-state, much as it has in some other rapidly urbanizing cities around the globe, due to the global economic downturn.

world-class city, put up private funds and spell out what the city should look like," says Simon O'Rourke, executive director of the Global Chicago Center at the Chicago Council on Global Affairs. "That's not necessarily a bad path, but it's a different path than the routes that New York or London have taken. New global cities can get things done quickly — if the money is there."

Abu Dhabi's Masdar Initiative, for example, remains on track despite the global recession, directors said this spring. The project is part of a strategic plan to make Abu Dhabi a world leader in clean-energy technology. "There is no question of any rollback or slowing down of any of our projects in the renewable-energy sector," said Sultan Ahmed Al Jaber, chief executive officer of the initiative, on March 16.[81] Last year the crown prince of Abu Dhabi created a $15 billion fund for clean-energy investments, which included funds for Masdar City.

Money is the front-burner issue during today's global recession. "Unless a country's overall economic progress is solid, it is very unlikely that a high proportion of city dwellers will see big improvements in their standard of living," says Harvard's Bloom. In the next several years, cities that ride out the global economic slowdown successfully will be best positioned to prosper when world markets recover.

In the longer term, however, creating wealth is not enough, as evidenced by conditions in Abu Dhabi's neighboring emirate, Dubai. Until recently Dubai was a booming city-state with an economy built on real estate, tourism and trade — part of the government's plan to make the city a world-class business and tourism hub. It quickly became a showcase for wealth and rapid urbanization: Dozens of high-rise, luxury apartment buildings and office towers sprouted up seemingly overnight, and man-made islands shaped like palm trees rose from the sea, crowded with multi-million-dollar second homes for jetsetters.

But the global recession has brought development to a halt. The real estate collapse was so sudden that jobless expatriate employees have been fleeing the country, literally abandoning their cars in the Dubai airport parking lot.[82]

Truly global cities are excellent in a variety of ways, says O'Rourke. "To be great, cities have to be places where people want to live and work." They need intellectual and cultural attractions as well as conventional features like parks and efficient mass transit, he says, and, ultimately, they must give residents at least some role in decisionmaking.

"It will be very interesting to see over the next 20 years which cities can increase their global power without opening up locally to more participation," says O'Rourke. "If people don't have a say in how systems are built, they won't use them."

Finally, great cities need creative leaders who can adapt to changing circumstances. Mumbai's recovery after last November's terrorist attacks showed such resilience. Within a week stores and restaurants were open again in neighborhoods that had been raked by gunfire, and international travelers were returning to the city.[83]

The Taj Mahal Palace & Tower was one of the main attack targets. Afterwards, Ratan Tata, grand-nephew of the Indian industrialist who built the five-star hotel, said, "We can be hurt, but we can't be knocked down."[84]

NOTES

1. Ben Sutherland, "Slum Dwellers 'to top 2 billion,'" BBC News, June 20, 2006, http://news.bbc.co.uk/2/hi/in_depth/5099038.stm.

2. United Nations Population Fund, *State of World Population 2007: Unleashing the Potential of Urban Growth* (2007), p. 6.

3. UN-HABITAT, *State of the World's Cities 2008/2009* (2008), p. xi.

4. UN-HABITAT, *op cit.*, p. 90.

5. *Ibid.*, p. 92.

6. *Ibid.*, pp. 90-105.

7. Anna Tibaijuka, "The Challenge of Urbanisation and the Role of UN-HABITAT," lecture at the Warsaw School of Economics, April 18, 2008, p. 2, www.unhabitat.org/downloads/docs/5683_16536_ed_warsaw_version12_1804.pdf.

8. For background see Peter Katel, "Ending Poverty," *CQ Researcher*, Sept. 9, 2005, p. 733-760.

9. For details, see www.endpoverty2015.org. For background, see Peter Behr, "Looming Water Crisis," *CQ Global Researcher*, February 2008, pp. 27-56.

10. Tobias Just, "Megacities: Boundless Growth?" Deutsche Bank Research, March 12, 2008, pp. 4-5.

11. Commission on Legal Empowerment of the Poor, *Making the Law Work for Everyone* (2008), pp. 5-9, www.undp.org/legalempowerment/report/Making_the_Law_Work_for_Everyone.pdf.

12. Angel Rabasa, *et al.*, "The Lessons of Mumbai," *RAND Occasional Paper*, 2009, pp. 1-2, www.rand.org/pubs/occasional_papers/2009/RAND_OP249.pdf.

13. Wieland Wagner, "As Orders Dry Up, Factory Workers Head Home," *Der Spiegel*, Jan. 8, 2009, www.spiegel.de/international/world/0,1518,600188,00.html; Malcolm Beith, "Reverse Migration Rocks Mexico," *Foreign Policy.com*, February 2009, www.foreignpolicy.com/story/cms.php?story_id=4731; Anthony Faiola, "A Global Retreat As Economies Dry Up," *The Washington Post*, March 5, 2009, www.washingtonpost.com/wp-dyn/content/story/2009/03/04/ST2009030404264.html.

14. For background, see David Masci, "Emerging India, *CQ Researcher*, April 19, 2002, pp. 329-360; and Peter Katel, "Emerging China," *CQ Researcher*, Nov. 11, 2005, pp. 957-980.

15. For background, see Mary H. Cooper, "Exporting Jobs," *CQ Researcher*, Feb. 20, 2004, pp. 149-172.

16. Ji Yongqing, "Dalian Becomes the New Outsourcing Destination," *China Business Feature*, Sept. 17, 2008, www.cbfeature.com/industry_spotlight/news/dalian_becomes_the_new_outsourcing_destination.

17. Thomas L. Friedman, *The World Is Flat: A Brief History of the Twenty-First Century*, updated edition (2006), pp. 24-28, 463-464.

18. Priya Deshingkar and Claudia Natali, "Internal Migration," in *World Migration 2008* (2008), p. 183.

19. Views expressed here are the speaker's own and do not represent those of his employer.

20. Martin Ravallion, Shaohua Chen and Prem Sangraula, "New Evidence on the Urbanization of Global Poverty," World Bank Policy Research Working Paper 4199, April 2007, http://siteresources.worldbank.org/INTWDR2008/Resources/2795087-1191427986785/RavallionMEtAl_UrbanizationOfGlobalPoverty.pdf.

21. For background on the *hukou* system, see Congressional-Executive Commission on China, "China's Household Registration System: Sustained Reform Needed to Protect China's Rural Migrants," Oct. 7, 2005, www.cecc.gov/pages/news/hukou.pdf; and Hayden Windrow and Anik Guha, "The Hukou System, Migrant Workers, and State Power in the People's Republic of China," *Northwestern University Journal of International Human Rights*, spring 2005, pp. 1-18.

22. Wu Zhong, "How the Hukou System Distorts Reality," *Asia Times*, April 11, 2007, www.atimes.com/atimes/China/ID11Ad01.html; Rong Jiaojiao, "Hukou 'An Obstacle to Market Economy,' " *China Daily*, May 21, 2007, www.chinadaily.com.cn/china/2007-05/21/content_876699.htm.

23. "Scientific Outlook on Development," "Full text of Hu Jintao's report at 17th Party Congress," section V.5, Oct. 24, 2007, http://news.xinhuanet.com/english/2007-10/24/content_6938749.htm.

24. Wu Zhong, "Working-Class Heroes Get Their Day," *Asia Times*, Oct. 24, 2007, www.atimes.com/atimes/China_Business/IJ24Cb01.html.

25. "Internal Migration, Poverty and Development in Asia," *Briefing Paper no. 11*, Overseas Development Council, October 2006, p. 3.

26. Clare T. Romanik, "An Urban-Rural Focus on Food Markets in Africa," The Urban Institute, Nov. 15, 2007, p. 30, www.urban.org/publications/411604.html.

27. UN-HABITAT, *op. cit.*, pp. 24-26.

28. "How Shifts to Smaller Family Sizes Contributed to the Asian Miracle," *Population Action International*, July 2006, www.popact.org/Publications/Fact_Sheets/FS4/Asian_Miracle.pdf.

29. Edson C. Tandoc, Jr., "Says UP Economist: Lack of Family Planning Worsens Poverty," *Philippine Daily Inquirer*, Nov. 11, 2008, http://newsinfo.inquirer.net/breakingnews/nation/view/20081111-171604/Lack-of-family-planning-worsens-poverty; Blaine Harden, "Birthrates Help Keep Filipinos in Poverty," *The Washington Post*, April 21, 2008, www.washingtonpost.com/wp-dyn/content/story/2008/04/21/ST2008042100778.html.

30. Kenneth Fletcher, "Colombia Dispatch 11: Former Bogotá Mayor Enrique Peñalosa," Smithsonian.com, Oct. 29, 2008, www.smithsonianmag.com/travel/Colombia-Dispatch-11-Former-Bogota-mayor-Enrique-Penalosa.html.

31. Charles Montgomery, "Bogota's Urban Happiness Movement," *Globe and Mail*, June 25, 2007, www.theglobeandmail.com/servlet/story/RTGAM.20070622.whappyurbanmain0623/BNStory/lifeMain/home.

32. Bus Rapid Transit Planning Guide, 3rd edition, Institute for Transportation & Development Policy, June 2007, p. 1, www.itdp.org/documents/Bus%20Rapid%20Transit%20Guide%20%20complete%20guide.pdf.

33. Project details at www.masdaruae.com/en/home/index.aspx.

34. Awad and Schuler remarks at Greenbuild 2008 conference, Boston, Mass., Nov. 20, 2008.

35. "Green Dreams," Frontline/World, www.pbs.org/frontlineworld/fellows/green_dreams/; Danielle Sacks, "Green Guru Gone Wrong: William McDonough," *Fast Company*, Oct. 13, 2008, www.fastcompany.com/magazine/130/the-mortal-messiah.html; Timothy Lesle, "Cradle and All," *California Magazine*, September/October 2008, www.alumni.berkeley.edu/California/200809/lesle.asp.

36. Shannon May, "Ecological Crisis and Eco-Villages in China," *Counterpunch*, Nov. 21-23, 2008, www.counterpunch.org/may11212008.html.

37. Rujun Shen, "Eco-city seen as Expensive 'Green-Wash,'" *The Standard* (Hong Kong), June 24, 2008, www.thestandard.com.hk/news_detail.asp?we_cat=9&art_id=67641&sid=19488136&con_type=1&d_str=20080624&fc=8; see also Douglas McGray, "Pop-Up Cities: China Builds a Bright Green Metropolis," *Wired*, April 24, 2007, www.wired.com/wired/archive/15.05/feat_popup.html; Malcolm Moore, "China's Pioneering Eco-City of Dongtan Stalls," *Telegraph*, Oct. 19, 2008, www.telegraph.co.uk/news/worldnews/asia/china/3223969/Chinas-pioneering-eco-city-of-Dongtan-stalls.html; "City of Dreams," *Economist*, March 19, 2009, www.economist.com/world/asia/displaystory.cfm?story_id=13330904.

38. Details at www.tianjinecocity.gov.sg/.

39. "LEED Projects and Case Studies Directory," U.S. Green Building Council, www.usgbc.org/LEED/Project/RegisteredProjectList.aspx.

40. Remarks at Greenbuild 2008 conference, Boston, Mass., Nov. 20, 2008.

41. Population Reference Bureau, "Urbanization," www.prb.org; Tertius Chandler, *Four Thousand Years of Urban Growth: An Historical Census* (1987).

42. Lewis Mumford, *The City In History: Its Origins, Its Transformations, and Its Prospects* (1961), pp. 417-418.

43. Frederick Engels, *The Condition of the Working Class in England* (1854), Chapter 7 ("Results"), online at Marx/Engels Internet Archive, www.marxists.org/archive/marx/works/1845/condition-working-class/ch07.htm.

44. Population Reference Bureau, *op. cit.*

45. Robert A. Caro, *The Power Broker: Robert Moses and the Fall of New York* (1975).

46. Jane Jacobs, *The Death and Life of Great American Cities* (1961).

47. Mumford, *op. cit.*, pp. 454-455.

48. Joshua Kurlantzick, "The Big Mango Bounces Back," *World Policy Journal*, spring 2000, www.worldpolicy.org/journal/articles/kurlant.html; UN-HABITAT, *op. cit.*, pp. 74-76.

49. BBC News, "Interactive Map: Urban Growth," http://news.bbc.co.uk/2/shared/spl/hi/world/06/urbanisation/html/urbanisation.stm.

50. Licia Valladares and Magda Prates Coelho, "Urban Research in Latin America: Towards a Research Agenda," MOST Discussion Paper Series No. 4 (undated), www.unesco.org/most/valleng.htm#trends.

51. Jose de Gregorie, "Sustained Growth in Latin America," Economic Policy Papers, Central Bank of Chile, May 2005, www.bcentral.cl/eng/studies/economic-policy-papers/pdf/dpe13eng.pdf.

52. UN-HABITAT, *op cit.*, pp. 70-74.

53. Hernando de Soto, *The Mystery of Capital: Why Capitalism Triumphs in the West and Fails Everywhere Else* (2000), excerpted at http://ild.org.pe/en/mystery/english?page=0%2C0.

54. Deepak Kindo, "Microfinance Services to the Urban Poor," *Microfinance Insights*, March 2007; World Bank, "10 Years of World Bank Support for Micro-credit in Bangladesh," Nov. 5, 2007; "Micro Finance Gaining in Popularity," *The Hindu*, Aug. 25, 2008, www.hindu.com/biz/2008/08/25/stories/2008082550121600.htm.

55. Michael Richardson, "Clinton Warns APEC of 'Digital Divide,'" *International Herald Tribune*, Nov. 16, 2000, www.iht.com/articles/2000/11/16/apec.2.t_2.php.

56. Abigail Keene-Babcock, "Study Shows Half the World's Population With Mobile Phones by 2008," Dec. 4, 2007, www.nextbillion.net/news/study-shows-half-the-worlds-population-with-mobile-phones-by-200.

57. "Millennium Development Goals Report 2008," United Nations, p. 48, www.un.org/millenniumgoals/pdf/The%20Millennium%20Development%20Goals%20Report%202008.pdf.

58. Robyn Dixon, "Zimbabwe Slum Dwellers Are Left With Only Dust," *Los Angeles Times*, June 21, 2005, http://articles.latimes.com/2005/jun/21/world/fg-nohomes21.

59. Ewen MacAskill, "UN Report Damns Mugabe Slum Clearance as Catastrophic," *Guardian*, July 23, 2005, www.guardian.co.uk/world/2005/jul/23/zimbabwe.ewenmacaskill.

60. Freedom House, "Freedom in the World 2008: Zimbabwe," www.freedomhouse.org/uploads/press_release/Zimbabwe_FIW_08.pdf.

61. "Crisis Reveals Growing Finance Gaps for Developing Countries," World Bank, March 8, 2009, http://web.worldbank.org/WBSITE/EXTERNAL/NEWS/0,,contentMDK:22093316~menuPK:34463~pagePK:34370~piPK:34424~theSitePK:4607,00.html.

62. "Swimming Against the Tide: How Developing Countries Are Coping with the Global Crisis," World Bank, background paper prepared for the G20 finance Ministers meeting, March 13-14, 2009, http://siteresources.worldbank.org/NEWS/Resources/swimmingagainstthetide-march2009.pdf.

63. "Major Victories for City Priorities in American Recovery and Reinvestment Act," U.S. Conference of Mayors, Feb. 23, 2009, www.usmayors.org/usmayornewspaper/documents/02_23_09/pg1_major_victories.asp.

64. Carter Dougherty, "Chinese Premier Injects Note of Optimism at Davos," *The New York Times*, Jan. 29, 2009, www.nytimes.com/2009/01/29/business/29econ.html?partner=rss.

65. Jamil Anderlini and Geoff Dyer, "Downturn Causes 20m Job Losses in China," *Financial Times*, Feb. 2, 2009, www.ft.com/cms/s/0/19c25aea-f0f5-11dd-8790-0000779fd2ac.html.

66. Joe McDonald, "World Bank Cuts China's 2009 Growth Forecast," The Associated Press, March 18, 2009.

67. "Bill and Melinda Gates Urge Global Leaders to Maintain Foreign Aid," Bill and Melinda Gates Foundation, Jan. 30, 2009, www.gatesfoundation.org/press-releases/Pages/2009-world-economic-forum-090130.aspx.

68. Mark Landler and David E. Sanger, "World Leaders Pledge $1.1 Trillion to Tackle Crisis," *The New York Times*, April 4, 2009, www.nytimes.com/2009/04/03/world/europe/03summit.html?_r=1&hp.

69. "Is Demolition the Way to Go?" World Bank, www.worldbank.org/urban/upgrading/demolition.html.

70. "What Is Urban Upgrading?" World Bank, www.worldbank.org/urban/upgrading/what.html.

71. For more information, see "Urban Poor Fund," *Shack/Slum Dwellers International*, www.sdinet.co.za/ritual/urban_poor_fund/.

72. Neal R. Peirce, "Gates Millions, Slum-Dwellers: Thanksgiving Miracle?" *Houston Chronicle*, Nov. 22,

2007, www.sdinet.co.za/static/pdf/sdi_gates_iupf_neal_peirce.pdf.

73. "Statement at the African Ministerial Conference on Housing and Urban Development," UN-HABITAT, Abuja, Nigeria, July 28, 2008, www.unhabitat.org/content.asp?cid=5830&catid=14&typeid=8&subMenuId=0.

74. Michael Meyer, *The Last Days of Old Beijing* (2008), pp. 54-55; Richard Spencer, "History is Erased as Beijing Makes Way for Olympics," *Telegraph* (London), June 19, 2006, www.telegraph.co.uk/news/worldnews/asia/china/1521709/History-is-erased-as-Beijing-makes-way-for-Olympics.html; Michael Sheridan, "Old Beijing Falls to Olympics Bulldozer," *Sunday Times* (London), April 29, 2007, www.timesonline.co.uk/tol/news/world/asia/china/article1719945.ece.

75. Meyer, *op. cit.*, pp. 45, 52.

76. Solomon J. Greene, "Staged Cities: Mega-Events, Slum Clearance, and Global Capital," *Yale Human Rights & Development Law Journal*, vol. 6, 2003, http://islandia.law.yale.edu/yhrdlj/PDF/Vol%206/greene.pdf.

77. Slum Rehabilitation Authority, "Dharavi Development Project," www.sra.gov.in/htmlpages/Dharavi.htm; Porus P. Cooper, "In India, Slum May Get Housing," *Philadelphia Inquirer*, Sept. 22, 2008.

78. Mukul Devichand, "Mumbai's Slum Solution?" BBC News, Aug. 14, 2008, http://news.bbc.co.uk/2/hi/south_asia/7558102.stm.

79. Henry Chu, "Dharavi, India's Largest Slum, Eyed By Mumbai Developers," *Los Angeles Times*, Sept. 8, 2008, www.latimes.com/news/nationworld/world/la-fg-dharavi8-2008sep08,0,1830588.story; see also Dominic Whiting, "Dharavi Dwellers Face Ruin in Development Blitz," Reuters, June 6, 2008, http://in.reuters.com/article/topNews/idINIndia-33958520080608; and Mark Tutton, "Real Life 'Slumdog' Slum To Be Demolished," CNN.com, Feb. 23, 2009, www.cnn.com/2009/TRAVEL/02/23/dharavi.mumbai.slums/.

80. Unless otherwise cited, this section is based on "The 2008 Global Cities Index," *Foreign Policy*, November/December 2008, www.foreignpolicy.com/story/cms.php?story_id=4509.

81. T. Ramavarman, "Masdar To Proceed with $15 Billion Investment Plan," *Khaleej Times Online*, March 16, 2009, www.khaleejtimes.com/biz/inside.asp?xfile=/data/business/2009/March/business_March638.xml&section=business&col=; Stefan Nicola, "Green Oasis Rises From Desert Sands," *Washington Times*, Feb. 2, 2009, www.washingtontimes.com/themes/places/abu-dhabi/; Elisabeth Rosenthal, "Gulf Oil States Seeking a Lead in Clean Energy," *The New York Times*, Jan. 13, 2009, www.nytimes.com/2009/01/13/world/middleeast/13greengulf.html.

82. David Teather and Richard Wachman, "The Emirate That Used to Spend It Like Beckham," *The Guardian*, Jan. 31, 2009, www.guardian.co.uk/world/2009/jan/31/dubai-global-recession; Robert F. Worth, "Laid-Off Foreigners Flee as Dubai Spirals Down," *The New York Times*, Feb. 12, 2009, www.nytimes.com/2009/02/12/world/middleeast/12dubai.html; Elizabeth Farrelly, "Dubai's Darkening Sky: The Crane Gods are Still," *Brisbane Times*, Feb. 26, 2009, www.brisbanetimes.com.au/news/opinion/dubais-darkening-sky-the-crane-gods-are-still/2009/02/25/1235237781806.html.

83. Raja Murthy, "Taj Mahal Leads India's Recovery," *Asia Times*, Dec. 3, 2008, www.atimes.com/atimes/South_Asia/JL03Df01.html.

84. Joe Nocera, "Mumbai Finds Its Resiliency," *The New York Times*, Jan. 4, 2009, http://travel.nytimes.com/2009/01/04/travel/04journeys.html.

BIBLIOGRAPHY

Books

Meyer, Michael, *The Last Days of Old Beijing: Life in the Vanishing Backstreets of a City Transformed*, Walker & Co., 2008.
An English teacher and travel writer traces Beijing's history and describes life in one of its oldest neighborhoods as the city prepared to host the 2008 Olympic Games.

Silver, Christopher, *Planning the Megacity: Jakarta in the Twentieth Century*, Routledge, 2007.
An urban scholar describes how Indonesia's largest city grew from a colonial capital of 150,000 in 1900 into a megacity of 12-13 million in 2000, and concludes that overall the process was well-planned.

2007. State of the World: Our Urban Future, World-watch Institute, Norton, 2007.
Published by an environmental think tank, a collection of articles on issues such as sanitation, urban farming and strengthening local economies examines how cities can be healthier and greener.

Articles

"The 2008 Global Cities Index," *Foreign Policy,* November/December 2008, www.foreignpolicy.com/story/cms.php?story_id=4509.
Foreign Policy magazine, the Chicago Council on World Affairs and the A.T. Kearney management consulting firm rank the world's most "global" cities in both industrialized and developing countries, based on economic activity, human capital, information exchange, cultural experience and political engagement.

"Mexico City Bikers Preach Pedal Power in Megacity," The Associated Press, Dec. 28, 2008.
Bicycle activists are campaigning for respect in a city with more than 6 million cars, taxis and buses.

Albright, Madeleine, and Hernando De Soto, "Out From the Underground," *Time,* July 16, 2007.
A former U.S. Secretary of State and a prominent Peruvian economist contend that giving poor people basic legal rights can help them move from squatter communities and the shadow economy to more secure lives.

Bloom, David E., and Tarun Khanna, "The Urban Revolution," *Finance & Development,* September 2007, pp. 9-14.
Rapid urbanization is inevitable and could be beneficial if leaders plan for it and develop innovative ways to make cities livable.

Chamberlain, Gethin, "The Beating Heart of Mumbai," *The Observer,* Dec. 21, 2008, www.guardian.co.uk/world/2008/dec/21/dharavi-india-slums-slum-dog-millionaire-poverty.
Eight boys growing up in Dharavi, Asia's largest slum, talk about life in their neighborhood.

Osnos, Evan, "Letter From China: The Promised Land," *The New Yorker,* Feb. 9, 2009, www.newyorker.com/reporting/2009/02/09/090209fa_fact_osnos.
Traders from at least 19 countries have set up shop in the Chinese coastal city of Guangzhou to make money in the export-import business.

Packer, George, "The Megacity," *The New Yorker,* Nov. 13, 2006, www.newyorker.com/archive/2006/11/13/061113fa_fact_packer.
Lagos, Nigeria, offers a grim picture of urban life.

Schwartz, Michael, "For Russia's Migrants, Economic Despair Douses Flickers of Hope," *The New York Times,* Feb. 9, 2009, www.nytimes.com/2009/02/10/world/europe/10migrants.html?n=Top/Reference/Times%20Topics/People/P/Putin,%20Vladimir%20V.
Russia has an estimated 10 million migrant workers, mainly from former Soviet republics in Central Asia — some living in shanty towns.

Reports and Studies

"Ranking of the World's Cities Most Exposed to Coastal Flooding Today and in the Future," Organization for Economic Cooperation and Development, 2007, www.rms.com/Publications/OECD_Cities_Coastal_Flooding.pdf.
As a result of urbanization and global climate change, up to 150 million people in major cities around the world could be threatened by flooding by 2070.

"State of World Population 2007," U.N. Population Fund, 2007, www.unfpa.org/upload/lib_pub_file/695_filename_sowp2007_eng.pdf.
A U.N. agency outlines the challenges and opportunities presented by urbanization and calls on policy makers to help cities improve residents' lives.

"State of the World's Cities 2008/2009: Harmonious Cities," UN-HABITAT, 2008.
The biennial report from the U.N. Human Settlements Programme surveys urban growth patterns and social, economic and environmental conditions in cities worldwide.

For More Information

Chicago Council on Global Affairs, 332 South Michigan Ave., Suite 1100, Chicago, IL 60604; (312) 726-3860; www.thechicagocouncil.org. A nonprofit research and public education group; runs the Global Chicago Center, an initiative to strengthen Chicago's international connections, and co-authors the Global Cities Index.

Clean Air Initiative for Asian Cities, CAI-Asia Center, 3510 Robinsons Equitable Tower, ADB Avenue, Ortigas Center, Pasig City, Philippines 1605; (632) 395-2843; www.cleanairnet.org/caiasia. A nonprofit network that promotes and demonstrates innovative ways to improve air quality in Asian cities.

Institute for Liberty and Democracy, Las Begonias 441, Oficina 901, San Isidro, Lima 27, Peru; (51-1) 616-6100; http://ild.org.pe. Think tank headed by economist Hernando de Soto that promotes legal tools to help the world's poor move from the extralegal economy into an inclusive market economy.

Overseas Development Institute, 111 Westminster Bridge Road, London SE1 7JD, United Kingdom; (44) (0)20 7922 0300; www.odi.org.uk. An independent British think tank focusing on international development and humanitarian issues.

Shack/Slum Dwellers International; (27) 21 689 9408; www.sdinet.co.za. The Web site for the South Africa-based secretariat of an international network of organizations of the urban poor in 23 developing countries.

UN-HABITAT, P.O. Box 30030 GPO, Nairobi, 00100, Kenya; (254-20) 7621234; www.unhabitat.org. The United Nations Human Settlements Programme; works to promote socially and environmentally sustainable cities and towns.

World Bank, 1818 H Street, N.W., Washington, DC 20433, USA; (202) 473-1000; http://web.worldbank.org. Two development institutions with 185 member countries, which provide loans, credits and grants to middle-income developing countries (International Bank for Reconstruction and Development) and the poorest developing countries (International Development Association)

Voices From Abroad:

DAVID DODMAN

Researcher, International Institute for Environment and Development, England

Cities aren't to blame for climate change.
"Blaming cities for climate change is far too simplistic. There are a lot of economies of scale associated with energy use in cities. If you're an urban dweller, particularly in an affluent country like Canada or the U.K., you're likely to be more efficient in your use of heating fuel and in your use of energy for transportation."

Toronto Star, March 2009

BABATUNDE FASHOLA

State Governor Lagos, Nigeria

Megacities create many challenges.
"Because of human activities there will be conflict and there will be the issue of security, everybody fighting for control, and these are some of the challenges that come with the status of a megacity. It is really a status that creates certain challenges that the government must respond to."

This Day (Nigeria), November 2007

JONATHAN WOETZEL

Director, McKinsey & Company, Shanghai

Migration to China could cause problems.
"The fact that 40 to 50 per cent of [Chinese] cities [by 2025] could be made up of migrant workers is a real wake-up call. Smaller cities in particular are going to face a growing challenge if they are to provide equal access to social services."

Irish Times, March 2008

Cagle Cartoons, La Prensa, Panama/Arcadio Esquivel

THE WORLD BANK

Singapore does it right.
"Improving institutions and infrastructure and intervening at the same time is a tall order for any government, but Singapore shows how it can be done. . . . Multi-year plans

were produced, implemented and updated. For a city-state in a poor region, it is also not an exaggeration to assert that effective urbanization was responsible for delivering growth rates that averaged 8 per cent a year throughout 1970s and 1980s."

World Development Report 2009

THORAYA AHMED OBAID

Executive Director, U.N. Population Fund

Informal work has value.
"Many of tomorrow's city dwellers will be poor, swelling the ranks of the billion who already live in slums, but however bad their predicament, experience shows that newcomers do not leave the city once they have moved. . . . They are also remarkably productive. Economists agree that informal work makes a vital contribution to the urban economy and is a key growth factor in developing countries."

The Guardian (England), July 2007

ZHU TONG

Environmental Scientist, Peking University

Different air standards cause confusion.
"Different countries vary in their air quality standards, and the WHO does not have a binding set of standards.

China's national standards are not as high as those in developed countries, which has led to disagreements, confusion or even misunderstandings."

South China Morning Post, July 2008

SUDIRMAN NASIR

Lecturer, University of Hasanuddin, Indonesia

Opportunities lead to migration.
"The lack of job and economic opportunities in rural areas justifies migration to the cities as a survival strategy. It is a rational choice made by villagers because cities generally have more jobs to offer. It's impossible to reduce urbanization through the repressive approach."

Jakarta Post (Indonesia),
October 2008

5

Aging Infrastructure

Marcia Clemmitt

Steam explodes from a burst pipe near Manhattan's Grand Central Station on July 18, 2007. One person was killed and several injured. Throughout the country, many facilities and systems are 50-100 years old, and engineers say they have been woefully neglected. Now lawmakers are debating whether aging infrastructure merits higher taxes or other measures, such as turning more highways into privately managed toll roads.

From *CQ Researcher*, September 28, 2007.

On Aug. 1, 24-year-old Gary Babineau was driving across the I-35 West bridge in Minneapolis when it collapsed, plunging more than 100 vehicles into the Mississippi River and killing 13 people.

After falling about 30 feet, Babineau's pickup truck dangled over the edge of a bridge section as cars hurtled past him into the water. "The whole bridge from one side of the Mississippi to the other just completely gave way," Babineau told CNN. "I stayed in my car until the cars quit falling for a second, then I got out real quick." He and other survivors then helped children in a school bus scramble off the bridge.[1]

The fatal collapse brought to mind other recent infrastructure failures — including the aging underground steam pipe that burst in New York City two weeks earlier, killing a pedestrian and injuring several others. More important, the collapse raised concern about the condition of the nation's dams, water and sewer lines, electric power networks and other vital systems. Many were constructed decades ago, during a 75-year building boom, and are nearing the end of their intended lifespan, engineering groups say.

"The steam pipe that blew up in New York was over 80 years old," says David G. Mongan, president-elect of the American Society of Civil Engineers (ASCE).[2]

Indeed, because of increasing user demand and years of neglected maintenance, the U.S. infrastructure overall rates a near-failing grade of "D" from the ASCE. The group says a $1.6-trillion, five-year investment is needed to bring facilities up to snuff.[3]

Many Bridges Are "Structurally Deficient"

Twelve percent of all bridges in the United States — nearly 75,000 structures — are structurally deficient, according to the Department of Transportation. In four states — Oklahoma, Iowa, Pennsylvania and Rhode Island — more than 20 percent of the bridges are deficient.

Percentage of Structurally Deficient Bridges by State, 2006

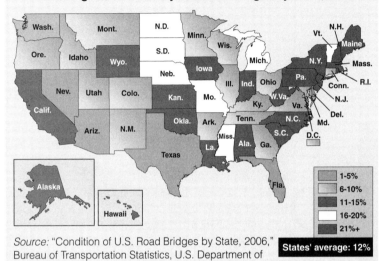

1-5%
6-10%
11-15%
16-20%
21%+

States' average: 12%

Source: "Condition of U.S. Road Bridges by State, 2006," Bureau of Transportation Statistics, U.S. Department of Transportation

Much of the existing U.S infrastructure was built in the 1930s, '40s and '50s and today carries loads that "are magnitudes beyond" what its builders anticipated, he says.

As the Water Environment Foundation (WEF) puts it: "A hundred years ago, Teddy Roosevelt was president, crossword puzzles hadn't been invented, Las Vegas had a population of 39 people and your sewer system was brand new." The nonprofit advocacy group seeks to focus attention on infrastructure that's mainly out of sight and out of mind until a catastrophic event like a bridge collapse.

Infrastructure consists of the structures and systems that "we can't do without," says Paula R. Worthington, a lecturer in economics at the University of Chicago's Harris School of Public Policy.

While vital, infrastructure is also easy to ignore. In fact, a good definition of infrastructure could be "all the things that we take for granted somebody is taking care of," says Linda Kelly, the WEF's managing director of

public communications and the former deputy director of the Portland, Ore., water system.

But Americans have not been taking good care of their infrastructure, many analysts say. For one thing, politicians generally believe they gain more political capital from new projects than from maintaining and upgrading old systems, even heavily used ones.

Washington "is a classic case," says Heywood Sanders, a professor of public administration at the University of Texas, San Antonio. "There are a great number of older highways" in the nation's capital that need fixing, disastrously deteriorating school buildings and more, Sanders says. "But what you've got is a new convention center and a brand-new ballpark. In a city that needs a great many things, those are the things that happen."

Focusing public attention on the need for maintenance funds "unfortunately takes some kind of major problem," says Rob Villee, executive director of the Plainfield Area Regional Sewerage Authority in Middlesex, N.J. The result is that few infrastructure agencies "do proactive maintenance." In every town, many interests fight for a piece of the public budget, "and until [a sewer] backs up into the house of somebody important," sewer maintenance seldom commands attention and dollars, he says.

Ownership issues also work against proper maintenance and improvements to privately owned infrastructure, such as the electric system, says Richard Little, director of the Keston Institute for Public Finance and Infrastructure Policy at the University of Southern California (USC).

Since government-imposed ownership rules were removed for electrical utilities during the 1990s, "the new owners of transmission capacity" — power lines — "aren't in the electricity-generation business," says Little. Such owners may have little financial incentive to upgrade their systems, he says. "When the system was vertically integrated" — with the same companies owning both power-generation facilities and transmission lines — "there was a stronger business reason for keeping it up." Today, however, "the great national transmission grid is not as integrated as we think" — and potentially more vulnerable to failures such as blackouts.

As the Minneapolis bridge collapse starkly showed, neglect comes with a price.

After the accident, a construction-industry official told the *Minneapolis Star-Tribune* that some workers at the Minnesota Department of Transportation had been "deathly afraid that this kind of tragedy was going to be visited on us." Some "were screaming" to have "fracture-critical" bridges like I-35 West "replaced" sooner than the state had budgeted for.[4]

Bridges aren't the only infrastructure sector that is collapsing. The increasing frequency of sinkholes that swallow people and property is evidence of deteriorating wastewater infrastructure, says Kelly. When an underground sewer pipe springs a leak, soil seeps into the crack and is carried away, and eventually "the soil can't support heavy cars or a building," she explains.

Last December, a 64-year-old Brooklyn, N.Y., woman carrying groceries home was injured when she fell into a five-foot-deep sinkhole that opened under the sidewalk. The same month, a 30-foot-deep sinkhole shut down a stretch of California's famed Pacific Coast Highway near Malibu, while in Portland, Ore., a sinkhole swallowed a 40-foot-long sewer-repair truck. A few months earlier, a 2-year-old boy in Irving, Texas, may have disappeared into a sinkhole while playing in a park; the child was never recovered.[5]

Dams are another growing concern. At least 23 have failed in the past four years, including Ka Loko Dam in Kauai, Hawaii, which collapsed in March 2006 killing seven people and causing at least $50 million in property and environmental damage.[6]

And the spate of air-traffic delays that stranded thousands of vacation travelers just this summer is directly due to a lack of important upgrades to the air-traffic control system, says the ASCE's Mongan. Airports can't land as many planes as they could because outdated radar tracking systems make it unsafe to space planes as closely as modern GPS tracking systems would allow, he says.

Virtually all infrastructure analysts say upgrades and maintenance require more funding, but increasing taxes to raise the money is sparking hot debate in Washington. As early as the 1930s, states introduced fuel taxes to pay for road construction, and the main federal source of highway funds today is an 18.4-cents-per-gallon gasoline tax, last increased in 1993.[7]

"I consider it ludicrous that the United States has the lowest gas taxes in the world," says Lt. Gen. Hank Hatch, a former chief of the U.S. Army Corps of Engineers who chairs the Board on Infrastructure and Environment at the National Research Council. "If we had a higher one, we could do amazing things."

But the Bush administration and some conservatives oppose any tax increases.

"Increasing federal taxes and spending would likely do little, if anything, to address either the quality or performance of our roads," Secretary of Transportation Mary E. Peters told the House Transportation Committee on Sept. 5. The occasion was a hearing on legislation sponsored by Committee Chairman James Oberstar, D-Minn., to raise the federal gas tax to 23.3 cents to create a bridge-maintenance trust fund.[8]

Later, President George W. Bush told Democratic and Republican backers of the increase that the real problem with highway upkeep is funding that lawmakers divert to low-priority pet projects. Bush opposes increasing the gas tax, he said, because it "could affect economic growth" negatively.[9]

With tax funds hard to come by, some highway and water agencies are opting for long-term lease agreements allowing private companies to operate and perhaps build facilities and collect tolls for their upkeep. Such "public-private partnerships" also are hotly debated.

Proponents praise the private sector's ingenuity and efficiency. "We need flexible solutions and, quite often, the most flexible minds are in the private sector," says Eli Lehrer, a senior fellow at the libertarian Competitive Enterprise Institute.

But most citizens feel more confident that their interests will be protected if local government manages infrastructure, said Wenonah Hauter, executive director of the advocacy group Food and Water Watch, which challenges private takeover of water systems. "They don't want a really important public service like water to be privatized," Hauter said. "They don't want the customer call center to be 1,000 miles away. They don't want their water rates going up."[10]

Federal Spending Cuts Shift Burden to States

The percentage of federal spending on transportation and water infrastructure has been decreasing since 1981, forcing cash-strapped states to pick up more of the expenses.

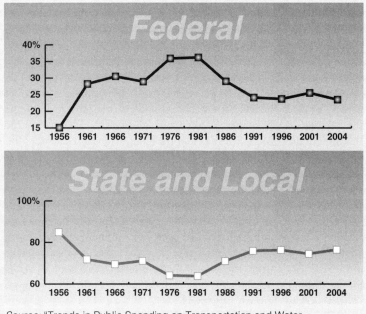

Percentage of Public Spending Spent on Infrastructure, 1956-2004

Source: "Trends in Public Spending on Transportation and Water Infrastructure, 1956 to 2004," Congressional Budget Office, August 2007

stress, water, sulfurous chemicals in the air in industrial areas and road salts, "it will get corrosion," he says. Water alone "is a very effective solvent, eating through paints and through steel," Baber says.

But even engineers are sometimes surprised by structural deterioration, says Ziyad Duron, a professor of engineering at Harvey Mudd College in Claremont, Calif. A few years ago, Duron was "leaning on a bridge in Massachusetts, and all of a sudden I found myself with one of the bolts in my hand."

Life-threatening events like dangerous sinkholes are on the rise, while the risk of other catastrophic events like dam and bridge failures is also increasing, some experts say.

The condition of many U.S. bridges is "quite scary" because many "are approaching the end of their useful life, which is typically 50 to 75 years," and "due to less than adequate maintenance over the years on some of these structures, anything could happen without warning," says Abi Aghayere, a professor of civil engineering at New York's Rochester Institute of Technology.

Dams are likely in worse condition than bridges, some engineers say.

Since 1998, the number of unsafe dams in the United States has increased by 33 percent, according to the American Society of Civil Engineers. The total number of dams whose failure could cause loss of life has risen from 9,281 to 10,094 over that period, largely because of population growth immediately downstream from dams and underfunding of government dam-safety agencies, according to the advocacy group Dam Safety Coalition.[11]

"Every moment of every day, unsafe dams form a vast reservoir of danger throughout America," warned journalist Gaylord Shaw, who won a 1978 Pulitzer Prize for a *Los Angeles Times* series investigating the nation's dams.

When it comes down to a choice between taxes and user fees like tolls, the public's first choice is "neither," says Little. "People would rather ride on a nice road for free than pay $6."

As voters, legislators and engineers contemplate solutions to crumbling highways and sewer lines, here are some questions being asked:

Does aging infrastructure endanger Americans?

No one argues the U.S. infrastructure is not deteriorating. But opinions vary about the amount of danger the deterioration poses.

"All materials deteriorate, and fatigue will hit every bridge eventually," says Thomas Baber, an associate professor of engineering at the University of Virginia. "If you put a bridge out there long enough," exposed to traffic

"When a dam fails . . . the events usually are viewed as local, transitory incidents rather than a symbol of a national problem," but "the cumulative hazard posed by unsafe dams is huge."[12]

And it's not just dams and bridges. The past year has seen a near-epidemic of sinkholes in most states, and the trend is likely to continue.

When underground sewer pipes break, the soil above falls into the crack and the "broken pipes whisk dirt away like a vacuum cleaner," said Thomas Rooney, CEO of Insituform Technologies, a pipe-repair company in Chesterfield, Mo. "When enough soil disappears above the pipe, but below a road or park or home, a sinkhole forms.

"All over America, engineers are telling city councils, water boards, sewer districts and other public agencies and officials about the dismal conditions of their water and sewer pipes," said Rooney. But "they would rather wait until the next catastrophe."[13]

Nevertheless, most of the infrastructure is basically safe, say many experts.

So-called "truss" bridges, like Minneapolis' I-35 West bridge, aren't dangerous in and of themselves, for example, says the University of Virginia's Baber. "We have been building truss structures for about 150 years, and by and large, they're very safe."

Furthermore, "We're much better today at monitoring" structures to catch problems before catastrophic failures, says Donald Vannoy, professor emeritus of civil engineering at the University of Maryland. "This failure in Minnesota is very strange and unusual."

"I don't think we're moving into an era of regular catastrophic failure, like a Minneapolis bridge every three months," says Little at the University of Southern California. In Minneapolis, "a certain bridge didn't get what it needed, and there was a failure."

The main effects of infrastructure aging are low-level, chronic problems, not catastrophes, many analysts say.

For example, if water quality deteriorates because of aging pipes in a region's water-supply system, "there's no explosion, or 100,000 people" suddenly inundated, as in a dam collapse, says Charles N. Haas, a professor of environmental engineering at Philadelphia's Drexel University. Nevertheless, what does result is "a low-level but continuous exposure" to chemical and biological hazards for hundreds of thousands of people, which may seriously harm the health of some, Haas says.

Water from the Ka Loko Reservoir rushes over an earthen dam that gave way on March 14, 2006, killing several people in Lilhue, Hawaii. It is one of 23 U.S. dams that have collapsed in the last four years.

Some undue alarm about aging infrastructure comes from the way infrastructure deficiencies are categorized and sold to the public and policy makers both by federal agencies and private groups, says Sanders at the University of Texas.

When engineers calculate totals of obsolete structures, the number usually includes both "functionally obsolete" facilities — those that aren't big enough to accommodate today's needs — and "structurally deficient" structures — those that are falling into disrepair, Sanders explains. Furthermore, a "structurally deficient" bridge "may have a bad roadway," which can be fixed by resurfacing and doesn't pose any danger of the bridge falling down, he says. It's important to sort out those categories and not simply assume that all "deficient" structures are actually dangerous, he says.

Should taxes be increased to overhaul the infrastructure?

As both publicly and privately owned infrastructure age, maintenance and replacement costs are inevitable, as are costs for monitoring their safety and reliability. Some analysts argue that current decision-making processes are so flawed that money raised by tax increases would be squandered.

Maintaining aging infrastructure undoubtedly costs more money than we have been spending, most analysts say.

Report Card Shows No Improvement

The nation's transportation infrastructure has not significantly improved since 2001, according to the American Society of Civil Engineers (ASCE). Much of the infrastructure has remained either structurally deficient or functionally obsolete, according to the ASCE. Moreover, in most instances, spending for maintenance, repairs and replacements has not met the group's requirements.

Infrastructure Grades, 2001 and 2005

Subject	2001 grade	2005 grade
Bridges	C	C
The percentage of the nation's structurally deficient or functionally obsolete bridges decreased from 28.5 to 27.1 percent from 2000 to 2003. However, it will cost $9.4 billion a year for the next 20 years to eliminate all deficiencies.		
Dams	D	D
Since 1998, the number of unsafe dams has risen by 33 percent to over 3,000. Federally owned dams are in good condition. It will cost $10.1 billion over the next 12 years to address all non-federal dams in critical condition.		
Drinking Water	D	D-
The United States faces an $11 billion annual shortfall to replace aging water facilities and comply with safe-drinking-water regulations. In 2005, federal funding for drinking water totaled $850 billion, 10 percent less than the total national requirement.		
National Power Grid	D+	D
Continual growth in electricity demand and investment in new power plants have not been matched by investments in new transmission facilities. Existing transmission capability leaves consumers vulnerable to blackouts. Maintenance spending has decreased by 1 percent annually since 1992.		
Roads	D+	D
Poor road conditions cost motorists $54 billion a year in operating costs and repairs. Americans spend 3.5 billion hours a year stuck in traffic, costing the economy $63.2 billion. Spending on transportation infrastructure currently totals $59.4 billion, well below the necessary $94 billion.		
Wastewater	D	D-
Aging wastewater systems discharge billions of gallons of untreated sewage into surface waters each year. The EPA estimates that $390 billion over the next 20 years will be required to replace existing systems, but in 2005 Congress cut funding for wastewater management for the first time in eight years.		

Source: American Society of Civil Engineers, www.asce.org/reportcard/2005/page.cfm? id=103

As in many other areas of life, with infrastructure age comes increasing responsibility, says Bernard Wasow, an economist and senior fellow at the liberal Century Foundation. "It's just like when your kids get older and need a college education. With time, come things you've got to pay for."

Furthermore, "compared to other nations like Japan, we do spend a smaller amount of [the gross domestic product]" on infrastructure, says Texas' Sanders.

In fact, it's the dauntingly high cost of properly maintaining the nation's vast infrastructure that has partly prevented the job from being done, says Little at the University of Southern California (USC). "We need to spend a couple of hundred billion dollars a year forever," and that prospect is too daunting for most policy makers to face, he says.

Many analysts say fuel taxes and other infrastructure-supporting taxes are too low, as are fees for infrastructure use, such as household water fees and highway tolls.

As an anti-tax movement has flourished over the past few decades, distrust of government and the belief that any tax is too high a tax have spread, says Jeffrey Buxbaum, a transportation consultant with Massachusetts-based Cambridge Systematics. Infrastructure maintenance has been stinted by "the legacy of 'No taxes' and 'The government isn't to be trusted,'" he says.

Furthermore, "there's a lack of understanding of how much people actually pay in the form of gas taxes," a common funding source for transportation infrastructure, says Buxbaum. In Massachusetts, for instance, the average person pays about "$150 a year" in state fuel taxes, "and if you wanted to raise it by a few cents" to pay for maintenance, "that would amount to less than $100 a year" per household, he says.

Anti-tax protests over the past couple of decades have all but paralyzed politicians on infrastructure, says Little.

"Even if they want to do the progressive thing, they worry because the anti-tax groups are going to get them."

"We've been spoiled in this country. We don't pay market rates for much of anything, and we have allowed the tax rebels to drive the agenda," says Little. "We have people in California in $100-million homes paying only hundreds of dollars in taxes. How silly is that?"

Many infrastructure-related fees also are too low, many analysts say.

"We aren't charging enough" for water to either residential or business users, for example, says Drexel University's Haas.

The federal gasoline tax and many state gasoline taxes are flat, cents-per-gallon taxes that have remained the same for years. Many economists argue that fuel taxes should be "indexed" to inflation or some other economic marker, simply to prevent them from losing value as all other costs in the nation rise — including the cost of maintaining roads and bridges.

Not only does a non-indexed tax lose its value over time, but the "unit-tax" structure of the current federal gas tax can actually cause tax revenues to drop when the price of gas rises, says Joel B. Slemrod, a professor of business economics and public policy at the University of Michigan. If a higher price leads people to buy less gas, then revenue drops from a cents-on-the-gallon tax, he explains.

Gas taxes "absolutely" should be indexed to rise with other prices, says Robert W. Poole Jr., director of transportation studies at the libertarian Reason Foundation in Los Angeles. "But I've talked myself blue in the face trying to convince" conservative colleagues of that, he says. "Indexing of the fuel tax is not a tax increase; it's just a way of keeping the value of the tax from completely deteriorating over time," says Poole.

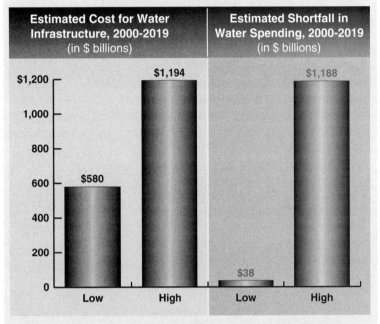

Shortfall Projected in Water Spending

The United States will need up to $1.1 trillion to meet future U.S. water infrastructure needs (left). However, Environmental Protection Agency analysts say if present funding trends continue, the U.S. could end up as much as $1.1 trillion short of that goal (right).

Estimated Cost for Water Infrastructure, 2000-2019 (in $ billions)	Estimated Shortfall in Water Spending, 2000-2019 (in $ billions)
Low: $580 High: $1,194	Low: $38 High: $1,188

Sources: "Water Infrastructure: Comprehensive Asset Management Has Potential to Help Utilities Better Identify Needs and Plan Future Investments," General Accounting Office, March 2004; Claudia Copeland and Mary Tiemann, "Water Infrastructure Needs and Investment: Review and Analysis of Key Issues," Congressional Research Service, June 13, 2007

New, highly targeted — but relatively painless — taxes also could meet some non-highway infrastructure needs, says Little. To pay for water infrastructure, "you could put a very small 1-cent-per-roll tax on toilet tissue or on soap. That would create a tremendous amount of money," he says. "We would need a responsible agency to dispense it well, however."

Nevertheless, the Bush administration strongly opposes any tax increases, including the gas-tax hike some members of Congress propose to finance a repair fund for aging bridges.

And one federal lawmaker goes so far as to argue that even cutting gas taxes to decrease the cost of driving in this era of high fuel prices would not harm infrastructure maintenance.

A sinkhole blocks a road in St. Cloud, Minn., on July 19, 2007. Sinkholes are often caused by deteriorating underground sewer pipes. When they spring a leak, soil seeps into the crack and is carried away, undermining roads and other sites above the pipes.

Rep. John "Randy" Kuhl, R-N.Y., has introduced legislation to cut the gas tax by 10 cents a gallon if the price of gas rises above $3. The tax cut wouldn't "hurt money that is directed to the Highway Trust Fund . . . as the lower gas prices will send more people to the pumps and generate similar revenue," said Kuhl in a statement.[14]

Even many who support higher taxes say new revenues might accomplish little without better priority-setting.

Maintenance of current infrastructure often loses out in the political process to flashy, perhaps unnecessary, new projects like ballparks or oversized bridges, says Texas' Sanders. "If you pour more money into a system that favors certain kinds of outcomes, you'll just continue to get the same outcomes."

Even when citizens vote for higher taxes to shore up infrastructure, lawmakers often reserve the option to shift the funding to other purposes, says Little.

In 2002, nearly 70 percent of California voters approved legislative Proposition 42 to allocate a portion of the state sales tax to transportation infrastructure. "But there was a kick-out clause," says USC's Little. "The governor could take the money and spend it for a non-transportation budget emergency" if he chose. "So even when you've had a designated [infrastructure] fund, it still gets robbed," he says.

About $2.5 billion of supposedly dedicated transportation funds has been diverted to other purposes under the state's Proposition 42 escape clause since 2002, according to Transportation California, an advocacy group seeking stronger protection for the funds.[15]

But even if infrastructure agencies can hold onto their funds, they should be required to make more thoughtful use of the money, said Robert Puentes, a fellow in the Metropolitan Policy Program at the centrist Brookings Institution.

"Billions of dollars of additional federal investments, without significant reform, will do precious little to fix our rusting bridges, expand our overcrowded transit systems, or unclog our ports," Puentes said. As a condition of approving any new funding, such as a gas-tax hike, "agencies should set annual performance objectives, and consequences should be established for . . . poor implementation," Puentes said.[16]

Should private companies run more of America's infrastructure?

In search of better financing and efficiency, governments around the United States and worldwide are turning roads, bridges and water systems over to private companies under long-term leases and other arrangements. Critics argue that social equity may be threatened, however, when for-profit operators aggressively raise fees to levels that threaten people's access to public facilities.

"Roads run by private companies tend to be kept up a little better because the companies are under contract and have to do certain things or they don't get paid," says Little, at USC's infrastructure institute.

Private groups "really do look at a road as a business," says Poole of the Reason Foundation. For example, while public agencies will immediately build all the on and off ramps they believe a highway will ever need, "a private company is more likely to "just build some, and leave the option of adding more later," speeding the building process and saving upfront dollars, he says.

A major reason for turning over infrastructure operation to a private enterprise that will collect fees for the service is governments' need to find new sources of funding, say privatization supporters.

"Cities, counties and states are maxing out their debt limits," and many can't pay for new infrastructure, says Richard Norment, executive director of the National Council for Public-Private Partnerships, a membership group. That's where the private sector can step in to help, he says.

"Public-private partnerships tap into a much broader and deeper range of funding sources" than are available to governments alone, says the Reason Foundation's Poole. Governments borrow in the municipal bond market, which has inflexible rules and requires money to be repaid on a fixed schedule, says Poole. Guaranteeing such fixed investor returns on an infrastructure project can become impossible "if a project misses its traffic target for five years," for example, he says.

Private companies, on the other hand, can "tap brand-new equity investment funds" whose investors are paid "only when the project is in the black," Poole explains.

But privatized infrastructure projects also have their downsides. In many cases, "governments may lose more than they gain," said Brookings' Puentes. "All that upfront cash looks sweet, but the long-term revenue stream is lost since all the toll receipts flow directly to the private operators. Governments also lose the option to borrow against those future revenues."[17]

Wasow of the Century Foundation questions whether the private sector will maintain its interest in infrastructure over the long haul. "Will private companies necessarily want to keep running infrastructure projects" as roads and structures age and require greater upkeep? he asks. "The first 10 years after something's constructed you've got low maintenance costs. But over time they'll rise," he says.

Furthermore, "what happens to fairness?" Wasow asks. "Everybody — left, right and center — basically believes that maintaining infrastructure is ultimately the province of government," since infrastructure like roads is, by definition, something that all residents need to go about their daily business, he says. "This means that a reasonable question to ask is, If government is not providing these goods that we all agree are public, what happens to fairness? Should everyone be required to pay private tolls" to use public facilities like water and bridges, even those who make very little money?

Experts on all sides of the issue generally agree that the details of a private-management contract can make or break it.

"The key thing" is making sure that private companies "actually take the risk," and not just rake in profits "while the public sector gets screwed" if the private managers fail or bail, says Lehrer of the Competitive Enterprise Institute. There should be "no explicit or implicit guarantee" that the government will bail out a private entity that gets into trouble managing an infrastructure asset, he says. "I believe the profit system is very good for society, but the flip side is that private

entities must be exposed to the loss" if they don't manage projects well.

The key to a project that succeeds is "picking your partners carefully," says Norment. In some high-profile private-management failures, contracts have been awarded for political reasons or through cronyism, he says. A Mexican city whose privatized water system collapsed had awarded the contract to a company owned "by a guy who'd never built a water project before, the brother-in-law of the governor," he says.

But while good contracts are crucial, good infrastructure-contracting practices are "probably hard for local governments to understand" today, says Shama Gamkhar, an associate professor of public affairs at the University of Texas, Austin. While the United States did have private toll roads in the 18th and 19th centuries, in recent memory U.S. toll roads have been operated by governments, as are most water systems. Today, however, privatization of toll-based infrastructure like roads and water is a new trend, and "people just learn [about contract design and management] on the job," she says. "There's not much experience to fall back on."

BACKGROUND

Meeting Needs

The late-19th through the mid-20th century was a time of massive infrastructure building in the United States, from interstate highways to sewer lines and water-treatment plants. And in the days when narrow, unpaved roads made travel a nightmare and untreated sewage contaminated rivers and other drinking-water sources, Americans weren't all that reluctant to ante up dollars for improvements.[18]

So vital was municipal infrastructure that water-treatment and power plants often were conceived as "objects of immense civic pride and sometimes monumental beauty," according to the advocacy group Environmental Defense. Buildings like the Boston Water Works were designed by top architects and became models of design for their communities, their styles copied by residential and commercial builders alike. The facilities "served as potent symbols of common purpose and progress in a young and rapidly growing nation," says the group.[19]

The need for clean drinking water to prevent disease spurred heroic infrastructure-building efforts around the

CHRONOLOGY

1900s–1960s *Federal government helps states build national transportation and water infrastructure.*

1908 Jersey City is first water district to chlorinate drinking water.

1916 Congress enacts Federal-Aid Highway Program, giving federal matching funds to states for road building.

1927 New York City and Jersey City are linked beneath the Hudson River by the Holland Tunnel, named for Clifford Holland, who invented the tunnel's fan system — including an 80-foot-diameter fan — that vents deadly car exhaust.

1940 First section opens on Pennsylvania Turnpike, the first U. S. highway with no cross streets, railroad crossings or traffic lights.

1956 President Dwight D. Eisenhower commits $25 billion to the national highway system, raising the federal funding share from 50 percent to 90 percent.

1965 Major power blackout in the Northeast spurs establishment of North American Electric Reliability Council (NAERC), a public-private consortium of power producers to set voluntary infrastructure standards for the electricity industry.

1970s *Federal role in infrastructure building peaks.*

1972 Clean Water Act spurs localities to enlarge water-treatment plants.

1977 President Jimmy Carter becomes an advocate for dam safety after a 78-year-old dam in his home state of Georgia collapses, killing 39 people.

1980s *Concern grows about aging infrastructure.*

1988 "Fragile Foundations" report by the National Council on Public Works Improvement recommends doubling infrastructure spending.

1990s–2000s *Federal funding is cut for highways and wastewater cleanup as engineers complain about neglected maintenance.*

1993 Sewage in Milwaukee's drinking water kills 100 residents.

2000 Milwaukee's Hoan Bridge partially collapses; no one is injured.

2001 Environmental Protection Agency (EPA) says $151 billion is needed over the next 20 years to upgrade drinking-water systems.

2003 Failure of Michigan's Silver Lake Dam causes $100 million in damage. . . . Electrical-transmission grid fails, blacking out 50 million customers in the Eastern U.S. and Canada for up to 24 hours and shutting down air traffic, mass transit and sewer and water systems. . . . EPA says $390 billion is needed to upgrade wastewater systems over 20 years.

2004 Failure of Mississippi's Big Bay Lake Dam destroys 100 homes. . . . NAERC declares "urgent need" for Congress to replace voluntary reliability standards for electric companies with mandates.

2005 Businesses in Taunton, Mass., close for a week after the 173-year-old, 12-foot-tall wooden Whittenton Mills Dam begins to buckle. . . . New Orleans floods when Hurricane Katrina overwhelms the inadequate levee system. . . . Chicago's Skyway toll bridge comes under private management. . . . More than 10 billion gallons of untreated sewage spill into Lake Erie because of broken pipes and overflows from overburdened local sewage systems in northern Ohio.

2006 Ka Loko Dam in Kauai, Hawaii, fails, killing seven people. . . . Three-hour power failure at a Washington, D.C., sewage-treatment plant spills 17 million gallons of raw sewage into Potomac River.

2007 An 80-year-old underground steam pipe bursts in Manhattan, killing one person. . . . A 95-year-old water pipe breaks in Seattle, cutting off residential water service and creating a sinkhole that swallows two cars. . . . I-35 West bridge over the Mississippi River collapses in Minneapolis at rush hour, sending dozens of cars into the water and killing 13 people. In public opinion poll a week later, two-thirds of the respondents oppose raising gas taxes to fix the nation's bridges.

country. At the turn of the 20th century, deadly waterborne diseases like cholera and typhoid killed many Americans, as untreated sewage contaminated drinking-water sources. In 1891, for example, 178 out of every 100,000 Chicago residents died of typhoid.[20]

In Chicago, Rudolph Hering, chief engineer for the water-supply system, carried out the massive project of digging a new channel to reroute the Chicago River away from its natural outlet, Lake Michigan, the source of the city's drinking water. Redirecting the Chicago — the dumping ground for the city's raw sewage and industrial waste — into rivers that drain to the Mississippi River immediately gave the city much cleaner drinking water.[21]

In the nation's drier regions, like Southern California, scarce water also led to massive infrastructure efforts. In 1905, Los Angeles voters approved a $1.5-billion bond issue to erect aqueducts to bring drinking water to the city from the Owens River, more than 230 miles north of the city.[22]

Even financially conservative leaders supported such infrastructure efforts. In 1956, for example, Republican President Dwight D. Eisenhower signed the Federal-Aid Highway Act, calling for states and the federal government to build a vast Interstate Highway System — 41,000 miles of high-quality roads to link the nation.[23] Spurred by his memory of a 1919 cross-country trip that took U.S. Army vehicles 62 days to travel from Washington, D.C., to San Francisco, hindered by rutted roads and sagging bridges, Eisenhower committed the federal government to assume 90 percent of the cost.[24]

Infrastructure-building programs such as the Works Progress Administration and Civilian Conservation Corps, created as part of President Franklin D. Roosevelt's New Deal initiative in the 1930s and '40s, played key roles in "creating fixed assets for the nation," in the form of dams, bridges, post offices, parks and much more, says Michael Pagano, a professor of public administration at the University of Illinois, Chicago.

Not often considered in the budgets and agendas of such programs, however, was the inescapable fact that time brings more costs, Pagano says. "For the first 20 years, upkeep doesn't cost much," but after that the price of maintenance and replacement inevitably rises, often steeply, "and we just haven't ever incorporated those true costs into our thinking," he says.

Additional factors complicate today's infrastructure-upkeep problem. For one thing, infrastructure is owned and operated by many different entities, including the federal government, states, localities and private companies.

Perhaps surprisingly, about 85 percent of U.S. infrastructure is "owned and operated by the private sector," says Daniel Ostergaard, CEO of a homeland-security consultancy, Pelorus Enterprises, and a senior policy fellow at Western Carolina University's Institute for Economy and Future. About 68 percent of U.S. dams are privately owned, for example, according to the U.S. Army Corps of Engineers.[25]

Private ownership of so many public conveniences "poses a unique challenge for the federal government," which has no direct control over infrastructure like the electrical grid and telecommunications networks but nevertheless is ultimately held responsible for keeping Americans safe and productive, Ostergaard says.

Increasingly, though owned and operated separately, aspects of the national infrastructure rely on each other to function, Ostergaard points out. "We can't just look at the water supply on its own but have to look at the electrical grid," too, for example, since water systems need power to function. "You need a great deal of dialogue" to meet such challenges, and cooperative decision-making isn't easy to promote, he says. "If you look from a purely economic viewpoint, each system looks out for its own best interest."

Another threat to proper maintenance grows out of the fact that infrastructure benefits often cross geographic boundaries, and those who pay most to update or maintain infrastructure aren't necessarily those who benefit most. For example, there is a national benefit to having a well-maintained Interstate Highway System, even in sparsely populated areas, but must local residents shoulder costs for big roads that they themselves don't much need?

Water infrastructure is especially prone to such dilemmas. So-called watershed districts in some states — areas that drain into a specific bay, lake or river system — are government-established entities that have responsibility for water quality and flooding throughout the system. But is it fair to make upstream landowners pay for improvements that will only benefit those downriver? Bitter disagreements over this question have stalled many

Should America Take the Toll Road?

With roads aging, economists say tolls make sense.

The nation's first private toll road opened in 1794, spanning the 62 miles between Philadelphia and Lancaster. Private toll roads flourished in America's early days, as cash-strapped states turned to private investors to fund roads for farmers, merchants and manufacturers to carry goods to market.[1] Today, privately run toll roads may be making a comeback, as states look for ways to expand and maintain aging, overcrowded highway systems.

Over the past decade, states including California, Indiana, South Carolina, Texas and Virginia have entered agreements with private companies to build and/or operate toll roads, with varying degrees of success, and many more are contemplating such arrangements. In 2006, Chicago signed a 99-year lease with private operators to run the existing Chicago Skyway toll road.

In most agreements, the state retains ownership of the road, bridge or other structure, while a company leases it for a specified period — such as 50 years — agreeing to maintain it while collecting toll revenue.[2]

The draw for states is getting upfront cash — typically paid when the lease is signed — without tapping into the government treasury or borrowing on their own.

When private investors built the Southern Connector toll road around Greenville, S.C., "the state was able to get a $200-million federal interstate built without using precious state resources or using the state bond limit," said Pete Poore, communication director for the South Carolina Transportation Department.[3]

While private toll roads exist in many countries, most Americans are familiar only with some publicly run turnpikes and bridges erected during the interstate-highway building boom that began in the 1950s. Most of the tolls were eliminated once the roads were paid for. But with aging highway infrastructure needing critical maintenance as well as expansion, this is a new day, some transportation analysts say.

"In the past, tolling has been there to build a project, and theoretically you take it off when you've paid off the capital debt," says Jeffrey Buxbaum, a transportation consultant with Massachusetts-based Cambridge Systematics. "But the cost of a highway continues when the debt is paid off," and today's tolls would be permanent, not temporary, funding sources.

Economists have long thought a precisely calibrated, distance-based toll would have been the best means of paying for and maintaining interstate highways, "but it was just too difficult to collect," says Michael Pagano, a professor of public administration at the University of Illinois, Chicago. New technologies are making precise toll-collection feasible, however.

Future tolls also will likely feature "congestion pricing," says Pagano. Sensors in the pavement will "fine tune traffic on a highway" by triggering a rise in tolls — which will be posted

water projects since water-infrastructure efforts began flourishing in the 19th century, and they continue today.

"There's a responsibility for all residents in the watershed . . . to manage the watershed as a whole," even though some will pay for improvements from which they won't directly benefit, said John Hoopingarner, executive director of the Muskingum watershed district in northeastern Ohio, where debate rages over money for dam and reservoir repairs.[26]

But upstream residents often vigorously disagree. "It's unfair. It's unreasonable," said Tony Zadra, who owns a satellite-dish business in New Philadelphia, an upriver town. "People in the upper highlands aren't responsible for [flood] damage downstream."[27]

"You have a property-tax assessment that doesn't increase property value," said Scott Levengood, a farmer in another upriver town, Mineral City.[28]

Rust Never Sleeps

While funding for upkeep is seldom figured into construction budgets, civil engineers think a lot about the future in trying to design infrastructure to last, although the task is ultimately futile.

"All bridges are going to deteriorate," says the University of Virginia's Baber. But "you use the best materials, the best design and the best maintenance you can afford, such on overhead signs — when traffic gets heavy, thus discouraging some drivers from entering the road, Pagano says.

California highways developed under public-private franchise agreements in San Diego and Orange County employ such technology today, according to Robert W. Poole Jr., director of transportation studies at the libertarian Reason Foundation in Los Angeles. "At any time during the day when traffic has built to a maximum, they'll up the rate by 25 cents per mile." The high-tech approach permits toll lanes in one congested California freeway to move at 65 mph even at rush hour, Poole says.

Many economists praise tolling as a way of ensuring that those who benefit from a highway are the same people who pay for it. Toll roads are a way to ensure that "people get what they pay for and pay for what they get," says Thomas A. Firey, managing editor of *Regulation* magazine, published by the libertarian Cato Institute. "Americans deep down really do appreciate fair pricing," so if highway tolls are clearly used to maintain a highway, "then they can probably accept that," he says.

Good lease agreements with private road managers can ensure that acceptance, says Poole. Private companies are "more aggressive in toll revenue — increasing the rates annually," for example, he says. "All the recent, highly publicized public-private partnerships like Chicago's Skyway have an annual index for raising tolls" by linking toll hikes to some measure of general economic change, such as the Consumer Price Index, he says.

Such indexing "wouldn't raise tolls much each year, but over 20 or 30 years the increases make a big difference" in the amount of revenue that could be applied to highway upkeep, Poole says. By contrast, the Indiana public toll

roads that were handed over to private management in 2006 "had not had an increase in 19 years," even as the roads deteriorated and the cost of maintenance rose, he says.

But critics of private toll roads argue there's too much room in leasing agreements for money to be shifted away from highway needs and that private companies have no reason to care about the general public that uses their roads.

In the past, "public toll roads built in the United States were designed to provide a high-quality ride for the lowest possible toll" to best serve the public, Gregory M. Cohen, president of the American Highway Users Alliance, told the House Highways and Transit Subcommittee in May.

Under private ownership, however, investors would most likely seek "the highest possible returns," shifting the purpose of toll roads from "maximizing the public good to maximizing profits for investors," Cohen said. "Under such a scenario, tolls are raised regularly, and the process is not subject to public or political review." [4]

[1] For background, see Daniel B. Klein and John Majewski, "Turnpikes and Toll Roads in Nineteenth-Century America," *Encyclopedia*, History of Economics Society, http://eh.net/encyclopedia/article/Klein.Majewski.Turnpikes.

[2] For background, see Robert W. Poole, Jr., "For Whom the Road Tolls," Reason Foundation Web site, February 2006, www.reason.org; Sylvia Smith, "U.S. Public-Private Agreements Have Mixed Record," *The Times of Northwest Indiana*, Jan. 23, 2006, www.thetimesonline.com/articles/2006/01/23/news/top_news/73a0efca3665c38b862570fe001a1bee.txt.

[3] Quoted in Smith, *op. cit.*

[4] Gregory M. Cohen, "Highway Users' Perspectives on Public-Private Partnerships," testimony before House Subcommittee on Highways and Transit, May 24, 2007.

as regular painting. And you use as little road salt as you can to make [the structure] last as long as possible."

In the heyday of American highway building — the 1950s through the 1970s — state-of-the-art bridges were expected to last for around 50 years. But even "state of the art" is only as good as the times.

For example, "in the 1960s, [metal] fatigue wasn't as well understood as it is today," a factor that likely played a role in the I-35 West bridge collapse, says the University of Maryland's Vannoy.

The bridge "probably wouldn't have been built in the exact same way today," says Baber. The design was fine, based on "what we knew in 1967 but not quite right

given what we know in 2007. Right now, we aim to design for 75 years," and more structural redundancy is incorporated, he adds. "You don't see many bridges now with only two load-carrying members. You're more likely to see five or six."

Part of improving upkeep involves learning how to build better in the first place, but research funds aren't always adequate for some important but overlooked infrastructure, such as water systems, some engineers say.

The federal Environmental Protection Agency (EPA) devotes under $10 million a year to drinking-water research, and even taking all private and public research funders together, "I'd be surprised if you get close to $100 million"

Pedestrians crowd New York City's Queensboro Bridge to Queens on Aug. 14, 2003, after a power blackout crippled the city and much of the Northeastern United States and Canada.

annually, says Drexel University's Haas. By contrast, hundreds of millions of dollars is probably spent every year to research technology related to the nation's electrical grid, he says.

One of the toughest infrastructure-design problems is predicting future usage. For bridges, "it's very difficult to predict traffic trends more than five or six years in advance," says Baber. "Plus, sometimes the bridge attracts traffic," a particularly difficult thing for planners to foresee, he says. "This has happened to a lot of interstate bridges."

"People in the early 1950s did not envision the 21st century," says USC's Little. For example, the inability of planners to accurately see into the future led designers to focus highway and public-transit systems mainly on accommodating transportation between suburbs and central cities, he says. Today, however, the growing prevalence of suburb-to-suburb travel is helping make the transportation system obsolete.

"We also never anticipated the huge growth in imports," which requires not only expanded ports but highway and rail systems to carry a huge proportion of the country's goods inland, Little says.

Also unanticipated in highway design was the new model for stocking large retail stores that freight-hauling companies and retailers like Wal-Mart and Dell Computer have developed over the past few decades, Little says.

Instead of building large warehouses to store goods awaiting shipment, industry now keep much of the nation's

freight cargo on trucks traveling the highways at all times. The resulting huge increase in truck traffic wears down roads that were never built for such constant, heavy loads.[29]

"Trucks are responsible for virtually 100 percent of the damage to the roads" because of their high weight per axle, says transportation consultant Buxbaum.

The trucking problem isn't complex to fix, theoretically, but it would involve a major — expensive — overhaul, says the Reason Foundation's Poole. "One idea that has a lot of promise is a truck-only toll lane" equipped with special "high-strength pavement," he says.

Paying It Forward

Between the mid-1950s and today, overall infrastructure spending has risen annually. But funding hasn't kept up with aging and the rapid development of new demands and technologies. Faulty priority-setting processes also cause problems.

So-called pork-barrel spending — inserted into congressional bills as "earmarks" — is a big problem, says the Reason Foundation's Poole. Ostensibly, members of Congress direct funding to specific local projects to please constituents. But "when I talk to [state transportation] directors, they say the projects they get in the federal bills are . . . way, way down the list," Poole says.[30]

The water pipes and roadways we use most are local, giving Congress little obvious role in those major infrastructure sectors. A federal role comes in when "externalities" — benefits and burdens connected to infrastructure — extend to people outside the region, explains Ghamkar of the University of Texas.

The federal role has applied mostly to new construction, she says. Cars and trucks drive across all states, including the less populous ones in the middle of the country, but sparsely populated areas could not be expected to build national-scale highways on their own, so Congress stepped in.

In a similar way, the Clean Water Act of 1972 acknowledged the federal role in assuring that both upstream and downstream communities get clean drinking water. Because upstream communities dump wastewater into rivers that supply drinking water to people downstream, Congress offered federal grants to improve water-treatment plants everywhere to improve water quality regionally.

Some other infrastructure, such as ports, and air-traffic control, for example, is primarily a national responsibility.

Between 1956 and the mid-1970s, federal spending on infrastructure increased by about 7 percent annually, compared to around 1 percent growth in state and local spending, according to the nonpartisan Congressional Budget Office. The federal share of infrastructure spending peaked in 1977, at 38 percent.[31]

Since then, primary responsibility for most government-funded infrastructure has shifted to states and localities. In 2004, the latest year for which complete data are available, the federal government spent $73.5 billion, or about 24 percent, of the total $312 billion in infrastructure spending in the United States. States and localities spent $238.7 billion. Of the total, $143.6 billion went to project construction, while the remaining $168.7 billion funded operation and maintenance, a proportion that's remained relatively stable for the past two decades, despite infrastructure aging.

About 45 percent of federal funds for maintenance and operation go to run the nation's air-traffic control system, and 60 percent of federal construction funds pay for highway projects. Total spending to build capital projects has grown by about 2 percent per year since 1981, while spending on maintenance and operation has risen 2.1 percent.[32]

While states and localities do the bulk of infrastructure funding and planning, Congress periodically modifies federal law to shore up vital systems. For example, the National Dam Safety Act of 2006 offered grants to improve states' dam-safety programs in response to reports that the number of deteriorating dams is increasing, along with the proportion of the population living in the flood path of a shaky dam.[33]

The bill stopped short of offering federal funding for repairs. Dam safety remains primarily a state and private-sector responsibility. The federal government owns only about 4 percent of the nation's dams, and states have primary oversight responsibility for dams, 68 percent of which are privately owned.[34]

Other infrastructure — such as water and sewage systems and the electrical and telecommunications systems, which are privately owned — is funded by user fees. But charging fees high enough to support upgrades is difficult in those sectors as well.

Utilities constantly face the question — Should we patch or replace infrastructure? says New Jersey sewerage Director Villee. "Logically," that decision would be based "on some cost ratio, like, 'If patching exceeds 50 percent we will replace it,' " Villee says "Unfortunately, factors other than logic often take precedence. Money and politics are two of the major players."

It's like having a 10-year-old car with a transmission problem, Villee says. "Logic says get a new car," but "money says we can't afford that. So you roll the dice, fix the transmission and gamble that you can extend the life of the car until you can pay for a new one. That is the game most utilities play. We defer maintenance and capital improvements to keep rates at a politically acceptable level."

CURRENT SITUATION

Bridge Tax?

Since the Minnesota bridge collapse, Congress has been mulling a tax increase for bridge repair, but President Bush opposes it.

House Transportation and Infrastructure Committee Chairman Oberstar is circulating a plan to hike the federal gas tax by five cents per gallon to repair some 6,000 "structurally deficient" bridges, and Congress is expected to discuss the proposal this fall.

But more taxes won't help, said Transportation Secretary Peters at a Sept. 5 hearing. "It is not that we don't have the money," she said, "it's where we're spending" it.[35]

Democratic and some Republican lawmakers say more money is needed and that congressional "earmarking" of funds to specific projects — criticized by many, including the White House — has increased bridge safety.

Ohio Rep. Steven C. LaTourette, a Republican moderate, said that two structurally deficient bridges in his district are being repaired thanks to congressional earmarks. "To say that all things are not on the table," including a tax hike, "cheats the American motoring public, and I would hope that the administration would rethink its position," LaTourette said.[36]

Academic analysts say a more stable long-term funding source and a means to ensure that money is dedicated to the highest-priority problems are also needed.

The gas-tax boost would be "a nice little stopgap solution," says the University of Illinois' Pagano. But as cars' fuel efficiency increases "revenue collections would still fall" under the plan, he points out.

Funding Programs Discouraged Smart Planning

Upkeep was often ignored.

Local economies and home values depend on infrastructure maintenance, but even programs like federal grants for infrastructure building often have ignored the need for continued upkeep.

"We depend vitally on infrastructure services, and ignoring them can cause trouble for communities" down the line, says Richard Little, director of the Keston Institute for Public Finance and Infrastructure Policy at the University of Southern California.

If a community lets its infrastructure — water, sewer and transportation — languish while neighboring communities don't, "pretty soon businesses will say, 'Let's go somewhere else,'" as potholed roads and sewer overflows mount up, says Little. "People will go to a newer place where there don't seem to be the same problems. Housing values drop, so we all have a real vested interest in maintenance," he says.

Federal grants have helped communities build big projects, such as massive water-treatment plants and 10- or 12-lane roads and bridges, for example. But building big may mean ignoring equally important priorities.

The federal Clean Water Act of 1972 offered grants to encourage communities to improve water-treatment plants, says Linda Kelly, managing director of public communications for the Water Environment Foundation (WEF), a nonprofit advocacy group. The law worked, up to a point, she says.

"People got very excited about putting big water plants in. My own utility had 15 little, bitty wastewater plants and consolidated them into four," says Kelly, former deputy general manager of wastewater treatment in Portland, Ore. Meanwhile, localities were left on their own to oversee — and often ignore — thousands of miles of underground pipes, which are the main source of water-system troubles today, she says. "The big plants were new in the 1970s, but the infrastructure in the ground is upwards of 100 years old."

With federal grants available for big projects — and sometimes not available for smaller projects to cover the same needs — many communities over the years have opted to build the biggest ones they could, whether that was the smartest choice or not.

In one classic care of "overbuilding," in 1976 in Pittsburgh, the large Birmingham Bridge replaced the Brady Street Bridge, which, though only a third the size, was nevertheless "adequate" for the site, says Joel A. Tarr, professor of history and policy at Carnegie-Mellon University's Heinz School of Public Policy and Management.

Planned as part of a larger highway system that never materialized, the bridge was reconfigured for local use.

The bridge remains too large for the neighborhood traffic it carries and its redesigned on and off ramps twist and turn to link the bridge with local streets it was originally meant to bypass.

"Why is it so big? Because that's the only way they could get funding," says Tarr.

Similar structures abound nationwide, says Michael Pagano, professor of public administration at the University of Illinois, Chicago. Cities and states should have asked, "Do we need 12-lane roads?" Pagano says. Instead, many localities draw up the grandest plans they can to snag federal grants that often favor the biggest projects. Under the Clean Water Act, the federal government would pay 75 percent of the cost, Pagano says. "So the obvious response was, 'Hell, I'll build the biggest plant I can get.'"

Federal grants also sometimes encourage infrastructure neglect, says Heywood Sanders, a professor of public administration at the University of Texas, San Antonio. If a city can get federal funds for a major overhaul, it's easy for local officials to neglect routine maintenance for which they'd have to spend their own money, he says.

"The other big problem with federal funding is the transfer of money among the states," says Robert W. Poole Jr., director of transportation studies at the libertarian Reason Foundation in Los Angeles. The grant formula "was created to get interstate highways built" through sparsely populated regions like Montana that didn't need the highways for their own use. That meant that low-population, low-growth areas get considerably more money than they would if grants were based on population numbers, he says.

But as infrastructure ages, current highway needs run in exactly the opposite direction, Poole says. Today's top transportation need is for upgrades and expansion in the top 25 urban areas, all located in states that get less than the average per-capita share of federal grants, he says.

Within states, a similar problem makes it hard to direct funds to the high-population areas with roads most in need of expansion and heavy-duty maintenance, says Poole. For political reasons, "you have to share the money among all the legislative districts," no matter how little some may need the funds.

Over the years, Congress has made a few attempts to shift more grant money to high-population states but the Senate — where low-density states have equal representation with high-density states — has successfully fought such efforts, Poole says. "There's not much chance" formulas will change in the foreseeable future, he says.

Are toll roads the best way to maintain highways and bridges?

YES — Robert W. Poole Jr.
Director of Transportation Studies,
The Reason Foundation

From testimony before House Subcommittee on Highways and Transit,
Feb. 13, 2007

To properly maintain of our highways and bridges, we should be spending $6 billion more every year. And to improve the system, to cope with increases in auto and truck travel, we should be spending $51 billion more every year.

The existing state and federal fuel tax and highway trust-fund system seems to be unable to meet these investment needs. Neither the Congress nor most state legislatures have increased fuel taxes to levels that would even offset increases in fuel efficiency and the ravages of inflation, let alone cope with increased travel demand. So increasingly, states are turning to toll finance and public-private partnerships (PPPs). . . .

The newest trend is the long-term concession model, in which an investor-owned company will finance, design, build, operate, modernize and maintain a highway project, financing its expenditures from toll revenues. What this model is all about is extending the investor-owned utility concept from network industries like electricity and telecommunications to the network industry of limited-access highways. This model is what built most of the postwar toll motorway systems in France, Italy, Portugal and Spain, and the trend has more recently spread to Australia, Latin America, Canada, Britain, Germany and other countries.

PPPs offer access to large, new sources of capital; the ability to raise larger sums for toll projects and shift risk from taxpayers to investors.

Long-term concessions are a good vehicle for organizing multi-state projects such as truck-only toll lanes to serve major shipping routes. These projects need to be developed in a unified manner, but individual states are not well-positioned to develop such unified projects; concession companies are.

Comparing the typical U.S. state-run toll agency with the typical European or Australian toll road company, it's clear that the latter are far more customer-oriented, more innovative and generally more commercial. Many state-operated toll agencies are run by short-term political appointees rather than by career toll-road professionals. . . .

One of the most important advantages of investor-owned toll-road companies is their motivation to innovate to solve difficult problems or improve their service, such as by varying tolls to discourage traffic congestion.

None of the transactions that have occurred or are being planned — either for existing toll roads or for new ones — involves the sale of any roads. The government remains the owner at all times, with the private partner carrying out only the tasks spelled out for it.

NO — Bill Graves
President, American Trucking
Associations (ATA)

From testimony before House Subcommittee on Highways and Transit,
May 24, 2007

We strongly believe that while private financing of highway infrastructure may play a limited role in addressing future transportation needs, certain practices may generate unintended consequences whose costs will vastly exceed their short-term economic benefits. We are very concerned about attempts by some states to carve up the most important segments of the highway system for long-term lease. . . .

Highway user fees should be reasonably uniform in application among classes of highway users and be based chiefly on readily verifiable measures of highway and vehicle use. ATA believes that fuel taxes meet the above criteria, while tolls fail on certain critical points.

Fuel-tax evasion is relatively low compared to other highway user fees. Tolls, on the other hand, are often easily evaded, usually by motorists using alternative, less safe routes that were not built to handle high levels of traffic. There are significant capital and operating costs associated with collecting tolls, while fuel taxes are relatively inexpensive to administer.

Private toll-road operators need not be concerned about the social impacts of toll rates on low-income workers or on the costs to businesses that depend on the highway. Nor do private operators care about the extent of traffic diversion to lesser quality, usually less safe, roads. Their sole concern is to maximize the toll road's profitability. . . .

Privatization boosters point to caps on toll-rate increases that have been a standard part of privatization agreements. However, the two major lease agreements that have been completed in the United States — the Indiana Toll Road and Chicago Skyway — have been accompanied by very large initial rate increases combined with caps on future increases. . . .

It has been suggested that these massive toll-rate escalations are unrealistic because, as has been demonstrated on other facilities, including the Ohio Turnpike, raising the toll rate too high forces significant traffic off the highway. However, the lessee will set a toll rate to a level that maximizes profitability, not traffic.

Indeed, a recent financial report by [Australia-based toll-road developer Macquarie Infrastructure Group] revealed that while traffic on the Indiana Toll Road's barrier system — jointly operated by Macquarie and Spain-based Cintra Concesiones de Infraestructuras de Transport — actually declined by 1.6 percent between July 2006 and March 2007, and increased by just 0.2 percent on the ticket system, revenues shot up by a whopping 46.2 percent due to large toll-rate increases.

AP Photo/Pool

A helicopter prepares to drop a sandbag in an attempt to plug the breached London Avenue Canal levee in New Orleans in the wake of flooding caused by Hurricane Katrina in September 2005.

On Aug. 6, President Bush signed a bill sponsored by the Minnesota congressional delegation to waive the $100-million-per-state limit on federal funding for emergency highway reconstruction and allow up to $250 million in funds for the Minnesota bridge.

How the measure will play out is in doubt, however, since actual funds would only be approved as part of highway appropriations legislation, and Bush has already said he'll veto the "irresponsible and excessive" $104.4 billion appropriations measure that's moving through Congress.[37]

Other Proposals

Debate also rages over the Water Resources Development Act of 2007, a bill that in its current form authorizes — but does not actually appropriate — about $21 billion in

funding for projects to be undertaken by the U.S. Army Corps of Engineers.[38]

President Bush has threatened to veto the bill, which he and other critics call an expensive mishmash of pork projects.[39]

Some of the bill's earmarks authorize "a series of costly projects that benefit the rich and influential," said Ronald D. Utt, a senior research fellow at the conservative Heritage Foundation. "Notwithstanding continuing concern" over flood protection for cities like New Orleans, "this Congress appears intent on diverting taxpayer dollars . . . to water-sports and other low-priority schemes."[40]

Some congressional Republicans, including self-described fiscal conservatives like Sen. James M. Inhofe of Oklahoma, top-ranking Republican on the Senate Environment and Public Works Committee, strongly oppose Bush's veto threat.[41]

Congress has also held hearings this year on the idea of turning more infrastructure over to private companies for management. "The battle has been joined" over the value of privately operated toll roads, with the Bush administration a strong proponent, says the Reason Foundation's Poole.

Some key Democrats have been highly skeptical, however. In a May 10 letter to state officials, Transportation Committee Chairman Oberstar and Rep. Peter DeFazio, D-Ore., warned against "rushing" into public-private partnerships (PPPs) and said their committee would undo any such agreements "that do not fully protect the public interest." In June, however, the lawmakers softened their stance, saying that "under the right circumstances and conditions," PPPs can be efficient and effective.[42]

Also in the legislative mix, though receiving little attention, is a proposal by Sens. Christopher J. Dodd, D-Conn., and Chuck Hagel, R-Neb., for an independent federal entity, the National Infrastructure Bank. It would analyze infrastructure projects costing $75 million or more and report to Congress on how to prioritize and pay for them.[43]

The Minnesota bridge collapse spurred quick action by many state and local governments to step up monitoring and repair of aging bridges. On Aug. 29, the Missouri Legislature approved a plan to repair 802 bridges in the next five years, about four times as many as previously contemplated. Tennessee will inspect bridges annually, up

A car rests against a tree near Purvis, Miss., after a dam holding back Big Bay Lake collapsed, flooding more than 50 homes on March 13, 2004. There are 10,094 dams in the United States whose failure could cause loss of life, according to the American Society of Civil Engineers.

from the two-year inspection cycle federal law requires. Wisconsin will install stress sensors to monitor the state of 14 bridges that are more than 50 years old.[44]

In general, states are making better progress than the federal government on improving decision-making processes, says Poole. In California, a state Transportation Commission with members appointed by government bodies with various missions sets priorities. "There is some politics still, but they do a reasonably good job," says the Reason Foundation's Poole.

Some state and local leaders are spotlighting infrastructure needs. Atlanta Mayor Shirley Franklin conducted an aggressive public-awareness campaign on the city's long-neglected water system, "and now the community is funding it," says the Water Environment Foundation's Kelly.

But public support may not be as tough a sell as many believe, says transportation consultant Buxbaum.

"Washington state has passed two gas tax increases" in just the past few years, after the state "built more accountability and transparency" into the highway-construction process, he says.

Buxbaum acknowledges that funding may be easier to get in the West, where infrastructure is still being built. Eastern states must mainly fund repairs, and "that's not as sexy," he says.

OUTLOOK

Threats Increase

Infrastructure problems won't get easier to resolve as systems age, population grows and developments like global warming change the very nature of the challenge.

But while problems continue to simmer, most analysts believe the public interest sparked by the Minnesota bridge collapse will be fleeting. "I've learned that the half-life of the public attitude on this issue is very short," says former Corps of Engineers chief Hatch.

Nevertheless, technological developments may make prioritizing maintenance tasks easier, says Harvey Mudd's Duron, who has developed sensors to measure internal threats to a structure's stability that inspectors can't pick up visually.

Such sensors could be attached to structures at all times, at regularly scheduled times throughout the year, or during stressful times — such as during repairs, when the I-35 West bridge collapsed — Duron says. Technology is making it possible to get "a real-time assessment of changing conditions" that can trigger structural failure, and the cost is dropping, he says. Armed with that information, engineers will be better able to explain to policy makers which projects are highest priority, Duron says.

But while technology may help, other changes will increase infrastructure strains.

Climate change will likely trigger more extreme storms and floods, including massive floods in mountainous regions caused by the melting of natural "ice dams" that form glacial lakes today, according to the International Rivers Network. "The world's more than 45,000 existing large dams have not been built to allow for a rapidly intensifying hydrological cycle," says a 2005 article in the group's journal, *World Rivers Review.*[45]

More regions may face drought as climate changes, and that will require attention to water-system deficiencies, says Nancy Connery, an infrastructure consultant in Woolwich, Maine, who chaired the congressionally created National Council on Public Works Improvement in the 1980s. "So much water is lost today, so many leaks and so much flushed down the toilet," she says. "This is a very expensive problem, and one we'll have to face sooner than we imagine."

The future will demand "dramatically new ideas" about infrastructure, perhaps even a new version of the early 20th-century era when infrastructure building was seen as heroic, says Connery.

For example, the myriad small drinking-water systems around the country might be re-envisioned as "regional, networked operations" that share an expert staff, Connery says. But attaining such efficiencies of scale would require new incentives for agencies to inform the public about their operations and to cooperate with each other, she says.

As an example of the innovative thinking she hopes to see more of, Connery cites a small company that tried to run fiber-optic cable carrying broadband Internet house to house alongside existing sewer lines. The plan ultimately stalled after Hurricane Katrina hit their planned roll-out city, New Orleans, in 2005. Nevertheless, the scheme represents "the kind of imaginative idea that could build excitement," she says. "There's so much more that's possible."

Infrastructure "is not about engineering, and it's not about financing," says Little at USC's infrastructure institute. "It's about what we want to leave to our grandchildren, and that's more than blue sky and green trees. It's the infrastructure that allows us to live," he says. "Neglecting it is a failure of imagination."

NOTES

1. For background, see "Driver Who Survived Bridge Collapse: 'I Can't Believe I'm Alive,' " CNN.com, Aug. 3, 2007, www.cnn.com/2007/US/08/02/bridge .survivors/index.html.

2. For background, see James Barron, "Steam Blast Jolts Midtown, Killing One," *The New York Times*, July 19, 2007, p. B4.

3. For background, see "Report Card for America's Infrastructure," American Society of Civil Engineers, www.asce.org/reportcard.

4. Quoted in Laurie Blake, *et al.*, "MnDOT Feared Cracking in Bridge but Opted Against Making Repairs," [Minneapolis] *Star Tribune*, Aug. 3, 2007, p. 1A, www.startribune.com.

5. For background, see William Yardley, "U.S. Faces a Sinkhole Epidemic As Its Century-Old Water and Sewer Infrastructure Leaks and Erodes," *The New York Times*, Feb. 8, 2007, p. A19; Chris Mayer, The Sinkhole Syndrome, *The Daily Wealth blog*, May 8. 2007, www.dailywealth.com; Thomas Rooney, "The Looming Sinkhole Crisis," March 28, 2007, *Los Angeles Times*, p. A21.

6. "The Need for a National Dam Rehabilitation Program," Dam Safety Coalition, www.damsafety coalition.org.

7. For background, see Robert Puentes and Ryan Prince, "Fueling Transportation Finance: A Primer on the Gas Tax," Brookings Institution Center on Urban and Metropolitan Policy, March 2003, www .brookings.org.

8. Quoted in Frederic J. Frommer, "Push to Raise Gas Tax for Bridget Repairs," The Associated Press, Sept. 6, 2007, http://ap.google.com.

9. "President Bush Discusses American Competitiveness Initiative During Press Conference," transcript, White House press conference, Aug. 9, 2007, www .whitehouse.gov/news/releases/2007/08/200708 09-1.html.

10. Quoted in Megan Tady, "A Win in the Water War," *In These Times* Web site, Aug. 1, 2007, www.inthese times.com.

11. Dam Safety Coalition, *op. cit.*

12. Gaylord Shaw, "The Enormous U.S. Dam Problem No One Is Talking About," *The Christian Science Monitor*, Jan. 3, 2006, p. 9.

13. Thomas Rooney, "Fixing Failing Pipes Is a Public Health Issue," *The Chief Engineer* Web site, www .chiefengineer.org.

14. "Kuhl Reintroduces Gas Price Relief Bill," press release, http://kuhl.house.gov/News/Document Print.aspx?DocumentID_65980.

15. For background, see "Transportation California Is Working to Close the Proposition 42 Loophole," Transportation California, www.transportationca.com/ displaycommon.cfm?an=1&subarticlenbr=156.

16. Robert Puentes, "Don't Raise that Gas Tax . . . Yet!" position statement, Aug. 22, 2007, www.brookings.edu.

17. Robert Puentes, "Cashing in on the BP Beltway," op-ed originally published in the *Hartford Courant*, March 1, 2007, www.brookings.edu/views/op-ed/puentes/20070301_beltway.htm.

18. For background, see "Trends in Public Spending on Transportation and Water Infrastructure, 1956 to 2004," Congressional Budget Office, August 2007, www.cbo.gov; Kate Asher, *The Works: Anatomy of a City* (2005); Joel A. Tarr, ed., *Devastation and Renewal: An Environmental History of Pittsburgh and its Region* (2005).

19. Michael Singer, Ramon J. Cruz and Jason Bregman, "Infrastructure and Community," Environmental Defense, 2007.

20. "Reversal of the Chicago River," Of Time and the River Web site, Illinois Department of Natural Resources, www.oftimeandtheriver.org. For background, see Richard L. Worsnop, "Water Resources and National Water Needs," *Editorial Research Reports*, 1965, Vol. II, *CQ Researcher Plus Archives*, www.cqpress.com.

21. "Water Supply and Distribution History II — Early Years," Greatest Engineering Achievements of the 20th Century, National Academy of Engineering, www.greatestachievements.org.

22. "Water Supply and Distribution III — Thirsty Cities," Greatest Engineering Achievements of the 20th Century, National Academy of Engineering, www.greatestachievements.org.

23. For background, see David Hosansky, "Traffic Congestion," *CQ Researcher*, Aug. 27, 1999, pp. 729-752; W. Street, "Interstate Highway System at 25," *Editorial Research Reports 1981*, Vol. II; M. Packman, "New Highways," *Editorial Research Reports 1954*, Vol. II; and B. W. Patch, "Federal Highway Aid and the Depression," *Editorial Research Reports 1932*, Vol. II, all available at *CQ Researcher Plus Archives*, www.cqpress.com.

24. Daniel Schulman and James Ridgeway, "The Highwaymen," *Mother Jones*, January/February 2007, www.motherjones.com.

25. Dam Safety Coalition, *op. cit.*

26. Quoted in Robert Wang, "District Raises Taxes Without a Vote," *The Canton* [Ohio] *Repository*, Aug. 26, 2007, p. 1A.

27. Quoted in *ibid.*

28. *Ibid.*

29. For background, see Kathy Koch, "Truck Safety," *CQ Researcher*, March 12, 1999, pp. 209-232.

30. For background, see Marcia Clemmitt, "Pork-Barrel Politics," *CQ Researcher*, June 16, 2006, pp. 529-552.

31. "Trends in Public Spending on Transportation and Water Infrastructure, 1956 to 2004," Congressional Budget Office, August 2007, www.cbo.gov.

32. *Ibid.*

33. Dam Safety Coalition, *op. cit.*

34. *Ibid.*

35. Quoted in Kathryn A. Wolfe, "Funding to Repair Bridges Caught in Ideological Gap," *CQ Today*, Sept. 5, 2007.

36. Quoted in *ibid.*

37. *Ibid.*

38. For background, see David Hosansky, "Reforming the Corps," *CQ Researcher*, May 30, 2003, pp. 497-520.

39. For background, see Avery Palmer, "No Conflict Seen in Water Resources Bill, Earmarks and Ethics Measure," *CQ Today*, Sept. 4, 2007.

40. Ronald D. Utt, *The Water Resources Development Act of 2007: A Pork Fest for Wealthy Beach-Front Property Owners*, Heritage Foundation, May 15, 2007, www.heritage.org/Research/Budget/wm1458.cfm.

41. Palmer, *op. cit.*

42. Quoted in Ken Orski, "Committee Chairs Soften Stance Against Public-Private Transportation Deals," *Budget and Tax News*, The Heartland Institute, August 2007, www.heartland.org.

43. "Bill Proposes National Infrastructure Bank," *WaterWeek*, American Water Works Association, Aug. 3, 2007, www.awwa.org.

44. Judy Keen, "States Act Swiftly on Bridge Repairs," *USA Today*, Sept. 3, 2007, p. 1A.

45. Patrick McCully, "And the Walls Came Tumbling Down: Dam Safety Concerns Grow in Wake of Failures, Changing Climate," *World Rivers Review*, June 2005, www.irn.org.

BIBLIOGRAPHY

Books

Ascher, Kate, *The Works: Anatomy of a City*, **Penguin Press, 2005.**
The executive director of the New York City Economic Development Corporation explains how the city's complex infrastructure works and what maintenance engineers and planners do to keep it running.

Tarr, Joel A., ed., *Devastation and Renewal: An Environmental History of Pittsburgh and Its Region*, **University of Pittsburgh Press, 2005.**
Essays assembled by a Carnegie Mellon University professor of history and policy detail the conflicting roles of money, politics, industry and the environment in shaping the infrastructure of Pittsburgh and the surrounding region.

Articles

Duke, Kenny, "If the Feds Can't Fix the Bridge, Should We?" *The Cincinnati Post*, **Aug. 29, 2007, http://news.cincypost.com/apps/pbcs.dll/article?AID=/20070829/NEWS01/708290365.**
A Kentucky state senator proposes a new state finance authority with the power to sell bonds and impose tolls to fund the huge rebuilding projects required by the aging national highway system, such as bridges over the Ohio River.

Hughes, John, and Angela Greiling Keane, "Bridge Disaster Fuels Push to Raise Tax for Repairs," *Bloomberg.com*, **Aug. 20, 2007, www.bloomberg.com/apps/news?pid=20601103&sid=aUfj43QPplT8&refer=us.**
The recent bridge collapse in Minneapolis puts new pressure on federal lawmakers and 2008 presidential candidates to offer plans for future infrastructure funding and priority setting.

Shaw, Gaylord, "The Enormous U.S. Dam Problem No One Is Talking About," *The Christian Science Monitor*, **Jan. 3, 2006.**
A long-time reporter on dam safety argues that state and federal neglect has led to catastrophic dam failures in the past and threatens to allow more in the future.

Reports and Studies

Hargen, David T., and Ravi K. Karanam, *16th Annual Report on the Performance of State Highway Systems*, **The Reason Foundation, June 2007.**
A libertarian think tank specializing in transportation issues state-by-state rankings of road performance, capacity and funding.

Drinking Water Distribution Systems: Assessing and Reducing Risks, **Committee on Public Water Supply Distribution Systems, National Research Council, 2006.**
A national expert panel pinpoints the top priorities in maintaining and upgrading drinking-water systems and describes how new technologies may increase safety.

The Fuel Tax and Alternatives for Transportation Funding, **Transportation Research Board, 2006.**
A national expert panel examines the history and potential of fuel taxes as the primary funding source for transportation infrastructure and concludes that direct user fees are a better option for the future.

2006 Long-Term Reliability Assessment: The Reliability of the Bulk Power Systems in North America, **North American Electric Reliability Council, October 2006.**
The industry council that sets voluntary standards for electrical-power delivery finds that in the next decade electricity demands will far outstrip planned maintenance and capacity-building by power-generation and transmission companies.

Privatization of Water Services in the United States: An Assessment of Issues and Experience, **Committee on Privatization of Water Services in the United States, National Research Council, 2002.**
A national expert panel summarizes the history of U.S. water and wastewater utilities and dissects pros and cons of various privatization schemes.

Report Card for America's Infrastructure 2005, **American Society of Civil Engineers, March 2005, www.asce.org/reportcard/2005/page.cfm?id=203.**
The most recent in a series of periodic infrastructure assessments by a public-works engineers' group analyzes

infrastructure health sector by sector and state by state and references local media coverage of infrastructure issues. The ASCE gives the overall U.S. infrastructure a grade of "D."

Surface Transportation: Strategies Are Available for Making Existing Road Infrastructure Perform Better, **Government Accountability Office, July 2007.**
Congress' nonpartisan auditing office concludes that greater private-sector involvement, expansion of user

tolls and management reforms including the setting of performance measures would improve America's roads.

Trends in Public Spending on **Transportation and Water Infrastructure, 1956 to 2004, Congressional Budget Office, August 2007.**
Congress' nonpartisan financial-analysis office describes historical patterns in federal and state infrastructure spending for dams, mass transit, railways, air-traffic control and other systems.

For More Information

American Association of State Highway and Transportation Officials, 444 N Capitol St., N.W., Suite 249, Washington, DC 20001; (202) 624-5800; www .transportation.org/. Represents state highway departments.

American Public Works Association, 1275 K St., N.W., Suite 750, Washington, DC 20005; (202) 408-9541; www.apwa.net. Provides information and analysis on infrastructure-related public policy.

American Society of Civil Engineers, 1801 Alexander Bell Dr., Reston, VA 20191-4400; (800) 548-2723; www .asce.org/. Issues a periodic report card on U.S. infrastructure needs and updates a list of infrastructure-related news stories.

American Water Works Association, 6666 W. Quincy Ave., Denver, CO 80235; (303) 794-7711; www .awwa.org. Provides information and public-policy analysis.

Federal Highway Administration, U.S. Department of Transportation, 1200 New Jersey Ave., S.E., Washington, DC 20590; (202) 366-065-; www.fhwa.dot.gov/. Monitors bridge and highway safety and transportation funding needs.

Greatest Engineering Achievements of the Twentieth Century, National Academy of Engineering; www

.greatachievements.org. Web site that details the modern history of infrastructure systems including roads and water systems.

Keston Institute for Public Finance and Infrastructure Policy, School of Policy, Planning, and Development, Marshall School of Business, University of Southern California, Ralph and Goldy Lewis Hall 232, Los Angeles, CA 90089-0626; (213) 740-4120; www.usc.edu/schools/ sppd/keston/index.php. Provides research and analysis on California and national infrastructure issues.

National Council for Public-Private Partnerships, 2000 14th St. North, Suite 480, Arlington, VA 22201; (703) 469-2233; http://ncppp.org/. Organization of businesses and public officials interested in joint initiatives to provide public services.

Reason Foundation, 3415 S. Sepulveda Blvd. Suite 400, Los Angeles, CA 90034; (310) 391-2245; www .reason.org/index.shtml. Libertarian think tank that analyzes transportation-infrastructure problems and issues reports on highways.

Water Environment Federation, 601 Wythe St., Alexandria, VA 22314-1994; (800) 666-0206; www .wef.org/Home. Provides information and public-policy advocacy on water-quality issues

6

Mass Transit Boom

Thomas J. Billitteri

To ease traffic congestion in Manhattan, Mayor Michael R. Bloomberg has proposed a "congestion-pricing" scheme to charge motorists to drive into the most crowded sections of the city on weekdays. The approach has been used in London and Stockholm, Sweden, and is getting close attention in the United States. Above, 42nd Street on Thursday, June 7, 2007.

AP Photo/Richard Drew

From *CQ Researcher*, January 18, 2008.

Tampa officials think they might have the answer to a big headache for travelers: getting to and from the airport without getting tangled in traffic gridlock.

Last fall, Tampa officials showed a video animation of a six-car electric train whisking airport passengers along a 3.5-mile track to their terminal. If built, the train could link to a possible rail network connecting downtown Tampa to St. Petersburg 25 miles away.

Tampa Mayor Pam Iorio, a big supporter of building passenger rail service, urged people to compare the airport system's estimated cost — $190 million to $235 million — to the enormous sums spent to improve the region's Interstate highways.

"In the long run, this is cheaper," she said. Moreover, it would be "congestion-proof."[1]

Similar zeal for public transit is spreading nationwide. Pressed by population growth, rising gas prices, global warming and dizzying levels of traffic congestion, cities are pouring unprecedented amounts of money into "light-rail" systems, commuter trains, rapid-transit buses and other forms of public transportation.

Meanwhile, new ideas and technologies are helping to alleviate congestion in traffic-choked metropolitan areas. "Smart card" fare-collection systems allow electronic transfers among buses, subways and other transit modes. Online travel-planning tools, such as Google Transit and hopstop.com, enable commuters to navigate around cities. Car-sharing networks like Zipcar offer quick short-term access to vehicles when needed, reducing the need for car ownership. Planners are fashioning specially wired "e-burbs," such as La Plata, Md., in suburban Washington, D.C., to ease communication with remote headquarters and make it

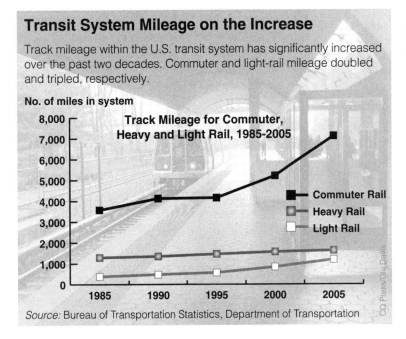

Transit System Mileage on the Increase

Track mileage within the U.S. transit system has significantly increased over the past two decades. Commuter and light-rail mileage doubled and tripled, respectively.

No. of miles in system

Track Mileage for Commuter, Heavy and Light Rail, 1985-2005

- Commuter Rail
- Heavy Rail
- Light Rail

1985 1990 1995 2000 2005

CQ Press/Olu Davis

Source: Bureau of Transportation Statistics, Department of Transportation

Soaring vehicle ownership also fuels congestion. Roughly 30 million vehicles were added to the national fleet between 1990 and 2000, and more than 13 million of those were in households that already had two or more vehicles.[7] In 2000, three of every four commuters got to work by driving alone.[8] Many of those drivers were immigrants of working age (25-45) — people who are on the roads, commuting to jobs.

Some light-rail systems are designed to help invigorate urban areas with "transit-oriented development" — upscale, walkable mixed-use neighborhoods built around transit stations. In 2001 a new streetcar system in Portland, Ore., spurred the transformation of a down-at-the-heels industrial zone, kicking off a surge of interest in streetcars that has spread from Albuquerque, N.M., and Sacramento, Calif., to Columbus, Ohio, and Kenosha, Wis.[9]

Today, 30 to 50 cities are planning, designing or building streetcar projects, according to Charles Hales, a former Portland city commissioner who led that city's streetcar revival. "It's not a fad," declares Hales, now a transit consultant for cities, "or if it is, it's going to be one that lasts a long time."

Advocates cite a recent rise in transit ridership as evidence drivers are ready to park their cars — at least occasionally — and take public transportation. After hitting bottom in the 1970s, trips on trains, trolleys, buses and other transit bounced up and down in a narrow range until the mid-1990s, then began to trend upward. (*See graph above.*) So-called unlinked * passenger trips totaled 9.8 billion in 2005, the most recent year for which data are available, compared with 7.8 billion in 1995, according to the American Public Transportation Association.[10]

easier for workers to telecommute — a move that takes cars off the road.[2]

In addition, the Bush administration has been promoting toll lanes and other "congestion-pricing" tools as part of a broad "congestion initiative" aimed at mitigating gridlock in the nation's transportation systems.[3]

Perhaps the most notable trend, though, is an explosion in urban rail projects, including streetcars and other "light-rail" systems, typically electrically powered trains that share at least part of the right-of-way with cars. (*See "Glossary," p. 150.*) From 2002 through 2006, for instance, 921 new light-rail cars were delivered — up 75 percent from the previous five years. Deliveries of heavier commuter-rail cars rose by more than 200 percent.[4]

Growing traffic congestion is a major problem driving the transit boom. The Texas Transportation Institute estimates that congestion cost drivers 4.2 billion in lost hours and 2.9 billion gallons of wasted fuel in 2005 — the equivalent of 105 million weeks of vacation and 58 fully loaded supertankers.[5] Easing congestion not only relieves aggravated drivers and saves gas but also improves business. A study of the San Francisco Bay Area found that every 10 percent rise in commuting speed increased work output by 1 percent.[6]

---

* "Unlinked" passenger trips denote the number of passengers who board public transportation vehicles. Passengers are counted each time they board vehicles no matter how many vehicles they use to travel to their destination.

The association's president, William W. Millar, says transit's growth has important policy implications. "Public transit helps us meet the needs of people and solve problems that are important at all the levels — to meet national goals like reduction in greenhouse gases, reduce our reliance on foreign energy sources, you name it," he says. It also helps local communities support economic growth and deal with sprawl and a burgeoning elderly population, he adds.

But not all urban transportation experts are so enthusiastic. Critics argue that investing in expensive projects makes little sense outside of traditional urban megalopolises like the New York region, which alone accounts for about 35 percent of the nation's transit ridership. Despite the recent uptick in ridership, they point out, transit accounts for only a fraction of overall urban travel and ridership remains far below the World War II-era peak, when trips approached 25 billion per year.

The rush to build light rail comes in for especially harsh criticism. "There's a huge amount of money wasted on building rail," says Jonathan Richmond, an urban transportation consultant who has written widely on the subject. "It has pathetically low ridership and very little to show for it."

Some argue, too, that local leaders have created unrealistic expectations that transit systems will make urban life easier. "Transit has been sold as a way to solve congestion, air quality and other environmental problems and make places more livable," says Genevieve Giuliano, senior associate dean for research and technology at the University of Southern California's School of Policy, Planning and Development. Under most circumstances — notably, outside of very high-density corridors where demand exceeds the capacity of buses operating at the shortest possible intervals — rapid bus service is as effective as rail transit and far less expensive to build, she says.

Buses Are Top Public Transportation Mode

More than 20 million so-called unlinked* bus rides were taken during the average weekday in 2005, constituting nearly 60 percent of all U.S. public-transportation trips. Heavy rail was a distant second with just under 10 million rides, about 29 percent.

Average Weekday Unlinked Passenger Trips, 2005

Mode	Average weekday unlinked trips	Percent of total
Bus	20.1 million	59.7%
Commuter rail	1.5 million	4.3%
Ferryboat	225,000	0.7%
Heavy rail	9,626,000	28.6%
Light rail	1,304,000	3.9%
Other rail	114,000	0.3%
Paratransit	427,000	1.3%
Trolleybus	367,000	1.1%
Vanpool	61,000	0.2%
Total	**33,641,000**	**100.1%**

Note: Percentages do not total 100 due to rounding; unlinked trips do not add to total due to rounding.

* Unlinked passenger trips are the number of passengers who board public transportation vehicles. Passengers are counted each time they board vehicles

Source: "Public Transportation Fact Book," 58th ed., American Public Transportation Association, May 2007

The list of urban ills that transit is expected to solve is "very long," says Giuliano. "And, unfortunately, it could not possibly live up to that list. But you need the list to get the political support to fund it."

Transit projects also stir passionate debate between "smart growth" enthusiasts — who advocate reducing sprawl by encouraging high-density, close-in development along transit corridors — and those who call such efforts social engineering. "The notion that government agencies should be forcing people into situations because of a belief in how people ought to live in cities is crazy," says Robert Bruegmann, author of the controversial book *Sprawl: A Compact History*, which argues that mobility, choice and privacy are much easier for most people to find in sprawling areas than in densely populated ones.

With the population growing and with most people wedded to their cars, transit will remain an "insignificant factor" on the transportation scene, "short of some completely unforeseen turn of events," says Bruegmann, an expert on urban planning at the University of Illinois, Chicago. "The only real way for transit to work is to completely change our cities," he says. "There's simply no evidence that will occur."

But developers in places like Charlotte, N.C., are betting on a growing demand for public transportation as well as places to live and work near transit lines. They are investing more than $1 billion in projects near stations planned for the region. "We always saw transit as a means, not an end," Planning Director Debra Campbell said. "The real impetus for transit was how it could help us grow in a way that was smart. This really isn't even about building a transit system. It's about place-making. It's about building a community."[11]

As cities continue to build and expand public-transit systems, here are some of the questions being asked by transit supporters and critics:

Will spending more on transit ease congestion?

Of all the benefits touted by public-transportation supporters, none resonates with the public as much as the idea that transit might reduce the mayhem on traffic-choked roads. "Congestion is a scourge on the United States," declares Millar of the American Public Transportation Association. He adds, "A comprehensive public transportation system . . . helps to reduce congestion and saves energy."[12]

It's an oft-repeated mantra among transit advocates.

"I never got caught in a traffic jam on I-96 15 years ago," U.S. Rep. Vernon J. Ehlers, a Michigan Republican from the Grand Rapids area, was quoted by the Michigan Land Use Institute, a "smart-growth" advocacy organization. "Today, you drive in every morning and it's jammed up. . . . With the increase in traffic, what do you think is going to happen? We'll need light rail in 15 years. Public transit is very important for our future."[13]

But transportation specialists hotly debate the notion that public transit can curb traffic congestion. "Attempts to cope with rising traffic congestion by shifting more people to public transit are not going to work," argues Anthony Downs, a senior fellow at the Brookings Institution, a Washington think tank. "The automobile is and will remain a better form of movement for most people in spite of congestion."[14]

The author of the 1992 book *Stuck in Traffic* and the 2004 sequel *Still Stuck in Traffic*, Downs notes that only a fraction of commuting is done by public transit, a proportion that drops even more if New York is excluded. "In 2000 transit provided about 46.6 billion miles of movement while passenger miles traveled [in cars, small trucks and SUVs] . . . totaled about 4 trillion," Downs said. "In fact, transit's share of all passenger miles traveled in the U.S. from 1985 through 2000 averaged only 1.26 percent."[15]

Others also doubt the ability of transit — particularly expensive rail projects — to make a significant dent in congestion in a large urban region. While transit can reduce congestion on some high-density traffic corridors, says Michael D. Meyer, a professor of civil and environmental engineering at the Georgia Institute of Technology and former director of transportation planning and development for Massachusetts, most indicators show it can provide "an almost insignificant impact on congestion" across a metropolitan region.

"If you talk to the elected officials behind the scene," Meyer adds, they will often say they need to build transit systems "because . . . you can't be a world-class city unless you have a rail system, you need to be prepared for a future where gas may be God knows how many dollars per gallon and you need to be more sustainable." But "deep down," Meyer says, most realize that transit "isn't going to reduce congestion" significantly throughout a region.

But transit advocates see things differently. "How did we get into the problem of road congestion?" Millar says. "We spent . . . trillions of dollars building the 4 million miles of public road we have today. You simply cannot build your way out of congestion. Yes, there will be cases when roads need to be expanded or new roads need to be built, but it is a more balanced, multimodal approach that is ultimately going to give us the long-term solutions that we desire. For something like congestion, it's always easy to take a look at the short term and immediate cost and forget that you get a long-term benefit."

Todd Litman, executive director of the Victoria Transport Policy Institute, a research organization in British Columbia that studies international transportation and land use policies, says high-quality rail transit has several "congestion-reduction benefits." It tends to attract passengers who would otherwise drive, reducing congestion on roads running parallel to transit systems.

It stimulates transit-oriented development, thereby reducing vehicle travel. And, it can lower "travel-time costs" incurred by people who shift to transit.

"Even if transit takes more minutes," according to Litman, "many travelers consider their cost per minute lower than driving if transit service is comfortable . . . allowing passengers to relax and work. . . ."[16]

Cities with high-quality transit systems benefit in other ways as well, Litman argues. Energy consumption, pollution and traffic fatalities drop substantially, as do parking-related costs, he says. "The research . . . shows very clearly that households save money by living in a city that has high-quality rail transit," Litman says.

Yet some urban transportation experts argue that even with congestion, cars can be faster and more flexible than rail transit, which operates on fixed routes and schedules.

"If you think in terms of the value of time as being one of the great factors in people's thinking, then public transit is going to have to compete to meet people's time needs", says Alan E. Pisarski, a transportation consultant and the author of a series of statistical reports on commuting trends published by the Transportation Research Board, part of the National Academy of Sciences. "Typically that's one of the weakest areas, in terms of getting people where they want to go when they want to go."

Randal O'Toole, a senior fellow at the Cato Institute, is blunter. "Light rail and streetcars may be cute, but they are S-L-O-W," wrote O'Toole, a longtime transit critic. "Portland's fastest light-rail line averages 22 miles per hour. Portland's streetcar goes about 7 miles per hour. I am waiting to see a developer advertise, 'If you lived here and rode transit home from work, you'd still be sitting on the train.'"[17]

But transit advocates say such analysis is misguided as it pertains to streetcars and congestion. Hales, the former Portland city commissioner, says that some transit projects — including Portland's streetcar line — are actually not meant to diminish congestion, but rather to increase it. The aim, he says, is to boost population density in downtown areas by attracting residents, shoppers and office workers to transit-oriented neighborhoods, making it easy for them to circulate among stops on the streetcar line.

Before Portland added the streetcars to its Pearl District in 2001, Hales says, the neighborhood had fewer

New streetcars in Kenosha, Wis., run on electricity on tracks alongside cars. Madison, Wis., is considering streetcars similar to those in Kenosha.

than half a dozen businesses and only a couple of hundred residential units. Now the streetcar has helped transform the Pearl District into a trendy neighborhood with more than 250 commercial enterprises and 5,000 residences, he says. "So far, there's $3 billion of development within three blocks of the line. It's occurring at two to three times the density and pace that's happening in the rest of downtown."

It's that density and pace — not the lack of congestion — that city leaders wanted to generate with the streetcar line, says Hales, who now is helping to plan streetcars in Sacramento.

"In the United States, the streetcar has been about circulation in busy downtowns, or actually about making them busier," he says. "So I hope that they're causing congestion. That seems like an absurd thing to say, but what's absurd is that the only thing we're measuring when it comes to transit projects is their effect on road congestion. That's a very limited view."

Should government spend less on roads and more on transit?

Linked to the debate over congestion is the question of whether more government money should be flowing to transit projects.

Total government spending on transit grew about 80 percent in inflation-adjusted terms between 1980 and 2004, faster than the 12 percent growth in passenger trips and 24 percent growth in passenger miles traveled on transit, according to the Congressional Research Service.

"It is often pointed out that while transit spending [amounted in 2004] to about 16 percent of all government highway and transit spending and about 14 percent of federal highway and transit capital expenditure . . . only about 2 percent of all trips are made by this mode.

"Even for commuting trips, for which transit is better suited, transit accounts for only 5 percent nationwide, a share that has changed little over the past two decades. Only in two cities, New York and Chicago, does the transit share rise above 10 percent. The effect, according to transit critics, is to shortchange highway spending, thereby causing highway conditions and performance, including highway congestion, to be worse than they would otherwise be."[18]

Many transit advocates argue, however, that the government's transportation funding priorities have been shortsighted. For decades, they say, the government's bias toward funding roads has encouraged sprawling development patterns that have limited Americans' mobility — a problem that is likely to grow more acute as the population ages and people look for alternatives to driving.[19]

"Why do we have [sprawling] development today? Because we followed for 80-some years a single-minded policy of subsidizing the automobile and the road system," says Millar of the American Public Transportation Association. "So you get what you pay for."

"This year we will spend close to $2 trillion on transportation — that's public and private spending," he adds. "Eighty percent of that will be spent on the highway network and private automobiles and things like that. We are simply underinvested in public transit, so that in most communities in America public transit is not a viable option for most Americans."

Public-transportation advocates also cite what they see as a variety of economic benefits from funding transit systems. For instance, investing in transit creates new jobs and can raise real estate values, especially near stations, they say.

David Lewis, senior vice president of HDR/Decision Economics, a division of HDR Engineering, told a congressional subcommittee in 2007 that in Washington, D.C., for the average commercial property of about 30,500 square feet, "each 1,000-foot reduction in walking distance to a Metrorail station increases the value of a commercial property by more than $70,000."

"Transit creates statistically measurable economic value for communities, with benefits extending to both transit users and nonusers," he said.[20]

But critics of transit argue that far from being tilted too far toward highway spending, Washington bureaucrats have actually gone too far in promoting transit.

The Cato Institute's O'Toole argued that "the federal government has created a system that promotes wildly extravagant spending on mass transit and on rail lines in particular."

"[R]ail transit poses three major threats to regional transit service," he wrote. Overruns in construction costs "often force agencies to raise fares or cut service"; rail construction tends to put transit agencies "so heavily in debt that, during recessions and periods of low tax revenue, they are forced to make large cuts in service"; and "rail lines must be rebuilt about every 30 years, and reconstruction costs nearly as much as the original construction."[21]

O'Toole, who is director of the Thoreau Institute, a group in Oregon that says it "seeks ways to protect the environment without regulation, bureaucracy or central control," also argued that current laws give transit and labor unions power to veto federal grant projects. That, he contended, is a "bargain [that] favors high-cost transit systems over low-cost bus systems."

Transit agencies could contract out all their service to provide better service at lower cost, according to O'Toole, but "any plans by transit agencies to do so without a state mandate would be opposed by transit unions and thus would make the agencies ineligible for federal funds."

Worse, O'Toole argued, the Environmental Protection Agency (EPA) subsidizes "anti-highway activist groups to participate in transportation planning initiatives" and ties the funds to mandates for air-quality improvement projects. Both the anti-auto groups and the EPA guidelines, he contended, "favor rail transit over new roads. Most cities would never consider building new rail systems without federal incentives to waste money. In fact, buses can provide the same level of service as trains for far less money."[22]

In a detailed rebuttal of O'Toole's analysis, Litman of the Victoria Transport Policy Institute calls it "outdated and biased, looking backward at the last century . . . rather than looking forward toward the changing transportation needs of the next century."

Although highways showed high annual return on investment during the 1960s when the Interstate Highway System was developed, Litman wrote, this has since declined significantly, a decline likely to continue because the most cost-effective projects have been implemented. Thus, he added, it "makes sense to invest less in roadways and more in public transit to maximize economic returns."[23]

Do toll lanes and other "congestion-pricing" schemes work?

In traffic-choked New York City, Mayor Michael R. Bloomberg last year proposed a controversial method for easing congestion and generating money for transit: Charge motorists to drive into the most crowded sections of Manhattan on weekdays.[24]

Bloomberg's proposal is a form of "congestion pricing," an approach that has been used in London and Stockholm and that is getting close attention in the United States — including strong support from the Bush administration.

Congestion pricing can take many forms, from high-occupancy toll (HOT) lanes to higher tolls during peak traffic hours to fees for driving into certain congested areas of cities. It is similar to the idea behind utility usage: consumers pay for what they use and sometimes pay more when demand is high. "I think there's perception roads are free, but we're paying one way or another," points out Paul Larrousse, director of the National Transit Institute at Rutgers University.

Congestion pricing can be used to manage traffic flows in order to relieve congestion, to encourage the use of mass transit and to generate revenue for transportation projects, including train or bus systems. Transportation experts say taxpayers and local politicians object to congestion pricing less when it is applied to new highways rather than being imposed on existing ones.

Supporters of congestion pricing say it eases bottlenecks on busy traffic corridors and speeds commutes for transit riders who share the road with autos. Grace

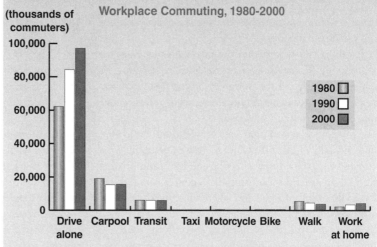

Solitary Commuting Is Most Popular

Nearly 100 million commuters drove alone to work in 2000 — more than a 50 percent increase over the previous 20 years. Carpooling and public transit have remained relatively constant.

Workplace Commuting, 1980-2000
(thousands of commuters)

Source: "Commuting in America III: The Third National Report on Commuting Patterns and Trends," Transportation Research Board, 2006

Crunican, director of the Seattle Department of Transportation, calls congestion pricing "a good tool to manage and rationalize our system."

In Washington state, tolling operations began last summer on the Tacoma Narrows Bridge, using high-speed, nonstop electronic toll collection to help pay for bridge construction, maintenance and operation. This spring the state is expected to open nine miles of HOT lanes on busy State Road 167 using the same technology, with pricing varying with traffic demand.[25]

Elsewhere, congestion pricing has helped ease bottlenecks, encouraged people to shift to transit and raised money for transportation, according to a 2006 report by the U.S. Department of Transportation (DOT).

For example, it said the number of vehicles with more than three passengers rose 40 percent within the first three months of opening priced express lanes on California's SR-91, while ridership on buses and a nearby rail line remained steady. Along Interstate 15 HOT lanes in San Diego, revenues generated by toll-paying drivers helped pay for transportation improvements that contributed to a 25 percent increase in bus ridership, the DOT report said.[26]

"We're faced with increasing growth in population and employment, and there's nowhere near enough [money for roads] to handle the demand, says Meyer, the Georgia Tech professor. The only "clear option," he adds, is to adopt some form of congestion pricing, an approach being considered in his own city of Atlanta, where — despite a large rail system — traffic backups are among the worst in the nation.

Transportation Secretary Mary E. Peters made similar arguments in a newspaper op-ed column last year, in which she criticized the notion of raising gasoline taxes to pay for building and maintaining roads, bridges and other transportation infrastructure.

"In addition to breeding wasteful spending, the gas tax does virtually nothing to reduce the explosion in highway congestion," she wrote, reflecting the Bush administration's long aversion to raising fuel taxes. "Gas taxes are levied regardless of when and where someone drives, creating a misperception that highways are 'free.' "

Peters continued, "[C]harging directly for road use holds enormous promise both to generate large amounts of revenue for reinvestment and to cut congestion. Ultimately, it will allow political leaders to reduce reliance on or even cut the inefficient array of fuel taxes, sales taxes and property taxes that are being funneled into transportation systems nationwide."[27]

But critics of congestion pricing argue that pricing schemes are no substitute for higher fuel taxes to finance crucial maintenance on America's aging roads and bridges.[28] Moreover, they say, congestion pricing hits poor and middle-class commuters the hardest.

"Proponents of congestion pricing say those who don't want to pay or cannot afford to pay increased commuting costs have other choices," Bill Graves, CEO of the American Trucking Associations and a former Republican governor of Kansas, wrote in a newspaper column last year. "But many low-income motorists cannot change their work hours or child-care needs. Not everyone has access to public transit, which can take longer and is less reliable than traveling by car. The motorist's alternative to paying more at the toll booth is to find another route that is time-consuming and merely shifts congestion to other roads and neighborhoods."[29]

Rep. Anthony Weiner, D-N.Y., who represents sections of the boroughs of Queens and Brooklyn, called the Bloomberg congestion-pricing scheme a regressive tax on working middle-class families and small-business owners. "While I applaud the mayor for focusing on a long-term sustainability plan for the city, in this case the cure seems to be worse than the disease."[30]

BACKGROUND

Transit's Golden Age

Like a trolley running on hilly terrain, transit in America has had its steep ups and downs over the years.

The first horse-drawn street railways began service in New York in 1832, and the service had expanded to Cincinnati, Baltimore, Philadelphia and other cities well before the Civil War.[31] Cable cars came on the scene in 1873 in San Francisco and soon appeared elsewhere.[32]

Then in 1888 came a huge advance in public transit: the electric streetcar.[33]

"During the remainder of the golden age of mass transit" in the late 1800s and early 1900s, "the electric streetcar reigned supreme as the common man's magic carpet," wrote transportation expert George M. Smerk. "It was the shaper of cities. Electric lines were much cheaper to build than cable lines and much less costly to operate than animal-powered railways. They were also tokens of progress for most cities and, as such, many lines were built that were uneconomic, merely to show that a city was progressive."[34]

Seattle's new streetcar begins its inaugural run from downtown on Dec. 12, 2007. The 1.3-mile line serves the developing area around the Fred Hutchinson Cancer Research Center. A streetcar passes one of the line's 11 stops every 15 minutes.

CHRONOLOGY

1800-1920 *Early transit services begin on the East Coast.*

1832 Horse-drawn street railways introduced in New York City.

1873 San Francisco starts cable car service.

1880s Electric streetcars introduced.

1892 First Chicago elevated line opens.

1904 New York begins subway service.

1920-1940s *After losing ground to the automobile, transit rebounds.*

1926 Peacetime ridership on public transportation hits 17.2 billion.

1939 General Motors' "Futurama" exhibit at New York World's Fair features automated superhighways.

1940s World War II industrialization and rationing of rubber and gas spur surge in transit ridership to record 23.4 billion passenger trips.

1950s-1960s *Growth of suburbs leads millions of Americans to buy cars and abandon public transportation.*

1961 President John F. Kennedy calls mass transportation a key factor "in shaping community development."

1964 Congress enacts Urban Mass Transportation Act.

1968 Federal government creates Urban Mass Transportation Administration.

1970s-1980s *Transit enters the modern age as big cities begin ambitious urban rail operations.*

1970s Recession and high inflation hit the nation; ridership on public transit reaches an historic low.

1970 National Environmental Policy Act requires environmental impact statements for transit and highway projects that receive federal money.

1972 San Francisco launches first computer-controlled heavy-rail transit agency.

1976 First segment of Metrorail system opens in Washington, D.C., area.

1979 Metropolitan Atlanta Rapid Transit Authority (MARTA) opens its first line.

1981 San Diego Trolley helps to start light-rail renaissance.

1984 Miami completes first part of Metrorail.

1990s *U.S. strengthens role of local planning organizations in charting future needs.*

1990 Americans with Disabilities Act requires transit agencies to serve people with disabilities.

1990 Los Angeles County opens initial light-rail segment.

1990 Clean Air Act imposes tough pollution standards on transit buses.

1991 Landmark Intermodal Surface Transportation Efficiency Act gives states new flexibility in use of transportation funds.

1995 Ridership in public transit begins to show a gradual increase

2000-Present *Policy makers put new focus on reducing congestion.*

2007 Gasoline prices exceed $3 per gallon. . . . Texas Transportation Institute study says traffic congestion creates a $78 billion annual drain on the economy. . . . Interstate 35 West bridge over Mississippi River in Minneapolis collapses, putting renewed focus on highway infrastructure. . . . Congressional Budget Office says highway account in Highway Trust Fund could run out of money by fiscal 2009.

2008 Washington's Metrorail imposes largest fare increase in its history.

New Transit Projects Raise Questions

Do they ignore the needs of less-affluent riders?

As cities rush to embrace new transit projects and congestion-pricing ventures, some experts worry that the poor may be shortchanged. Among the concerns:

- That tax-financed commuter-rail projects may benefit wealthier people, while bus services heavily used by poor people who don't own cars or have jobs near rail stops may suffer;
- That fare policies typically favor peak-hour long-distance commutes to downtowns and other white-collar destinations over shorter, off-peak trips common to low-income people juggling second- and third-shift jobs, child-care duties and other necessities;
- That light-rail systems are often intended to attract discretionary riders — an approach that may come at the expense of improving transportation services generally, including for the poor.

"Transit has two objectives," says Genevieve Giuliano, senior associate dean for research and technology at the University of Southern California's School of Policy, Planning, Policy and Development. "One is solving congestion and air-quality problems. The other is about basic mobility. By putting our eggs in the congestion and air-quality basket, we've made people who need mobility worse off. If we actually paid attention to the quality and availability of service, we'd be doing well toward both of those objectives. But we're going in the wrong direction."

In some localities, grass-roots advocates have taken up the call for greater equity in local transit.

In Los Angeles, the powerful Bus Riders Union gained a federal consent decree a little over a decade ago that forced the city to expand bus service.

In part, too, the equity issue has surfaced because of the way cities have developed. Central cities once were dominated by low-income and working-class residents, but rising urban real estate values and job creation in sprawling suburbs have pushed many of those people into the far reaches of metro areas. That makes their transit needs different from those who commute to downtown professional jobs.

"There's massive gentrification at the center of many cities, very often centered around these transit stops," says Robert Bruegmann, a professor at the University of Illinois, Chicago, who studies urban planning and sprawl. "If you're wealthy enough and you've got a job in the central business district, it provides a wonderful choice."

But, adds Bruegmann, "the lower middle class increasingly has moved out to the outer edge" of cities and relies on autos or buses to get to jobs that frequently are scattered throughout metro areas.

Even bus service, which Bruegmann says can be "long, arduous and uncomfortable," doesn't always meet the needs of the poor and can add to a city's traffic and pollution problems. One solution, he says, is to put more money into "on-demand transit" that allows patrons to summon vans or other transport vehicles exactly when and where they are needed.

In the 1920s the nation's post-World War I economy boomed, and motorized vehicles began to take center stage. Buses became a popular mode of transit. At the same time, the car culture was becoming a central feature of U.S. society, fueling a rivalry between private mobility and public transit that grew more intense as time went on.

By 1929, more than 23 million private and commercial automobiles were registered in the United States — or roughly one car for every five Americans.[35] In prosperous cities such as Detroit and Los Angeles, automobiles were the most common means of transportation for most families.[36]

With more and more people traveling by car, transit's golden age was receding in the rear-view mirror. Then, as the Great Depression (1929-1939) battered the economy, transit ridership plunged. Suddenly tens of thousands of Americans had no jobs to travel to, and leisure trips were a luxury few could afford.

Meanwhile, transit hit another bend in the tracks. Electric utilities had for years provided money and

Some transit experts worry that city transit buses in Los Angeles, above, and other cities will receive less funding than tax-financed commuter-rail projects.

The issue of transit equity can put local politicians in a difficult spot. On one hand, they have a responsibility to ease traffic and pollution problems, and they may also see new systems such as light rail as a way to project a modern, progressive image of their cities. But they also have a duty to serve the transportation needs of all citizens,

including those who may never step foot in a trolley or train.

A few years ago, the *Los Angeles Times* noted the juggling act that faced Los Angeles Mayor Antonio Villaraigosa as he sought to deal with the city's massive transportation challenges. "The mayor wields considerable power over local transit decisions . . . but that power comes fraught with political peril," the newspaper editorialized.

"Invariably the [Metropolitan Transportation Authority board on which the mayor serves] has to choose between pleasing the powerful Bus Riders Union by maintaining and expanding bus service or pleasing business interests and wealthier constituents by expanding the rail system."[1]

Villaraigosa promised to do both, but seeking transit equity hasn't been easy. Last year the *Times* noted that the Metropolitan Transportation Authority was building two rail projects, the Expo Line to Culver City and the Gold Line extension to East Los Angeles, at a $1.5 billion price tag. The MTA said that while rail accounted for only about 17 percent of the city's transit ridership, it was growing.

But critics weren't buying the rail projects. "You see how crowded the buses are, and yet . . . the Gold Line at 4 in the afternoon is practically empty," Joel Kotkin, a Los Angles resident, told the newspaper. "Obviously, the buses are in demand much more than the more expensive stuff, so why aren't we putting more money into the buses?"

Added Kotkin, the author of *The City: A Global History*, "It seems to be unconscionable we could be raising fares so a few yuppies from Santa Monica can go downtown on the subway."[2]

[1] "The Politics of Power: Pumped-up public transit," *Los Angeles Times*, Aug. 13, 2005, p. 18B.

[2] Rong-Gong Lin II and Francisco Vara-Orta, "Transit fare hikes called unwise," *Los Angeles Times*, April 28, 2007, p. 1A.

management expertise to transit systems, but that trend faded after Congress passed the Public Utility Holding Company Act of 1935. The law forced the power companies to start shedding their transit subsidiaries and weakened transit's financial and management underpinnings.[37]

With the advent of World War II, transit ridership turned around. Suddenly, America was back on the job, with factory workers boarding streetcars, subways and buses to get to defense plants making bullets, ships and

airplanes. The government rationed gasoline as well as rubber used in car tires, prompting the fortunate few who owned automobiles to keep them parked. Transit ridership soared to an all-time high of 23.4 billion trips in 1946.[38]

But the transit boom was short-lived. In the postwar economic revival, Americans abandoned transit in droves, choosing instead to get behind the wheel. By 1960, transit ridership had plunged to 9.3 billion trips — 40 percent of its wartime high — eventually falling to an all-time low in 1972 of 6.5 billion trips.[39]

Can a Daily Transit Pass Save the Planet?

Skeptics say claimed benefits are hyped.

Among the many arguments that advocates make for transit, impact on the environment is at or near the top of the list.

"The most powerful weapon you can use to combat global climate change may be a daily transit pass," the American Public Transportation Association (APTA) declared last September in announcing a new study on reducing greenhouse gases.

But critics argue that transit's environmental benefits are vastly overstated. "No big deal," Wendell Cox, a prominent transit critic, wrote in response to transit's claimed role in cutting greenhouse gases.[1]

The study found that in comparison to other household actions that limit carbon dioxide, taking public transportation can be more than 10 times greater in reducing that greenhouse gas.[2]

"A solo commuter switching his or her commute to existing public transportation in a single day can reduce their CO_2 emissions by 20 pounds, or more than 4,800 pounds in a year," the study concluded.

It also said transit helps support higher-density land uses that reduce vehicle travel while helping cut household carbon dioxide emissions.

"The carbon footprint of a typical U.S. household is about 22 metric tonnes per year," the study concluded. "Reducing the daily use of one low-occupancy vehicle and using public transit can reduce a household's carbon footprint between 25 [and] 30 percent."

In testimony to a congressional panel in spring 2007, APTA president William W. Millar said a separate study concluded that public transportation reduces petroleum consumption by 1.4 billion gallons of gasoline annually.[3] That savings results from the fact that transit carries multiple passengers per vehicle, reduces traffic congestion and does not rely exclusively on petroleum to power its fleets, Millar said.

"The transportation sector is the largest consumer of petroleum in the United States — accounting for 67 percent of America's petroleum consumption and 28 percent of our greenhouse gas . . . emissions," Millar stated. "If we are serious about reducing America's 'addiction to oil' and reducing [greenhouse-gas] emissions, then we must also reduce transportation-related petroleum consumption. This will require a multi-pronged approach that must include expanded public transportation use."

Millar told the panel that Congress should take a variety of legislative steps to promote public transportation use, including increasing federal support for transit agencies to buy buses that use new fuel- and pollution-reduction technology, and extending tax credits for alternative fuel vehicles past a scheduled 2009 expiration.

But transit critics argue that public transportation's role in reducing pollution and saving energy is overblown.

Several trends accounted for the downturn — some of them subsidized by the federal government. During the 1950s and '60s, millions of families — often headed by veterans using low-interest government loans — bought homes and moved to the suburbs, places ill-served by transit systems.[40] Along with suburban sprawl came the nation's huge investment in roads, most notably the Interstate Highway System inaugurated during the Eisenhower administration. Automobile registrations doubled in less than a generation from about 40 million in 1950 to 80 million in 1967. In 1973, they broke the 100-million mark and kept climbing, despite an oil embargo, rocketing gas prices and recession.[41]

Meanwhile, other changes in American life discouraged transit ridership. The postwar workweek fell to five days, reducing work travel. While downtowns continued to be major employment hubs, many new jobs sprang up in outlying areas not easily accessible by transit. Retailing shifted from Main Street to suburban malls. Television's growing popularity kept people at home and reduced outings to the movies. And many inner-city neighborhoods, particularly in the Northeast, became blighted, accelerating flight to the suburbs and reducing transit use even more.

An Urban Problem

Not everyone liked the shift to an auto culture. Criticism of cars swelled in the 1950s. In his book on sprawl,

Rail is not "the environmental panacea its advocates promise," contends Randal O'Toole, director of the Thoreau Institute and a senior fellow at the Cato Institute, a Washington think tank. "Light rail may seem to use less energy and emit less pollution than buses or cars. But rail lines must be supplemented by feeder buses that tend to run much emptier than the corridor buses the rail lines replaced. Empty buses mean high energy use and pollution per passenger, so the transit system as a whole ends up consuming more energy and producing more pollution, per passenger, than if it ran only buses."

O'Toole also criticized transit advocates who "brag that transit produces less carbon monoxide than autos. But carbon monoxide is no longer a serious environmental threat. Today's problems are nitrogen oxides, particulates and greenhouse gases. Diesel buses, and rail cars whose electric power comes from burning coal, produce far more of these pollutants than today's automobiles."[4]

Taking aim at the APTA study released in September, Cox said on the Thoreau Institute's Web site that "a full cost accounting of greenhouse gas emissions" would include "emissions from construction of transit and highway systems, construction of vehicles, extraction of fuel for electricity generation and refining, disposal of vehicles and other materials, vehicle maintenance and administrative support."

Cox conceded that without transit use, more congestion would occur near the cores of the largest downtown areas, such as Manhattan and Chicago's Loop. But, he wrote, "the impact would be slight" elsewhere, in "places like Portland,

Phoenix and perhaps Paducah . . . where the great bulk of the nation's traffic-congestion delay occurs."

"[R]elatively tiny (and low-cost) improvements to automobiles will do far more to reduce [greenhouse gas] emissions without reducing people's mobility or forcing people to change their travel habits," Cox wrote.[5]

But Millar has a different view.

"While it is good public policy to require more fuel-efficient automobiles, increasing the use of transit can have a more immediate impact on our nation's transportation fuel consumption," he said. "It could take 20 to 30 years to see a complete turnover of the vehicle fleet. A household does not need to go to the expense of buying a new vehicle to make a difference. They can simply take advantage of the nation's existing bus or rail services to dramatically reduce their carbon footprint."[6]

---

[1] Wendell Cox, "Transit's Role in Reducing Greenhouse Gases: No Big Deal," accessed at http://ti.org/antiplanner/?p=257.

[2] American Public Transportation Association, "Public Transportation Use Substantially Reduces Greenhouse Gases, According to New Study," news release, Sept. 26, 2007. The study is Todd Davis and Monica Hale, "Public Transportation's Contribution to U.S. Greenhouse Gas Reduction," Science Applications International Corp., September 2007.

[3] The study is ICF International, "Public Transportation and Petroleum Savings in the U.S.: Reducing Dependence on Oil."

[4] Randal O'Toole, "Dispelling Transit Myths," *Charlotte Observer*, Oct. 12, 2007, p. 8A. The article is from remarks O'Toole prepared for a John Locke Foundation forum in Charlotte.

[5] Cox, *op. cit.*

[6] American Public Transportation Association, *op. cit.*

Bruegmann of the University of Illinois at Chicago wrote: "Led by upper-middle-class residents of central cities in the Northeast . . . this group took a passionate dislike not just to the automobile but to an entire worldview that they believed supported it. For them the automobile was symptomatic of an individualistic, consumerist society run amuck."[42]

To some degree, these sentiments took hold. By the 1960s, many cities were starting to rethink the idea of autos as a solution to their transportation needs, William D. Middleton, a transportation historian and journalist, wrote in a history of rail transit in America. "While the development of expressways and freeways had encouraged and facilitated a massive shift of urban population to the suburbs,

no amount of road building ever seemed to be enough to meet the growing demand that it created. More and more, too, cities began to recognize the destructive effects of massive highway construction on the urban community."[43]

Pressure also was growing for the federal government to subsidize the struggling urban transit systems. In 1961 President John F. Kennedy signed the Omnibus Housing Act, which provided limited funds for loans and grants for public transportation. In signing the act, Kennedy said mass transportation was "a distinctly urban problem and one of the key factors in shaping community development."[44]

The next year, Kennedy asked Congress to establish a program to help cities build and maintain public transportation systems. "To conserve and enhance values in existing urban areas is essential," Kennedy said in a message to Congress. "But at least as important are steps to promote economic efficiency and livability in areas of future development. Our national welfare therefore requires the provision of good urban transportation, with the properly balanced use of private vehicles and modern mass transport to help shape as well as serve urban growth."[45]

The year after Kennedy's assassination, President Lyndon B. Johnson signed into law the Urban Mass Transportation Act, establishing permanent federal support for transit.[46]

In the 1970s, some of America's largest cities began building big "heavy-rail" systems that changed not only travel habits for tens of thousands of residents and visitors but also the urban landscape itself. San Francisco's Bay Area Rapid Transit District (BART) started passenger service on its regional metro system in 1972; the system now covers 104 miles. The first segment of Washington's Metrorail system opened in 1976, and Atlanta opened the first of its "MARTA" metro system lines in 1979.[47]

The Ronald Reagan administration did not share the Kennedy era's interest in the health and welfare of urban transit systems, however. Reagan sought to reduce federal spending through budget cuts and privatization of programs traditionally supported by government. "The Reagan administration made it clear that it wanted to do away with what it deemed to be the 'unseemly federal role in mass transportation,' " transportation expert Smerk wrote.[48]

Still, Congress ensured that money for rail project was available. "The reason for the interest of Congress is proof of the dictum of longtime Speaker of the House Thomas P. "Tip" O'Neill [D-Mass.] that all politics is local politics," Smerk wrote. " . . . [T]he simple and straightforward fact is that the federal mass-transit program touches virtually every congressional district and at least some of the constituents of every senator."[49]

Light Rails

Not all systems relied on federal money, though. In 1981, using only local money, San Diego became the first U.S. city to open a new light-rail system, using existing tracks.[50] Other cities also opened light-rail lines — Buffalo in 1984, Portland in 1986 (using money from a canceled freeway project) and then Sacramento and San Jose in California.[51] Seattle began a downtown trolleybus tunnel, and Los Angeles started building its subway system.[52]

Transit continued growing steadily in the 1990s, with new emphasis on "intermodalism" — combining various forms of transport, such as roads, rail, buses and ships.

The landmark Intermodal Surface Transportation Efficiency Act of 1991 gave states and localities flexibility to shift federal highway funds to transit projects. Seven years later the law's successor legislation, the Transportation Equity Act for the 21st Century, enabled states and local authorities to shift $8.5 billion from highways to transit — but only $40 million from transit to highways, Rep. James Oberstar, D-Minn., chairman of the House Transportation and Infrastructure Committee, said in 2003. He added, "99.5 percent of the time, states and local authorities choose to flex funds from highways to transit."[53]

By the turn of the 21st century, cities were clamoring to build or upgrade big transit networks and create smaller systems, such as streetcar lines, to help revitalize urban neighborhoods. In 2005, as part of a Transportation Department reauthorization bill, Congress enacted a program to finance projects costing up to $250 million in which the federal portion is $75 million or less. Under that "Small Starts" program transit advocates saw a bright future for projects — such as streetcar systems — designed not just to move people but also to promote smart growth and spark economic development in urban neighborhoods.

Transit and urban planning proponents have complained, though, that the Federal Transit Administration has erected high hurdles for streetcar funding and is using Small Starts to emphasize rapid-transit bus routes over rail. The actions reflect the Bush administration's efforts to focus on easing highway gridlock rather than long-term urban planning.

The administration has "a very arduous and arcane process" for project evaluation with criteria that favor cost- and travel-time savings and congestion relief, says Hales, the former Portland city commissioner. But, he adds, "Does the federal government care about how Americans settle on the landscape and how they live? People are willing to pay handsomely to live in a more sustainable way. If the answer is 'yes,' then the transit issue is one place where the federal government can make a huge difference."

Hales says cities like Portland have come up with much of the money themselves for their streetcar projects, relying largely on local tax money.

"I don't see states and localities falling over themselves to come up with 50 percent of the cost of new highways," he says. "But here are cities waving wads of dollar bills [for streetcar projects], saying, 'We'll pay at least half of these things if [the federal government] will just say yes'. So in terms of leveraging federal dollars, transit projects in general and urban streetcar projects in particular, win hands down if the test is putting local money where the mouth is."

Yet, some analysts question the cost-effectiveness of light-rail projects. Researchers from the St. Louis Federal Reserve Bank wrote that "light rail is kept afloat by taxpayer-funded subsidies that amount to hundreds of millions of dollars each year."

"If light rail is not cost-efficient, nor an effective way to reduce pollution and traffic congestion, nor the least costly means of providing transportation to the poor, why do voters continue to approve new taxes for the construction and expansion of light-rail systems?" they wrote in 2004. Then they answered their own question: One reason is that although the benefits of light rail are highly concentrated, the costs are spread over the tax-paying population. They wrote: "The direct benefits of a light-rail project can be quite large for a relatively small group of people, such as elected officials, environmental groups, labor organizations, engineering and architectural firms, developers and regional businesses, which often campaign vigorously for the passage of light-rail funding."

In St. Louis, they wrote, light rail ran about $6 per taxpayer annually — a sum modest enough to attract voter support even if a transit system is financially inefficient. "A large group of taxpayers facing relatively minimal costs can be persuaded to vote for light rail based on benefits shaped by the interested minority, such as helping the poor, reducing congestion and pollution and fostering development. Even if these benefits are exaggerated and the taxpayer realizes the cost-ineffectiveness of light rail, it is probably not worth the $6 for that person to spend significant time lobbying against light rail."[54]

But transit supporters say rail transit does pay off. A 1999 study underwritten by private-sector business members of the American Public Transit Association found major economic benefits to transit investment. The study concluded, for instance, that in the year following each $10 million in transit capital funding, 314 jobs were created, business sales rose $32 million for each $10

million in transit operations spending, and more than $15 million was saved in transportation costs to highway and transit users for every $10 million invested in transit in major metropolitan areas.[55]

And according to Litman, of the Victoria Transport Policy Institute, the St. Louis analysis ignored many benefits of rail transit and understated the costs of automobile travel on the same corridors.

"[It] would not be cost effective to provide light rail transit service everywhere," Litman wrote, but "when all costs and benefits are considered, rail transit is often the most cost-effective way to improve transportation on major urban travel corridors."[56]

CURRENT SITUATION
Budget Woes

The current transit debates are occurring at a time when gasoline prices are rising, local and federal budgets are limited and policymakers increasingly are concerned about curbing climate change.

This past fall, for example, Congress debated a climate-change bill that would limit carbon emissions and auction the right to emit them, earmarking some of the revenues for transit projects. Others are calling for more of the burden for congestion and new infrastructure to be borne by automobile drivers, by using congestion-pricing and privatizing some roads and bridges — which essentially means charging tolls.

For instance, faced with a $1.8 billion financing gap for road improvements, Indiana negotiated a $3.85 billion deal with a foreign consortium to lease and operate the Indiana Toll Road for 75 years.[57] In Florida, more than 90 percent of new roads since the early 1990s have been toll roads, according to a state Transportation Department spokesman.[58]

Transit funds are limited because the Highway Trust Fund — which provides 80 percent of the federal portion of transit funding and is financed with gasoline taxes — is running out of money. The shortfall is blamed on a variety of causes, including a growing demand for infrastructure projects, an overcommitment of transportation spending by Congress, greater auto fuel efficiency (which reduces fuel-tax revenues) and spiraling infrastructure-construction costs.

A Mass Transit Glossary

Aerial Tramway — Unpowered passenger vehicles suspended from a system of aerial cables and propelled by separate cables attached to the vehicle suspension system. The cable system is powered by engines or motors at a central location not on board the vehicle.

Automated Guideway Transit — Guided transit vehicles operating singly or multi-car trains with a fully automated system (no crew on transit units). Service may be on a fixed schedule or in response to a passenger-activated call button. Automated guideway transit includes personal rapid transit, group rapid transit and people-mover systems.

Bus — Rubber-tired vehicles operating on fixed routes and schedules on roadways, powered by diesel, gasoline, battery or alternative fuel engines.

Commuter Rail — Urban passenger train service for local short-distance travel operating between a central city and adjacent suburbs.

Monorail — Guided transit vehicles operating on or suspended from a single rail, beam, or tube. Monorail vehicles usually operate in trains.

Light Rail — Lightweight passenger rail cars operating singly (or in short, usually two-car, trains) on fixed rails in right-of-way that is not separated from other traffic for much of the way. Light-rail vehicles are driven electrically with power being drawn from an overhead electric line via a trolley or a pantograph.

Heavy Rail — High-speed, passenger rail cars operating singly or in trains of two or more cars on fixed rails in separate rights-of-way from which all other vehicular and foot traffic are excluded.

Source: Federal Transit Administration

The Congressional Budget Office projected last fall that if annual spending continued at authorized levels, the transit account would have enough revenue to cover expenditures until 2012, but the highway account would be exhausted in fiscal 2009.[59] The Senate Finance Committee and the Transportation Department have been considering ways to shore up the fund.[60]

Federal money pays for about half of the $13 billion a year spent on transit construction and equipment, and about 5 percent of operating costs, with the rest of operating costs covered by state and local funds and fare-box revenue. Still, transit supporters are watching the fund carefully.

"We'll be OK until Congress gets around to the next [transportation] authorization bill" in 2009, says Jeffrey Boothe — a Washington lawyer who chairs the New Starts Working Group, a coalition that backs federal funding for transit projects — unless lawmakers move money from the transit account to the highway account as a stopgap measure.

In recent months policymakers and federal officials have been debating what to do about the nation's aging bridges and other infrastructure — prompted in part by last year's Interstate 35 West bridge collapse in Minneapolis. The gasoline tax is central to the debate.

House Transportation Committee Chairman Oberstar wants to raise the federal gasoline tax, which has remained at 18.4 cents per gallon since 1993.[61] He has proposed raising the tax by 5 cents and dedicating the revenue to a new bridge-maintenance fund.[62]

Rep. Peter DeFazio, D-Ore., who chairs the committee's Highways and Transit Subcommittee, also wants a gas-tax hike. "There is a tremendous cost to doing nothing," he said. "We have been treading water, and now we are beginning to sink."[63]

In January a divided National Surface Transportation Policy and Revenue Study Commission urged an increase of up to 40 cents per gallon in federal gas taxes over five years to help fix aging bridges and roads and expand transit, but dissenters — including Transportation Secretary Peters, the commission's chairwoman — disagreed, saying tolls and private investment are better options.

"A dramatic increase in the gas tax does not stand a snowball's chance in hell of passing Congress," said Rep. John Mica, R-Fla., the top Republican on the House Transportation and Infrastructure Committee.[64]

But President Bush opposes any hike in gas taxes, as do fiscal conservatives. "The last thing we should do is

Is "congestion pricing" a good strategy?

YES
Jeffrey N. Shane
Under Secretary for Policy,
U.S. Department of Transportation

From testimony before Subcommittee on
Highways and Transit, June 7, 2007

Taxing fuel consumption rather than road usage disconnects the price travelers pay for using the transportation system — and thus their decisions about when and how much to use it — from the true [cost] of travel. Today a U.S. automobile driver pays the equivalent of about 2-3 cents per mile in federal and state gas taxes.

Yet, when that driver uses a congested roadway during rush hour, he or she imposes between 10 and 50 cents per mile — and in some cases even more — in costs upon the other drivers stuck in traffic by taking space on the highway and exacerbating congestion.

Similarly, gas-tax charges for off-peak travel are not adjusted to reflect the lower costs of such travel. Moreover, the enormous cost savings potentially available from highway pricing are even closer than previously believed. Research in recent years confirms that very small reductions in the number of vehicles using a congested highway facility can produce significant increases in traffic speeds. . . .

By substantially increasing traffic speeds and preventing gridlock, pricing can substantially increase facility "throughput." Counterintuitively, this means that an initial diversion of drivers actually allows for *more* customers to be served in a given time period. . . .

The benefits of congestion pricing extend beyond simply enhancing the speed of travel and the efficiency of highways. Road pricing encourages the use of mass transit, and by reducing traffic delays it can enable the operation of high-speed, reliable, commuter transit services such as bus rapid transit. . . .

Pricing will improve fuel economy and reduce greenhouse gas emissions by cutting out stop-and-go movement and idling. Pricing will encourage more sustainable land-use patterns by providing transparent signals about the true costs of real estate development on the outskirts of major cities.

Finally, congestion-based user charges can dramatically improve project-planning processes by providing clear signals as to where and when the benefits of expanding capacity are likely to exceed the costs of providing that capacity.

As prices rise, the case for adding new lanes or roads becomes increasingly obvious, to say nothing of the new supply of revenues from pricing that can be used to finance the improvements. . . .

NO
James J. Baxter
President, National Motorists
Association

From "Toll Roads: The Slippery Slope,"
www.motorists.org

Conservative and libertarian organizations have been on a campaign to convince the public that the solution to America's traffic problems, primarily congestion, is toll roads.

The arguments for toll roads are laced with references to "free-market principles," "proper pricing," "supply and demand" and "economic incentives." Most of these discussions have become so obfuscated with nonsensical ruminations that important realities are ignored.

A real market-based system has willing sellers, willing buyers and reasonably unfettered competition among sellers and among buyers. The limited role of government in this system is to make sure everyone operates under the same rules. . . .

Ultimately, sellers base their prices on their costs and the demand of buyers who want to buy their products or services. Competing sellers can drive the price down. Competing buyers can drive the price up. . . .

Any highway of any consequence falls flat . . . when it comes to market principles. First, highway corridors are not assembled by willing buyers in competition with other willing buyers who must negotiate with willing (and unwilling) sellers who are also in competition with one another. The "state" identifies the corridor it wants, establishes what it considers to be a politically and judicially acceptable price and condemns the land of those sellers who disagree. This is "market principles" figuratively at the end of a gun barrel.

In the case of so-called "private" toll roads, the state [exclusively] grants its eminent domain . . . authority to the toll road owner. Does this seem like an unfettered, private, market-based system? . . .

Toll road advocates argue that those who use the system the most will pay the most. . . . [B]ut who determines what the buyers should pay? Is it competing sellers of similar services? Do the buyers really have viable alternatives to buy highway services from other sources? . . .

[N]ew highways are not being delayed for lack of money. There are billions of gas-tax dollars being siphoned off for non-highway purposes, or covering the federal deficit. New highways aren't being built because there is significant political opposition to new highways. . . .

Toll roads are an inefficient, counterproductive component of our highway system. They foster corruption, political patronage and detract from needed improvements on the rest of the highway system. . . .

To reduce traffic congestion, certain lanes on I-394 in St. Louis Park, Minn., are restricted around-the-clock to toll-payers, bus riders, carpoolers and motorcyclists. Experts estimate that congestion cost U.S. drivers 2.9 billion gallons of wasted fuel in 2005 — the equivalent of 58 fully loaded supertankers.

raise the federal gas tax, which would give members of Congress a bigger slush fund for earmarks," said Rep. Jeff Flake, R-Ariz.[65]

Transportation Secretary Peters told the House Transportation and Infrastructure Committee that an increase in federal taxes and spending "would likely do little, if anything, without a more basic change in how we analyze competing spending options and manage existing systems more efficiently." She also cited a "disturbing evolution" in the federal transportation program, with more than 6,000 earmarks in the 2005 funding bill, which added up to a "truly staggering" $23 billion.[66]

The fate of the Highway Trust Fund remains unclear. Some observers think it is unlikely that whoever wins next year's presidential election will walk into the White House in early 2009 and raise the federal gasoline tax to

shore up the fund. On the other hand, a funding crisis could spur Washington to pass a stopgap measure to keep the fund from running dry.

"There's nothing like a good crisis to get people's attention," says Meyer, the Georgia Institute of Technology professor. In any event, he adds, "something will have to happen. If nothing else, the construction industry is incredibly powerful. If they're not building those roads and transit systems and all those things they make money on, there will be pressure brought to bear on Congress."

Local Support

The shortfall in federal transportation funds is likely to push states and localities to come up with more money for transit systems, which would mean persuading voters to pay higher sales or gas taxes or tolls.

Boothe, the Washington lawyer, says voters have approved 70 percent of transit-related ballot initiatives in the past five years. "There's a fair amount of support at the local level," he says. "We hope that doesn't cause a withdrawal of funds at the federal level."

Last fall's campaign season underscored the strong — but not always universal — support for transit-related ballot initiatives. In Charlotte, N.C., voters in Mecklenburg County overwhelmingly turned aside an effort to repeal a half-cent transit sales tax that generated $70 million in 2006, allowing the Charlotte Area Transit System to continue with an ambitious plan to expand rail and bus service.[67]

But in the Seattle area, voters in King, Snohomish and Pierce counties rejected the largest transportation tax proposal in Washington state's history. It would have raised the sales tax to 9.4 percent and boosted car-license fees in order to add 50 miles of light rail (at a cost of $30.8 billion), 186 miles of new highway lanes ($16.4 billion) and provide money for a new bridge.[68] Some observers blame the measure's defeat on its high cost and the fact that it combined highway and rail spending, which may have turned off transit supporters who chafe at seeing more highway lanes and cars.

Crunican, the Seattle transportation director, is optimistic about transit in her region. She notes that growth in average vehicle miles traveled in the Puget Sound region leveled off to zero in the past five years and that vehicle ownership statewide has fallen 20 percent in 20 years.

But in last fall's vote, some Seattle-area voters showed that they are carefully judging current transit projects and being cautious about further expansion. "I want to see how the [light-rail line linking downtown Seattle with the Seattle-Tacoma International Airport] goes before we put up 50 more miles of it," teacher Amy Larson said in explaining why she voted against the tax measure.[69] The 15.6-mile Sea-Tac line is scheduled to open in 2009.

Meanwhile, transit projects continue to spread. Dallas, Denver, Orlando, Phoenix, Salt Lake City and Sacramento are building or expanding transit systems, as are other cities.[70] "Everybody talks about smart growth now," said Robert Dunphy, senior resident fellow for transportation and infrastructure at the Urban Land Institute. "These cities understand that transit is a huge part of that."[71]

In Seattle, local leaders are working on several fronts to expand public transit, encourage development near stations and reduce car traffic. Besides the airport line, which is expected to carry 40,000 riders a day, a new streetcar line opened in December to serve a newly developed South Lake Union area, a former industrial zone that planners are making into a biotech hub for the region.

Last year the City Council voted to require Seattle, when building a new road or maintaining an existing one, to try to provide for as many travel modes as possible, including bike lanes, sidewalks and transit. Plus, Seattle-area voters recently passed a measure to boost funding for bus services, the city established a program to provide space for shared cars and it helped start a trip-planning service that seeks to reduce drive-alone commutes. Seattle also has eased the parking-space requirements for developments around light-rail stations and other urban centers.

"If you provide more parking, it just encourages people to drive," said John Rahaim, the city's planning director.[72]

As with many cities, Seattle sees transit as part and parcel of a larger plan that aims not only to bring sanity to the roadways but also to produce a healthier environment and a more economically vibrant economy.

"We're a metropolitan area, and we're trying to manage congestion," says Crunican. "If you're adding new jobs, which we're doing, and you're adding new housing units, which we're doing, you should expect more activity. And then the question is, can you leverage some of that activity onto greenhouse-friendly trips."

Besides, she says, "We're also an overweight society in general, and there's nothing wrong with healthier lifestyles."

OUTLOOK
Proactive Planning

With traffic congestion building, greenhouse gases growing and large numbers of Americans seeking sidewalk-friendly urban neighborhoods, public transit clearly seems to be on a roll. Even so, obstacles lie on the tracks.

For instance, transportation problems need regional solutions, but political and taxing jurisdictions typically stop at city or county borders. Tim Lomax, who heads the national congestion studies undertaken by the Texas Transportation Institute, warned in congressional testimony in 2007 against a "patchwork of solutions to large interregional problems with little to no continuity."

"We already recognize regional and in some cases national consequences flowing from any of a number of transportation problems."[73]

Within localities conflict among proponents of various transportation modes — such as buses, rail and highways — can lead to decision-making gridlock. Better financing techniques, stronger management and greater political courage are needed to bring down the "separate silos" that characterize metropolitan transportation networks and integrate them into smooth-running systems, says Joseph M. Giglio, a business professor at Northeastern University with extensive experience in transportation issues.

"Transit has its own operating mode, financing and engineering basis. And highways do. But the commonality is the customer," he says.

Transit will also have to move in lockstep with land-use planning, experts say. Otherwise, systems designed to reduce sprawl and ease congestion could have the perverse effect of making those problems worse.

And that risk doesn't exist only within cities. "In California, sprawl could increase several orders of magnitude if high-speed train services come to the Central Valley, connecting Bakersfield to [Los Angeles] and Fresno to San Francisco," warned Robert Cervero, chair of the Department of City and Regional Planning at the University of California, Berkeley.

Expanding rail services between metropolitan areas and even between states underscores the need for "proactive state land-use planning and management . . . if the unintended sprawl-inducing consequences of these investments are to be avoided," he wrote.[74]

Ultimately, the outlook for public transit seems mixed. On the one hand, population growth, global warming, traffic gridlock and the desire for new kinds of close-in development suggest significant demand for rail lines, rapid buses and other kinds of transit. On the other hand, tight financing, sprawl and Americans' reluctance to leave their cars present significant obstacles.

In the end, cities face difficult choices in how to allocate their precious transportation dollars.

As Pisarski, the author of the Transportation Research Board's exhaustive studies on commuting, says, "One question I always ask is, what percent of a problem am I solving with what percent of my resources?"

NOTES

1. Steve Huettel, "Airport board takes light rail for a virtual ride," *The St. Petersburg Times*, Nov. 2, 2007, wwww.sptimes.com.

2. For background see Kathy Koch, "Flexible Work Arrangements," *CQ Researcher*, Aug. 14, 1998, pp. 697-720.

3. In 2006, the U.S. Department of Transportation began a broad initiative, the "National Strategy to Reduce Congestion on America's Transportation Network," to help state and local governments develop strategies to deal with congestion. Approaches related to road congestion include "Urban Partnership Agreements" with metro areas that in part encompass plans for congestion-pricing demonstrations and expansion of rapid bus services. For background, see: http://transportation.house .gov/Media/File/Highways/20070607/SSM_HT_ 6-7-07.pdf.

4. American Public Transportation Association, "Public Transportation Fact Book," 58th Edition, May 2007, p. 19. Data are from *Railway Age*, 2006 totals are preliminary.

5. Press release, "Annual study shows traffic congestion worsening in cities large and small," Texas Transportation Institute. Data are from the institute's 2007 Urban Mobility Report, based on 2005 data, the latest available.

6. Robert Cervero, "Economic Growth in Urban Regions: Implications for Future Transportation,"

prepared for Forum on the Future of Urban Transportation, Eno Transportation Foundation, Washington, D.C., December 2006, p. 14.

7. Alan E. Pisarski, "Commuting in America III," Transportation Research Board, 2006, p. 38.

8. *Ibid.*, p. 62.

9. For background, see Alan Greenblatt, "Downtown Renaissance," *CQ Researcher*, June 23, 2006, pp. 553-576.

10. American Public Transportation Association, *op. cit.*, p. 12; 2005 data are preliminary.

11. Zach Patton, "Back on Track," *Governing*, June 2007.

12. "Statement on Texas Transportation Institute's Congestion Report by American Public Transportation Association President William W. Millar," www.apta .com, Sept. 17, 2007.

13. Andy Guy, "Looking for Modern Transit," Great Lakes Bulletin News Service, Michigan Land Use Institute, Jan. 27, 2006. For background, see Mary H. Cooper, "Smart Growth," *CQ Researcher*, May 28, 2004, pp. 469-492.

14. U.S. General Accounting Office, "Surface Transportation: Moving Into the 21st Century," May 1999, p. 24.

15. Anthony Downs, "How Real Are Transit Gains?" *Governing*, March 2002.

16. Todd Litman, "Smart Transportation Investments II: Reevaluating the Role of Public Transit for Improving Urban Transportation," Victoria Transport Policy Institute, Sept. 10, 2007.

17. Randal O'Toole, "Debunking Portland: The Public Transit Myth," TCSdaily.com, Aug. 15, 2007.

18. William J. Mallett, "Public Transit Program Issues in Surface Transportation Reauthorization," Congressional Research Service, Sept. 10, 2007.

19. By 2025, a fifth of Americans will be 65 or older, many of them unable to drive, the American Public Transportation Association states in its "Public Transportation Fact Book," May 2007. It cites an AARP/Surface Transportation Policy Project study that found that half of non-drivers age 65 and over stay home on any give day in part because they don't have transportation options. The study cited is

Linda Bailey, Surface Transportation Policy Project, "Americans: Stranded without Options," April 2004.

20. Testimony before House Committee on Transportation and Infrastructure, Subcommittee on Highways and Transit Implementation of New Starts and Small Starts Program, May 10, 2007.

21. Randal O'Toole, "A Desire Named Streetcar: How Federal Subsidies Encourage Wasteful Local Transit Systems," Cato Institute, Jan. 5, 2006.

22. Cato Institute news release, "Federal Subsidies Derail Local Train Systems," Jan. 5, 2006.

23. Todd Litman, "Responses to 'A Desire Named Streetcar,' Victoria Transport Policy Institute, Feb. 1, 2006.

24. Michael M. Grynbaum, "New York Pitches 'Congestion Pricing' to Federal Officials,' *The New York Times*, June 26, 2007, p. 4B.

25. Testimony of Craig J. Stone, deputy administrator, Washington State Department of Transportation's Urban Corridors Office, U.S. House of Representatives Committee on Transportation and Infrastructure, Subcommittee on Highways and Transit, "Congestion and Mobility Hearing," June 7, 2007.

26. Federal Highway Administration, U.S. Department of Transportation, "Congestion Pricing: A Primer," December 2006.

27. Mary E. Peters, "The Folly of Higher Gas Taxes," *The Washington Post*, Aug. 25, 2007, p. A15.

28. For background, see Marcia Clemmitt, "Aging Infrastructure," *CQ Researcher*, Sept. 28, 2007, pp. 793-816.

29. Bill Graves, "Add roads, not tolls," *USA Today*, www.usatoday.com, Feb. 27, 2007.

30. Press release from office of Anthony D. Weiner, "Weiner Applauds Mayor for Thinking Big, But Says Put the Brakes on Regressive Congestion Tax," April 21, 2007.

31. William D. Middleton, *Metropolitan Railways: Rapid Transit in America* (2003), pp. 1-2.

32. Brian J. Cudahy, *Cash, Tokens and Transfers: A History of Urban Mass Transit in North America* (1990), p. 22.

33. George M. Smerk, *The Federal Role in Urban Mass Transportation* (1991), p. 35.

34. *Ibid.*

35. Federal Highway Administration, www.fhwa.dot.gov/ohim/summary95/mv200.pdf.

36. Robert Bruegmann, *Sprawl: A Compact History* (2005), p. 130.

37. Smerk, *op. cit.*, p. 43.

38. American Public Transportation, *Public Transportation Fact Book 2007*, p. 11.

39. American Public Transportation Association, *op. cit.*

40. The 1944 GI Bill of Rights provided low-interest home loans for veterans. For background, see Peter Katel, "Wounded Veterans," *CQ Researcher*, Aug. 31, 2007, pp. 697-720.

41. Federal Highway Administration, *op. cit.*

42. Bruegmann, *op. cit.*, p. 130.

43. Middleton, *op. cit.*, p. 107.

44. Federal Transit Administration, "The Beginnings of Federal Assistance for Public Transportation," accessed at www.fta.dot.gov.

45. *Ibid.*

46. Middleton, *op. cit.*, p. 107.

47. *Ibid.*, p. 243.

48. Smerk, *op. cit.*, pp. 6-7.

49. *Ibid.*, p. 241.

50. Cudahy, *op. cit.*, p. 202; and Middleton, *op. cit.*, p. 151.

51. *Ibid.*, p. 152.

52. Smerk, *op. cit.*, p. 241.

53. Remarks of James Oberstar, "Intermodal Transportation: The Potential and the Challenge," Center for Transportation Studies, University of Minnesota, March 16, 2003, accessed at www.cts.umn.edu/Events/ObserstarForum/203/Speech.html.

54. Molly D. Castelazo and Thomas A. Garrett, "Light Rail: Boon or Boondoggle?" Federal Reserve Bank of St. Louis, 2004.

55. Cambridge Systematics Inc. with Economic Development Research Group, "Public Transportation and the Nation's Economy," October

1999. The study was underwritten by the private sector business members of the American Public Transit Association, the predecessor of the American Public Transportation Association, Washington, D.C.

56. Todd Litman, "Evaluating Public Transit Benefits in St. Louis," Victoria Transport Policy Institute, July 27, 2004.

57. Jim Abrams, The Associated Press, "Frozen gas tax leads to toll roads," www.usatoday.com, May 20, 2007.

58. *Ibid.*

59. Statement of Robert A. Sunshine before the Committee on the Budget, U.S. House of Representatives, "Public Spending on Surface Transportation Infrastructure," Oct. 25, 2007.

60. Abrams, *op. cit.*

61. Humberto Sanchez and Lynn Hume, "Report on Traffic's Economic Drain Prompts Calls for Gas Tax Hike," *The Bond Buyer*, Sept. 19, 2007, p. 33.

62. Jim Snyder, "Democrats, White House diverge on gas tax," *The Hill*, Sept. 6, 2007.

63. Sanchez and Hume, *op. cit.*

64. The Associated Press, "Transit Panel Urges Gas Tax Increase," *The New York Times*, Jan. 15, 2008.

65. Kevin Bogardus, "Flake joins Bush administration in opposition to gas tax increase," *The Hill*, Sept. 7, 2007, p. 13. For background, see Marcia Clemmitt, "Pork Barrel Politics," *CQ Researcher*, June 16, 2006, pp. 529-552.

66. Statement of Mary E. Peters before House Committee on Transportation and Infrastructure, Sept. 5, 2007.

67. Steve Harrison, "Tax supporters, foes surprised by margin of victory," *Charlotte Observer*, Nov. 7, 2007, p. 1A.

68. Larry Lange, "Proposition 1: Voters hit the brakes," *Seattle Post Intelligencer*, Nov. 7, 2007, updated Nov. 9, 2007.

69. *Ibid.*

70. Patton, *op. cit.*

71. *Ibid.*

72. Keith Schneider, "Seattle and Other Cities' Mantra: Improve Transit, Reduce Traffic," *The New York Times*, Oct. 24, 2007.

73. Testimony before House Committee on Transportation and Infrastructure Subcommittee on Highways and Transit, "The Many Dimensions of America's Congestion Problem — And a Solution Framework," June 7, 2007.

74. Cervero, *op. cit.*, p. 17.

BIBLIOGRAPHY

Books

Bruegmann, Robert, *Sprawl: A Compact History*, University of Chicago Press, 2005.
An urban planning expert at the University of Illinois, Chicago, argues that many problems blamed on sprawl, such as traffic congestion, "are, if anything, the result of the slowing of sprawl and increasing density in urban areas."

Cudahy, Brian J., *Cash, Tokens, and Transfers: A History of Urban Mass Transit in North America*, Fordham University Press, 1990.
Cudahy spans American transit history from horse-drawn rail cars to automated transit systems.

Middleton, William D., *Metropolitan Railways: Rapid Transit in America*, Indiana University Press, 2003.
This oversize book by a noted authority traces the history of rapid transit and includes a useful appendix that maps metro and light-rail transit lines in major North American cities.

Smerk, George M., *The Federal Role in Urban Mass Transportation*, Indiana University Press, 1991.
The director of the Institute for Urban Transportation at Indiana University traces the long history of transit policy and explores both its successes and failures in intricate detail.

Articles

Bernstein, Sharon, and Francisco Vara-Orta, "Near the rails but still on the road," *Los Angeles Times*, June 30, 2007.

This article analyzes the results of the Los Angeles region's efforts to wean people away from autos through transit-oriented residential development.

Patton, Zach, "Back on Track: Sprawling Sun Belt cities discover a new way to grow," *Governing*, June 2007.
While focusing on Charlotte, N.C.,'s ambitious transit plans, Patton writes: "Sun Belt cities from Orlando to Phoenix are building out light-rail systems, in an historic break from the car-bound past."

Pucher, John, "Renaissance of Public Transport in the United States?," *Transportation Quarterly*, winter 2002.
A professor in the Department of Urban Planning at Rutgers University traces developments in public transit during the 1990s.

Reports and Studies

Hennessey, Bridget, Jason Jordan, Mary Karstens and Stephanie Vance, "Transportation Finance at the Ballot Box," Center for Transportation Excellence, 2006.
The report provides details on transportation ballot measures since 2000, plus five local case studies.

Maguire, Meg, Kevin McCarty and Anne Canby, "From the Margins to the Mainstream: A Guide to Transportation Opportunities in Your Community," Surface Transportation Policy Partnership, Final Edition, 2006.
Planning, community design and transportation options for communities are among the topics covered.

Heffernan, Kara, ed., "Preserving and Promoting Diverse Transit-Oriented Neighborhoods," Center for Transit Oriented Development: A collaboration of the Center for Neighborhood Technology, Reconnecting America, and Strategic Economics, October 2006.
A study sponsored by the Ford Foundation offers recommendations for creating more mixed-income, mixed-race housing near transit stations.

"Mobility 2030: Meeting the Challenges to Sustainability," World Business Council for Sustainable Development, 2004.
A report based on the work of a dozen international automotive and energy companies concludes "that the way people and goods are transported today will not be sustainable if present trends continue."

"National Strategy to Reduce Congestion on America's Transportation Network," U.S. Department of Transportation, May 2006.
The plan calls for more-efficient bus systems, new private-investment opportunities in transportation infrastructure, a reduction in freight bottlenecks and other steps to relieve congestion.

Pisarski, Alan E., "Commuting in America III," Transportation Research Board, The National Academies, 2006.
The third report in a series going back 20 years gives a detailed snapshot of commuting patterns and trends.

"Public Transportation: Benefits for the 21st Century," American Public Transportation Association, 2007.
The report surveys in great detail what it calls "the benefits that public transportation brings to individuals, communities and our nation as a whole."

"Public Transportation Fact Book," 58th Edition, American Public Transportation Association, May 2007.
This thick compendium of transit data covers modes ranging from trolleys to ferryboats and vanpools.

Davis, Todd, and Monica Hale, "Public Transportation's Contribution to U.S. Greenhouse Gas Reduction," Science Applications International Corp., September 2007.
This technical study examines the growth in pollution from vehicles and the potential role of public transportation in reducing it.

For More Information

American Public Transportation Association, 1666 K St., N.W., Suite 1100, Washington, DC 20006; (202) 496-4800; www.apta.com. Represents public bus and commuter rail systems and others involved in transit.

Center for Transportation Excellence, 1640 19th St., N.W., #2, Washington, DC 20009; (202) 234-7562; www .cfte.org. Policy research center on public transportation.

Community Transportation Association of America, 1341 G St., N.W., 10th Floor, Washington, DC 20005; (800) 891-0590; www.ctaa.org. Advocates for effective public and community transportation and improved mobility.

Federal Transit Administration, 1200 New Jersey Ave., S.E., 4th & 5th Floors — East Building, Washington, DC 20590; (202) 366-4043. Administers federal funding for public transit systems.

Reason Foundation, 3415 S. Sepulveda Blvd., #400, Los Angeles, CA 90034; (310) 391-2245. www.reason .org. Research organization that studies market-oriented transportation policies.

Reconnecting America, 436 14th St., Suite 1005, Oakland, CA 94612; (510) 268-8602; www.reconnecting america.org. Advocates integrating transit into communities and hosts the Center for Transit-Oriented Development.

Surface Transportation Policy Partnership, 1707 L St., N.W., Suite 1050, Washington, DC 20036; (202) 466-2636; www.transact.org. Nonprofit coalition that advocates transportation options that improve public health, the economy, the environment and social equity.

Taxicab, Limousine & Paratransit Association, 3200 Tower Oaks Blvd., Suite 220, Rockville, MD 20852; (301) 984-5700; www.tlpa.org. Trade association for taxi companies, airport shuttles and other passenger transporters.

University Transportation Center for Mobility, Texas Transportation Institute, Texas A&M University System, 3135 TAMU, College Station, TX 77843-3135; (979) 845-2538; http://utcm.tamu.edu.Studies congestion management and other transportation issues.

Victoria Transport Policy Institute, 1250 Rudlin St., Victoria, BC V8V 3R7 (Canada); (250) 360-1560; www .vtpi.org. Independent research organization that produces useful background on transportation issues.

7

Property Rights

Kenneth Jost

Nissan President Carlos Ghosn celebrates with employees at the opening of the company's assembly plant in Canton, Miss., in May 2003. Advocates for municipalities and states say eminent domain enables private companies to build facilities like the Nissan plant, which provide jobs and crucial tax revenues. Critics say the burden of land condemnation mostly falls on racial and ethnic minorities, the elderly and the poor.

From *CQ Researcher*,
March 4, 2005 (updated May 15, 2006).

Susette Kelo thinks of the run-down 19th-century Victorian cottage that she bought for $52,000 in 1997 as her "diamond in the rough."

The clapboard house in New London, Conn., had been vacant for 10 years. Weeds and overgrown brush covered the porch. But Kelo loved the view of the Thames River and New London Harbor and the close-knit, working-class Fort Trumbull neighborhood, where she had lived as a youngster.

Nine years later, Kelo's house has been lovingly renovated, but the neighborhood has changed just as dramatically. Now Kelo also can see a modernistic global drug-research facility, celebrated when Pfizer opened it in 2001 as a much-needed shot in the arm for the financially distressed city.

But if Kelo looks in another direction, she mostly sees desolation. The old houses from her childhood are almost all gone. A city-chartered development company demolished them under the power of eminent domain with grand hopes of turning the bull-dozed land into upscale commercial and residential developments and public space.

The city and the New London Development Corp. (NLDC) say the planned developments will help revitalize the one-time whaling center, badly hurt by the loss of manufacturing jobs to the Sun Belt or beyond and the migration of residents to the surrounding suburbs. Indeed, officials predict the developments will produce up to 4,000 new jobs and $1 million or more annually in property taxes for the city of 26,000.

But Kelo and eight other owners are refusing to clear out. In a legal challenge that went all the way to the U.S. Supreme Court,

Some Courts Bar Condemnation to Boost Taxes

Cash-strapped cities seeking economic-development projects increasingly are using their power of eminent domain to condemn property to help developers assemble large tracts of land for commercial or residential ventures. But property owners are fighting back, and nine state supreme courts so far have forbidden cities from condemning property just to increase the tax base.

How State Supreme Courts Have Ruled On Condemnations to Boost Tax Revenues

Not permitted	Permissible under certain circumstances	Permissible
Arkansas	Delaware	Connecticut
Florida	Massachusetts	Kansas
Illinois	New Hampshire	Maryland
Kentucky		Minnesota
Maine		New York
Michigan		North Dakota
Montana		
South Carolina		
Washington		

Source: Institute for Justice, Sept. 17, 2004

they claim the NLDC is abusing the well-established power of eminent domain by taking property not to benefit the public but to transfer their cherished homes to private interests.

"They're trying to take the land away from us and give it to a private developer who can build something and pay more taxes than we can," Kelo says. "If they can do that to us, they can do it to anybody anywhere."

The Supreme Court case — *Kelo v. City of New London* — was the most ambitious of many recent challenges to the growing use of the power of eminent domain, which traditionally has been used to build government facilities such as roads or schools.[1] Lately, however, governments have been using eminent domain to facilitate private economic development. Critics say the practice violates the Fifth Amendment of the Bill of Rights, which permits the "taking" of private property for "public use" as long as the government pays the owner "just compensation."

State and local government groups say eminent domain has been used since Colonial times to benefit private development and is needed more than ever today to help struggling cities. They point to well-recognized urban landmarks — including New York City's former World Trade Center — as products of cities' use of eminent domain.

"It's a tool that the Constitution grants us," says David Parkhurst, principal legislative counsel for the National League of Cities, which filed a brief on New London's side in the Supreme Court case. "It's a powerful tool, and it's one that [the league] believes must be used prudently."

Critics, however, say using eminent domain for private economic development goes beyond what the Framers of the Constitution envisioned — and that its use in New London and other cities has been anything but prudent.

"The fundamental question is whether there is going to be any limit to eminent domain under the Fifth Amendment," says Scott Bullock, a lawyer with the Washington-based Institute for Justice, a libertarian law office that represented Kelo before the Supreme Court. Under the cities' view, he says, any property can be taken if it can be put to a more "economically beneficial" use.

"If that is accepted, then that does sound the death knell of the 'public use' requirement," Bullock concludes. "Every home will be more economically beneficial, as they use the term, if used as a Home Depot."

"That's kind of a scare tactic," counters Laura Lucero, a lawyer in New Mexico with the American Planning Association, which filed a brief on New London's side. "I don't think you see city councils and local legislative bodies swooping down on any property owner. What they're doing is very methodically preparing a plan and addressing the needs of the entire community through a planning process that is open, that all property owners can participate in, to see what the problems are and what some of the solutions might be."

An Institute for Justice report, however, counts more than 10,000 condemnations filed or threatened for the benefit of or use by private parties over the five-year period 1998-2002. The hundreds of cases described in the institute's report make clear that the use of eminent domain for economic development is common — and commonly controversial. Municipal governments readily resort to eminent domain to help make way for sports stadiums or arenas, to save and renovate historic properties, to provide parking or other support for public venues and — most controversially perhaps — to help companies or developers assemble large tracts of contiguous land for profit-making commercial or residential ventures.

Cash-strapped cities often work hand in glove with the developers in hopes of boosting the property-tax base. Home or business owners who stand in the way of the supposed progress often get short shrift from their elected representatives or the various redevelopment authorities set up to facilitate such plans.

"Eminent domain for private use happens all over the country," the report concludes, "and local governments and developers regularly force residents and businesses out by threatening eminent domain."[2]

For the Supreme Court, the *Kelo* case represented the first detailed re-examination of the use of eminent domain in urban settings since a controversial 1954 decision that upheld the bulldozing of thousands of homes and businesses in a supposedly "blighted" section of Washington, D.C.[3] In the half-century since then, "urban renewal" has come to be viewed more critically because of its effect on established neighborhoods and minority and other low-income groups.

In addition, a diverse property-rights movement has emerged to challenge actions at all levels of government that limit what home, business or land owners can do with their property.[4] The Supreme Court has given property owners partial victories in a few of those cases.

Property rights advocates saw *Kelo* as a chance for a major victory, but the court's ruling proved instead to be a major disappointment. By a 5-4 vote, the court in June 2005 rejected any federal constitutional prohibition on use of eminent domain for private economic development. "Promoting economic development is a traditional and long accepted function of government," Justice John Paul Stevens wrote for the majority.

Institute for Justice

Mississippi property owner Lonzo Archie Jr. successfully fought state efforts to take his home and 24 acres to enable Nissan to build a new truck manufacturing plant in Canton. Nissan redesigned the facility so Archie could keep his land.

The ruling prompted a strong dissent, written by Justice Sandra Day O'Connor, and touched off waves of criticism from politicians and the general public. Property-rights advocates emphasized the court's acknowledgment that states could themselves limit the use of eminent domain and immediately stepped up lobbying in state capitals and in Washington for legislative restrictions on the practice.

As municipal governments, planning groups and property-rights advocates consider the Supreme Court's decision, here are some of the major questions being debated:

Should local governments use eminent domain to acquire private property for economic development?

When New York and New Jersey drew up plans more than 40 years ago for the World Trade Center, the enabling legislation authorized the Port of New York

A City Reborn . . . or Neighborhood Destroyed?

When the New London, Conn., City Council considered the proposed redevelopment of the Fort Trumbull neighborhood, Councilman Lloyd Beachey saw the project not as an economic boon for the city but a personal tragedy for the home and business owners to be displaced.

In a crowded high school auditorium on Jan. 18, 2000, Beachey explained his vote against the plan by listing some of the working-class families who would be forced to move. "I said I was voting in their favor so they could keep their homes," Beachey recalls today.

But there was no stopping his colleagues' desire to upgrade the area adjacent to the Pfizer pharmaceutical company's big research facility, then under construction. With the promise of $70 million in bond financing from the state's Department of Community and Economic Development, the council voted 6-1 to approve a plan calling for a hotel, marina, new residences and public spaces on 90 acres.

The council designated the city-chartered New London Development Corp. (NLDC) to oversee the plan and to use the governmental power of eminent domain to acquire property from any home or business owners who declined to sell.

Six years later — after setbacks and delays for the project and a legal challenge then pending before the U.S. Supreme Court — local opposition appears to be stronger. A poll of New London residents conducted in December 2004 for the local newspaper, *The Day*, found that a majority — 53 percent — opposed the use of eminent domain for the Fort Trumbull redevelopment compared to 39 percent in favor.[1]

The court fight began with a suit filed in Connecticut Superior Court in December 2000 by six families and a small real-estate partnership that owned 15 of the 115 parcels designated for redevelopment. In interviews before the Supreme Court arguments, several residents spoke fondly about the neighborhood and critically of the effort to take their homes for private development. "This is just government-sanctioned thievery as I see it," said Matthew Dery, a home-delivery sales manager for the newspaper.

"We feel like what they want this property for is totally wrong," said Michael Cristofaro, a computer engineer whose nephews now want to remain in his parents' former home. "They're giving it to somebody else."

Both Dery and Cristofaro have long family ties to the neighborhood and the city's Italian-American community. Another of the plaintiffs, Bill von Winkle, has owned three buildings in the neighborhood since 1984, all now rented out as investment properties. One of the buildings housed the Fort Trumbull Deli, which von Winkle took over from an Italian-American family.

Today, the neighborhood — essentially, a peninsula at the mouth of the Thames River and New London Harbor — is almost all rubble. "It's pretty desolate," says lead plaintiff Susette Kelo, a nurse whose quaintly

Authority to use eminent domain to assemble the property. Landowners to be displaced challenged the project in court, but New York's highest court unanimously upheld the port authority's right to take private property to promote the port's "economic well-being."[5]

Now, more than four years after the 9/11 terrorist attacks destroyed the twin towers, a massive rebuilding program is under way. And the government-chartered Lower Manhattan Development Corporation again expects to use what critics call the "despotic power" of eminent domain in the reconstruction. *

---
* More than 200 years ago, Justice William Paterson, sitting as a circuit justice, wrote in *Vanhorne's Lessee v. Dorrance* (1795) that the "despotic power" of taking private property "exists in every government" and that "government could not subsist without it."

State and local governments, planning groups and others say the World Trade Center exemplifies a practice well established in the United States at least since the construction of the Erie Canal in the early 19th century. "It's very clear that early on in our constitutional jurisprudence the Supreme Court recognized that eminent domain can be used for economic ends," says Timothy Dowling, a lawyer with Community Rights Counsel, a Washington-based public-interest law firm that helps state and local governments defend land-use laws.

Some property-rights advocates dispute that reading of U.S. history. "Throughout the 19th and most of the 20th century, it's simply not true that public use was anything that the legislature said it wanted it to be," says Ilya Somin, an assistant professor at George Mason University School of Law in Arlington, Va.

decorated Victorian cottage overlooks the harbor.

Attorneys representing the city countered that New London contended that the holdout property owners were putting their interests above the city's need for jobs and tax revenue that the development plan will generate. "Plaintiffs would have us be in the thrall of one or two residents who don't agree with the plan," says Edward O'Connell, the private attorney who represents NLDC.

The plaintiffs all professed optimism in advance of the Supreme Court arguments in February 2005. When the court ruled in the city's favor in June, officials voiced satisfaction, but Kelo vowed to continue resisting. "They're going to have to drag me out of here kicking and screaming," she told the *Hartford Courant.*[2]

The resistance has proved to be availing. Despite the legal victory, the city and NLDC made no immediate moves to evict the dissident owners, citing the political controversy and financial uncertainties resulting from the protracted fight. "Winning took so long," Mayor Jane Glover told *The New York Times* in November 2005, "that the plan may not be as viable in 2005 or 2006 or 2007."[3]

Matthew Dery and his wife Susan are fighting to save their New London home.

City council elections in November also brought in two new members who wanted to try a new approach. With a new political climate, the council in February 2006 voted 7-0 to instruct the city's legal director to determine whether the development plan could be revised to allow the remaining half-dozen property owners to cluster their properties on a single block in the neighborhood.

"For the first time in this ongoing saga we are considering and asking our attorneys to explore the possibility of occupancy on the peninsula as a way of settling the dispute," Mayor Beth Sabilia, who rotated into the position in January, told the *Times.* The plan would likely require Kelo to move her house to allow for construction of the planned road. Still, Kelo called the proposal "a step in the right direction."[4]

---

[1] The poll of 600 residents was conducted for the newspaper in December 2004 by Research 2000 of Rockville, Md. The margin of error was plus or minus 4 percent.

[2] Lynne Tuohy, "High Court: City Can Seize Homes to Boost Economy," *The Hartford Courant,* June 24, 2005, p. A1.

[3] Quoted in William Yardley, "After Eminent Domain Victory, Disputed Project Goes Nowhere," *The New York Times,* Nov. 21, 2005, p. A1.

[4] William Yardley, "Compromise in Connecticut Property Seizure Case," *The New York Times,* Feb. 8, 2006, p. B5.

Somin, who wrote a brief supporting *Kelo,* says eminent domain historically has been used to take land for the government itself to own or to be given to a closely regulated public utility, such as railroads. "It was only in the last 40-50 years that courts have gone away from that to a large extent," he says.

Property-rights advocates say barring the use of eminent domain for private economic developments would fulfill the basic purpose of the Fifth Amendment's "Takings Clause" to protect private-property rights except when the taking is for governmental purposes. "Private takings are unconstitutional," Bullock says. "You can't have economic development at the expense of constitutional rights."

Critics also say that many of the projects that rely on eminent domain fall short of their promised goals or fail

to even make it to completion. In the most notorious example, the city of Detroit cleared much of the working-class Poletown neighborhood in the late 1970s to make way for a General Motors automotive assembly plant that the company said would employ 6,000 people; the eventual number was far lower.

"As often as not, these projects flop miserably because there's no market for them," says Los Angeles lawyer Michael Berger, a longtime property-rights advocate who wrote a brief on Kelo's side for the National Association of Home Builders. "If private development won't go in on its own, then there's probably something wrong with the development in terms of what the city wants to do with it."

Government and planning groups acknowledge the harsh effects of eminent domain on home or business

Controversy in New London

1990 Connecticut Office of Planning and Management designates New London a "distressed municipality."

1996 Naval Undersea Warfare Center, located on Fort Trumbull peninsula, closes; had employed up to 1,500 people in 1980s.

1997 New London Development Corp. (NLDC) is revived; originally created in 1978.

January 1998 Connecticut State Bond Commission authorizes $5.3 million in bonds to support planning and property acquisition on Fort Trumbull peninsula. State bonds eventually total $70 million.

February 1998 Drugmaker Pfizer Inc. announces plan to develop global research facility on site adjacent to Fort Trumbull neighborhood.

April 1998 New London City Council approves preparation of development plan for Fort Trumbull area by NLDC.

January 2000 City Council adopts NLDC development plan covering about 90 acres adjacent to Pfizer facility and

Fort Trumbull State Park; NLDC begins purchasing properties.

October 2000 NLDC votes to use eminent domain to acquire remaining properties from owners who declined to sell.

December 2000 Six families and one business file suit in Connecticut Superior Court challenging use of eminent domain to acquire their properties for development.

Early 2001 Pfizer begins moving staff into new research facility.

March 2002 Judge Thomas Corradino upholds taking of properties of three plaintiffs but bars use of eminent domain for time being to acquire properties of four others; both sides appeal to Connecticut Supreme Court.

March 2004 Connecticut Supreme Court rejects property owners' challenge

June 2005 U.S. Supreme Court rejects property owners' challenge in 5-4 decision.

2006 New London City Council approves plan to allow property owners to remain on Fort Trumbull peninsula.

---

owners. But they say that — as in New London — the costs are justified by the greater public good for the city and its other residents.

"I have a great deal of sympathy for the plight of some of the landowners," says Dowling, "but that has to be balanced against the thousands of unemployed in New London who will be offered jobs as a result of the development."

As a practical matter, government and planning groups say, eminent domain is often the only way for cities to assemble the large tracts that developers can find more readily in suburban or exurban areas. "The land supply in New York City, for example, is so

limited that the only way they're going to be able to redevelop, to bring revitalization efforts to fruition, is by using eminent domain," says Lucero of the planning association.

Moreover, says the League of Cities' Parkhurst, political and financial realities make cities reluctant to invoke eminent domain except for well-planned projects. "I can't imagine that cities are going to push for pie-in-the-sky projects if you have tremendous business and financial opposition to the project."

In fact, California land-use expert William Fulton says property-rights advocates already have caused municipal governments to be warier about using eminent domain.

"The property-rights lawyers are having a psychological effect," says Fulton, an author and newsletter publisher who also serves on Ventura, Calif.'s City Council. "They're causing the government to think twice and holding the line."

Do redevelopment plans disproportionately hurt minority and disadvantaged groups?

In its heyday, urban renewal brought redevelopment to central-city districts by clearing great swaths of supposedly blighted neighborhoods — forcibly relocating huge numbers of African-Americans in the process. From 1949 to 1963, non-whites comprised nearly two-thirds of the residents — 63 percent — displaced by urban-renewal condemnations.[6] To many, urban renewal amounted simply to "Negro removal."

Today, critics say that economically disadvantaged groups — racial and ethnic minorities, low- to moderate-income whites, and the elderly — continue to bear the brunt of urban redevelopments that are designed to benefit private companies and well-to-do residents. "It's a reverse Robin Hood notion — taking from the less advantaged and giving to the more advantaged," says James Ely, a professor at Vanderbilt Law School in Nashville, Tenn., and leading academic supporter of the property-rights movement.

Municipal and planning groups acknowledge past abuses, but today they say economic redevelopment helps rather than hurts lower-income population groups by creating jobs and providing revenues to finance needed public services. "The millions of dollars provided by revitalization projects can mean more jobs and more money for vital government services across the board," the National League of Cities writes in its brief in the *Kelo* case.

"Most of the abuses occurred a long, long time ago," says Dowling. "There are situations today where minority groups are among the biggest cheerleaders for these kinds of projects."

Now mostly gone, New London's Fort Trumbull neighborhood was home to much of the city's Italian-American population during most of the 20th century. Among the *Kelo* case plaintiffs, Wilhelmina Dery, who turned 87 in February, lives with her husband Charles on the same parcel of land where she was born to Italian immigrant parents in 1918.

Susette Kelo, with Institute for Justice attorney Scott Bullock, addresses the media following arguments before the U.S. Supreme Court on Feb. 22, 2005, in her suit to block New London, Conn., from taking her home and others for a private development. A court decision is expected in June. "If they can do that to us, they can do it to anybody anywhere," she says.

Attorney Bullock says the case illustrates that minority and working-class communities continue to be most affected by eminent domain. "Those are the ones that governments and developers are going to target," Bullock says. "They're not going in to tony neighborhoods and proposing doing things like this, because they know the consequences of doing so."

O'Connell, the development corporation's attorney, in fact, describes Fort Trumbull as a marginal area. "This was not an historic neighborhood, not a thriving, middle-class neighborhood," he says.

Pfizer's decision to build a new facility on abandoned industrial sites adjacent to Fort Trumbull created a unique opportunity for economic development to benefit the whole city, O'Connell says.[7] "The city seized the opportunity to do this," O'Connell says. "They would have been derelict if they had not seized this opportunity."

The holdout homeowners all flinch at the unflattering descriptions of the neighborhood. "It was a great place to grow up," says the Derys' son Matthew, who lives with his wife and son in a house on the same parcel as his parents.

In any event, Dery says, the city should have "revitalized the neighborhood if that's what they wanted to do. Why tear it down?"

> **"*Kelo* is a fairly well-balanced case. There are longtime neighbors about to be thrown out of their homes because the government wants economic development, and on the other hand, there is economic distress in the city."**
>
> — *Steven Eagle,*
> *Professor of Law,*
> *George Mason University*

O'Connell added to the holdouts' resentments by telling *The New York Times* that the goal of the development was to change the city's demography. "We need to get housing at the upper end, for people like the Pfizer employees," the *Times* quoted O'Connell as saying. "They are the professionals, they are the ones with the expertise and the leadership qualities to remake the city — the young, urban professionals who will invest in New London, put their kids in school and think of this as a place to stay for 20 or 30 years."[8]

Asked later about his comment, O'Connell says, "It clearly wasn't one of the goals [of the development] to replace one class of people with another." But he also acknowledges that — in contrast to some development plans elsewhere — New London is not requiring the developer to offer affordable housing or give preference to displaced residents who might want to purchase some of the new homes once they are built.

Advocates for municipalities point to other cities' use of eminent domain to acquire land needed for private companies to build revenue-producing facilities, such as a speedway in Kansas City, Kan., and a Nissan plant in Canton, Miss. Dowling says projects such as those "overwhelmingly benefit the most in need by putting a paycheck in the hands of the unemployed and enhancing public services for the poor."

Among the groups supporting the New London homeowners, however, are two major civil rights organizations, the NAACP and the Southern Christian Leadership Conference. "The burden of eminent domain has and will continue to fall disproportionately upon racial and ethnic minorities, the elderly and the economically disadvantaged," the two groups argue in a brief for which they also were joined by AARP, the senior-citizens' lobby. The brief notes that legal aid lawyers are currently challenging redevelopment projects in three New Jersey cities — Atlantic City, Camden and Mt. Holly — on grounds that they would disproportionately displace Latino or African-American homeowners or businesses.[9]

Planning groups, however, insist that the days of mass clearances of minority groups are gone. "The federal government doesn't go around pushing projects like that any more," says Thomas Merrill, a professor at Columbia University School of Law in New York City, who helped write a brief for the planning association in Kelo's case. "What has emerged is a much more targeted approach that focuses much more on individual projects that would have focused economically beneficial effects on distressed areas."

Should courts limit use of eminent domain for private development?

When it cleared the way for urban renewal in Washington, D.C., in 1954, the Supreme Court said the judiciary had only "an extremely narrow" role in reviewing governmental exercise of the power of eminent domain. The Michigan Supreme Court took the same view in 1981 when it upheld the use of eminent domain in Detroit's Poletown neighborhood to make way for the GM auto plant.[10]

In July 2004, however, the Michigan court explicitly repudiated its prior ruling when it blocked the use of eminent domain for a planned development adjacent to the Detroit Metropolitan Wayne County Airport. Instead, the court adopted the view of the dissenting justices in the *Poletown* case: Courts must make an "independent determination of what constitutes a public use for which the power of eminent domain may be utilized."[11]

Property-rights advocates say most courts have been — and continue to be — guilty of what Vanderbilt Professor Ely calls "supine behavior" in reviewing governmental exercise of eminent domain.

"We no longer have judicial deference; we have judicial abdication," says Ely, who joined a brief supporting *Kelo*. "Courts are making almost no serious attempt to examine what is being done by way of eminent domain at all, and that is less than faithful to the constitutional command."

Berger, the Los Angeles lawyer, says the Connecticut Supreme Court made the same mistake in upholding the New London condemnations. "When they say virtually anything goes — which is what *Kelo* holds — they're going too far," he says. "There is no public use in *Kelo*. There is no public use in a lot of cases that have been trying to push the boundaries of that concept."

Merrill, however, argues that courts cannot be more precise in defining what constitutes a legitimate public use. "History suggests that judicial efforts to limit the definition of public use are doomed to failure," Merrill says. "It's very hard in some verbal formula to capture [all the government uses for eminent domain]. We can't anticipate the kinds of circumstances that will arise in the future."

Municipal representatives also insist that decisions about the use of eminent domain are for legislative and executive officials, not the courts. "What the opponents seek is to bypass the legislative process," says Parkhurst of the League of Cities. "Eminent domain is an authority that is vested in the legislative branch."

Bullock, however, says the New London case illustrates how the political process is tilted against landowners who fight eminent-domain actions. "You have a small number of property owners who face abuse by a combination of political forces and private forces — and private forces that have quite a lot of power and influence, corporations like Pfizer and large developers," he says.

"The very reason we have a Bill of Rights," he adds, "is to protect against abuses of the political process."

But Parkhurst says the political process itself protects against any abuses of eminent domain. "If there's a problem, the public has the opportunity to vote out those who made choices they didn't like and to address these issues in the sunshine of public hearings," he says.

In *Kelo*, the Institute for Justice lawyers asked the Supreme Court to rule categorically that eminent domain cannot be used for private economic development or at least that takings for private development are subject to some level of heightened judicial scrutiny. Lawyers for New London argued that neither position was supported by Supreme Court precedent or constitutional language.

Whatever the legal arguments, one expert generally sympathetic to property-rights claims saw *Kelo* as a good vehicle for the Supreme Court to decide the issue. "*Kelo* was a fairly well-balanced case," says Steven Eagle, a law professor at George Mason University. "There are longtime neighbors about to be thrown out of their homes because the government wants economic development, and on the other hand there is economic distress in the city."

BACKGROUND

Public Uses

The government's power to acquire private property by eminent domain and put it to public use has been recognized in America since Colonial times. Private property was often transferred to other private entities for construction or development. The requirement that government compensate private owners for the property seized also dates to the Colonial era and over time became enshrined in the federal and in state constitutions. Courts have carefully scrutinized the need for compensation and the amounts paid, but have only rarely second-guessed governments' justifications for taking the property.[12]

Eminent domain has long been viewed as an inherent governmental power, so well established that the Framers of the Constitution saw no need to affirmatively authorize its use. Instead, the Bill of Rights — the 10 amendments added to the Constitution two years after ratification — merely sets two conditions on the use of eminent domain. The Fifth Amendment provides that private property shall not "be taken for public use, without just compensation." The provision, drafted by James Madison, was approved by Congress with no debate. Several states added similar provisions to their own constitutions over the next several decades.

The "public use" condition has never been understood to require that the government maintain ownership of the acquired property. In Colonial times, an ironworks was allowed to cut timber on adjacent private property in order to maintain an access road. "Mill acts" passed by Colonial and early state legislatures allowed private grist mills to build dams that flooded upstream properties in order to power waterwheels. From the early 19th century, state governments condemned land for private companies to build canals and, later, railroads.

CHRONOLOGY

Before 1900 *Right to take private property for public use under eminent domain recognized in America from Colonial times on; Bill of Rights incorporates requirement of just compensation for property owners.*

1789-1791 Congress writes and states ratify the Bill of Rights; "Takings Clause" in Fifth Amendment requires "just compensation" when private property is "taken for public use."

1833 Supreme Court rules Takings Clause applies only to takings by federal government, not states.

1897 Supreme Court rules that under 14th Amendment Takings Clause extends to state and local governments.

1900-1950 *"Regulatory taking" doctrine created by Supreme Court.*

1922 Supreme Court strikes down Pennsylvania law limiting underground mining; says regulation that goes "too far" may constitute taking of property.

1949 National Housing Act provides federal funding for clearing "blighted" urban areas.

1950s-1960s *Eminent domain used widely in urban renewal.*

1954 Supreme Court upholds use of eminent domain to take properties in "blighted" neighborhoods for urban renewal (*Berman v. Parker*).

1961 Urbanologist Jane Jacobs strongly criticizes urban renewal for destroying established city neighborhoods.

1970s-1980s *Property-rights movement gains traction, but makes limited headway in courts.*

1981 Michigan Supreme Court upholds use of eminent domain to take Detroit's Poletown neighborhood for auto assembly plant; General Motors falls short of promised jobs.

1984 U.S. Supreme Court again upholds broad definition of "public use" in ruling on Hawaii land-redistribution scheme.

1988 President Ronald Reagan issues executive order requiring "takings analysis" of any new federal regulation; order is largely ignored in subsequent administrations.

1990s *Supreme Court sets some limits on regulatory takings; use of eminent domain for private development challenged in some state courts.*

1992 Supreme Court says property owner entitled to compensation if regulation destroys all "economically viable" use of property in ruling favoring South Carolina beachfront owner.

1994 Supreme Court limits local governments' ability to require public use of private land as condition for development.

1996 Institute for Justice takes on eminent-domain issue in case pitting widow in Atlantic City, N.J., against casino mogul Donald Trump; among its victories is a 1998 ruling blocking seizure of property.

2000-Present *Some state courts rethink eminent domain; U.S. Supreme Court backs broad use, draws widespread criticism.*

2002 Illinois Supreme Court blocks condemnation of private business for racetrack parking lot, calls for "restraint" in using eminent domain.

2004 Connecticut Supreme Court upholds condemnations in New London's Fort Trumbull neighborhood for planned development. . . . Michigan Supreme Court overturns *Poletown* decision, blocking condemnations for business park near Detroit airport. . . . Oregon voters approve Measure 37 to compensate landowners for restrictions on development.

2005 U.S. Supreme Court ruling in *Kelo v. City of New London* backs use of eminent domain for private economic development; 5-4 decision is widely criticized; over next year, more than 20 states pass laws to limit use of eminent domain.

Often, the power of eminent domain was delegated directly to railroad companies, to use as they saw fit. Critics today stress that the private entities in these cases generally operated as common carriers or public utilities; but in some cases eminent domain was used solely for private benefit — as, for example, in constructing a rail line to an individual farm or business.

The need for compensation was also recognized as early as Colonial times as a necessary concomitant of eminent domain. In the course of one opinion, the Supreme Court in 1798 commented that when public projects are built on private property, "justice is done" by paying landowners "a reasonable equivalent."[13] Many states included compensation requirements in their constitutions; in other states, courts recognized the need for compensation as established by common law.

Still, as Professor Ely notes, financially strapped states often sought to avoid or minimize payment of compensation to landowners whose properties were adversely affected by public improvements. In one such case, the owner of a Baltimore wharf sought compensation for what today might be called a "regulatory taking" after the city diverted water from his wharf while undertaking other harbor improvements. In a decision that was to stand for 64 years, the Supreme Court in 1833 ruled against the wharf owner, holding that the Fifth Amendment's requirement under the Takings Clause that a property owner be awarded "just compensation" for his land applied only to the federal government, not to the states.[14]

The post-Civil War era of industrialization and national expansion saw greater attention to property rights from the Supreme Court, but no retrenchment from the broad discretion allowed to state and federal governments in the use of eminent domain. As one legal historian has written, the late-19th and early-20th centuries were the "heyday of expropriation as an instrument of public policy designed to subsidize private enterprise."[15] In 1897, however, the Supreme Court did decide that under the 14th Amendment, the states, like the federal government, had to compensate landowners for property taken under eminent domain.[16]

A quarter-century later, the court also for the first time recognized that land-use regulations might trigger a need for compensation. The 1922 ruling favored a Pennsylvania coal company that claimed a state law

Baltimore's blighted Inner Harbor was transformed by developer James Rouse into the popular Harborplace development using land acquired by the city through eminent domain.

limiting underground mining destroyed the value of its mineral rights on a site. In striking down the state law, the high court said a regulation becomes a taking if it goes "too far" — a vague phrasing that has since defied more precise definition.[17]

Urban Renewal

Eminent-domain condemnations grew in number and scope in the mid- and late-20th century, especially in cities. With legislative and financial support from the federal government, cities engaged in "urban renewal" — redevelopment policies aimed at ridding central cities of supposedly blighted residential and commercial neighborhoods and replacing them with better housing and more attractive commercial centers. Over time, critics pointed out that the presumed benefits for cities often came at significant costs to residents, especially minority and low-income groups. The courts, however, posed hardly any obstacles to the use of eminent domain if city or state governments deemed the proposed redevelopments to constitute a public use.

The federal government laid the foundation for urban renewal with the landmark Housing Act of 1949, which funded large-scale clearances of "blighted" urban areas to promote the stated goals of "a decent home and suitable living environment for every American." Cities used eminent domain to buy up homes and businesses and turn the properties over to redevelopment agencies. In

Hawaii Law Tests "Regulatory Takings" Doctrine

Hawaii legislators were trying to keep the price of gasoline down in 1997 when they capped the amount of rent a major oil company could charge an independent service-station operator. Chevron U.S.A. challenged the law in federal court, claiming it amounted to an unconstitutional taking of property without just compensation.

In a pair of surprising decisions, a lower federal court and the federal appeals court for Hawaii and other Western states agreed. The April 2004 ruling by the 9th U.S. Circuit Court of Appeals cheered property-rights advocates, who have long argued that courts should curtail governments' ability to pass laws or take executive actions that restrict an owner's use of his land — which they call "regulatory takings."

On appeal, however, the Bush administration and 27 states sided with Hawaii, warning that the ruling, if upheld, would hamper governments' abilities to pass regulatory legislation and expose governments to substantial costs of litigation and possible compensation to property owners. And in a significant decision, the U.S. Supreme Court in May 2005 agreed. The ruling in *Lingle v. Chevron U.S.A.* unanimously upheld Hawaii's law and in the process somewhat relaxed the standard for determining whether a government regulation amounts to an unconstitutional taking of property.

The Fifth Amendment to the U.S. Constitution specifies that the government cannot physically "take" private property without compensation. In 1922, the Supreme Court went further when it struck down a Pennsylvania coal mine safety statute. In an opinion by Justice Oliver Wendell Holmes, the court said a law regulating the use of property might constitute a taking requiring compensation to the owner if it "goes too far."[1]

The court has done little to explain Holmes' cryptic comment in the 80-plus years since the decision. In a historic preservation case involving New York City's Grand Central Terminal, the court in 1978 laid out three factors for judges to use considering regulatory-takings claims: the "character" of the government action, the "economic impact" of the regulation and "particularly" its impact on "investment-backed expectations."[2] Application of that test normally results in the upholding of government regulations.

Two years later, in rejecting a takings claim in a zoning case, the court — perhaps inadvertently — set out another, seemingly stricter test by saying that land-use regulations must "substantially advance legitimate governmental

some cases, redevelopment meant new housing — though only rarely for low-income residents. In other cases, urban renewal brought now-familiar public spaces like San Francisco's Yerba Buena Park or mixed private-public developments such as Baltimore's Inner Harbor.

The Supreme Court ruled on the constitutionality of using eminent domain for these purposes when the owners of a small District of Columbia department store challenged the condemnation of their property as part of a slum-clearance plan in the city's southwest quadrant. Most of the housing in the area was substandard and beyond repair, evidence showed. But the storeowners said their commercial property should not be taken and turned over to a private agency for private use. Unanimously, the justices in 1954 rejected the challenge.

"The concept of the public welfare is broad and inclusive," Justice William O. Douglas wrote in *Berman v. Parker.* The court, he said, would not "reappraise" the project or review the specific boundary lines. The property owners' rights would be "satisfied," he concluded, when they received the "just compensation" required under the Fifth Amendment for the taking.

A critique of urban renewal began to emerge by the 1960s, notably in Jane Jacobs' searing attack in *The Death and Life of American Cities* (1961). Jacobs, recognized today as a leading scholar on urban policy, argued that "urban renewal" typically destroyed established neighborhoods and scattered the people who lived there — most of them poor. Today, many elements of the critique are widely accepted. Urban renewal "rid the cities of some of their worst slums," University of Michigan goals."[3] The court repeated that phrasing in various property-rights opinions over the next two decades.

Chevron's lawyers picked up the phrase in challenging Hawaii's service-station rent-control law. The act capped the amount of rent that oil companies could charge to lessee-dealers at 15 percent of the dealer's profits on gasoline sales plus 15 percent of gross sales on other products. Hawaii legislators said capping rents would protect competition in the retail gasoline market by preventing major oil companies from driving out independent station operators. Currently, about half of the state's 300 service stations are owned directly by the oil companies.

In challenging the law, Chevron put an economic expert on the stand who said the law would not affect gasoline prices — and thus would not advance the public interest. The state offered its own expert with a different view. U.S. District Judge Susan Oki Mollway in Honolulu agreed with Chevron's expert. In a 2-1 opinion, so did the 9th Circuit. Both rulings said the law failed to "substantially advance" the state's goal of keeping gas prices down.

In its decision, the high court held that the "substantially advances" test does not apply in cases challenging government regulations as unconstitutional takings of property. Justice Sandra Day O'Connor acknowledged, in effect, that the "regrettably imprecise" standard had become "ensconced" in the court's jurisprudence by mistake. The test was not useful, she said, because it did not focus on "the magnitude or character of the burden" imposed on a property owner nor on the distribution of the regulatory burden among property owners.

On that basis, O'Connor continued, "the 'substantially advances' formula is not a valid takings test." Instead, regulations other than those involving permanent physical occupation or complete destruction of economic value should be judged under the test set out in the 1978 case. All justices joined O'Connor's opinion, but Justice Anthony M. Kennedy wrote in a brief concurrence that a regulation still might be subject to challenge as "so arbitrary or irrational as to violate due process."

Property rights advocates voiced disappointment with the ruling. The decision "jettisoned" part of the regulatory takings analysis, Douglas Kmiec, a conservative constitutional law expert at Pepperdine University Law School in Malibu, Calif., commented afterward. But the American Planning Association, which filed a brief supporting Hawaii, praised the decision. The ruling "makes it very clear that while a regulation can be a taking, it is equally clear that the court's standard is high," said Paul Farmer, the group's executive director.

---

[1] The case is *Pennsylvania Coal Co. v. Mahon*, 260 U.S. 393 (1922). For a comprehensive treatise, see Steven J. Eagle, *Regulatory Takings* (3d. ed.), forthcoming 2005.

[2] The decision is *Penn Central Transportation Co. v. City of New York*, 438 U.S. 104 (1978).

[3] The decision is *Agins v. City of Tiburon*, 447 U.S. 255 (1980).

Professor Robert Fishman wrote in 2000, "but the federal bulldozer also leveled many close-knit neighborhoods." The efforts to re-create the "vibrant" feel of urban neighborhoods or revitalize downtown commercial districts generally proved unavailing, he said.[18]

The emerging critique appeared to have little effect, however, on court decisions. In 1981 the Michigan Supreme Court brushed aside any constitutional objections to Detroit's plan to raze Poletown's 1,300 homes and 140 businesses and turn the land over to General Motors for an automobile plant. The city was using eminent domain, the 5-2 majority wrote, "to accomplish the essential public purposes of alleviating unemployment and revitalizing the economic base of the community." Any private benefit, the majority added, was "merely incidental."

Three years later, the U.S. Supreme Court again approved a broad interpretation of the public uses permitted in eminent-domain condemnations by upholding a Hawaii land-redistribution scheme. To reduce concentration of land ownership, the Hawaii law used eminent domain to acquire property from large landowners and sell it to the tenants. Writing for a unanimous court in *Hawaii Housing Authority v. Midkiff*, Justice Sandra Day O'Connor upheld the law, saying it was not a "purely private taking" but an effort "to attack certain perceived evils of concentrated property ownership in Hawaii — a legitimate public purpose."[19]

By the end of the 1980s, any limits on the public use needed to justify eminent domain had all but disappeared. "In practice, 'public use' has long been defined so broadly that it is almost no barrier at all," Jennifer

Eminent domain was used 40 years ago to assemble the land for New York's World Trade Center. Now, nearly four years after terrorist attacks destroyed the twin towers, eminent domain again is likely to be used in the massive reconstruction planned.

Nedelsky, a University of Toronto law professor, wrote in 1991. The *Poletown* and *Midkiff* decisions demonstrated courts' willingness to let legislatures determine what constituted a public use. Legal commentators, she said, grappled with compensation issues, but "almost none" of them dealt with the question of defining public use.[20]

Rights Revival?

A fledgling property-rights movement began to form in the 1970s and gained some momentum during the conservative era of Ronald Reagan's presidency in the 1980s. The movement drew financial support from some major business lobbies, intellectual strength from the growing "law and economics" school in legal academia, and public visibility from grass-roots protests by small land or business owners depicting themselves as victims of overreaching government regulation.

The Reagan administration gave the movement a paper victory in 1988 by issuing an executive order requiring government agencies to carry out a "takings" analysis before issuing any new regulations. Both Presidents George H. W. Bush and Bill Clinton left the executive order on the books, but largely ignored it.[21]

Beginning in the late 1980s, the Supreme Court gave landowners a series of partial victories in property-rights cases. In the most important, the court in 1992 ruled that a South Carolina beachfront owner was entitled to compensation because a coastal-protection law deprived him of any "economically viable" use of the property. Two years later, the court held that local authorities in Oregon could require a landowner or developer to set aside parts of their property for public use only if there is a "rough proportionality" between the conditions and the harm from the proposed development.[22]

The regulatory-takings decisions signaled no retreat, however, from the broad discretion given to government in eminent-domain cases. In 1992, for example, the high court backed the Interstate Commerce Commission's decision upholding the right of Amtrak, the government-chartered passenger railroad corporation, to acquire track from a private freight company and turn it over to a rival railway. The agency's decision that the condemnation would serve a public purpose by facilitating Amtrak's rail service was not irrational, the majority said in the 6-3 decision.[23]

Property-rights advocates mobilized in the 1990s around a variety of issues, including so-called eminent-domain abuse, but made only limited headway with their most ambitious proposals. Supreme Court rulings gave property owners some grounds to challenge "regulatory takings" under land-use and environmental laws, and to contest local agencies' efforts to require public use of private land as a condition of development. A measure that would have required broader compensation for regulatory takings died in Congress, however. Meanwhile, some state courts were proving receptive to eminent-domain challenges. But the Supreme Court steered clear of the issue until the *Kelo* case.

The Institute for Justice first took on the eminent-domain issue in late 1996 by representing an elderly Atlantic City, N.J., woman against an effort by real estate mogul Donald Trump and a New Jersey state agency to seize her home for use as a parking lot for one of Trump's

Atlantic City casinos.[24] Two years later, a New Jersey judge blocked the seizure, saying any public use was "overwhelmed by the private benefit." Over the next several years, the organization scored some other victories. Representing a Canton, Miss., homeowner, it helped dissuade a state agency in April 2002 from condemning his property for Nissan to use as a parking lot for its auto-manufacturing plant. In another case, it won a ruling in 2003 from the Arizona Court of Appeals blocking the city of Mesa from acquiring the site of an automobile brake shop in order to turn the property over to a hardware store for expansion.

The institute had no luck with the *Kelo* case in Connecticut courts, but supreme courts in two other states were meanwhile signaling a change in the judicial climate on eminent domain by backing property-owners' challenges to condemnations for the benefit of private entities.

In April 2002 the Illinois Supreme Court blocked a state development authority from seizing a private auto recycling facility for use as a parking lot for a nearby auto racetrack built several years earlier on eminent-domain acquired land.

"The power of eminent domain is to be exercised with restraint, not abandon," the majority wrote in *Southwestern Illinois Development Authority (SWIDA) v. National City Environmental, L.L.C.*[25]

Then, four months after the Connecticut high court ruling in the *Kelo* case, the Michigan Supreme Court gave eminent-domain critics a major victory by overturning the *Poletown* decision. In blocking the seizure of land to be used for a planned 1,300-acre business and technology park adjacent to the Detroit Metropolitan Wayne County Airport, the high court called the *Poletown* ruling "a radical departure from fundamental constitutional principles." The proposed condemnations "do not advance a 'public use,'" the majority wrote in *County of Wayne v. Hathcock.*[26]

CURRENT SITUATION

Controversial Decision

The Supreme Court's decision upholding the taking of property for private economic development is continuing to stir strong criticism across the country despite

efforts by city officials and planners to defend the practice as a vital tool for financially hard-pressed municipalities.

The justices themselves were closely divided in the 5-4 ruling. For the majority, Stevens cited Supreme Court precedents dating from the late 19th century upholding taking of private property for economic purposes. "[T]here is no basis for exempting economic development from our traditionally broad understanding of public purpose," he wrote. Three liberal-leaning justices joined Stevens' opinion — David H. Souter, Ruth Bader Ginsburg, and Stephen G. Breyer — along with the moderate-conservative Anthony M. Kennedy.

In a strongly written dissent, O'Connor said the decision amounted to abandoning a "long-held, basic limitation on government power," and effectively deleted the words "public use" from the Takings Clause. "Under the banner of economic development," she wrote, "all private property is now vulnerable to being taken and transferred to another private owner, so long as it might be upgraded — i.e., given to an owner who will use it in a way that the legislature deems more beneficial to the public — in the process." The court's most stalwart conservatives joined O'Connor's opinion: Chief Justice William H. Rehnquist and Justices Antonin Scalia and Clarence Thomas.

In his opinion, Stevens emphasized positive elements of the New London plan, calling it "comprehensive" and "carefully formulated." In a significant concurrence, Kennedy also highlighted the city's compliance with "elaborate procedural requirements" and the broad economic benefits projected from the development. He warned that closer judicial scrutiny would be required for property transfers "intended to confer benefits on particular, favored private entities, and with only incidental or pretextual public benefits. . . ."

Polls conducted in two New England states immediately after the ruling registered lopsided public opposition. In Connecticut itself, a Quinnipiac University poll found that 89 percent of those surveyed opposed the taking of private property for private uses, even if it was for the public economic good, compared to 8 percent who supported the practice. A University of New Hampshire poll similarly found 93 percent opposed to the taking of private land for private development. Tellingly, 61 percent of those surveyed in the Connecticut poll said they

Randy Bailey's brake shop would have been taken by Mesa, Ariz., and transferred to a hardware store that wanted the location, but the Arizona Court of Appeals unanimously blocked the city on Oct. 1, 2003.

strongly or somewhat opposed the use of eminent domain for traditional government purposes, such as roads or schools.[27]

Property rights advocates say opposition to the court's ruling shows no sign of abating. "The only people who support the decision are city officials, planners and developers," says Institute of Justice attorney Bert Gall. "But this is an issue where everyone else is lined up against them, because the American dream doesn't include having someone take your home so that someone else can make more money."

Supporters of the ruling acknowledge the popular backlash, but also question whether the public is well informed about the issues. "There's something going on," says John Echeverria, director of the Georgetown Environmental Law and Policy Institute in Washington, who helped write a brief supporting New London. "But I'm not sure the public has been presented the question whether, for example, the District of Columbia should be permitted to build a new stadium on South Capitol Street [even] if one homeowner refuses to sell."

In legal terms, Echeverria calls the high court ruling "completely unremarkable." "I don't think any competent lawyer with relevant experience was surprised by the

outcome," he says. But property rights advocate Ely at Vanderbilt insists the ruling goes beyond the court's previous rulings on eminent domain. "Once you allow this kind of analysis, almost any property can be taken and put to a higher use," he says.

In his opinion, Stevens said courts should not "second-guess" local officials' determinations as to what property was needed for development projects. But in a bar association speech in Las Vegas only two months after the ruling, Stevens acknowledged the public backlash. After saying he thought development should be guided by market forces instead of political decisions, Stevens continued, "The public outcry that greeted (the ruling) is some evidence that the political process is up to the task of addressing such policy concerns."[28]

Multiple Issues

Property rights advocates are hailing the passage of laws in more than 20 states — and the consideration of bills in many others — aimed at curbing the use of eminent domain. City officials, planning groups and environmentalists say the laws may prove to have only limited effect, but could hurt cities if they block worthwhile redevelopment projects.

Meanwhile, property rights advocates in at least six states are hoping to follow Oregon's lead in approving ballot initiatives aimed at freeing property owners from land-use controls that reduce the value of their property or compensating them for the difference. Critics say the Oregon measure — approved in November 2004 — is interfering with land use controls needed to protect the public.

In the most common eminent domain reform, at least 12 states have responded directly to the *Kelo* decision by restricting the governmental power to take private property to use for economic development, transfer to a private entity or generate additional tax revenue. In a second common approach, several states have tightened the definition of "public use" of the property being taken to mean possession, occupation or enjoyment by the public at large. In addition, several states have passed laws specifying the definition of "blight" needed to justify use of eminent domain.

Less commonly, some states have included procedural reforms, such as requiring greater public notice, more public hearings and approval by elected governing

Should courts limit the use of eminent domain for private economic development?

YES
Ilya Somin
Assistant Professor of Law, George Mason University School of Law

Written for *CQ Researcher*, February 2005

Courts should not allow government to condemn property merely because it might further "economic development." Such takings allow the wealthy and politically connected to help themselves to their neighbors' land, and rarely provide any real economic benefits to the public.

Under the U.S. and most state constitutions, government may take private property only for a "public use." Traditionally, this was interpreted as allowing condemnation of property only to carry out necessary governmental functions, such as to build public roads. The public-use test thus forbade most takings that transferred private property to other private hands.

Unfortunately, many recent state court decisions have authorized private-to-private condemnations in order to promote "economic development." This rationale is almost a blank check for abuse. It leads to notorious cases such as the 1981 *Poletown* decision, in which the Michigan Supreme Court upheld a condemnation that expelled 4,200 people from their homes so General Motors could build a new factory. As the Michigan court explained recently in overruling *Poletown*, the "economic benefit" rationale "would validate practically any exercise of the power of eminent domain on behalf of a private entity." Property rights are "perpetually threatened by the expansion plans of any large [business]." Homeowners and nonprofit property owners are particularly vulnerable. Because they make little or no profit from their property, it can always be argued that a business could use their land to better promote "development."

Moreover, economic-development takings usually fail to provide the economic benefits they promise. General Motors claimed its Poletown factory would create more than 6,000 jobs, yet the plant employed less than half that many. It is likely that more jobs were lost from Poletown's destruction than were created by the factory — a typical result of such takings.

In practice, the political power of those who gain from a taking is a much stronger influence on condemnation decisions than any potential economic benefit. Therefore, economic-development takings often victimize the poor and politically weak for the benefit of the wealthy and powerful, with little regard for any broader public interest.

If a business really can use a property more efficiently than its current owners, it usually can buy it on the open market. Most of America's factories, office buildings and malls were built without resort to condemnation. Cities have other ways to promote development, including tax incentives and regulatory reform. Most important, economic growth is best promoted if citizens can develop their own property without fear of losing it.

NO
David Dana
Professor of Law, Northwestern University School of Law

Written for *CQ Researcher*, February 2005

Why do exercises of eminent domain similar to the Kelo case make so many of us uncomfortable? It's not because they are purportedly justified by a desire for economic growth, because condemning land to extend or build a road is generally justified on the grounds of anticipated economic growth.

Nor can our discomfort derive from the fact that such an exercise of eminent domain often greatly benefits a corporation such as Pfizer. Again, condemning land to build a new road or expand an airport provides some landowners, businesses or airlines more economic benefits than the rest of society.

The source of our discomfort also cannot be that the developments at issue in *Kelo*-type exercises of eminent domain will not be open to the public, and hence will not be physically of public use. After all, the U.S. Supreme Court (or any court) would never block a state or federal government's condemnation of land to build a nuclear-waste dump in an area particularly well-suited, geologically, to that use, as long as the government had tried to buy the site in a market transaction. Yet the nuclear-waste dump presumably would not be open to the general public.

My suspicion is that the source of the discomfort is the same as the suspicion that runs throughout federal and state law regarding local zoning: That local governmental decision-making is often insufficiently transparent and thus susceptible to capture by powerful actors, such as large developers. Federal and state politics are also open to "undue influence" or "capture," but they generally involve more diverse people than the politics of any given locality, and, hence, are of lesser concern to the courts.

But if undue influence of cash-rich corporations/developers is the root of our discomfort with *Kelo*-type exercises of eminent domain, then the answer is for the courts to insist that every such exercise be openly debated under formally adopted guidelines and reasonably well-tailored to achieve the public use identified by the agency that condemned the property. The U.S. Supreme Court could advance this agenda by extending to eminent domain the nexus and reasonable-proportionality requirements it has applied to regulatory exactions. In my view, a preferable route for our federalism-avowing Supreme Court would be to leave this issue to those courts that are on the frontlines in policing distortions and failures in local politics — that is, the state courts.

Kansas Speedway

The $224 million Kansas Speedway was built in 2001 on 1,200 acres acquired through eminent domain. The speedway was expected to have a $170 million annual economic impact on the Kansas City area and create 65 full-time jobs.

bodies. A few states have passed laws requiring above-market compensation for the taking of an owner's principal residence. And Ohio passed a one-of-a-kind measure imposing a moratorium on use of eminent domain for economic development through 2006 and creation of a legislative task force to study the issue.

State courts also are weighing in on the issue. In May 2006, the Oklahoma Supreme Court became the tenth state tribunal to bar use of eminent domain for economic development under state constitutional provisions.[29]

In many states, the proposals have drawn broad support from Republicans traditionally supportive of property rights as well as from Democrats responsive to working-class and minority groups. "It's become a totally nonpartisan issue," says Larry Morandi, director of state policy research for the National Conference of State Legislatures.

In New Mexico, however, Gov. Bill Richardson, a Democrat, vetoed a one-sentence bill passed by the Democratic-controlled legislature that would have barred use of eminent domain for economic development. Three states — Florida, Michigan and New Hampshire — will vote on legislatively approved constitutional amendments in November 2006.

"Basically, every state that was in session in 2006 had some sort of eminent domain bill that they were

considering," says Institute for Justice attorney Gall. The only exception was Delaware, which passed a modest reform measure in 2005. No legislation had passed, however, in California and New York, two big states that have made extensive use of eminent domain for economic development in the past.

League of Cities attorney Parkhurst says the reform measures "have not been as extreme as property rights advocates would have liked." But he says the post-*Kelo* backlash has made city officials "hyper-cautious on approaching eminent domain issues."

Property rights advocates also want Congress to step into the issue by prohibiting the use of federal funds on any project that takes private property for economic development. The House in November 2005 passed a bill by a vote of 376-38 that would bar federal funds for such projects for a two-year period, but it was still awaiting action in the Senate as of mid-May 2006.

Meanwhile, in the state where the *Kelo* case originated, Connecticut lawmakers adjourned in May without acting on a measure that Institute for Justice attorneys called inadequate in any event. With Democrats controlling both chambers, House Republicans were hoping for a direct vote to bar use of eminent domain for economic development; Senate Democrats had crafted a narrower bill combining some procedural and compensation reforms. Democratic division even on the lesser bill kept the Senate bill from a vote, however, and House leaders saw no reason to bring any bill to a vote in the lower chamber either.[30]

On a related front, property rights advocates in at least six states — California, Colorado, Idaho, Montana, Nevada and Washington — are seeking the needed signatures to qualify ballot initiatives comparable to Oregon's successful initiative, Measure 37. Adopted with 61 percent of the vote in November 2004, the Oregon measure allows landowners to file claims for so-called regulatory takings — the diminished value of their property due to land-use controls. The Oregon Supreme Court upheld the measure in February 2006.

Oregon lawmakers provided no funds to pay the so-called Measure 37 claims. So the main effect of the initiative has been to free property owners of restrictions on development, especially in rural areas.

OUTLOOK

Changed Environment?

When Bridgeport, Conn., invoked eminent domain to acquire waterfront land for a planned redevelopment, the owners of the 100-year-old Pequonnock Yacht Club fought back — first by asking officials to be allowed to remain in their location and then by challenging the condemnation in court.

The development plans fell through, but the city persisted in its effort to acquire the property — only to be rebuffed by the Connecticut Supreme Court. "Just because the property may be desirable to the [city]," the court said in a unanimous opinion in February 2002, "does not justify its taking by eminent domain."

The ruling is one of many instances of successful legal or political resistance to eminent-domain condemnations cited by an April 2003 Institute for Justice report. Two years later, however, the same Connecticut court upheld New London's condemnation of the Fort Trumbull neighborhood properties for a similarly ambitious redevelopment plan — which the holdout property owners and others warn may fall through just as the Bridgeport project did.

The political and legal environment for such condemnation efforts, however, has changed since the U.S. Supreme Court's 1954 decision giving municipalities virtual carte blanche in urban renewal, at least in "blighted" areas. "Municipal governments are so accustomed to having a high degree of control over urban land markets that it's unimaginable that it could be any different," says planning expert Fulton. "But more and more resistance is cropping up."

Legal battles succeed more often than in the past, but courts still give substantial deference to local governments' decisions about whether a project constitutes a "public use" and whether particular properties need to be taken for the project. In advance of the *Kelo* decision, most legal observers were predicting that the U.S. Supreme Court would rule as it eventually did: in favor of broad use of eminent domain if authorized by the appropriate local governing body or redevelopment authority. But none of them were predicting the widespread, vocal opposition that the ruling has provoked.

League of Cities attorney Parkhurst puts a positive spin on the reaction. "It's shined a spotlight on comprehensive economic development, which is a good thing," he says. "Increasing public participation, ensuring that municipal officials get the word out. And a lot of grandmothers still have their homes. Bulldozers have not plowed over as many homes as we'd been led to believe."

Still, some big-city leaders, including New York Mayor Michael Bloomberg, warn that restricting use of eminent domain will hamper economic development. "You would never build any big thing any place in any big city in this country if you didn't have the power of eminent domain," Bloomberg said during a groundbreaking ceremony on May 2 in Times Square. *The New York Times'* account of the event noted that Times Square was redeveloped in part through government condemnation of private property.[31]

Institute for Justice attorney Gall discounts the warning. "In those states that pass strong legislation, you're going to see that you can have economic development without use of eminent domain," Gall says. "That myth is going to be disproved." But he warns that states that do not restrict eminent domain "will continue to see cities and towns emboldened" to take property for private development.

Meanwhile, the outlook is uncertain for the possible compromise in New London that would allow Kelo and the other holdouts to continue living on the Fort Trumbull peninsula. Institute for Justice attorneys complain that the deal calls for the city to keep title to the properties, while state officials say there may be legal problems in reconfiguring the development plan. For her part, Kelo sees one bright spot: "At least we're all going to be discussing the issue in the open."[32]

NOTES

1. The case number is 04-108. Supreme Court docket information, a transcript of the argument and a link to the parties' opposing legal briefs can be found at www.supremecourtus.gov. For the Connecticut Supreme Court decision, see *Kelo v. City of New London*, 843 A.2d 500 (Conn. 2004).

2. Dana Berliner, "Public Power, Private Gain," Institute for Justice, April 2003 (www.ij.org).

3. The D.C. case is *Berman v. Parker*, 348 U.S. 26 (1954).

4. For background, see Kenneth Jost, "Property Rights," *CQ Researcher*, June 16, 1995, pp. 513-536.

5. The case is *Courtesy Sandwich Shop, Inc. v. Port of New York Authority*, 12 N.Y.2d 379 (1963).

6. Bernard J. Frieden and Lynne B. Sagalyn, *Downtown Inc.: How America Rebuilds Cities* (1989), p. 28, cited in Brief of Jane Jacobs as *Amica Curiae* in Support of Petitioners, *Kelo v. City of New London*, 04-108.

7. For background, see Mary H. Cooper, "Environmental Justice," *CQ Researcher*, June 19, 1998, pp. 529-552.

8. Quoted in Iver Peterson, "There Goes the Old Neighborhood, to Revitalization," *The New York Times*, Jan. 30, 2005, Sec. 1, p. 29 (metropolitan edition).

9. For coverage, see Charles Toutant, "Alleging Race-Based Condemnation," *New Jersey Law Journal*, Aug. 2, 2004.

10. The case is *Poletown Neighborhood Council v. City of Detroit*, 304 N.W.2d 455 (Mich. 1981). For a strongly critical account, see Jeanie Wylie, *Poletown: Community Betrayed* (1989).

11. The case is *County of Wayne v. Hathcock*, 684 N.W.2d 765 (Mich. 2004).

12. Background drawn in part from James W. Ely Jr., *The Guardian of Every Other Right: A Constitutional History of Property Rights* (2d ed.), 1998. See also Polly J. Price, *Property Rights: Rights and Liberties Under the Law* (2003).

13. The case is *Calder v. Bull*, 3 U.S. 386 (1798).

14. The case is *Barron v. Baltimore*, 32 U.S. 243 (1833).

15. Harry Scheiber, "Property Law, Expropriation and Resource Allocation," cited in Jennifer Nedelsky, *Private Property and the Limits of American Constitutionalism* (1991), p. 226.

16. The case is *Chicago, Burlington & Quincy Railroad v. City of Chicago*, 166 U.S. 226 (1897).

17. The case is *Pennsylvania Coal Co. v. Mahon*, 260 U.S. 393 (1922).

18. Robert Fishman, "The American Metropolis at Century's End: Past and Future Influences," *Housing Policy Debate*, Vol. 11, No. 1 (2000).

19. The citation is 467 U.S. 229 (1984).

20. Nedelsky, *op. cit.*, pp. 232-233.

21. For a brief historical overview, with citations to other sources, see Steven J. Eagle, *Regulatory Takings* (3d ed.), forthcoming, 2005. Executive Order No. 12630, 3 C.F.R. 554 (March 15, 1988). The text appears in Eagle, *op. cit.*, pp. 1137-1154.

22. The cases are *Lucas v. South Carolina Coastal Council*, 505 U.S. 1003 (1992); *Dolan v. City of Tigard*, 512 U.S. 374 (1994).

23. The case is *National Railroad Passenger Corporation v. Boston & Maine Corp.*, 503 U.S. 407 (1992).

24. Information about this and subsequent cases is available on the Institute for Justice's Web site: www.ij.org.

25. The citation is 786 N.E.2d 1 (Ill. 2002). For coverage, see Jim Getz, "Despite Ruling, Agency Plans to Condemn Swansea Lodge," *The St. Louis Post-Dispatch*, April 8, 2002, p. B1.

26. The citation is 684 N.W.2d 765 (Mich. 2004). For coverage, see John Gallagher, "Poletown Seizures Are Ruled Unlawful," *The Detroit Free Press*, July 31, 2004.

27. See Quinnipiac University Poll, July 28, 2005 (www.quinnipiac.edu/x11385.xml?ReleaseID=821); Granite State Poll, University of New Hampshire, July 20, 2005 (www.unh.edu/survey-center/sc07 2005.pdf).

28. Associated Press, Aug. 22, 2005.

29. The case is *Board of County Commissioners of Muskogee County v. Lowery*, May 9, 2006. Other states listed by the Institute of Justice with similar rulings are Arkansas, Florida, Illinois, Kentucky, Maine, Michigan, Montana, South Carolina and Washington.

30. Ted Mann, "In Legislature, Prospect Fading for Revisions to Eminent Domain," *The* (New London) *Day*, May 3, 2006.

31. Diane Cardwell, "Bloomberg Says Power to Seize Private Land Is Vital to Cities," *The New York Times*, May 3, 2006, p. B1.

32. Yardley, *op. cit.*, Feb. 8, 2006.

BIBLIOGRAPHY

Books

Eagle, Steven J., *Regulatory Takings* **(3d ed.), Lexis, 2005.**
A professor at George Mason University School of Law comprehensively covers the intersection of property rights and government regulation from the writing of the Constitution to the Supreme Court's first enunciation of the doctrine of "regulatory takings" in the 1920s through the birth and growth of the modern property-rights movement.

Ely, James W., Jr., *The Guardian of Every Other Right: A Constitutional History of Property Rights* **(rev. ed.), Oxford University Press, 1998.**
A professor of law and history at Vanderbilt University surveys property law in America from Colonial times through the 1990s. Includes notes, 13-page bibliographical essay.

Epstein, Richard A., *Takings: Private Property and the Power of Eminent Domain,* **Harvard University Press, 1985.**
The well-known University of Chicago law professor argues in this influential and controversial book that a wide range of government actions, including zoning laws, rent control, workers' compensation laws and progressive taxation, unconstitutionally infringe on property rights.

Fullilove, Mindy Thompson, *Root Shock: How Tearing Up City Neighborhoods Hurts America, and What We Can Do About It,* **One World/Ballantine, 2004.**
A professor of clinical psychiatry and public health at Columbia University critically examines the psychological and social effects of neighborhood "displacement" on individuals and communities. Includes notes, 24-page bibliography.

Kemp, Roger L. (ed.), *Community Renewal through Municipal Investment: A Handbook for Citizens and Public Officials,* **McFarland, 2003.**
The city manager of Vallejo, Calif., provides 38 case studies of what he calls "state-of-the-art practices" in municipal investment aimed at enhancing the quality of life and improving economic development.

Meltz, Robert, Dwight H. Merriam and Richard M. Frank, *The Takings Issue: Constitutional Limits on Land-Use Control and Environmental Regulation,* **Island Press, 1999.**
The authors, all attorneys, provide an accessible, objective and authoritative examination of the background and current issues surrounding regulatory takings. Includes summaries of key Supreme Court takings decisions and a flow-chart detailing how a court might analyze a land-use takings claim.

Price, Polly J., *Property Rights: Rights and Liberties under the Law,* **ABC-Clio, 2003.**
A professor at Emory University School of Law traces property-law development from Colonial times to the present. The book includes excerpts from some of the Supreme Court's major property-law decisions and a chronology, table of cases and four-page bibliography.

Siegan, Bernard H., *Property and Freedom: The Constitution, the Courts, and Land-Use Regulation,* **Transaction, 1997.**
A professor at the University of San Diego School of Law writes approvingly of Supreme Court decisions since 1987 that have been more protective of private property than earlier zoning and land-use precedents. Includes detailed notes. Siegan is also the author of an historical account, *Property Rights: From Magna Carta to the Fourteenth Amendment* (Transaction, 2001).

Articles

Greenhouse, Linda, "Justices Will Hear a Property Rights Case Contesting the Limits of Eminent Domain," *The New York Times,* Sept. 29, 2004, p. A21.
Seven property owners take their case to the U.S. Supreme Court after the Connecticut Supreme Court upheld the right of New London, Conn., to take the land.

Moran, Kate, "City to Assess State of Fort Trumbull Development; Eminent Domain Lawsuit Not Only Source of Frustration," *The* [New London] *Day,* Sept. 30, 2004.
The story describes the various financial and other issues surrounding the proposed New London, Conn., redevelopment plan immediately after the U.S. Supreme

Court decision to review the suit filed by a group of homeowners challenging the use of eminent domain for the project. The reporter covered the case in depth throughout the legal proceedings.

Tuohy, Lynne, "High Court to Test Seizure of Homes," *The Hartford Courant*, Feb. 20, 2005, p. A1.
The story provides thorough background on the New London, Conn., eminent-domain case in advance of arguments before the U.S. Supreme Court. An accompanying sidebar details the views of the dissident homeowners and the effects the case has had on their lives ("In Fort Trumbull, Holdouts Stick Together").

Reports and Studies

Berliner, Dana, *Public Power, Private Gain*, Institute for Justice, April 2003.
The report by the leading advocacy group working to limit eminent domain counted some 10,000 instances over a five-year period in which the power was invoked or threatened to take private property for the use or benefit of another private entity.

For More Information

American Planning Association, 1030 15th St., N.W., Suite 750 West, Washington, DC 20036; (202) 872-0611; 20005-1503; www.planning.org. A public interest and research organization committed to urban, suburban, regional, and rural planning.

Cato Institute, 1000 Massachusetts Ave., N.W., Washington, DC 20001-5403; (202) 842-0200; www.cato .org. A research organization that supports "the traditional American principles of limited government, individual liberty, free markets and peace."

Institute for Justice, 901 N. Glebe Rd., Suite 900, Arlington, VA 22203; (703) 682-9320; www.ij.org. The nation's "only libertarian public interest law firm" pursues "cutting-edge litigation in the courts on behalf of individuals whose most basic rights are denied by the government."

National Association of Home Builders, 1201 15th St., N.W., Washington, DC 20005; (202) 266-8200; www .nahb.org. A trade association that helps promote the policies that make housing a national priority.

National League of Cities, 1301 Pennsylvania Ave., N.W., Suite 550, Washington, DC 20004; (202) 626-3000; www .nlc.org. The oldest and largest national organization representing U.S. municipal governments seeks to "strengthen and promote cities as centers of opportunity, leadership, and governance."

New London Development Corporation, 165 State St., Suite 313, New London, CT 06320; (860) 447-8011; www.nldc.org. A nonprofit community-development group committed to improving the city's economic health and quality of life.

8

Downtown Renaissance

Alan Greenblatt and Charles S. Clark

Lunchtime crowds pack Atlanta's Fairlie-Poplar Historic District for weekly concerts. Across the country, once moribund downtown areas have become clean, chic and expensive, thanks in part to new convention centers, stadiums and performing-arts complexes. But some critics say downtowns' newfound popularity will fade as affluent city dwellers start families and move to the suburbs. Meanwhile, they say, low-income residents are being forced out of gentrifying neighborhoods.

Noel St. John

From *CQ Researcher*,
June 23, 2006 (updated September 27, 2010).

One fine May afternoon, Sam Kleckley was sitting in downtown Greenville, S.C., enjoying watching people meandering across the new pedestrian bridge overlooking the waterfalls cascading down the Reedy River. Nodding toward a wedding party posing for pictures, he said, "It's amazing the number of people who came here for prom pictures, too."

The chance for photo ops is new in downtown Greenville. A few years ago, a large vehicular bridge blocked the view of the falls. Today it's gone, and the 18-month-old pedestrian bridge and the park surrounding it are the city's leading tourist attraction.

But they're not the only draw in a downtown that suddenly finds itself crowded with shoppers and folks hunting for places to eat. Main Street, which had only four restaurants 20 years ago, now boasts more than 75. There's a busy performing-arts center, and the new minor league ballpark just up the street has largely silenced local complaints about the home team's quirky name, The Drive. And the number of downtown residential units has jumped 50 percent in the last five years.

"It is phenomenal," says Kleckley, owner of a restaurant with an impressive river view. "Ten years ago, this area was like a slum."

Greenville's revitalization *is* phenomenal, but it's far from unique. After decades of decline, America's downtowns are making a comeback. From Phoenix to Philadelphia, from Memphis to Minneapolis, once derelict areas have become clean, chic and expensive.

"If you look at the numbers, there's no question that downtowns are coming back and are healthy in ways that we never expected," says David Feehan, president of the International Downtown Association.

183

Suburbs Outpacing Central Cities

Suburbs throughout the United States are growing rapidly, especially in the South and West. In contrast, central cities are growing more slowly. In the Midwest, however, they are declining.

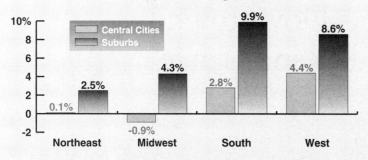

Population Change in Central Cities and Suburbs of Large Metropolitan Areas, 2000-2004
(By percent change)

Source: The Brookings Institution, "Living Cities Census Series," September 2005

Greenville suffered many of the same woes that befell other American cities after World War II, when an explosion of cars and road building lured city dwellers to the suburbs. Even today, Greenville accounts for only 56,000 residents in a sprawling county of 400,000.

But central business districts were never meant as places to live. They were where people went to work and shop. And they were famous for their huge department stores, women's-wear shops and, improbable as it may seem, car dealers. But the retail outlets and car dealerships soon followed their customers to the suburbs, where giant malls began rising in the 1940s. By 2000, downtown retail sales accounted for less than 5 percent of the nation's total, says Feehan.

Office workers still came downtown to shop, since many jobs remained in the cities, even through the worst of times. But casual visitors stayed away: Parking was scarce and expensive, many retail outlets had closed and crime became a major concern, particularly after a crack epidemic left drug addicts, homelessness and panhandlers in its wake. Cities in the 1970s and '80s were "places of crime and danger," says Paul Levy, president of the Philadelphia Center City District.

Downtowns had become the empty center of the metropolitan donut. But while suburban population and job

growth continue to outpace downtowns, central cities are experiencing an undeniable, if perhaps fragile, renaissance. A strong economy and better policing techniques, as pioneered in New York City, have helped bring crime way down. Violent crimes dropped by 32 percent between 1995 and 2004, according to the FBI. [1]

Moreover, says Feehan, between 1995 and 2005 major crimes declined 58 percent in U.S. cities. Business-improvement districts (BIDs) such as Levy's, invested heavily in sprucing up appearances, which helped downtowns look cleaner and safer. Many BIDs imposed levies or even helped pass tax increases that paid for new convention centers, stadiums and performing-arts complexes.

Movies and television shows like "Ally McBeal" and "Sex and the City" began depicting urban living as the lifestyle choice of hip, single, young adults. "The cultural change reflected demographic change," says Levy, "and these things are reinforcing each other."

Today, many young people aspire to live in cities because that's where the action is. For a generation that grew up knowing only the vast, anonymous spaces of shopping malls and suburban sprawl, downtowns feel richer in history and a sense of place. "People are looking for denser social experiences, a greater sense of civic life," says Alison Isenberg, a Rutgers University historian and author of the 2004 book *Downtown America*. "That's something that's very hard to find in suburbs."

Fifteen or 20 years ago, feasibility studies suggested no one would want to live downtown. But after a few developers took a risk and began converting abandoned old buildings into condos, the "loft" spaces became an important new trend.

"In the studies, no one could get it in their minds what it was like to live downtown," says Richard T. Reinhard, managing director of urban development and public infrastructure at the Urban Land Institute. "Yet when the product was put on the market, people discovered it was something that they really liked."

The lofts, coffee shops and hookah bars that now are common in many contemporary downtowns are catnip to young people. Older folks whose children are grown — so-called empty nesters — also find themselves drawn back to city living. Many baby boomers, it seems, find they no longer need 5,000-square-foot homes in suburban cul-de-sacs and instead prefer to walk to work or to downtown attractions.

Some worry that the influx of middle- and upper-income residents is driving out long-term, low-income residents. But others say that busier downtowns, which were never primarily residential areas, are a boon. Downtowns that once were barren after 6 o'clock are now bustling at night with tourists or residents with more disposable income than children. In Greenville, ballgames, outdoor concerts and other events draw people downtown and encourage them to loiter at restaurants and cafes. "There's something going on every night from Wednesday on," says Kleckley, the restaurant owner.

Many cities now rely on a similar formula of attractions and leisure spending, leading some critics to warn that downtowns are becoming Disneyfied versions of themselves — all with the same chain restaurants and not enough sustainable business activity of substance, such as legal and professional services. Downtowns certainly don't command the same dominant share of either jobs or

Downtown Revival Lagging in Some Cities

Only five downtown areas are fully developed in the United States, including Boston and Chicago, according to a Brookings Institution study. Another five are on the verge of taking off, and a baker's dozen are emerging. However, St. Louis and Detroit are among a dozen cities experiencing population declines.

Status of Downtowns in Major Cities

Fully Developed — Large, densely settled, sustained positive household growth in past three decades; highly educated, relatively affluent populace has highest rates of homeownership.

Boston	Lower Manhattan	Philadelphia
Chicago	Midtown Manhattan	

Emerging — Located primarily in the South and West, smaller and far less dense than fully developed downtowns; only experienced growth in the 1990s and are much less affluent; show promise of becoming fully developed if high household growth rates continue.

Atlanta	Cleveland	Memphis	Portland, Ore.
Baltimore	Denver	New Orleans	San Diego
Charlotte	Los Angeles	Norfolk	San Francisco
			Seattle

About to Take Off — Larger than emerging downtowns but slightly less dense; experienced greater losses in households between 1970-1990 than emerging downtowns but made a comeback in the '90s with higher rates of homeownership and educational attainment; relatively more affluent than emerging downtowns.

Chattanooga	Miami	Washington, D.C.
Dallas	Milwaukee	

Slow-Growing — Majority are in the South and West; the smallest and least dense of all the downtown categories. Experienced growth in the 1990s after significant losses in the previous two decades; generally lower average education attainment rates and less affluence than cities above.

Albuquerque	Boise	Indianapolis	Pittsburgh
Austin	Colorado Springs	Lafayette	Salt Lake City
	Columbus, Ohio	Phoenix	

Declining — Primarily in the Midwest and South, these downtowns are smaller and have less density; all lost households in each of the last three decades and by 2000 had just 65 percent of the households they had in 1970; small percentage of downtown residents have bachelor's degrees.

Cincinnati	Detroit	Mesa, Ariz.	San Antonio
Columbus, Ga.	Jackson, Miss.	Minneapolis	Shreveport
Des Moines	Lexington, Ky.	Orlando	St. Louis

Source: The Brookings Institution, "Living Cities Census Series," September 2005

City Shoppers Find Plenty of Merlot, But No Diapers

The Park Slope section of Brooklyn is now stroller infested, a prime place for parents wanting to raise their children in a leafy, upscale neighborhood. It is still adjusting, however, to its new demographics, with well-publicized disputes between parents and the childless as more and more places become child-friendly — even taverns.[1]

But the neighborhood hasn't fully given itself over to the prerogatives of parents. For one thing, there aren't enough disposable diapers. Eager shoppers are known to form long lines at the few places that carry the products whenever a delivery is expected.

Even in cities that have thriving downtown office and entertainment districts filled with crowded restaurants and condo and loft dwellers, retail has been slow to follow. Downtowns and their big department stores dominated retail during the first half of the 20th century, but only a paltry amount of goods are sold downtown today. "Even the office worker" — once the most loyal group of downtown shoppers — "has to be competed for against the suburban mall," says Alison Isenberg, author of *Downtown America*.

Shopping in urban areas is a lot different than in the suburbs, where well-stocked big-box and warehouse stores come equipped with lifetime supplies of groceries, household goods and other sundry items that are either hard to find in the inner city or are sold after a high markup in small convenience stores.

But that may be changing, at least in some places. Wal-Mart, the world's largest retailer, announced in April that it would open 50 stores in blighted urban areas over the next couple of years.[2] Its rival, Target, has already opened stores in several urban malls, including a two-story location in its hometown of Minneapolis. Even supermarkets, which have been fleeing urban settings since the 1970s, are returning.[3]

People may not want to drive very far to buy the goods and services that they need on a daily basis, such as groceries and dry cleaning. But, as with live entertainment or sports, suburbanites have become willing to come downtown for "destination shopping" — unique boutiques that have items that can't be found anywhere else, or stores that make shopping into an event.

"You don't go to Williams-Sonoma just to buy a frying pan," says David Feehan, president of the International Downtown Association. "It's all about the experience. They can teach you how to prepare French meals."

But author Joel Kotkin, a skeptic about the extent of downtown revivals, is dubious that downtown retail is going to make a dent in suburban sales. "It's very difficult in American cities now to find a unique anything," he says. "Why go to a Gap in Harvard Square when there's a Gap in every shopping mall?"

Although downtowns have found it tough to attract retail outlets, that is only natural, says Christopher B. Leinberger, a visiting fellow at the Brookings Institution. Retailers are followers of real estate, he says, reluctant to enter downtown markets until there is enough population in place to support them.

"The housing must be in place before a grocery can build a store," he says. "As a downtown redevelops, there are not enough households initially to justify the conventional grocery store."

Limitations on land present special challenges for big stores, especially for parking. But there are enough people moving into some downtowns to more than justify the headaches. In Manhattan, for example, more than 40 cash registers at the 59,000-square-foot Whole Foods store at Columbus Circle, on the Upper West Side, barely keep up with the crowds at lunch time and during the evening rush hour.[4]

"Grocery stores in particular are finding urban locations exceedingly profitable due to less shelf space devoted to low-profit paper goods, like diapers, and more space for more profitable take-out food for busy professional households," Leinberger concluded in a Brookings research brief.[5]

---

[1] Chris Erikson, "Lowering the Bar," *The New York Post*, Dec. 20, 2005, p. 42.

[2] Abigail Goldman, "Wal-Mart Plans Stores in Ailing Urban Areas," *Los Angeles Times*, April 5, 2006, p. C3.

[3] Alan Ehrenhalt, "The Grocery Gap," *Governing*, April 2006, p. 9.

[4] Teri Karush Rogers, "Turning Supermarkets Into Restaurants, Too," *The New York Times*, Aug. 28, 2005, p. 3:24.

[5] Christopher B. Leinberger, "Turning Around Downtown: Twelve Steps to Revitalization," Brookings Institution, March 2005, p. 19.

retail sales they once did. Indeed, the Census Bureau stopped tracking downtown retail sales in 1977 because the number had become such a small percentage of overall metropolitan sales — just 4 percent compared with 50 percent in 1920. Thus, rather than being revitalized, downtowns are being reinvented, Isenberg suggests.

Despite the naysaying, there's no question that dozens of American downtowns are livelier places than they were just a few years ago. "If we're filling up the buildings and we're attracting middle- and upper-income people and we're having lively streets and restaurants, where's the problem?" wonders Feehan. "I don't see it."

As people contemplate the changing nature of downtowns and their future, here are some of the questions they're debating:

Are downtowns making a sustainable comeback?

Greenville has drawn people back downtown using several methods that have become popular with city governments: It helped build a large hotel for business meetings, a pair of large performing-arts venues and the new ballpark. Those attractions provided anchors for downtown development along Main Street, encouraging both people and retailers to return to the area.

Although many downtowns today clearly are healthier than they were a few years ago, many experts fear their success is not built on solid foundations. Because many reviving downtowns rely heavily on entertainment, skeptics wonder how long such "urban theme parks" will remain popular. And downtown growth — in terms of business, retail and residential — still represents only a fraction of the continued oceanic swelling of American suburbs.

"The numbers are pretty overwhelming that what is happening in downtowns is real but very, very small compared to suburbs," says Joel Kotkin, a senior fellow at the New America Foundation and author of several books and studies about cities. "Perhaps most troubling, there is not a huge amount of job growth in most of the traditional downtowns, even though we have a strong [nationwide] expansion. My sense is that many cities are becoming more residential, in part, because the office demands are not there."

Pittsburgh Cultural Trust (both)

Transformation in Pittsburgh

In the 1980s, the Harris Theater was one of many X-rated attractions in downtown Pittsburgh. Today the dramatically revitalized central city features a dozen theaters and performance spaces and numerous art galleries.

Downtowns might be able to survive as "Disneylands for adults," as Kotkin calls them, but some analysts worry they'll lose their shine over time. New downtown residents are overwhelmingly young professionals who may very well move back to the suburbs soon after starting families because, while public schools in many large cities have shown measurable

Top Cities Are Fun, Hip and Affordable

The cities that Americans most want to live in feature good values in home prices, reasonable costs of living, high quality of life, access to quality health care and a strong economy, according to a survey by Kiplinger's Personal Finance. Here are the top 10 cities on the magazine's list of the 50 most desirable cities:

1. *Nashville, Tenn.* — Affordable homes, mild climate, lively entertainment scene.

2. *Minneapolis-St. Paul, Minn.* — Hip and progressive atmosphere with a Midwestern sensibility, multiple cultural outlets, professional teams in all four major sports, a dozen universities and colleges and a diverse economy.

3. *Albuquerque, N.M.* — Resort-town ambience, boomtown economy but reasonable prices.

4. *Atlanta, Ga.* — Vibrant city with a rich history, good health care, hip cultural scene and genteel neighborhoods shaded by magnificent dogwood and magnolia trees.

5. *Austin, Texas* — State capital features a medley of culture, history and politics, including the University of Texas, the Zachary Scott Theater and the Umlauf Sculpture Garden and Museum.

6. *Kansas City* — Straddling the Kansas and Missouri state line, offers stately houses, downtown suburbs, world-class museums and barbecue.

7. *Asheville, N.C.* — A virtually franchise-free downtown with fine cuisine, unique crafts, live-music venues, fine arts and beautiful mountain views.

8. *Ithaca, N.Y.* — In the scenic Finger Lakes region, liberal home of Cornell University; farms provide rich assortment of organic products.

9. *Pittsburgh, Pa.* — Undergoing an ongoing renaissance; distinctive neighborhoods, tree-lined streets, glittering skyscrapers, upscale shops and a diversified economy.

10. *Iowa City, Iowa* — Oasis on the prairie bursting with creative and intellectual energy, including an annual jazz festival, a Shakespeare festival and the home of the University of Iowa.

Source: "50 Smart Places to Live," Kiplinger's Personal Finance, *June 2006*

and planning at MIT. "That's the big litmus test even for people who are big city lovers — the quality of the public schools, outdoor space, the ability to pick up the things you need without having to take a large chunk out of your day."

Indeed, says Meg Boyco, a loft dweller in downtown St. Louis, having to drive miles to buy groceries or rent videos gets old fast. "It seems nice, but are people going to grow old here?" she asked. "Is it going to be people moving in and out for three years at a time, while they get established and then bump into the suburbs?"[2]

However, downtown boosters note that even in their heyday, downtowns weren't home to very many people. And they don't think downtowns will ever return as singularly important economic centers. But that doesn't mean urban centers can't become healthier.

"Some people are saying that downtown revitalization is a myth because the numbers aren't growing like in the suburbs," says Feehan, of the International Downtown Association. "Of course not — it's a built area."

And even if they only appeal to a limited subset of people — young professionals and empty nesters — that's still a sizable, growing market as baby boomers retire and the 25-to-35-year-old cohort expands. After all, points out Christopher B. Leinberger, a visiting fellow at the Brookings Institution's Metropolitan Policy Program, three-quarters of U.S. households do not have school-age children.

"Clearly, downtowns play a central role in the identity of a region," says Lee Munnich, director of the state and local policy program at the University of Minnesota's

improvement of late, they remain poor performers compared to suburban schools.

"Clearly, cities can maintain a certain amount of vitality with empty nesters and young professionals, but to sustain their health there has to be more infrastructure," says Lorlene Hoyt, a professor of urban studies

Hubert H. Humphrey Institute of Public Affairs. "They're still major employment centers, and they're increasingly a place where people are choosing to live and spend their leisure time."

Cities long sought magic bullets — such as sports arenas or free parking — to solve their downtown woes. "The history of downtowns contains a lot of false optimism," says Otis White, an Atlanta-based consultant to cities. "There was always a search for an easy solution to fixing downtowns, but they were in the grip of bigger forces than beautification can deal with."

Since then, says Rutgers historian Isenberg, cities have realized that no one thing — whether retail, residential or entertainment — is going to restore downtowns. Rather, the mix of attractions will need regular updating and maintenance, just as shopping centers and industrial parks do, and downtowns will have to be adaptable. And unlike the urban-renewal movement of the 1950s and '60s — when entire neighborhoods were destroyed, hundreds of acres at a time, to make way for new developments — planners today "envision more incremental progress," she argues.

"There is no, one, stable set of ideas, no one stable set of needs that can be met downtown," Isenberg says. "What we see as aesthetically pleasing today, or what we want to see downtown, will be different in 30 years."

Does gentrification hurt longtime residents?

Much of the recent downtown revitalization has been fostered by tax breaks. Cities often agree to forego a percentage of property taxes to get more attractive properties built. In Houston's rapidly gentrifying Third Ward, however, Texas state Rep. Garnet Coleman is using the same tax-financing arrangements to put limits on growth.

A board he partially controls has been buying up land in order to keep it away from developers who want to tear down low-cost housing and replace it with high-priced condominiums. He's also trying to impose restrictive deeds and covenants on existing properties to ensure that they are used only for rental housing in perpetuity.

"We can give tax abatements out the wazoo for lofts and condominiums," Coleman told *Governing* magazine. "The question is . . . whether we are willing to

Milwaukee's popular River Walk blossomed from the city's once-undeveloped waterfront in the late 1990s. It now features condominiums, restaurants and entertainment.

spend the same money on people who need a nice, affordable, clean place to live."[3]

While Coleman's tactics are unusual, his motivation is not. As middle- and upper-income people move into downtowns, there has been widespread concern that lower-income residents will be priced out of their longtime neighborhoods.

In May the Los Angeles City Council approved a one-year moratorium on conversions of 14,000 single-room occupancy (SRO) hotel rooms, which generally serve the poor, into high-end condos. It is also considering a broader slowdown on residential redevelopment.

"Landlords were evicting tenants so they could flip those properties," says Eva Kandarpa, an aide to Councilwoman Jan Perry, who sponsored the ordinance. "We wanted to stop that until we could come up with a comprehensive plan for more affordable housing."

Columbia University urban-planning professor Lance Freeman lauds the goal of trying to get more affordable housing built but says trying to halt gentrification won't achieve that aim. In a 2005 study, Freeman concluded that residents of gentrifying neighborhoods were no more likely to move than residents of non-gentrifying neighborhoods. Older neighborhoods tend to have a high turnover in any event, he found, but improvements in gentrifying areas — such as increased jobs and falling

Getty Images/Mark Wilson

A critic of the Supreme Court's controversial *Kelo v. New London* decision makes his position clear at a Senate Judiciary Committee hearing last year. The court ruled that New London, Conn., could force homeowners to sell their land to make way for a $350 million pharmaceutical factory.

crime rates — were likely to be a boon to long-term residents, who then are more inclined to stay.[4]

Freeman concedes, however, that lower-income residents may feel the wealthier newcomers change the fabric of the community, and renters may be forced out if the affordable housing stock is limited. Even so, cities that do not gentrify will be no better off, he says.

"It's hard to argue that cities are better off if housing is affordable because no one wants to live there," he says.

Similarly, Duke University economist Jacob Vigdor, who has studied gentrification in Boston, says gentrification is a symptom, not the cause of housing-affordability problems. In other words, residents are often displaced because land values throughout a regional market are going up — not just in their neighborhood — which encourages new development that in turn attracts new people.

No one is going to go to the expense of renovating an old warehouse, Vigdor says, until property values have already climbed enough to justify the investment.

"People assume that the arrival of yuppies [young urban professionals] causes price escalation," he says. "But when the prices start to go up, that's what gets developers' juices flowing."

In addition, since unused, old warehouses — along with schools, jails, office buildings and even grain elevators — often are converted into urban housing, that means no one is being displaced, say some downtown boosters. If no one was living there previously, how can they be forced out?

"A lot of downtowns historically have not had much in the way of housing," Freeman says. "If you add housing to the downtown, and no one was living there previously or it was predominantly manufacturing, then you wouldn't expect much displacement."

But such analyses don't sit well with longtime residents of New York's Harlem or San Francisco's Mission District, who feel their neighborhoods are being overrun by latte-sippers who are driving up property costs and forcing them out. To prevent that, many cities require developers of high-end projects to create a certain number of affordable-housing units.

"Lower-class housing and work-force housing are diminishing," says Donald J. Borut, executive director of the National League of Cities. "Where cops and teachers can afford to live — it's not a small issue."

"Atlanta is gentrifying at a very substantial rate," says Larry Keating, a professor of city and regional planning at Georgia Institute of Technology, who recently chaired a gentrification task force for the City Council. "The displacement [of low-income renters] is substantial."

While urban improvements enhance a city's overall tax base, he says, they reduce the amount of affordable housing, forcing poor residents to the city's fringes or the suburbs, tearing apart their social networks.

"Absolutely, people are being displaced," says Brookings' Leinberger. He recommends policies to help transfer some of cities' growing wealth into programs to subsidize affordable housing.

He mordantly recalls a multi-panel cartoon that illustrates some of the negative social dynamics associated with gentrification. The first panel shows a white couple moving out to the suburbs during the 1950s and extolling their good fortune. The second shows an African-American couple moving to the suburbs during the 1990s and feeling equally lucky to be leaving the city.

CHRONOLOGY

1940s-1960s *Downtowns lose business and cities lose population to suburbs.*

1948 Downtown's share of retail trade — nearly one-third before the Great Depression — falls to 11 percent.

1949 Housing Act provides federal funds to help cities acquire and clear slum and blighted property for private redevelopment.

1961 Jane Jacobs publishes *The Death and Life of Great American Cities*, arguing that small, dense mixed-use neighborhoods are more vital and safer than huge developments.

1965 Congress creates Department of Housing and Urban Development (HUD), the first Cabinet-level agency devoted to urban problems.

1968 Assassination of civil rights leader the Rev. Martin Luther King Jr. sparks rioting in 125 cities, killing 39 and damaging 2,600 buildings.

1970s-1980s *Federal government scales back its commitment to urban programs; cities begin attracting specialty shops and new customers.*

1973 President Richard M. Nixon freezes most HUD programs to control costs and address allegations of mishandled funds.

1974 Congress approves Community Development block grants for city infrastructure improvements.

1975 President Gerald R. Ford refuses federal aid to financially ailing New York City, prompting *Daily News* headline, "Ford to City: Drop Dead."

1976 Developer James Rouse opens Faneuil Hall Marketplace in historic Boston building, beginning string of urban "festival" markets.

1977 Community Development Reinvestment Act requires lenders to invest in their areas of service.

1984 *Newsweek* declares "The Year of the Yuppie" in response to the growing number of affluent white-collar workers in some cities.

1987 President Ronald Reagan abolishes revenue sharing, which distributed federal funds to states and cities.

1990s-2000s *The nation's improving economy helps revive cities that provide professional or technological services; cities succeed in developing a mix of attractions that lure some downtown inhabitants.*

1991 Driven partly by the crack cocaine epidemic of the late 1980s, the U.S. homicide rate peaks at 9.8 per 100,000 population, largely affecting urban areas.

1992 U.S. Conference of Mayors leads thousands in March on Washington, proposes "Marshall Plan for the Cities" to be paid for with $35 billion in new federal funds. . . . Baltimore opens Camden Yards stadium, a much-imitated home for baseball's Orioles that is integrated with its downtown, its bustling harbor and the city's mass-transit system.

1993 Congress rejects President Bill Clinton's $16 billion economic-stimulus package for cities.

1995 Clinton creates urban-empowerment and enterprise zones in cities receiving federal funds and tax incentives for development and social services.

2000 Eight of the 15 cities that had been among the nation's 15 largest in 1950 have lost population for the fifth census in a row.

2004 Chicago opens its downtown Millennium Park, a $475 million, 24-acre sculpture garden.

2005 President George W. Bush's budget would slash Community Development Block Grants. . . . U.S. Supreme Court upholds cities' ability to take control of private property through eminent domain in *Kelo v. New London* case. . . . Hurricane Katrina devastates New Orleans.

2006 During the first five months of the year, 23 state legislatures pass bills to restrict cities' use of eminent domain. . . . Federal housing officials announce that more than 5,000 public housing units in New Orleans will be razed in favor of mixed-income developments.

2009

January — President Obama takes office during a severe economic downturn but with a solid base of urban voters and a willingness to use federal power to steer resources to cities.

May 5 — Former NBA basketball star Dave Bing is elected mayor of Detroit.

Sept. 14 — Bing launches strategic plan to remake Detroit's downtown, including projects to convert abandoned residential property to farmland.

Dec. 16 — Cleveland-area Cuyahoga County Land Reutilization Corporation (CCLRC) reaches agreement with mortgage giant Fannie Mae allowing CCLRC to acquire properties from Fannie's inventory of foreclosed homes.

2010

Jan. 13 — CCLRC transforms its first property into a community garden.

Jan. 15 — CCLRC receives $40 million from U.S. Department of Housing and Urban Development (HUD) to rehabilitate homes for resale to low- and middle-income families.

April 22 — CCLRC receives $400,000 from U.S. Environmental Protection Agency to help assess environmental contamination in industrial, residential and commercial sites.

July 2 — CCLRC reaches agreement with HUD in which HUD's foreclosed properties in Cuyahoga County appraised for $20,000 or less can be transferred to the land bank for $100.

Oct. 13-15 — Cleveland scheduled to host CCLRC conference on the reclamation of vacant properties.

The last panel shows the white couple returning happily to the city, saying, "It worked."

Should greater restrictions be placed on government use of eminent domain to acquire land?

Some recent downtown development, especially major projects covering many acres, has been fostered by cities using their power of eminent domain — the process of condemning private land for public use.

The Constitution forbids governments from "seizing" private property without compensating its owners, but cities have long used eminent domain — or condemnation — to force owners to sell when it is determined that the land is needed for the public's benefit. Although governments usually buy property through normal real estate transactions, they sometimes use eminent domain to take control of large parcels of land rather than having to deal with scattered holdouts reluctant to sell.

In the past, local governments used eminent domain to acquire land for public infrastructure, such as roads, bridges, railroads or schools. But during the urban-renewal movement that flourished from the 1940s to the 1960s, they began using eminent domain for economic purposes, taking over blighted sections of towns — often occupied primarily by African-Americans or poor residents — that were ripe for redevelopment.

Recently, cash-strapped cities have begun using their powers of eminent domain again to promote economic development by condemning commercially viable properties or middle-income homes to make way for pricier hotels, retail shops or condominiums. The higher-end use of the land will bring in greater tax revenues, the cities argue, thus benefiting the common good. For example, Greenville employed eminent domain to acquire rundown riverfront warehouses for a large hotel, office, condo and artists' studio complex.

CBS' "60 Minutes" highlighted a city that went so far as to redefine "blighted" to include park-side homes with only a single-car garage so middle-class homes could be condemned to make way for upscale condos with a park view. In Minnesota, a car dealership was forced to sell out five years ago to make way for Best Buy's $160 million corporate headquarters in suburban Richfield.

"We cannot understand how giving our property to a multibillion-dollar company like Best Buy serves a 'public purpose' as the law mandates," said Barbara Jerich, general counsel for Walser Automotive Group.[5]

Cities and developers, however, point out that a big electronics headquarters, for example, generates more

"Walkable Urbanity" Livens Up the Burbs

The population of Sugar Hill, Ga., about 40 miles north of Atlanta, has tripled over the last decade, leading local officials to try to think of new ways to improve things. When they polled townspeople about the changes they would most like to see, the answer was overwhelming: They wanted a lively, pedestrian-friendly downtown.

Sugar Hill is now building itself a downtown — from scratch — along a road that will be lined with 15-foot-wide sidewalks. Developers are eager to start filling in the area with stores and restaurants.

"They wanted that hometown, downtown walking area, and that's what the mayor and council have said they'll have," says City Manager Bob Hail. "We are not renovating. We are doing the 'build it and they will come.' "

Sugar Hill is not the first place in the area to try to create instant urbanism. Many communities within the sprawling 17-county metro Atlanta region have decided they need town centers, both to provide a distinct identity for their communities and to afford residents the pleasures of a walkable downtown shopping and entertainment district without having to drive into the big city.

"Deprived by the difficulty of driving to social and cultural activities, people are bringing those activities to the suburbs," says Michael M. Sizemore, whose firm designed a downtown for Smyrna, 35 miles west of Sugar Hill. "When they do, it starts to provide the anchor or catalyst for revitalizing their downtowns."

The suburbs are associated with strip malls and other signs of sprawl, but some observers predict they will increasingly become convenient, urban-style gathering places. "There is so much pent-up demand for walkable urbanity that it cannot all be satisfied in the traditional downtown," says Christopher B. Leinberger, an urban strategist and developer.

Even more common than the creation of new downtowns is the phenomenon of older suburbs attempting to revitalize central business and shopping districts — often located near mass-transit lines — that had long been neglected. In Decatur, which sits along Atlanta's eastern border, the shopping district is undergoing extensive renovation, and the first new downtown residential units are being built since the Great Depression, all within easy walking distance of a stop on Atlanta's citywide rail system.

"The 1950s and 60s suburban ideal was you don't want to live anywhere near a storefront, you want to get as far away as possible from commercial development," said Brian J. Nickerson, director of the Michaelian Institute for Public Policy and Management at Pace University in New York City. "Now, you want to live above the storefront."[1]

In many suburbs, old-fashioned shopping malls are giving way to "town centers" or "lifestyle centers" — shopping complexes that mimic some of the qualities of the walkable downtowns. In some cases, this amounts to a direct swap. In Centennial, Colo., the 1974-vintage Southglenn Mall will be replaced with a development called The Streets at Southglenn that will feature — in addition to about 100 stores — sidewalk cafes, shaded walkways and little nooks for relaxing.

More than 60 lifestyle centers will open around the country this year and next, compared with just one traditional covered mall, according to the International Council of Shopping Centers.[2] "In both suburban downtowns and new town developments, you've got civic leaders and developers trying to replicate the success of urban downtowns," says Brad Segal, president of Progressive Urban Management Associates, a development-consulting firm in Denver.

Segal questions the staying power of the new shopping developments, warning they offer too many of the same chain stores and have a homogeneous, cookie-cutter feel as a result. Urban "downtowns have a competitive advantage in terms of organic qualities that have evolved over time — they have 100 or 200 years of history, and you can see it," he says. "These new lifestyle centers are really a product of 2006."

For now, though, it is clear that many suburbs covet sophisticated little shopping areas of their own. Perhaps the new downtown designers in Sugar Hill will be able to pull a page from Smyrna's successful urban playbook. Retail sales and property values there have increased so much that the city has been able to lower its property tax rates every year since construction of the downtown began in the late 1980s.

"For about a half-mile all around it, there are all kinds of development," Sizemore says. "If you create a place that's great for everybody, starting with the kids, everybody wants to be there, and they're willing to pay for it."

[1] Debra West, "Adding More Urban to Suburbia," *The New York Times*, May 14, 2006, Section 14WC, p. 1.

[2] Thaddeus Herrick, "Fake Towns Rise, Offering Urban Life Without the Grit," *The Wall Street Journal*, May 31, 2006, p. A1.

San Diego's PETCO Park, a new open-air stadium built in the East Village area near the historic Gaslamp Quarter, is part of a comprehensive plan to revitalize the city's aging downtown.

income and jobs than a car dealer and a few dozen homes, benefiting the entire community. Losing such a moneymaker due to the intransigence of a single property owner would have been a big blow to the area, said the project's supporters.

Nevertheless, the practice has stirred up stiff resistance among affected landowners, who claim cities are "stealing" private land to sell it to rich developers at reduced rates. When a city condemns land, it normally only pays the appraised value for the land — usually lower than the price developers would have to pay on the open market. If a redevelopment project is such a wise investment, argue affected landowners, developers should just buy the land on the open market.

The simmering controversy burst into the open in 2005, when the U.S. Supreme Court ruled in *Kelo v. New London* that New London, Conn., could legally force landowners in the "distressed municipality" to sell their land to make way for a $350 million pharmaceutical factory. Fifteen homeowners didn't want to sell, but in a 5 to 4 decision the Supreme Court ruled that the increased potential economic activity generated by the plant justified the city's taking of the land. Swelling the tax base amounted to a "public purpose," the court ruled.[6]

"Promoting economic development is a traditional and long accepted function of government," Justice John Paul Stevens wrote. "Clearly, there is no basis for exempting economic development from our traditionally broad understanding of public purpose."[7]

But in her dissenting opinion Justice Sandra Day O'Connor wrote: "Under the banner of economic development, all private property is now vulnerable to being taken and transferred to another private owner, so long as it might be upgraded. The specter of condemnation hangs over all property. Nothing is to prevent the state from replacing any Motel 6 with a Ritz-Carlton, any home with a shopping mall or any farm with a factory."

If eminent domain was not a sexy topic before, *Kelo* turned it into one, stirring up a hornet's nest of opposition in cities across the country. "I was down about the decision for about 20 minutes," recalls Scott Bullock, a senior attorney with the libertarian Institute for Justice in Arlington, Va., who argued New London landowner Susette Kelo's case before the court. Then he saw O'Connor's passionate dissent and realized she had handed him a gift. "I read the dissenting opinions and realized that there's a real opportunity here to take what was a terrible decision and turn it into something that was very positive for property owners."

Indeed, both conservatives and liberals opposed the decision. Conservatives disliked the apparent expansion of governmental power over private property. Liberals — recalling the massive displacement of poor communities during the urban-renewal movement — feared the practice could be used to once again force low-income citizens from their homes to make way for the wealthy.

Before the decision, nine state supreme courts had already forbidden the use of eminent domain to build revenues or employment.[8] In fact, Justice Stevens explicitly pointed out that states have the power to curb the use of eminent domain — and many have quickly done

San Diego Convention and Visitors Bureau

so. In the past year, two-dozen states have passed new restrictions on the use of eminent domain, and bills to restrict the practice have been introduced in Congress and nearly every state legislature. Initiatives are on the ballot in four states, and petitions are circulating in California and eight other states to put it before voters in November, according to the American Planning Association.

"What I don't like is where somebody has a higher and better use in their minds, and they give the land to a private developer," says Indiana state Rep. David Wolkins, who sponsored a bill that would discourage the practice by narrowing the state's definition of blight and forcing redevelopment agencies to pay ousted owners 150 percent of the appraised value of a property.

Similar arguments were made in Iowa, where the legislature this year voted to restrict the use of eminent domain to areas that are 75 percent blighted. But developers and local officials say that's a bad idea, because areas targeted for redevelopment will have to decline further before a city can step in to improve them. They cite the example of downtown Des Moines, which was legally declared a slum 30 years ago — dominated by dilapidated buildings, abandoned stores and seedy hotels. The city has since helped foster an impressive renaissance, using eminent domain to make way for several office and retail complexes and other projects that have increased the taxable value of the area by more than $1 billion.

"We would not have the development activity we have within the downtown core right now if we didn't have eminent domain," says Councilwoman Christine Hensley, who represents the area. The legislature went overboard in reaction to anti-*Kelo* emotions, she says. Sounding emotional herself, she adds, "It pisses me off." Perhaps responding to such reasoning — if not the emotion — Gov. Tom Vilsack vetoed the eminent-domain bill.

Indianapolis Mayor Bart Peterson says eminent domain should be left intact because it is self-regulating — taking private property is usually so controversial public officials don't do it unless it's absolutely necessary. "Elected officials rightly know they cannot go around taking property at will," he says.

If they didn't know it before, they've certainly gotten the message since *Kelo*. Ironically, the decision didn't

Blossoming Cities

(Top): Architect Santiago Calatrava designed a recent addition to the Milwaukee Art Museum, right. New condos are rising nearby. (Middle): Several big projects in Phoenix, including expansion of the Convention Center, are pumping new life into the city. (Bottom): New York's Harlem has undergone a dramatic revival that has seen the arrival of new businesses and residents and restoration of the world-famous Apollo Theater.

expand local governments' powers; it merely affirmed them. But in so doing, the court set the stage for a political backlash that has left many cities with more limited tools for promoting economic development.

In that regard, says the National League of Cities' Borut, "It was like winning the Super Bowl and then not having a team."

BACKGROUND

Industrial Age

America's cities grew rapidly as the country industrialized in the late 19th century, and millions left their farms or their home countries and poured into American downtowns. Between 1790 and 1890, the total U.S. population grew 16-fold — but the nation's urban population grew to 139 times its 1790 size.[9]

Downtowns were often referred to as the cities' heart, with streetcars bringing workers in each morning and carrying them home each night. Not every town had a skyscraper or an opera house, but they all had commercial Main Streets, points out author Isenberg in *Downtown America*.[10] Downtowns also served as a melting pot for the cities — the one area where people from all over came and felt welcome.

"The central business district was the one bit of turf common to all," writes historian Jon C. Teaford. "Along the downtown thoroughfares, wealthy financiers passed by grubby beggars, rubbed shoulders with horny-handed porters and draymen and jostled for space with clerks and stenographers."[11]

Downtowns were also home to railroad and ferry terminals, department stores and often the cities' sole business and financial districts. As late as 1890, downtowns were often the only part of town with electricity.[12] They were compact, crowded places for industry and shopping, often occupying less than a square mile but generating more trade than the rest of the city combined. And they generated a huge percentage of urban property-tax valuations — more than 20 percent in St. Louis, for example, and almost half in Cincinnati.[13]

Downtowns in the early 20th century also became great manufacturing centers, and it was convenient to have lawyers, accountants and other professional services nearby. Convenience also drew women shoppers downtown, where they could find everything they wanted in one of the mammoth department stores that dominated retail sales. Novelist William Kennedy recalls "booming, bustling" downtown Albany, where "crowds were six abreast on the sidewalks at high noon and all day Saturday,

City of Greenville

Newly revitalized Greenville, S.C., turned the Reedy River and its scenic falls into the city's most popular attraction. Main Street, which had only four restaurants 20 years ago, now boasts more than 75. There's also a performing-arts center and a new minor league ballpark just up the street.

when all the trolley cars were crowded, and you had to stand in line to get into the movies."[14]

By 1925, the 18 cities with populations of more than 400,000 had grown by an average of 71 percent since the dawn of the century. Los Angeles had ballooned by 609 percent; Detroit had more than tripled.[15] As cities grew more crowded, many families became willing to ride an hour to distant neighborhoods or out to the country to avoid living under or over another family. As a result, cities desperately needed rapid transit, especially as automobile traffic began to clog downtown streets.

Many cities talked of building subways to deliver every resident to within a half-mile of his job, but few invested the large sums required. By the late 1920s, New York and Boston boasted more than 90 percent of the nation's subway traffic.[16]

Moving on Out

Faced with congestion and high downtown land values, industry began to move out of the central cities by the late 1920s, first to peripheral neighborhoods and then to suburbs. In suburban Dearborn, Mich., Ford's River Rouge facility — the largest factory in the world when it opened in 1928 — was more than double the size of downtown Detroit. Secondary business districts also began to spring up, with some professional firms moving their administrative offices out and banks beginning to set up branch offices.

Retailers soon followed suit. Because a central-city location no longer guaranteed proximity to shoppers, a proliferation of chain stores moved into the suburbs. Joseph Appel, president of Wanamaker's department store, wrote in 1928 that it was time for the store to go to its customers rather than try "to force them to come to us."[17]

The Great Depression of the 1930s, which hit inner cities disproportionately hard, accelerated the trend outward. Hotels and other downtown properties fell widely into receivership, and more office buildings were being torn down during the decade than were going up. Desperate owners tore down tall buildings, replacing them with one- or two-story parking lots, in order to decrease their tax burdens and generate some income. Chicago's land value dropped by as much as 78.5 percent from 1930 to 1935, while New York City's assessed values by 1939 had dropped below 1889 levels.[18] *Business Week* declared in 1940: "Every American city of 6,000,000 or 6,000 population shows symptoms of identical dry rot at its core."[19]

By the end of World War II, central-business-district organizations had sprung up in most cities to lobby for tax and zoning policies that would promote downtowns as places worth visiting. They studied how to improve transportation and even the idea of banning downtown traffic, but the forces favoring the decentralization of commerce were ultimately much stronger.

After the war, even though the nation's economy boomed, downtowns stagnated. The newly built parking lots didn't generate jobs, and new freeways meant that more and more downtown land was devoted to traffic and parking and less to trade. Congestion remained a problem, prompting many big businesses to follow heavy industry to the suburbs.[20] Several insurance companies moved from New York to leafy Westchester County, just north of Manhattan, as did General Foods, Standard Oil and other large corporations. Cargill, the country's largest grain trader, left Minneapolis for Lake Minnetonka.[21] In 1948, 80 percent of the new manufacturing, retail and wholesale jobs were being created in the suburbs.[22]

That year, in fact, downtowns' share of the nation's retail trade, which had been nearly one-third in 1929, plummeted to just 11 percent.[23] (The first regional shopping center had been built in Los Angeles a year earlier.)

Over the next six years, retail sales downtown climbed by just 1.6 percent while increasing 32.3 percent in suburbs.[24]

As the president of the TG&Y variety store chain declared, "We do not think the housewives (who are our main customers) will drive miles and miles to get downtown when they can obtain the same merchandise in better facilities in the suburbs."[25]

Urban "Jungles"

During the early 1950s, 84 percent of the nation's population growth occurred in the 168 metropolitan areas, but less than 2 percent was in central cities.

"The upper and middle classes were moving to the periphery and the suburbs," writes MIT urban historian Robert M. Fogelson in his 2001 book *Downtown*. "But the lower class, many of whose members belonged to one or another of the nation's ethnic and racial minorities, were staying put — some because they did not want to move, others because they could not afford to."[26]

As downtown retailers lost their best customers, private interests sought to raze the slums in the inner city to make way for large-scale development. Local governments hoping for increased property assessments were eager to help them. A 1955 *Life* magazine article, headlined "An Encroaching Menace," captured the tone of their plea: "The slums of Chicago each year have pushed closer to the heart of the city. Some of the worst came only six blocks from the glittering skyscrapers. There a newly aroused and desperate city stopped them."[27]

States such as New York and New Jersey gave private companies the power of eminent domain, authorizing them to acquire land for redevelopment. Congress got involved, passing the Housing Act of 1949, which further spurred urban clearance and redevelopment. In theory, private initiatives were supposed to improve and rebuild low-income housing, but that rarely happened. By 1961, 126,000 residential units had been demolished but only 28,000 built to replace them.[28] A study that year found that in 60 cities that had undertaken urban-renewal projects, 60 percent of the dispossessed simply relocated to other substandard housing.[29]

During the 1960s, Presidents John F. Kennedy and Lyndon B. Johnson dramatically expanded the scope of federal urban policy. In 1965, Johnson created the Department of Housing and Urban Development (HUD), the first

Are downtowns undergoing a real renaissance?

YES
David Feehan
President, International Downtown Association

Written for *CQ Researcher*, June 2006

The evidence is irrefutable: Downtowns in the United States have made a remarkable, perhaps historic, comeback. After decades of decline, disinvestment and near abandonment, American downtowns are experiencing what can only be called a renaissance.

This remarkable phenomenon is not without its critics and cynics. The most prominent of these, however, blithely ignore the overwhelming body of evidence and instead engage in sensationalistic arguments based on highly selective data and flawed reasoning. Often they compare downtown growth with suburban growth, which is a bit like comparing a minivan and a sports car — they both are gasoline-powered vehicles with four wheels, but with decidedly different purposes and ancestries.

Let's look at the facts: In the early 1990s, an economist studying downtown's economic importance found that it contributed more than $19 in tax revenues to various taxing bodies for every dollar in services it consumed. City managers, finance directors and other city officials have confirmed that these numbers are reasonably representative of most downtowns and central cities in the United States. Clearly, downtown is the economic engine that pulls the city's train. Strong downtowns make stronger core cities possible, which in turn helps to support regional economic health.

The downtown office market is showing strength and resiliency. Occupancy rates nationally since 1990 have favored downtowns over suburbs. The downtown housing market is strong and has grown explosively in many cities, including cities of every size and region — from New York, Philadelphia and Washington to Miami, Los Angeles and Seattle; and from Memphis to Des Moines to Fort Worth to Albuquerque. People want to live downtown and will pay a premium to do so.

Dining, entertainment, sports, meetings and conventions and tourist attractions have all expanded in downtowns. Crime is at historic lows. Downtown public spaces not only look better but also are managed better than ever through a plethora of public-private partnerships and business-improvement districts.

Downtowns are stronger than at any time in the past 50 years, and as downtowns continue to improve they provide the resources cities need to improve neighborhoods, schools and services. The downtown renaissance is little more than a decade old, and it may take another decade or two for urban neighborhoods to catch up. But now, with revitalized downtowns, they may have the resources and opportunity to do so. Few would argue that this is a very important goal.

NO
Joel Kotkin
Irvine Senior Fellow, New America Foundation

Written for *CQ Researcher*, June 2006

Even amidst a strong economic expansion, the most recent census data reveal a renewed migration out of our urban centers. This gives considerable lie to the notion, popularized over a decade — particularly among the media — that cities are enjoying a historic rebound.

In 1999 *The Economist* suggested "Americans [are] abandoning their love affair with far-flung suburbs and shopping malls." The recovery in some downtowns, suggested Jonathan Fanton, president of the MacArthur Foundation, heralded a new "urban renaissance."

But this may be more wishful thinking than reality. Since 1950 more than 90 percent of all growth in U.S. metropolitan areas has been in the suburbs. Nor is this trend showing any sign of turning around. Census data show that since 2000 even healthy urban centers like New York, Boston, Portland, Ore., and San Francisco have experienced slowing or declining population growth. Meanwhile, suburbs in those regions and elsewhere have been capturing an ever-expanding percentage of both people and jobs.

The simple fact is that most Americans — including 86 percent of all Californians, according to a recent survey — express a great preference for single-family homes, which for most means choosing suburbia. Unless there is some radical and unexpected change, most new population growth and expansion of the built environment (which is estimated to grow 50 percent by 2030) will occurr in the suburbs, particularly in the South and West — places dominated by low-density, automobile-dependent growth.

The tapering housing bubble has created a false notion of an urban renaissance driven by, among other things, empty nesters returning to the city. In many urban cores, from New York to San Diego, large numbers of condo units — in some cases upwards of a third — have been bought not by new urbanites but by speculators. So we have the odd phenomenon of more housing units, at higher costs, but fewer full-time residents.

Instead of luring the "hip and cool" with high-end amenities, cities should address issues that concern businesses as well as middle-class families. These include such basic needs as public safety, maintenance of parks, improving public schools and cutting taxes — in other words, all those unsexy things that contribute to maintaining a job base and upward mobility.

Cities can't thrive merely as amusement parks for the rich, the nomadic young and tourists. To remain both vital and economically relevant, they must remain anchored by a large middle class, and by families and businesses that feel safe and committed to the urban place.

Cabinet-level position to address the problems of urban America. Its first major initiative — Model Cities — sought to include community wishes in comprehensive rebuilding plans.

But inner cities continued to become islands of ethnicity due to "white flight" to the suburbs. Between 1960 and 1970, the white population of the 20 largest Northeastern and Midwestern cities fell by more than 2.5 million, or 13 percent. The decline was even more precipitous in the 1970s, dropping by another 4 million, or 24.3 percent.[30] Meanwhile, the black share of central city populations shot up 725 percent from 1960 to 1968.[31]

The urban riots of the late 1960s and early '70s made matters worse. Anecdotal and newspaper accounts suggested that rioters in Los Angeles, Harlem, Washington and elsewhere targeted white merchants they felt had long cheated them economically. Whatever the rationale, riots certainly did not help urban America's fortunes.

As Rutgers University's Isenberg writes, "certainly people were less likely to make shopping excursions with riot threats hanging in the air."[32] Suburbanites began to think of downtown as a dangerous no-man's land. In 1969, a *Newsweek* cover report looked at "The Sick, Sick Cities."

With the central cities continuing to lose jobs, many local leaders despaired. St. Louis Mayor A. J. Cervantes declared in 1968: "We just can't make it anymore."

New Orleans Mayor Moon Landrieu echoed the sentiment: "The cities are going down the pipe."

HUD Secretary George Romney said in 1972, "The whole social web that makes living possible [in the cities] is breaking down into a veritable jungle."[33]

A year later, President Richard M. Nixon froze most HUD programs following allegations the funds were being mishandled. He folded Model Cities and other urban-renewal programs into Community Development Block Grants, which gave localities wide discretion over the types of programs that could be funded. Cities foundered financially, as exemplified by New York City's $726 million budget deficit in 1975. President Gerald R. Ford's refusal to aid the city led to the memorable New York *Daily News* headline, "Ford to City: Drop Dead," which Ford believed cost him the 1976 election.

Hitting Bottom

Ford's opponent, Jimmy Carter, created new grant programs to send money directly to neighborhoods, rather than passing it through lower levels of government. During his first year in office, Congress approved the Community Development Reinvestment Act, which required banks to invest funds in the communities they served.

Many of Carter's programs for cities, though, were dismantled by his successor, Ronald Reagan. In fact, Reagan was following a Carter administration advisory panel that recommended helping city residents move to the suburbs. The federal government's role should be "to assist communities to adjust to redistributional trends, rather than attempt to reverse them," the commission concluded."[34]

Reagan eliminated Carter's Office of Neighborhoods and cut programs for cities by nearly a quarter during his first two years in office. He ended federal revenue sharing, by which Washington sent funds to other levels of government to spend as they saw fit.

Without the federal government to help them out, city and business leaders decided they were responsible for improving the lot of the cities. Many businesses were willing to pay additional assessments in order to clean up downtowns and make them safer. The first business-improvement district (BID) was created in New Orleans in 1975, and BIDs became widespread in the 1980s.

Cities also welcomed their first good retail news in decades with the creation of "festival marketplaces" — shopping areas built in historic districts or among the ruins of old industrial sites, including Ghirardelli Square in San Francisco, the Inner Harbor in Baltimore and Faneuil Hall in Boston. Although often criticized as Potemkin villages — pockets of prosperity that did little for the wider city surrounding them — they were successful and widely imitated. They appealed to the nostalgia many people felt for the downtowns of yore — before crime, congestion and despair overran the cities. The American city, as Isenberg points out, had become a commodity to be marketed rather than a place in decline to be ignored.

At the same time, the National Trust for Historic Preservation's Main Street program began encouraging downtown business owners in small communities to properly restore their storefronts as a way to use the charm of a community's historic ambience to revive struggling local economies. Scores of communities across the country have benefited from the downtown face-lifts under Trust guidance, helping them battle the often overpowering competition from regional malls and discounters.[35]

Some cities, such as New York, Denver and Houston, even enjoyed job growth during the 1980s with the rise of the service sector, but older industrial cities such as Detroit, Philadelphia and Baltimore were left behind. Jobs continued their exodus to the suburbs. During a three-year period, Atlanta's suburbs gained twice as many jobs as the city; the suburbs of St. Louis, Chicago and San Francisco gained five times as many jobs as those cities, and Detroit's suburbs outstripped the city by nearly 700 percent.[36]

The cities, meanwhile, continued to struggle, having fallen into a downward spiral. Whites who fled the cities during the 1960s grew increasingly reluctant to come to downtowns that had become scenes of poverty, crime and drug abuse — particularly given the crack epidemic of the 1980s.

Likewise, homelessness became a headline issue, as the share of the nation's poor who lived in central cities had increased by a third since 1960.[37] In 1992, *Business Week* declared, "The breeding ground for economic misery is the American city."[38]

The sense of urban uncertainty continued into the booming 1990s despite falling crime rates, a growing economy and a set of exceptionally gifted mayors, including Rudolph Giuliani of New York, Ed Rendell of Philadelphia and Richard M. Daley of Chicago.

Even Rendell, after a highly praised tenure during which he pulled Philadelphia back from the brink of bankruptcy, said as he left office in 1998, "Forget all the good things I've done. Philadelphia is dying."[39]

CURRENT SITUATION

Success Stories

Rendell's pessimism aside, his city has thrived in recent years. Or, at least its center city has. The downtown is now home to a thriving arts district anchored by the massive Kimmel Center. Condos around Rittenhouse Square are in great demand, and a city that once had no outdoor cafes now has 167. The prosperity that surrounds the downtown area is starting, slowly, to spread to blighted areas around it.

Levy, of the Philadelphia Center City District, argues that rather than being caught in a vicious downward cycle, as they were for decades, cities are starting to recover.

Levy and some other urban observers say that cities, ironically, have the federal government to thank, because when the government turned its back on the cities, local officials realized they could only depend on themselves. "The withdrawal of federal agencies has done more for the cities than all previous federal activities combined," says MIT's Hoyt. "Now you have business-improvement districts, universities and hospitals partnering with cities and raising resources in creative ways."

The federal government today is only minimally interested in helping cities. For the past two years the Bush administration has tried to slash funding for Community Development Block Grants — the last major source of federal grants for local governments — and to merge it with other economic-development programs within the Commerce Department. Although the program still exists, city and county lobbyists aren't optimistic that it will remain robust. The administration also wants to eliminate the Section 8 rental-assistance program and Hope VI grants to cities to rebuild housing.

"The federal doctor doesn't make house calls anymore," says Levy. Cities have relatively few champions in GOP-dominated Washington. Urbanites historically do not vote for Republicans.

"It's hard to think of urban constituencies to whom the Republicans owe anything," says Michael S. Greve, director of the American Enterprise Institute's Federalism Project.

So cities are pulling up their bootstraps and doing for themselves. Using BIDs, downtown employers collect taxes to pay for the services they once sought from government. "They allowed people to tax themselves extra to get signage, plantings, additional police services," says urban consultant White. "The rise in property values has more than covered whatever people have paid in taxes."

In the 1990s, cities tried various schemes to draw people back downtown, spending billions on new sports stadiums and convention centers. With his 1997 book, *The Rise of the Creative Class*, Richard Florida convinced many civic leaders that the path to prosperity lies not in granting tax breaks to businesses but in presenting the right blend of social and cultural amenities to attract well-educated workers.

However, none of the ideas proved to be a magic bullet.[40] Sports stadium promoters' promises of thousands of new jobs and millions in additional city revenues rarely panned out, but the improvement ideas did begin to rouse central cities from their long slumber and pessimism.[41]

Cities entered into partnerships with the private sector to construct multi-million-dollar projects. Government used its eminent-domain power to amass land, secured tax-exempt financing and provided fast-track approvals. Private partners determined what the market wanted, and together they built convention centers, performing-arts facilities, hotels and other ambitious projects that began to attract people back downtown, albeit in fits and starts.

Cities eventually learned how to attract people with money. Consider the sprawling desert city of Phoenix. Having grown from 100,000 people in 1950 to more than 1 million today, it is a classic Sun Belt town, better known for ranch-resort tourism than for downtown vitality. It has no distinguishing topography and little historical cachet.

"Phoenix had sprawled out to the suburbs and pretty much abandoned the central city," says City Councilman Claude Mattox. Left behind were "the homeless, vagrants and prostitutes."

But today, with new baseball, basketball and hockey facilities, two major new museums and two concert halls, an upscale retail complex and a $600 million expansion of the convention center, Phoenix draws tens of thousands of people downtown every night. Convinced that sports and tourism weren't enough to make downtown healthy, city leaders have also promoted residential construction and gave the planned site of a new football stadium to a big biomedical campus.

"Over the last two or three years, the residential part is starting to kick in, creating quite a vibrant area," says Maricopa County Administrator David R. Smith.

In March, city voters approved an $878 million bond package to help fund a wide variety of projects, most aimed at revitalizing downtown. Eventually, a chunk of Arizona State University will move into the city from suburban Tempe, drawing 15,000 students, faculty and administrators downtown.

Phoenix's success story has been replicated in many other cities. Although the specific details may differ, downtowns have become chic places for young professionals and empty nesters to buy low-maintenance lofts and condos, surrounded by a mix of outdoor cafes, entertainment options and plenty of people-watching. For instance, Washington, D.C.'s Seventh Street corridor — next door to Chinatown — had historically been an

Getty Images/David McNew

Suburban houses rise next to a dairy farm east of Los Angeles. Despite odors, flies and pollution from hundreds of dairy farms in the surrounding Chino Basin, the quest for affordable, new homes draws a steady stream of immigrants from the city.

important shopping district. But a decade ago it was rundown and lined with vacant buildings. In 1997, a new basketball arena was opened up nearby, followed by a popular museum and dozens of restaurants — including one with an $18 million interior.

On a recent Friday night, patrons browsed in a bookstore before curtain time at the neighboring Shakespeare Theater. Teenagers watched a "bucket drummer" banging on seven upside-down plastic tubs. Small kids won tee shirts and balloon hats from a radio station's street festival. Inside a new retail alley designed to look like old cast-iron storefronts, a line snaked round and doubled back on itself at a cineplex showing thrillers, cartoons, hip-hop comedies and independent films.

Buffalo's BID sponsors a downtown concert series that now draws 8,000 to 12,000 people a week. Detroit has had more housing starts than any other jurisdiction in Michigan in the last two years. A developer in Nashville is building a 65-story, luxury condo tower.[42]

Cities and their private partners have learned to integrate stadiums and ballparks into neighborhoods in ways that encourage people to walk around and see other things. As a result, downtowns are animated after the 9 to 5 workday, and retailers have added five or six hours to their business day.

However, downtowns are still relatively small potatoes in the broader economic scheme of things. Few central cities have attracted more than a few thousand new residents, while suburbs — including new towns sprouting up on the far metropolitan fringe — continue to draw millions. Attracting just 2 percent of the city's population to live downtown remains an elusive goal almost everywhere.

But downtowns have always been primarily places for commerce, and the fact that so many people with high disposable incomes are either living downtown or visiting regularly represents an impressive turnaround.

Cities still have a long way to go in some fundamental areas, such as lowering the disparities in wealth between loft-dwellers and the poor and providing higher-quality education. But Levy argues that rather than being caught in a vicious downward cycle, as they were for decades, cities are starting to build on their increasing strengths and attractiveness.

"I don't think we're going to have downtowns dominating regions like they did in 1900," he says, "but we're long past the point where downtowns are embarrassments to their regions."

OUTLOOK

Multicentered Regions

Levy of the Philadelphia Center City District and many others speak of "multicentered regions," in which commerce is spread among many business districts. Brookings fellow Leinberger says while sprawling cities like Los Angeles and Atlanta were once the model of urban development, Washington now represents the future.

Washington's Metro system, he says, has fostered a series of thriving downtown commercial districts scattered along the subway lines — not just around the downtown Seventh Street area but in suburbs such as Bethesda and Silver Spring in Maryland and Arlington and Alexandria in Virginia. Most building permits now being issued in the region, Leinberger says, are for attached properties rather than the stand-alone projects that define sprawl.

Kotkin, the New America Foundation fellow who is perhaps the leading debunker of downtown cheerleading, argues that America's future lies in the suburbs, just as it has for decades. Downtowns may be attracting a few more people, but they represent a paltry share of the nation's population growth, he says.

"I'm not saying it's not real, but it's not significant," Kotkin says. "Most real-estate bankers and analysts — not,

of course, developers and their PR people — will tell you the condo market is overbuilt."

Even downtown boosters are concerned that center cities won't attract a stable, long-term population until the public schools improve. Test scores are up even in some tough districts, such as Chicago, Boston and Philadelphia, but inner-city schools as a rule cannot compete with private or suburban schools. Until they can, only small numbers of affluent parents will raise their families in or around downtowns.

"The quality of school systems is actually an economic-development tool," says Steve Moore, president of the Washington DC Economic Partnership. "You want people to stay for years and raise their kids here."

Moore points out, however, that cities have become "cool for a particular kind of person," if not for parents of school-age children. Brad Segal, a development consultant in Denver, thinks downtowns will benefit from demographic trends that will lead to increased numbers of those particular kinds of persons — both young workers without children and older adults with grown children — who have been repopulating center cities.

Segal also believes that more people will be drawn to downtowns and inner suburbs because of the same factors that kicked off the gentrification trend of the 1970s — they're fed up with long commutes, congestion and the rising cost of gasoline. "Urban living is a far more resource-efficient way of life," Segal says. "The ability to recapture time is a huge factor that will move people more toward urban living. The long-term economics of resource depletion are going to push us back into cities whether we like it or not."

Despite recent spikes, however, gas prices eat up a smaller portion of personal spending than they did back in 1981. And most cities, despite their glitzy, new downtown neighborhoods, are still losing population, or at least population share, to the suburbs.

"When they talk about 5,000 units in downtown L.A., does anyone understand what that means in a region of 15 million people?" asks Kotkin. "Some of these downtowns are going to have a lot of nomadic people."

UPDATE

Since taking over as mayor of Detroit in May 2009, former pro-basketball star Dave Bing has been captaining an aggressive zone defense of the Motor City's crumpled image. The blighted picture includes a once-proud auto industry in federal receivership, a crime rate seared in the national consciousness in photos of abandoned homes burning on Halloween, a formerly gleaming football stadium sold for a paltry $583,000[43] and a Detroit suburb named in a recent study as the nation's worst city for job seekers.[44]

This September, Bing launched as his administration's top priority a long-term urban land-use initiative aimed at stabilizing neighborhoods, boosting development and attracting new residents. The focus of his Detroit Strategic Framework Plan will be to "right-size" the decaying city through the unusual strategy of clearing abandoned inner-city properties and turning the land into urban "farms." Beginning with a series of community meetings to enlist citizen support over the next year, the multifaceted plan would proceed over five to 10 years with a combination of classic downtown revitalization tools such as exploiting historical and cultural resources, encouraging public transit and embracing environmental sustainability.[45] The envisioned new green spaces and agricultural enterprises would do double duty by shrinking the area that must be covered, for example, by law enforcement and garbage pickup services.

There is, however, a key obstacle: No money is available for the effort — unless philanthropists step in. "When I look at the focus of this," Bing said, "we've still got to talk about how we create jobs . . . how it's going to impact public safety, how it's going to impact education and finally, financial stability. It's not an overnight plan."[46]

Still, at least one bright spot shimmers on Detroit's horizon. Last April, conservationists who created the city's Campus Martius Park, a 2.5-acre green space shaped from a previously desolate downtown parcel, received a prestigious national award and $10,000 from the Urban Land Institute for an "outstanding example of a public open space that has catalyzed the transformation of the surrounding community."[47]

Other cities also are trying to grapple with blight and economic decline. In the Cleveland area, for example, the Cuyahoga County Land Reutilization Corporation (CCLRC) has formed a partnership with such agencies as the Department of Housing and Urban Development (HUD), Environmental Protection Agency and mortgage giant Fannie Mae to make it easier for people to buy foreclosed homes and to protect the surrounding community.[48]

Established in December 2008 in response to mounting foreclosures and a residential exodus, the CCLRC — or County Land Bank — works closely with area cities to determine how demolished properties can be turned into small parks and other public resources. In January, CCLRC acquired its first property, which is set to become a neighborhood garden. The land bank currently has 60 properties set for demolition.

In December 2009, CCLRC reached an agreement with Fannie Mae to halt the sale of low-value properties to speculators. Now, properties valued at $25,000 or less can be acquired from Fannie and resold to low- and middle-income families or redeveloped. Pilot projects are under way in Minneapolis/St. Paul, Phoenix and other cities.

CCLRC also secured $40 million from HUD to help stabilize neighborhoods suffering from high rates of foreclosure and home abandonment. In addition, CCLRC is working with the Cleveland Housing Network to provide first-mortgage financing to people trying to buy homes through lease-purchase agreements.[49]

While Cleveland, Detroit and other blighted cities are taking steps to redevelop themselves, the recession has upset even short-term downtown-revitalization plans. Since the fall of 2008, the economic downturn has cost millions of Americans jobs and houses while depriving local governments of funds for planning and development.

The city centers that have survived — or fared the least poorly — during the economic earthquake are those with "clearly diversified land use that includes office, retail, residential [components] as well as a good pedestrian fabric," says Paul Levy, president and CEO of the Central City District, a business improvement area in Philadelphia. Downtowns in places such as Philadelphia, New York City, San Francisco and Portland, Ore., for the most part "hold up better than suburban office districts further out from the center." Levy says that harder-hit cities such as Phoenix, Atlanta and Miami have higher office vacancy rates, and he notes that the home vacancy rate, just 7 percent in Philadelphia, is as high as 40 percent in Phoenix, Atlanta and Las Vegas.

The downtowns that have held up usually have a three-legged approach, Levy adds: They have diversified to attract tourism, conventions and business travelers. Detroit and Las Vegas, by contrast, "are single-industry towns."

An inevitable rise in fuel prices in coming years favors inner-city growth that is less auto-dependent, Levy says. Another urban-friendly trend is cultural and demographic. Americans who were young in the 1990s experienced a largely positive view of cities — one in which single women walk alone at night — from romanticized renderings in TV shows such as "Seinfeld," "Friends" and "Ally McBeal," as well as from movies such as "You've Got Mail," Levy says. "Those images have predisposed those in their 20s to early 40s to think urban. That's in contrast to the influence of the scary portrait of New York City that spread in the 1970s via the film 'The French Connection,'" about heroin smuggling. On top of that, he adds an "overlay of interest in sustainability" among today's 20- and 30-somethings.

Many urban planners' visions for downtowns have stressed an orchestrated effort to lure residents from a dependency on the automobile in favor of public transit and walkable space. But those values do not apply in many localities around the country, asserts Joel Kotkin, an author and scholar on social trends who is a Distinguished Presidential Fellow in Urban Futures at Chapman University in Orange, Calif.

"We've been putting lots of money into transit for a long time, and there's not much evidence that it helps downtowns," he says. "Yes, light rail helps with some real estate investment, but look at the [glutted] condo market in Los Angeles, Phoenix or Miami. It would be a bleeding sore for many cities," he adds, noting that in cities such as Dallas, fewer than 2 percent of employees work downtown.

Revitalizing downtowns cannot work "if there are no jobs," Kotkin continues. And the growth and investment in jobs is still occurring more in the middle-class suburbs than in the burned-out inner cities, where the work force tends to possess fewer skills and education.

Not all analysts are so optimistic about the suburbs. William H. Lucy, an urban planning professor at the University of Virginia, argues that the spate of home foreclosures in suburban America has combined with demographic trends to give new impetus to downtown growth. In *Foreclosing the Dream: How America's Housing Crisis Is Reshaping Our Cities and Suburbs*, published in February 2010 by the American Planning Association, he cites higher rates of foreclosures in new suburbs and exurbs than in cities. And he reports that the number of households in the 30-to-45 age group has declined by 3.4 million since 2000, reducing demand for large suburban houses. The stereotypical "white flight exodus" from central cities, he writes, has been reversed in most large metropolitan areas. "Changing demographics and consumer attitudes coupled with political support for compact development, transit investments and awareness about climate change all point to a dramatic shift in development patterns."[50]

The recession's impact on the balance between suburbia and the inner cities was laid out in an Urban Land Institute study released in January 2010. Scholar John K. McIlwain noted that middle-aged and older members of the baby-boom generation, many of whom are trapped in houses that lost value in the mortgage crisis, are more likely than younger people to stick to suburbia, while members of the more mobile Generation Y are more likely to gravitate toward walkable, close-in communities.

"All of these groups have some characteristics that reflect a desire to live in more pedestrian-friendly, transit-oriented, mixed-use environments that de-emphasize auto dependency, whether the location is urban or suburban," he writes. "Economic and land constraints make it impossible for urban infill development to accommodate all the housing demand represented by all the demographic groups." As a result, suburban development "must adapt or it will be obsolete."[51]

The Obama administration, soon after taking office in 2009, was greeted by a Brookings Institution study recommending that it retool federal agencies to confront changing demographics affecting the nation's suburban-urban mix. The study documented a slowdown in domestic migration because of the recession; a trend among recent immigrants to pick suburban locations over urban ones; an aging baby-boomer population that will stick to suburbs; and widening gaps in income and education levels among ethnic groups.

The study's authors noted that "even as the nation enters an extended period of economic uncertainty, the continued demographic dynamism of our metropolitan areas raises key policy and program issues" for the

Obama administration. "Steps to implement the administration's economic-recovery package wisely, pursue immigrant integration alongside immigration reform, close educational achievement and attainment gaps, combine the planning of transportation and housing, and provide needed support to low-income workers and families should take account of our constantly evolving and changing metropolitan populations," they wrote.[52]

Kotkin, however, says any high priority that Obama might give to urban revitalization will be short-lived. For the most part, the administration has focused stimulus package aid to job creation, aid to homeowners facing foreclosure and long-term infrastructure funding for transit projects such as high-speed rail. Since the 2008 election, everything has been stacked for Obama and the urban vote, but this will be over in November," he says, adding that the vast majority of Congress comes from low-density, non-urban districts. "Only 3 to 5 percent of the population takes transit," he says. "Why would someone in suburban Kansas City want to subsidize high-speed rail to take people from Milwaukee to Madison or from Tampa to Orlando? It's an attempt to engineer history that won't work."

Cities need to "heal themselves," he says, "and become more economically competitive" without help from the suburbs and the federal government.

NOTES

1. Terry Frieden, "FBI: Violent crime rate drops again," CNN.com, Oct. 17, 2005, www.cnn.com/2005/LAW/10/17/crime.rate/. For recent coverage, see Rick Lyman, "Surge in Population in the Exurbs Continues," *The New York Times*, June 21, 2006, p. A10.

2. Quoted in Matt Sepic, "St. Louis Escapes Its Rust-Belt Past," National Public Radio, May 17, 2006.

3. John Buntin, "Land Rush," *Governing*, March 2006, p. 26.

4. Lance Freeman, "Displacement or Succession?: Residential Mobility in Gentrifying Neighborhoods," *Urban Affairs Review*, 2005, p. 463.

5. Scott Carlson, "Richfield Wins Court Battle to Condemn Car Dealership Site," *St. Paul Pioneer Press*, Jan. 20, 2001, p. 1C.

6. For background see Kenneth Jost, "Property Rights," *CQ Researcher*, March 4, 2005, pp. 197-220.

7. Linda Greenhouse, "Justices Uphold Taking Private Property for Development," *The New York Times*, June 24, 2005, p. A1.

8. Avi Salzman and Laura Masnerus, "For Homeowners, Anger and Frustration at Court Ruling," *The New York Times*, June 24, 2005, p. A20.

9. Arthur M. Schlesinger Jr., "The City in American Civilization," in *American Urban History* (1969), p. 35.

10. Alison Isenberg, *Downtown America: A History of the Place and the People Who Made It* (2004), p. 7.

11. Jon C. Teaford, *The Twentieth Century American City*, 2nd ed. (1993), p. 17.

12. Robert M. Fogelson, *Downtown: Its Rise and Fall, 1880-1950* (2001), p. 13.

13. *Ibid.*, p. 193.

14. William Kennedy, *O Albany!* (1983), p. 8.

15. Robert A. Beauregard, *Visions of Decline: The Postwar Fate of U.S. Cities* (1993), p. 75.

16. Fogelson, *op. cit.*, p. 109.

17. *Ibid.*, p. 199.

18. Isenberg, *op. cit.*, p. 129.

19. *Ibid.*, p. 142.

20. For background, see "Business Migrates to the Suburbs," *CQ Researcher*, Nov. 14, 1986.

21. Fogelson, *op. cit.*, p. 387.

22. Michael A. Burayidi, ed., *Downtowns: Revitalizing the Centers of Small Urban Communities* (2001), p. 1.

23. Fogelson, *op. cit.*, p. 223.

24. Isenberg, *op. cit.*, p. 174.

25. *Ibid.*, p. 178.

26. Fogelson, *op. cit.*, p. 318.

27. Isenberg, *op. cit.*, p. 188.

28. Herbert J. Gans, "The Failure of Urban Renewal," in *American Urban History*, *op. cit.*, p. 568.

29. *Ibid.*, p. 569.

30. W. Dennis Keating *et al.*, eds., *Revitalizing Urban Neighborhoods* (1996), p. 207.

31. Beauregard, *op. cit.*, p. 171.

32. Isenberg, *op. cit.*, p. 239.

33. Beauregard, *op. cit.*, p. 201.

34. For background, see Charles S. Clark, "Revitalizing the Cities," *CQ Researcher*, Oct. 13, 1995, pp. 897-920.

35. For background see Richard L. Worsnop, "Historic Preservation," *CQ Researcher*, Oct. 7, 1994, pp. 865-888.

36. Beauregard, *op. cit.*, p. 231.

37. *Ibid.*, p. 259.

38. Christopher Farrell and Michael Mandel, "The Economic Crisis of Urban America," *Business Week*, May 18, 1992, p. 38.

39. Quoted in William H. Hudnut, *Cities on the Rebound* (1998), p. 1.

40. William Fulton, "The Panacea Patrol," *Governing*, October 2004, p. 62.

41. Alan Ehrenhalt, "Ballpark Dreaming," *Governing*, November 2004, p. 6.

42. Lisa Chamberlain, "Creating Demand for City Living in Nashville," *The New York Times*, June 21, 2006, p. C10.

43. Mark Guarino, "New Tale of Detroit's Woe: Pontiac Silverdome Sold for $583,000," *The Christian Science Monitor,* Nov. 18, 2009, www.csmonitor.com/Business/2009/1118/new-tale-of-detroits-woe-silverdome-sold-for-583000

44. Joel Kotkin, "The Worst Cities for Jobs: No. 1: Warren-Troy-Farmington Hills, Michigan," Forbes.com, cited on ABC News, May 2, 2010, http://abcnews.go.com/print?id=10510368.

45. Suzette Hackney and Naomi R. Patton, "Bing: City Needs Detroiters' Help," *Detroit Free Press,* Aug. 18, 2010, www.freep.com/article/20100817/NEWS01/100817031/Bing-s-land-use-plan-to-reshape-Detroit.

46. *Ibid.*

47. Urban Land Institute press release, April 16, 2010.

48. Cuyahoga County Ohio Land Bank, www.cuyahogalandbank.org.

49. Jim Rokakis, "Cuyahoga County Land Bank Is Fighting Back Against the Foreclosure Crisis," *Plain Dealer* (Ohio), July 13, 2010, www.cleveland.com/opinion/index.ssf/2010/07/cuyahoga_county_land_bank_is_f.html.

50. American Planning Association press release.

51. Urban Land Institute press release, "Housing in America: The Next Decade," Jan. 27, 2010.

52. William H. Frey, Alan Berube, Audrey Singer and Jill H. Wilson, "Getting Current: Recent Demographic Trends in Metropolitan America," Brookings Institution, March 2009, www.brookings.edu/reports/2009/03_metro_demographic_trends.aspx.

BIBLIOGRAPHY

Books

Fogelson, Robert M., *Downtown: Its Rise and Fall, 1880-1950*, Yale University Press, 2001.
An MIT professor of urban studies and history examines how downtowns lost their retail dominance.

Isenberg, Alison, *Downtown America: A History of the Place and the People Who Made It*, University of Chicago Press, 2004.
A Rutgers University historian examines downtowns during the 20th century, with particular attention to how retail trends reflected broader racial and economic issues.

Articles

Boddy, Trevor, "Vancouverism vs. Lower Manhattanism," Archnewsnow.com, Sept. 20, 2005.
The architecture critic for the *Vancouver Sun* explains how the downtown population of the British Columbia city doubled over the past 15 years, making it the highest residential density urban area in North America.

Buntin, John, "Land Rush," *Governing*, March 2006, p. 26.
Residential development is taking off around downtown Houston and other cities, but some feel that the government should intervene to preserve old neighborhoods.

Chan, Sewell, "Standard & Poor's Upgrades City's Credit Rating to Best Ever," *The New York Times*, May 23, 2006, p. B1.
A major bond-rating agency upgraded New York City's debt rating, citing surging tax revenues, new money for school construction and a new retiree health-insurance trust fund.

DiMassa, Cara Mia, and Roger Vincent, "Retailers Not Sold on Grand Avenue," *Los Angeles Times*, April 25, 2006, p. A1.
A leading architect and influential civic boosters are promoting new office and condo towers along Grand Avenue in Los Angeles but failing to lure high-end retailers back.

Hampson, Rick, "Studies: Gentrification a Boost for Everyone," *USA Today*, April 19, 2005, p. 1A.
Studies suggest gentrification drives comparatively few low-income residents from their homes, but anecdotal testimony indicates the poor are being priced out of their homes.

Leroux, Charles, and Ron Grossman, "Putting the 'Chic' Back in Chicago," *Chicago Tribune Magazine*, Feb. 5, 2006, p. 10.
Areas such as North Kenwood/Oakland, which had long struggled, have suddenly become fashionable.

MacGilless, Alec, "Region's Job Growth a Centrifugal Force," *The Washington Post*, June 18, 2006, p. A1.
Job and population growth in the National Capital Area continue to be much stronger in suburbs far from Washington, to the dismay of planners who wished for more density and better integration with transit.

Maler, Kevin, "Suburbs Want Downtowns of Their Own," *The New York Times*, April 30, 2006, Sec. 11, p. 10.
An increasing number of suburbs around Minneapolis-St. Paul are building their own downtowns.

Mehren, Elizabeth, "States Acting to Protect Private Property," *Los Angeles Times*, April 16, 2006, p. A1.
In response to a Supreme Court decision allowing cities to take control of properties for private development, all but three states have considered legislation to curb the practice.

Montgomery, Lori, "Education Becoming Top Issue for D.C.," *The Washington Post*, May 24, 2006, p. A1.
Business leaders with a stake in Washington's economic revival argue that healthy public schools are vital.

Mui, Ylan Q., "Wal-Mart to Enter Urban Markets," *The Washington Post*, April 5, 2006, p. D1.
The leading retailer announces it will build stores in more than 50 blighted urban areas.

Reports and Studies

Birch, Eugenie L., "Who Lives Downtown," *Living Cities Census Series*, Brookings Institution, November 2005.
An analysis of 44 cities finds that downtown populations are growing after decades of decline.

Freeman, Lance, "Displacement or Succession?: Residential Mobility in Gentrifying Neighborhoods," *Urban Affairs Review*, 2005, p. 463.
A Columbia University urban-planning professor finds that gentrification plays a minor role, if any, in displacing poor city dwellers.

Kotkin, Joel, "The New Suburbanism: A Realist's Guide to the American Future," The Planning Center, November 2005.
Despite urban planners' love for central cities, suburbs will continue as the stage for America's future growth.

Leinberger, Christopher B., "Turning Around Downtown: Twelve Steps to Revitalization," The Brookings Institution, March 2005.
A consultant lays out the template for revitalizing downtowns, from initial planning through housing strategy to attracting retail.

For More Information

International Downtown Association, 1025 Thomas Jefferson St., N.W., Suite 500 West, Washington, DC 20007; (202) 393-6869; www.ida-downtown.org. The association provides information and support to business-improvement districts.

Metropolitan Policy Program, Brookings Institution, 1775 Massachusetts Ave., N.W., Washington, DC 20036; (202) 797-6139; www.brookings.edu/metro. The think tank's urban program issues studies and supports scholars whose work can help communities grow in sustainable ways.

National League of Cities, 1301 Pennsylvania Ave., N.W., Suite 550, Washington, DC 20004; (202) 626-3000; www .nlc.org. The nation's oldest and largest association representing municipal governments.

National Trust for Historic Preservation, 1785 Massachusetts Ave., N.W., Washington, DC 20036; (202) 588-6219; www.mainstreet.org. Sponsors educational activity and advocates for neighborhood conservation, preservation law and downtown Main Street initiatives.

Urban Land Institute, 1025 Thomas Jefferson St., N.W., Suite 500 West; Washington, DC 20007; (202) 624-7000; www.uli.org. Initiates research into trends in land use and property development.

9

Housing the Homeless

Peter Katel

Leida Ortiz was getting by. She lived with her sister and both of their children in an apartment in Worcester, Mass. Then, in the spring of 2007, her factory-worker father was diagnosed with stomach cancer, so Ortiz moved back into the home her parents owned to help her mother care for her father.

After he died, in December of that year, Ortiz and her mother couldn't afford the mortgage payments on the house. A move back to her sister's didn't work out, so Ortiz and her two children began sharing an apartment with a roommate. But she wasn't making enough from her part-time job as a nursing assistant to kick in her $400 share of the rent.

The roommate asked her and her 11-year-old son, Joseph, and 5-year-old daughter, Angelina, to leave.

"I became homeless in July," Ortiz said. "I cried every night, wondering if my kids were going to end up in different schools somewhere else. We were living out of our bags. We didn't know where we were going to end up next. The kids, they see that you're stressed, they get stressed. They see you putting yourself to sleep every night crying."

Speaking at a Capitol Hill briefing held by an advocacy group in early December, Ortiz recounted a happy ending to her family's two-week stay at a motel. She urged the assembled housing advocates and congressional staffers to work to expand the "prevention and rapid rehousing" program that she credited for her family's rescue.

Now working three part-time jobs, the 30-year-old Ortiz hardly fits the picture of "homeless" that hit the national consciousness in the early 1980s — seemingly unemployable people suffering

Nursing assistant Leida Ortiz is working three part-time jobs and getting back on her feet after becoming homeless in July and living with her two children in a motel room for two weeks. At a recent briefing on Capitol Hill, she urged housing advocates to work to expand the emergency housing program that helped her family.

From *CQ Researcher*,
December 18, 2009.

California Has Largest Homeless Population

Nearly 160,000 people in California are homeless, more than twice as many as New York, the state with the next-largest homeless population. Seventeen states have more than 10,000 homeless people, while 11 states have fewer than 2,000.

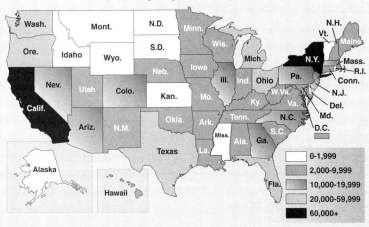

Homeless Population by State
(on a single night in January 2008)

☐	0-1,999
◻	2,000-9,999
◻	10,000-19,999
◼	20,000-59,999
■	60,000+

Source: "The 2008 Annual Homeless Assessment Report to Congress," U.S. Department of Housing and Urban Development, July 2009

mental illness or addiction or both. But in an economic climate shadowed by massive unemployment, some experts see working families facing threats to their housing stability that easily can escalate into homelessness, as in Ortiz's case. "When you're going into a recession starting with a limited supply of affordable housing, with families who are precariously housed and at risk, it's the perfect storm for families," says Mary K. Cunningham, a housing specialist at the nonpartisan Urban Institute think tank.

In 2008, homelessness among people in families rose by 9 percent over the number from the previous year, the U.S. Department of Housing and Urban Development (HUD) reported in an annual survey on homelessness.[1]

Overall, about 1.6 million people slept in homeless shelters or other temporary housing in the United States in 2008, the report said.[2] Whether that rough estimate shows an increase or decrease from the 1980s can't be determined, Cunningham says, given the vast differences in methodology from then until now.

Whatever the case, housing advocates are united in the belief that government action can eliminate homelessness

once and for all. Conservatives tend to be more skeptical, though ideology isn't a reliable guide to views on homelessness.

"It is immoral," Cheh Kim, a staff member for Sen. Christopher Bond, R-Mo., told the Capitol Hill briefing. "People need to understand that anybody can slip into homelessness. Just go into shelters and talk to people and realize that a lot of them were middle-income, or owned small businesses, and because of one little thing in their life, they just fell down."

To be sure, Kim's overall view was that Congress has been responding effectively to the persistence of homelessness. A major piece of evidence: a $1.5 billion appropriation in mid-2009 for a new Homelessness Prevention and Rapid Re-Housing Program (HPRP).

But Joel Segal, a staffer for Rep. John Conyers, D-Mich., argued at the briefing that congressional attitudes remain an obstacle to a definitive solution to homelessness. "A majority of people in Congress do think that homeless people want to be homeless," Segal told Kim and the rest of those present. "That's who they see in the streets pushing the baskets. Trust me on this — they do not know who's in those shelters, because most members of Congress are raising money from very wealthy donors.' "

Notwithstanding the staffers' emphasis on shelters, the growing consensus among advocates for the homeless is that a danger exists of policy makers focusing too heavily on shelters. That approach, they say, would effectively mean continuing to channel mentally unstable and chronically homeless people into shelters instead of expanding a newer strategy of building permanent facilities designed to meet their needs. And families in unstable housing situations — perhaps "doubled up" in relatives' homes — should be kept out of shelters in the first place.

"What we've learned over the past 10 years is that building up a bigger shelter system is a sort of self-fulfilling prophecy," says Nan Roman, president of the National Alliance to End Homelessness.

A number of sources report rising housing instability among families. HUD experts studying present-day trends see a link between the economic crisis and the growing number of families in shelters.[3] The National School Boards Association said in January 2009 that 724 of the country's nearly 14,000 school districts had already served 75 percent or more of the number of homeless students they'd served during the 2007-2008 school year.[4]

Districts track the trend because the Education for Homeless Children and Youth Act requires schools to provide the same level of education to students without fixed addresses as to all other children and youth. Schools can also use grants made under the law to provide homeless students with medical and dental care and other services.

A constellation of other laws authorizes programs designed for the "chronically" homeless, for households who can't afford decent housing and for veterans without homes.

This year, Congress added new forms of assistance, including the Homeless Emergency Assistance and Rapid Transition to Housing (HEARTH) Act for families facing imminent loss of housing or recently made homeless. The law also promotes the construction of so-called "supportive housing" for the long-term homeless, who need mental health services and similar services along with roofs over their heads.

Meanwhile, about 2 million families nationwide receive substantial help in paying their rents under the Section 8 Housing Choice Voucher Program, in place since 1974 and revamped in 1998. For many housing advocates, Section 8 vouchers represent a speedy way to expand the supply of affordable housing, the lack of

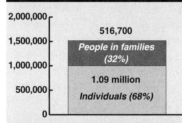

Total No. of Homeless

About 1.6 million persons used a shelter or transition housing, including half a million individuals in families.

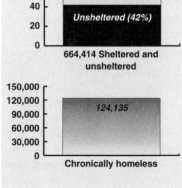

Over the Course of a Year
(Oct. 2007-Sept. 2008)

516,700
People in families (32%)

1.09 million
Individuals (68%)

At a Single Point in Time
(one night in January 2008)

Sheltered (58%)

Unsheltered (42%)

664,414 Sheltered and unsheltered

124,135

Chronically homeless

Source: Department of Housing and Urban Development, July 2009

which they view as a major contributor to homelessness.

Some conservative policy experts say the problem isn't a shortage of affordable housing but deeply rooted poverty — a condition they call ill-suited for resolution by housing subsidies. "The idea that housing is unaffordable and that we've done nothing about it — give me a break," says Howard Husock, vice president of the Manhattan Institute for Policy Research, a New York think tank. "What we've done to make housing more affordable over the past 30 years is so extensive that I would inquire of advocates what more they would have government do."

Even so, HUD, which administers three of those programs, calculates that a family with one full-time, minimum-wage worker can't afford a two-bedroom apartment anywhere in the country.[5]

As a practical matter, a one-earner family means a household headed by a single mother — the population segment that by all accounts is the most economically and socially vulnerable to deep poverty. The HUD annual report says that families in shelters are typically headed by a single mother.[6]

Ortiz, the once-homeless single mother in Worcester, Mass., says that she was able to start turning her life around only after her city's housing program helped her find an $850-a-month apartment, which she pays for with the help of a $700 monthly subsidy from the "rapid rehousing" program.

Before that, she says. "I couldn't get more work hours because of my kids getting out of school at 4:10. I didn't have anybody reliable enough to drop them off for me or pick them up if I did get a full-time job, and after-school programs cost so much."

Homeless in Nation's Capital Face Cold Winter

Funding cuts may reduce number of beds in shelters.

Mark Raymond is worried. He says funding cuts will prevent his organization's huge 1,350-bed shelter in Washington — among America's largest — from adequately serving homeless men and women in the nation's capital.

"Lots of programs that were started last year and this year are not to be funded next year," says Raymond, director of administrative offices at the Community for Creative Non-Violence.

In late September, Clarence Carter, director of the city's Department of Human Services, announced a $12 million cut in homeless-services funding for fiscal 2010. D.C. Council member Tommy Wells, D-Ward 6, contended the cut could be as large as $20 million. [1] Either way, homeless shelters say they will have to scramble to find enough beds for the lethally cold hypothermia season.

The current economy has forced more people onto the streets, including more families in which jobs have been lost and no savings exist. The slow housing market means an increasing number of electricians and construction workers are unemployed. [2] Half the homeless adults in Washington don't receive regular income, including Social Security and disability checks. The 20 percent who are employed have a median monthly income of $524.

According to a January 2009 survey, 6,228 homeless people live in shelters or transitional housing in the District, a 3 percent increase over 2008. [3] In July the total included 703 homeless families and more than 1,400 homeless children. Last year, homelessness among families across the nation rose 9 percent but 25 percent in the District. [4]

The number of teenagers without a place to live is also rising. But so is awareness of their plight. Recently, rappers Flava Flav, once homeless himself, and Chuck D., of the band Public Enemy, shared a Thanksgiving meal with the young residents at the Sasha Bruce House in Washington, which features programs for children ages 11-17. Typically, youths are reunited with their families or transitioned into more permanent care. Counseling services are provided, particularly as children without families transition into adulthood.

The two entertainers encouraged the youngsters to stay in school. "It takes three times as much to get your education later as now, so do it now," Chuck D told the teens crowded around him. Later, Public Enemy performed, and Flava Flav stressed the importance of volunteerism. "If you're successful and can't talk to younger people in need, you got a problem," he said.

During his term, former Mayor Anthony A. Williams called for an end to homelessness by 2014. [5] A major component of his "Homeless No More" plan, now being implemented by current Mayor Adrian M. Fenty, is providing housing and financial support to those most at risk of becoming homeless. In early December, the District distributed $7.5 million in federal stimulus money to house homeless families and help struggling families remain in their homes. The money, from federal Homeless Prevention and Rapid Re-Housing funds awarded to the District in July, will help

Once she and her family got a place of their own, she found a friend who could pick up the children twice a week, allowing Ortiz to work two part-time jobs as a nursing assistant, and one in a party-supply store. In addition, she's studying for the GED, planning to then enroll in medical-technology training.

"Things are slowly falling into place for me," she says. "A shelter would have been no way for my kids to live. It's not the same as having your house."

As homeless advocates and public officials struggle with rising numbers of homeless families, here are questions being debated:

Can government end homelessness?

Homelessness has remained a social and political issue since it surfaced in the late 1970s and exploded in the early '80s.

The fact that more than a million and a half people every year experience homelessness makes plain that all

680-800 households.[6] Those who have been homeless the longest and those with the most severe disabilities will be housed first. Proponents of the plan say programs in Denver, San Francisco, and Portland, Ore., have proven that providing housing and counseling is more humane and cost-effective than putting people in shelters.

Martha Burt and Sam Hall — researchers at the Urban Institute, a Washington think tank — endorse Fenty's focus on permanent supportive housing, but they caution he needs to keep the momentum going if homelessness is to be ended in the next four years.[7] However, Michael Ferrell, executive director of the District of Columbia Coalition for the Homeless, says ending homelessness by 2014 is "very highly unlikely" and calls for a multipronged approach.

"The first prong has to be prevention strategies, and quite frankly, that's preferable to addressing the problem on the back end," he says. Homeless individuals and families should be rehoused as soon as possible, he explains, but the long-term goal should be to provide enough rental assistance or subsidies for up to 12 months to prevent homelessness from occurring in the first place.

But Raymond cautions against shifting the focus away from shelters. "So many people need subsidized housing," he says, "that there is a year-and-a-half, two-year waiting list. Shelters are absolutely still necessary."

The shift towards permanent supportive housing instead of shelters, however, is a national trend. Philip F. Mangano, until recently executive director of the U.S.

A homeless man settles in at a Metro station in Washington, D.C., in May 2009. More than 6,000 homeless people live in shelters or transitional housing in the District.

Interagency Council on Homelessness, had focused on getting people out of shelters and into homes. "When you ask the consumer what they want, they don't simply say a bed, blanket and a bowl of soup," he said. "They say they want a place to live. We have resources being provided to us at record levels. If you look at the numbers for chronic homelessness, we're winning."[8]

— *Emily DeRuy*

[1] Darryl Fears, "Officials Squabble, Service Providers Scramble; No Matter How You Do the Math, Advocates Say, Less Money Means More People on Streets," *The Washington Post*, Oct. 6, 2009, p. B2.

[2] Mary Otto, "A Growing Desperation; Housing, Economic Slumps May Portend Rise in Ranks of Region's Homeless, Survey Shows," *The Washington Post*, Jan. 25, 2008, p. B1.

[3] "A Summary of the 2009 Point in Time Enumeration for the District of Columbia," The Community Partnership for the Prevention of Homelessness, www.community-partnership.org/docs/TCP%20 Fact%20Sheet%20Point%20in%20Time%202009.pdf.

[4] "In the News," Washington Legal Clinic for the Homeless, www.legal clinic.org/about/inthenews.asp.

[5] Anthony A. Williams, "Homeless No More: A Strategy for Ending Homelessness in Washington, D.C. by 2014," U.S. Department of Health and Human Services, www.hrsa.gov/homeless/statefiles/dcap.pdf.

[6] Darryl Fears, "District to Disburse $7.5M in Stimulus Money to Help Homeless," *The Washington Post*, Nov. 30, 2009.

[7] Martha Burt and Sam Hall, "What It Will Take to End Homelessness in D.C.," The Urban Institute, July 13, 2008, www.urban.org/publicat ions/901185.html.

[8] Derek Kravitz, "Homelessness Official Wins Praise with Focus on Permanent Housing; Detractors Cite Mangano's Frequent Travel, Including Trips Abroad," *The Washington Post*, Dec. 30, 2008, p. A13.

the attention focused on the problem over the past three decades hasn't eliminated it. To some conservatives, the persistence of homelessness despite myriad government programs suggests they may be doing more to perpetuate the problem than to solve it — if a solution is possible at all, which some conservatives doubt.

Nevertheless, conservatives don't automatically reject government programs, especially those aimed directly at people shuttling between the street and

shelters. In fact, the government committed itself to ending "chronic" homelessness in 10 years when Republican George W. Bush was in office (*See p. 216*).

Housing advocates on the liberal side argue for expanding that goal to ensure that no families suffer loss of their homes, or, in the worst-case scenario, get help in acquiring new housing. That strategy is embodied in the expansion of the McKinney-Vento Homeless Assistance Act that President Obama signed into law in May. It provides "homelessness prevention" aid to families living in unstable housing conditions — moving in with relatives, for example.

Now, the housing advocates are pushing for more funding, arguing that as more families benefit, builders will respond. "The government can stimulate the housing market in a way to allow homeless people to become housed," says Linda Couch, deputy director of the National Low Income Housing Coalition. She advocates expanding government subsidies designed to make housing affordable for low-wage workers.

Responses that go beyond helping individuals cope with financial emergencies are also well within government's capability, Couch argues. "We know how to build housing," she says. "It's not rocket science, it's just too expensive for people earning the minimum wage, or even two times the minimum wage. Work doesn't pay enough."

Conservative analysts don't necessarily reject strategies designed to boost the purchasing power of low-wage workers. But they argue that such measures shouldn't be lumped in with responses to homelessness.

"Government should strive to end homelessness of single individuals — people who live on the street, who have mental illness and substance abuse problems," says Husock, at the Manhattan Institute. People who aren't on the street but who face housing crises, he argues, can be helped more effectively by programs that don't limit assistance to housing subsidies. "Let's say a blue-collar, two-parent family has been hurt by this recession," Husock says. "Why would we want to say, 'Here's a chit for housing?' All you can use that for is to rent an apartment from a landlord who is willing to take you. Why wouldn't we say we are increasing unemployment insurance, or the value of the earned-income tax credit, and you can use that money as you see fit? If you want to live with his parents for a year while you save, why wouldn't you have that choice?"

But the line isn't hard and fast between policy experts who are skeptical of government's capacity to end all homelessness, and those who argue that government programs can prevent homelessness as well as rescue the homeless from the street.

Roman has no preference for housing-only assistance over other kinds of aid. "Housing affordability has an income dimension and a supply dimension," she says. "You could make housing cheaper or figure out some

way to supplement people's income through vouchers or tax credits — however you want to do it."

The bottom line, Roman says, is that the government can rescue long-term homeless people from the streets, even while ensuring that people who have homes don't lose them. "Do I think homelessness can be ended? Yes," she says. "People will always have housing crises, but I don't think there's any particular reason we can't end homelessness. I remember a time when we didn't really have homelessness."

Policy experts who advocate reducing government's efforts at social engineering doubt that politicians and bureaucrats can achieve anything close to a definitive result. "I don't think government can end homelessness," says Michael D. Tanner, a senior fellow at the Cato Institute, a libertarian think tank.

But government could protect more people from homelessness by making affordable housing more available, argues Tanner, who specializes in domestic policy. County and city governments could modify zoning restrictions that, for instance, prohibit apartment building construction in some localities.

Should the definition of homeless include people in unstable housing situations?

The ways in which laws and policies define a condition also specify who will — and who won't — benefit from programs designed as remedies.

"Homeless" might seem to be an easily defined term. But some argue for expanding its definition to those with housing, albeit in unstable situations. Skeptics question whether that would blunt the effectiveness of programs designed to get unsheltered people off the streets.

The activists who first drew attention in the late 1970s to the homeless were advocating on behalf of the lost souls on skid rows in virtually every city, the looked-down-upon people often described as hoboes, vagrants and bums. They slept in parks, bus stations or cardboard boxes in alleys or — at best — ultra-cheap hotels known as "flop houses" or "cage hotels" (featuring cubicles with wire-mesh roofs to prevent stealing).

At about the same time, concerns were also raised about veterans of the recently ended Vietnam War. Then came the recession of 1981-1982, and worries about homelessness began to focus on people who'd never been homeless before but were losing their houses after losing

Most Sheltered Homeless People Are Men

Nearly two-thirds of the people living in shelters in 2008 were men. One-fifth were under age 18, and 43 percent were disabled.

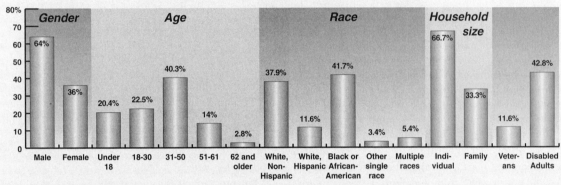

Percentage of All Sheltered Homeless Persons, 2008

Source: "The 2008 Annual Homeless Assessment Report," U.S. Department of Housing and Urban Development, July 2009

their jobs. (The unemployment rate rose to 10.8 percent in December 1982, compared to 10.0 percent this November.)[7]

Citing an apparent connection between economic trends and threats to the housing stability of working Americans, some housing program advocates began arguing for a more expansive definition of homelessness.

But HUD, the federal agency most directly involved in the issue today, defines the term literally: A homeless person is someone who "lacks a fixed, regular and adequate nighttime residence," and who spends nights in a shelter of some kind, including places not designed for that use.[8]

That definition, however, doesn't control all federal law on homelessness. When it comes to public school students, the 2000 McKinney-Vento Homeless Assistance Act, which created most homelessness-related programs, effectively defines homelessness more expansively. Children who can enroll in programs for helping homeless children and youth include those who are sharing housing with others because of economic hardship; who are living in hotels, trailer parks or campgrounds out of necessity; who are awaiting foster care placement or those whose parents are migrant workers.[9]

The Runaway and Homeless Youth Act uses a still-broader definition. It makes young people eligible for transitional housing if they're 16-21 years of age, or for short-term shelter if under 18 and not living with relatives.[10]

As these interpretations of the word show, defining the term is the critical step in deciding who can benefit from government programs. "It's a waste of breath to argue with people who want an expansive definition that makes it look like we should do more, and with the others who want a restricted agenda so it makes it look like we should do less," says Christopher Jencks, a professor of social policy at Harvard University's Kennedy School of Government. "Both sides have agendas."

At the same time, Jencks favors the approach of housing advocates who want government to issue more housing subsidies. "I'm not sure that making the number bigger is the way to go," he says. "Do we want to say that 4 million people are homeless?"

Some housing advocates argue that a broader definition of homelessness applied to all government programs would, in fact, reflect reality. "We believe that everyone has a right to a home," says Couch of the National Low-Income Housing Coalition. "In my mind that doesn't include a van, or a garage or couch-surfing. It would be a real shame, after all we've learned about the importance of stable housing if, in response to the spike in family homelessness, we started building shelters."

Couch adds that HUD officials, along with lawmakers who specialize in housing issues, understand that building more facilities designed for the street-dwelling homeless population wouldn't respond adequately to the housing instability that threatens families who may have roofs over their heads but may also have to change lodgings frequently. "I think reason will prevail," Couch says. "People in housing know that homelessness is solved by housing."

Some of those who favor narrowing the scope of anti-homelessness programs argue that defining homelessness beyond the plain meaning of the word opens the door to unfocused strategies.

"In Hong Kong they talk about 'street sleepers,'" says Husock of the Manhattan Institute. "It's a very accurate description, and a useful one to distinguish them from people who are sharing accommodations with other family members."

People who are doubled-up clearly experience stress, Husock acknowledges. But it doesn't resemble the perils faced by people in the streets. "We should not confuse that issue with the problems faced by very-low-income people," he says. "Two or three generations under one household roof — it's not a common-sense definition of homelessness."

But even some who agree that the definition of homeless should be kept narrow also advocate that people at risk of becoming homeless — and currently bedding down at a relative's or friend's house where they're "doubled up" — should get assistance under homelessness prevention programs. That approach wouldn't require expanding the definition of "homeless."

"There are lots of people who are literally homeless," says Roman of the National Alliance to End Homelessness. "A substantial percentage of them are not sheltered at all. That's who is homeless. People who are doubled up and at risk of homelessness, we would not be in favor of calling homeless."

Are housing subsidies the best way to help families facing homelessness?

Since 1974, the Section 8 Housing Choice Voucher program has been the major federal provider of housing for low-wage workers. Its rental subsidy means recipients don't have to pay more than 30 percent of their income for housing. Through the voucher, the government pays the difference between that 30 percent and the monthly rent.

About 2 million U.S. households currently receive subsidies, which go to poor families who can document their inability to rent decent housing. But most cities also maintain waiting lists, some of them years long, because demand for vouchers outstrips supply. Overwhelmingly, housing experts say, the biggest share of vouchers go to households headed by single mothers, who make up the greatest share of low-income families threatened by housing instability. Vouchers may be simple in concept, but Section 8 isn't simple in operation. "The system is governed by hundreds of pages of regulations and guidance that make the program, some argue … difficult to administer," the Congressional Research Service (CRS) reported last year.[11]

The program owes its complexity to its dual mission. Section 8 was designed to provide decent housing to poor people, with the longer-range aim of helping them climb out of poverty. But affordable housing alone may not be enough for some people to make that climb. Recognizing the key role of education in giving young people a chance at a better future, the so-called "portability" feature of Section 8 allows voucher recipients to live wherever a landlord will accept them (the feature also allows families to move to another state for a job).

"Portability offers the possibility for families with vouchers to move from areas of high concentrations of poverty, poor schools, and little opportunity to areas with low concentrations of poverty, good schools and more opportunity," the CRS report said. It added, "Researchers and advocates for low-income families have argued that the mobility potential of portability has not been fully reached. They argue for more funding for mobility counseling and performance standards that encourage mobility efforts."[12]

Some housing advocates argue that expanding the long-established program offers the fastest way to open affordable housing to more families. Rep. Maxine Waters, D-Calif., is sponsoring a bill to add 150,000 more vouchers next year. The National Low-Income Housing Coalition, which is backing the legislation, sees the legislation as the first step toward a larger goal of doubling the number of vouchers to 4 million by 2020.

"We know that vouchers solve homelessness," says Couch, at the National Low-Income Housing Coalition.

"Often, homeless families need nothing other than a voucher. They don't need transportation or job training. Vouchers are a surefire way not only to prevent homelessness but also to get people out of that situation as quickly as possible."

An expansion is especially needed now, Couch argues, because the recession is hitting low-wage households so hard. "Typically, about 10 percent of people cycle off the program every year," she says. "But in the recession, what we've seen is that, because people's incomes aren't going up, they're staying in the program longer than normal. The waiting lists in a lot of places are frozen."

Not all those who object to the proposed expansion oppose vouchers on principle. Rep. Barbara Capito, R-W. Va., the ranking Republican on the House Financial Services' Housing and Community Opportunity Subcommittee, voted against the Waters bill in the House Financial Services Committee. "It's a critical program, particularly at a time of economic challenge," Capito says. "I'd like to see the vouchers work better for people, but I'm concerned the Section 8 could swallow up the HUD budget."

Capito says adding 150,000 vouchers would lessen the housing agency's ability to deal with other issues, including substandard housing, which she calls a serious problem in her district. But the cost of the proposed voucher expansion is "way out of control," she says.

Deeper objections to Section 8 focus on what critics call the program's tendency to make beneficiaries dependent on the vouchers. "It makes much more sense to supplement the earnings of those at the low end of the income scale," says the Manhattan Institute's Husock. "It's much

Housing Issues Central to Homelessness

Lack of affordable housing is seen as the biggest cause of homelessness — and the main solution — by officials from a majority of 27 U.S. cities surveyed. Most of the officials also called for permanent housing for the disabled and better-paying jobs.

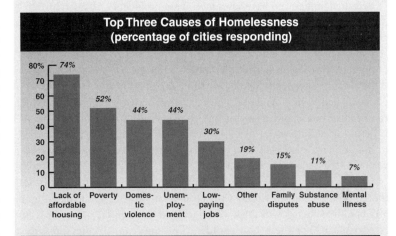

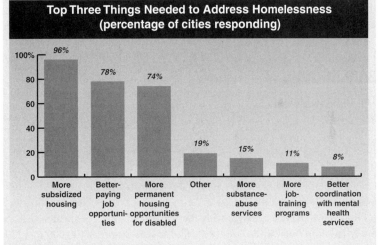

Source: "Hunger and Homelessness Survey," United States Conference of Mayors, December 2009

more efficient. If people have cash in their pocket, they can find something to rent."

Built into Husock's preferred approach is that recipients of income supplements would, by definition, have incomes — that is, they would have jobs. People suffering unstable housing who don't have jobs have other problems that aren't best solved by simply subsidizing apartments for them, he argues. Job training or help in job-seeking would be of more help. "Housing as a solution to the problem of poverty — it's not self-evident to me why that would be the best solution."

People who deal with individuals' housing problems agree to some extent with Husock's categorizations. "There are families who have substance-abuse problems, domestic violence, extreme disability issues such as a child with cerebral palsy," says Marta Beresin, a staff attorney with the Washington Legal Clinic for the Homeless. But she adds that a number of families in these circumstances couldn't be helped by income supplements tied to employment. "There are families where the head of household may not qualify for disability benefits but may have a lot of issues that make it difficult to hold down a steady job — domestic violence, mental health, kids with lot of health issues."

Those conditions, Beresin agrees, spring from deeply rooted poverty. But she differs with Husock on how to give families afflicted with these woes a toehold on a better existence. For these households, "The only way they're ever going to get out of a shelter is with a housing subsidy."

BACKGROUND

The Right to Shelter

The sight of homeless people in big cities began to arouse public concern in the late 1960s and post-Vietnam War era when social activism was at its peak. At the end of the decade, a New York lawsuit played a key role in the emergence of homelessness as a national issue with legal and political dimensions.

Robert M. Hayes, a lawyer with the white-shoe Wall Street law firm Sullivan & Cromwell, filed a class action lawsuit against the city and state in 1979 on behalf of homeless men — represented by six homeless plaintiffs — demanding a right to shelter. Some shelter space was available, but government policy at the time was to deny shelter in order to pressure homeless people to find temporary housing on their own.[13]

In 1979, Judge Andrew R. Tyler of the New York Supreme Court (equivalent to district courts in other states) ruled that the U.S. and New York constitutions required that shelter space be available for every homeless man.

Technically, the ruling applied only to homeless men in the skid row area of New York known as the Bowery. But after the judge made his initial ruling to the case, Hayes and government lawyers settled the suit by agreeing that government was obliged to provide shelter for all men with no homes (women were included later). Underscoring the urgency of the homelessness issue, Robert Callahan, who led the list of named plaintiffs, died on the street before the settlement was reached.

The August 1981, court-approved agreement led to a vast expansion of shelter space in New York. When Hayes had gone to court, shelter space was scattered around the cheap, dormitory-style hotels known as "flophouses." By 1988, when demand for shelter reached a peak, city refuges could house as many as 10,000 people in 24 shelters. The accommodations went far beyond a place to sleep, meals and bathing facilities. The shelters also offered health care, mental health counseling, drug rehabilitation and job-training programs.

By 1981, homeless men and women were fixtures in cities across the country, often camping out in downtown areas and parks. Many were former residents of mental institutions who were turned out and left on their own after a wave of "deinstitutionalizations" prompted by horror stories about conditions in institutions. Some scholars say that President Ronald W. Reagan's administration further added to the ranks of the homeless by drastically cutting back on the number of recipients of federal disability payments, among them people too mentally ill to work. The administration also cut federal funds for public housing.[14]

New York's growing homeless population inspired activists and lawyers elsewhere. Pinning down the numbers proved difficult. Jencks, at Harvard University's Kennedy School, estimated that the nation's homeless population grew from 100,000 in 1980 to 200,000 in 1984 to 400,000 in 1987-1988.[15]

Mitch Snyder, a Washington-based advocate for the homeless, had put the number of homeless at 2 million to 3 million, but he later acknowledged the estimate had "no meaning, no value."[16]

Snyder dedicated himself to awakening the national conscience and challenging the political system. Starting in the late 1970s, he had begun organizing demonstrations designed to call attention to the unmet needs of homeless men and women in the streets of the nation's

CHRONOLOGY

1978-1980s *As homelessness grows into a major social and political-legal problem, advocates win important legal rights for those lacking permanent housing.*

1978 Washington, D.C., activist Mitch Snyder leads a takeover of the National Visitors' Center by the homeless, forcing the city to open more shelter space.

1979 Wall Street lawyer Robert M. Hayes sues New York City and state, demanding a right to shelter for homeless men; initial ruling in case named for homeless plaintiff Robert Callahan is favorable to the homeless.

1981 Callahan dies while sleeping on the street.... In a landmark agreement, New York settles the case by agreeing to provide shelter for everyone who is homeless.

1982 Philadelphia law guarantees the homeless a right to shelter.... As deep recession brings unemployment, homelessness surges.

1983 Callahan agreement is amended to apply to women.

1984 After more attention-getting protests organized by Snyder and fellow activists, Washington voters pass the nation's first referendum guaranteeing overnight shelter to homeless people.

1987 President Ronald W. Reagan signs into law the McKinney (later renamed McKinney-Vento) Homeless Assistance Act, which becomes the major source of federal funds to help the homeless.

1990s *Persistent homelessness leads academics and think-tank analysts to crunch data in an effort to understand causes and possible cures and leads the Bill Clinton administration to step up its rhetoric on the issue.*

1993 Martha R. Burt of the Urban Institute concludes that a shortage of affordable housing for working Americans clearly is one cause of the long-running homelessness crisis.... Homeless 43-year-old Yetta M. Adams freezes to death outside Washington, D.C., headquarters of the U.S. Department of Housing and Urban Development (HUD).

1994 Partly in response to Adams' death, the Clinton administration unveils a plan to reduce homelessness by one-third.

1998 Congress revamps Section 8 housing voucher program to require that vouchers for rental assistance go to very poor families.

2000s *Idea that government can eliminate homelessness gains strength, but the economic crisis at the end of the decade threatens to deepen the problem.*

2002 George W. Bush administration vows to end chronic homelessness in 10 years.

2003 Administration hands out $48 million in grants to programs designed to get chronically homeless people off the streets.

2007 HUD count shows number of chronically homeless dropped since 2006 by about 30,000 to approximately 124,000.... Service providers begin warning of the potential for massive homelessness among Iraq-Afghanistan veterans.

2008 As recession grips the nation, progress on reducing the ranks of the chronically homeless halts; number remains essentially flat from previous year.... Bush creates National Housing Trust Fund, designed to finance affordable housing.

2009 Family homelessness is up 9 percent, apparently due to recession, with veterans slightly overrepresented among the homeless.... National School Boards Association reports growth in student homelessness in more than 700 school districts.... President Barack Obama signs law creating new Homelessness Prevention and Rapid Re-Housing program, funded with $1.5 billion. . . . U.S. Conference of Mayors says about three-quarters of a group of cities show rise in family homelessness and decline or leveling off of homelessness among individuals.... Advocacy groups launch drive to push Congress to appropriate another $1 billion to the program for fiscal 2010-2011.

Scotland's Homeless and the Right to Housing

Long-term housing soon will be available to almost everyone.

Scotland probably comes closer than any other country to implementing a right to housing for the homeless, according to American homeless advocates.[1] Since 1977, legally enforceable rights to housing have been on the books in Scotland, as well as England and Wales. But until recently the right was limited to "priority" categories of the most vulnerable people — families with children, the elderly, disabled and those displaced in natural disasters, among others.[2]

In 2003, Scotland forged ahead of the rest of Britain and greatly expanded the kinds of homeless individuals for whom the government has a duty to provide accommodation, including single adults. Scotland's uniquely expansive definition of homelessness "has no equivalent anywhere in Europe," according to Tom Mullen, a professor of law at the University of Glasgow.[3]

By 2012 the right to long-term permanent housing will extend to virtually all homeless people in Scotland under the revised law. In the interim, local authorities have a legal duty to provide immediate temporary shelter for all homeless persons and long-term permanent housing for a greatly expanded class of priority groups.

In 2004, the priority-need category was expanded to include homeless youth ages 16-17; 18-20-year-olds in danger of sexual or financial exploitation or drug abuse; adults discharged from prison, the armed forces or a hospital; adults with personality disorder, and those at risk from domestic abuse, violence or harassment.

"On paper we have the most progressive homelessness legislation in Europe, if not, possibly, the world," concedes Chris Campbell, deputy chief executive of the Scottish Council for Single Homeless, an umbrella group for homeless-service organizations.

But the challenge of making it work on the ground, he says, includes "changing public attitudes about the deserving vs. the undeserving: Someone's been on the waiting list paying their rent on time: Should they come before or second to someone who in their eyes is going to squander that tenancy with a drug issue?"

Homeless advocates say the tension comes essentially over allocating a scarce, desirable resource — public housing,

which doesn't carry the same stigma as in the United States — and finding enough government money to increase the supply of affordable housing.

In 2005, a government-appointed monitoring group found that a shortage of affordable housing was a major obstacle to implementing the new law.[4] Towns short of housing have resorted to sending families to bed and breakfasts or towns up to 200 miles away, according to homeless advocates.

The shortage has produced one of the most commonly heard criticisms of the law. "Imagine a small town in Scotland with a family which has been there quite a long time and has made an application to move into social [public] housing. They see someone who is not from that area getting housing in front of them — quite legitimately because they're homeless. That can cause a problem," says Graeme Brown, director of Shelter Scotland, a homeless advocacy and advice organization.

Reluctance among some local government officials to shift toward the statute's more inclusive definition of those eligible for help has also been cited by government monitors as impeding the law's goals.[5]

Before passage of the 2003 act, those who did not fit into priority categories were entitled only to advice and assistance — not housing — which some observers viewed as a way of rationing scarce housing.[6]

Another rationing device was the lower-priority status the law gave to "intentional homelessness." The category was developed in response to local authorities' fears that large numbers of people would give up their existing accommodation to secure a better house under the legislation. After 2012, those deemed "intentionally homeless" are the only remaining group entitled only to temporary, not permanent, housing.[7]

Immediately after passage of the act, the number of homeless applications surged — a 34 percent increase in 2005-06 over the beginning of the decade. Some experts attribute the rise to more people becoming aware they were now eligible for help.

Homelessness figures in 2008-09 show a slight increase, but the steep rise seen earlier in the decade has now leveled off, coinciding with policy changes making housing rights available to more single adults, according to the Scottish government.[8]

"To be fair, local government has gotten better at preventing homelessness," Brown says. "The highly visible homeless sleeping on the streets that we saw 10 years ago in Edinburgh and Glasgow has declined."

Two innovative Scottish programs hold out hope of keeping people in their homes in these times of rising foreclosures — which hit 6,500 households last year. Under the 2003 law, a lender who is about to foreclose on a homeowner or a landlord about to evict a tenant must inform the local government authority immediately. The idea is to give officials time to prevent eviction or find alternative housing.

Scotland has also pioneered an innovative mortgage-to-rent scheme, since imitated by England and Wales. Local nonprofit groups funded by government purchase a house that is about to be foreclosed upon and rent the house back to the residents. With funding limited, however, it will help only 250-300 of the 4,500 households that may be repossessed this year, according to the Scottish government.

In a recent law journal article on the 2003 legislation, attorney Eric S. Tars of the National Law Center on Homelessness and Poverty, in Washington, D.C., applauded a Scottish applicant's ability to sue if local government has not met its statutory duty to provide him housing — a right denied to Americans.[9]

But in Scotland's far less litigious society, suits are rare. If someone comes to Shelter Scotland for help after their local authority has wrongly denied them housing, "we find that almost always the [local] council will back down" after they are contacted, Gavin Corbett, Shelter Scotland's head of policy, said in an e-mail. Shelter could threaten the council with a judicial review of its decision in a higher court, but it rarely comes to that.

The lack of litigiousness may reflect greater social consensus around the issue of homelessness in Scotland than even in the rest of Great Britain, says Brown. "Culturally and politically, even in these post-industrial days, Scotland

Homeless people live under a bridge along the River Clyde in Glasgow, Scotland. Scotland has greatly expanded the government's obligation to house the homeless.

Getty Images/Christopher Furlong

is still more of a nation concerned about their fellow citizens," he says in his lilting Scottish brogue. Speaking by phone from Edinburgh, where it was raining, he added, "This is a northern European country; you need a roof over your head."

The law's ultimate success hinges on whether local governments manage to house the expanded universe of citizens who will qualify for help by the law's target date of 2012 — still an open question, homeless advocates say.[10]

— *Sarah Glazer*

[1] Eric S. Tars and Caitlin Egleson, "Great Scot!" *Georgetown Journal on Poverty Law & Policy*, winter 2009, pp. 187-216, www.nlchp.org/view_report.cfm?id=314.

[2] The 1977 act, enacted under a Labor government, applied to all of Great Britain. Homeless rights under the act were reduced later under Conservative governments in 1979-1997 in England and Wales, but not Scotland, and largely restored under Labor in 2002.

[3] Tom Mullen, "The Right to Housing in Scotland," Homeless in Europe, European Federation of National Organizations Working with the Homeless, autumn, 2008. The law is the Homelessness, Etc. (Scotland) Act of 2003, www.feantsa.org/files/Month%20Publications/EN/Magazine_Homeless_in_Europe_EN/Homeless%20in%20Europe_Autumn08_EN.pdf.

[4] *Ibid.*

[5] *Ibid.*, and Tars and Egleson, *op. cit.*, p. 203.

[6] Mullen, *op. cit.*

[7] *Ibid.*, p. 197. However, temporary housing can last up to one year, with further help after that.

[8] E-mail from Scottish Housing and Support Division.

[9] Tars and Egleson, *op. cit.*, p. 215. The law provides a legally enforceable duty on the local government to meet the housing needs of its residents. Applicants unhappy with a decision may seek judicial review. However, in a judicial review a court cannot substitute its own opinion for that of the decision makers. It can strike down a decision on the grounds that the decision maker has exceeded or abused powers or failed to perform the duty delegated or entrusted or exhibited bias. (E-mail from Scottish Housing and Support Division.)

[10] Local authorities have targets to increase their numbers of priority-need assessments until all of those assessed as homeless have the same rights. Statistics published by the Scottish government in September indicate local authorities have increased their priority assessments to 83 percent of homeless households across Scotland.

capital, often sleeping on steam-heat exhaust grates located near federal buildings.

Headline-grabbing protests that Snyder sparked — as a leader of a onetime anti-Vietnam War organization, the Community for Creative Nonviolence — included a December 1978 takeover of the National Visitors Center, near Union Station, by homeless people. The action forced the city to provide more shelter space.[17]

In November 1981 — three months after the New York settlement — Snyder led a group of about 150 activists and homeless people in building and occupying a tent camp they called "Reaganville" in Lafayette Park, across from the White House. In naming the camp after President Reagan, the activists were trying to evoke the Great Depression, when the jobless and homeless built camps they called "Hoovervilles," after President Herbert Hoover.

The next year, Philadelphia enacted an ordinance that also guaranteed the right to shelter, and in 1984 Washington finally acted. Partly in response to Snyder's and other protests, Washington voters in 1984 passed the nation's first referendum measure guaranteeing "adequate overnight shelter" to homeless people — a statutory equivalent of the New York legal agreement.[18]

Beyond Shelter

The major federal response to rising homelessness came in the form of the Stewart B. McKinney Homeless Assistance Act, which Reagan signed in 1987. (It was retitled in 2000 as the McKinney-Vento Homeless Assistance Act.)[19]

The law authorized programs designed to expand or upgrade shelters and created a series of initiatives aimed at meeting other needs of the homeless population, including: HUD homeless assistance grants for emergency shelters; supportive housing for disabled people and SRO (single-room occupancy) rehabilitation; Veterans Administration and Department of Labor programs for homeless veterans who needed medical care and job-seeking help; Health and Human Services grants and medical care; and Education Department programs for homeless children and youth.[20]

The 1987 law made up the biggest part of the federal attempt to cope with homelessness, but some separate programs had already existed, and others were created later. These included services to homeless youth, provided under a 1974 law; grants to homelessness-prevention projects in local communities, authorized by a 1983 law; a series of programs aimed at homeless veterans, created over several years; and a Social Security Administration program begun in fiscal 2003 designed to help chronically homeless people apply for disability payments.

As Congress legislated, policy experts at universities and think tanks were trying to determine the size of the homeless population and its sub-groups and whether socioeconomic changes played a part in the growth of homelessness. They zeroed in on changes in the housing market, the job market and care of the mentally ill.

By the early 1990s, a consensus had formed among liberals and centrists that the decreasing availability of affordable housing was the root cause of non-chronic homelessness among families and others.

"There is an absolute shortage of appropriate rental units to accommodate poorly housed families," wrote Martha R. Burt, a scholar at the Urban Institute think tank, in a 1993 book that analyzed voluminous data on housing availability, cost and other factors. She found, however, that families made up perhaps as little as 12 percent, of the homeless population.[21]

The bulk of the homeless were single men, almost all weighed down by mental illness, addiction or both — disabilities that had led to long periods of reliance on shelters or the streets. It was these chronically homeless who had been largely responsible for drawing attention to the issue.

They continued to do so, even in death. On Nov. 29, 1993, a homeless woman named Yetta M. Adams, 43, died of exposure on a bench outside the Washington headquarters of HUD Secretary Henry G. Cisneros, prompting new government attention.

In response, the Clinton administration launched a wave of spending — grants totaling $11 million to 187 homeless-assistance programs in 44 states. And in May 1994, the administration unveiled a plan aimed at reducing chronic homelessness by one-third.

Ending Homelessness

The Clinton plan didn't fulfill the expectations created by its announcement. Some programs took effect, said Donald Whitehead, executive director of the National Coalition for the Homeless, but "many other initiatives were never implemented, [and] HUD ended up with no real, substantial increase in new funding."[22]

Nonetheless, the idea took hold that the government could do more than simply respond to homelessness. In 2000, the National Alliance to End Homelessness released a 10-year plan to eliminate homelessness. "Housing has become scarcer for those with little money," the organization said. "Earnings from employment and from benefits have not kept pace with the cost of housing for low income and poor people. Services that every family needs for support and stability have become harder for very poor people to afford or find."[23]

The plan centered on mobilizing government and private organizations to provide housing and related services designed to reverse the conditions that the alliance saw as the core of the problem.

But the new Bush administration took a narrower approach. In 2002 it set a goal of ending chronic homelessness in 10 years. To carry it out, the administration revived the Interagency Council on Homelessness, which had been formed in 1987 but fell into inactivity in the 1990s.[24]

In a series of other actions designed to meet the 10-year goal, the administration in 2003 made grants totaling $48 million to programs designed to help chronically homeless people get jobs, permanent housing, substance-abuse treatment and mental health services.[25]

Over the following years, the Bush administration maintained its focus on the chronically homeless. For example, in evaluating grant applications for building housing for the chronically homeless, HUD gave preference to state and local agency applicants that had developed 10-year plans of their own.

Six years after the Bush administration launched its 10-year campaign, chronic homelessness seemed to be diminishing. From 2006 to 2008, for instance, the national one-night count of homeless people that HUD conducts every January showed a decrease from 155,623 to 124,135 chronically homeless people both in shelters and in other locations, such as streets and bus stations. (Despite the seeming precision of those numbers, HUD'S "point-in-time" count is an estimate, given the difficulty of locating every single homeless person on a single night.)[26]

From 2007 to 2008, however, HUD's count of the chronically homeless was virtually unchanged.[27]

"Ending chronic homelessness has been a national policy objective that has been supported by significant

Tracy Munch (above) and her fiancé were evicted last February from the house they were renting in Adams County, Colo., after the owner stopped paying his mortgage. They managed to borrow enough money to rent another house for themselves and their four children, but not in time to avoid eviction.

investments in developing permanent supportive housing," HUD said in its report, which was released this year. "For several years communities have reported declines in the number of persons experiencing chronic homelessness."[28]

Meanwhile, some organizations advocating a push to eliminate homelessness in all its forms were working to expand the definition of "homelessness." The goal was to enlarge the community of people who would benefit from programs aimed at the people who weren't included in the "chronic" segment of the homeless population.

In 2008, Rep. Gwen Moore, D-Wis., introduced a bill to expand the McKinney-Vento law's definition of "homeless" to include individuals or families who would "imminently lose" their housing and couldn't afford a new house or apartment, plus anyone fleeing domestic violence or another threat to life.

Moore's bill would also have authorized community programs to serve families with children, or children on their own, who were defined as homeless in other laws. The effect would have been to include people who had experienced prolonged periods without stable housing, and could be expected to remain in that condition because of chronic disabilities, chronic physical or mental health problems, addiction, histories of domestic violence, or multiple barriers to employment.

The legislation passed the House, but the Senate took no action on the measure.[29]

War and Recession

In the last two years of the Bush administration the economic and political climate in which politicians and advocates debated and crafted anti-homelessness measures was changing fast.

The foreclosure crisis that started in 2007, with millions of homeowners beginning to default on mortgages, led to the Wall Street meltdown and what economists began calling the Great Recession.[30]

The same HUD report that showed a decline in the number of chronically homeless people also seemed to contain an early warning about families. The report showed that the number of homeless people in families increased from 2007 to 2008 by 43,000, to 516,724, a 9 percent jump. And the number of families in shelters with children rose from 130,968 in 2007 to 159,142. "The most common demographic features of sheltered family members are that adults are women, children are young, the family identifies itself as belonging to a minority group, and the family has two or three members," the report said.[31]

The statistics confirmed anecdotal reports that had been circulating among advocates for low-income families. As a result, the advocacy organizations were able to bolster the argument they'd been making for increasing homelessness assistance and prevention funds to individuals and families who fell outside the "chronically homeless" category. Until then, says Roman of the National Alliance to End Homelessness, "We didn't have the data."

Economic conditions alone would have been enough to suggest that the ranks of the homeless would include growing numbers of low-income households hit by job loss or cutbacks in working hours. But another factor was present as well — the appearance of a new cohort of combat veterans. As men and women began returning from Iraq and Afghanistan, many in the veterans' and housing policy communities began warning against a repetition of what many believed to be a plague of homelessness among Vietnam vets.

Researchers in the 1990s had concluded that homeless veterans of the Southeast Asia war were not as numerous as many had thought.[32] Still, the reality of any veterans from the new century's wars wandering streets or sleeping in shelters was widely considered a reflection of failure by government's veteran-care and social services agencies. "We're beginning to see, across the country, the first trickle of this generation of warriors in homeless shelters," Phil Landis, chairman of Veterans Village of San Diego, a residence and counseling center, told *The New York Times* in 2007. "But we anticipate that it's going to be a tsunami."[33]

So far, no tidal wave has hit. But the HUD annual report does show that veterans account for 11.6 percent of the adult population that uses shelters, but a lesser share — 10.5 percent — of the national adult population. "The estimated number of homeless veterans should be watched closely," the report adds, "as the number of veterans returning from recent combat increases during the next few years."[34]

CURRENT SITUATION
Fund Drive

Housing advocacy groups are campaigning for increased federally funding for homelessness programs. But many are pessimistic due to the state of the economy, the growing government deficit and the Obama administration's growing list of priorities, including the newly announced Afghanistan troop surge.

At the same time, the gravity of the economic crisis may persuade politicians that homelessness has become more than a niche issue. "I can count on one hand the number of staffers who are actually invested, passionate, care about housing," Kim, the aide to Missouri Republican Sen. Bond, told a Capitol Hill briefing in early December organized by the National Alliance to End Homelessness. He added, "Now with the foreclosure crisis, there are probably people who are a little more sensitive to it."

Alliance president Roman went even further. Enactment earlier in the year of the Homelessness Prevention and Rapid Rehousing Program (HPRP) — designed to help families avoid losing their housing — marked a major shift in government strategy, she said. "We may actually come out of this difficult period with a better homelessness system than we went into it with, if we're able to take advantage of the opportunity presented by HPRP."

Should homelessness be redefined by HUD to include more youths and families?

YES
Phillip Lovell
Vice President for Education, Housing, and Youth Policy First Focus

Written for *CQ Researcher*, Dec. 15, 2009

"Not homeless enough." That's the message sent to over 550,000 children who are considered homeless by the Department of Education and other agencies but are not homeless enough for the Department of Housing and Urban Development (HUD). Yes, you read that correctly. A child can be homeless enough for one federal agency, but not for another.

Increasingly, the homeless are families who lose their homes and temporarily "double up" with others or stay in motels, often because shelters are full. They do not live in "unstable housing situations." They have lost their homes, cannot afford another apartment and do not know where or when their next move will take place. No one staying in this type of temporary, often unsafe, situation can be said to have a home. Denying this fact is disastrous.

In 2007, a youth whom I will call John became homeless. Desperate, he accepted an offer to stay with an adult for two months. John was raped repeatedly and, as a result, contracted HIV.

When I met John, he looked like a normal kid. He was receiving a scholarship to help him go to college and was bright, articulate and smiling. He did not look homeless. But he was no less homeless, vulnerable or deserving of federal support.

The president recently signed legislation making modest improvements to the HUD definition. Now, a family in a doubled up or motel situation is considered homeless if they can only stay in their housing for 14 days. Additionally, families can be considered homeless if they are fleeing situations where the health and safety of children are jeopardized.

Neither provision would have helped John. He stayed in his doubled up situation until another temporary situation became available — well above the 14-day maximum. And the only way he would qualify for assistance under the health and safety clause is by being raped. This is unacceptable.

In the end, this is about our children. This is about keeping them safe and making sure they have the basic necessities of life. Congress must change HUD's definition of homelessness to reflect reality. A narrow definition masks the real problems facing our communities. Homelessness cannot be defined away.

It will be some time before Congress considers this issue again. In the meantime, HUD is required to issue regulations on the newly passed definition of homelessness. For all those who may follow in John's footsteps, let us hope HUD does so in a way that protects as many children, youth and families as possible.

NO
Howard Husock
Vice president for policy research Manhattan Institute for Policy Research and author, America's Trillion-Dollar Housing Mistake: The Failure of American Housing Policy

Written for *CQ Researcher*, Dec. 15, 2009

Without doubt, the collapse of the U.S. housing market has caused hardship. Owners are stuck with homes worth less than the price they paid. Others have moved in with parents and extended families. We cannot, however, address our housing situation clearly by using emotional descriptions as arguments for a vast expansion of subsidized housing — which would be both difficult to afford and, just as significantly, ill-advised social policy.

The term "homelessness" dates to the early Reagan administration, when two trends overlapped. The deinstitutionalization of those suffering from mental illness or alcohol and substance abuse problems — begun as a liberal policy in the 1960s — utterly failed. Many people wound up living on the streets, becoming the public image of "homelessness." At the same time, reductions in public assistance forced some very low-income (primarily single-parent) households to double-up with relatives or live in more crowded conditions. Such households never fit the common-sense definition of homeless — known in Britain as "street-sleeping." But advocates of subsidized housing began to include them in estimates of homelessness — and, in some cities, they began to be admitted in large numbers to public group-living quarters (the very term "shelters" perpetuated the image that such households were living on the street). Those households also received priority for a rapidly expanding housing-voucher program, which allowed them to pay public housing rents for private apartments. This, in turn, ballooned the Section 8 voucher program — to the point that its budget now surpasses that for cash welfare assistance.

Now those who want to further expand such housing assistance are using the foreclosure and delinquency spike as a rationale for expanding that same housing-voucher program — by using the image of the recession-strapped working family as the new face of homelessness. Such problems are being addressed through federal efforts to modify loans and other methods. Doubling the size of the housing-voucher program is not likely even to reach such families.

Far better to continue to take steps to help the truly homeless — the mentally ill who should be assisted through housing combined with social services — and to adjust the voucher program by converting it to a cash payment expansion of the Earned Income Tax Credit. Let's help those of low income but not by costly, ineffective and inaccurately labeled remedies.

AFP/Getty Images/Jewel Samad

Homeless people pitch camp beside a Las Vegas street last April. Across the nation, another group of people is joining the growing number of low-income households hit by job loss and homelessness: men and women returning from the wars in Iraq and Afghanistan.

Accordingly, Roman and her allies are urging Congress to add another $1 billion to the HPRP, on top of the $1.5 billion appropriated earlier this year.

They also want lawmakers to allocate $1 billion to the National Housing Trust Fund (NHTF), created by a 2008 law to provide funds to build or rehabilitate rental housing for households with very low incomes. The request is in line with a plan endorsed by the Obama administration for fiscal 2010-2011. "We will work with Congress to identify a financing source for the Housing Trust Fund, which will help provide decent housing for families hardest hit by the current economic downturn," HUD Secretary Shaun Donovan said in October.[35]

Rep. Barney Frank, D-Mass., chairman of the House Banking Committee, and Sen. Jack Reed, D-R.I., a member of the Housing, Transportation, and Community Development Subcommittee, have introduced bills to make the $1 billion allocation.

In the last month of 2009, the National Low-Income Housing Coalition was drumming up a grassroots campaign to pressure lawmakers into committing themselves to the trust fund legislation. "Our goal is to create an early-December blizzard of phone calls from all over in a compressed period of time to demonstrate strong and urgent support for an initial infusion of money for the NHTF," the coalition told its members.[36]

Advocacy groups are also pressing for the appropriation of $2.4 billion under the Homeless Emergency Assistance

and Rapid Transition to Housing (HEARTH) Act. Enacted in 2009, but without funding for 2009-2010, HEARTH authorizes homeless-assistance grants and supportive housing for homeless people with disabilities.

In addition, with the Temporary Assistance to Needy Families (TANF) system up for reauthorization in 2010, housing advocates are asking Congress to add funding for states with effective strategies against family homelessness. TANF was created under the Clinton administration as a new version of welfare aid to families with children.

Metropolitan Trends

Several big and medium-size cities are showing the same trend in homelessness that HUD reported in mid-2009. Homelessness among single individuals is declining or remaining flat, but more families are losing their homes, the U.S. Conference of Mayors reported in early December.[37]

"The recession and a lack of affordable housing were cited as the top causes of family homelessness in the surveyed cities," the organization said.[38]

The survey covered 27 cities from October 2008 to Sept. 30, 2009, including Boston, Chicago, Dallas and Los Angeles, as well as Gastonia, N.C., Louisville and St. Paul, Minn., among the smaller cities. About three-fourths of the cities reported an uptick in family homelessness — ranging from 1 percent in Salt Lake City to 41 percent in Charleston, S.C. Seventy-four percent of the municipal governments reported a lack of affordable housing as the top cause of homelessness.

Developments among families stood in sharp contrast to the trend for individuals. In 64 percent of the responding cities (16 cities), individual homelessness was reported decreased or at the same level as the previous year. Norfolk, Va., reported the highest increase, of 18 percent.

However, the survey isn't a precision instrument, as the Conference acknowledged. For instance, Los Angeles reported a 68 percent decline in family homelessness, basing that result on censuses it conducted in 2007 and 2009. "The steep decline … conflicts with anecdotal evidence from Los Angeles homeless service providers, who say the number of families seeking shelter has swelled recently because of the recession."

And the reported national drop in individual homelessness has at least one major exception. In New York, which didn't participate in the survey, lawyers representing homeless men and women took city government to court in early December, charging failure to live up to the landmark Callahan agreement of 1981. The city isn't keeping up with demand for shelter space, lawyers for the Legal Aid Society and the Coalition for the Homeless charged.

"The extreme situation now is reminiscent of problems that we haven't seen in years," Steven Banks, attorney in chief for Legal Aid, told *The New York Times*. "It's a failure to plan, and it's having dire consequences for vulnerable women and vulnerable men."[39]

A motion by the lawyers cited reports by monitors for the coalition. For example, they said two shelters in late September hadn't provided beds for 15 men. At another shelter in late October, 52 men slept in chairs or on the floor; 14 men were bused to shelters with beds, but 38 were left bedless for the night. At yet another shelter, two women slept on a dining room table.

Robert V. Hess, the city's commissioner of homeless services, called the motion "alarmist." He told *The Times*: "We've seen an uptick in demand, so our system, as you might expect, is a little tight. We're confident that we'll continue to be able to meet demand and meet our obligations throughout the winter."[40]

Capacity in the adult shelter system was at 99.6 percent on Dec. 8, Hess told *The Times*. The shelters held 4,934 men and 2,041 women that day. Not included were military veterans in short-term housing; chronically homeless people who've entered a program designed for them; and 30,698 people in families who were in short-term housing set aside for them.

Concerning the monitors' reports, Hess said that some of those without beds had refused them, or had arrived at shelters after 2 a.m. Of a report that some women were taken by bus to a shelter where they had less than five hours to sleep, Hess called the account "potentially correct."

Small-Town Woes

Homelessness is often considered a big-city phenomenon, but it's hitting rural communities and small towns as well.

"More companies are downsizing or closing," says Kay Moshier McDivitt, adviser to the Lancaster County Coalition to End Homelessness, in the heart of Pennsylvania's Amish country. "Now our demand has increased beyond our ability to respond."

Employment prospects in the area, a major tourist destination, are dominated by low-wage service jobs, which leave little cushion against job loss. Some service workers spend up to 75 percent of their incomes for housing, McDivitt says.

Speaking at the December Capitol Hill briefing organized by the National Alliance to End Homelessness, McDivitt said that in October and November of 2009 the coalition had received 1,500 requests for help paying rent or mortgages — a 400 percent increase over 2008. "Most of our families when they first become homeless spend a year or more moving among family and friends. By the time we see our families, they have often been homeless for a year or more, with lots of instability. They are ready for permanence and stability."

Demand for help has risen so sharply the coalition is setting up its first family shelters. Until now, McDivitt said, HPRP funds have enabled the county to help families pay rent so they never become homeless. But, she adds, "We expect family homelessness is going to increase."

A slightly less pessimistic assessment came from Kathy Wahto, executive director of Serenity House of Clallam County, Wash., which helps the homeless in Port Angeles, northeast of Seattle.

There, despite persistent poverty, a state-funded homelessness-prevention program had helped lower homelessness by about 40 percent over the past three years. But the recession has cut a major source of revenue for that program — document recording fees on real estate transactions. "That's $200,000 in revenue we're not going to have," Wahto said.

HPRP partly made up for the loss with an $89,000 infusion. "The ending of homelessness in our county was in sight," Wahto said. "We don't want to go backwards."

OUTLOOK

"Modestly Positive" Trends

Housing advocates who've been pushing for years to expand homelessness services tend toward optimism about the medium-term future.

"If you had asked me last year if we would have $1.5 billion for HPRP, I would have said no," says the Urban Institute's Cunningham. "A lot of positive things are coming out of the present administration."

She concedes that homelessness programs are competing for money and attention in a time of crisis on several fronts. But it's within the administration's reach to go a long way toward eliminating homelessness, she says. "If you look at the research, the bottom line is, we know how to end homelessness. We just need the political will to do it."

Husock of the Manhattan Institute takes a somewhat more skeptical view, though not an entirely bleak one. "I would guess we would be closer to the status quo than any kind of big change," he says. But he says he's encouraged by the openness of HUD Secretary Donovan to programs in Atlanta and elsewhere that combine housing assistance with work requirements of the kind that transformed the welfare system.

"To me, Atlanta is pointing the way to the future," Husock says. Overall, he says, "The trend has been modestly positive."

The Cato Institute's Tanner takes a dimmer view, based on what he calls continuing attachment to regulatory controls that he argues slows construction of affordable housing. "I don't see any policy to expand the availability of low-income housing through eliminating rent control or zoning regulations."

That aside, he argues that the extent of homelessness over the next decade will largely be determined by the state of the economy. "If you get long-term economic growth, you'll get a lower number of people homeless because they lost their jobs."

On that point at least, virtually everyone agrees.

"How about you give me a prediction about where we'll be on the unemployment rate in 10 years," says Jencks of Harvard's Kennedy School of Government. "I would love to believe we won't be in this fix."

One nuance to the question, though, is that providing more services to homeless people may not result in an immediate reduction in their numbers. "Conservatives tend to argue, and they're not completely off-base, that when you do more, you're going to get more homeless people," Jencks says. "I don't take that as defeat. A lot of people are living in terrible circumstances, and if you give them the opportunity not to live with a belligerent brother-in-law, they will. Is that a waste? I don't think so."

Among those who deal daily with the heartaches and complexities of individual and family housing crises, the depth of the economic crisis leads to caution in forecasting when a homelessness turnaround might occur.

"A number of people are falling into poverty, and a number of governments are being hit by the recession and having to cut programs," says Beresin of the Washington Legal Clinic for the Homeless. "It takes a long time to bounce back from all that — not to mention that we've decided to send 30,000 more troops into Afghanistan."

In Washington, Beresin notes, some construction projects for affordable housing have been stopped in their tracks because a city government program that provides funding is itself short of revenue, which comes from a real-estate transaction tax. "D.C. definitely can't do it alone," she says. "It needs federal dollars, and if those aren't going to be there because the government is prioritizing other things, we don't have much control over that."

Still and all, among advocates who deal with Congress, the prevailing mood tends toward optimism. "In 10 years, I think there will be fewer homeless people," says Roman of the National Alliance to End Homelessness. "We've learned a lot about how to run a much better homeless system. We could probably get about half the way to ending homelessness with that."

The other half may be harder to solve. "The affordable housing crisis is the driver," she says. "When we didn't have that gap, we didn't have homeless people. People have lots of problems, but they used to be able to afford a place to live, and now they can't."

NOTES

1. "The 2008 Annual Homeless Assessment Report to Congress," U.S. Department of Housing and Urban Development, July 2009, p. v, www.hudhre.info/documents/4thHomelessAssessmentReport.pdf. HUD reported on 2008 in mid-2009; the 2009 report is scheduled for release in 2010.

2. *Ibid.*

3. "Affordable Housing," U.S. Department of Housing and Urban Development, Dec. 3, 2009, www.hud.gov/offices/cpd/affordablehousing/.

4. Ellie Ashford, "Districts Cope With Rising Numbers of Homeless Students," School Board News, National School Boards Association, January 2009, www.nsba.org/HPC/Features/AboutSBN/SbnArchive/2009/

January-2009/Districts-cope-with-rising-numbers-of-homeless-students.aspx.

5. "Affordable Housing," *op. cit.*

6. "The 2008 Annual Homeless Assessment," *op. cit.*, p. 31.

7. "Labor Force Statistics from the Current Population Survey," U.S. Bureau of Labor Statistics, updated monthly, http://data.bls.gov/PDQ/servlet/Survey OutputServlet.

8. "Federal Definition of Homeless," U.S. Department of Housing and Urban Development, March 3, 2009, www.hud.gov/homeless/definition.cfm.

9. Libby Perl, *et al.*, "Homelessness: Targeted Federal Programs and Recent Legislation," Congressional Research Service, Jan. 15, 2009, p. 2, http://web.mit .edu/lugao/MacData/afs.lugao/MacData/afs/sipb/con trib/wikileaks-crs/wikileaks-crs-reports/RL30442.pdf.

10. *Ibid.*

11. Maggie McCarty, "Section 8 Housing Choice Voucher Program: Issues and Reform Proposals in the 110th Congress," Congressional Research Service, p. 3, http://wikileaks.org/leak/crs/RL34002 .pdf.

12. *Ibid.*, p. 10.

13. Details of the lawsuit and its effects are drawn from Kim Hopper, *Reckoning With Homelessness* (2003), pp. 186-191; Lyn Stolarwski, "Right To Shelter: History of the Mobilization of the Homeless as a Model of Voluntary Action," *Nonprofit and Voluntary Sector Quarterly*, 1988, http://nvs.sagepub.com/cgi/ reprint/17/1/36.pdf; Robin Herman, "Pact Requires City to Shelter Homeless Men," *The New York Times*, Aug. 27, 1981, p. A1; Charles Kaiser, "A State Justice Orders Creation of 750 Beds for Bowery Homeless," *The New York Times*, Dec. 9, 1979.

14. For background, see Charles S. Clark, "Mental Illness," *CQ Researcher*, Aug. 6, 1993, pp. 673-696. Chris Koyanagi, "Learning From History: Dein-stitutionalization of People With Mental Illness as Precursor to Longterm Care Reform," Kaiser Commission on Medicaid and the Uninsured, August 2007, p. 8, www.kff.org/medicaid/upload/7684.pdf.

15. Christopher Jencks, *The Homeless* (1994), pp. 16-17. For background, see William Triplett, "Ending Homelessness," *CQ Researcher*, June 18, 2004, pp. 541-564.

16. *Ibid.*, pp. 1-2.

17. Paul W. Valentine, "Street People in Visitor Center Vex U.S.," *The Washington Post*, Dec. 7, 1978, p. B1; Paul W. Valentine, "City Agrees to Provide More Homeless Shelters," *The Washington Post*, Dec. 16, 1978, p. D1.

18. Sandra G. Boodman, "City Softens Opposition to Shelter Initiative," *The Washington Post*, Nov. 8, 1984, p. A58.

19. Except where otherwise indicated, this subsection is drawn from Perl, *et al.*, *op. cit.*

20. *Ibid.*

21. Burt, *op. cit.*, pp. 16-17.

22. Quoted in Triplett, *op. cit.*

23. "A Plan, Not a Dream: How to End Homelessness in Ten Years," National Alliance to End Homelessness, June 1, 2000, www.endhomelessness.org/content/ article/detail/585.

24. Maggie McCarty, *et al.*, "Homelessness: Recent Statistics, Targeted Federal Programs, and Recent Legislation," Congressional Research Service, May 31, 2005, pp. 17-18, www.fas.org/sgp/crs/misc/ RL30442.pdf.

25. *Ibid.*, pp. 17-18.

26. "The 2008 Annual Homeless Assessment Report to Congress," *op. cit.*

27. *Ibid.*

28. *Ibid.*, p. 5.

29. HR 7221, *CQ Billtrack*, Nov. 17, 2008.

30. For background, see Marcia Clemmitt, "Mortgage Crisis," *CQ Researcher*, Nov. 2, 2007, pp. 913-936; Peter Katel, "Straining the Safety Net," *CQ Researcher*, July 31, 2009, pp. 645-668.

31. "The 2008 Annual Homeless Assessment Report to Congress," *op. cit.*, pp. 31, 42.

32. For background, see Peter Katel, "Wounded Veterans," *CQ Researcher*, Aug. 31, 2007, pp. 697-720.

33. Quoted in Erik Eckholm, "Surge Seen in Number of Homeless Veterans," *The New York Times*, Nov. 8, 2007, www.nytimes.com/2007/11/08/us/08vets.html.

34. "The 2008 Annual Homeless Assessment Report to Congress," *op. cit.*, p. 28.

35. "Administration Calls on Congress to Approve Key Housing Measures," U.S. Department of Housing and Urban Development, press release, Oct. 29, 2009, http://treas.gov/press/releases/tg336.htm.

36. "Please Call Congress December 1 or 2 for NHTF Money," National Low Income Housing Coalition, undated, http://capwiz.com/nlihc/issues/alert/?alertid=14407651.

37. "Hunger and Homelessness Survey: A Status Report on Hunger and Homelessness in America's Cities, a 27-City Survey," United States Conference of Mayors, December 2009, www.usmayors.org/pressreleases/uploadsUSCMHungercompleteWEB2009.pdf.

38. "U.S. Cities See Sharp Increases in the Need for Food Assistance; Decreases in Individual Homelessness," United States Conference of Mayors, Dec. 8, 2009, www.usmayors.org/pressreleases/uploadsRELEASE-HUNGERHOMELESSNESS2009FINALRevised.pdf.

39. Quoted in Julie Bosman, "Advocates Say City is Running Out of Beds for the Homeless," *The New York Times*, Dec. 10, 2009, www.nytimes.com/2009/12/10/nyregion/10homeless.html?_r=1&ref=nyregion.

40. Quoted in *ibid.*

BIBLIOGRAPHY

Books

Burt, Martha R., *Over the Edge: The Growth of Homelessness in the 1980s*, Russell Sage Foundation, 1993.
One of the leading scholars of homelessness wrote an early and influential analysis of its causes and extent.

Hopper, Kim, *Reckoning With Homelessness*, Cornell University Press, 2003.
Homelessness can be approached historically, through first-hand observation or anthropologically; one anthropologist blended all three approaches.

Husock, Howard, *America's Trillion-Dollar Housing Mistake: The Failure of American Housing Policy*, Ivan R. Dee, 2003.
A policy expert for the conservative-leaning Manhattan Institute critically analyzes federal subsidized-housing programs as a strategy that has promoted dependency instead of independence and social advancement.

Jencks, Christopher, *The Homeless*, Harvard University Press, 1994.
Writing from a perspective that remains relevant today, an influential policy scholar examines the causes and possible remedies for homelessness.

Articles

Bazar, Emily, "Tent cities filling up with casualties of the economy," *USA Today*, May 5, 2009, p. A1.
Money troubles are driving thousands of homeless people into tent encampments around the country, a national newspaper reports.

Chong, Jia-Rui, "Some vets of recent wars find homelessness at home," *Los Angeles Times*, June 29, 2009, p. A4.
A growing number of Iraq-Afghanistan combat veterans are winding up homeless, often because of the psychological effects of their battlefield experiences.

Eckholm, Erik, "More Homeless Pupils, More Strained Schools," *The New York Times*, Sept. 6, 2009, p. A1.
School systems are scrambling to meet the needs of children and youth living in various types of temporary housing, ranging from trailers in campgrounds to friends' and relatives' homes.

Fears, Darryl, "15 Homeless People Get Apartments Next Month," *The Washington Post*, Sept. 29, 2009, p. B4.
As part of a nationwide policy to provide "supportive housing" to chronically homeless people, Washington is moving forward with a plan to provide permanent housing for mentally ill people who had been living on the street.

Patterson, Thom, "U.S. seeing more female homeless veterans," CNN, Sept. 25, 2009, www.cnn.com/2009/LIVING/09/25/homeless.veterans.
As growing numbers of women return from the front lines, some are joining the ranks of homeless male veterans.

Rubin, Bonnie Miller, "Homeless, unless you count storage space," *Los Angeles Times*, Nov. 15, 2009, p. A12.
A reporter finds a Chicago-area family fallen on hard times whose illegal home is a storage locker, except on rare occasions when they can rent a motel room for a night.

Urbina, Ian, "Recession Drives Surge in Youth Runaways," *The New York Times*, Oct. 26, 2009, p. A1.
The number of teenagers living on their own — usually in perilous circumstances — is growing because of family stresses aggravated by the economic crisis.

Reports

"The 2008 Annual Homeless Assessment Report to Congress," U.S. Department of Housing and Urban Development, July 2009, www.hudhre.info/documents/4thHomelessAssessmentReport.pdf.
The federal government's annual study provides a wealth of statistics and analysis.

Cunningham, Mary K., "Preventing and Ending Homelessness — Next Steps," Urban Institute, February 2009, www.urban.org/publications/411837.html.
A longtime specialist provides a detailed summary of programs and recommends further measures.

DeHaven, Tad, "Three Decades of Politics and Failed Policies at HUD," Cato Institute, Nov. 23, 2009, www.cato.org/pub_display.php?pub_id=10981.
A budget analyst for the libertarian think tank recounts the history of scandals at the main federal agency in charge of program to alleviate homelessness.

Duffield, Barbara and Phillip Lovell, "The Economic Crisis Hits Home: The Unfolding Increase in Child and Youth Homelessness," National Association for the Education of Homeless Children and Youth, First Focus, December 2008, www.naehcy.org/dl/TheEconomicCrisisHitsHome.pdf.
Children's rights organizations examine the growth in homelessness and unstable housing among young people.

Perl, Libby, *et al.*, "Homelessness: Targeted Federal Programs and Recent Legislation," Congressional Research Service, Jan. 15, 2009, http://wikileaks.org/leak/crs/RL30442.pdf.
Specialists for Congress' research arm provide a wealth of detail about legislation designed to reduce homelessness.

For More Information

Manhattan Institute for Policy Research, 52 Vanderbilt Ave., New York, NY 10017; (212) 599-7000; www.manhattan-institute.org. A conservative leaning think tank on urban issues that tends to be skeptical about federal housing and homelessness policies.

National Alliance to End Homelessness, 1518 K St., N.W., Suite 410, Washington, DC 20005; (202) 638-1526; endhomeless.org. Works on legislation and program design and publishes research on causes and effects of homelessness.

National Center on Homelessness Among Veterans, U.S. Department of Veterans Affairs, 810 Vermont Ave., N.W., Washington, DC 20420; (800) 827-1000; www1.va.gov/Homeless/. Publishes information on federal homeless programs as well as research on veterans and homelessness.

National Coalition for the Homeless, 2201 P St., N.W., Washington, DC 20037; (202) 462-4822; www.national

homeless.org/index.html. Helps organize voter-registration drives for the homeless and other national campaigns.

National Law Center on Homelessness & Poverty; 1411 K St., N.W., Suite 1400, Washington, DC 20005; (202) 638-2535; www.nlchp.org. Pursues judicial and legislative remedies to problems tied to homelessness.

U.S. Department of Housing and Urban Development, 451 7th St., S.W., Washington, DC 20410; (202) 708-1112; http://portal.hud.gov/portal/page/portal/HUD/topics/homelessness. Publishes detailed data on homelessness and government programs.

Urban Institute, 2100 M St., N.W., Washington, DC 20037; (202) 833-7200; www.urban.org/housing/index.cfm. A nonpartisan think tank that studies homelessness and policies designed to reduce or end it.

10

Domestic Poverty

Thomas J. Billitteri

Hispanic day laborers negotiate with a potential employer in Homestead, Fla. As low-skilled immigrants, many living below the poverty line, move to the South and Midwest to work in meatpacking and other industries, debate intensifies over immigration's impact on native-born Americans at the bottom of the income scale. Newly released Census data for 2006 show that 36.5 million Americans — including nearly 13 million children — lived below the federal poverty line of $20,614 in income for a family of four.

From *CQ Researcher*,
September 7, 2007.

Marilyn Bezear, a 52-year-old single parent in Harlem who lost her husband to cancer, was living in run-down public housing and working two jobs last winter, cleaning offices and doing clerical work for a temp agency.

"Together, after taxes, I bring home up to $300 a week," she told a congressional panel in February. "With this I pay my rent, food, telephone and payments for the loan that I took out for my daughter to go to college." When the temp agency has no work, Bezear scrambles for ways to meet expenses, like working the late shift at a bowling alley and "getting home at 4:30 in the morning."

Bezear added: "I am just one of many who live through these struggles. . . . Wages, education, training and health care are a necessity. I hope my testimony did not fall on deaf ears."[1]

It's a hope that many of America's poorest citizens would no doubt echo. Despite a relatively stable economy, an overhaul of the welfare system a decade ago and billions spent on programs for the needy, poverty remains pervasive and intractable across the nation.

Conservatives say solutions must emphasize personal responsibility, higher marriage rates and fewer out-of-wedlock births, while liberals blame the negative effects of budget cuts for anti-poverty programs, tax cuts benefiting the wealthy and the need for more early-childhood-development programs. The Democratic Congress has made poverty a priority issue. And a number of presidential candidates are focusing either squarely on poverty or more generally on ideas to narrow the growing gap between the rich and poor.

Newly released Census data for 2006 show that 36.5 million Americans — about one in eight — lived below the federal poverty line of $20,614 in income for a family of four. More than

233

South Is Most Impoverished Region

Almost all the Southern states have poverty levels exceeding the national average of 12.3 percent of residents living in poverty. Mississippi leads the nation with a poverty rate of 20.6 percent. New Hampshire has the lowest rate, 5.4 percent.

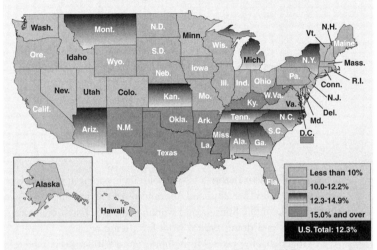

Percentage of People in Poverty by State, 2006

Less than 10%
10.0-12.2%
12.3-14.9%
15.0% and over

U.S. Total: 12.3%

Source: "Historical Poverty Tables," U.S. Census Bureau, 2007

- The gap between rich and poor is growing. In 2005, the average income of the top 1 percent of U.S. households rose $102,000 (adjusted for inflation), but the bottom 90 percent saw incomes rise $250, according to economists Thomas Piketty and Emmanuel Saez.[6] And the top 1 percent got the biggest share of national income since 1928.[7]

- The chance an average American family will see its income plummet at least 50 percent is roughly two-and-a-half times that of the 1970s.[8]

- At some time, most Americans will live at least one year below the poverty line, according to sociologists Mark R. Rank and Thomas A. Hirschl.[9]

Such trends have helped push poverty and broader issues of inequality and economic insecurity onto the national stage in ways not seen for decades. Two years ago, televised images of squalor in post-Katrina New Orleans refocused the nation's attention — at least temporarily — on poverty. More recently, the subprime mortgage debacle, higher gas prices and spiraling medical costs have edged millions of middle-class Americans closer to economic ruin. Meanwhile, Main Street angst is growing over globalization, which has contributed to the elimination of one-sixth of U.S. factory jobs in the past six years.[10]

Jacob S. Hacker, a political scientist at Yale University and author of the 2006 book *The Great Risk Shift: The Assault on American Jobs, Families, Health Care, and Retirement — And How You Can Fight Back*, says poverty is on the nation's radar for reasons that go beyond high-profile events like Katrina.

"Poverty is something the middle class cares about when it looks down and sees itself poised on the financial precipice," he says. The middle class is looking up, too, at those in the top income strata, and "there's a lot more discussion about [income] inequality." And finally, many middle-class Americans "have a deep concern about the fact that we're such a rich nation, and yet children and

a third of them are children, and 3.4 million are 65 and older. And while the nation's poverty rate declined for the first time this decade, from 12.6 percent in 2005 to 12.3 percent last year, the number of children without health insurance rose to 11.7 percent in 2006.[2]

Indeed, among "rich" nations, the United States ranked second — behind Mexico — in poverty at the turn of the 21st century.[3]

"An astonishing number of people are working as hard as they possibly can but are still in poverty or have incomes that are not much above the poverty line," said Peter Edelman, a law professor at Georgetown University who was co-chairman of a poverty task force this year for the Center for American Progress, a Washington think tank.[4]

A number of indicators underscore the depth and breadth of American poverty:

- Those in "deep," or severe, poverty, with incomes of half or less of the official poverty threshold, number over 15 million — more than the populations of New York City, Los Angeles and Chicago combined. Severe poverty hit a 32-year high in 2005, according to McClatchy Newspapers.[5]

Gap Between Rich and Poor Widened

The top 1 percent of income households earned about 20 percent of the nation's total income in 2005, its highest share since 1929. From 2004 to 2005, the average income of such earners increased by $102,000, after adjusting for inflation. By contrast, the average income of the bottom 90 percent rose by $250.

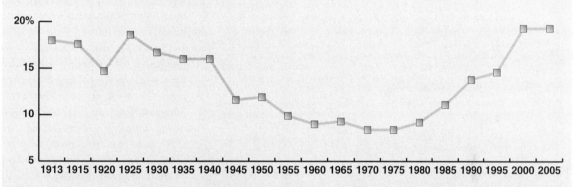

Share of Total Pre-tax Income Held by Top 1 Percent of Earners

Source: Thomas Piketty and Emmanuel Saez, based on IRS data; in Aviva Aron-Dine, "New Data Show Income Concentration Jumped Again in 2005: Income Share of Top 1% Returned to Its 2000 Level, the Highest Since 1929," Center on Budget and Policy Priorities, March 29, 2007

hardworking adults who moved into the labor market after welfare reform are struggling to get by."

While politicians in both major parties have spoken to concerns about middle-class vulnerability, Democrats have been focusing squarely on poverty and inequality, blending appeals for middle-class protections with rhetoric reminiscent of the 1960s "War on Poverty."

Since assuming control of Congress in January, Democrats have held several hearings on poverty, hunger and economic threats to the needy. Rep. Charles B. Rangel, D-N.Y., chairman of the powerful House Ways and Means Committee, declared this spring that "with the exception of getting the hell out of the Middle East, I can't think of anything more patriotic that we can do than eliminate poverty."[11]

In the 2008 presidential race, Sen. Hillary Clinton, D-N.Y., has accused the Bush administration of making the middle class and working families into "invisible Americans,"[12] while Sen. Barack Obama, D-Ill., alluding to his work as a community organizer in Chicago, has said poverty "is the cause that led me to a life of public service."[13] Former Sen. John Edwards, D-N.C., has staked his campaign on the poverty issue, calling it "the great moral issue of our time."[14]

Among other contenders, Mayor Michael Bloomberg of New York — who dropped his affiliation with the Republican Party in June — has been among the most outspoken on poverty. On Aug. 28, the billionaire founder of Bloomberg News, who is thought to be considering a third-party presidential bid, proposed a sharp expansion in the Earned Income Tax Credit (EITC), which provides tax relief to the working poor, and called on politicians of both parties to move beyond ideology to overcome poverty. Bloomberg proposed roughly doubling the number of Americans eligible to benefit from the EITC to 19.7 million people.[15]

"We are beginning to hear a chorus of voices urging action on poverty," Rep. Jim McDermott, D-Wash., chairman of the House Ways and Means Subcommittee on Income Security and Family Support, said in April.[16]

Edelman, at the Center for American Progress, echoed the point. "There's a rising concern in the country about inequality," he said. "There's concern about giveaways to the really wealthy, and there's concern about economic insecurity. The poverty issue is embedded in that."[17]

Nevertheless, it remains unclear how far voters will go in supporting new programs for the poor. A mere 1 percent of respondents to a Gallup Poll in June ranked

Democratic Candidates' Stands on Poverty

 Joseph Biden voted for the Fair Minimum Wage Act of 2007, which raised the minimum wage from $5.15 an hour to $7.25 an hour. Biden broke with his party to vote in favor of the Bankruptcy Abuse Prevention and Consumer Protection Act of 2005, which makes it harder for people to erase debt by declaring bankruptcy.

 Hillary Clinton accuses the Bush administration of turning the middle class into "invisible Americans," and says if she is elected president, "they will no longer be invisible." In 2002, Clinton was criticized by liberal groups for supporting an increase in the work requirement for welfare; she said that she supported the measure because it was tied to $8 billion in funding of day care for welfare recipients. She advocated for welfare reform under her husband's administration. As a senator, Clinton voted for an increase in the federal minimum wage.

 Christopher Dodd says that one of his policy priorities influenced by Catholic social teachings and the emphasis on the common good is "creating safety nets for the disadvantaged." As a senator, one of Dodd's priorities has been helping children, and he has authored numerous child care bills. Dodd has favored increases in the federal minimum wage.

 John Edwards has made reducing poverty the signature issue of his campaign, calling it "the great moral issue of our time." He has set a goal of ending poverty in 30 years by lifting one-third of the 37 million currently impoverished Americans above the poverty line each decade through a higher minimum wage, tax cuts for low-income workers, universal health care and housing vouchers for poor families.

 Mike Gravel says America's war on drugs must end because it "does nothing but savage our inner cities and put our children at risk." Gravel proposes to help end poverty by creating a progressive tax system in which consumers of new products would be taxed at a flat rate. This would encourage Americans to save, Gravel says. This proposed system would replace the income tax and Internal Revenue Service.

 Dennis Kucinich advocates ending the war in Iraq and using the money saved to fight domestic poverty, calling homelessness, joblessness and poverty "weapons of mass destruction." In July 2007, Kucinich said that he was in favor of reparations for slavery, saying, "The Bible says we shall and must be repairers of the breach. And a breach has occurred. . . . It's a breach that has resulted in inequality in opportunities for education, for health care, for housing, for employment."

 Barack Obama In the Illinois Senate, Obama helped author the state's earned income tax credit, which provided tax cuts for low-income families. Obama has supported bills to increase the minimum wage. In *The Audacity of Hope*, Obama describes what he calls America's "empathy deficit," writing that a "stronger sense of empathy would tilt the balance of our current politics in favor of those people who are struggling in this society."

 Bill Richardson As governor of New Mexico, Richardson took steps to combat poverty in the state, one of the nation's poorest. He eliminated the tax on food and offered tax breaks to companies paying above the prevailing wage. Richardson has backed a living wage in the state and created tax credits for the creation of new jobs.

Source: This information first appeared on www.pewforum.org. Reprinted with permission from the Pew Forum on Religion & Public Life and Pew Research Center.

the "gap between rich and poor" as the most important economic problem, and only 5 percent named "poverty, hunger and homelessness" as the most important "non-economic" problem.[18]

Likewise, Edwards has trailed his rivals for the Democratic nomination and even failed to capture much support from voters who are struggling financially. In a survey of independent voters, 40 percent of respondents in households earning less than $20,000 said they would not vote for Edwards if he were the Democratic nominee.[19]

The public's fickle interest in the poor has been evident in the two years following Hurricane Katrina, which produced some of the starkest and most widely disseminated images of urban poverty in American history.

"After Katrina, with its vivid images, a lot of people who have been working in the area of poverty reduction were excited. They said, 'now we have some visible images, now people will get excited, and we can push this anti-poverty platform,'" says Elsie L. Scott, president of the Congressional Black Caucus Foundation. "That lasted a month maybe, that excitement. Now that people in New Orleans have been dispersed around the country, people want to forget about it. They don't want to admit we have this kind of poverty in the United States."

Policy experts say it would be unfortunate if Middle America fails to recognize how much poverty undermines the nation's overall well-being. Childhood poverty alone saps the United States of $500 billion per year in crime and health costs and reduced productivity, according to Harry J. Holzer, a professor of public policy at Georgetown University.[20]

Rising poverty should be a concern even among those who don't see a moral obligation to aid the poor, experts warn. "The global competitiveness of the U.S. economy suffers if workers are too poor to obtain an education and modern job skills, the government loses tax revenue and spends more on public assistance because of poverty, and communities fall victim to urban decay, crime, and unrest," notes a recent study on severe poverty in the *American Journal of Preventive Medicine*.[21]

Yet, the American public has always had a tendency to blame the poor for their ills, some poverty experts lament. "There is a common perception that the problem with the poor folks in the United States is a problem with values," said Dalton Conley, chairman of the Department of Sociology at New York University. "It's not a values deficit at all; it's really a resource deficit."[22]

And that deficit can be steep. "Most Americans would be shocked to know that full-time male workers, at the median, earned no more in 2005 than they did in 1973" after taking inflation into account, says Sheldon H. Danziger, a professor of public policy at the University of Michigan. And that wage stagnation came amid a boom in productivity in the 1990s, he adds.

"There's a tendency for people to blame the poor for their own circumstances," Danziger says. "And I don't think anybody would blame full-time male workers."

As Congress, policy experts and presidential candidates consider what to do about poverty, here are some of the questions they are asking:

Is extreme poverty growing?

In Savannah, Ga., not far from the lush parks and antebellum mansions of the city's fabled historic district, poverty runs wide and deep.

More than one-fifth of Savannah's residents live below the federal poverty line, and that's not the worst of it.* "We have six census tracts with over a

Republican Candidates' Stands on Poverty

 Sam Brownback voted for the 1996 welfare reform bill that required more work for recipients and placed limits on the amount of time they could receive benefits. He says poverty can best be addressed by encouraging people to get married, get a job and not have children out of wedlock. He has promoted a "marriage development account program" to help married couples get training, buy a car, get an education or purchase a house. Brownback has voted against increasing the minimum wage.

 Rudolph Giuliani advocates requiring welfare recipients to work or engage in job training to receive benefits. New York City's welfare rolls were cut by more than half while Giuliani was mayor, and he touts his overhaul of the city's welfare system as one of his major successes. During his 2000 senate campaign, Giuliani indicated that he would support an increase in the minimum wage if studies showed it would not reduce the number of available jobs.

 Mike Huckabee says one of his priorities is to address poverty because it's "consistent with me being pro-life." He calls his desire to fight poverty a "faith position" rather than a political position. He says it is impossible to address poverty without "prioritizing stable homes and families."

 Duncan Hunter says tax cuts are the best tool for reducing poverty because they enable the poor to save and support their families. He advocates what he calls a "Fair Tax," which would replace the national income tax with a national retail sales tax. As part of his anti-poverty agenda, he supports tariffs on Chinese imports to help preserve American manufacturing jobs.

 John McCain voted for a 1996 welfare reform bill that required more work for recipients and placed limits on the amount of time they could receive benefits. Although McCain voted for a bill to increase the federal minimum wage in February 2007, he has historically voted against minimum wage increases, arguing that they can hurt small businesses.

 Ron Paul In May 2007, Paul asserted that "subsidies and welfare" only provide poor people with "crumbs," while "the military-industrial complex and the big banks" receive "the real big welfare," further impoverishing the middle class and the poor. Paul opposes foreign aid, writing that "the redistribution of wealth from rich to poor nations has done little or nothing to alleviate suffering abroad."

 W. Mitt Romney As Massachusetts governor, Romney proposed a plan requiring more people to work in order to receive state welfare benefits, bringing Massachusetts policy in line with federal welfare reforms. He supports increasing the minimum wage to match inflation but vetoed a bill to raise it in Massachusetts, saying it called for increases that were too extreme and too abrupt.

 Tom Tancredo The Colorado Congressman advocates moving from an income-based tax to a consumption-based tax, which he says would create an "explosion of job opportunities and economic growth" that would benefit all sectors of society, particularly the poor. He also supports repealing the 16th Amendment and establishing a flat, national sales tax to alleviate the burden on American companies and "put billions back into the economy."

 Fred Thompson In May the actor and former U.S. senator criticized programs that would "redistribute the income among our citizens" as "defeatist." A policy of lowering taxes, he said, would stimulate economic growth and "make the pie bigger." In 1999 he voted against an increase in the minimum wage. He also voted to reduce taxes on married couples in 2000. He has yet to officially declare his candidacy.

Source: This information first appeared on www.pewforum.org. Reprinted with permission from the Pew Forum on Religion & Public Life and Pew Research Center.

---

* Many people who study domestic poverty criticize the way the government measures poverty, arguing the standard federal poverty index does not accurately count the poor. Presidential candidate John Edwards is among those who call for reform of the poverty measure. His Web site states that it "excludes necessities like taxes, health care, child care and transportation" and "fails to count some forms of aid including tax credits, food stamps, Medicaid and subsidized housing. The National Academy of Sciences has recommended improvements that would increase the count of people in poverty by more than 1 million." See also, for example, Reid Cramer, "The Misleading Way We Count the Poor: Alternatives to Our Antiquated Poverty Measure Should Consider Assets," New America Foundation, September 2003, and Douglas J. Besharov, senior scholar, American Enterprise Institute, testimony before House Subcommittee on Income Security and Family Support, "Measuring Poverty in America," Aug. 1, 2007.

TANF Assistance on the Decline

The number of households receiving financial support through the Temporary Assistance for Needy Families (TANF) program has declined every fiscal year since 1996. A monthly average of just over 4 million households received TANF assistance in 2006, less than a third of the number of recipients 10 years earlier.

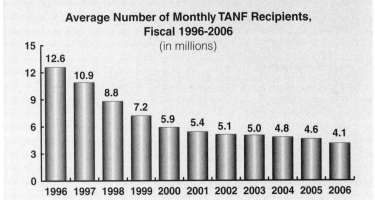

Average Number of Monthly TANF Recipients, Fiscal 1996-2006
(in millions)

Source: "2008 Budget in Brief," Department of Health and Human Services, 2007

50-percent poverty rate," says Daniel Dodd, who directs a project that enlists Savannah's business community in helping the poor.

Savannah is hardly unique. At least one neighborhood of "concentrated" poverty — often defined as a place where at least 40 percent of residents live below the poverty line — exists in 46 of the nation's 50 biggest cities, according to Alan Berube, a fellow in the Metropolitan Policy Program of the Brookings Institution, a think tank in Washington.[23]

McClatchy Newspapers concluded this year that 43 percent of the nation's 37 million poor people live in severe poverty — sometimes called "extreme" or "deep" poverty. Severe poverty reflects those with incomes of less than half the federal poverty threshold — in other words, under $9,903 for a family of four and $5,080 for an individual in 2005.

"The number of severely poor Americans grew by 26 percent from 2000 to 2005," McClatchy reported. "That's 56 percent faster than the overall poverty population grew in the same period."

The rise in severe poverty extends beyond large urban counties to suburban and rural areas. "Severe poverty is worst near the Mexican border and in some areas of the

South, where 6.5 million severely poor residents are struggling to find work as manufacturing jobs in the textile, apparel and furniture-making industries disappear," McClatchy noted. "The Midwestern Rust Belt and areas of the Northeast also have been hard hit as economic restructuring and foreign competition have forced numerous plant closings. At the same time, low-skilled immigrants with impoverished family members are increasingly drawn to the South and Midwest to work in meatpacking, food processing and agricultural industries."[24]

In Illinois, the rate of extreme poverty is the highest in the hard-hit Midwest, with more than 700,000 people in such straits, according to the Heartland Alliance for Human Needs & Human Rights, an advocacy group in Chicago. A family of four living in extreme poverty in Bellevue, Ill., would have monthly expenses of $2,394 but monthly income of only $833, the group says.[25]

But some researchers see little or no evidence that severe poverty is on the rise. Robert Rector, a senior policy analyst at the conservative Heritage Foundation, said "he's seen no data that suggest increasing deprivation among the very poor," according to the McClatchy report.

Rector "questioned the growth of severe poverty, saying that census data become less accurate farther down the income ladder. He said many poor people, particularly single mothers with boyfriends, underreport their income by not including cash gifts and loans."[26]

Such skeptical views extend beyond the severely poor. "While real material hardship certainly does occur, it is limited in scope and severity," Rector told a congressional panel this year. "Most of America's 'poor' live in material conditions that would be judged as comfortable or well-off just a few generations ago. Today, the expenditures per person of the lowest-income one-fifth . . . of households equal those of the median American household in the early 1970s, after adjusting for inflation."[27]

In fact, many more consumer items are within reach of a wider segment of the population — even the poor — than they were 30 or 40 years ago, thanks in part to globalization and the spread of discount retailers. But the cost of necessities such as health care and shelter have exploded, taking a much higher proportion of income than they once did.

Indeed, while the poor may have more material goods than in the past, many analysts say poverty is much more complicated than comparisons with earlier eras might suggest.

"On the one hand, the poor have vastly more consumer goods than a generation ago — TVs, cars, washing machines, dishwashers in many cases," says Hacker of Yale University. "But at the same time, if you think about where they are relative to middle-class Americans, to say nothing of those at the top, they're much further behind."

A major portion of the spending done by poor people is for basics, especially housing, transportation, child care and health care, and the poor have had a tough time keeping up with those costs, Hacker says. What's more, "the consumption of the poor is supported by higher levels of debt that can leave them extremely vulnerable."

And those most vulnerable are people who live in severe poverty. From 2000 to 2004, its prevalence rose sharply. The risk of extreme poverty is significantly higher for children than adults, and it is higher for African-Americans and Hispanics than for whites or Asian-Americans, according to the study in the *American Journal of Preventive Medicine.*

"Millions of Americans, overrepresented by children and minorities, have entered conditions of extreme poverty," the study said. "After 2000, Americans subsisting under these conditions grew as a class more than any other segment of the population."[28]

Reducing severe poverty is a daunting challenge that has spurred an outpouring of policy proposals from all sides of the political spectrum.

In Savannah, Dodd's project — called Step Up, Savannah's Poverty Reduction Initiative — represents one of the nation's most ambitious local anti-poverty efforts. Formed in 2004, it is a collaboration of more than 80 organizations representing business, local government, nonprofit organizations, neighborhood groups and others. It receives donations from several major foundations as well as other sources, including businesses.

Step Up's methods include asking employers and business executives to role play for a few hours what impoverished residents experience every day. "These things are quite eye-opening for a lot of people," Dodd says. The

Step Up Savannah, one of the nation's most ambitious local anti-poverty efforts, is a collaboration of organizations from business, government, education and the nonprofit sector that helps residents of high-poverty neighborhoods become self-sufficient.

Courtesy Step Up Savannah

"poverty simulation" exercise reveals "how frustrating the system is to navigate if you're making minimum wage, if you don't have the skills, and how hard it is to keep a job with what you're getting paid. There's transportation obstacles, crime," and other impediments.[29]

The exercise "provides a common frame of reference for the community and demystifies myths" about poverty, adds Dodd, who points out that welfare reform has led to a 70 percent reduction in government subsidies for the city's poor in the past seven years.[30]

Step Up's goals include expanding poor people's access to good jobs and quality health care, training them for career-level positions and expanding access to the EITC.

The effort grew from a realization that "we hadn't had a decline in poverty in 30 years," Dodd says. "People realized we'd thrown millions of dollars at this but hadn't had the impact we needed to have."

For all the project's earnestness, though, it remains unclear whether Step Up will succeed. "What I always tell people," says Dodd, "is we don't have it all figured out yet."

Has welfare reform reduced entrenched poverty?

In August 1996, President Bill Clinton's signature ended a six-decade practice of guaranteeing cash assistance to the poor. A new system required most people who get aid to work within two years of receiving it. The revised law also limited most aid to a total of five years. And it turned over to states and localities much of the control over how federal poverty money is dispensed.[31]

More then a decade later, experts are still debating whether the poor are better off.

Ron Haskins, a former Ways and Means Committee staff member who played a key role in the welfare overhaul, has written that "above all, welfare reform showed that work — even low-wage work — provides a more durable foundation for social policy than handouts."[32]

"Before welfare reform," Haskins, now a senior fellow at the Brookings Institution, said last year, "the main goal of state welfare programs was simply to give out money. But now the message families receive when they apply for welfare is that they need a job, that the 'welfare' program is there to help them find one and that they can receive cash benefits for a maximum of five years. As a result, welfare rolls plunged by over 60 percent, as many as 2 million mothers entered the labor force, earnings for females heading families increased while their income from welfare payments fell, and child poverty declined every year between 1993 and 2000. By the late 1990s, both black child poverty and poverty among children in female-headed families had reached their lowest levels ever."

Even after four years of increased child poverty following the 2001 recession, Haskins said, the rate of child poverty was still 20 percent lower than in 1993.

Haskins went on to say that "the success of welfare reform was created both by welfare reforms itself and by the work-support programs that provided tax credits, health insurance, nutrition supplements and child care to low-income working families."[33]

Yet, despite what many see as its positive effects, welfare reform remains a mixed bag. It is not clear, for example, to what degree welfare reform itself, along with its time limits on benefits, caused poverty rates to fall and work rates to rise.

"Welfare reform, and in particular the onset of time limits, arrived in the midst of an extremely tight labor market and a flourishing economy," says Katherine Newman, a professor of sociology and public affairs at Princeton University.

"So how much the shift toward work was attributable to the pull of a growing economy and [demand for] labor is very hard to sort out," she continues. "My sense is that welfare reform had something to do with it, but it's hardly the whole story. A lot had to do with favorable market conditions."

The Center on Budget and Policy Priorities, a Washington think tank, last year noted, among other negative trends, that while child poverty declined in the 1990s, as Haskins pointed out, it nonetheless rose sharply after 2000, as did the number of children living in severe poverty.[34] (*See sidebar, see p. 240.*)

Many anti-poverty advocates say even though welfare reform put more people to work, further steps are needed to ensure that families can climb out of poverty and stay there, and that poor children are protected.

Timothy M. Smeeding, director of the Center for Policy Research at Syracuse University, says welfare reform "turned the welfare poor into the working poor. You've got more self-respect, you're earning it, but the effect on kids is mixed." He calls for a system that will "make work pay," where "you go out and you work, you show the effort, you put in 1,000 hours, and we'll find a way to make sure you've got $15,000 or $20,000 and you're not poor."

In Wisconsin — where some of the earliest efforts at welfare reform took place — the rate of growth in the number of people living in poverty was higher in 2003-2004 than in any other state.[35] Richard Schlimm, executive director of the Wisconsin Community Action Program Association, a statewide association of community-action and anti-poverty groups, says welfare reform simply "has not worked," in reducing poverty in his state.

"Certainly it was the right thing to do, to get people working," Schlimm says. "But I've always believed poor people want to work, and they prefer work over welfare.... We successfully achieved the elimination of welfare, but I maintain that we had the wrong goal. The goal was to reduce poverty, and if we kept that in our sights we would have focused a whole lot [more] funding on that than we did."

Would more government spending on poverty help?

While welfare reform encouraged work and reduced government caseloads, many experts say the fight against poverty has only begun.

Some argue that reducing poverty depends in large measure on the poor exercising greater personal responsibility. "While it is often argued that the U.S. devotes far fewer resources to social welfare spending than other rich nations, the facts show otherwise," Rector of the Heritage Foundation said. "The good news is that remaining poverty can readily be reduced further, particularly among children. There are two main reasons that American children are poor: Their parents don't work much, and fathers are absent from the home."[36]

Others say more government spending on anti-poverty programs is the key. Schlimm, at the Wisconsin Community Action Program Association, says that to reduce poverty, the nation needs political leadership coupled with "a massive investment" in affordable housing, accessible health care, education and job creation for the poor. "Let's face it, we have committed massive investments in Iraq," he says, "and [with] half of that — even a fourth of that — focused on poverty in the United States, we could make remarkable strides."

Smeeding, the Syracuse University policy researcher, says U.S. poverty could be cut by a third to a half with an outlay of $45 billion to $60 billion a year, focused on three things: child care for working mothers, guaranteed child support for mothers who have established paternity with fathers who can't or won't pay because of disability or prison, and an expansion of the EITC.

Lawrence Mead, a professor of politics at New York University, advocates a stick-and-carrot approach with low-income men. "In 2005, there were more than 7 million poor men ages 16 to 50 in the United States, and only half of them worked at all," Mead wrote. "Among black men in poverty, nearly two-thirds were idle, and their employment has fallen steadily in recent decades."

Mead proposes using the child-support and criminal-justice systems to promote work among poor males. "Right now, these institutions depress male work levels by locking men up and by garnishing their wages if they do work," he wrote. "But they could be used to promote work. For example, men in arrears on their child support could be assigned to government-run work programs, as could parolees with employment problems. These men — about 1.5 million each year — would have to show up and work regularly — on penalty of going to jail. Both groups might also receive wage subsidies. The combination might instill more regular work habits."

Mandatory work for 1.5 million men would run $2 billion to $5 billion annually, according to Mead. "In return, governments could collect more in child support and spend less on incarceration."[37]

"Everyone recognizes that men are the frontier," Mead says. The ultimate goal, he says, should be to both reward and enforce work in ways the current system doesn't do now.

While spending on new programs is one approach to fighting poverty, some argue the solution isn't more outlays for anti-poverty programs but rather a mix of free-market capitalism and charity.

"Despite nearly $9 trillion in total welfare spending since Lyndon B. Johnson declared [the] War on Poverty in 1964, the poverty rate is perilously close to where it was when we began, more than 40 years ago," wrote Michael D. Tanner, director of health and welfare studies for the conservative Cato Institute think tank.

"Clearly we are doing something wrong. Throwing money at the problem has neither reduced poverty nor made the poor self-sufficient. . . . [I]f we have learned anything by now, it is that there are limits to what government programs — even reformed ones — can do to address the root causes of poverty.

Observers have known for a long time that the surest ways to stay out of poverty are to finish school; not get pregnant outside marriage; and get a job, any job, and stick with it. That means that if we wish to fight poverty, we must end those government policies — high taxes and regulatory excess — that inhibit growth and job creation. We must protect capital investment and give people the opportunity to start new businesses. We must reform our failed government school system to encourage competition and choice. We must encourage the poor to save and invest.

More importantly, the real work of fighting poverty must come not from the government, but from the engines of civil society. . . . [P]rivate charities are far more effective than government welfare programs."[38]

BACKGROUND

Warring on Poverty

Concerns about work, hardship and who deserves help go back to the roots of the Republic. The Virginia Assembly of 1619 decreed that a person found guilty of idleness would be forced to work under a master "til he shewe apparant signes of amendment."[39]

In the 19th century, poorhouses sprang up to accommodate a growing tide of desperate people flooding the cities from the countryside. Poverty flourished along with widespread indifference to the plight of the needy. After the Civil War the journalist and political economist Henry George called the United States a place where "amid the

CHRONOLOGY

1950s–1960s *Many Americans enjoy a post-war economic boom, but poverty persists. Poverty rate is 22.4 percent in 1959.*

1962 Michael Harrington's book *The Other America* helps spur President Lyndon B. Johnson's War on Poverty. . . . Welfare program is renamed Aid to Families with Dependent Children (AFDC).

1964 Congress establishes permanent food stamp program. . . . Federal government develops income thresholds to define poverty in American society.

1965 Congress enacts Medicaid to provide health care to low-income people.

1967 Congress establishes the Work Incentive Program, requiring states to establish job-training programs for adults receiving welfare.

1969 President Richard M. Nixon calls hunger in America an "embarrassing and intolerable" national shame.

1970s *The energy crisis, recessions and industrial restructuring put new strains on the poor.*

1975 Congress approves Earned Income Tax Credit (EITC), partly to offset the burden of Social Security taxes on low-income families and to provide an incentive to work.

1980s *Poverty programs of the 1960s and '70s come under scrutiny from the Reagan administration.*

1981 Congress cuts cash benefits for the working poor and lets states require welfare recipients to work.

1988 President Ronald Reagan signs Family Support Act, requiring states to implement education, job training and placement programs for welfare recipients.

1990s *Clinton administration pushes Congress to pass massive welfare reforms.*

1992 Democratic presidential candidate Bill Clinton pledges to "end welfare as we know it."

1993 Clinton expands EITC.

1996 Congress ends 60-year welfare entitlement program, passing a reform law that imposes work requirements and puts time limits on cash benefits.

1997 Federal minimum wage rises to $5.15 an hour.

1997 State Children's Health Insurance Program (SCHIP) is created.

1999 The government of British Prime Minister Tony Blair introduces a plan to end child poverty in Britain by 2020, spurring calls for a similar effort in the United States.

2000s *Hurricane Katrina devastates Gulf Coast, putting spotlight on poverty.*

2000 Federal poverty rate falls to 11.3 percent, lowest since 1974.

2004 Federal appeals court upholds the "living wage" law in Berkeley, Calif., rejecting the first major challenge to civic ordinances requiring contractors to pay above-poverty wages. . . . Poverty rate climbs to 12.7 percent

Aug. 29, 2005 Hurricane Katrina hits New Orleans.

2006 Congress reauthorizes Temporary Assistance for Needy Families (TANF) as part of Deficit Reduction Act.

2007 McClatchy Newspapers analysis finds that percentage of poor Americans living in severe poverty reached a 32-year high in 2005. . . . Congress spars with the Bush administration over expansion of SCHIP. . . . House Ways and Means Committee hearings focus on poverty and inequality. . . . Democratic presidential candidate John Edwards takes a three-day, 1,800-mile "Road to One America" poverty tour. . . . Federal minimum wage rises for the first time in a decade to $5.85 an hour; it goes to $6.55 in summer 2008 and $7.25 in summer 2009. . . . Poverty rate falls to 12.3 percent.

greatest accumulations of wealth, men die of starvation, and puny infants suckle dry breasts."[40]

Later came the first rudimentary efforts to measure poverty. In 1904 the social worker Robert Hunter set what might have been the first national poverty line — $460 per year for a five-member family in the Northern industrial states and $300 for a family in the South.[41]

In the post-World War I boom years, some Americans enjoyed unprecedented comfort and wealth, but poverty wracked much of the nation. Between 1918 and 1929, some 10 million families were poor. By 1933, in the depths of the Great Depression, a fourth of the labor force was without jobs, and an estimated 15 million families — half the American population — lived in poverty.[42]

World War II jump-started the U.S. economy, and in the 1950s and early '60s many Americans enjoyed middle-class prosperity. But not all saw their living standards rise. Poverty persisted and grew, much of it concentrated in the rural South, Appalachia and the gritty urban cores of the industrial North. Many Americans blamed the poor for their plight, dismissing racism, educational inequality and other entrenched societal ills as major factors in perpetuating poverty.

In 1962 Michael Harrington wrote in his groundbreaking book *The Other America: Poverty in the United States:*

"There are sociological and political reasons why poverty is not seen; and there are misconceptions and prejudices that literally blind the eyes. . . . Here is the most familiar version of social blindness: 'The poor are that way because they are afraid of work. And anyway they all have big cars. If they were like me (or my father or my grandfather), they could pay their own way. But they prefer to live on the dole and cheat the taxpayers.'"

"This theory," Harrington went on, "usually thought of as a virtuous and moral statement, is one of the means of making it impossible for the poor ever to pay their way. . . . [T]he real explanation of why the poor are where they are is that they made the mistake of being born to the wrong parents, in the wrong section of the country, in the wrong industry or in the wrong racial or ethnic group. Once that mistake has been made, they could have been paragons of will and morality, but most of them would never even have had a chance to get out of the other America."[43]

By 1962, more than a fifth of Americans were living in poverty. Harrington's book helped spur Washington to act.[44]

A few months before his assassination, President John F. Kennedy directed his Council of Economic Advisers to study domestic poverty and recommend ways to fight it.[45]

Kennedy's successor, President Lyndon B. Johnson, followed through, declaring in his first State of the Union address, on Jan. 8, 1964, "unconditional war on poverty in America." Later that year Congress established the Office of Economic Opportunity, which attacked poverty through a phalanx of new programs, from Head Start — a school-readiness effort — to Job Corps, a training program for teens and young adults.[46] Johnson's fight against poverty also included a wide range of "Great Society" programs, from the 1964 Food Stamp Act to Medicare and Medicaid.

The War on Poverty persisted under the Nixon administration, which broadened the Food Stamp program and saw the passage of the Supplemental Security Income program for disabled people, among others. Even so, President Richard M. Nixon sought to dismantle the Office of Economic Opportunity, disbursing many of its programs among various federal agencies. The office was finally closed by President Gerald R. Ford in 1975.

Under Attack

By the 1980s and the start of the Reagan administration, poverty programs were under full-scale attack. The poverty rate, which dipped to just over 11 percent in the early 1970s, hit 15.2 percent in 1983. Conservatives, impatient with the Johnson-era philosophy of federally funded social aid for the poor, charged that the government's expensive programs were making poverty and dependence worse rather than better.

"[S]ome years ago, the federal government declared War on Poverty, and poverty won," Reagan famously said in his 1988 State of the Union address. "Today the federal government has 59 major welfare programs and spends more than $100 billion a year on them. What has all this money done? Well, too often it has only made poverty harder to escape. Federal welfare programs have created a massive social problem. With the best of intentions, government created a poverty trap that wreaks havoc on the very support system the poor need most to lift themselves out of poverty: the family."

The Reagan administration argued "that the social policies enacted in the 1960s and '70s had undermined the functioning of the nation's basic institutions and, by encouraging permissiveness, non-work and welfare dependence, had led to marital breakup, non-marital childbearing and the erosion of individual initiative," according to the

Military Families Face Financial Strain

"This spring our caseload doubled."

Meredith Leyva's work with military families recently has led her to a troubling conclusion: Poverty is growing among the ranks of deployed service members, especially those who have been seriously injured in Iraq or Afghanistan.

"This spring our caseload of both military families and wounded warriors doubled," says Leyva, who is the founder of Operation Homefront, a Santa Ana, Calif., charity that helps military families through 31 chapters nationwide. And, adds Leyva, whose husband is a Navy physician, "We saw a significant change in the types of cases. We're now seeing many more complicated and high-dollar crises that are compounded by deployment after deployment."

Operation Homefront served approximately 1,700 families of wounded service members in 2006, Leyva says, and "over half and possibly more were living in poverty."

As for the 1.5-million-member military as a whole, however, little if any hard data exist on the extent of poverty in military families during the current conflict. Much of the government information on issues like food stamp use among military families predates the war.

Indeed, the financial health of military families can be a highly complicated and nuanced issue to analyze, even leaving aside the struggles of those dealing with catastrophic injury. "By any traditional measure of

Meredith Leyva, founder of Operation Homefront.

poverty..., military families are a lot better off than their civilian peers based on such things as age and education," says Joyce Raezer, chief operating officer of the National Military Family Association, a policy advocacy group in Alexandria, Va.

Still, she says some military families may be on the "financial edge," often because "they're young and financially inexperienced" and perhaps "prey for financial predators." Others may be strained by relocation demands that put them in temporary financial straits, she says.

"My sense is that you don't have folks living in poverty so that day in and day out things are inadequate," says Raezer. "But it can be episodic, where they're strapped for cash because of the military lifestyle, financial inexperience and predators."

Most military families are ineligible for food stamps because the military housing allowance puts them over the eligibility threshold, Raezer notes.

Even so, in fiscal 2006 food-stamp redemptions at military commissaries rose about $2.3 million over the previous year, to $26.2 million. While it was not clear what caused the increase, three military stores affected by Hurricane Katrina and other storms accounted for more than 80 percent of the increase.[1]

In May, U.S. Reps. James McGovern, D-Mass., and Jo Ann Emerson, R-Mo., introduced a bill that would expand

University of Michigan's Danziger and Robert H. Haveman, a professor of economics and public affairs at the University of Wisconsin.

"The Reagan philosophy was that tax cuts and spending cuts would increase the rate of economic growth, and that the poor would ultimately benefit through the increased employment and earnings that would follow such growth," they wrote. "However, a deep recession in the early 1980s increased poverty, and the subsequent

economic growth did not 'trickle down.' Although the economy expanded for many years in the 1980s, the wage rates of low- and medium-skilled male workers did not. On the other hand, the earnings of those in the upper part of the income distribution grew rapidly."[47]

Welfare Reform

The 1980s laid the groundwork for the radical shift in anti-poverty policy that was to come during the Clinton spending for federal nutrition programs, including a provision that would exclude combat-related military pay from income calculations for food-stamp eligibility.[2]

National Guard and active-duty families can feel financial strain differently. Lt. Col. Joseph Schweikert, state family program director for the Illinois National Guard, says "there are definitely families that go through financial hardships, sometimes due to deployments. But it varies from soldier to soldier, family to family. Some make more while deployed."

Nonetheless, at least 30 percent of Guard soldiers suffer a financial loss when deployed, he says.

Because the Guard offers a college-scholarship program, many young soldiers enlist, get a degree and then enter a well-paying career field. When they are mobilized, their pay may drop sharply. "It causes the family to go through a lot of hardships," Schweikert says, especially if the soldier doesn't have savings or a spouse's income to rely on.

Still, he suggests, many Guard members can be more stable financially than active-duty troops. Guard soldiers tend to be older and to have established civilian careers. Moreover, a working spouse will not have had to uproot periodically from a job, as often happens within the active-duty forces.

"In active duty, a lot of time you have to transfer from base to base, and it's hard to establish a long-term career," Schweikert says.

Nonetheless, military families in both the Guard and regular forces may find it hard to avoid financial ruin, especially in cases of serious injury suffered in war.

When a soldier is deployed, a spouse may have to pay others to do jobs the soldier performed at home, such as

Wounded soldiers and their families attend a get-together sponsored by the Texas chapter of Operation Homefront at Brooke Army Medical Center at Fort Sam Houston.

mowing the lawn and maintaining the car, Leyva says. And if a soldier is wounded, she says, "his pay immediately drops while the expenses skyrocket." Often, a spouse takes leave from a job or quits altogether to be at the wounded soldier's bedside or to help the soldier through rehabilitation, spending long days or weeks away from home.

"Service members were never paid well," Leyva says, "but these extraordinary crises certainly overwhelm."

Leyva fears that poverty among veterans will skyrocket in the wake of the current war, as it did after the Vietnam conflict. "I think we're going to see a whole new generation of disabled veterans that are sort of the mirror images of the Vietnam veterans," she says. "It's as much about mental as physical wounds," she says, and it could lead to a new "generation of poverty."

---

[1] Karen Jowers, "Storms May Have Spurred Jump in Food-Stamp Use," *Air Force Times*, July 5, 2007, www.navytimes.com.

[2] The Feeding America's Family Act, HR 2129.

---

era. In 1993 Clinton pushed through a record expansion of the Earned Income Tax Credit. Then, Clinton signed the Personal Responsibility and Work Opportunity Reconciliation Act of 1996 — otherwise known as the Welfare Reform Act.

The move to overhaul welfare outraged some. Georgetown University's Edelman resigned from the Clinton administration in protest. In a blistering critique, Edelman wrote that the measure would lead to

"more malnutrition and more crime, increased infant mortality and increased drug and alcohol abuse" and "increased family violence and abuse against children and women."[48]

But others have praised the reform measure. What the Clinton bill did, a *Boston Globe* columnist opined on the act's 10th anniversary, "was end the condescending attitude that the poor were incapable of improving their situation, and that 'compassion' consisted of supplying money

Did Recent Reforms Help Needy Families?

Bush administration tightened TANF work requirements.

Mention welfare reform to a political observer, and it is Bill Clinton who typically comes to mind. It was candidate Clinton who pledged to "end welfare as we know it" and President Clinton who signed the landmark welfare reform act into law in 1996.

But the Bush era also has engineered significant reforms in the welfare system, changes that could have far-reaching effects on the nation's poor.

The most important came with last year's congressional reauthorization of Temporary Assistance for Needy Families (TANF), the federal block-grant program that replaced the old welfare system.

The reauthorization strengthened work requirements and closed a loophole so that separate state-funded TANF programs have to be included in work-participation calculations.

"In effect, the Bush administration and Congress put teeth back into TANF work requirements but set difficult benchmarks for state programs that are working with adult populations experiencing many barriers to employment," Scott W. Allard, an assistant professor of political science and public policy at Brown University, noted recently.[1]

Others looking back on more than a decade of welfare reform worry the recent changes in the welfare rules could make poverty trends worse. Two analysts at the Center on Budget and Policy Priorities, Sharon Parrott, director of the center's Welfare Reform and Income Support Division, and senior researcher Arloc Sherman, argue that even though changes in TANF a decade ago "played a role in reducing poverty and raising employment rates during the 1990s, our safety net for the poorest families with children has weakened dramatically."[2]

Among the trends they pointed to: child poverty fell in the 1990s, but began rising after 2000, and the number of children in "deep" poverty rose; the number of jobless single mothers receiving no government cash assistance has risen significantly, and TANF now helps a far smaller share of families that qualify for the program than it used to help.

Last year's reauthorization could weaken the safety net even more, the two analysts suggested. Welfare reauthorization requires states to place a much bigger portion of their TANF caseloads in work activities and restricts the kind of activities that can count toward state work-participation requirements, Parrott and Sherman noted. "In many cases,

indefinitely to women who had children, but no husbands or jobs." The bill "replaced deadly condescension with respect."[49]

Still, while welfare caseloads plummeted, poverty persisted, even among those who joined the labor force.

"Basically, things are better than most people thought," Danziger says today. "On average, welfare recipients did much better moving from welfare to work, in part because the minimum wage was increased in 1997, the Earned Income Tax Credit expanded so much in the early '90s, states put so much into child-care subsidies, and the State Children's Health Insurance Program (SCHIP) came in. But the poverty rate among single mothers remains very high, and there's nothing new on the horizon."

Danziger noted in a 2006 paper that as many as 30 percent of single mothers who left welfare and took jobs are out of work in any given month.[50]

Advocates point out that it is possible to make real gains against poverty — and not just gains in cutting welfare caseloads. They point to big strides against child poverty in Britain, where in 1999 Prime Minister Tony Blair pledged to end child poverty by 2020.

"Elusive Dream"

But in cities and towns across America, President Johnson's 1964 pledge "not only to relieve the symptom of poverty but to cure it and, above all, to prevent it" remains an elusive dream.[51]

The loss of manufacturing jobs — and the stability and safety net they once provided — is a big reason the dream remains out of reach.

In Wisconsin, a state of 5.6 million people, the poverty rate shot from 8.2 percent to 11 percent over five years, says the Wisconsin Community Action Program state programs designed to address two of the biggest problems that have emerged over TANF's first decade — that parents who leave welfare for work often earn low wages and have unstable employment, and that many families with the greatest barriers to employment are being left behind — will no longer count toward states' work requirements," they wrote.

"In fact, the cheapest and easiest way for a state to meet the new work rules would simply be to assist fewer poor families, especially the families with barriers to employment who need the most help."

On top of that, the amount of basic federal block-grant funds for states has not been adjusted since 1996 and has lost 22 percent of its value to inflation, Parrott and Sherman wrote.

Some observers are more sanguine about the course of welfare reform. Writing in a "point-counterpoint" format with Parrott and Sherman, Lawrence Mead, a professor of politics at New York University and an architect of welfare reform, describes it as an "incomplete triumph." He says reform achieved its two main goals: Work levels rose sharply among poor mothers, the main beneficiaries of welfare. And caseloads plummeted.

Still, Mead says that the reform effort has had limitations. For one thing, he says, it did not create a system that promotes work on an ongoing basis through a combination of government incentives and emphasis on personal responsibility. He notes that 40 percent of those who have left welfare have not gone to work, and many welfare recipients have moved in and out of jobs.

Nor did welfare reform ensure that people leaving welfare for jobs will have enough income to live on, Mead says. "The situation has improved, but not enough."

And welfare reform did not adequately address the employment challenges among poor men, many of whom are fathers in welfare families, Mead says.

Nonetheless, Mead is hopeful the limitations of welfare reform can be addressed at least partly through engagement by the poor in the political process. Because more of the poor are working or moving toward work, they are in a stronger position to demand changes, such as payment of living wages, than they were under the old entitlement system of welfare, Mead says.

First, though, the poor must assert themselves both on the job and in the political sphere, he says.

"Finally," he writes, "what reform enforced was not work, but citizenship."[3]

---

[1] Scott W. Allard, "The Changing Face of Welfare During the Bush Administration," *Publius*, June 22, 2007.

[2] Sharon Parrott and Arloc Sherman, "Point-Counterpoint," in Richard P. Nathan, editor, "Welfare Reform After Ten Years: Strengths and Weaknesses," *Journal of Policy Analysis and Management*, Vol. 26, No. 2, 2007.

[3] Lawrence Mead, "Point-Counterpoint," in *ibid.*

Association's Schlimm. "I'm 58 and have lived in Wisconsin all my life, and it's very unusual to see those kinds of numbers," he says. It is the "loss of good jobs, manufacturing jobs" that is to blame.

"A lot of Wisconsin's good jobs support the auto industry," he continues. "And we're a paper-making state. Many of the papermakers moved. . . . When I got out of college, you could go to a paper mill, and if it didn't work out, you could drive a couple of blocks down the street and find work with another company. In 1968 they paid $6 to $7 an hour. Now they pay $25. They're very coveted jobs. But there aren't as many of them. The economy hasn't been able to replace those very good jobs."

What matters most in the fight against poverty, many advocates contend, is leadership and political will.

The No. 1 problem is leadership, says David Bradley, executive director of the National Community Action Foundation. "We're not talking billions of dollars. We're talking receptivity to looking at ideas."

Bradley notes that the Johnson-era Office of Economic Opportunity was a laboratory for anti-poverty innovations. "For many years we've not had the federal government willing to fund and be experimental in partnering in new ideas on poverty. A lot of ideas start at the grass roots. I see incredible projects out there but no mechanism to duplicate them nationwide."

At the same time, Bradley laments that some in both political parties believe none of the ideas from the 1960s are worth keeping. "I find it frustrating that some candidates who are talking about poverty view anything that's gone on previously as not successful or not innovative or creative enough," he says. "If you're a program that started in 1964 or 1965, that doesn't mean by definition that you're still not innovative in your community."

Bradley is cautiously optimistic that a renewed commitment to fighting poverty is afoot in the nation. Political leaders in both parties are talking about the issue and the government's role in bringing about solutions, he points out.

But that will happen, Bradley says, only if solutions are not overpromised, the effort is bipartisan, innovation and creativity are part of the approach, sufficient government money is available and, "most important, if there is a general acceptance that the federal government wants to be a positive partner."

"It can be a partner that requires accountability," he says, "but a partner nevertheless."

CURRENT SITUATION

Presidential Race

It remains unclear how much traction the poverty theme will have in the 2008 presidential race. But as the campaign began moving into high gear this summer, poverty — and what to do about it — has been high on the list of priorities among several leading Democratic candidates, most notably Edwards and Obama.

Edwards has set the ambitious goal of cutting poverty by a third within a decade and ending it within 30 years. Echoing President Johnson's Great Society program, Edwards proposes a "Working Society" where "everyone who is able to work hard will be expected to work and, in turn, be rewarded for it."

To attack poverty, Edwards is pushing more than a dozen ideas, from raising the minimum wage, fighting predatory lending and reducing teen pregnancy to creating a million temporary "stepping stone" jobs for those having difficulty finding other work.

Obama has his own long list of proposals. He also backs a transitional jobs program and a minimum-wage increase, for example, along with such steps as improving transportation access for the working poor and helping ex-prisoners find jobs.

But deeper differences exist in the two candidates' approaches. "Edwards has focused on the malignant effects of the concentration of poverty in inner cities," *The Washington Post* noted. "He has argued for dispersing low-income families by replacing public housing with a greatly expanded rental voucher program to allow families to move where there are more jobs and better schools." Obama, on the other hand, has "presented a sharply different overall objective: fixing inner-city areas so they become places where families have a shot at prospering, without having to move."[52]

Part of what is noteworthy about the Edwards and Obama proposals is that they exist at all. Many Democratic candidates, including Sen. Clinton, have focused on the plight of the middle class rather than the poor. "Since the late 1980s," the columnist E. J. Dionne Jr. noted, "Democrats have been obsessed with the middle class for reasons of simple math: no middle-class votes, no electoral victories."[53]

With the exception of recent comments by former Republican Bloomberg of New York, GOP rhetoric on poverty has not been nearly as prevalent as the Democrats'. In January, President Bush acknowledged that "income inequality is real," suggesting his administration might be poised to do more on poverty and perhaps get ahead of Democrats on the issue.[54] But more recently the administration has resisted congressional efforts to expand the SCHIP program, which benefits poor children.

Meanwhile, Republican presidential hopeful Mitt Romney echoed the longstanding conservative criticism of Democrat-backed social policies, declaring that Democrats are "thinking about big government, big welfare, big taxes, Big Brother."[55]

Anti-Poverty Proposals

In recent months several think tanks and advocacy groups have turned out policy proposals for reducing poverty. In April the liberal Center for American Progress advanced a dozen key steps to cut poverty in half in the next decade, including raising the minimum wage to half the average hourly wage, expanding the EITC and Child Tax Credit, promoting unionization, guaranteeing child-care assistance to low-income families and creating 2 million new housing vouchers "designed to help people live in opportunity-rich areas."

The center's main recommendations would cost roughly $90 billion annually — "a significant cost," it conceded, "but one that is necessary and could be readily funded through a fairer tax system." Spending $90 billion a year "would represent about 0.8 percent of the nation's gross domestic product, which is a fraction of the money spent on tax changes that benefited primarily the wealthy in recent years."

Should immigration be reduced to protect the jobs of native-born poor?

YES

Steven A. Camarota
Director of Research, Center for Immigration Studies

From testimony prepared for House Judiciary Committee, May 9, 2007

There is no evidence of a labor shortage, especially at the bottom end of the labor market where immigrants are most concentrated. . . . There is a good deal of research showing that immigration has contributed to the decline in employment and wages for less-educated natives. . . . All research indicates that less-educated immigrants consume much more in government services than they pay in taxes. Thus, not only does such immigration harm America's poor, it also burdens taxpayers. . . .

While the number of immigrants is very large . . . the impact on the overall economy or on the share of the population that is of working age is actually very small. And these effects are even smaller when one focuses only on illegal aliens, who comprise one-fourth to one-third of all immigrants. While the impact on the economy . . . may be tiny, the effect on some Americans, particular workers at the bottom of the labor market may be quite large. These workers are especially vulnerable to immigrant competition because wages for these jobs are already low, and immigrants are heavily concentrated in less-skilled and lower-paying jobs. . . .

It probably makes more sense for policymakers to focus on the winners and losers from immigration. The big losers are natives working in low-skilled, low-wage jobs. Of course, technological change and increased trade also have reduced the labor market opportunities for low-wage workers in the United States. But immigration is different because it is a discretionary policy that can be altered. On the other hand, immigrants are the big winners, as are owners of capital and skilled workers, but their gains are tiny relative to their income.

In the end, arguments for or against immigration are as much political and moral as they are economic. The latest research indicates that we can reduce immigration secure in the knowledge that it will not harm the economy. Doing so makes sense if we are very concerned about low-wage and less-skilled workers in the United States. On the other hand, if one places a high priority on helping unskilled workers in other countries, then allowing in a large number of such workers should continue.

Of course, only an infinitesimal proportion of the world's poor could ever come to this country even under the most open immigration policy one might imagine. Those who support the current high level of unskilled legal and illegal immigration should at least do so with an understanding that those American workers harmed by the policies they favor are already the poorest and most vulnerable.

NO

Gerald D. Jaynes
Professor of Economics and African-American Studies, Yale University

From testimony before House Subcommittee on Immigration, Citizenship, Refugees, Border Security, and International Law, May 3, 2007

We can acknowledge that immigration probably hurts the employment and wages of some less-educated citizens and still conclude immigration is a net benefit for the United States. The most methodologically sound estimates of the net effects of immigration on the nation conclude that the United States, as a whole, benefits from contemporary immigration. Properly measured, this conclusion means that during a period of time reasonably long enough to allow immigrants to adjust to their new situations, they produce more national income than they consume in government services.

Confusion about this issue is caused by some analysts' failure to make appropriate distinctions between immigration's impact on specific local governments and groups and its impact on the whole nation. Although benefits of immigration — such as lower prices for consumer and producer goods and services, greater profits and tax revenues — accrue to the nation as a whole, nearly all of the costs for public services consumed by immigrants are borne by localities and specific demographic groups. . . . Even so, inappropriate methods of analysis have led some analysts to overstate the costs of immigration even at the local level. . . .

On average, Americans receive positive economic benefits from immigration, but, at least in the short run, residents of particular localities and members of certain groups may lose. . . .

Democratic concepts of justice suggest the losses of a few should not override the gains of the many. Democratic concepts of justice also demand that society's least-advantaged members should not be paying for the immigration benefits enjoyed by the entire nation. A democratic society benefiting from immigration and debating how to reshape its immigration policies should also be discussing social policies to compensate less-skilled workers through combinations of better training, relocation and educational opportunities. . . .

[T]he evidence supports the conclusion that from an economic standpoint immigration's broader benefits to the nation outweigh its costs. An assessment of the effects of immigration on the employment prospects of less-educated native-born workers is that the effect is negative but modest, and probably is significant in some specific industries and geographic locations. . . . However, it is just as likely that the relative importance of less-educated young native [workers'] job losses due to the competition of immigrants is swamped by a constellation of other factors diminishing their economic status.

The Urban Institute estimated that four of the center's recommendations — on the minimum wage, EITC, child tax credit and child care — would cut poverty by about a fourth. Moreover, it said, both child poverty and extreme poverty would fall.[56]

A Brookings Institution proposal to "reinvigorate the fight for greater opportunity" includes seven recommendations for the next U.S. president, from strengthening work requirements in government-assistance programs, promoting marriage and funding teen pregnancy-prevention efforts to subsidizing child care for low-wage workers, increasing the minimum wage and expanding the EITC.

"We need a new generation of anti-poverty policies that focus on requiring and rewarding work, reversing the breakdown of the family and improving educational outcomes," the proposal states. The $38.6 billion per year cost should not be incurred, the authors say, unless it "can be fully covered by eliminating spending or tax preferences in other areas."[57]

Many advocates emphasize the need to help poor people build their assets, such as savings accounts and home equity, as a way of propelling them out of poverty. Also key, they say, is the need to spend more on early-childhood programs to help keep youngsters from falling into poverty in the first place.

"Universal high-quality early childhood education is the single most powerful investment we could make in insuring poverty doesn't strike the next generation," says Newman of Princeton University.

Tax Policy

Proposals to adjust federal tax policy to help lift the poor into the economic mainstream are among those getting the most attention. Much of the discussion has focused on expansion of the child and earned income tax credits.

A letter sent to members of Congress last spring by hundreds of advocacy groups urged expansion of the child credit, which can reduce the tax liability of families with children. "The current income threshold — in 2007, it is $11,750 — excludes 10 million children whose families are too poor to claim the credit," the letter stated. "The threshold keeps rising with inflation, increasing the tax burden on the poor and dropping many families from the benefit altogether."

The letter added that according to the Tax Policy Center, operated by the Urban Institute and Brookings Institution,

"half of all African-American children, 46 percent of Hispanic children and 18 percent of white children received either no Child Tax Credit or a reduced amount in 2005 because their families' earnings were too low."[58]

Along with the child credit, the EITC is widely cited as ripe for expansion.

Created in 1975 to protect low-wage workers from rising payroll taxes, the credit has been expanded several times, under both Republican and Democratic administrations. More than 20 million families benefit from more than $40 billion in credits today, according to Brookings' Berube. Most of those eligible for the credit have children under age 18 living at home and earn less than $35,000, according to Berube. In 2004 the average claimant received a credit of about $1,800.[59]

While claims of abuse have been leveled at the tax credit, it has generally been popular across the political spectrum because it encourages work, helps the needy and does not levy a cost on wealthier taxpayers.[60]

But anti-poverty advocates say the tax credit could be even more effective by making it easier for families with two earners to get the credit and extending it to single workers in their late teens and early 20s.[61]

"Childless adults are the only group of working tax filers who begin to owe federal income taxes before their incomes reach the poverty line," says the letter to members of Congress. Workers in that category got an average credit of only $230 last year, the letter said. "Increasing the amount of the credit for low-income workers not living with children would increase work incentives and economic security for millions of Americans working in low-wage jobs."

Making poor people aware of the tax credit is also an obstacle that must be overcome, advocates say. Many people who are eligible for the credit don't claim it, sometimes because of language or educational barriers.

Dodd, at Step Up in Savannah, says the Internal Revenue Service said $10 million to $12 million in credits go unclaimed in his city alone.

States and Localities

As federal policymakers wrestle with the poverty issue, states and localities are making inroads of their own. Mayor Bloomberg has been promoting a plan to pay poor families in New York up to $5,000 a year to meet such goals as attending parent-teacher meetings, getting medical checkups and holding full-time jobs. Patterned after a Mexican initiative, the plan aims to help poor families make better long-range decisions and break cycles of poverty and dependence that can last generations.[62]

Other efforts are afoot in the states. A proposed bill in the California Assembly, for example, would establish an advisory Childhood Poverty Council to develop a plan to reduce child poverty in the state by half by 2017 and eliminate it by 2027.[63]

Not all such steps pan out, though. In 2004, Connecticut passed legislation committing the state to a 50 percent reduction in child poverty by 2014, but child poverty has risen since then, an official of the Connecticut Association for Community Action complained this summer, blaming the failure to enact a state-funded EITC.[64]

As states seek ways to reduce the number of poor within their borders, they also are trying to adjust to the stiffer work requirements that Congress enacted last year when it reauthorized welfare reform.[65]

The new rules are forcing some states to adapt in creative ways. In California, for example, where less than a fourth of welfare recipients work enough hours to meet federal requirements, officials are moving some teenage parents, older parents and disabled people into separate programs paid entirely by state funds so they aren't counted in federal work-participation calculations.

Arkansas, on the other hand, has been sending monthly checks to the working poor. "Arkansas eventually aims to artificially swell its welfare population from 8,000 families to as many as 11,000 and raise the work-participation rate by at least 11 percent," according to a press report. "Officials hope the extra cash will also keep the workers employed."[66]

The tougher work rules have upset poverty advocates, who argue they damage efforts to help those most vulnerable or lacking in skills to prepare for the job market. "Some of the changes made it almost impossible in some ways for people to use the system to get out of poverty," said Rep. McDermott, the Washington Democrat.[67]

But others defend the approach. "The bottom line is that the only real way to get out of poverty is to find a job," said Rep. Wally Herger, a California Republican who chaired the House subcommittee that worked on last year's reauthorization. "There's always the line, 'Well, some people can't do it.' What that's really doing is selling those people short."[68]

OUTLOOK

Ominous Signs

The outlook for real progress against domestic poverty is mixed, especially in the near term.

On one hand, concerns about poverty, income inequality and declining mobility are playing a bigger role on the national scene than they have in years. The kind of political momentum that spurred the War on Poverty in the 1960s may be emerging again — albeit in a more muted fashion and with a different set of policy proposals.

But big obstacles remain, especially funding. Congress would face difficult fiscal choices if it sought to enact any major anti-poverty program, many analysts point out. Even the Democratic majority, which has long pushed for more spending for social programs, would face major barriers.

"The Democrats have committed to pay-as-you-go budgeting, so I don't think we'll have a major push on anti-poverty [programs] or on programs designed to help the poor and middle class" over the next four to eight years, says Yale's Hacker. "That's part of the reason for the public's frustration — we're hamstrung by the budgetary situation."

At the same time, a number of ominous developments have been occurring that suggest the poor will have an even rougher time financially than they have in recent years. The explosion in mortgage foreclosures, rising prices for basics like gasoline and milk and the ever-present threat of recession and layoffs all conspire most heavily against those with the fewest resources. Recently, job growth and expansion in the service sector have both been weaker than expected, indicating tougher times ahead for those on the economic margins.

Coupled with the uncertain economic outlook is the unresolved issue of immigration. Some analysts are less concerned about illegal immigrants taking low-paying jobs from native-born Americans as they are about the chance that immigrant groups will become mired in permanent poverty because of out-of-wedlock births and other social problems.

"In the long term," says Mead of New York University, "overcoming poverty probably does depend on restricting immigration" to 1970 levels. Curbing immigration, he says, not only would make more entry-level jobs available to native-born men — the group that Mead sees as a priority for anti-poverty action — but also help keep a new underclass from developing even as the nation struggles to reduce poverty in the established population.

As scholars and activists look ahead, some express optimism, as Lyndon Johnson once did, that poverty not only can be substantially reduced but actually eliminated. Others note that Johnson's vow to eliminate poverty raised expectations that were never satisfied.

"I think the poor are always going to be with us," says Bradley of the National Community Action Foundation. "Can we substantially reduce poverty? Yes. But the [idea] that somehow certain programs are going to eradicate poverty in America is just unrealistic."

NOTES

1. Testimony before House Ways and Means Subcommittee on Income Security and Family Support, "Hearing on Economic Opportunity and Poverty in America," Feb. 13, 2007.

2. Figures reflect U.S. Census Bureau data for 2006. For background, see Kathy Koch, "Child Poverty," *CQ Researcher*, April 7, 2000, pp. 281-304.

3. Timothy M. Smeeding, testimony before House Ways and Means Subcommittee on Income Security and Family Support, "Hearing on Economic Opportunity and Poverty in America," Feb. 13, 2007. The study is based on Smeeding's calculations from the Luxembourg Income Study.

4. Quoted in Bob Herbert, "The Millions Left Out," *The New York Times*, May 12, 2007, p. A25.

5. Tony Pugh, "U.S. Economy Leaving Record Numbers in Severe Poverty," McClatchy Newspapers, Feb. 22, 2007, updated May 25, 2007.

6. Aviva Aron-Dine, "New Data Show Income Concentration Jumped Again in 2005," Center on Budget and Policy Priorities, March 29, 2007, www.cbpp.org/3-29-07inc.htm.

7. David Cay Johnston, "Income Gap Is Widening, Data Shows," *The New York Times*, March 29, 2007, p. C1.

8. "Panel Study of Income Dynamics; Cross-National Equivalent File," Cornell University. Cited in John Edwards, Marion Crain and Arne L. Kalleberg, eds., *Ending Poverty in America: How to Restore the American Dream* (2007), The New Press, published in conjunction with the Center on Poverty, Work and Opportunity, University of North Carolina at Chapel Hill. Data are from Jacob S. Hacker, "The Risky Outlook for Middle-Class America," Chapter 5, p. 72.

9. Mark R. Rank, "Toward a New Understanding of American Poverty," *Journal of Law & Policy*, Vol. 20:17, p. 33, http://law.wustl.edu/Journal/20/p17Rankbookpage.pdf.

10. Steven Greenhouse, "A Unified Voice Argues the Case for U.S. Manufacturing," *The New York Times*, April 26, 2007, p. C2.

11. Katrina vanden Heuvel, "Twelve Steps to Cutting Poverty in Half," Blog: Editor's Cut, *The Nation*, April 30, 2007, www.thenation.com/blogs/edcut?pid=190867.

12. Patrick Healy, "Clinton Vows Middle Class Will Not Be 'Invisible' to Her," *The New York Times*, March 11, 2007, www.nyt.com.

13. Quoted in Alec MacGillis, "Obama Says He, Too, Is a Poverty Fighter," *The Washington Post*, July 19, 2007, p. 4A.

14. Jackie Calmes, "Edwards's Theme: U.S. Poverty," *The Wall Street Journal Online*, Dec. 28, 2006.

15. Edward Luce, "Bloomberg urges US to extend anti-poverty scheme," *FT.com* (*Financial Times*), Aug. 29, 2007.

16. "McDermott Announces Hearing on Proposals for Reducing Poverty," press release, House Ways and Means Subcommittee on Income Security and Family Support, April 26, 2007.

17. Mike Dorning, "Will Poverty Make Political Comeback?" *Chicago Tribune*, June 3, 2007, p. 4.

18. Gallup Poll, June 11-14, 2007.

19. Jon Cohen, "Despite Focus on Poverty, Edwards Trails Among the Poor," *The Washington Post*, July 11, 2007, p. 7A.

20. Testimony before House Committee on Ways and Means, "Hearing on the Economic and Societal Costs of Poverty," Jan. 24, 2007.

21. Steven H. Woolf, Robert E. Johnson and H. Jack Geiger, "The Rising Prevalence of Severe Poverty in

America: A Growing Threat to Public Health," *American Journal of Preventive Medicine*, Vol. 31, Issue 4, October 2006, p. 332.

22. Quoted in "Statement of Child Welfare League of America," House Ways and Means Subcommittee on Income Security and Family Support, "Hearing on Economic Opportunity and Poverty in America," Feb. 13, 2007. According to the statement, Conley's comment came in an ABC television profile of poverty in Camden, N.J., broadcast in January 2007.

23. Testimony before House Ways and Means Subcommittee on Income Security and Family Support, Feb. 13, 2007. Berube said concentrated poverty is defined by Paul Jargowsky of the University of Texas-Dallas as neighborhoods where at least 40 percent of individuals live below the poverty line.

24. Pugh, *op. cit.*

25. Nell McNamara and Doug Schenkelberg, *Extreme Poverty & Human Rights: A Primer* (2007), Mid-America Institute on Poverty of Heartland Alliance for Human Needs & Human Rights. For the Bellevue data, the report cites Pennsylvania State University, "Poverty in America (n.d.) Living Wage Calculator," retrieved Nov. 15, 2006, from www.livingwage.geog.psu.edu/.

26. Pugh, *op. cit.*

27. Testimony before House Ways and Means Subcommittee on Income Security and Family Support, Feb. 13, 2007.

28. Woolf, *et al.*, *op. cit.*

29. Peter Katel, "Minimum Wage," *CQ Researcher*, Dec. 16, 2005, pp. 1053-1076.

30. Sarah Glazer, "Welfare Reform," *CQ Researcher*, Aug. 3, 2001, pp. 601-632.

31. Dan Froomkin, "Welfare's Changing Face," www.Washingtonpost.com/wp-srv/politics/special/welfare/welfare.htm, updated July 23, 1998.

32. Ron Haskins, "Welfare Check," *The Wall Street Journal*, July 27, 2006, accessed at www.brookings.edu.

33. "Interview: Welfare Reform, 10 Years Later," *The Examiner*, Aug. 24, 2006, accessed at www.brookings.edu.

34. Sharon Parrott and Arloc Sherman, "TANF at 10: Program Results are More Mixed Than Often

Understood," Center on Budget and Policy Priorities, Aug. 17, 2006.

35. Wisconsin Council on Children & Families, "Wisconsin Ranks First in Growth in Poverty: Census Bureau Reports," press release, Aug. 30, 2005. See also testimony of Richard Schlimm, House Ways and Means Committee, "Hearing on the Economic and Societal Costs of Poverty," Jan. 24, 2007.

36. Testimony before House Subcommittee on Income Security and Family Support, Feb. 13, 2007.

37. Lawrence Mead, "And Now, 'Welfare Reform' for Men," *The Washington Post*, March 20, 2007, p. 19A.

38. Michael D. Tanner, "More Welfare, More Poverty," *The Monitor* (McAllen, Texas), Sept. 8, 2006.

39. Proceedings of the Virginia Assembly, 1619.

40. Henry George, "Progress and Poverty," first printed in 1879. Quoted in H. B. Shaffer, "Persistence of Poverty," *Editorial Research Reports*, Feb. 5, 1964, available at *CQ Researcher Plus Archive*, www.cqpress.com.

41. Gordon M. Fisher, "From Hunter to Orshansky: An Overview of (Unofficial) Poverty Lines in the United States from 1904 to 1965-Summary, March 1994, retrieved at http://aspe.hhs.gov/poverty/papers/htrssmiv.htm.

42. *CQ Researcher, op. cit.*

43. Michael Harrington, *The Other America: Poverty in the United States* (1962), pp. 14-15.

44. U.S. Census data show the poverty rate for individuals was 22.2 percent in 1960; 21.9 percent in 1961; 21 percent in 1962; 19.5 percent in 1963; and 19 percent in 1964. For families the rate ranged from 20.7 percent to 17.4 percent in that period.

45. See H. B. Shaffer, "Status of War on Poverty," in *Editorial Research Reports*, Jan. 25, 1967, available at *CQ Researcher Plus Archive*, www.cqpress.com.

46. Marcia Clemmitt, "Evaluating Head Start," *CQ Researcher*, Aug. 26, 2005, pp. 685-708.

47. Sheldon H. Danziger and Robert H. Haveman, eds., *Understanding Poverty* (2001), Russell Sage Foundation and Harvard University Press, pp. 4 and 5.

48. Peter Edelman, "The Worst Thing Bill Clinton Has Done," *The Atlantic Monthly*, March 1997.

49. Jeff Jacoby, "Wefare Reform Success," *The Boston Globe*, Sept. 13, 2006, p. 9A.

50. Sheldon H. Danziger, "Fighting Poverty Revisited: What did researchers know 40 years ago? What do we know today?," *Focus*, University of Wisconsin-Madison, Institute for Research on Poverty, Spring-Summer 2007, p. 3.

51. Lyndon B. Johnson, "Annual Message to Congress on the State of the Union," Jan. 8, 1964.

52. MacGillis, *op. cit.*

53. E.J. Dionne Jr., "Making the Poor Visible," *The Washington Post*, July 20, 2007, p. A19.

54. Mary H. Cooper, "Income Inequality," *CQ Researcher*, April 17, 1998, pp. 337-360.

55. www.mittromney.com.

56. Mark Greenberg, Indivar Dutta-Gupta and Elisa Minoff, "From Poverty to Prosperity: A National Strategy to Cut Poverty in Half," Center for American Progress, April 2007, www.americanprogress.org/issues/2007/04/poverty_report.html.

57. Ron Haskins and Isabel V. Sawhill, "Attacking Poverty and Inequality," Brookings Institution, Opportunity 08, in partnership with ABC News, February 2007, www.opportunity08.org/Issues/OurSociety/31/r1/Default.aspx.

58. Coalition on Human Needs, "Nearly 900 Organizations Sign Letter to Congress in Support of Expanding Tax Credits for the Poor," May 25, 2007, www.chn.org. The letter, dated May 24, 2007, was accessed at www.chn.org/pdf/2007/ctceitcletter.pdf.

59. Alan Berube, "Using the Earned Income Tax Credit to Stimulate Local Economies," Brookings Institution, www.brookings.org.

60. Adriel Bettelheim, "The Social Side of Tax Breaks," *CQ Weekly*, Feb. 5, 2007.

61. *Ibid.*

62. Diane Cardwell, "City to Reward Poor for Doing Right Thing," *The New York Times*, March 30, 2007, p. 1B.

63. The bill is AB 1118.

64. David MacDonald, communications director, Connecticut Association for Community Action, letter to the editor of the *Hartford Courant*, June 27, 2007, p. 8A.

65. Clea Benson, "States Scramble to Adapt To New Welfare Rules," *CQ Weekly*, June 25, 2007, p. 1907.

66. *Ibid.*

67. *Ibid.*

68. *Ibid.*

BIBLIOGRAPHY

Books

Danziger, Sheldon H., and Robert H. Haveman, eds., *Understanding Poverty, Russell Sage Foundation and Harvard University Press, 2001.*
Writings on domestic poverty range from the evolution of anti-poverty programs to health policy for the poor. Danziger is a professor of social work and public policy at the University of Michigan, Haveman, a professor of economics and public affairs at the University of Wisconsin, Madison.

DeParle, Jason, *American Dream: Three Women, Ten Kids, and a Nation's Drive to End Welfare*, Viking Adult, 2004.
A reporter looks at the effort to overhaul the American welfare system through the lives of three former welfare mothers.

Edwards, John, Marion Crain and Arne L. Kalleberg, eds., *Ending Poverty in America*, New Press, 2007.
Co-edited and with a conclusion by Democratic presidential candidate Edwards, this collection of articles reflects a progressive economic agenda.

Haskins, Ron, *Work Over Welfare: The Inside Story of the 1996 Welfare Reform Law*, Brookings Institution Press, 2006.
A former Republican committee staffer and a chief architect of welfare reform, Haskins tells the story of the political debates leading up to the historic welfare overhaul.

Articles

Bai, Matt, "The Poverty Platform," *New York Times Magazine*, June 10, 2007.
Taking a close look at presidential candidate John Edwards' focus on the poor, Bai says "the main economic debate in Democratic Washington" focuses on "the tools

of economic policy — taxes, trade, welfare — and how to use them."

Dorning, Mike, "Will Poverty Make Political Comeback?" *Chicago Tribune,* **June 3, 2007.**
Since the 1960s, Dorning notes, "leading presidential candidates generally have not focused on the plight of the poor as a central issue."

Reports and Studies

Congressional Budget Office, "Changes in the Economic Resources of Low-Income Households with Children," May 2007.
This study charts income changes among the poor from the early 1990s.

Children's Defense Fund, "The State of America's Children 2005."
Marian Wright Edelman, founder and president of the Children's Defense Fund, writes, "Far less wealthy industrialized countries have committed to end child poverty, while the United States is sliding backwards."

Greenberg, Mark, Indivar Dutta-Gupta and Elisa Minoff, "From Poverty to Prosperity: A National Strategy to Cut Poverty in Half," Center for American Progress, April 2007.
The think tank's Task Force on Poverty says the United States should set a goal of halving poverty over the next decade.

Harrison, David, and Bob Watrus, "On Getting Out–and Staying Out–of Poverty: The Complex Causes of and Responses to Poverty in the Northwest," Northwest Area Foundation, 2004.
An estimated 2 million people live in poverty in the Northwest, more than 900,000 of them in severe poverty.

McNamara, Nell, and Doug Schenkelberg, "Extreme Poverty & Human Rights: A Primer," Heartland Alliance for Human Needs & Human Rights, 2007.
A guidebook explains how human rights advocacy can combat both global and domestic poverty.

Meyer, Bruce D., and James X. Sullivan, "Three Decades of Consumption and Income Poverty," National Poverty Center Working Paper Series, September 2006.
The study examines poverty measurement in the United States from 1972 through 2004 and how poverty rates have changed over the years.

Rector, Robert, "How Poor Are America's Poor? Examining the 'Plague' of Poverty in America," Heritage Foundation, Aug. 27, 2007.
A senior research fellow at the conservative think tank writes that " 'the plague' of American poverty might not be as 'terrible' or 'incredible' as candidate [John] Edwards contends."

Toldson, Ivory A., and Elsie L. Scott, "Poverty, Race and Policy," Congressional Black Caucus Foundation, 2006.
The four-part report explores affordable-housing policy, wealth-accumulation needs and strategies for reducing poverty and unemployment.

Woolf, Steven H., Robert E. Johnson and H. Jack Geiger, "The Rising Prevalence of Severe Poverty in America: A Growing Threat to Public Health," *American Journal of Preventive Medicine,* **October 2006.**
Woolf, a professor of family medicine, epidemiology and community health at Virginia Commonwealth University and lead author of this study, says the growth in severe poverty and other trends "have disturbing implications for society and public health."

For More Information

Center for American Progress, 1333 H St., N.W., 10th Floor, Washington, DC 20005; (202) 682-1611; www.americanprogress.org. A liberal think tank that issued a report and recommendations on poverty this year.

Coalition on Human Needs, 1120 Connecticut Ave., N.W., Suite 312, Washington, DC 20036; (202) 223-2532; www.chn.org. An alliance of organizations that promote policies to help low-income people and others in need.

Economic Policy Institute, 1333 H St., N.W., Suite 300, East Tower, Washington, DC 20005-4707; (202) 775-8810; www.epi.org. A think tank that studies policies related to the economy, work and the interests of low- and middle-income people.

Heritage Foundation, 214 Massachusetts Ave., N.E., Washington, DC 20002-4999; (202) 546-4400; www.heritage.org. A conservative think tank that studies poverty and other public-policy issues.

Institute for Research on Poverty, University of Wisconsin-Madison, 1180 Observatory Dr., 3412 Social Science Building, Madison, WI 53706-1393; (608) 262-6358; www.irp.wisc.edu. Studies the causes and consequences of poverty.

Mid-America Institute on Poverty, 2085 S. LaSalle St., Suite 1818, Chicago, IL 60640; (312) 660-1300;

www.heartlandalliance.org. A research arm of Heartland Alliance, which provides services for low-income individuals.

National Community Action Foundation, 810 First St., N.E., Suite 530, Washington, DC 20002; (202) 842-2092; www.ncaf.org. Advocates for the nation's community-action agencies.

Step Up, Savannah's Poverty Reduction Initiative, 428 Bull St., Suite 208, Savannah, GA 31401; (912) 232-6747; www.stepupsavannah.org. A coalition of more than 80 local business, government and nonprofit organizations seeking to reduce poverty.

U.S. Census Bureau, 4600 Silver Hill Road, Suitland, MD 20746; www.census.gov. Maintains extensive recent and historical data on poverty and demographics.

University of North Carolina Center on Poverty, Work and Opportunity, UNC School of Law, Van Heck-Wettach Hall, 160 Ridge Road, CB #3380, Chapel Hill, N.C. 27599-3380; (919) 962-5106; www.law.unc.edu/centers/poverty/default.aspx. A national forum for scholars, policymakers and others interested in poverty, established by presidential candidate John Edwards.

Urban Institute, 2100 M St., N.W., Washington, DC 20037; (202) 833-7200; www.urban.org. Studies welfare and low-income families among a range of issues.

11

Mortgage Crisis

Marcia Clemmitt and Charles S. Clark

This house in Pasadena, Calif., is among thousands around the country being sold after the owners defaulted on their mortgages. An estimated 2.2 million borrowers will lose their homes to foreclosure, largely because they had subprime mortgages. Congress and the Bush administration are debating how to help borrowers keep their homes and whether tough, new lending standards are warranted.

From *CQ Researcher*,
November 2, 2007 (updated August 9, 2010).

When retired Chicago office administrator Delores King refinanced her house in 2004, she didn't expect to end up with "a mortgage that's thousands of dollars more than I started with" and payments that "have nearly doubled in two years."

"I have refinanced before, but I've never seen anything like this," King told a Senate Banking panel earlier this year.[1]

King's loan became unaffordable after its initial low interest rate reset to a higher rate and several unexpected, extra fees kicked in. King says her mortgage broker "rushed me through" the loan closing and never explained the mortgage's unusual features. King is one of millions of Americans in mortgage trouble in 2007, and her tale of an apparently "easy" loan that turns catastrophic is all too common, Eric Stein, senior vice president of the Center for Responsible Lending, in Durham, N.C., told a House subcommittee in September.

An estimated 2.2 million families will lose their homes to foreclosure because of a spate of "reckless" mortgage lending in recent years, Stein said. Today's foreclosure levels are the "worst they've been in at least 25 years," said Stein. Moreover, he said, "Millions of other families . . . will be hurt by declines in property values spurred by nearby foreclosures."[2]

The worst problems are concentrated in areas with slow economies, where cheap land encouraged a building frenzy, and in popular places like Phoenix and Florida, where floods of retirees and other new residents heated up the housing market.

Lower-income people are most at risk, but others will also feel pain. "Executives who built second homes out in the Carolinas" with 2- or 3-percent-interest loans that are about to reset to higher

Subprime Foreclosures Affect All Regions

In most of the states, 11-15 percent of the subprime mortgage loans made in 2006 will be foreclosed. In at least a half-dozen states, the failure rate is projected at up to 24 percent. The nation is experiencing the highest foreclosure rate since the Great Depression, according to the Center for Responsible Lending.

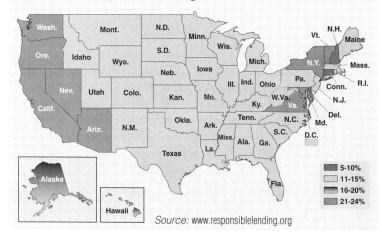

5-10%
11-15%
16-20%
21-24%

Source: www.responsiblelending.org

Several large investment funds and banks have already taken billion-dollar hits from losses on defaulting mortgages. Last summer big investment bank Bear Stearns put up over $3 billion to save one of its hedge funds that faced huge losses on mortgage investments.[5] Late last month financial giant Merrill Lynch announced an $8-billion loss on mortgage securities, over $3 billion more than the company had anticipated only weeks earlier.[6]

A combination of easy money, loose lending standards and real-estate bidding wars that sent home prices soaring contributed to today's problems.

The current crisis comes from a "confluence of factors, and if you looked at each individually, it wouldn't be a big problem," says Robert Rainish, a professor of finance at the University of New Haven.

rates "will have trouble, too," says Robert Schultz, a home-building consultant in Boca Raton, Fla.

Still in question is whether the crunch will spread beyond housing and drag the nation into recession.

"I think the worst is over," wrote Jeremy Siegel, a professor of finance at the Wharton School, in early October. "Everyone is going to say, 'There is going to be a big bomb and . . . a hedge fund . . . is going to go under' " because it invested in mortgage-backed securities that are now defaulting. "Well, we haven't heard anything recently and . . . no news is good news. We are slowly returning to normal here."[3] Others see deeper housing troubles and recession ahead.

"A recession happens every decade, but this is going to be bigger" than usual "because the debt is so extreme," says Peter Cohan, president of a management-consulting and venture-capital firm in Marlborough, Mass. Builders will be hard hit as well as "insurance, furniture, paint and building-supply companies," he says.

Mortgage lenders and insurers are taking big losses, and some — including New Century Financial, the country's second-largest subprime lender — have gone bankrupt as recent loans began defaulting and the housing market slows.[4]

The development in the 1990s of investment instruments known as mortgage-backed securities tempted even cautious investors to buy mortgages, Rainish says.

The so-called securitization of mortgages boosted homeownership by enabling banks and other lenders to sell mortgages, thus raising capital to make additional housing loans. With so much mortgage money available, however, "an incredible ramp-up" of riskier mortgages occurred "in a very short period," says Rainish.

The highest-risk mortgages — known as subprimes — were usually offered to people with poor credit histories at higher interest rates than ordinary mortgages. "Virtually nonexistent before the mid-1990s, subprimes accounted for a fifth of all new mortgages by 2005," said Robert J. Shiller, a Yale University professor of economics and finance.[7]

By 2006, another formerly limited mortgage class was being offered to people with poor credit scores — often without requiring documented proof of income — as lenders sought to write as many mortgages as possible to boost their own bottom lines. Virtually unheard of a decade earlier, subprime and so-called Alt-A loans accounted for $1 trillion of the nation's mortgage debt by 2006, says Rainish.

"People who didn't qualify for credit to rent could get credit to buy a house," says real-estate developer Robert Sheridan, of River Forest, Ill.

Many of the new loans had no or very low down payments and were adjustable-rate mortgages (ARMs) with low initial interest rates that would have to be refinanced later, when rates were much higher.

"You couple easy money with the fact that a lot of people were not astute enough to understand" the risks involved in their loans, and "it was a train wreck waiting to happen," says Schultz.

Compounding the problem, the high number of would-be new buyers drove house and condo prices far above what was traditionally thought to be affordable. And the easy mortgage money encouraged hopeful homeowners as well as speculators as they bid up prices to unprecedented levels.

Pre-boom, median home prices typically equaled about 2.5 times the buyer's median income. Today, they're about 4.5 times income, and much higher in some regions, says Rainish. "That's a housing bubble."

Mortgages Are Widely Purchased

Mortgages held by homeowners are sold to institutional investors in many sectors of the U.S. economy and abroad. The large number of investors, and the fact that many know little about the mortgage market, has led lenders to greatly increase the number and riskiness of mortgages they offer.

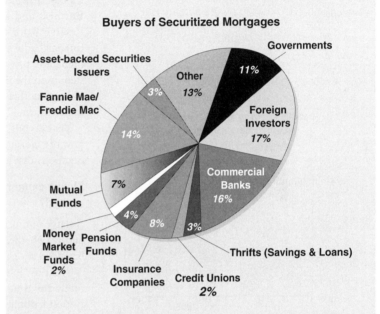

Buyers of Securitized Mortgages

Governments 11%
Foreign Investors 17%
Commercial Banks 16%
Thrifts (Savings & Loans) 3%
Credit Unions 2%
Insurance Companies 8%
Pension Funds 4%
Money Market Funds 2%
Mutual Funds 7%
Fannie Mae/ Freddie Mac 14%
Asset-backed Securities Issuers 3%
Other 13%

Source: "Mortgage Liquidity du Jour: Underestimated No More," Credit Suisse, March 12, 2007; Federal Reserve

Trouble was inevitable when we simultaneously "made home ownership the American dream and then allowed prices to grow way beyond the rate of growth of the rest of the economy," says Corey Stone, CEO of Pay Rent, Build Credit, an Annapolis-Md.-based company that helps consumers repair bad credit histories.

"The average American today can't afford to buy a home at current prices," says Robert Hardaway, a professor of law at the University of Denver. "The average home in California costs $500,000. You can't afford that home." But easy initial mortgage terms made many buyers believe they could, which led to today's record defaults and foreclosures.

Now Congress is contemplating restrictions on risky mortgages.

For example, regulators should impose an " 'ability-to-repay' standard" for all loans made to people with poor credit histories, Martin Eakes, CEO of the Center for Responsible Lending, told the Senate Banking Committee in February. ARMs "now make up the vast majority of subprime loans, and they have predictable and devastating consequences for . . . homeowners," who may lose their houses when interest rates change, he said.[8]

The Federal Reserve Board (the Fed) — which governs the nation's banking system and money supply — has cut interest rates on bank-to-bank loans to encourage lenders and investors spooked by rising mortgage-default rates to get back in the financial game.

Lower Fed rates would not directly translate into lower mortgage interest. However, by making it easier for banks to get money, "the Fed is signaling, 'Let's restore confidence and get the economy started again,'" says Philip Ashton, an assistant professor of urban planning and policy at the University of Illinois, Chicago.

Housing Costs Swamp Millions of Families

The number of working families paying more than half their income for housing nearly doubled from 1997 to 2005. The increase reflects the rise in housing prices and the larger number of low-income people who obtained mortgages.

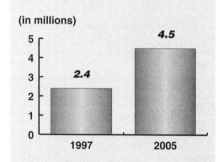

Families Paying More Than Half Their Income for Housing

(in millions)

Source: "The Housing Landscape for America's Working Families," Center for Housing Policy, August 2007

The rate cuts get mixed reviews as a strategy to ease the mortgage mess and credit freeze, since many experts partly blame low Fed interest rates in the early 2000s for helping fuel recent excesses.

Meanwhile, states, localities and the federal government — as well as private lenders and the giant Federal National Mortgage Corporation (Fannie Mae) — are making funds and loans available to help struggling homeowners stay put. For example, in hard-hit Cleveland, Cuyahoga County will fund loans to struggling homeowners using $3 million in penalties collected for late payment of property taxes.[9]

And under pressure to stop the bleeding, the nation's biggest mortgage lender, Countrywide Financial Corp.,

announced in October that it will restructure about 82,000 mortgages to make them more affordable.[10]

But some economists criticize such "bailouts" as unwise tinkering with economic markets.

"Individuals need to be responsible for their own borrowing," says Marvin Goodfriend, a professor of economics at Carnegie Mellon University's Tepper School of Business and a research economist with the Federal Reserve Bank of Richmond. That means much more financial education for everyone, he says. The government, the private sector, and nonprofit groups should step up to the task but haven't yet, he says. "People need to hear another voice besides the voice that's saying, 'No money down.'"

As nervous homeowners and investors wait to see how the mortgage crunch plays out, here are some of the questions that are being asked:

Should certain kinds of risky home loans be banned?

As large numbers of mortgages go into default, Congress debates whether some mortgage-lending practices should be ended altogether.

"At least in the vast majority of situations, and definitely any time federal money is involved," some of the riskiest lending practices should be banned, says Robert Losey, chairman of the Department of Finance at American University in Washington, D.C. For example, "there should be a requirement for significant down payments" for most loans, a tradition that's gotten lost, Losey says. "If someone makes no down payment, they have nothing to risk" and are more likely to walk away from the mortgage if the going gets tough, he says.

Some recent mortgages also have limited requirements for borrowers to document their income and assets — or don't require them at all.

"Oversight should limit or eliminate no-doc [no-documentation] loans," says Sandra Phillips, an assistant professor of finance at Syracuse University. "There should have been a crackdown on these lenders who were originating mortgages based on nonexistent and inflated equity," she says.

It's also become common practice for lenders to certify that borrowers are equipped to pay off adjustable-rate mortgages (ARMs) based on whether they have enough income to pay the loans' initial, low "teaser" rates. Critics call for ARMs to be sold only to borrowers who show they will be able to make payments when interest resets to a higher rate.

The Treasury Department and other federal agencies recommended in October 2006 eliminating ARMs that certify only that borrowers can pay the low, initial rates. According to the agencies, analysis "of borrowers' repayment capacity should include an evaluation of their ability to repay the debt by final maturity at the fully indexed rate."[11]

But many in the mortgage industry protest that strict rules will stifle innovation in lending and keep many people from getting mortgages.

"While it may sound reasonable to require that all borrowers contending for" ARMs "be qualified at the fully indexed rate . . . such an approach will lock some borrowers out of the home of their dreams and deprive them of lower payments," Douglas O. Duncan, senior vice president for research and business development at the Mortgage Bankers Association, told a Senate panel in February. "The magic of today's market is that the widest range of borrowers can get the widest spectrum of loans."[12]

"We cannot agree that underwriting to the fully indexed rate is the correct standard in all situations," said Sandor Samuels, an executive managing director of Countrywide Financial. Many "homeowners who will need to refinance will not be able to qualify under such a standard," and "many first-time homebuyers who can currently purchase a home will no longer . . . qualify . . . under the proposed guidelines," he said. "This will materially reduce housing demand . . . and delay the housing recovery."[13]

The National Association of Mortgage Brokers (NAMB) "believes the problem of rising foreclosures is complex and will not be corrected by simply removing products from the market," said NAMB President Harry Dinham.

Indeed, the availability of subprime mortgages helped push homeownership to an all-time high of about 69 percent of families in the last few years.[14]

Rules can be significantly tightened without banning some kinds of mortgages altogether, many analysts say.

"I would change the way people [in the mortgage industry] get compensated," for example, says Cohan, the management-consultant and venture capitalist.

Greg Giniel's house in Arizona's Queen Creek housing development in is in foreclosure, but he hopes to buy it back in November. Many borrowers got in trouble because they were saddled with high-risk, high-interest "subprime" mortgages, which are usually offered to people with bad credit histories. However, subprimes were also pushed on many people with good credit.

Instead of paying commissions up front, which gives brokers and some lenders' representatives incentive to push buyers into mortgages whether they can afford them or not, "I'd put half the commission in escrow," Cohan says. If the mortgage "maintained value for 10 years, then brokers would get the money." But if the mortgage "collapsed, then the money would go to pay the cost of their mistakes."

"Reducing the incentive for volume" by decreeing that commissions can't be based on the number of deals a broker or salesperson arranges would help limit bad mortgages, says Syracuse University's Phillips.

"You need to regulate and supervise the mortgage brokers," says Phillips. To do that, federal laws would have to be reinterpreted or rewritten to allow regulation of brokers, she says. "Right now, they're in the cracks" and unregulated.

Risky loans proliferate partly because current disclosure rules don't require lenders to give borrowers clear, understandable information about exactly what their mortgage provisions mean, says the University of New Haven's Rainish. Today's rules about what lenders must tell borrowers "were made before anybody conceived of the current market," with its proliferation of complex mortgages, he says.

Subprime Loans Can Have Abusive Terms

A high percentage of subprime loans carry prepayment penalties and adjustable interest rates that are due to reset in two to three years. More than a third of the loans were issued based on little or no documentation of the borrower's income.

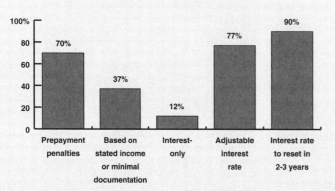

High-Risk Characteristics of Abusive Subprime Loan

Source: Testimony of Michael D. Calhoun, President, Center for Responsible Lending, before the Senate Banking Subcommittee on Housing, Transportation and Community Development, June 26, 2007

"Borrowers need a one-page summary that explains exactly what their mortgage entails," says Cohan. "Nobody reads these 65-page things" that current disclosure rules require, he says.

Should the government "bail out" borrowers caught in the mortgage meltdown?

Some analysts are encouraging states and the federal government to loosen the rules governing government-guaranteed mortgage programs to include homeowners in default and provide loan funds to help homeowners refinance. The Bush administration, congressional Democrats and several state governments back at least limited bailout plans, but some economists say any bailout encourages "bad behavior" to continue.

"Bailouts are terrible because they create moral hazard" — the tendency of people to make more bad choices in the future because they didn't have to face consequences of earlier choices, says Goodfriend of Carnegie Mellon University and the Richmond Federal Reserve Bank.

Even if bailouts are labeled as being for homeowners, it's lenders — many of whom engaged in risky and even predatory practices — who largely will benefit, some analysts say.

In August, President Bush announced a plan to open up Federal Housing Administration loans to some people struggling in the mortgage crisis. But, while the president "claims the bailout is for deserving homeowners, the thinly veiled policy changes are obviously meant to ensure that lenders are not defaulted on," commented the investment Web site eFinanceDirectory.com.[15]

Investors who carelessly speculated in high-risk securities would also be winners if fewer mortgages go into default, and the government should not prop them up, some financial analysts say.

"A borrower bailout and an investor bailout are synonymous," said Paul Jackson, a real-estate analyst for the mortgage blog Housing Wire. Furthermore, allowing people who can't afford their mortgages to get new ones for the same properties doesn't fix the fundamental problem — "millions of borrowers who simply can't afford a mortgage on the property they're now in," he said.[16]

Those who hope for a quick and simple bailout will be disappointed, says Illinois real-estate developer Sheridan. Because housing values won't quickly rebound, "federal legislation to help buyers hold on would have to be in place for a long time," he says.

Nevertheless, "there's a natural tendency by Congress and the executive branch to throw money at problems," so bailouts are likely inevitable, says American University's Losey. "But only the people who would qualify for loans anyway should have the opportunity to row their way out," he says.

"People are going to be hurt, but that doesn't mean we should subsidize them for buying a home they couldn't afford," Losey says. "There's no reason to say, 'Now we'll let you stay in that home.'"

Thirty percent or more of buyers in the recent, hot real-estate market "were speculators — non-occupying buyers" who bought homes with easy-to-get mortgages, then tried to "flip" them for a profit as prices rose, says Rainish, at the University of New Haven. Speculators "should not be bailed out," he says. If the government "is going to do a bailout, they need to be sure that only home-occupying buyers get assistance."

"We should not be bailing out people who invested in real estate, but it would be easy enough to separate speculators from owners," says Sheridan. "Just find out who's living in the house. Send them a letter. Show me the bills that come there."

Nevertheless, the sheer size of the foreclosure mess probably requires action, especially since government has stepped into similar crises as rescuer, says Rainish. "The government is trying to come up with a way for credit institutions to refinance these loans, but the question is how far they're willing to go," he says. "They spent $150 billion on the savings & loan crisis" of the late 1980s.[17] "And there's not much reason they can't do something similar to mitigate today's level of foreclosure," he says.

"You will have to say to some people, 'No matter how we restructure the financing, you can't afford the house,'" Rainish says. "But others can handle a restructured loan."

However, he adds, "You can't disentangle helping borrowers and lenders." But he argues that "it's not a bad idea to help the lenders. If lenders are going to come back in the game ever again, you have to help them. Otherwise, you won't have a market."

Left out of the Bush bailout are lower-income people, especially in minority neighborhoods, many of whom were deceived by predatory lenders into taking on more expensive loans than they realized, says Syracuse University's Phillips. "The irony of the proposal is that it only goes to upper-income people with good credit," she says. "I don't think we should leave out the population targeted for predatory loans," she says.

Community-advocacy groups working in neighborhoods hit by predatory lending "are doing a pretty good job helping people find a way to make the payments," says Phillips. A group she works with in Syracuse has helped many people stay in their homes, she says.

Number of Foreclosures to Double

The failure rate of recent subprime loans is expected to double, affecting 2.2 million borrowers. As housing prices decline, fewer delinquent borrowers have the equity needed to refinance their loan or sell their home to avoid foreclosure.

Chance of foreclosure for loan made in 2005 and 2006:
20 percent (vs. 10% for loans made in 2002)

Cost of foreclosures to borrowers:
Up to $164 billion

Number of foreclosed or soon-to-be-foreclosed loans:
2.2 million

Source: "Losing Ground: Foreclosures in the Subprime market and Their Cost to Homeowners," Center for Responsible Lending, December 2006

Sen. Charles E. Schumer, D-N.Y., has proposed legislation giving $300 million to community groups that specialize in foreclosure prevention. "This seems like a cost-effective investment to me," said Schumer. "It will save billions in spillover foreclosure costs."[18]

It wouldn't be difficult to provide assistance only to people saddled with predatory loans because the details of those abusive loans are a dead giveaway, says Phillips. "Looking at the loan agreement, in predatory loans you will see substantial charges [not found in other mortgages], and the fees will be high. There will be restrictions on refinancing."

Will the mortgage crisis trigger a larger financial crisis in the United States and elsewhere?

Most everyone agrees that people holding subprime mortgages — mostly low-income borrowers with poor credit — are defaulting and losing their homes. How far subprime fallout will spread in the economy, however, is sharply debated.

"The real bears in this market believe housing will lead the economy into recession," said John Burns, a real-estate consultant in Irvine, Calif. "Thus far, these bears are wrong. The housing market peaked in June 2005 and, two years into the downturn, economic growth is still positive. Unemployment remains very low . . . and consumers have started ramping up their credit-card debt again."[19]

Furthermore, the housing market itself is in good shape, according to Lawrence Yun, senior economist at the National Association of Realtors. "Although sales are off from an unsustainable peak in 2005, there is a historically high level of home sales . . . this year," he said. "One out of 15 American households is buying a home."[20]

"The speculative excesses have been removed from the market, and home sales are returning to fundamentally healthy levels, while prices remain near record highs, reflecting favorable mortgage rates and positive job gains," Yun said.

"Housing is only about 5 percent of the economy," said columnist Ben Stein at Yahoo! Finance. "If it falls by 15 percent, that would represent a fall-off [in the total economy] of about 0.75 percent. That's not trivial, but it's also not the stuff of which recessions are made."[21]

Eight out of the 10 U.S. recessions since World War II "were preceded by sustained and substantial problems in housing, and there was a more minor problem in housing prior to the 2001 recession," points out Edward E. Leamer, professor of management, economics and statistics at the University of California, Los Angeles.[22]

Nevertheless, "this time troubles in housing will stay in housing," Leamer said. "An official recession cannot occur without job loss, but . . . outside of manufacturing and construction there is little or no job loss. . . . Though this is largely uncharted territory, it doesn't look like manufacturing is positioned to shed enough jobs to generate a recession."[23]

But other analysts are less hopeful.

Some large financial entities, such as hedge funds and institutional investors like pension funds, bought risky packages of subprime mortgages, which are now defaulting at high rates. Worse, some have borrowed a lot of money against these securities, which they can't pay back, spreading the financial pain farther, says financial consultant Cohan. Just how far isn't clear because "we have an unknown amount of money that's been borrowed against these securities, and nobody is willing to mark the [value] truthfully," Cohan says.

The mortgage meltdown is a replay of similar events in the 1970s and '80s, says home-building consultant Schultz, However, "the results are bigger this time because prices were higher."

Adjustable-rate loans will reset to higher interest rates over the next two years, "so during that time people will be wondering, 'How do I move from my home? Can I take such a big loss?' " says the University of New Haven's Rainish. "The resulting uncertainty will freeze up the whole system, and the economy could go into shock."

Retirement funds and other investors who buy mortgage-backed securities "now don't know how to value part of their portfolio," Rainish says. "How do you manage your portfolio if you can't put a value on it? . . . Some of them will go under. If you want to sell these securities, you'll have to sell them at 10 or 15 percent below their real value."

Harvard Professor of Economics Martin Feldstein, a former chairman of the Council of Economic Advisers, said, "If house prices now decline" to traditional levels, "there will be serious losses of household wealth and resulting declines in consumer spending. Since housing wealth is now about $21 trillion, even a 20-percent . . . decline would cut wealth by some $4 trillion and might cut consumer spending by $200 billion or about 1.5 percent of GDP. The multiplier consequences of this could easily push the economy into recession."[24]

BACKGROUND

Losing Homes

The beloved 1946 movie "It's a Wonderful Life," starring Jimmy Stewart and Donna Reed, revolves around the struggle of a small-town banker to help workers hold onto their homes in hard times. The movie provides the traditional image most Americans have of the mortgage business — "there's an S&L [savings & loan] and a borrower, and they know each other," says management consultant and venture-capitalist Cohan.

Today, that picture is way out of date, says Cohan. "There are many, many more players than there used to be," and what happens to mortgages in one U.S. town "has ripples that spread out into the national and even international economy," he says. Moreover, mortgage debt is a much larger piece of each home-owning American's financial picture than in the past.[25]

Before the Great Depression of the 1930s, local savings institutions like banks made mortgage loans, and a mortgage lasted for five to 10 years, after which the outstanding principal had to be paid, or the loan had to be refinanced.

During the Depression, however, as employment and house values plummeted, lenders worried about losing money and refused to refinance mortgages. As a result, lenders repossessed many homes when owners failed to make the big final payment. At the height of the Depression, almost 10 percent of homes were in foreclosure.

The federal government began a series of interventions that gradually changed the way home loans are made. The first such program — the Home Owners' Loan Corporation (HOLC), established in 1933 — bought defaulted mortgages from banks and other lending institutions and returned the houses to owners who'd been foreclosed upon, with new mortgages.

The new HOLC loans lasted 20 years and had fixed interest rates. The new mortgages also were fully amortizing — that is, borrowers paid off both principal and interest for the life of the loan and didn't face a large "balloon" payment of the remaining principal when the 20 years was up.

HOLC was disbanded in 1936. But Congress continued to enact laws to ease access to homeownership over the next several decades.

Because the government didn't want to be in the business of holding the HOLC mortgages, in 1936 Congress created the Federal Housing Administration (FHA) to sell mortgage insurance. To encourage private investors to buy packages of government-originated HOLC loans, borrowers paid premiums into an FHA insurance pool that would protect investors from losses if homeowners defaulted.

Beginning in 1938, Congress created several entities authorized to invest in packages of mortgages in order to free up money at traditional lending institutions, such as banks, so they could offer more mortgages. The Federal National Mortgage Association (known as Fannie Mae) opened in 1938, and the Federal Home Loan Mortgage Corporation (Freddie Mac) was created in 1970 to provide competition for Fannie Mae. Over the years, Fannie's and Freddie's mandate expanded from purchasing government-originated loans to purchasing mortgages from private institutions.

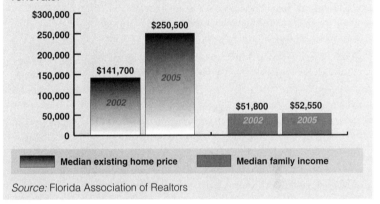

Florida Housing Prices Outraced Income Gains

Reflecting a nationwide trend, the median sales price of a single-family home in Florida increased 77 percent from 2002 to 2005 while incomes remained flat. As the cost of owning a home skyrocketed, more people turned to risky adjustable-rate or interest-only mortgages; many took on second mortgages to pay other bills or renovate.

Median existing home price: $141,700 (2002), $250,500 (2005)
Median family income: $51,800 (2002), $52,550 (2005)

Source: Florida Association of Realtors

U.S. home ownership — and the mortgage debt that goes with it — has grown over the years. In 1949, total mortgage debt equaled only 20 percent of total household income in the United States. By 2001, mortgage debt equaled 73 percent of income.

Selling Mortgages

While Fannie Mae and other government-initiated programs spurred home ownership, today's commercial mortgage market wasn't created until the 1990s, when more private investors became interested in buying up packages of home mortgages that were sold as financial assets — "securitized." The influx of private money into the housing market helped trigger today's foreclosure problems for subprime loans.

For decades, most private investors were reluctant to invest in packaged mortgages — mortgage-backed securities — "because they would have been bearing the full risk" should homeowners default, as a few inevitably will, says Jay Hartzell, an associate professor of real-estate finance at the University of Texas, Austin.

During the 1990s, however, financial institutions became more adept at "structuring" the securities: slicing up a single mortgage package — totaling hundreds or thousands of loans — into several investment vehicles, or tranches, with a range of risk.

CHRONOLOGY

1930s-1970s *After thousands of Americans lose their houses during the Great Depression, the federal government establishes programs to support home ownership.*

1933 Federal Home Owners Loan Corporation (HOLC) repurchases foreclosed homes, reinstates former mortgages.

1936 Federal Housing Administration (FHA) is created to insure HOLC mortgages so that investors will buy them.

1938 Federal National Mortgage Association — Fannie Mae — is founded as a "government-sponsored enterprise" to invest in mortgages, freeing up funds for lenders to make more home loans.

1944 Veterans' Bill of Rights creates a home-loan program for veterans.

1968 Truth in Lending Act passes, requiring lenders to informer borrowers about key terms in their loans. . . . Fannie Mae becomes a private, shareholder-owned company.

1970 Freddie Mac (Federal Home Loan Mortgage Corporation) joins Fannie Mae as a "secondary mortgage market," freeing up lenders' cash to offer more loans.

1974 Congress enacts Equal Credit Opportunity Act to stem lending discrimination against minority borrowers and others. . . . Real Estate Settlement Procedures Act requires lenders to give "good-faith estimates" of mortgage closing costs.

1980s-1990s *Adjustable-rate, interest-only and low down-payment mortgages become popular, spurring private investors to buy mortgage-backed securities. . . . Loans purchased by FHA, Fannie Mae and Freddie Mac decrease as a proportion of housing market.*

1989 First Bush administration and Congress act to bail out the savings and loan industry after S&Ls around the country make bad investments and collapse.

1992 Federal Reserve Bank of Boston concludes that low-income and minority neighborhoods face abusive lending practices and bias from borrowers.

2000s *House prices rise faster than inflation or incomes, and many homeowners take on second mortgages to pay other bills. Investors pour cash into the housing market, leading lenders to offer subprime mortgages, some of which don't document borrowers' incomes. Risky lending and soaring prices create a home-foreclosure crisis.*

2003 New mortgages are written worth $4 trillion.

2004 Federal Reserve Bank raises interest rates, causing a 26 percent drop in new home loans.

2005 Federal Reserve Chairman Alan Greenspan says that "without calling the overall national issue a [housing] bubble, it's pretty clear that it's an unsustainable underlying pattern." . . . Average house price grows more than three times faster than disposable income. . . . Delinquent payments and foreclosures rise. . . . House prices increase 49 percent over 2004 in Las Vegas; 43 percent in Phoenix. . . . Subprime loans make up 20 percent of new mortgages, up from 8 percent in 2003. . . . Forty percent of existing mortgages are refinanced.

2006 New Fed Chairman Ben S. Bernanke says housing market will "cool but not change very sharply." . . . New home construction drops. . . . Mortgage lender Ownit Mortgage Solutions files for bankruptcy. . . . Housing-finance giant Fannie Mae pays $400-million fine on accounting-fraud charges. . . . Risky new mortgages, like interest-only loans and loans that don't require documentation of the borrowers' income account for 13 percent of new mortgages, up from 2 percent in 2003.

2007 Mortgage lenders including New Century Financial, the second-largest subprime lender, file for bankruptcy. . . . Standard & Poor's and other securities-rating agencies downgrade securities backed by subprime mortgages. . . . Mortgage-market problems cause earnings to fall at major investment banks like Bear Stearns and Goldman Sachs; Merrill Lynch posts an $8-billion loss in the third quarter. . . . IDK, a German bank, slashes its earnings targets due to heavy losses on U.S. subprime investments. . . . In May, foreclosure filings are up 90 percent from May 2006.

Dec. 6 — President Bush announces a plan to temporarily freeze the mortgage terms of a limited number of debtors holding adjustable-rate mortgages.

2008

March 1-June 18 — More than 400 people, including buyers, sellers and others across the industry, are arrested for mortgage fraud in a nationwide FBI sting.

March 6 — Mortgage Bankers Association says 7.9 percent of mortgage loans are past due or in foreclosure, an all-time high.

March 16 — JP MorganChase acquires Bear Stearns after credit-default swaps push Bear into dire straits. Federal Reserve provides $30 billion as backing for the deal.

June 18 — Sen. Christopher Dodd, D-Conn., proposes housing bailout to the Senate that would assist troubled subprime mortgage lenders.

July 30 — President Bush signs Housing and Economic Recovery Act to aid subprime borrowers.

Sept. 7 — Federal government takes over Fannie Mae and Freddie Mac.

Sept. 15 — Lehman Brothers files for bankruptcy protection after collapse from credit-default swaps.

Sept. 17 — Federal Reserve lends $85 billion to AIG to keep it from bankruptcy following decline in value of credit-default swaps stemming from mortgage crisis.

Sept. 25 — FDIC seizes Washington Mutual, and its banking assets are sold to JP MorganChase. WaMu's home-loan division closed nearly half of its offices in December 2007 following subprime losses.

Oct. 3 — President Bush signs the Emergency Economic Stabilization Act, creating $700 billion Troubled Asset Relief Program (TARP) to purchase failing bank assets, primarily mortgage-backed securities.

Nov. 12 — Treasury Secretary Paulson abandons plan to purchase toxic assets under TARP. Remaining $140 billion in the fund allocated for recapitalizing financial companies.

Nov. 24 — Federal government agrees to rescue Citigroup after stock plummets 60 percent in one week.

2010

April 16 — SEC sues Goldman Sachs for failure to disclose information on mortgage-backed collateralized debt obligations that were allegedly "designed to fail" in 2007.

May 12 — RealtyTrac reports that nationwide foreclosures dropped from the previous year for the first time since January 2005.

July 15 — Goldman settles SEC charges for $550 million.

July 21 — President Obama signs Dodd-Frank Wall Street Reform and Consumer Protection Act, enacting widespread changes in the country's financial services industry; law sets standards for residential loans and curbs predatory lending.

July 29 — More than one in every 100 homes were in foreclosure during the first six months of 2010, according to RealtyTrac.

Elderly, Rural and Minority Borrowers Are Easy Targets

Lenders add extra fees, omit key information.

Some mortgage lenders have taken advantage of the housing boom to saddle borrowers with loans they can't afford, especially in minority neighborhoods.

It's easy to take advantage of people when it comes to mortgages, says Robert Schultz, a Boca Raton, Fla., home-building consultant. Some lenders have pushed loans that were too good to be true, taking advantage of many borrowers' lack of financial savvy, "much like the credit-card industry trolls through college campuses and preys on kids' taste for instant gratification and the fact that they're not skilled in the ways of finance," says Schultz.

Higher interest "subprime" mortgages are generally offered to borrowers with poor credit. High interest rates on such loans protect lenders against the much higher probability that people with bad credit histories will default. But some lenders not only deceive borrowers about the true nature of the loans they're getting but also add in extra fees. Furthermore, in minority and rural communities, borrowers often are targeted for extremely expensive loans even though their incomes and credit histories would qualify them for lower-cost mortgages.

Some mortgage brokers have steered people into loans they clearly couldn't afford simply "because [the brokers] get the fees up front," says Sandra Phillips, an assistant professor of finance at Syracuse University. "Brokers got credit for volume, so the more you did, the more you got paid by banks."

In today's complex mortgage market, it's easy to slip costly loan provisions past borrowers, says Meghan Burns, co-founder of OfferAngel, a Scottsdale, Ariz., company that reviews and clarifies the terms of a mortgage offer for consumers. Federal rules about what lenders must disclose to borrowers "came out years ago, but meanwhile about 300 mortgage products have come out that weren't dreamed of" when the disclosure rules were written, says Burns.

"A house loan is much more complicated than a car loan, for example," and the disclosure rules make it easy for lenders to simply slip in some hair-raising provisions, she says. For example, lenders aren't required to flatly state in writing whether a mortgage carries a prepayment penalty — which socks the borrower with a substantial fee if they try to sell or refinance a property before a specified number of years have elapsed, says Burns.

Some brokers falsify borrower information on loan applications, sometimes with the borrowers' consent, sometimes without it, says real-estate developer Robert Sheridan, of River Forest, Ill. Lenders reassured borrowers that "we'll help you cook the books" to qualify for a loan, "and if people said they were worried about taking out too big a loan, they said, 'Don't worry! You can refinance!'" says Sheridan. But the reassurance about refinancing often wasn't true, he says. Prepayment penalties prevent borrowers from refinancing, and refinancing doesn't work if home prices don't rise, he says.

"More than ever, I'm seeing junk fees — unnecessary charges that lenders add to borrowers' bills to pad their own profits — and bigger junk fees than ever before," says Carolyn Warren, author of *Mortgage Ripoffs and Money*

"You take the same loan package, and you say the first 10 percent of the [mortgage] payments go to investors in this security — and it becomes the triple-A-rated, safest security in which the investors will always get paid," regardless of how many borrowers default, explains Rainish of the University of New Haven. That top-level security provides the lowest dollar payouts, but the payment is guaranteed, no matter what the level of default on the loans as a whole.

Then successive layers of security risk are carved out — each with a lesser guarantee of being paid in full but with a higher payout if they do, he says.

"Once people are able to buy the amount of the risk they want, more become willing to invest," says Hartzell.

"Nobody who was risk-averse" would buy mortgage-backed securities before the risk was segmented, explains Rainish. Once selling mortgage packages with different

Savers. "A document-preparation fee! It's ridiculous," Warren says. "As if, otherwise, they weren't going to prepare documents at the end! It's like a restaurant charging you for a napkin. When I see a $695 processing fee, that's price gouging."

In addition, "a whole group of people inappropriately has been steered to more expensive loans" than they actually qualified for, says Corey Stone, CEO of Pay Rent, Build Credit, an Annapolis, Md., company that helps people rehabilitate bad credit histories.

Most people who've been steered to the worst loans are the nation's most vulnerable people — elderly, rural and minority residents who have less access to traditional financial institutions like banks than other Americans.

"The accumulated home equity and limited incomes of older homeowners have made them a primary target for predatory lending," said Jean Constantine-Davis, senior attorney for the AARP Foundation, a research group operated by the large seniors' lobby AARP. Predatory lenders often target elderly homeowners with pitches to refinance their homes to get extra cash to pay bills, she said.[1]

"One gentlemen, an 86-year-old stroke victim in a wheelchair, had a tax return that described him as a computer programmer who made $30,000 a year," said Constantine-Davis. Brokers and lenders had worked together to fabricate his and other tax returns to make it appear that elderly people "could afford mortgages whose monthly payments, in some cases, exceeded their incomes. Because our clients had owned their homes for decades, they had equity, and that was all the lender cared about."

Rural residents, who have limited access to banks, are among those heavily targeted by predatory lenders, according to the University of New Hampshire's Carsey Institute. In 2002, for example, rural borrowers were 20 percent more likely than urban residents to have mortgages that would sock them with large prepayment penalties if they paid off the loans or tried to refinance them.[2]

Minority borrowers are the most likely to have mortgages with oppressive terms, and many minority borrowers are pushed into expensive, subprime loans even though their incomes and credit histories qualify them for better interest rates.

In a study based on 2005 data, both African-Americans and Hispanics of all income levels were at least twice as likely to have high-cost loans as whites.[3]

In 2005, 52 percent of mortgages to blacks, 40 percent of mortgages to Hispanics, and only 19 percent of loans to whites were high-cost loans, said the Rev. Jesse L. Jackson.[4]

In New York City, 44 percent of mortgages in middle-income, predominantly black neighborhoods were subprime, compared to only 15 percent of the loans in economically comparable white neighborhoods, according to a 2002 study conducted for Sen. Charles E. Schumer, D-N.Y. "In other words, a significant proportion of black residents in New York City are being unnecessarily channeled into more expensive financing," said the report.[5]

This past summer the National Association for the Advancement of Colored People (NAACP) filed a class-action suit against more than a dozen mortgage companies — including Ameriquest, H&R Block's Option One, and Bear Stearns investment bank's Encore Credit — alleging "systematic, institutionalized racism in making home-mortgage loans."[6]

---

[1] Jean Constantine-Davis, testimony before the Senate Committee on Banking, Housing and Urban Affairs, Feb. 7, 2007.

[2] "Subprime and Predatory Lending in Rural America," Policy Brief No. 4, Carsey Institute, University of New Hampshire, fall 2006.

[3] "NAACP Subprime Discrimination Suit," *Mortgage News Daily*, July 16, 2007, www.mortgagenewsdaily.com.

[4] Testimony before Senate Committee on Banking, Housing and Urban Affairs, Feb. 7, 2007.

[5] "Capital Access 2002: Lending Patterns in Black and White Neighborhoods Tell a Tale of Two Cities, www.senate.gov/~schumer/SchumerWebsite/pressroom/special_reports/cap%20access%202002.pdf.

[6] "NAACP Subprime Discrimination Suit," *op. cit.*

---

risk levels became widespread practice, however, "we have all this money flowing in" to housing lenders, he says. "We've created a money machine."

But the machine had flaws, says Rainish. Investors didn't really know how risky a buy they were making, a fact that has already led some investment funds to fail and now threatens further instability in financial markets. Bad mortgage loans, which in the past would have affected only a local bank or S&L, now have potential repercussions around the world.

"This is what happened [last summer] with two of [investment bank] Bear Stearns' hedge funds, which placed highly leveraged bets on packages of subprime-mortgage derivative products," says the British financial Web site Market Oracle. "When the value and creditworthiness of these bond packages . . . was cut due to the subprime

Home Values Always Go Up, Right?

Millions of Americans are discovering otherwise.

Between 1890 and 1997, inflation-adjusted house prices in the United States stayed roughly flat. But since around 1998, they've climbed each year, rising about 6 percent annually above inflation, according to Yale University Professor of economics and finance Robert J. Shiller.[1]

This unprecedented housing boom has helped create an urban myth — that home prices always rise, say economists. That idea is in for a severe test, however, as a wave of defaults on home mortgages builds, and the housing market undergoes huge changes.

Over the past several years, many Americans have used novel loan types — such as adjustable-rate mortgages (ARMs) and interest-only mortgages — to buy "more house" than they would have thought they could afford. Such loans have artificially low payments for the first several months or years, and borrowers gamble that, when it comes time for payments to rise, they can refinance into a different loan on the strength of their now much higher home value or sell the house for a profit.

Office manager Chaundra Carnes and her husband Michael, a winery production manager, purchased a $950,000 house just north of San Francisco in 2005 with a $700,000 interest-only mortgage. In the past, the couple's combined $100,000-a-year salary would have been considered far too low to afford the house, but their interest-only loan has low payments and they figured that, before higher payments came due, they'd be able to refinance or sell the house at a profit, as they had with three previous homes.[2]

"The only risk is if housing values go down," Chaundra said at the time. "And I guess that's a risk we're willing to take. And I think a lot of other people are too. So we're not alone."[3]

Today, however, the downside of that risk is around the corner, financial analysts say.

U.S. home prices peaked in the first quarter of 2006 and have since fallen 3.4 percent, said Shiller. Although that drop doesn't seem severe, "when there are declines, they may be muted at first" because "home sellers tend to hold out for high prices when prices are falling," Shiller said. "The 17 percent decline in the volume of U.S. existing home sales since the peak in volume of sales in 2005 is evidence that this is happening now."

It should have been clear that the recent, drastic run-up in house prices couldn't continue forever, because people don't have unlimited funds to spend on housing, even though easy mortgage terms made it seem they did, say some real-estate experts.

"The mismatch between income gains and higher real-estate values in some cities is particularly striking," said Jonathan Miller, CEO of the Manhattan-based real-estate appraisal firm Miller Samuel. "How can someone earning $70,000 a year afford a $500,000 home? They can't over the long run."[4]

The price boom began in metropolitan areas of California, the Northeast, and Florida, then spread inland, said Sheila C. Bair, chairman of the Federal Deposit Insurance Corporation. But "while home prices were effectively doubling in . . . boom markets, median incomes grew much more slowly, severely reducing the affordability of

defaults . . . the effect . . . was to virtually wipe out the total value of the funds that had been rated as low risk."[26]

Security risk was determined based on historical models predicting that between 5 and 10 percent of the mortgages would default, says Rainish. "But fraud and the lack of adequate underwriting" — documenting borrowers' finances and income to be sure they could make the payments — "changed the results," he says. "Investors did not anticipate that the underwriting standards would be changed to the degree they have been."

Determining risk involves seeing how many mortgages have defaulted in the past, then adding any important new factors into your calculation, says Yildiray Yildirim, an associate professor of finance at Syracuse. As the mortgage market heated up, "they didn't use the correct models" to gauge risk, and "some hedge funds and others trading these securities don't even have" a predictive model, he says. "If they see something they think will make money, they go after it."

Among the overlooked factors was how many subprime borrowers — most of whom have poor credit and low home ownership, despite the benefit of historically low interest rates," she said.[5]

But while recent prices may not be strictly "affordable" for the average American, easy mortgage terms blinded many to that reality and led to real-estate bidding wars that drove up prices all over. Good old-fashioned optimism, plus greed, played a role.

For most people who get into trouble, "it's not so much that they shouldn't have bought a house but that they shouldn't have bought such an expensive house," says Seattle-based Carolyn Warren, author of *Mortgage Ripoffs and Money Savers*. "Instead of tailoring their house demands to their budget, they fell in love with a house and then had to take a teaser rate to afford it, and then hope," she says.

Real-estate speculators also helped to drive up prices, says home-building consultant Robert Schultz, of Boca Raton, Fla. In earlier housing booms, flipping — buying a house in order to quickly sell it for a higher price — was relatively rare, says Schultz. But in the 2000s boom, flipping ran rampant. "The loans were so much easier to get this time," says Schultz.

"The number of pure speculators" was much higher than reported: "30 or 40 percent is my gut feeling," says real-estate developer Robert Sheridan, of River Forest, Ill.

With so many bidders in the game, it's no wonder that prices were driven sky-high, Schultz and Sheridan say.

The fact that house and condo prices have soared compared to the rest of the economy has been hidden by the way the government reports statistics, says University of Denver Professor of Law Robert Hardaway. "There was a purposeful 1983 decision to take house prices out" of the *Consumer Price Index* (CPI), he says.

"The decision was rationalized this way: People don't buy houses every year, so the cost of houses shouldn't be factored into the annual rise of the cost of living," Hardaway says. "But they do buy every six or seven years," he says.

At the same time, with speculators buying up houses they didn't plan to live in, rental properties flooded the market, driving rents down — and rents do get counted in the CPI, Hardaway says. "This makes it seem as if the price of living is rising even more slowly, but this is fraudulent. In fact, the real inflation rate is 15 percent when you put in housing."

Perhaps the most pernicious effect of skyrocketing prices was that it increased the temptation to borrow against homes' value to finance other wants. But if prices fall, a homeowner can end up unable to move without taking a huge loss and paying interest on their original loan many times over.

"Don't use your house as a piggybank for financing inessential things," says Warren. "You need to preserve your precious home equity or you'll end up like the 70-year-old who said to me, 'My bills are killing me! Can I do a debt consolidation?' He had [borrowed so many times on his house that he had] a mortgage of $350,000 even though he'd bought his house 30 years ago for $40,000."

The bottom line on home values is this, says Robert Losey, chairman of the Department of Finance at American University in Washington, D.C., where home prices have skyrocketed: "What goes up doesn't have to come down, but it usually does."

[1] Robert J. Shiller, "Understanding Recent Trends in House Prices and Home Ownership," paper presented to Federal Reserve Bank of Kansas City symposium, Jackson Hole, Wyo., September 2007.

[2] Quoted on "NOW," Public Broadcasting Service, Aug. 26, 2005, www.pbs.org/now/transcript/transcriptNOW134_full.html.

[3] *Ibid.*

[4] Jonathan J. Miller, "Unraveling the Pyramid of Bad Practices," Soapbox blog, Dec. 19, 2005, http://soapbox.millersamuel.com/?p=119.

[5] Testimony before House Financial Services Committee, Sept. 5, 2007.

incomes — default on their loans after low "teaser" interest rates on their ARMs expired, Yildirim says.

Insecure Securities

Current accounting standards also encouraged non-bank lenders to write unusually risky mortgages, making it harder for investors to discern the true value of the mortgage-backed securities, says John D. Rossi, associate professor of accounting at Moravian College in Bethlehem, Pa.

A mortgage is essentially a liability for a lender until it's paid off in full, and traditionally it would be listed as such on lenders' account books, where auditors and potential creditors could use it to judge organizations' financial health. However, once a non-bank mortgage lender has "sold" mortgages to investors, current rules allow the lender to erase them from its books, even if the securities were sold on the promise that the lender would absorb some losses, should the mortgages default, Rossi explains.

How to Avoid Mortgage Troubles

Do's and don'ts for would-be homeowners.

Using common sense and being skeptical of hype can help you avoid mortgage trouble, experts say. Among the housing do's and don'ts:

- **Don't be in a hurry to buy.** "If you're going to move in two or three years, you should rent," says Robert Losey, chairman of the Department of Finance at American University in Washington, D.C. Switching houses carries "quite substantial transition costs" — as much as 3 to 4 percent of a home's value, he says.
- **Don't tap into home equity for non-essential purposes.** Second mortgages can mean trouble if home prices fall or you need to move. "You should think of your home as the place you live in, not something you should make money on," says Margaret Mann, head of the restructuring and insolvency practice at Heller Ehrman, a San Francisco law firm.
- **Shop for a house based on what you can afford.** "If buyers would tailor their desires to their budgets," home prices wouldn't rise sky high and lenders wouldn't offer dangerous mortgages like adjustable-rate and interest-only loans, says Carolyn Warren, author of *Mortgage Ripoffs and Money Savers.* Too often, "a person gets preapproved by a lender for $350,000, but the real-estate agent comes back and asks to get them approved for $399,000," saying "they really want this sunken Jacuzzi," says Warren. That means a riskier loan and a skyward jump in local home prices, she says.
- **Remember that a lender's "good faith estimate" is just that, an estimate,** says Meghan Burns, co-founder of OfferAngel, a Scottsdale, Ariz., company that checks out mortgages for prospective home buyers. "The borrower takes it as gospel, thinking the estimate is a contract, but it's not," she says. "If you have somebody who's trying to lure you in" to a bad loan, "that's the bait in the bait-and-switch."
- **Watch for the signs** of predatory lenders, such as encouraging borrowers to lie about their income or assets to get a bigger loan; charging fees for unnecessary services; pressuring borrowers to accept higher-risk mortgages like interest-only loans; pressuring people in need of cash to refinance their homes; and using high-pressure sales tactics.[1]

---

[1] U.S. Department of Housing and Urban Development, www.hud.gov/offices/hsg/sfh/buying/loanfraud.cfm.

Being able to take loans off their books increased the likelihood that lenders would engage in shoddier underwriting and make riskier loans, says Rossi. "Most likely it made them a lot less diligent," he says.

Securities-ratings agencies, like Standard & Poor's and Moody's Investors Service, rate securities based on risk. But the rating system broke down in the past few years, especially for mortgage-backed securities, many financial analysts say.

Based on the history of mortgage-backed securities, ratings agencies were listing subprime mortgage-backed securities as "A" grade — safe investments — when they were actually "B" grade — high risk, says Rainish. "The ratings agencies have been blindsided as much as others. They were pricing in a different world," he says.

Other analysts say ratings agencies and investors bear much of the blame for their woes.

"Wall Street and rating agencies, rather than state regulators or even lenders, largely decide what types of borrowers obtain subprime loans and how the loan products . . . are designed," Kurt Eggert, a professor at Chapman University School of Law in Orange, Calif., told the Senate Subcommittee on Securities, Insurance and Investments in April. But "unlike government agencies, ratings agencies work . . . in their own financial self-interest and . . . at the behest of investors and do not have the mandate to ensure consumer protection," he said.[27]

"In the end, Wall Street creates a demand for particular mortgages; underwriting criteria for these mortgages [are] set to meet this demand and [the] underwriting criteria, not the mortgage originator, [dictate] whether a consumer qualifies for this particular loan product," said Harry Dinham, president of the National Association of Mortgage Brokers.[28]

After lenders package mortgages into securities, ratings agencies "put a piece of gold wrapping paper around them," says venture capitalist Cohan. The agencies have a conflict of interest because "the investment banks shop the packages around and give the fee to the [agency] that gives the best rating," he says.

"I would be amazed if there weren't massive litigation" by investors against the ratings agencies down the line, says Illinois real-estate developer Sheridan. "They were advising clients how to put lipstick on the pig," and, "at a minimum, they sure didn't ring the fire alarm bell very quickly."

Ratings agencies reject such accusations.

The "issuer-pays business model" does have "potential conflicts of interest," acknowledged Michael Kanef, managing director of Moody's Investors Service Group, to the House Subcommittee on Capital Markets, Insurance, and Government-Sponsored Enterprises on Sept. 27. However, "we believe we have successfully managed" the conflicts by not paying analysts based on revenue earned by companies they rate, posting ratings methodologies on a public Web site, and having a separate analysis team monitor all rated securities on an ongoing basis."[29]

Easy Money

More private investors willing to invest in mortgage-backed securities gave lenders an incentive to make more loans. Easy money — and new 1990s technology that allowed financial institutions to automate credit checks and vary interest rates in real time — led lenders to create mortgages that made home ownership seem more affordable.

Investors' interest in mortgage-backed securities increased after the 1990s technology boom went bust, says Ashton, the assistant professor of urban planning and policy at the University of Illinois. With investors wary of stocks and lenders "figuring out ways to help more and more people afford homes, suddenly the subprime mortgage market looked like a good place to park your capital," he says.

Non-U.S. investment also has flowed into housing. In the developing economies of China and India, "people save a lot of income, they're unsure about their future" and that money needs to be invested, says economist Goodfriend. Oil-producing countries flush with cash from rising oil prices have provided another pot of housing investment, he says.

Finally, to keep the overall economy moving, Federal Reserve Bank Chairman Alan Greenspan kept interest rates at historically low levels for three years, until June 2004, when he began raising them again. Although the Fed sets interest rates only for bank-to-bank money transfers, other lenders take their cue from the Fed rate, and mortgage interest also hit historic lows.

In the 1970s and '80s, interest rates in double digits were the norm, soaring to over 20 percent in 1980. In the 1990s, interest on a 30-year, fixed-rate mortgage hovered between 7 percent and 9 percent. Beginning in 2003, however, rates dropped below 6 percent and have hovered at around 6 percent since, according to the mortgage-information Web site Lender 411.[30]

The Federal Reserve "wanted to prevent inflation, but in doing that they made homeownership dirt cheap," says the University of New Haven's Rainish.

Low interest rates created a surge in mortgage demand between 2001 and 2003, especially for refinancings that allowed homeowners to lower their interest payments and tap into extra cash at the same time, said Emory W. Rushton, senior deputy comptroller and chief national bank examiner in the U.S. Office of the Comptroller of the Currency.

Surging demand prompted "lenders to expand their operations to boost capacity" and "attracted new market participants, often lenders with little business experience or financial strength," and a flood of new, risky mortgages ensued, Rushton told the Senate Banking Committee in March.[31]

As a result, "Lots of people in the United States who have no money — they are called subprime borrowers — borrowed 100 percent of the value of a house right at the top of a housing market which has since fallen sharply," wrote Paul Tustain, founder of a British investment-information Web site, BullionVault.com. With higher interest and a lower home value, many of these people can't make their new payments or refinance their houses.[32]

"The whole system allowed the frailty of human nature to triumph," says home-building consultant Schultz. "It took away all the restraints."

CURRENT SITUATION
Widespread Pain

Beginning in late 2006 and continuing this year, the wheels came off the mortgage bus. The number of people defaulting — falling behind — on payments, then losing

Should the federal government impose stricter rules on the mortgage industry?

YES
Sen. Christopher J. Dodd, D-Conn.
Chairman, Senate Committee on Banking,
Housing and Urban Affairs

From a statement to the committee, Oct. 3, 2007

Today we are facing a serious meltdown in the subprime mortgage market. This crisis is the equivalent of a slow-motion, 50-state Katrina, taking people's homes one by one, devastating their lives and destroying their communities. As a result, 2.2 million families are in danger of losing their homes to foreclosures at a cost of over $160 billion in hard-earned home equity that should have been available to finance college educations, pay health-care expenses or [act] as a cushion against uncertainty.

President Bush and his administration need to get fully engaged. They need to press subprime servicers and lenders to modify loans into long-term, affordable mortgages. Where modifications are not possible, the administration must work with Fannie Mae and Freddie Mac to refinance troubled borrowers on fair and affordable terms.

In April, I convened a Homeownership Preservation Summit where a number of the largest subprime lenders and servicers pledged to do these modifications. Unfortunately, a recent report tells us that just 1 percent of subprime adjustable-rate mortgages have been modified. This is wholly inadequate, and the administration must work with us to press the lenders and servicers to live up to their obligation.

While we are focused today on how we can rescue homeowners that have been victimized by predatory practices, we are also mindful that we need to prevent these kinds of abuses in the future.

The federal regulators — the cops on the beat — must be far more aggressive in policing the markets. The Federal Reserve [Board] noted as early as 2003 that problems were developing. Yet, not until it came under intense pressure from the Congress did the Federal Reserve agree to meet its obligation under the Homeownership and Equity Protection Act to prohibit unfair or deceptive mortgage practices. The board has the power to put an end to many of the practices that have gotten us into this mess today. They ought to exercise that power, and they ought to do it comprehensively and quickly.

In addition, a number of us have introduced or outlined anti-predatory-lending legislation. Let me say, the measure of any legislation must be that it creates high lending standards for the subprime market, and it must include remedies and penalties sufficient to ensure those standards are adequately enforced. Today's crisis is a market failure. Legislation must reengineer that market so that it works to create long-term, sustainable and affordable homeownership.

NO
Rep. Tom Price, R-Ga.
Member, House Committee on Financial
Services

From a statement to the committee, Sept. 5, 2007

As anyone paying attention can tell you, we're seeing a dramatic increase in the actual number of foreclosures. To put the current "crisis" in perspective, according to the Mortgage Bankers Association in the first quarter of 2007 there are about 44 million mortgages in the U.S. and less than 14 percent of them are subprime. And only about 13 percent of those subprime mortgages are late on payments, with the majority of late payers working through their problems with the banks.

With approximately 561,857 mortgages in foreclosure — up from roughly 517,434 from the fourth quarter of 2006 — the subprime "meltdown" has given us an increase of 44,423 foreclosures. This still represents a small percentage of the number of home mortgages.

One of the main reasons we have seen a rise in foreclosures is that during the housing boom of the last few years, consumers with a higher credit risk qualified for mortgages. Now that those riskier loans are resetting to higher interest rates — a trend that will continue until April of 2008 — a credit crunch is occurring for home buyers. It will take time to determine which of the mortgage-backed securities contain "bad" loans and which don't, partially because the entire securitization process is relatively new and hasn't faced a challenge of this size.

A comprehensive consumer-advocacy-driven predatory-lending bill is not the answer. It is tantamount to fighting the last war and will only make the markets more skittish, as they have to react to new underwriting standards and liability issues, making the situation worse, not better. This would harm all consumers!

By the time a new "anti-predatory-lending" law goes into effect in the marketplace, this problem will already have changed, and we will be left with strict, national underwriting standards that will prohibit various loan products and banish a number of consumers to the rental market forever. This is not a goal that is responsible.

The American economy has more than enough liquidity and is plenty strong enough to weather this bump in the road. Congress should stay out of the way while the market corrects itself or it will only make matters worse. We saw last week just how strong the market is when the Commerce Department reported that the gross domestic product — the broadest measure of economic health — expanded at an annual rate of 4 percent in the April-June quarter, significantly higher than the 3.4-percent rate the government had initially estimated.

homes to foreclosure, is rising sharply. Some lenders have gone bankrupt, and some recent investors in mortgage-backed securities have seen their investments quickly become worthless.

The financial industry and its regulators "got complacent" as mortgage loans got riskier and riskier, says the University of New Haven's Rainish. "It wasn't until sometime in 2006 that some of this stuff was starting to smell. Prior to that, nobody really got the gist of the excess that was taking place. But in the latter half of 2006, the most recent securities that were sold defaulted almost immediately," he says.

Midwestern states like Ohio are "national leaders in foreclosures," says the University of Chicago's Ashton. These areas have been in economic hard times for years, as the auto and steel industries waned, says Rainish. "You're seeing an implosion of income" at the same time as cash-flush lenders offered risky loans, he says. "People wanted to fix up, so they refinanced" with ARMs. "Then there was reset [of interest to higher rates], and they lost their equity."

The presence of foreclosed homes in a neighborhood affects everybody there, Rainish says. "Nobody can sell a home, even when they need to. You freeze the whole market. On a personal level, it's tragic."

"Even though we talk about people walking away from homes" and in some cases losing only a little cash since they made small — or no — down payments, "the foreclosure keeps you from buying a home later, and there are legal and moving costs associated with foreclosure, too," says Ashton.

While Chicago is not one of the hardest-hit areas, "there were still a lot of subprime loans for moderate-to-middle-income households in African-American neighborhoods," Ashton says. "It may be years — if ever — before they can get back into a home."

In Florida, Nevada, parts of California and some other sought-after locales, "flippers" — real-estate speculators — are big players in the ongoing crisis, says Ashton. "We've got flippers and speculators simply walking away" from properties, since the loan cost them little in the first place, Ashton says. That leaves lenders holding the bag, he says.

Some banks are ending up as owners of condos whose developers couldn't sell the majority of units before housing sales slowed, says Sheridan.

Banks aren't permitted to permanently manage residential properties, so they must sell them, he says. Meanwhile, "residents who've already bought in are locked

Auctioneer Travis Toth, right, accepts bids for a foreclosed home on the steps of the Los Angeles County courthouse in Norwalk, Calif., on March 16, 2007. To help struggling homeowners stay put, the nation's biggest mortgage lender, Countrywide Financial Corp., is restructuring about 82,000 mortgages to make them more affordable.

into a property that isn't being cared for, whose value is deteriorating and which is likely to become a rental property," which is not what they plunked their money down for, says Sheridan. "The homeowner is not in a happy situation."

The selling and reselling of mortgage-loan packages to ever-more-distant investors may make it harder for some people facing foreclosure to work out a payment plan to keep their homes.

"How do you do a workout when nobody knows who owns what?" says Rainish. In the past, mortgages sold to a secondary market were in a big portfolio with Fannie Mae or Freddie Mac, organizations that are in the business of helping people stay in their houses. "Now the mortgages are owned by investment funds, by foreigners; they've been sold and resold," he says. "How are they going to deal with the workout? We don't know."

Nevertheless, "there still will be in almost every case a local institution that is the servicer" of the loan, says American University's Losey. "They don't have the same vested interest in working it out" as they did when local lenders held onto mortgages. Nevertheless, "I don't know that this means there will be that many more defaults or not," he says. "There should still be pressure from the institutions that own the securities to work out a logical deal."

Interest-Rate Cut

Debate rages over whether the government should bail out homeowners and whether strict new rules for mortgage lending should be created.

The first major action at the national level came from the Federal Reserve Board.[33]

In August and then again in September and late October, new Fed Chairman Ben S. Bernanke dropped key interest rates that make it easier for banks to lend money.[34] The moves came after the world's banks and other financial institutions began tightening credit, spooked by billion-dollar losses suffered by some banks and investment funds that had found their newly purchased mortgage-backed securities to be worthless. Banks became reluctant to loan to anyone, including other banks, because no one knows which institutions are holding the riskiest mortgage-backed securities.

But "the Federal Reserve's solution to the bubble" of rising house prices driven by easy money "is to keep the bubble going as long as possible," says Hardaway of the University of Denver, a critic of the move.

"It's like 17th-century Tulipmania in Holland," when high demand for the showy flowers led hundreds of frenzied speculators into the market, hoping to make a killing, Hardaway says. After prices for single bulbs rose to hundreds of dollars, the mania abruptly stopped as bidders worried that prices could not get any higher. Almost overnight, the price collapsed, bankrupting many middle-class people.[35]

"The Fed's policy is just like Holland: 'Let the mania continue, because if it stops, nobody else will be able to buy tulips,'" says Hardaway. "Better to let the bubble burst now," he argues. "That would flush out all excesses, like the 4-to-5-percent teaser [interest] rate, which is offered to people knowing they won't be able to afford it when it triples."

Others say the rate cut won't solve the problem but could keep it from worsening. "There's sludge in the system" as investors back away from securitized higher-risk mortgages, and "the Fed is reliquifying the system so banks can carry some new debt," says Rainish.

Government Role

Congress, the Bush administration, and several states are contemplating or have already acted to aid struggling homeowners and keep the housing market afloat.

Massachusetts, New York, Ohio, Pennsylvania, New Jersey and Maryland will build loan funds to help homeowners refinance. Ohio, and Pennsylvania will sell bonds to raise funds, for example.[36]

The federal Office of Federal Housing Enterprise Oversight (OFHEO) gave the green light Sept. 19 for Fannie Mae and Freddie Mac to increase the amount of mortgage loans they invest in by 2 percent annually, as private investors pull back.

The move was a big deal, given recent concerns about financial fraud at the two mortgage giants. In May 2006, OFHEO capped the size of Fannie Mae's portfolio after investigators said some Fannie Mae executives — since departed — had manipulated accounts to show higher earnings to get bonuses. Fannie Mae paid a $400-million fine in 2006. And in September Freddie Mac paid a $50-million fine to settle its own charges of accounting fraud.[37] Nevertheless, the Fannie Mae and Freddie Mac upticks aren't considered large enough to jumpstart the slowing housing market.

Alternative legislation introduced in October by Sen. Schumer and House Financial Services Committee Chairman Rep. Barney Frank, D-Mass., would do more and also would assist current owners trying to hold onto homes. It would raise investment caps for both Fannie Mae and Freddie Mac by 10 percent for six months and direct 85 percent of the money to refinancing subprime mortgages, mostly for low-income borrowers.[38]

Critics of the bill, including the Bush administration, argue that it would be a costly distraction from what they see as a need to reform Fannie and Freddie.

"Frank must know that a temporary increase in the portfolio limits . . . will reduce the pressure for comprehensive reform," said Peter J. Wallison, a resident fellow at the free-market-oriented American Enterprise Institute think tank.[39]

The administration supports another Democratic initiative — eliminating the tax that kicks in for a homeowner when a lender forgives some mortgage debt after a house is sold or a loan is restructured.

"Say you take out a $310,000 mortgage to buy a house and then you find you can't keep up the payments and the house gets sold for $250,000," says developer Sheridan. "The bank may, out of a sense of compassion, and because they can't collect the $60,000 shortfall anyway, simply write it off." That sounds like good news for the strapped consumer, but under current law that money becomes taxable income at tax rates as high as 30 or 40 percent, he says. "That's a $15,000 bill you won't have the money to pay."

Congressional Democrats and the White House have recommended eliminating the tax. Democrats would end the tax permanently and cut tax breaks for sales of some vacation and rental properties to pay it. The White House wants a temporary elimination and would retain the other tax breaks.[40]

President Bush also has announced a new Federal Housing Administration program, FHASecure, to offer FHA-insured loans to creditworthy borrowers who are delinquent on their mortgages. Delinquent borrowers were ineligible in the past.[41]

Congress also is debating new consumer protections. In September the House Financial Services Committee approved a bill giving several additional federal agencies a watchdog role over mortgage lending.[42] Several states, including Massachusetts, Maine, Minnesota and North Carolina, now require mortgage brokers to scrutinize would-be borrowers more carefully to ensure they can afford their loans.[43]

OUTLOOK

Hitting Bottom

One thing about fallout from the mortgage crisis is not in doubt: Washington will tighten some rules, says American University's Losey. "Congress reacts to crises," he says.

But the changes will come against a backdrop of stark financial pain and an end to giddy times in which people believed that house values would rise forever.

It will be two years or more before all existing ARMs reset, and only then will the extent of home losses be known, says the University of New Haven's Rainish. "For the subprime mortgage holders, the American dream will be crushed," he says. "Even many who have been making full payments won't be able to refinance because of pre-payment penalties" in many subprime mortgages.

He predicts the housing market will be slow for the next two to three years. "The investment community will take a $100-$200 billion haircut, and many people will be hurt. Consumption growth will be slowed."

To emerge from the other side of this crisis, we need house prices to contract 20 percent or even as much as 40 percent, says the University of Chicago's Ashton.

"That's not a painless process," as many homeowners may end up owing more than their houses are worth, Ashton says. Owners with ARMs as their first or second mortgages must either make huge monthly mortgage payments when rates reset or try to refinance. But most won't be able to get a new loan for the full amount of their debt, since falling prices will slash their equity.

"We may hit bottom [on home prices] in early 2009, and maybe 2010 in some markets," says Sheridan. "There'll be a long period of prices staying down."

Most if not all subprime borrowers would have been unable to seek loans except under the conditions of the past few years, "so now that whole demand has gone away," possibly permanently, says Margaret Mann, head of the restructuring and insolvency practice at San Francisco-based law firm Heller Ehrman.

"Builders have almost stopped building," and a glut of housing inventory sits in some markets, says Florida home-building consultant Schultz. In South Florida, for example, three to four years' worth of condo inventory already sits empty, he says. "I doubt that the demand will ever be back to the level of 2007. A lot of regional and national builders will have to scale back."

Commercial real estate could be next to go bust. New, empty office buildings with large construction debts and vacant retail malls are being reported around the country, according to Michael Shedlock, an investment consultant for SitkaPacific Capital Management, in Prairie Grove, Ill.

"Here we are, right near the tip top in commercial real-estate insanity where no price was too high to pay for a building on the silly belief that property values would continually rise," said Shedlock. "Given how rapidly investor psychology is changing in this sector, it won't take much now to send it over the edge."[44]

Furthermore, many analysts say it's only a matter of time before a new boom of risky loans and investments occurs again, followed by inevitable bust.

"People's memories are usually good for five to 10 years," says Hardaway at the University of Denver. "For that period of time, maybe they'll remember they should look at the collateral."

UPDATE

The outlook for the American housing industry in the summer of 2010 remained gloomy, with high foreclosure rates continuing to plague many regions and home sales sliding, despite a plunge in mortgage rates to a 50-year low. Fears of a double-dip recession crept higher.

One in 12 mortgages is seriously delinquent, and one in 10 is past due, according to the National Consumer Law Center. That translates to 4.56 million mortgage loans in default or some stage of foreclosure in June, according to LPS Applied Analytics, slightly fewer than in May. [45] Nevada, Arizona and Florida had the highest foreclosure rates, according to the business service RealtyTrac, while California, Florida, Michigan, Illinois and Nevada accounted for more than half of all U.S. foreclosures. [46] Nationwide, 154 of 206 metropolitan areas with at least 200,000 residents reported an annualized increase in foreclosures between January and June, RealtyTrac said.[47]

One Ohio homeowner became so desperate he bulldozed his $350,000 home to avoid having his bank foreclose on the property.[48]

The rising foreclosure rate has bolstered the rental market. MPF Research in Carrollton, Texas, said more people are renting as home purchases decline and younger residents look for places to live. The number of occupied apartments rose by 215,000 in the nation's 64 largest markets in the first half of the year, nearly twice as many units as were added throughout 2009, MPF said.[49]

New Home Sales Drop

Congress tried to stimulate housing sales with a first-time homebuyer tax credit, enacted in 2008 and expanded in 2009. But after the credit expired on April 30, 2010, new single-family home sales in May dropped more than 18 percent below the rate a year earlier, indicating that the tax credit's boost lacked staying power.[50] The inventory of unsold homes increased by 2.5 percent in June, according to the National Association of Realtors, and reached its highest level since August 2009.

Home sales, a traditional engine of economic growth, have failed to provide much firepower to the nation's overall recovery from recession. The July Economic Outlook report from Fannie Mae's Economics and Mortgage Analysis Group noted that the country had "shifted into a lower gear in economic expansion," with projected 2010 growth rates falling from 3.2 percent to 2.8 and housing losing its traditional stimulative effect. "We believe that residential investment will have a neutral effect on economic growth this year, which makes the current recovery quite unusual," wrote Fannie Mae chief economist Doug Duncan. "Housing has historically played a significant role in leading the country out of recession."[51]

The housing outlook "remains very uncertain," Yelena Shulyatyeva, an analyst at BNP Paribas. "Only when jobs start being created at a sufficient pace will potential home buyers get back to the market, and home sales return to sustainable healthy levels."[52]

Action in Congress

Efforts on Capitol Hill to address many of the underlying causes of the recession, including abuses in the mortgage-lending field, have done little to quell consumer unease and stimulate home sales.

When President Barack Obama signed the Dodd-Frank Wall Street Reform and Consumer Protection Act into law on July 21, 2010, the measure was hailed as the most far-reaching financial reform legislation in more than seven decades. Two years in the making, the legislation was a response to the history-making financial system meltdown (expected by only a few Wall Street insiders) that had at its core a housing bubble. The crisis that gathered in the fall of 2008 slashed housing and stock prices worldwide and eventually cost U.S. households $17 trillion, according to May 2010 congressional testimony by Treasury Department chief economist Alan Krueger.[53]

Major elements of the multi-pronged Wall Street Reform and Consumer Protection Act will affect businesses and financial firms. Most relevant to existing and aspiring homeowners, the law created a Bureau of Consumer Financial Protection within the Federal Reserve to regulate mortgages and credit cards, and included new restrictions on the selling of adjustable-rate mortgages. The bill requires mortgage companies to verify that borrowers can repay loans; penalize irresponsible lenders; end penalties for paying off a mortgage ahead of schedule; and broaden consumers' ability to access their credit scores.[54]

The law did not, however, overhaul mortgage giants Fannie Mae and Freddie Mac, the government-sponsored enterprises that for decades have made mortgage money more available by bundling mortgages and selling them to investors. The government took over both Freddie Mac and Fannie Mae in September 2008, at a cost to taxpayers of almost $150 billion. Despite pleas from Republicans (who for the most part opposed the overall Dodd-Frank bill), Democratic leaders shied away from fixing Freddie and Fannie because it would be "too complicated."[55] In general Democrats favor the mission of these two quasi-public entities in making more mortgage money available, while Republicans tend to oppose their competing with private lenders.[56]

Republican Critics

The Dodd-Frank bill drew heavy criticism from key Republicans. Sen. Bob Corker, R-Tenn., who spent months working on the financial reforms only to vote against the final product, blasted it in a July 15 press release: "Housing and mortgage finance policies — the root causes of the meltdown and the greatest symptoms of the correction — were left largely unaddressed in the bill," Corker said. "There is no doubt that we needed to address consumer protection, but instead of doing so appropriately, this bill creates a mammoth new government agency with dangerous, unchecked powers and enormous taxpayer monies at its disposal."

The Fairfax, Va.-based National Association of Mortgage Brokers expressed its disappointment that the law will mean "higher costs to the consumers and continued job loss for small businesses in the mortgage industry." In a statement, NAMB President William Howe complained that "consumers will only have two choices at the closing table: to come up with thousands of dollars to pay for closing costs out of their pocket . . . or to roll all of their closing costs into their interest rate."

In an interview, Howe said Congress had overreacted in limiting the conditions under which a lender can offer an adjustable-rate mortgage. "What if I want to retire in five years and move north? I'd do a five-year ARM because it would be worth it to" get a lower mortgage rate for a few years, he said. ARMs got a bad name in recent years when some borrowers were encouraged to select pay options that eventually put them in negative

High foreclosure rates plague many parts of the United States in the aftermath of the 2008 meltdown on Wall Street, and a nationwide housing slump continues despite a drop in mortgage rates to a 50- year low. One in 10 mortgages — a total of more than 4.5 million loans — is past due; Nevada, Florida and Arizona had the highest foreclosure rates in June.

financial footing, he added. "But had the housing market not dropped, ARMs would have been a non-issue."

Kathleen Day, spokesperson for the Center for Responsible Lending, said the NAMB's complaints are a "scare tactic" from a group that is "whining because the law ends a lot of tricks the mortgage industry used to price-gouge consumers, which torpedoed the economy." She applauded the new law for ending "hidden explosion" and "teaser rates" for ARMs and subprime mortgages whose major purpose, she said, was less to boost homeownership than to get consumers to keep

Marc Joseph, the owner of Foreclosures 'R Us realty company, displays a map showing foreclosed properties to prospective buyers as they motor down a canal during a foreclosure boat tour last year in Cape Coral, Fla.

refinancing to deliver profits to the lending industry. "Nine out of 10 of those who got bad subprime mortgages already owned their home," she says.

Consumer Protection Bureau

Day also supports the new Bureau of Consumer Financial Protection that has prompted much opposition from regulation-wary Republicans. Previously, multiple entities with responsibility for consumer protection, such as the Federal Deposit Insurance Corp., the Comptroller of the Currency, Office of Thrift Supervision and the Federal Reserve, were "cheerleaders for the industry, and the banks shopped for the most lenient one," she says. "Now the [consumer-protection bureau] will have all consumer regulation concentrated in one place."

Much of the law's impact will be determined by the myriad regulations to be written over the next few years. That is one reason the National Association of Realtors worked closely with Congress to shape the bill, winning, for example, an exemption for agents, brokers and other real estate professionals from regulation by the new consumer bureau. But it lost its bid to remove from the bill new limits on the number of "points" or fees that lenders can charge mortgage consumers at settlement.

Despite the financial gloom and a new frugality trend that, Census Bureau data suggest, favors renting, Americans haven't given up on the dream of home ownership.[57] The Fannie Mae National Housing Survey, conducted between December 2009 and January 2010, polled homeowners and renters to assess their confidence in homeownership as an investment, the current state of their household finances, views on the U.S. housing-finance system and overall confidence in the economy. It found that two-thirds of Americans (65 percent) still prefer owning a home.[58]

NOTES

1. Delores King, testimony before Senate Committee on Banking, Housing and Urban Affairs, February 2007.

2. Eric Stein, testimony before House Judiciary Subcommittee on Commercial and Administrative Law, Sept. 25, 2007.

3. "What's Ahead for Financial Markets?" Knowledge@ Wharton electronic newsletter, Oct. 3, 2007, http://knowledge.wharton.upenn.edu.

4. David Cho, "Huge Mortgage Lender Files for Bankruptcy," *The Washington Post*, April 3, 2007, p. A1.

5. "Subprime Mess Hits Wall Street Again," *Mortgage News Daily*, www.mortgagenewsdaily.com, June 25, 2007.

6. Doug Noland, "Structured Finance Under Duress," *Asia Times online*, Oct. 30, 2007, www.atimes.com/atimes/Global_Economy/IJ30Dj02.html.

7. Robert J. Shiller, "Understanding Recent Trends in House Prices and Home Ownership," paper presented at the Jackson Hole symposium of the Federal Reserve Bank of Kansas City, September 2007.

8. Martin Eakes, testimony before Senate Committee on Banking, Housing and Urban Affairs, Feb. 7, 2007.

9. For background see J.W. Elphinstone, "Mortgage Bailouts Run Into Opposition," The Associated Press, *The Salt Lake Tribune online*, Sept. 29, 2007, www.sltrib.com/realestate/ci_7038862.

10. Les Christie, "Countrywide Wins Over Critics," CNNMoney.com, Oct. 24, 2007, http://money.cnn.com/2007/10/24/real_estate/Countrywide_plan_wins_support/index.htm?postversion=2007102416.

11. For background, see "Interagency Guidance on Nontraditional Mortgage Product Risks," Office of

Thrift Supervision, Department of the Treasury, October 2006, www.ots.treas.gov/docs/2/25244.pdf.

12. Douglas G. Duncan, testimony before Senate Committee on Banking, Housing and Urban Affairs, Feb. 7, 2007.

13. Sandor Samuels, testimony before Senate Committee on Banking, Housing and Urban Affairs, March 22, 2007.

14. "Home Ownership Rates," Danter Co., www.danter.com/statistics/hometown.htm.

15. "Why Bush's Mortgage Bailout Plan Is a Bad Idea," *eFinanceDirectory.com*, Sept. 4, 2007.

16. "Mortgage Fallout: Interview With Housing Wire," *eFinanceDirectory.com*, Sept. 6, 2007.

17. For background see "Behind the S&L Crisis," *Editorial Research Reports*, 1988, Vol. II, *CQ Researcher online*; and "S&L Bailout: Assessing the Impact," *Editorial Research Reports*, 1990, *CQ Researcher online.*.

18. "Schumer, Others Propose First Major Legislation to Deal with Subprime Crisis as Weakening Housing Market Threatens Economy," press release, office of Sen. Charles Schumer, May 3, 2007, http://schumer.senate.gov.

19. "The Truly Bearish Case Isn't Playing Out," John Burns Real-Estate Consulting Web site, July 2007, www.realestateconsulting.com.

20. "Improvement in Mortgage Market Bodes Well for Housing in 2008," press release, National Association of Realtors, Oct. 10, 2007.

21. Ben Stein, "How Speculators Exploit Market Fears," Yahoo! Finance, Aug. 2, 2007, http://finance.yahoo.com.

22. Edward E. Leamer, "Housing and the Business Cycle," paper presented at the Jackson Hole symposium of the Federal Reserve Bank of Kansas City, September 2007.

23. *Ibid.*

24. Martin Feldstein, "Housing, Housing Finance, and Monetary Policy," remarks presented at the Jackson Hole symposium of the Federal Reserve Bank of Kansas City, September 2007.

25. For background see Richard K. Green and Susan M. Wachter, "The American Mortgage in Historical and International Context," *Journal of Economic Perspectives*, fall 2005, pp. 92-114.

26. Nadeem Walayat, "Hedge Fund Subprime Credit Crunch to Impact Interest Rates," The Market Oracle: Financial Markets Forecasting and Analysis, July 31, 2007, www.marketoracle.co.uk.

27. Kurt Eggert, testimony before Senate Subcommittee on Securities, Insurance and Investments, April 17, 2007.

28. Quoted in *Ibid.*

29. Michael Kanef, testimony before House Subcommittee on Capital Markets, Insurance, and Government Sponsored Enterprises, Sept. 27, 2007.

30. Mortgage Rates: A Historical Look at Mortgage Interest Rates, Lender 411, www.lender411.com/mortgage-articles/index_desc.php?art _id=37.

31. Emory W. Rushton, testimony before U.S. Senate Committee on Banking, Housing, and Urban Affairs, March 22, 2007.

32. Paul Tustain, "Bear Stearns and MBS Hedge Funds: What Are the Real Risks Today?" Financial Sense University, June 23, 2007, www.financialsense.com/fsu/editorials/tustain/2007/0623.html.

33. For background see David Masci, "The Federal Reserve," *CQ Researcher*, Sept. 1, 2000, pp. 673-688.

34. For background see Martin Crutsinger, "Fed Approves Cut in Discount Loan Rate," The Associated Press, Yahoo! Finance Web site, Aug. 17, 2007, http://biz.yahoo.com/ap/070817/fed_interest_rates.html.

35. For background see "Tulip Mania," *Encyclopaedia Britannica online*, 2007.

36. For background see "$500 Million-Dollar Bailout Extended to U.S. Mortgage Borrowers," eFinance-Directory Web site, July 24, 2007, http://efinance-directory.com.

37. For background see Kathleen Day, "Study Finds 'Extensive' Fraud at Fannie Mae," *The Washington Post*, May 24, 2006, p. A1.

38. For background see Benton Ives, "Short-Term Foreclosure Fix Could Cloud Long-Term Regulatory Overhaul," *CQ Today*, Oct. 15, 2007, www.cq.com.

39. Quoted in *ibid.*

40. For background see Richard Rubin, "Tax Relief Plan for Struggling Homeowners Would Exclude the Wealthy," *CQ Today*, Oct. 2, 2007, www.cq.com.

41. For background, see "Fact Sheet: New Steps to Help Homeowners Avoid Foreclosure," White House Web site, Aug. 31, 2007, www.whitehouse.gov/news/releases/2007/08/20070831-4.html.

42. For background, see Michael R. Crittenden, "Measure Outlines Expansion of Financial Protections for Consumers," *CQ Today*, Sept. 18, 2007, www.cq.com.

43. Amy Scott, "States Crack Down on Mortgage Market," Marketplace, National Public Radio, Oct. 19, 2007.

44. Michael Shedlock, "Commercial Real Estate Abyss," Mish's Global Economic Trend Analysis blog, Sept. 13, 2007, http://globaleconomicanalysis.blogspot.com.

45. Robbie Whelan, "Housing Glut Is Likely to Build," *The Wall Street Journal*, July 27, 2010.

46. Douglas A. McIntyre, "A Little Relief in Foreclosure Rates," 24/7 Wall St., May 13, 2010, http://247wallst.com/2010/05/13/a-little-relief-in-foreclosure-rates/#ixzz0uXgjfQGl.

47. Lynn Adler, "Foreclosures Up in 75 percent of Top U.S. Metro Areas," *Los Angeles Times*, July 29, 2010.

48. Associated Press in *Las Vegas Review-Journal*, Feb. 22, 2010.

49. Alejandro Lazo, "Home prices tick up 1.3% in May," *Los Angeles Times*, July 28, 2010, http://articles.latimes.com/2010/jul/28/business/la-fi-home-prices-20100728.

50. Nicole Duarte, "TIGTA Report on Housing Credit Fraud Confirms Analysts' Fears," *Tax Notes Today*, June 24, 2010.

51. www.fanniemae.com/newsreleases/2010/ 5097 .jhtml?p=Media&s=News+Releases&searchid= 1280259527495.

52. Sudeep Reddy, "Home Data Slide Again As Tax Credit Expires," *The Wall Street Journal*, Aug. 3, 2010.

53. Jay Heflin, "Financial Crisis Cost Households $17 trillion, Treasury Official Says," *The Hill*, May 3, 2010.

54. Jill Jackson, "Wall Street Reform: A Summary of What's In the Bill," CBS News, www.cbs news.com/8301-503544_162-20008835-503544. html.

55. Brian M. Carney, "Fan and Fred and the Problem of Narrative," op-ed, *The Wall Street Journal*, July 26, 2010.

56. See Franklin D. Raines, "Poor Credit Judgments Sank Fannie and Freddie," letter, *The Wall Street Journal*, Aug. 3, 2010.

57. Conor Dougherty, "Migration Data Suggest Homeowners Becoming Renters," *The Wall Street Journal*, May 10, 2010.

58. www.fanniemae.com/newsreleases/2010/ 4989 .jhtml?p=Media&s=News+Releases&searchid= 1280259347878.

BIBLIOGRAPHY

Books

Gramlich, Edward M., and Robert D. Reischauer, *Subprime Mortgages: America's Latest Boom and Bust*, Urban Institute Press, 2007.
Two experts recount the history of the subprime-mortgage market and suggest reforms. Gramlich once chaired the Federal Reserve's Consumer and Community Affairs Committee; Reischauer is president of the Urban Institute.

Schwartz, Alex F., *Housing Policy in the United States: An Introduction*, Routledge, 2006.
An associate professor of housing policy at New School University describes the housing-finance system.

Articles

Morgenson, Gretchen, "Can These Mortgages Be Saved?" *The New York Times*, Sept. 30, 2007, Sec. 3, p. 1.
Many borrowers in trouble say mortgage lenders aren't helping them to keep their homes.

Rokakis, Jim, "The Shadow of Debt," *The Washington Post*, Sept. 30, 2007, p. B1.
A once-tranquil Cleveland neighborhood becomes crime-infested after predatory lending leads to massive foreclosures.

Smith, David, "HUD Homes Go Cheap," *Journal & Courier* [Lafayette, Indiana], September 16, 2007, http://m.jconline.com.
The Department of Housing and Urban Development has bought so many foreclosed Indiana properties it is now the state's largest home seller.

Wargo, Brian, "Cancellations of New-Home Purchases Climb," *In Business Las Vegas*, Sept. 21-27, 2007, edition, www.inbusinesslasvegas.com.
Many Nevada homebuyers are canceling sales. Meanwhile, the National Association of Hispanic Real Estate Professionals is trying to protect Latinos from predatory lending.

Reports and Studies

"Ask Yourself Why . . . Mortgage Foreclosure Rates Are So High," *Common Cause*, 2007.
A citizens' group argues that $210 million in campaign funds and lobbying costs spent by the mortgage-lending industry has made Congress unwilling to curb industry practices.

"Mortgage Liquidity Du Jour: Underestimated No More," Credit Suisse, March 2007.
A large investment bank concludes dangers lurk in all sectors of the mortgage market, not just subprime loans.

Subprime and Predatory Lending in Rural America, Policy Brief No. 4, Carsey Institute, University of New Hampshire, fall 2006.
Affordable housing groups say many rural residents fall prey to predatory lenders, partly because they have little access to mainstream banks.

Essene, Ren S., and William Apgar, "Understanding Mortgage-Market Behavior: Creating Good Mortgage Options for All Americans," Joint Center for Housing Studies, Harvard University, April 2007.
Researchers conclude many consumers can't accurately evaluate the many mortgages that have sprung up.

Larson, Michael D., "How Federal Regulators, Lenders, and Wall Street Created America's Housing Crisis," Weiss Research, July 2007.
A financial analyst describes what house prices, foreclosures and other data reveal about the housing crisis and argues federal regulators underestimated the problems.

Murphy, Edward Vincent, "Alternative Mortgages: Risks to Consumers and Lenders in the Current Housing Cycle," Congressional Research Service, Dec. 27, 2006.
A CRS analyst describes how alternative mortgages have trapped some homeowners.

Schloemer, Ellen, et al., "Losing Ground: Foreclosures in the Subprime Market and Their Cost to Homeowners," Center for Responsible Lending, December 2006.
Analysts predict 2.2 million subprime borrowers will lose their houses in the current crisis.

Helpful Web Sites

How to avoid predatory lenders: www.hud.gov/offices/hsg/sfh/buying/loanfraud.cfm.

How to calculate how much house you can afford, whether to buy or rent: www.hud.gov/buying/index.cfm.

What you should know about mortgage brokers: http://homebuying.about.com/od/findingalender/qt/0407LoanOffRep.htm.

Definitions of terms connected with home buying: www.statefarm.com/bank/sr_center/morgloss.asp.

Explanations of mortgage terms and advice about various types of loans: http://michaelbluejay.com/house/loan.html.

For More Information

Carsey Institute, University of New Hampshire, 73 Main St., Huddleston Hall, Durham, NH 03824; (603) 862-2821; http://carseyinstitute.unh.edu. Researches housing and other economic issues in rural America.

Center for Responsible Lending, 302 West Main St., Durham, NC 27701; (919) 313-8500; www.responsiblelending.org. Provides information on predatory lending and other abusive practices.

Fannie Mae, 3900 Wisconsin Ave., N.W., Washington, DC 20016; (800) 732-6643; www.fanniemae.com/index.jhtml. The government-sponsored, shareholder-owned corporation buys mortgages in the secondary market to provide capital for the mortgage industry.

Freddie Mac, 8200 Jones Branch Dr., McLean, VA 22102-3110; (703) 903-2000; www.freddiemac.com/index.html. The government-sponsored company supports the mortgage market.

Housing, Housing Finance, and Monetary Policy, 2007 Symposium of the Federal Reserve Bank of Kansas City, http://www.kc.frb.org/home/subwebnav.cfm?level=3&theID=10982&SubWeb=10658. The symposium on the mortgage crisis features papers presented by leading economists, including Federal Reserve Chairman Ben S. Bernanke.

Joint Center for Housing Studies, Harvard University, 1033 Massachusetts Ave., 5th Floor, Cambridge, MA 02138; (617) 495-7908; www.jchs.harvard.edu/index.

htm. Provides information and research on U.S. housing issues.

Mortgage Professor's Web Site, www.mtgprofessor.com/. The University of Pennsylvania's Wharton School of Business provides financial education and policy analysis written by a businessman who is professor emeritus of finance at the University of Pennsylvania's Wharton School.

National Association of Mortgage Brokers, 11325 Random Hills Rd., Suite 360, Fairfax, VA 22030; (703) 342-5900; www.namb.org/namb/Default.asp. Provides information on the mortgage industry, including legislative proposals.

National Association of Realtors, 500 New Jersey Ave., N.W., Washington, DC 20001-2020; (800) 874-6500; www.realtor.org. Provides and analyzes its own data on housing-market trends.

National Mortgage News Online, www.nationalmortgagenews.com/. The independent news outlet covers mortgage-related news.

Office of Federal Housing Enterprise Oversight, 1700 G St., N.W., 4th Floor, Washington, DC 20552; (202) 414-3800; www.fhfa.gov. Oversees Fannie and Freddie and provides data and research on housing.

U.S. Department of Housing and Urban Development, 451 7th St., S.W., Washington, DC 20410; (202) 708-1112; www.hud.gov/. Provides information about mortgages, home buying and related federal programs.

12

Immigration Debate

Alan Greenblatt and Charles S. Clark

A Mexican farmworker harvests broccoli near Yuma, Ariz. With the number of illegal immigrants in the U.S. now over 12 million — including at least half of the nation's 1.6 million farmworkers — tougher enforcement has become a dominant theme in the 2008 presidential campaign. Meanwhile, with Congress unable to act, states and localities have passed hundreds of bills cracking down on employers and illegal immigrants seeking public benefits.

Getty Images/David McNew

From *CQ Researcher*,
February 1, 2008 (updated September 27, 2010).

ohn McCain, the senior senator from Arizona and the leading Republican candidate for president, has been hurt politically by the immigration issue.

McCain would allow illegal immigrants to find a way eventually to become citizens. The approach is seen by many Republican politicians and voters (and not a few Democrats) as akin to "amnesty," in effect rewarding those who broke the law to get into this country. Legislation that he helped craft with Sen. Edward M. Kennedy, D-Mass., and the White House went down to defeat in both 2006 and 2007.

McCain rejects the approach taken by House Republicans during a vote in 2005 and favored by several of his rivals in the presidential race — namely, classifying the 12 million illegal immigrants already in this country as felons and seeking to deport them. This wouldn't be realistic, he says, noting not only the economic demands that have brought the foreign-born here in the first place but also the human cost such a widespread crackdown would entail.

On the stump, McCain talks about an 80-year-old woman who has lived illegally in the United States for 70 years and has a son and grandson serving in Iraq. When challenged at Clemson University last November by a student who said he wanted to see all illegal immigrants punished, McCain said, "If you're prepared to send an 80-year-old grandmother who's been here 70 years back to some other country, then frankly you're not quite as compassionate as I am."[1]

As the issue of illegal immigrants reaches the boiling point, however, and as he gains in the polls, even McCain sounds not

California Has Most Foreign-Born Residents

California's nearly 10 million foreign-born residents represented about one-quarter of the national total in 2006 and more than twice as many as New York.

Foreign-Born Individuals by State, 2006*

	Over 1 million
	500,000-999,999
	200,000-499,999
	100,000-199,999
	0-99,999

* Includes legal and illegal immigrants

Source: Migration Policy Institute

Complaints about illegal immigrants breaking the law or draining public resources have become a daily staple of talk radio programs, as well as CNN's "Lou Dobbs Tonight."

In a high-profile speech in August 2007, Newt Gingrich, a former Republican House Speaker, railed about two suspects in a triple murder in New Jersey who turned out to be illegal immigrants. He argued that President Bush should call Congress into special session to address the matter, calling himself "sickened" by Congress being in recess "while young Americans are being massacred by people who shouldn't be here."

Gingrich said Bush should be more serious about "winning the war here at home, which is more violent and more dangerous to Americans than Iraq or Iran."[4]

Concerns about terrorism have also stoked fears about porous borders and unwanted intruders entering the country.

quite so compassionate as before. In response to political pressures, McCain now shares the point of view of hard-liners who say stronger border security must come before allowing additional work permits or the "path to citizenship" that were envisioned by his legislation.

"You've got to do what's right, OK?" McCain told *The New Yorker* magazine recently. "But, if you want to succeed, you have to adjust to the American people's desires and priorities."[2]

Immigration has become a central concern for a significant share of the American public. Immigrants, both legal and illegal, are now 12.6 percent of the population — more than at any time since the 1920s.

Not only is the number of both legal and illegal immigrants — now a record 37.9 million — climbing rapidly but the foreign-born are dispersing well beyond traditional "gatekeeper" states such as California, New York and Texas, creating social tensions in places with fast-growing immigrant populations such as Georgia, Arkansas and Iowa.[3]

"Whenever I'm out with a [presidential] candidate at a town hall meeting, it's the exception when they do not get a question about immigration — whether it's a Democratic event or a Republican event," says Dan Balz, a veteran political reporter at *The Washington Post.*

With no resolution in sight to the immigration debate in Congress, the number of immigrant-related bills introduced in state legislatures tripled last year, to more than 1,500. Local communities are also crafting their own immigration policies. (*See sidebar, p. 296.*)

In contrast to the type of policies pursued just a few years ago, when states were extending benefits such as in-state tuition to illegal immigrants, the vast majority of current state and local legislation seeks to limit illegal immigrants' access to public services and to crack down on employers who hire them.

"For a long time, the American public has wanted immigration enforcement," says Ira Mehlman, media director of the Federation for American Immigration Reform (FAIR), which lobbies for stricter immigration limits.

"Is there a rhetorical consensus for the need for immigration control? The answer is clearly yes," Mehlman says. "When even John McCain is saying border security and enforcement have to come first before the amnesty he really wants, then there is really a consensus."

While most of the Republican presidential candidates are talking tougher on immigration today than two or three years ago, Democrats also are espousing the need for border security and stricter enforcement of current laws. But not everyone is convinced a majority of the public supports the "enforcement-only" approach that treats all illegal immigrants — and the people that hire them — as criminals.

"All through the fall, even with the campaign going on, the polls consistently showed that 60 to 70 percent of the public supports a path to citizenship," says Tamar Jacoby, a senior fellow at the Manhattan Institute who has written in favor of immigrant absorption into U.S. society.

There's a core of only about 20 to 25 percent of Americans who favor wholesale deportation, Jacoby says. "What the candidates are doing is playing on the scare 'em territory."

But over the last couple of years, in the congressional and state-level elections where the immigration issue has featured most prominently, the candidates who sought to portray themselves as the toughest mostly lost.

Some analysts believe that, despite the amount of media attention the issue has attracted, anti-immigrant hard-liners may have overplayed their hand, ignoring the importance of immigrant labor to a shifting U.S. economy.

"To be energized we need new workers, younger workers, who are going to be a part of the whole economy. We don't have them here in the United States," Sen. Kennedy told National Public Radio in 2006.

Fastest-Growing Foreign-Born Populations

Foreign populations at least tripled in 10 states since 1990. In North Carolina foreign-born residents increased by a record 534 percent.

Percentage Increases in Foreign-Born Individuals, 1990-2006

State	Percentage
North Carolina	534%
Georgia	497%
Nevada	454%
Arkansas	432%
Tennessee	400%
Utah	359%
Nebraska	353%
South Carolina	352%
Colorado	344%
Arizona	334%

1990
2006

0   200,000   400,000   600,000   800,000   1,000,000

Number of Immigrants in State

* Includes legal and illegal immigrants

Source: Migration Policy Institute

"We need to have the skills of all of these people," he continued. "The fact is, this country, with each new wave of immigrants, has been energized and advanced, quite frankly, in terms of its economic, social, cultural and political life. I don't think we ought to fear it, we ought to welcome it."[5]

Polls have made it clear that the Republican Party, which is seen as generally tougher on the issue, is losing support among Hispanics — the fastest-growing segment of the population.

"The Bush strategy — enlightened on race, smart on immigration — developed in Texas and Florida with Jeb Bush — has been replaced by the Tancredo-Romney strategy, which is demonizing and scapegoating immigrants," said Simon Rosenberg, a Democratic strategist, "and that is a catastrophic event for the Republican Party."[6] Jeb Bush, the president's brother, served two

A prospective employer in Las Vegas holds up two fingers indicating how many day laborers he needs. One of the few pieces of immigration legislation still considered to have a chance in Congress this year is the SAVE Act, which would require all employers to use an electronic verification system to check the legal status of all workers.

terms as governor of Florida, while Colorado Rep. Tom Tancredo and former Massachusetts Gov. Mitt Romney each sought this year's GOP presidential nomination.*

There is a well-known precedent backing up Rosenberg's argument. In 1994, Pete Wilson, California's Republican governor, pushed hard for Proposition 187, designed to block illegal immigrants from receiving most public services. The proposition passed and Wilson won reelection, but it turned Hispanic voters in California against the GOP — a shift widely believed to have turned the state solidly Democratic.

"While there might be some initial appeal to trying to beat up on immigrants in all different ways, it ultimately isn't getting to the question of what you do with 12 million people," says Angela Kelley, director of the Immigration Policy Center at the American Immigration Law Foundation, which advocates for immigrants' legal rights. "It isn't a problem we can enforce our way out of."

But it's not a problem politicians can afford to ignore. There will be enormous pressure on the next president and Congress to come up with a package that imposes practical limits on the flow of illegal immigrants into the United States. Doing so while balancing the economic interests that immigrant labor supports will remain no less of a challenge, however.

_____
* Tancredo dropped out in December, and Romney has been trailing McCain in the primaries.

That's in part because the immigration debate doesn't fall neatly along partisan lines. Pro-GOP business groups, for example, continue to seek a free flow of labor, while unions and other parts of the Democratic coalition fear just that.

"The Democrats tend to like immigrants, but are suspicious of immigration, while the Republicans tend to like immigration but are suspicious of immigrants," says Frank Sharry, executive director of the National Immigration Forum, a pro-immigration lobby group.

"Republicans want to deport 12 million people while starting a guest worker program," he says. "With Democrats, it's the reverse."

During a Republican debate in Florida last December, presidential candidate and former Massachusetts Gov. Mitt Romney took a less draconian position, moving away from his earlier calls to deport all illegals. "Those who have come illegally, in my view, should be given the opportunity to get in line with everybody else," he said. "But there should be no special pathway for those that have come here illegally to jump ahead of the line or to become permanent residents or citizens."[7]

One of the loudest anti-immigration voices belongs to Republican Oklahoma state Rep. Randy Terrill, author of one of the nation's toughest anti-immigration laws, which went into effect in December 2007. "For too long, our nation and our state have looked the other way and ignored a growing illegal immigration crisis," he said. "Oklahoma's working families should not be forced to subsidize illegal immigration. With passage of House bill 1804, we will end that burden on our citizens."[8] Among other things, the law gives state and local law enforcement officials the power to enforce federal immigration law.

As the immigration debate rages on, here are some of the specific issues that policy makers are arguing about:

Should employers be penalized for hiring illegal immigrants?

For more than 20 years, federal policy has used employers as a checkpoint in determining the legal status of workers. It's against the law for companies to knowingly hire illegal immigrants, but enforcement of this law has been lax, at best.

Partly as a result — but also because of the growing attention paid to illegal immigrants and the opportunities that may attract them to this country — the role of business in enforcing immigration policy has become a major concern.

"I blame 90 percent on employers," says Georgia state Sen. Chip Rogers. "They're the ones that are profiting by breaking the law."

The Immigration and Customs Enforcement agency has pledged to step up its efforts to punish employers who knowingly hire undocumented workers. In response, an Electrolux factory in Springfield, Tenn., fired more than 150 immigrant workers in December after Immigration and Customs Enforcement (ICE) agents arrested a handful of its employees.

Last year, ICE levied $30 million in fines and forfeitures against employers, but arrested fewer than 100 executives or hiring managers, compared with 4,100 unauthorized workers.[9]

One of the few pieces of immigration legislation still considered to have a chance in Congress this year is the SAVE Act (Secure America With Verification Enforcement), which would require all employers to use an electronic verification system to check the legal status of all workers. The House version of the bill boasts more than 130 cosponsors.

Employers are also being heavily targeted by state and local lawmakers. More than 300 employment-related laws addressing illegal immigrants have been recently passed by various levels of government, according to the U.S. Chamber of Commerce.

"There is still this general consensus that although the current employer-sanctions regime hasn't worked, the point of hire is the correct place to ensure that the employee before you is legally here," says Kelley, of the American Immigration Law Foundation.

But for all the efforts to ensure that businesses check the legal status of their workers — and to impose stiffer penalties on those who knowingly hire illegal immigrants — there is still considerable debate about whether such measures will ultimately resolve the problem.

Critics contend there is no easy way for employers to determine legal status. For one thing, documents often are faked. Dan Pilcher, spokesman for the Colorado Association of Commerce and Industry, notes that during a high-profile ICE raid on the Swift meatpacking plant in Greeley in December 2006, many of the arrests were for identity theft, not immigration violations, since so many illegal immigrants were using Social Security numbers that belonged to other people.

"Even when those numbers are run through the system, the computers didn't pick up anything," Pilcher says. "Until that system [of verification] is bulletproof, it doesn't work to try to mandate that businesses be the front line of enforcement."

Concerns about the verification systems in place are shared across the ideological spectrum. "We're now 21 years after the enactment of employer sanctions, and we still haven't come up with a system that allows for instant verification," says Mehlman, at the Federation for American Immigration Reform. "If Visa and MasterCard can verify literally millions of transactions a day, there's no reason we can't have businesses verify the legal status of their employees."

"When you look to employers to be the ones that are going to have damages imposed for hiring someone who is not properly documented, the first thing you have to do is give me a program so I can make sure the person is legal for me to hire," says Bryan R. Tolar, director of marketing, education and environmental programs for the Georgia Agribusiness Council.

So far, though, there is no such system. The Department of Homeland Security's E-Verify system, which grew out of a pilot program, is the new checking point of choice. In fact, federal contractors will soon be required to check the residency status of employees using E-Verify. As of Jan. 1, a new state law requires all employers in Arizona to use the E-Verify system.

But such requirements have drawn lawsuits from both business groups and labor unions, who complain that E-Verify is based on unreliable databases. Tom Clark, executive vice president of the Denver Metro Chamber of Commerce, complains that E-Verify is not accurate and worries therefore that the employer sanctions contained in the Arizona law could lead to serious and unfair consequences.

Under the law, companies found guilty of hiring an illegal worker can lose their business licenses for 10 days; for second offenses they are at risk of forfeiting their licenses entirely. "Do you know the [power] that gives you to take out your competitors?" Clark asks.

Supporters of tougher employer sanctions say the databases are getting better all the time. Mark Krikorian, executive director of the Center for Immigration

Immigration Is on the Rise

The number of foreign-born people in the United States has nearly quadrupled since 1970, largely because of changes in immigration laws and increasing illegal immigration (top). The increase has pushed the foreign-born percentage of the population to more than 12 percent (bottom).

Number and Percentage of Foreign-Born Individuals in the U.S., 1900-2005

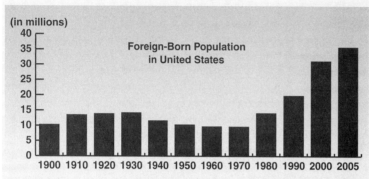

Source: Audrey Singer, "Twenty-first Century Gateways: Immigrant Incorporation in Suburban America," Metropolitan Policy Program, Brookings Institution, April 2007

them at a juncture when verification methods remain in doubt could create greater problems.

"Until you create an effective verification system, employer sanctions will drive the problem further underground and advantage the least scrupulous employers," Sherry says.

Can guest worker programs be fixed?

The United States has several different programs allowing foreigners to come into the country for a limited time, usually to work for specific "sponsoring" employers, generally in agriculture. But most of these programs have been criticized for being ineffective — both in filling labor demands and ensuring that temporary workers do not become permanent, illegal residents.

The best-known guest worker program, the H-2A visa program for visiting agricultural workers, has been derided by farmers as cumbersome and time-consuming, preventing them from timing their hiring of workers to growing and harvesting seasons. Farmers use H-2A visas only to cover an estimated 2 percent of farmworkers.

Instead, growers turn to the black market for undocumented workers. At least half of the nation's 1.6 million farmworkers — and as many as 70 percent by some estimates — are immigrants lacking documentation.[10]

Still, growers' groups have complained about labor shortages as border security and regulation of employers are tightening. Some growers in the Northwest last fall let cherries and apples rot because of a shortage of workers, and some in North Carolina did not plant cucumbers because of a fear they wouldn't find the workers to harvest them.[11]

Three federal agencies — Homeland Security, State and Labor — have been working in recent months to

Studies, says E-Verify needs to be made into a requirement for all American employers. Once they are handed a working tool, he says, all businesses need to follow the same rules.

"Legal status is a labor standard that needs to be enforced just like other labor standards," he says. "Holding business accountable to basic labor standards is hardly revolutionary."

The National Immigration Forum's Sharry agrees that employers "need to be held to account for who they hire." But he warns that imposing stiff penalties against craft regulations to speed the H-2A visa process. But farmworker advocates worry that the sort of changes the administration has been contemplating could weaken labor protections for workers. Some critics of lax immigration policy complain, meanwhile, that the H-2A changes would allow employers to skirt a process designed to limit the flow of immigrant workers.

Changes adopted by or expected from the administration could weaken housing and wage standards that have traditionally been a part of temporary-worker programs, which date back to World War II, according to Bruce Goldstein, executive director of Farmworker Justice, a group that provides legal support to migrant workers.

Those changes would make a bad situation for farmworkers worse, Goldstein contends. "The government has failed to adopt policies that adequately protect workers from abuses and has failed to enforce the labor protections that are on the books," Goldstein says.

The Federation for American Immigration Reform's Mehlman criticizes the proposed changes for "trying to tip the balance in favor of employers."

"There's no evidence that we have a labor shortage in this country," Mehlman says. "You have businesses that have decided they don't want to pay the kind of wages American workers want in order to do these kinds of jobs."

Whether there is an overall labor shortage or not, clearly the numbers don't add up in agriculture. Officials with several immigration-policy groups note that the number of people coming to work in this country outnumber the visas available to new, full-time workers by hundreds of thousands per year.

"The only way we can provide for the labor needs of a growing and very diverse agriculture industry is to make sure there's an ample workforce to do it," says Tolar, at the Georgia Agribusiness Council. "Americans have proven that they're not willing to provide the work that needs doing at a wage agriculture can support."

Five years ago, a bipartisan group of congressmen, working with farmworkers, growers and church groups, proposed a piece of legislation known as the AgJobs bill. The attempt at a compromise between the most directly interested players has been a part of the guest worker and immigration debates ever since.

The bill would allow some 800,000 undocumented workers who have lived and worked in the U.S. for several years to register, pay a fine and qualify for green cards (proof of legal residency) by working in agriculture for three to five more years. It would also streamline the H-2A visa application process.

Legal Immigration Has Steadily Increased

The number of legal immigrants has risen steadily since the 1960s, from about 320,000 yearly to nearly 1 million. The largest group was from Latin America and the Caribbean. (In addition to legal entrants, more than a half-million immigrants arrive or remain in the U.S. illegally each year.)

Average Annual Number of Legal U.S. Immigrants by Region of Origin, 1960-2005

Legend:
- Latin America and the Caribbean
- Asia
- Europe and Canada
- Other

Period	Total	Latin America and the Caribbean	Asia	Europe and Canada	Other
1960-69	321,000	39%	11%	49%	1%
1970-79	429,000	41%	33%	24%	3%
1980-89	624,000	41%	38%	13%	8%
1990-99	978,000	54%	29%	16%	4%
2000-05	951,000	41%	32%	18%	9%

* Percentages may not total 100 due to rounding.

Source: "Economic Mobility of Immigrants in the United States," Economic Mobility Project, Pew Charitable Trusts, 2007

More Immigrants Moving to Suburbs

The gap between the number of immigrants who live in inner cities and suburbs widened significantly from 1980-2005. By 2005 more than 15 million foreign-born people were in suburbs, or three times as many in 1980. The number in cities doubled during the same period. Demographers attribute the popularity of the suburbs to their relative lack of crime, lower cost and better schools.

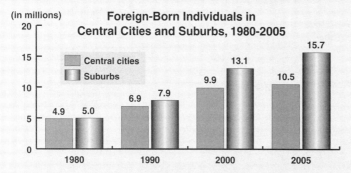

(in millions)

Foreign-Born Individuals in Central Cities and Suburbs, 1980-2005

Central cities
Suburbs

1980	1990	2000	2005
4.9 / 5.0	6.9 / 7.9	9.9 / 13.1	10.5 / 15.7

Source: Audrey Singer, "Twenty-first Century Gateways: Immigrant Incorporation in Suburban America," Metropolitan Policy Program, Brookings Institution, April 2007

Although it won Senate passage as part of a larger immigration bill in 2006, the current version of AgJobs has not gained traction due to complaints that it would reward illegal immigrants and employers with what amounts to "get out of jail free" cards.

In November 2007, Sen. Dianne Feinstein, D-Calif., announced that she would not seek to attach AgJobs as an amendment to a larger farm bill, due to strong opposition to legislation seen as helping illegal immigrants. "We know that we can win this," Feinstein said in a statement. But, she conceded, "When we took a clear-eyed assessment of the politics . . . it became clear that our support could not sustain these competing forces."

Feinstein vows to try again this year. But Krikorian, of the Center for Immigration Studies, which favors reduced immigration, counters that guest worker programs in any form are not the right solution. "They still imagine there's a way of admitting low-wage illegals and not have immigration consequences," he says. "It's a fantasy."

"Guest worker programs don't work anyway," he adds. "There's nothing as permanent as a temporary worker."

The American Immigration Law Foundation's Kelley speaks for many on the other side of the debate who argue that it's not enough to conclude that guest worker programs are problematic. Workers from other countries are going to continue to come into this country, she notes.

"We need somehow to replace what is an illegal flow with a legal flow," Kelley says. "We have a guest worker program now — it's called illegal immigration."

Should illegal immigrants be allowed to attend public colleges and universities?

Miami college students Juan Gomez, 18, and his brother Alex, 20, spent a week in jail in Fort Lauderdale last summer. They were both students at Miami Dade College but faced deportation as illegal immigrants. They had come to the United States from Colombia when they were toddlers.

In handcuffs while riding to the detention center, Juan managed to type out a text message to a friend on his cell phone. The friend set up a Facebook group that in turn led 3,000 people to sign petitions lobbying Congress on the brothers' behalf.

In response, Rep. Lincoln Diaz-Balart, R-Fla., and Sen. Christopher Dodd, D-Conn., introduced legislation to prevent their deportation. As a courtesy to Congress, immigration officials delayed their deportation for two more years.[12]

But the brothers may still face deportation, because Congress failed to pass the DREAM (Development, Relief and Education for Alien Minors) Act. The bill would protect students from deportation and allow young adults (up to age 30) to qualify for permanent legal status if they completed high school and at least two years of college or military service.

On Oct. 24, 2007, the Senate voted 52-48 to end debate and move to a vote on final passage — eight votes short of the 60 needed under Senate rules to end a filibuster. Opponents of the measure claimed it was an unfair plan to grant amnesty to illegal immigrants.

The debate over illegal immigration has regularly and heatedly intersected with questions about education for illegal immigrants: Do young people deserve a break even if their parents skirted the law in bringing them to this country? Should illegal immigrants be barred from publicly supported colleges?

The courts have made it clear that states must provide elementary and secondary educations to all comers, including illegal immigrants. But higher education is another matter entirely.

Ten states have passed legislation in recent years granting in-state tuition to children of illegal immigrants. Most passed their laws during the early years of this decade, before immigration had become such a heated political topic.

Similar proposals in other states have died recently, with critics charging that it would be wrong to reward people who are in the country illegally with one of American society's dearest prizes.

"It is totally unfair if you're going to grant in-state tuition to illegal aliens in Georgia and charge out-of-state tuition to someone from Pennsylvania," says Phil Kent, national spokesman for Americans for Immigration Control.

Katherine "Kay" Albiani, president of the California Community Colleges board, stepped down last month along with two other board members in response to criticism from Republican legislators. The board had voted unanimously last year to support legislation that would have allowed illegal immigrants to qualify for student financial aid and community-college fee waivers.

"We have the best benefit package of any state for illegal immigrants, so they come here," complained California Senate GOP leader Dick Ackerman.[13]

Some argue that illegal immigrants should be barred not only from receiving tuition breaks but also from attending public colleges and universities altogether. Public institutions of higher education, after all, are subsidized by taxpayers, and therefore all students — including illegal immigrants — receive an indirect form of aid from state or local governments.

"Every college student is subsidized to the tune of thousands of dollars a year," says Krikorian, of the Center for Immigration Studies. "They are taking slots and huge amounts of public subsidies that would otherwise go to Americans or legal immigrants."

"Our view is that they shouldn't be there in the first place, and they certainly shouldn't be subsidized by taxpayers," says Mehlman of FAIR. "The typical illegal immigrant isn't coming to the U.S. for higher education. But

After living in Clarion, Iowa, for nine years, undocumented Mexican immigrant Patricia Castillo, right, and her family were deported for entering the country illegally. Townspeople like Doris Holmes and her daughter Kelli threw a fund-raiser to help the Castillos pay their legal bills.

once you're here, if the state says we'll subsidize your college education, that's a pretty good incentive to stay here."

Others argue that banning students because their parents chose to break the law would be a mistake. "We are a better country than to punish children for what their parents did," former Arkansas Gov. Mike Huckabee said during the Nov. 28 CNN/YouTube GOP presidential debate. Huckabee says he opposes the congressional DREAM Act, but his opponents in the primary campaign have pointed out his former support as governor for in-state tuition for longtime illegal residents.

Beyond the question of whether it's fair to punish students for decisions their parents made, some argue it would be a mistake to deprive illegal immigrants of educational opportunities. A college education may be an extra inducement for them to stay in this country, but the vast majority are likely to remain in this country anyway.

"If these are people who are going to live here for the rest of their lives, we want them to be as educated as possible," says the Manhattan Institute's Jacoby.

The American Immigration Law Foundation's Kelley agrees. She describes the DREAM Act as a reasonable compromise, saying it would protect students but wouldn't give illegal immigrants access to scholarships or grants. She argues that states that do offer in-state tuition rates to illegal immigrant students have not seen "a huge influx" of them.

AP Photo/The Messenger/Cynthia Kaneshiro

CHRONOLOGY

1920s *Hard economic times and public concern about the nation's changing ethnic makeup prompt Congress to limit immigration.*

1921-1929 Congress establishes immigration quota system, excluding Asians and Southern and Eastern Europeans.

1924 U.S. Border Patrol is created to block illegal immigrants, primarily Mexicans.

1940s-1950s *Expansion of U.S. economy during World War II attracts Mexican laborers. U.S. overhauls immigration laws, accepts war survivors and refugees from communist countries.*

1942 Controversial Bracero guest worker program allows Mexicans to work on American farms.

1952 Landmark Immigration and Nationality Act codifies existing quota system favoring Northern Europeans but permitting Mexican farmworkers in Texas.

1960s-1970s *Civil Rights Movement spurs U.S. to admit more Asians and Latin Americans.*

1965 Congress scraps national quotas, gives preference to relatives of immigrants.

1980s *Rising illegal immigration sparks crackdown.*

1986 Apprehension of a record 1.7 million illegal Mexican immigrants prompts lawmakers to legalize undocumented workers and for the first time impose sanctions on employers.

1990s-2000s *Congress again overhauls immigration laws amid national-security concerns.*

1993 Middle Eastern terrorists bomb World Trade Center; two had green cards.

1994 California voters pass Proposition 187, blocking illegal immigrants from receiving most public services; three years later it is largely declared unconstitutional.

1996 Number of illegal immigrants in U.S. reaches 5 million.

Sept. 11, 2001 Attacks on World Trade Center and Pentagon focus new attention on porous U.S. borders.

2004 The 9/11 Commission points to "systemic weaknesses" in border-control and immigration systems.

2005 Congress passes Real ID Act, requiring proof of identity for driver's licenses. . . . President Bush calls for a "temporary worker" program excluding "amnesty" for illegal immigrants. . . . House passes bill to classify illegal immigrants as felons and deport them.

2006 On April 20, Homeland Security Secretary Michael Chertoff announces a federal crackdown on employers who hire illegal aliens. . . . On May 1, hundreds of thousands of immigrants demonstrate across the country to call for legal status. . . . On Nov. 7, 69 percent of Hispanic voters support Democrats in congressional races, according to exit polls.

2007 On May 9, churches in coastal cities provide "sanctuaries" for undocumented families. . . . On May 17, President Bush and a bipartisan group of senators announce agreement on a comprehensive bill to strengthen border protection and allow illegal immigrants eventual access to citizenship. . . . On Aug. 10, the administration calls for more aggressive law enforcement, screening of new employees by federal contractors and firing of workers whose Social Security numbers don't match government databases. . . . On Oct. 24, the Senate fails to end debate on a proposal to protect illegal immigrants who are attending college from deportation. . . . On Dec. 26, Bush signs spending bill calling for 700 miles of "reinforced fencing" along U.S.-Mexico border.

Jan. 1, 2008 Arizona law holding employers responsible for checking legal status of workers is the most recent of hundreds of punitive, new state immigration laws. . . . On Jan. 22, Michigan stops issuing driver's licenses to illegal immigrants. . . . Implementation of Real ID Act, slated to go into effect in May, is postponed.

Dec. 15, 2009 Congressional Hispanic Caucus joins 100 House cosponsors to introduce Comprehensive Immigration Reform for America's Security and Prosperity Act of 2009. It goes nowhere.

April 23, 2010 Arizona enacts tough anti-immigration legislation giving police broad powers to detain anyone suspected of being in the country illegally. Passage sparks worldwide protests and boycotts of state economy. President Obama says the law threatens "to undermine basic notions of fairness that we cherish as Americans, as well as the trust between police and our communities that is so crucial to keeping us safe."

July 6 U.S. Attorney General Eric Holder files suit challenging Arizona law.

July 27 U.S. District Court Judge Susan Bolton blocks portions of Arizona's law.

Aug. 24 Sen. John McCain, R-Ariz., wins primary after moving to the right on immigration enforcement.

Aug. 26 Republican Arizona Gov. Jan Brewer appeals district court's rejection of parts of crackdown law.

"Saying to students who have been raised here and by all accounts are American and are graduating in high numbers and are doing well — 'You can't advance and go any further' — doesn't make sense," Kelley says. "It would be helpful to our economy to have these kids get college degrees."

BACKGROUND

Earlier Waves

The United States was created as a nation of immigrants who left Europe for political, religious and economic reasons. After independence, the new nation maintained an open-door immigration policy for 100 years. Two great waves of immigrants — in the mid-1800s and the late-19th and early-20th centuries — drove the nation's westward expansion and built its cities and industrial base.[14]

But while the inscription on the Statue of Liberty says America accepts the world's "tired . . . poor . . . huddled masses," Americans themselves vacillate between welcoming immigrants and resenting them — even those who arrive legally. For both legal and illegal immigrants, America's actions have been inconsistent and often racist.

In the 19th century, thousands of Chinese laborers were brought here to build the railroads and then were excluded — via the Chinese Exclusion Act of 1882 — in a wave of anti-Chinese hysteria. Other Asian groups were restricted when legislation in 1917 created "barred zones" for Asian immigrants.[15]

The racist undertones of U.S. immigration policy were by no means reserved for Asians. Describing Italian and Irish immigrants as "wretched beings," *The New York Times* on May 15, 1880, editorialized: "There is a limit to our powers of assimilation, and when it is exceeded the country suffers from something very like indigestion."

Nevertheless, from 1880 to 1920, the country admitted more than 23 million immigrants — first from Northern and then from Southern and Eastern Europe. In 1890, Census Bureau Director Francis Walker said the country was being overrun by "less desirable" newcomers from Southern and Eastern Europe, whom he called "beaten men from beaten races."

In the 1920s, public concern about the nation's changing ethnic makeup prompted Congress to establish a national-origins quota system. Laws in 1921, 1924 and 1929 capped overall immigration and limited influxes from certain areas based on the share of the U.S. population with similar ancestry, effectively excluding Asians and Southern and Eastern Europeans, such as Greeks, Poles and Russians.[16]

But the quotas only swelled the ranks of illegal immigrants — particularly Mexicans, who needed only to wade across the Rio Grande River. To stem the flow, the United States in 1924 created the U.S. Border Patrol to guard the 6,000 miles of U.S. land bordering Canada and Mexico.

States Racing to Pass Restrictive Immigration Laws

Arizona, Georgia and Oklahoma seek to outdo Colorado.

Andrew Romanoff, the speaker of the Colorado House, offers a simple explanation for why his state enacted a sweeping immigration law in 2006.

"The immigration system is, by all accounts, broken," he says, "and the federal government has shown very little appetite for either enforcing the law or reforming the law."

In the absence of federal action on immigration, in 2007 every state in the nation considered legislation to address the issue, according to the National Conference of State Legislatures (NCSL). It released a study in November showing that states considered "no fewer than 1,562 pieces of legislation related to immigrants and immigration," with 244 passed into law in 46 states.[1] Both the number of bills and the number of new laws were three times higher than the totals in 2006.

When Colorado's law was enacted in 2006, it was considered perhaps the toughest in the country. It requires anyone older than 18 who is seeking state benefits to show identification proving legal status and requires employers to verify the legal status of workers. But it provides exemptions for certain types of medical care and was designed to hold harmless the children of illegal immigrants.

Colorado's approach has since been superseded by states such as Arizona, Georgia and Oklahoma, which have taken an even harder line. In fact, if there's one clear trend in state and local legislation, it's toward a stricter approach.

In Hazelton, Pa., a controversial set of laws has been held up by the courts. The ordinances would require businesses to turn employee information over to the city, which would then verify documents with the federal government. Prospective tenants would have to acquire a permit to rent by proving their legal right to be in the country.

"It used to be that state and local activity was all over the map," says Mark Krikorian, executive director of the Center for immigration Studies, which advocates reduced immigration. "Those that are loosening the rules now are the exception."

Georgia's law touches on every facet of state policy that relates to illegal immigrants. Under its provisions, state and local government agencies have to verify the legal residency of benefit recipients. Many employers will have to do the same whenever they make a hiring decision. And law enforcement agencies are given authority to crack down on human trafficking and fake documents.

Thousands of immigrants, both legal and illegal, have left Oklahoma following the November enactment of a law (HB 1804) that makes it a felony to knowingly transport illegal immigrants and requires employers to verify the immigration status of workers. It also limits some government benefits to those who can produce proof of citizenship.

Employers in numerous sectors, including hotels, restaurants and agriculture, have complained about labor shortages. But Republican state Rep. Randy Terrill, who wrote the law, says it will save the state money due to the abolition of public subsidies for illegal immigrants. "There's

After World War II, Congress decided to codify the scores of immigration laws that had evolved over the years. The landmark Immigration and Nationality Act of 1952 retained a basic quota system that favored immigrants from Northern Europe — especially the skilled workers and relatives of U.S. citizens among them. At the same time, it exempted immigrants from the Western Hemisphere from the quota system — except for the black residents of European colonies in the Caribbean.

Mass Deportation

The 1952 law also attempted to address — in the era's racist terms — the newly acknowledged reality of Mexican workers who crossed the border illegally. Border Patrol agents were given more power to search for illegal immigrants and a bigger territory in which to operate.

"Before 1944, the illegal traffic on the Mexican border . . . was never overwhelming," the President's Commission on Migratory Labor noted in 1951, but in significant evidence that HB 1804 is achieving its intended purpose," he said.[2]

States just a few years ago were debating the expansion of benefits for illegal immigrants, such as in-state tuition rates for college. But now politicians in most locales who appear to be aiding illegal immigrants in any way are widely castigated.

New York Gov. Eliot Spitzer, a Democrat, proposed in fall 2007 that illegal immigrants should be eligible for driver's licenses, arguing that would make them more likely to buy insurance. But the idea touched off a political firestorm not only in his state but also within the Democratic presidential campaign and he quickly backed down.

Early this year, Maryland Democratic Gov. Martin O'Malley called for his state to stop issuing driver's licenses to undocumented immigrants. (It's one of seven that currently do so.) "When you've got a New York governor getting clubbed over the head for trying to institute what Maryland has . . . you realize we are out of sync with the rest of the nation," said state House Republican leader Anthony J. O'Connell.[3]

Legislatures in at least a dozen states are already considering bills modeled on the get-tough approaches taken elsewhere. Legislators in states neighboring Oklahoma, for

A demonstrator in Tucson supports Proposition 200 on Dec. 22, 2004. The voter-approved Arizona law denies some public benefits to illegal immigrants.

instance, say that they feel pressure to introduce restrictive legislation, particularly from constituents in areas where immigrants who had lived in Oklahoma have relocated.

The fact that there's a sort of legislative arms race going on, with states trying to outdo each other on the immigration issue, has many people worried. A patchwork approach, with tough laws in scattered places driving some immigrants toward more lenient jurisdictions, is clearly not the way to resolve a national or even international issue such as immigration.

"Obviously, 50 different state immigration policies is ultimately unworkable," says Romanoff. "All of us much prefer a federal solution."

"The question is, how long should we wait? In Colorado we decided we could wait no longer."

[1] "2007 Enacted State Legislation Related to Immigrants and Immigration," National Conference of State Legislatures, Nov. 29, 2007, www.ncsl.org/print/immig/2007Immigrationfinal.pdf.

[2] Emily Bazar, "Strict Immigration Law Rattles Okla. Businesses," *USA Today*, Jan. 10, 2008, p. 1A.

[3] Lisa Rein, "Immigrant Driver ID Rejected by O'Malley," *The Washington Post*, Jan. 16, 2008, p. B1.

the past seven years, "the wetback traffic has reached entirely new levels. . . . [I]t is virtually an invasion."[17]

In a desperate attempt to reverse the tide, the Border Patrol in 1954 launched "Operation Wetback," transferring nearly 500 Immigration and Naturalization Service (INS) officers from the Canadian perimeter and U.S. cities to join the 250 agents policing the U.S.-Mexican border and adjacent factories and farms. More than 1 million undocumented Mexican migrants were deported.

Although the action enjoyed popular support and bolstered the prestige — and budget — of the INS, it exposed an inherent contradiction in U.S. immigration policy. The 1952 law contained a gaping loophole — the Texas Proviso — a blatant concession to Texas agricultural interests that relied on cheap labor from Mexico.

"The Texas Proviso said companies or farms could knowingly hire illegal immigrants, but they couldn't harbor them," said Lawrence Fuchs, former executive director of

Are Voters Ignoring Immigration?

Iraq War, other issues, may resonate more.

Immigration has emerged as a pervasive political issue, a part of seemingly every state and local campaign and presidential debate. "No issue has dominated the Republican presidential nomination fight the way illegal immigration has," *The Washington Post* reported in January.[1]

A poll conducted by the *Post* and ABC News in December found that more Republican voters in Iowa picked immigration as the first or second most important issue to them — 30 percent — than any other issue. Only 6 percent of Iowa Democrats rated the issue so highly.[2]

Yet illegal immigration has also emerged as a key concern in the Democratic contest. After Sen. Hillary Rodham Clinton, D-N.Y., gave conflicting answers during an October debate about her opinion of Democratic New York Gov. Eliot Spitzer's abortive plan to issue driver's licenses to illegal immigrants, her opponents attacked her. That moment has been widely characterized as opening up the first crack in the façade of her "inevitability" as the Democratic nominee.

"This is a real wedge issue that Democrats need to get right," wrote Stan Greenberg and James Carville, two prominent Democratic Party strategists.[3]

Despite the attention that the issue gets from both candidates and the media, however, there's as yet scant evidence that illegal immigration resonates as strongly with voters as other issues such as the economy, health care or the war in Iraq. "The bottom line is, to most people it's not a pocketbook issue," says Arizona pollster Jim Haynes, "and the pocketbook tends to be seminal in determining how somebody's going to end up voting."

In 2006, several House incumbents and candidates who made tough stances against illegal immigration the centerpiece of their campaigns went down to defeat, including Reps. J.D. Hayworth, R-Ariz., and Jim Ryun, R-Kan.

The track record for gubernatorial candidates who focused their campaigns on immigration was no better that year. Len Munsil in Arizona, Ernest Istook in Oklahoma and Jim Barnett in Kansas all ran against Democratic incumbents and tried to take advantage of their opponents' seeming vulnerability on the immigration issue. None won more than 41 percent of the vote.

Rep. Tom Tancredo, R-Colo., based his presidential campaign on his strong support for tougher immigration measures, but never broke out of the low single digits in polls before dropping out of the race in December.

It was also difficult for candidates to make immigration decisive at the ballot box during the off-year elections of 2007. Even in contests where the issue played a prominent role, it didn't have the influence many observers had predicted. In local contests in New York, for example, Democrats did not pay the predicted price for Spitzer's idea of issuing driver's licenses to illegal immigrants. Instead, they fared better.

In Virginia, Republicans made tough talk on immigration central to their plans for holding on to their threatened majority in the state Senate this past November. They ended up losing control of that body after a decade in power. Local Virginia elections told much the same story.

In Loudoun County, where arguments about illegal newcomers have been intense for several years, Sheriff Stephen Simpson lost a primary bid for renomination but came back to win as an independent against an opponent who had accused him of being soft on immigration. "I think it was hyped up quite a bit in the election, not just in my race but in the area," Simpson says.

In numerous other local contests in Virginia, the injection of immigration as a central concern not only failed to change the outcome but barely shifted the winner's share of the vote from previous elections.

the U.S. Select Commission on Immigration and Refugee Policy. "It was a duplicitous policy. We never really intended to prevent illegals from coming."

Immigration Reform

The foundation of today's immigration system dates back to 1965, when Congress overhauled the immigration rules, scrapping national-origin quotas in favor of immigration limits for major regions of the world and giving preference to immigrants with close relatives living in the United States. By giving priority to family reunification as a basis for admission, the amendments repaired "a deep and painful flaw in the fabric of American justice," President Lyndon B. Johnson declared at the time.

There were some races where opposition to illegal immigration was an effective political tactic. Tom Selders, the mayor of Greeley, Colo., lost after expressing sympathy for illegal immigrants snared in a federal raid on a local meatpacking plant. By showcasing immigration concerns, Republican Jim Ogonowski ran a surprisingly close race in an October special election in a Massachusetts congressional district that has long favored Democrats, although ultimately he lost.

"This issue has real implications for the country. It captures all the American people's anger and frustration not only with immigration but with the economy," said Rep. Rahm Emanuel of Illinois, chairman of the House Democratic Caucus and chief strategist for his party's congressional candidates in 2006. "It's self-evident. This is a big problem."[4]

But it has become surprisingly hard to outflank most candidates on this contentious subject. Last November's challenger to Charles Colgan, a Democratic state senator in Virginia, tried to paint him as soft, going so far as to distribute cartoons depicting Colgan helping people over the wall at the border. But Colgan countered by pointing out his votes in opposition to extending various benefits to illegal immigrants. "The first thing this nation must do is seal the border," he says. "We cannot let this influx continue." Colgan won reelection easily.

Why hasn't immigration, which is getting so much attention, proved to be a central concern when voters cast

Rep. Tom Tancredo, R-Colo., based his presidential campaign on his strong support for tougher immigration measures but got little traction and dropped out of the race in December 2007.

their ballots? For one thing, not everyone agrees on every proposal to make life tougher for illegal immigrants. And the GOP's hard line on immigration threatens to push Hispanic voters over to the Democratic Party.

But illegal immigration may be failing to take off as a voting issue not because of opposition to the hard-line proposals but because something like a consensus in favor of them has already emerged. It's a simple matter for any candidate to communicate a belief that border security should be tightened and that current laws should be more strictly enforced.

The emergence of that kind of consensus suggests that hard-liners have in fact won a good portion of their argument. In his statement announcing he was leaving the presidential race, Tancredo said, "Just last week *Newsweek* declared that 'anti-immigrant zealot' [Tancredo] had already won. 'Now even Dems dance to his no mas salsa tune.'"

[1] Jonathan Weisman, "For Republicans, Contest's Hallmark Is Immigration," *The Washington Post*, Jan. 2, 2008, p. A1.

[2] "What Iowans Care About," *The Washington Post*, Jan. 3, 2008, p. A11.

[3] Perry Bacon Jr. and Anne E. Kornblut, "Issue of Illegal Immigration Is Quandary for Democrats," *The Washington Post*, Nov. 2, 2007, p. A2.

[4] Jonathan Weisman, "GOP Finds Hot Button in Illegal Immigration," *The Washington Post*, Oct. 23, 2007, p. A7.

However, the law also dramatically changed the immigration landscape. Most newcomers now hailed from the developing world — about half from Latin America. While nearly 70 percent of immigrants had come from Europe or Canada in the 1950s, by the 1980s that figure had dropped to about 14 percent. Meanwhile, the percentage coming from Asia, Central America and the

Caribbean jumped from about 30 percent in the 1950s to 75 percent during the '70s.

In 1978, the select commission concluded that illegal immigration was the most pressing problem facing immigration authorities, a perception shared by the general public.[18] The number of border apprehensions peaked in 1986 at 1.7 million, driven in part by a deepening economic

A pro-immigrant rally in Atlanta draws a crowd on May 1, 2006. The nation's rapidly rising foreign-born population is dispersing well beyond "gatekeeper" states such as California and Texas to non-traditional destinations like Georgia, Arkansas and Iowa.

crisis in Mexico. Some felt the decade-long increase in illegal immigration was particularly unfair to the tens of thousands of legal petitioners waiting for years to obtain entry visas.

"The simple truth is that we've lost control of our own borders," declared President Ronald Reagan, "and no nation can do that and survive."[19]

In the mid-1980s, a movement emerged to fix the illegal-immigration problem. Interestingly, the debate on Capitol Hill was marked by bipartisan alliances described by Sen. Alan K. Simpson, R-Wyo., as "the goofiest ideological-bedfellow activity I've ever seen."[20] Conservative, anti-immigration think tanks teamed up with liberal labor unions and environmentalists favoring tighter restrictions on immigration. Pro-growth and business

groups joined forces with longtime adversaries in the Hispanic and civil rights communities to oppose the legislation.

After several false starts, Congress passed the Immigration Reform and Control Act (IRCA) in October 1986 — the most sweeping revision of U.S. immigration policy in more than two decades. Using a carrot-and-stick approach, IRCA granted a general amnesty to all undocumented aliens who were in the United States before 1982 and imposed monetary sanctions — or even prison — against employers who knowingly hired undocumented workers for the first time.

Changes in 1996

In the 1990s nearly 10 million newcomers — the largest influx ever — arrived on U.S. shores, with most still coming from Latin America and Asia.

Bill Clinton realized early in his presidency that the so-called amnesty program enacted in 1986 had not solved the illegal-immigration problem. And in the Border States, concern was growing that undocumented immigrants were costing U.S. taxpayers too much in social, health and educational services. On Nov. 8, 1994, California voters approved Proposition 187, denying illegal immigrants public education or non-essential public-health services. Immigrants'-rights organizations immediately challenged the law, which a court later ruled was mostly unconstitutional. But the proposition's passage had alerted politicians to the intensity of anti-illegal immigrant sentiment.[21]

House Republicans immediately included a proposal to bar welfare benefits for legal immigrants in their "Contract with America," and in 1995, after the GOP had won control of the House, Congress took another stab at reforming the rules for both legal and illegal immigration. But business groups blocked efforts to reduce legal immigration, so the new law primarily focused on curbing illegal immigration.

The final legislation, which cleared Congress on Sept. 30, 1996, nearly doubled the size of the Border Patrol and provided 600 new INS investigators. It appropriated $12 million for new border-control devices, including motion sensors, set tougher standards for applying for political asylum and made it easier to expel foreigners with fake documents or none at all.[22] The law also severely limited — and in many cases completely eliminated — non-citizens' ability to challenge INS decisions in court.[23]

But the new law did not force authorities to crack down on businesses that employed illegal immigrants, even though there was wide agreement that such a crack-down was vital. As the Commission on Immigration Reform had said in 1994, the centerpiece of any effort to stop illegal entrants should be to "turn off the jobs magnet that attracts them."

By 1999, however, amid an economic boom and low unemployment, the INS had stopped raiding work sites to round up illegal immigrant workers and was focusing on foreign criminals, immigrant-smugglers and document fraud. As for cracking down on employers, an agency district director told *The Washington Post*, "We're out of that business." The idea that employers could be persuaded not to hire illegal workers "is a fairy tale."[24]

Legal immigration, however, has been diminished by the government response to the terrorist attacks of Sept. 11, 2001. In fiscal 2002-2003, the number of people granted legal permanent residence (green cards) fell by 34 percent; 28,000 people were granted political asylum, 59 percent fewer than were granted asylum in fiscal 2000-2001.[25] But the growth of illegal immigration under way before 9/11 continued, with 57 percent of the illegal immigrants coming from Mexico.[26]

Due to the family-reunification provision in immigration law, Mexico is also the leading country of origin for legal immigrants — with 116,000 of the 705,827 legal immigrants in fiscal 2002-2003 coming from Mexico.[27] No Middle Eastern or predominantly Muslim countries have high numbers of legal immigrants, although Pakistan was 13th among the top 15 countries of origin for legal immigrants in 1998.[28]

Public Opinion

The combination of concerns about terrorism and the growing number of illegal immigrants — and their movement into parts of the country unused to dealing with foreign newcomers — made illegal immigration a top-tier issue.

In 2005, Congress passed the Real ID Act, which grew out of the 9/11 Commission investigations into how Arab terrorists burrowed into American society to carry out the Sept. 11, 2001. Of the 19 hijackers, 13 had obtained legitimate driver's licenses, said Rep. F. James Sensenbrenner Jr., R-Wis., author of the legislation. The commission called for national standards for the basic American identification documents: birth certificates, Social Security cards and driver's licenses. In states that adopt the strict requirements of the law — which begins to go into effect in May 2008 — license applicants will have to present

President George W. Bush announces the bipartisan compromise immigration deal he struck with Congress on May 17, 2007. The agreement would have granted temporary legal status to virtually all illegal immigrants. Despite the backing of most Democrats and several conservative Republicans, the package was defeated. Bush is flanked by Homeland Security Secretary Michael Chertoff, left, and Commerce Secretary Carlos Gutierrez.

ironclad proof of identity, which will be checked against federal and state databases.[29]

After the House in 2005 passed a punitive bill that would have classified illegal immigrants as felons, demonstrations in cities across the country drew hundreds of thousands of marchers during the spring of 2006. On May 1, hundreds of thousands more participated in what some billed as "the Great American Boycott of 2006." The idea was for immigrants, legal and illegal, to demonstrate their economic contribution to the country by staying away from their jobs on May Day.

In terms of numbers alone, the demonstrations of April and May were impressive. But they may also have spurred a backlash among some sectors of the public. "The size and magnitude of the demonstrations had some kind of backfire effect," John McLaughlin, a Republican pollster, told reporters after the first round of marches. "The Republicans that are tough on immigration are doing well right now."[30]

That turned out not to be the case come election-time, however. Some prominent critics of current immigration policy, including Republican Reps. Jim Ryun of Kansas and J.D. Hayworth of Arizona, went down to defeat in November 2006. Republicans in general paid a clear price among Hispanics for their tough stand. Exit polling in 2006 suggested that 30 percent of Hispanics voted for Republicans in congressional races that year, while Democrats garnered 69 percent. President Bush had taken

40 percent of the Hispanic vote in his reelection race two years earlier.[31] "I don't think we did ourselves any favors when we engaged the public in a major topic and didn't pass the legislation to deal with it," said Sen. Sam Brownback, R-Kan., who dropped out of the GOP presidential primary in October 2007.[32]

Perhaps partly in response, Republicans just after the 2006 elections selected as their new national chairman Florida Sen. Mel Martinez, a prominent Cuban-American who had served in the Bush Cabinet. The Federation for American Immigration Reform's Mehlman, then the outgoing party chairman, told reporters that he was concerned about where the party stood with Hispanics. "Hispanics are not single-issue voters, but GOP officials said the tone of the immigration debate hurt the party's standing with the fastest-growing minority group," *The Washington Post* reported.[33]

CURRENT SITUATION

Difficult Fix

Currently, immigration is the subject of countless legislative proposals at all levels of government. Congress under the new Democratic majority ushered in with the 2006 elections has generally considered more lenient legislation, but any proposal that seems to offer any sort of aid to illegal immigrants has failed to gain traction. In states and in many localities, meanwhile, hundreds of punitive bills have passed into law.

Amid much fanfare, President Bush and a bipartisan group of 10 senators announced an agreement on May 17, 2007, on a comprehensive compromise plan to tighten border security and address the fate of the nation's 12 million illegal immigrants. "The agreement reached today is one that will help enforce our borders," Bush said. "But equally importantly, it will treat people with respect. This is a bill where people who live here in our country will be treated without amnesty, but without animosity."[34]

The 380-page plan was worked out just in time to meet a deadline for the beginning of Senate debate on the issue. "The plan isn't perfect, but only a bipartisan bill will become law," said Sen. Kennedy.[35]

But immigration is the rare issue that cuts across partisan lines. Despite the backing of most Democrats, the Bush administration and conservative Republicans such as

Kennedy's negotiating partner, Sen. Jon Kyl, R-Ariz., the package went down to defeat. Supporters were unable to muster the support of 60 senators necessary even to bring it to a vote in the face of determined opposition.

The agreement would have granted temporary legal status to virtually all illegal immigrants, allowing them to apply for residence visas and citizenship through a lengthy process. They would have to wait for eight years before applying for permanent resident status and pay fines of up to $5,000; in addition, heads of households would be forced to leave the country and reenter legally.

But the process could not begin for any illegal aliens — and a new guest worker program would also be put on hold — until after a tough border crackdown had gone into effect. The deal called for the deployment of 18,000 new Border Patrol agents and extensive new physical barriers, including 200 miles of vehicle barriers, 370 miles of fencing and 70 ground-based camera and radar towers. In addition, funding would be provided for the detention of 27,500 illegal immigrants, and new identification tools would be developed to help screen out illegal job applicants.

Conservative opponents of the package in the Senate — as well as most of the 2008 GOP presidential hopefuls — derided it as an "amnesty" bill, giving an unfair citizenship advantage to people who had come into the country illegally.

But liberals and immigration advocacy groups also questioned the terms of the Senate proposal, particularly a change in visa applications. In contrast to the current system, which stresses family ties, a new, complex, point system would favor skilled, educated workers. About 50 percent of the points would be based on employment criteria, with just 10 percent based on family connections.

Even if the Senate had passed the bill, its prospects in the House would have been dim. Despite the change in partisan control of Congress, there was still less sentiment in the House than in the Senate for any bill that was perceived as giving a break to illegal aliens. "Unless the White House produces 60 or 70 Republican votes in the House, it will be difficult to pass an immigration bill similar to the Senate proposal," Rep. Rahm Emanuel, D-Ill., chairman of the House Democratic Caucus, said in May 2007.[36]

Those votes would have been tough to get. Some staunch critics of immigration policy were defeated in the

Would tighter border security curb illegal immigration?

YES
Mark Krikorian
Executive Director, Center for Immigration Studies

Written for *CQ Researcher*, Jan. 23, 2008

Border security is one piece of the very large controlling-immigration puzzle. But policing borders, including the use of physical barriers where necessary, has been integral to the preservation of national sovereignty for centuries. In our country, some two-thirds of the illegal population has snuck across the border with Mexico; the rest entered legally — as tourists, students, etc. — and never left.

As part of the development of a modern, national immigration system, Congress in 1924 created the U.S. Border Patrol. As illegal immigration grew to massive proportions in the late 1970s, the Border Patrol's work became something of a charade, with a handful of officers returning whatever Mexican border-jumpers they could nab and then watching them immediately turn around and try again.

The first step in closing that revolving door came in 1993 and 1994, when new strategies were implemented in San Diego and El Paso, where most illegal immigration occurred, to deter crossings altogether rather than simply chase after people through streets and alleys after they'd already crossed.

Over the past decade-and-a-half, the enforcement infrastructure at the border has grown immensely, but it is still laughably inadequate. Although the number of agents at the Southern border has tripled, to some 12,000, that still represents an average of no more than two agents per mile per shift.

Expanded fencing has also been part of this build-up. In the past, when the region on both sides of our Southern border was essentially empty, the limited fencing in place was intended simply to keep cattle from wandering off. Now, with huge metropolises on the Mexican side, serious fencing is being built — first in San Diego, where illegal crossings have plummeted as a result, and now along more than 800 additional miles of the border, though this is still a work in progress. In addition to these physical barriers, we have had for years additional security measures (deceptively labeled "virtual fencing"), such as motion sensors, stadium lighting and remote-controlled cameras.

But while border enforcement is a necessary element of immigration control, it is not sufficient. There are three layers of immigration security — our visa-issuing consulates abroad, the border (including legal entry points) and the interior of the country. Improvements at the border are essential, and many are already under way. The weakest link today is the interior, where efforts to deny illegal immigrants jobs, driver's licenses, bank accounts, etc., are being fought at every turn by the business and ethnic lobbyists who benefit from open borders.

NO
Douglas S. Massey
Professor of Sociology, Princeton University

From testimony before House Judiciary Subcommittee on Immigration, April 20, 2007

As envisioned under [the North American Free Trade Agreement], the economies of the U.S. and Mexico are integrating, and the rising cross-border movement of goods and services has been accompanied by migration of all sorts of people. Since 1986, the number of exchange visitors from Mexico has tripled, the number of business visitors has quadrupled and the number of intra-company transferees has grown 5.5 times.

Within this rapidly integrating economy, however, U.S. policy makers have somehow sought to prevent the cross-border movement of workers. We have adopted an increasingly restrictive set of immigration and border-enforcement policies. First, the Immigration Reform and Control Act of 1986 granted $400 million to expand the size of the Border Patrol. Then the 1990 Immigration Act authorized hiring another 1,000 officers. In 1993, these new personnel were deployed as part of an all-out effort to stop unauthorized border crossing in El Paso, a strategy that was extended to San Diego in 1994. Finally, the 1996 Illegal Immigration Reform and Immigrant Responsibility Act provided funds to hire an additional 1,000 Border Patrol officers per year through 2001.

In essence, the U.S. militarized the border with its closest neighbor, a nation to which it was committed by treaty to an ongoing process of economic integration. Rather than slowing the flow of immigrants into the U.S., however, this policy yielded an array of unintended and very negative consequences.

The most immediate effect was to transform the geography of border crossing. Whereas undocumented border crossing during the 1980s focused on San Diego and El Paso, the selective hardening of these sectors after 1993 diverted the flows to new and remote crossings. Undocumented Mexican migration was thus nationalized. The migrants got wise and simply went around built-up sectors. As a result, the probability of apprehension plummeted to record low levels. American taxpayers were spending billions more to catch fewer migrants.

And, rather than returning home possibly to face the gauntlet at the border again, Mexicans without documents remained longer in the U.S. The ultimate effect of restrictive border policies was to double the net rate of undocumented population growth, making Hispanics the nation's largest minority years before Census Bureau demographers had projected.

At this point, pouring more money into border enforcement will not help the situation, and in my opinion constitutes a waste of taxpayer money. We must realize that the solution to the current crisis does not lie in further militarizing the border with a friendly trading nation that poses no conceivable threat.

2006 elections, but for the most part they were replaced by newcomers who also took a hard line against illegal immigration. "This proposal would do lasting damage to the country, American workers and the rule of law," said Lamar Smith of Texas, ranking Republican on the House Judiciary Committee, in response to the deal between senators and the White House. "Just because somebody is in the country illegally doesn't mean we have to give them citizenship."[37] The House did not vote at all on comprehensive immigration legislation in 2007.

Federal Inaction

Not long after the Senate's comprehensive bill failed, the attempt to extend legal status to immigrants attending college also failed. The DREAM Act would have protected students from deportation and allowed young adults (up to age 30) to qualify for permanent legal status if they completed high school and at least two years of college or military service.

On Oct. 24, Senate supporters fell eight votes short of the 60 needed to end debate on the bill and bring it to a final vote. The following month, supporters of legislation to address the issue of temporary guest workers — the AgJobs bill — announced that the political climate had turned against them, and they would drop their efforts at least until 2008.

"Amnesty for illegal immigrants is dead for this Congress," says Krikorian of the Center for Immigration Studies. "When the pro-amnesty side couldn't even pass small measures like the DREAM Act and the AgJobs bill, there's little doubt that legalizing illegal immigrants is dead in the water at least until 2009."

Given the pressure on Congress to do something to address the topic, those lobbying for tougher restrictions remain optimistic that this year could see passage of the Secure America With Verification Enforcement Act. The SAVE Act would require all employers to use an electronic verification system to check the legal status of all workers.

In the absence of successful congressional action thus far, the Bush administration last August unveiled a package designed to break the stalemate. The strategy includes stepped-up work-site raids and arrests of fugitive illegal immigrants. The administration also created a new requirement for federal contractors to use the E-Verify system for screening the legal status of new employees.

In October, a federal judge issued a temporary injunction blocking a part of the Homeland Security package that would have required employers to fire workers whose Social Security numbers do not match information in government databases.

The Immigrations and Customs Enforcement agency in January announced a plan to speed the deportation of foreign-born criminals. Under current law, immigrants convicted of crimes are only deported after serving their sentences. ICE intends to work with states to create parole programs that would allow for the early release of non-violent offenders if they agreed to immediate deportation. The program would place a strain on federal detention centers but provide fiscal relief and bed space to state and local governments housing such prisoners. Last year, ICE sent 276,912 people back to their home countries, including many who were not arrested for crimes but had violated civil immigration statutes.[38]

OUTLOOK
Tough Talk

Immigration will clearly remain an important part of the political conversation in this country. The factors that have made it so prominent — the record number of immigrants, both legal and illegal, and their dispersal into parts of the country that had not seen large influxes of immigrants in living memory — show little sign of abating.

The course that any policy changes will take will depend on who wins the presidency. Attempts at addressing the issue in a comprehensive way in Congress failed, due to concerted opposition to the compromise package brokered between the Bush White House and a bipartisan group of senators. Since that time, more modest bills have not been able to advance.

That means the issue will not be resolved as a policy matter until 2009, at the earliest. Instead, it will remain a major theme of the presidential campaign. Immigration has become, perhaps, the dominant issue among the Republican candidates, as well as one that Democrats have had to address in several particulars.

In a December interview with *The Boston Globe*, Illinois Sen. Barack Obama, one of the Democratic front-runners, predicted that any Republican candidate, save for McCain, would center his race on two things — fear of terrorism and fear of immigration.[39]

But the immigration issue has not broken along strictly partisan lines. Krikorian of the Center for Immigration Studies predicts that even if the election results in a Democratic president and Congress, the broad policy trajectory will be toward further tightening of immigration policy.

"I don't care whether it's a new Democratic or a new Republican president, they're going to have to address it," says Kent, of Americans for Immigration Control. "The new president will have to toughen up the border."

Politicians of all stripes indeed now pay homage to the idea that border security must be tightened and that current laws need more rigorous enforcement. But debate is still hot over questions of how much to penalize illegal immigrants and employers — and whether efforts to do just that may ultimately prove counterproductive.

Mehlman of the Federation for American Immigration Reform says "the forces that have been trying to promote amnesty and lots of guest workers are not going to go away." Mehlman says that even if current campaign rhetoric generally supports the tough approach his organization favors, the dynamic of actually changing policies in 2009 and after may not change that much.

"It wouldn't be the first time a politician said one thing during the campaign and acted differently once in office," he says.

He notes that the business groups that encourage immigration have deep pockets, but he believes that "this is an issue that the American public is making a stand on."

The National Immigration Forum's Sharry counters that the policy debate has been hijacked by heated political rhetoric and that it's become difficult to discuss what would be the best solutions without accusations being hurled if a proposal sounds at all "soft" on illegal immigrants.

Nevertheless, he notes, most people do not support the toughest proposals that would treat illegal immigrants as felons and seek their mass deportation. "I suspect it's going to take one or perhaps two election cycles to figure out who does it help and who does it hurt," Sharry says. "My prediction is that the Republican embrace of the extreme anti-immigrant groups will be seen in retrospect as an act of slow-motion suicide."

Douglas S. Massey, a Princeton University sociologist, agrees that the politics of this issue may play out poorly over the long term for those proposing a serious crackdown. He notes that there have been many occasions in American history when "beating on immigrants" has been an expedient strategy, but he argues it's never played well successfully as a sustained national issue.

"It's not a long-term strategy for political success, if you look at the future composition of America," Massey says, alluding in particular to the growth in foreign-born populations.

The political debate clearly will have a profound influence on the policy decisions made on immigration in the coming years. But the underlying demographic trends are likely to continue regardless. "With the baby boomers retiring, we will need barely skilled workers more than ever," says Jacoby, of the Manhattan Institute, referring in part to health-care aides.

She argues that growth in immigration is simply an aspect of globalization. Although people are uncomfortable with change and tend to see its downsides first, she believes that people will eventually realize large-scale migration is an inevitable part of the American future.

"We're in a bad time, and our politics are close to broken," she says, "but eventually American pragmatism will come to the surface."

UPDATE

"People come here to have babies," Sen. Lindsey Graham, R-S.C., said on a Fox News show in July 2010 during a summer when immigration controversies swirled through Washington and the states. Graham introduced to the national discourse the term "drop and leave," a practice he says is common among illegal immigrants who enter the country and proceed to the nearest emergency room to give birth to their family's "anchor baby," who is automatically a U.S. citizen.[40]

Graham joined other Republicans who have been agitating for a constitutional amendment to alter the 14th Amendment to remove "birthright citizenship" for children of immigrants. Many of them know it would be an uphill battle to change a 142-year-old amendment designed primarily to ensure freedom for children of slaves — the Supreme Court has twice rejected similar proposals.[41] Politically, however, the proposal put wind in the sails of conservatives calling for stepped-up enforcement of immigration laws to seal porous U.S. borders, restore respect for the law and reduce the financial burden they say undocumented workers impose on state and local social programs.

But to immigrants' advocates, the proposal is a xenophobic distraction. "Our nation cannot revert to the shameful 'separate but equal' doctrine that justified segregation in America for over 50 years," said Ali Noorani, executive director of the National Immigration Forum, a Washington-based group that advocates on behalf of immigrants. "By denying the right to citizenship to children born on American soil, we will not only stifle the potential of success for countless Americans but we will betray the basic principles of equality envisioned by our Founding Fathers."[42]

About 340,000 of the 4.3 million babies born in the United States in 2008 — about 8 percent — have at least one undocumented immigrant as a parent, according to a study released in August by the Pew Hispanic Center.[43]

The proposal to change the 14th Amendment is opposed by 56 percent of Americans, according to a national poll by the Pew Research Center for the People and the Press, while 41 percent favor it.

Whether the anchor-baby issue endures or fades, it encapsulates the national divisions over proposed crackdowns on illegal immigration. These fissures have been on noisy display this year in Arizona, where in April Republican Gov. Jan Brewer signed the nation's toughest immigration enforcement law.

It makes the failure to carry immigration documents a crime and gives police broad powers to detain anyone suspected of being in the country illegally. "We have to trust our law enforcement," said Brewer, responding to demands from Arizonans fearful of being overrun by illegal immigrants committing crimes in their communities while the politically stalemated federal government sits idly by.[44] "What part of illegal don't you understand?" read countless protest signs carried by Arizonans supporting the crackdown when President Obama pounced on the law, saying it threatened "to undermine basic notions of fairness that we cherish as Americans, as well as the trust between police and our communities that is so crucial to keeping us safe."[45]

The plot thickened. Foreign governments, including Mexico, protested, and entertainers and civil rights groups began a boycott of Arizona businesses. U.S. Attorney General Eric Holder filed a lawsuit to block the law, and on July 27 U.S. District Judge Susan Bolton froze several of its components two days before they would have taken effect. In August, Gov. Brewer filed an appeal to the Ninth U.S. Circuit Court of Appeals.[46]

National polls showed a majority of Americans backing the Arizona crackdown, by 55 percent according to a July CNN/Opinion Research poll.

The Arizona debate, coupled with Congress' failure to take up immigration legislation, prompted an uptick in proposed state immigration bills around the country, according to the National Conference of State Legislatures. As of June 30, bills similar to Arizona's had been introduced in South Carolina, Pennsylvania, Minnesota, Rhode Island and Michigan.[47]

The political import of the issue was demonstrated in the August primary election for the Senate seat held by Sen. John McCain, R-Ariz. In 2007 McCain had worked with Democrats and the Bush administration in an unsuccessful attempt at comprehensive immigration reform. In 2010 he moved rapidly to the right in his ultimately successful campaign against conservative former U.S. Rep. J. D. Hayworth. McCain abandoned his past support for guest worker programs and stressed the enforcement approach.[48]

What is happening, according to Ira Mehlman, media director of the Federation for American Immigration Reform, which favors stricter immigration enforcement, is that "the enforcement of immigration law has become a higher priority for the public, as evidenced by the public support for the Arizona law and opposition to" the lawsuit by Attorney General Holder. "His suit is directed at other states in an attempt to intimidate them" so they won't follow Arizona's path, Mehlman says. "He's saying, 'We don't want immigration law enforced.'"

Noorani of the Immigration Forum says that what stands out from the polling is that "the country is asking why Congress hasn't fixed the broken immigration system."

Congress, however, has been unable to muster consensus even to take up omnibus immigration reform, and the Obama administration has not offered its own bill. The only recent action of note came on Aug. 12, when the Senate convened in a special session and passed by acclamation a bill just passed by the House providing $600 million for "emergency supplemental appropriations for border security."

One long-standing legislative item that proponents hope to move in a comprehensive package is the Development, Relief and Education of Alien Minors (DREAM) Act, introduced by Sen. Richard Durbin, D-Ill., and Rep. Howard Berman, D-Calif. Backed by many colleges and universities, it would help children of undocumented immigrants who have attended American public schools go on to higher education and emerge on a path to citizenship.

The American Association of Community Colleges said in an April 26 statement: "We call upon Congress to pass the DREAM Act and to further fulfill its responsibility to enact a national immigration policy that is clear, that is fair and that upholds our nation's founding principles as a land of sanctuary and opportunity." Opponents of the bill, who are organized in a group with a website called noamericandreamact.org, call it a bailout for illegal immigrants who will compete with native-born Americans for scarce slots at public universities.

The administration, meanwhile, has stepped up border enforcement, committing in May to send several hundred Army National Guard troops to Arizona. To help employers comply with the law on hiring, the Department of Homeland Security has launched a free, voluntary program called E-Verify, an Internet-based system that allows an employer, using information reported on an employee's Employment Eligibility Verification form, to determine the eligibility of that employee to work in the United States. More than 216,000 employers are enrolled in the program, and more than 13 million queries have gone through the system in fiscal 2010, as of July 31, 2010.[49]

More controversially, Homeland Security's Immigration and Customs Enforcement (ICE) in August was reported to have embarked on a systematic review of pending cases of immigration law violations and to be moving to dismiss a backlog of thousands that do not involve immigrants with serious criminal records.[50] An ICE spokesperson said the review is part of the agency's national strategy to prioritize the deportations of illegal immigrants who pose a threat to security and public safety. Critics, however, assailed the plan as another sign that the administration is trying to create a backdoor "amnesty" program.

Criticism of the Obama approach is not confined to conservatives. In July, lawyers at the pro-immigration American Immigration Council sued Homeland Security, seeking public release of records on enforcement of the H-1B visa program, which allows businesses temporarily to hire foreign workers with high-level skills. The concern is over a perceived increase in unannounced workplace visits by federal agents, as well as whether the Obama administration is holding to its announced "open government" initiative, in which it pledged to make the operations of federal agencies more transparent.

The future of the immigration debate revolves around the question of whether Congress, following the November midterm elections, will overcome political fractiousness and take up a bill that addresses key questions. They include what to do about the estimated 11.1 million undocumented immigrants living in the United States.[51] The questions also include how to stanch the continuing influx of foreigners illegally penetrating U.S. borders and how legally to meet the needs of industries such as agriculture, construction and domestic services that depend on immigrant workers.

"All indicators are that Congress' makeup will be different, with less likelihood for amnesty," says Mehlman. "Then the 2012 election starts, and there will likely be some pressure for more enforcement. Amnesty [for those who entered the country illegally] as a precondition [for a deal] is unacceptable," he says.

But Noorani predicts more compromise. "Early in 2011, before the presidential primaries, Republicans will be faced with a decision on whether to sue for peace on immigration," he says. "Only the most delusional political operative will think they can win the White House without significant numbers of Hispanic voters."

NOTES

1. Quoted in Ryan Lizza, "Return of the Nativist," *The New Yorker*, Dec. 17, 2007, p. 46. For more on immigrant families that face being split up, see Pamela Constable, "Divided by Deportation: Unexpected Orders to Return to Countries Leave Families in Anguish During Holidays," *The Washington Post*, Dec. 24, 2007, p. B1.

2. Quoted in Lizza, *op. cit.*

3. Ellis Cose, "The Rise of a New American Underclass," *Newsweek*, Jan. 7, 2008, p. 74.

4. William Neikirk, "Gingrich Rips Bush on Immigration," *Chicago Tribune*, Aug. 15, 2007, p. 3.

5. Jennifer Ludden, "Q&A: Sen. Kennedy on Immigration, Then & Now," May 9, 2006, NPR.org, www.npr.org/templates/story/story.php?storyId=5393857.

6. Lizza, *op. cit.*

7. "GOP Hopefuls Debate Immigration on Univision," www.msnbc.msn.com/id/22173520/.

8. David Harper, "Terrill Leads Way on Issue," *Tulsa World*, Oct. 30, 2007, www.TulsaWorld.com.

9. Julia Preston, "U.S. to Speed Deportation of Criminals Behind Bars," *The New York Times*, Jan. 15, 2008, p. A12.

10. "Rot in the Fields," *The Washington Post*, Dec. 3, 2007, p. A16.

11. Steven Greenhouse, "U.S. Seeks Rules to Allow Increase in Guest Workers," *The New York Times*, Oct. 10, 2007, p. A16.

12. Kathy Kiely, "Children Caught in the Immigration Crossfire," *USA Today*, Oct. 8, 2007, p. 1A.

13. Patrick McGreevy, "Gov's Party Blocks His College Board Choice," *Los Angeles Times*, Jan. 15, 2008, p. B3.

14. Unless otherwise noted, material in the background section comes from Rodman D. Griffin, "Illegal Immigration," April 24, 1992, pp. 361-384; Kenneth Jost, "Cracking Down on Immigration," Feb. 3, 1995, pp. 97-120; David Masci, "Debate Over Immigration," July 14, 2000, pp. 569-592; and Peter Katel, "Illegal Immigration," May 6, 2005, pp. 393-420, all in *CQ Researcher*.

15. For background, see Richard L. Worsnop, "Asian Americans," *CQ Researcher*, Dec. 13, 1991, pp. 945-968.

16. For background, see "Quota Control and the National-Origin System," Nov. 1, 1926; "The National-Origin Immigration Plan," March 12, 1929; and "Immigration and Deportation," April 18, 1939, all in *Editorial Research Reports*, available from *CQ Researcher Plus Archive*, http://cqpress.com.

17. Quoted in Ellis Cose, *A Nation of Strangers: Prejudice, Politics and the Populating of America* (1992), p. 191.

18. Cited in Michael Fix, ed., *The Paper Curtain: Employer Sanctions' Implementation, Impact, and Reform* (1991), p. 2.

19. Quoted in Tom Morganthau, *et al.*, "Closing the Door," *Newsweek*, June 25, 1984.

20. Quoted in Dick Kirschten, "Come In! Keep Out!" *National Journal*, May 19, 1990, p. 1206.

21. Ann Chih Lin, ed., *Immigration*, CQ Press (2002), pp. 60-61.

22. William Branigin, "Congress Finishes Major Legislation; Immigration; Focus is Borders, Not Benefits," *The Washington Post*, Oct. 1, 1996, p. A1.

23. David Johnston, "Government is Quickly Using Power of New Immigration Law," *The New York Times*, Oct. 22, 1996, p. A20.

24. William Branigin, "INS Shifts 'Interior' Strategy to Target Criminal Aliens," *The Washington Post*, March 15, 1999, p. A3.

25. Deborah Meyers and Jennifer Yau, "US Immigration Statistics in 2003," Migration Policy Institute, Nov. 1, 2004, www.migrationinformation.org/USfocus/display.cfm?id=263; and Homeland Security Department, "2003 Yearbook of Immigration Statistics," http://uscis.gov/graphics/shared/statistics/yearbook/index.htm.

26. Jeffrey S. Passel, "Estimates of the Size and Characteristics of the Undocumented Population," Pew Hispanic Center, March 21, 2005, p. 8.

27. Meyers and Yau, *op. cit.*

28. Lin, *op. cit.*, p. 20.

29. For background, see Peter Katel, "Real ID," *CQ Researcher*, May 4, 2007, pp. 385-408.

30. David D. Kirkpatrick, "Demonstrations on Immigration are Hardening a Divide," *The New York Times*, April 17, 2006, p. 16.

31. Arian Campo-Flores, "A Latino 'Spanking,'" *Newsweek*, Dec. 4, 2006, p. 40.

32. Rick Montgomery and Scott Cannon, "Party Shift Won't End Immigration Debate," *The Washington Post*, Dec. 17, 2006, p. A11.

33. Jim VandeHei, "Florida Senator Will Be a Top RNC Officer," *The Washington Post*, Nov. 14, 2006, p. A4.

34. Karoun Demirjian, "Bipartisan Immigration Deal Reached," *Chicago Tribune*, May 18, 2007, p. 1.

35. *Ibid.*

36. Robert Pear and Jim Rutenberg, "Senators in Bipartisan Deal on Broad Immigration Bill," *The New York Times*, May 18, 2007, p. A1.

37. Demirjian, *op. cit.*

38. Julia Preston, "U.S. to Speed Deportation of Criminals Behind Bars," *The New York Times*, Jan. 15, 2008, p. A12.

39. Foon Rhee, "Obama Says He Wants a Mandate for Change," www.boston.com/news/politics/political intelligence/2007/12/obama_says_he_w.html.

40. Elise Foley, "Graham Wants to Deny American-Born Babies Citizenship," *The Washington Independent*, July 29, 2010.

41. For a legal and historical discussion on birthright citizenship, see www.immigrationpolicy.org/per spectives/made-america-myths-facts-about-birth-right-citizenship.

42. National Immigration Forum press release, "Immigration Detour: GOP Attacks American Children Instead of Fixing Broken Immigration System," Aug. 11, 2010.

43. For the study "Unauthorized Immigrants and Their U.S.-Born Children," Aug. 11, 2010, see http://pewhispanic.org/reports/report.php?ReportID=125.

44. Randal C. Archibold, "Arizona Enacts Stringent Law on Immigration," *The New York Times*, April 23, 2010.

45. *Ibid.*

46. Warren Richey, "Why Judge Susan Bolton Blocked Key Parts of Arizona's SB 1070," *The Christian Science Monitor*, July 28, 2010.

47. National Conference of State Legislatures, "Arizona's Immigration Enforcement Laws," 2010, www.ncsl.org/?tabid=20263.

48. Robert Rische, "The 'Maverick' Survives Arizona Primary, but Incumbency Is Still Frowned upon from Florida to Alaska," *San Diego Examiner*, Aug. 25, 2010.

49. See www.dhs.gov/files/programs/gc_118522 1678150.shtm.

50. Susan Carroll, "Feds Moving to Dismiss Some Deportation Cases," *Houston Chronicle*, Aug. 24, 2010.

51. Hope Yen, "Illegal Immigration Population Down for 1st Time in 2 Decades," Associated Press, *Detroit Free Press,* Sept. 2, 2010.

BIBLIOGRAPHY

Books

Massey, Douglas S., ed., *New Faces in New Places: The Changing Geography of American Immigration*, Russell Sage Foundation, 2008.
A collection of academic pieces shows how the waves of recent immigrants have been dispersed across America by shifts in various economic sectors and how their presence in areas outside traditional "gateways" has led to social tension.

Myers, Dowell, *Immigrants and Boomers: Forging a New Social Contract for the Future of America*, Russell Sage Foundation, 2007.
A demographer suggests that rates of immigration already may have peaked and argues that rather than being stigmatized immigrants need to be embraced as a replacement workforce for an aging Anglo population.

Portes, Alejandro, and Ruben G. Rumbaut, *Immigrant America: A Portrait*, 3rd ed., University of California Press, 2006.
This updated survey by two sociologists offers a broad look at where immigrants settle, what sort of work they do and how well they assimilate.

Articles

Bacon, Perry Jr., and Anne E. Kornblut, "Issue of Illegal Immigration Is Quandary for Democrats," *The Washington Post*, Nov. 2, 2007, p. A4.
Immigration is a wedge issue that can work against Democratic presidential candidates and is perhaps the strongest card in the GOP's deck.

Bazar, Emily, "Strict Immigration Law Rattles Okla. Businesses," *USA Today*, Jan. 10, 2008, p. 1A.
Numerous business sectors in Oklahoma are complaining about worker shortages in the wake of a new state law that makes transporting or sheltering illegal immigrants a felony.

Goodman, Josh, "Crackdown," *Governing*, July 2007, p. 28.
States are reacting to immigration pressures largely by enacting new restrictions on illegal immigrants and the employers who hire them.

Greenhouse, Steven, "U.S. Seeks Rules to Allow Increase in Guest Workers," *The New York Times*, Oct. 10, 2007, p. A16.
Bush administration officials say they will allow farmers to bring in more foreign labor.

Kiely, Kathy, "Children Caught in the Immigration Crossfire," *USA Today*, Oct. 8, 2007, p. 1A.
A million young, illegal immigrants in the United States face potential deportation since the failure of a bill designed to grant permanent legal status to those who finish high school and at least two years of higher education.

Lizza, Ryan, "Return of the Nativist," *The New Yorker*, Dec. 17, 2007, p. 46.
How a hard line on immigration became central to the GOP Republican debate, taken even by candidates who had previously favored a more conciliatory approach.

Preston, Julia, "U.S. to Speed Deportation of Criminals Behind Bars," *The New York Times*, Jan. 15, 2008, p. A12.
A federal agency pledges to step up arrests of employers who knowingly hire illegal immigrants, while speeding deportation of immigrants who have committed crimes.

Sandler, Michael, "Immigration: From the Capitol to the Courts," *CQ Weekly*, Dec. 10, 2007, p. 3644.
The lack of action on Capitol Hill has encouraged scores of state and local jurisdictions to step in with immigrant-related legislation.

Weisman, Jonathan, "For Republicans, Contest's Hallmark Is Immigration," *The Washington Post*, Jan. 2, 2008, p. A1.
Illegal immigration has been a dominant issue in the GOP presidential primary contests.

Reports and Studies

"2006 Yearbook of Immigration Statistics," Department of Homeland Security, Sept. 2007, www.dhs.gov/xlibrary/assets/statistics/yearbook/2006/OIS_2006_Yearbook.pdf.
A wealth of statistical information about immigrant populations is presented, as well as enforcement actions.

"2007 Enacted State Legislation Related to Immigrants and Immigration," National Conference of State Legislatures, Nov. 29, 2007, www.ncsl.org/print/immig/2007Immigrationfinal.pdf.
Last year, every state considered legislation related to immigration, with more than 1,500 bills introduced and 244 enacted into law. The amount of activity "in the continued absence of a comprehensive federal reform" was unprecedented and represented a threefold increase in legislation introduced and enacted since 2006.

"2007 National Survey of Latinos: As Illegal Immigration Issue Heats Up, Latinos Feel a Chill," Pew Hispanic Center, Dec. 19, 2007; available at http://pewhispanic.org/files/reports/84.pdf.
The poll finds that the prominence of the illegal-immigration issue has Hispanics more concerned about deportation and discrimination but generally content with their place in U.S. society.

For More Information

American Immigration Council, 1331 G St., N.W., Suite 200, Washington, DC 20005-3141; (202) 507-7500; www .americanimmigrationcouncil.org. Seeks to increase public understanding of immigration law and policy, emphasizing the value of immigration to American society.

Center for Comparative Immigration Studies, University of California, 9500 Gilman Dr., Mail Code 0548, San Diego, La Jolla, CA 92093-0548; (858) 822-4447; www.ccis-ucsd .org. Compares U.S. immigration trends with patterns in Europe and Asia.

Center for Immigration Studies, 1522 K St., N.W., Suite 820, Washington, DC 20005-1202; (202) 466-8185; www .cis.org. The nation's only think tank exclusively devoted to immigration-related issues advocates reduced immigration.

Federation for American Immigration Reform, 25 Massachusetts Ave., NW, Suite 330, Washington, DC 20001; (202) 328-7004; http://fairus.org. A leading advocate for cracking down on illegal immigration and reducing legal immigration.

Metropolitan Policy Program, The Brookings Institution, 1775 Massachusetts Ave., N.W., Washington, DC 20036; (202) 797-6000; www.brookings.edu/metro.aspx. The think tank produces numerous reports on both immigration and broader demographics, including geographical mobility.

Migration Dialogue, University of California, Davis, 1 Shields Ave., Davis, CA 95616; (530) 752-1011; http:// migration.ucdavis.edu/index.php. A research center that focuses on immigration from rural Mexico and publishes two Web bulletins.

Migration Policy Institute, 1400 16th St., N.W., Suite 300, Washington, DC 20036; (202) 266-1940; www.migration policy.org. Analyzes global immigration trends and advocates fairer, more humane conditions for immigrants.

National Immigration Forum; 50 F St., N.W., Suite 300, Washington, DC 20001; (202) 347-0040; www.immigration forum.org. A leading advocacy group in support of immigrants' rights.